Economics:

Mainstream Readings and Radical Critiques

Third Edition

Economics:

Mainstream Readings and Radical Critiques

edited by

David Mermelstein

Polytechnic Institute of Brooklyn

Random House New York

Third Edition

987654321

Copyright © 1970, 1973, 1976 by Random House, Inc.

Library of Congress Cataloging in Publication Data
Mermelstein, David, 1933–   comp.
   Economics, mainstream readings and radical critiques.

   Includes bibliographical references.
   1. Economics—Addresses, essays, lectures.
I. Title.
HB171.5.M55 1976   330'.08   75–33870
ISBN 0–394–30108–0

Manufactured in the United States of America

Acknowledgments

Grateful acknowledgment is made to the following authors, publishers, and agencies for permission to reprint copyrighted material.

Roger Alcaly, "The Relevance of Marxian Crisis Theory." Reprinted by permission of the author.

Peter Barnes, "Those Soaring Food Prices" from *The New Republic*, October 12, 1974. Copyright © 1974 by The New Republic, Inc. Reprinted by permission of The New Republic, Inc.

Barbara Bergmann, "The Economics of Women's Liberation." Copyright © 1972 by Barbara Bergmann. Reprinted by permission of the author.

Raford Boddy and James Crotty, "Who Will Plan the Planned Economy?" excerpted from "Class Conflict, Keynesian Policies and the Business Cycle" from *Monthly Review*, October 1974, pp. 2–10. Copyright © October 1974 by Monthly Review Inc. Reprinted by permission of Monthly Review Press.

Robert A. Caro, "The Northern State Parkway and the Cross-Bronx Expressway: A Revealing Contrast," excerpted from *The Power Broker* by Robert A. Caro. Copyright © 1974 by Robert A. Caro. Reprinted by permission of Alfred A. Knopf, Inc. Portions of this book originally appeared in *The New Yorker*.

Hollis B. Chenery, "Restructuring the World Economy," excerpted from pp. 242–263 of *Foreign Affairs*, January 1975. Copyright © 1974 by Council on Foreign Relations, Inc. Reprinted by permission of *Foreign Affairs*.

Benjamin J. Cohen, "Toward a General Theory of Imperialism" from Chapter Seven, "Toward a General Theory of Imperialism," from *The Question of Imperialism: The Political Economy of Dominance and Dependence* by Benjamin J. Cohen. © 1973 by Basic Books, Inc., Publishers, New York.

The Committee for Puerto Rican Decolonization, "U.S. Capital in Puerto Rico: The Dollar Brings Destruction." Reprinted by permission of the Committee for Puerto Rican Decolonization.

James Crotty and Raford Boddy, "Who Will Plan the Planned Economy?" from *The Progressive*, February 1975, pp. 80–91. Copyright © 1975, The Progressive, Inc. Reprinted by permission from The Progressive, Madison, Wisconsin.

Matthew Edel, "Pogo Is Wrong (Pogo: 'We have met the enemy and he is us')" from *Boston After Dark*, December 7, 1971. Reprinted by permission of the Boston Phoenix.

S. R. Eyre, "Man the Pest: The Dim Chance of Survival" from *The New York Review of Books*, November 18, 1971 (tables, figures, and footnotes omitted). Reprinted by permission of the author.

Raymond S. Franklin and William K. Tabb, "The Challenge of Radical Political Economics," excerpted from *Journal of Economic Issues*, Vol. 7, No. 1 (March 1974), pp. 128–140 and 143–146. Reproduced by permission of the Association for Evolutionary Economics and the authors.

Milton Friedman, "The Distribution of Income" from pp. 161–179 of *Capitalism and Freedom* by Milton Friedman. Copyright © 1962 by The University of Chicago Press. Reprinted by permission of The University of Chicago Press, publishers.

John Kenneth Galbraith, "Consumption and the Household," excerpted from pp. 29–37 and 233–240 of *Economics and The Public Purpose* by John Kenneth Galbraith. Copyright © 1973 by John Kenneth Galbraith. Reprinted by permission of Houghton Mifflin Company.

Herbert Gintis, "Alienation from Work-Process and -Product" from *The Review of Radical Political Economics*, Vol. 4, No. 5 (Fall 1972), pp. 11–20. Reprinted by permission of the publisher.

David Gold, "James O'Conner's *The Fiscal Crisis of the State:* An Overview." Reprinted by permission of the author.

David M. Gordon, "Capital vs. Labor: The Current Crisis in the Sphere of Production." Copyright © David M. Gordon 1975. Reprinted by permission of the author.

C. Jackson Grayson, Jr., "Controls Are Not the Answer" from *Challenge*, November/December 1974. Copyright © 1974 by International Arts and Sciences Press, Inc. Reprinted by permission of International Arts and Sciences Press, Inc.

John G. Gurley, "Maoist Economic Development," excerpted from *America's Asia*, edited by Edward Friedman and Mark Selden. Copyright © 1969, 1970, 1971 by Random House, Inc. Reprinted by permission of Pantheon Books, a Division of Random House, Inc.

John Hardesty, "Economic Implications of Environmental Crisis," published by permission of Transaction, Inc., from *Society*, Vol. 12, No. 1. Copyright © 1974 by Transaction, Inc.

Stephen Hymer, "The Multinational Corporation and the Law of Uneven Development," excerpted from pp. 116–135 of *Economics and World Order* by J. N. Bhagwati. Copyright © 1972 by Macmillan Publishing Co., Inc. Reprinted by permission of Macmillan Publishing Co., Inc.

Carolyn J. Jacobson, "Women Workers: Profile of a Growing Force," excerpted from *American Federationist*, July 1974, pp. 9–14. Reprinted by permission of the AFL-CIO.

David Jenkins, "Industrial Democracy," excerpted from pp. 284–289 of *Job Power: Blue and White Collar Democracy* by David Jenkins. Copyright © 1973 by David Jenkins. Reprinted by permission of Doubleday & Company, Inc.

D. Gale Johnson, "Are High Farm Prices Here to Stay?" from *The Morgan Guaranty Survey*, August 1974, pp. 9–14. © 1974 by The Morgan Guaranty Trust Company of New York. Reprinted by permission of the Morgan Guaranty Trust Company and the author.

Charles P. Kindleberger, "Why World Bankers Are Worried," excerpted from *Challenge*, November/December 1794, pp. 20–22. Copyright © 1974 by International Arts and Sciences Press, Inc. Reprinted by permission of International Arts and Sciences Press, Inc.

Richard Kronish, "Responding to the OPEC: An Assessment of Oil Cartels" from *Socialist Revolution*, September/October 1973, pp. 28–46. Reprinted by permission of the Socialist Revolution.

Wilfred Lewis, Jr., "The Economics of Restraint," excerpted from *Social Policy*, Vol. 5, No. 4 (November/December 1974), pp. 4–9. © 1974 by Social Policy Corporation. Reprinted by permission of Social Policy Corporation, New York.

Carol Lopate, "Pay for Housework?" from *Social Policy*, Vol. 5, No. 3 (September/October 1974), pp. 27–31. © 1974 by Social Policy Corporation. Reprinted by permission of Social Policy Corporation, New York.

Harry Magdoff and Paul M. Sweezy, "Banks: Skating on Thin Ice," excerpted from *Monthly Review*, February 1975, pp. 1–21. Copyright © February 1975 by Monthly Review Inc. Reprinted by permission of Monthly Review Press.

S. Menshikov, "Millionaires and Managers," excerpted from Chapters Two through

Five of *Millionaires and Managers* by S. Menshikov. Copyright © 1965 by Progress Publishers, Moscow. Reprinted by permission of the author, the publisher, and the Copyright Agency of the U.S.S.R. (VAAP).

Randall Meyer, "The Role of Big Business in Achieving National Goals." This article was originally a speech delivered by the President of Exxon Corporation on November 26, 1974. Reprinted by permission of Exxon Corporation.

Raymond F. Mikesell, "More Third World Cartels Ahead?" excerpted from *Challenge*, November/December 1974, pp. 24–31. Copyright © 1974 by International Arts and Sciences Press, Inc. Reprinted by permission of International Arts and Sciences Press, Inc.

Herman P. Miller, "Inequality, Poverty, and Taxes," excerpted from *Dissent*, Winter 1975, pp. 40–49. Reprinted by permission of the publisher and author.

E. J. Mishan, "Crime and Traffic: A Parable and a Proposal" from pp. 66–73 of *Technology and Growth: The Price We Pay* by E. J. Mishan. © 1969 by E. J. Mishan. Excerpted and reprinted by permission of Praeger Publishers, Inc., New York, and Granada Publishing Limited.

Robert A. Mundell, "The Law of Economy" from *Man and Economics* by Robert A. Mundell. Copyright © 1968 by McGraw-Hill, Inc. Used with permission of McGraw-Hill Book Company.

Ralph Nader, "A Citizen's Guide to the American Economy," excerpted from *The New York Review of Books*, September 2, 1971. Reprinted with permission from *The New York Review of Books*. Copyright © 1971 Nyrev, Inc.

James O'Conner, "Suburban Exploitation of the City" from pp. 124–129 of *The Fiscal Crisis of the State* by James O'Conner. Reprinted by permission of the publisher, St. Martin's Press, Inc. "What Is Political Economy?", an unpublished article. Reprinted by permission of the author.

Andreas G. Papandreou, "The Myth of Market Capitalism," excerpted from pp. 12–26, 30–33, 35–37, and 39–40 of *Paternalistic Capitalism* by Andreas G. Papandreou. © Copyright 1972 by the University of Minnesota. Reprinted by permission of The University of Minnesota Press, Minneapolis.

Peter Passell and Leonard Ross, "Don't Knock the $2-Trillion Economy," excerpted from *The New York Times Magazine*, March 5, 1972. Copyright © 1972 by Peter Passell and Leonard Ross. Reprinted by permission of The Sterling Lord Agency, Inc.

Cheryl Payer, "The Lawyer's Typist: Variations on a Theme by Paul Samuelson" from *Monthly Review*, March 1974, pp. 44–48. Copyright © March 1974 by Monthly Review Inc. Reprinted by permission of Monthly Review Press.

Frances Fox Piven, "The Urban Crisis: Who Got What, and Why," excerpted from *The Politics of Turmoil: Essays on Poverty, Race and the Urban Crisis* by Richard A. Cloward and Frances Fox Piven. Copyright © 1974 by Richard A. Cloward and Frances Fox Piven. Reprinted by permission of Pantheon Books, a Division of Random House, Inc.

Michael Reich, "The Economics of Racism" from pp. 107–113 of *Problems in Political Economics* by David Gordon. Reprinted by permission of the author.

Michael Reich and David Finkelhor, "Capitalism and the 'Military-Industrial Complex': The Obstacles to 'Conversion,'" from *Up Against the American Myth*, by Thomas Christoffel et al. Reprinted by permission of Michael Reich, David Finkelhor (c/o International Creative Management), and Holt, Rinehart and Winston, Inc. Copyright © 1970 by Michael Reich and David Finkelhor.

Emma Rothschild, "G.M. in Trouble: The Vega Plant at Lordstown," excerpted from *Paradise Lost* by Emma Rothschild. Copyright © 1972 by Emma Rothschild. Reprinted by permission of Random House, Inc.

Paul A. Samuelson, "Defense Expenditure and Prosperity: An Important Digression" from *Economics* by Paul A. Samuelson. Copyright © 1971 by McGraw-Hill, Inc. Used with permission of McGraw-Hill Book Company. "Worldwide Stagflation: An Overview on the Eve of the Downturn," excerpted from pp. 3–9 of *The Morgan Guaranty Survey*, June 1974. Reprinted by permission of Marion C. Samuelson, Trustee. This article is an adaptation from a memorandum prepared for the West German Council of Economic Advisers.

Robert Samuelson, "Why Price Controls Stopped Working . . ." from *The Washington Monthly*, May 1974. Copyright by The Washington Monthly Co., Washington, D.C. Reprinted by permission of The Washington Monthly.

Charles L. Schultze, "Is Economics Obsolete? No, Underemployed" from *Saturday Review*, January 22, 1972, a special issue produced in cooperation with the Committee for Economic Development. Copyright © 1972 by Saturday Review, Inc. Reprinted by permission of Saturday Review, Inc.

Leonard Silk, "Economic Profession Debates Its Role" from "Paradox for Economists," *The New York Times*, October 30, 1974. © 1974 by The New York Times Company. Reprinted by permission.

Robert M. Solow, "The New Industrial State or Son of Affluence," excerpted from pp. 100–108 of *The Public Interest*, 9 (Fall 1967). Copyright © 1969 by National Affairs, Inc. Reprinted by permission of the publisher.

Thomas Sowell, "Capitalism Versus Socialism" from pp. 282–288 of *Economics: Analysis and Issues* by Thomas Sowell. Copyright © 1971 by Scott, Foresman and Company. Reprinted by permission of the publisher. "Race and the Market," excerpted from *Race and Economics* by Thomas Sowell. Copyright © 1975 by David McKay Co., Inc. Reprinted with permission of the publisher.

Thaddeus H. Spratlen, "The Record and Rhetoric of Black Economic Progress," excerpted from pp. 1–24 of *Review of Black Political Economy*, Vol. 4, No. 3 (September 1974). Reprinted by permission of the Review of Black Political Economy.

Alan Stone, "The Soul of Mammon: Corporate Responsibility and Capitalism" from *International Socialist Review*, December 1974. Copyright © 1974 by International Socialist Review. Reprinted by permission of the publisher.

Paul M. Sweezy, "Growing Wealth, Declining Power" from *Monthly Review*, March 1974, pp. 1–11. Copyright © March 1974 by Monthly Review Inc. "Toward a Program of Studies of the Transition to Socialism" from *Monthly Review*, February 1972. Copyright © 1972 by Monthly Review Inc. "Utopian Reformism" from *Monthly Review*, November 1973, pp. 1–11. Copyright © November 1973 by Monthly Review Inc. Reprinted by permission of Monthly Review Press.

William K. Tabb, "Capitalist State Planning Is Not Socialism." Reprinted by permission of the author.

Michael Tanzer, "The International Oil Crisis: A Tightrope Between Depression and War" from *The Energy Crisis* by Michael Tanzer. Copyright © 1975 by Michael Tanzer. Reprinted by permission of the Monthly Review Press.

URPE/PEA National Food Collective, "The Capitalist Food System: A Framework for Understanding Food Inflation." © Union for Radical Political Economics 1975. Reprinted by permission of Union for Radical Political Economics.

Howard M. Wachtel, "Looking at Poverty from a Radical Perspective," excerpted from *Political Economy: Radical vs. Orthodox Approaches*, edited by James Weaver. Reprinted by permission of the author.

Thomas Weisskopf, "Theories of American Imperialism: A Critical Evaluation," excerpted from *The Review of Radical Political Economics*, Vol. 6, No. 3 (Fall 1974), pp. 41–57. Reprinted by permission of the publisher.

Stephen W. Welch, "Zapping Labor: A Radical Perspective on Wage-Price Controls." Reprinted by permission of the author.

Personal Acknowledgments

Although I alone bear responsibility for the contents of this book—its format, editorial introductions, and choice of readings—I am grateful to David Curzon, Bob Dillon, David Gordon, and Michael Tanzer, who directed me to readings I would otherwise have overlooked. I would also like to acknowledge the help of Jim Bass, Lourdes Beneria, Louis Menashe, Julie Mermelstein, and especially Mary Margaret Hounsell. Because this book literally bears the imprint of what preceded it, my continuing gratitude extends to all who helped on its previous editions.

A number of readings in the present edition also appear in another volume that I have edited, *The Economic Crisis Reader* (New York: Vintage, 1975). For this reason, I would also like to thank those friends and colleagues who assisted me in that endeavor. Some of these readings also appear in *Radical Perspectives on the Economic Crisis of Monopoly Capital*, published by the Union for Radical Political Economics (1975). Special thanks go to URPE for permission to reprint these articles both in this volume and *The Economic Crisis Reader*. (Readers interested in joining this organization, receiving its newsletter and quarterly journal, or learning more about the Union for Radical Political Economics should write to: URPE, 41 Union Square, Room 201, New York, N.Y. 10003.)

I owe a different kind of debt to my students at the Polytechnic, where I have taught for fifteen years. It is to them that this book is dedicated, for they have shown me, in a way books could not, the enormous staying power and strengths of petite bourgeoisie consciousness—and how they are victimized by it.

DAVID MERMELSTEIN
MAY 1975

Preface to the Third Edition

Not long ago, complacency ruled America. It was easy then to ignore the Jeremiahs of the Left as long as real incomes continued to increase. Gradually, the social fabric began to unravel. Racism was confronted by a militant civil rights movement, and when moderates like Martin Luther King failed to secure needed reforms, more blacks either turned to revolutionary leaders like Malcolm X and Huey Newton—or vented their rage in destructive ghetto riots. Abroad, American troops were bogged down in what appeared to be an endless war in Vietnam. Everywhere there were strikes, demonstrations, protests, and violent disorders.

As the decade of the sixties drew to a close, many Americans were yearning to put these upheavals behind them. The election of Richard Nixon to the Presidency, the withdrawal of American troops from Vietnam (though the war itself continued), the disintegration or demise of the black and white revolutionary movements—these events and others rekindled optimism among many conservatives that America was returning to "normalcy." And normalcy of course meant getting on with the business of making money, the business of acquiring the symbols of status.

On the surface, then—Watergate aside—1972 and 1973 were good years, during which most of our leading politicians and economists continued to go through the postwar ritual of assuring and reassuring us that our economic system was basically sound. But behind the scenes were frantic efforts to shore up a crumbling international financial system. To the extent that optimistic projections had any basis at all during these years, they reflected the continuing presence of the post-World War II boom. That boom, unfortunately, is over. The reality of America as we enter the last quarter of this century is that of massive economic crisis, characterized so far by an unprecedented mix of inflation and unemployment.

The current depression—and that, not "recession," is likely to be the term historians will use to describe this epoch—has invalidated, or made obsolete or irrelevant, much of orthodox economics, especially its neo-Keynesian variant. More than that, it has led to a resurgence and revival of a powerful analytical alternative, the socialist analysis associated with the name of Karl Marx. As a result, the radical critique of mainstream economics has an urgency and cogency it previously lacked.

Once again, therefore, the quickening pace of events has prompted a considerable revision of this reader, the most important element of which is the inclusion of a major new section (approximately one quarter of the book) that explores the causes and consequences of the current crisis. In addition, new sections have been added, while those remaining from the previous edition have been thoroughly "pruned" and replaced by more appropriate material. No section has been left uncut or unrevised. The cumulative effect of these changes is that this third edition, like the second which preceded it, is virtually a new book.

In the preparing, I have again been made painfully aware of the many problems inherent in a reader of this type. Many appropriate articles have been omitted because of the necessity of conserving space; others had to be partially cut. Another difficulty is that individual readings, especially those with a Marxist orientation, often fall into several overlapping categories. Nonetheless, teachers using this edition should have little trouble in rearranging the material to fit their own needs and preconceptions. In general, I have tried to prepare this third edition with two kinds of potential instructors in mind: those who want to supplement a standard text with readings that represent different points of view, albeit weighted toward the radical side; and those who will use this kind of reader as an alternative to a standard text.

Given the crisis that besets our society, the need for public understanding of social issues has never been greater. But if this understanding is to be anything more than an intellectual exercise, it must provide the impetus for reconstructing our society along more sane, humanistic, and equitable lines. Whether this can be accomplished through reforms of the existing capitalist order, as mainstream economists believe, or will necessitate going beyond capitalism to new forms of social organization, as I and others who call for socialism maintain, only history will resolve. We do, however, have the option of being conscious human agents within this historical process. Ultimately, to be free we must understand the choices that lie before us. Then, and only then, can we responsibly begin to build a better social order.

Unfortunately, time may be running out. Either we achieve solutions soon, or we are likely to be engulfed by the fascistic and militaristic forces that capitalistic depressions touch off. These are sobering times.

DAVID MERMELSTEIN
MARCH 1975

Preface to the First Edition

Economics has developed into a highly professionalized discipline. Symbolic of this fact are its journals: mathematical, statistical, and depressingly dull. One might forgive orthodoxy its faults if it addressed itself to the central issues of our time. Unfortunately, it rarely does. Refinements in welfare economics where hypothetical constructs—indifference curves—are employed to justify hypothetical subsidies on the basis of hypothetical compensations so as to leave no one worse off could be considered harmless diversions were it not for the proliferation of actual subsidies that the wealthy use to extend their privileges.

Postwar economics textbooks, following the highly successful model provided by Paul A. Samuelson's earliest editions, have been marked by technical explications of orthodox theory, by sympathetic treatment of contemporary institutions, and by elaborate discussions of the technical aspects of orthodox policy alternatives. These presentations are embellished with multicolored charts and accompanied by lengthy workbooks and, more recently, by programmed texts.

For students who do not intend to become professional economists—and even, perhaps, for those who do—the typical textbook provides more than enough instruction in analytical technique. A reader designed to accompany introductory texts should not simply contain more elaboration and more examples of what is covered in the text. Instead, such a reader should challenge orthodoxy's assumptions, its complacent acceptance of existing institutions, and its judgments of what is and what is not important.

I would suggest, for example, that our teaching efforts are misguided if we discuss the alternate means to achieve full employment and a higher rate of growth without first showing that achievement of these objectives will bring about a better society. Growth for what purpose is the fundamental question of modern economics. The college student of today need only note the prevalence of ugly blighted cities, of the vast, progressive destruction of what were once surroundings of exquisite beauty, of glittering wealth amidst widespread deprivation and hunger, and, above all, of ever greater numbers of missiles, anti-missiles, and anti-missile missiles capable of unimaginable horrors to recognize that our system—called by some a mixed system, by others, monopoly capitalism—fails to use its resources intelligently and rationally.

Nor should our social institutions be evaluated by their efficacy in achieving goals that are not themselves valid. The ways in which these institutions—such as the banking system, the corporation, the university, and the institution of private property—create and perpetuate a highly unequal distribution of income, wealth, and power are largely ignored in contemporary economic writings.

In general, I am suggesting that contemporary economic texts do not make any serious effort to raise the relevant questions (not to speak of providing answers) concerning the fundamental nature of our society. Only perfunctorily do they indicate how the economic theory they uphold, even in conjunction with those economic institutions they extol, much less those they wish to create, can be used to direct mankind toward a better social order. In short, they do not demonstrate that contemporary economics speaks to the condition of twentieth-century man.

The readings in this volume attempt to redress this imbalance. The editor is guided by the view that "pure" economic analysis, which divorces its subject from its political context, does not merely perpetrate an unfortunate omission but rather a distortion of major proportions. While relevant readings of many political orientations have been included in this book, the majority have been deliberately chosen for their ability to provoke thought and challenge orthodoxy. Instead of simply juxtaposing liberal and conservative views, I have included a large number of New Left and socialist articles that provide alternatives to both wings of the mainstream. Most of the usual fields in economics are discussed; for example, microeconomics and macroeconomics, growth, monopoly, poverty, taxation, the balance of payments, and so forth. The main focus, however, is on economic policy, distributional justice, and what I would call the dynamics of socioeconomic relations. I hope to raise the appropriate questions concerning the social decay that is our lot to witness. It is my hope that we will not remain forever in a world where fear pervades our cities, war and military spending are central to our production, elitism forms our politics, and inequality rules our social relations.

Belief in the potentiality of man and concern for the value of human life have led a growing number of Americans to criticize contemporary capitalism. People should be able to live under institutions that they can control, and these institutions should enhance the meaning of individual life, not contribute to man's degradation and dehumanization. With the publication of this reader, I hope I have raised the level of dialogue between liberals and conservatives, on the one hand, and those like myself, who consider themselves socialists, on the other. Whatever one's system of values may be, if this reader can challenge students aware of economic issues for the first time, stimulate more sophisticated thinking, and create more worthwhile discussion about the workings of our society, it will be, for its editor, a personal success. For we all must agree, I assume, that a good society has yet to be created.

New York City   DAVID MERMELSTEIN

Contents

ℙ𝔸ℝ𝕋 𝟛 The Crisis of Depression

PART 4 Income, Wealth, and Power

PART 5 American Capitalism at the Crossroads

Economics:

Mainstream Readings and Radical Critiques

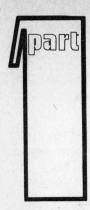

An Introduction to Political Economy

A century ago the field of academic specialization now called "economics" was known as "political economy." The difference reflects more than just semantics. As used by the classical French and British economists, the term "political economy" referred to a study of the social laws governing the production and distribution of goods, and thus social classes and their conflicts were the economist's legitimate concerns. Critics like Karl Marx also accepted this definitional framework. Indeed, the establishment of a new orthodoxy based on a subjective theory of value and marginalism can legitimately be considered a conservative reaction to the threat posed by Marx when he adapted classical assumptions to serve socialist ends.

The focus of modern bourgeois economics is generally narrower than in the past. Its primary concern is the analysis of equilibrium in "free" markets. Technique has been embraced for its own sake and the ability to further refine the general equilibrium model is considered a mark of a professional. This focus fills the needs of the ruling elite and of the giant corporations it controls. Economists qua economists no longer display much interest in questions that occupied their nineteenth-century predecessors. Issues involving class and power have been delegated to the disciplines of sociology and political science. Young academics who violate these jurisdictional boundaries are dismissed as dilettantes. To emphasize the social framework of their studies and to distinguish them from what they consider to be a vulgarization of economic inquiry, Marxist economists have continued to use the older term "political economy." It is interesting to note that the last few years have seen a revival of this latter term among some mainstream economists who appreciate the interdependence of economics and politics. Few would suggest, however, that this indicates any significant change in the overall focus or fundamental assumptions of orthodox economics.

Whatever its name, however, this discipline is controversial. How much so cannot be appreciated simply by studying mainstream literature. In the latter, debates, when they do exist, invariably take place within a shared social perspective. What should be at the core of the intellectual discourse—the basic assumptions about human beings and social institutions—is treated superficially or often omitted altogether. Fortunately, under the impact of radical criticism, students are occasionally being exposed to socialist analyses and socialist alternatives.

Section a contains an overview of some of the broader epistemological issues, while section b challenges our preconceptions of modern capitalism. Students should consider the critiques of capitalism in this and other sections of the book within a framework that compares the capitalism we have to the socialism that can be. (Socialism is discussed at greater length in Part 5.)

Contemporary Economics: An Overview

Unlike in the natural sciences, there is no body of economic knowledge that nearly all can agree on for a first course in economics or political economy. Economists do not even agree on the name of the discipline, never mind its scope and method! Students should not infer from this, however, that every economic thought thrown into the intellectual arena is of equal value. No doubt some are valid and others are not.

This section presents alternative overviews on where we are in the field of "economics." Leonard Silk, an economist with the *New York Times* (see Reading 1), provides a brief introduction to some of the controversies we shall come across throughout the book. This reading is followed by an introduction to the discipline of economics by a distinguished bourgeois economist, Robert A. Mundell (see Reading 2). In contrast is the Marxist approach offered in Reading 3 by Professor James O'Connor of San Jose State College, "What Is Political Economy?" These readings are

(in the former case) or could be (in the latter) opening chapters of a textbook on economics or political economy.

In recent years the orthodox perspective of Mundell and others has been increasingly under attack. Reading 4 by Charles Schultze, a former director of the Bureau of the Budget and author of a leading macroeconomic text, is an attempt to answer radical critics who believe conventional economics to be supportive of sexism, racism, imperialism, and a wide variety of other social ills. Schultze has little of substance to say about many of these problems, though he concedes modern economics has a number of failings. Schultze insists upon practical solutions of a technical nature to social problems, neglecting to note that pragmatism of this sort has brought us to our current impasse. Rather than consider new forms of social organization (for example, socialism) to deal with such problems as unemployment and pollution, he advocates political measures that change "the structure of incentives," thereby "forcing" corporations to behave "responsibly." But what if corporations control the very political instruments that are supposed to bring about reform? Radicals believe that they do and so remain skeptical of liberal programs similar to those advocated by Charles Schultze.

For a better understanding of the limits and shortcomings of orthodox economics—even when artfully applied by such eminent practitioners as Mundell and Schultze—it is useful to examine Reading 5 by Professors Raymond Franklin and William K. Tabb of Queens College (CUNY). This essay pulls together many of the criticisms radical economists have been making of mainstream economics.

Most of the issues touched upon in this introductory section are treated in more detail throughout the book. In fact, the radical selections can be thought of as both refutations of Mundell and Schultze and elaborations of Franklin and Tabb. Students may find it useful, therefore, to read this section once again at the end of the semester in order to grasp a number of the subtleties that may have been overlooked during a first reading.

1

Economic Profession Debates Its Role

Leonard Silk

The economics profession is caught in a curious and complicated paradox: The worse economic policy is, the worse the state of the economy; but the worse the economy, the more people turn to economists for solutions; and the more society turns to the economists to solve unsolved problems, the greater the sense of dissatisfaction and inadequacy within the economics profession.

This was the paradox that hung over the newly formed Eastern Economic Association last weekend at its inaugural convention in Albany. In a special panel on "economics for the fourth quarter of the 20th century," several leading economists tried to divine where both the world and the discipline of economics are heading.

Prof. James Tobin of Yale, a member of the Council of Economic Advisers under President John F. Kennedy, said that the agenda for economics derives from two inspirations—first, "exogenous" sources, i.e., troubles in the real world, such as wars, lines at gasoline stations, or double-digit inflation; and second, "endogenous" sources, i.e., the internal momentum of the science or nonscience of economics itself.

If economists pay too much attention to the endlessly changing outside problems, they run the risk of being faddish; if they concentrate too much on their internal intellectual problems, they run the risk of growing increasingly esoteric and irrelevant.

Professor Tobin suggested that a "golden age" occurs for economics whenever there is a convergence of the external and internal agenda. Such a convergence occurred at the end of the 18th century and early part of the 19th century, when "external" political and business controversies over international trade, economic development and the protectionist "corn laws" in Britain coincided with "internal" development of the theory of markets by the economists.

Another golden age for economics came in the nineteen-thirties, when the Great Depression came together with the theories of John Maynard Keynes on how the economy as a whole functions and the statistical work on national income of Simon Kuznets.

Is another golden age for economics ahead in the fourth quarter of this century? Professor Tobin was dubious. There is a lot of excitement among the economic theorists—especially the young ones—about abstract matters that seem more and more remote from the real-world problems that overlap economics and other disciplines: the population explosion, the shift of power to the oil-producing states, the growing conflict between the poor nations and the rich, world industrialization and hunger, threats to the environment, exhaustion of nonrenewable resources, dangers of a nuclear holocaust.

This divergence between the external and internal agenda, as Prof.

Robert Solow of the Massachusetts Institute of Technology put it, poses a dilemma for economists today: "Whether to have more and more to say about less and less, or whether to have less and less to say about more and more."

For his part, Professor Solow chose the former alternative, and suggested that it would be better for economists to aspire to be competent technicians—like plumbers, or, as Lord Keynes once put it, like dentists. But this is a choice that an increasing number of economists now regard as a fate worse than death, a "cop-out" from the world's really important problems.

Prof. John Kenneth Galbraith of Harvard, who was supposed to have been on the "last quarter of the century" panel in Albany but was summoned off to Mexico by its President, Luis Echeverria, has conceded that the economists "can, if they are determined, be unimportant; they can, if they prefer a comfortable home life and regular hours, continue to make a living out of the infinitely interesting gadgetry of disguise. . . .

"They will be socially more irrelevant than Keynes's dentist, for he would feel obliged to have a recommendation, were everyone's teeth, in conflict with all expectation, suddenly to fall out," Mr. Galbraith said.

The alternative, he has suggested, is for economists to enlarge their system, to have it embrace "the power they now disguise." This would make their domestic lives less passive, and might produce a reaction from those "whose power is now revealed and examined," as well as from those who find comfort in the fact that economists teach and discuss the wrong problems "or none at all."

Prof. Daniel Fusfeld of the University of Michigan and Prof. Robert Heilbroner of the New School for Social Research agreed with this Galbraithian critique of the profession. Professor Fusfeld said there was a growing isolation of the people who make political-economic decisions from the economists, who brought this upon themselves by their lack of realism.

For instance, he noted, there is great concern among the economists over the recycling of Arab oil profits, to the complete neglect of what he termed the real story: "How one elite rips off another, and how the second elite defends itself."

Thinking about the real problems of the last quarter of the century, Professor Fusfeld said he couldn't decide which of two books to start writing: "The Economics of an Equalitarian Social Order" or "The Economics of an Authoritarian Fascist World."

Professor Heilbroner of the New School said he saw five major issues ahead that called for fresh thinking by the economists:

- □ Inflation, "a chronic malady of industrial systems in which markets play a central role."
- □ Population and the environment, and the need for planning priorities, and control to prevent an environmental catastrophe.
- □ Corporate power—especially that of the multinational corporation—and how to identify and oversee it.
- □ The changing balance of power between the developed and developing nations, the growth of cartels, the spread of nuclear capabilities,

and the likelihood that autarchy—national self-sufficiency—will replace free trade.

☐ The danger that the world has passed an inflection point, and has entered a period like the decline of the Roman Empire, with everything starting to come apart—including past value systems.

Economics, said Mr. Heilbroner, was founded chiefly on the value of efficiency. But this fundamental value, too, may be disappearing. He noted that the quest for efficiency was not necessarily a constant in economics: "Buddhist economics," he said, "regards human labor not as an input to production but an output."

The more traditional economists, Professors Tobin and Solow, regarded all such talk as vague, if not soupy; found the existing use of economic tools, if limited, at least "productive," and urged the profession not to throw away its hard-won methodology.

Professor Solow said that people like to compare economists to the drunk who lost his key and kept looking for it under the street light, because at least he could see there. This, he suggested, was a joke on the people who tell the story; economists should keep looking where they have some light.

Professor Tobin said Yale knew how to produce "plumbers," that is, competent economic technicians, but it didn't know how to produce "philosopher-kings." He further cast doubt on the substantive value of the broad-gauged economic philosophers: "Any honest man or woman owes it to the reader to say why you should believe what I say," said Mr. Tobin. "Can it be proved empirically? Can it be observed?"

Specifically, those economists who like to talk about "power," he said, should produce an operationally useful definition of power; any economic journal would be glad to publish such an article. It hadn't been done, he suggested, because it was too difficult—and he himself had tried.

But is it really that hard? A rough working definition of power is that it is the ability of anybody to make somebody else do something that he may not want to do. Could this be measured in the case of the power of the oil cartel to levy higher prices on oil-consuming countries? In the case of a country to nationalize the property of a multinational corporation? In the case of a second country to prevent the first country from nationalizing the property of its multinationals?

Or are these problems that economists don't like because they don't fit neatly into the existing body of economic theory and analysis?

There is indeed great discontent within the economics profession over its inability to handle important and "dirty" problems—but this could prove to be intellectual labor pains. Is a new golden age about to be born? Or is it, rather, a time when economists can say, with the late, great comedian Will Rogers, "Things ain't as good as they used to be—but then they never were."

2

The Law of Economy

Robert A. Mundell

Economics is concerned with want and resources. It examines that aspect of individual and social action by which resources are used to reduce want. Because want is a state of mind, economics deals with *man*. Because resources constitute matter, economics deals with *nature*. Man and want, nature and resources—these are the universal actors in the drama of economics.

The ingredients of drama are in every economic problem, if by drama is meant as in the great tragedies of the theater, the confrontation of opposing forces. In economic problems there is always the confrontation of opposing forces: want and resources, desire and opportunity, man and nature, consumption and saving, supply and demand. The act of choice is but the final act, the denouement, where the romantic forces of desire are pitted against the realistic forces of opportunity.

There is no way of knowing whether man or nature is the more basic concept of economics. Man is part of nature, and therefore man is lesser. But nature is a postulate of man's perception, and therefore man is greater. Any attempt to establish the priority of one concept over the other meets with a metaphysical contradiction.

Want is basic to economics. It plays an essential role in the consumption process, and consumption is, as Adam Smith said, the sole end and purpose of all production. Without want there would be no basis for choice, no grounds for decisions, no purpose to consumption. Man would be a vegetable, purposeless and pointless. But want is indeed unlimited. It is ubiquitous, universal, and eternal. It springs from man's knowledge of himself, from the time he tasted the forbidden fruit. It springs from man's ignorance, from the primordial instincts that make him a biological entity. Want is a bottomless pit, and between the Garden of Eden and heaven its absence is not conceivable.

Resources derive from nature. They play the enabling role in the production process. Without resources nothing could live, and there would be no basis for perceiving the existence of anything else. There would be a nothingness, in itself beyond comprehension. But resources are limited. Matter is limited, and space is finite. Abundance of everything is a meaningless concept, beyond the purview of man and outside the objectivity of his existence. *Nothing* is unlimited.

Want, being a state of mind, is an attribute of subjective man, and so economics has an origin in the *psychological sciences*. Resources, being a state of nature, are an attribute of matter, and so economics has an origin in the *physical sciences*. The economic aspects of the sciences are joined in the transformation of matter into want elimination through the production and consumption of *goods*. The subjective and objective phenomena of life are joined in the economic concept of goods.

Resources constitute the class of all things that exist, wants the class of desired things that are lacking. Goods are desired things that exist, an overlapping of the class of wants with the class of resources.

Resources that are not desired, that are not capable of satisfying desires or eliminating wants, are not goods; and neither are desired things that do not exist. There is no useful sense in which a flea on the planet Mars can be considered a good, since it is not (as far as we know) desired, nor is there any useful sense in which immortality can be considered a good, since it does not exist.

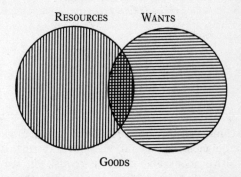

and consumption of *goods*. The subjective and objective phenomena of life

RESOURCES   WANTS

GOODS

Hunger is a want, and food is a resource. Hunger creates the desire for food. Thus the availability of food for reducing hunger, combined with the ability to eat it, implies that food is a good. Available food, drink, and shelter are goods that can eliminate hunger, thirst, and cold; a symphony concert is a good that can satisfy a listener's love of music; and a toy train is a good that can satisfy a child's taste for play.

The concept of a good in economics is a very broad one. A loaf of bread is a good; and so are a car, a house, a painting, a Beatles record, a bed, and a dog. So might be air, a date with a girl, a swim in the sea, a conversation with a genius, and a beautiful sunset.

There are many different types of goods in economics. There are

> *Free goods, scarce goods*
> *Goods made for market*
> *Public goods, private goods*
> *Goods made in Chile.*
>
> *There are necessaries, luxuries*
> *Snob goods of Veblen*
> *There are war goods, peace goods*
> *Goods sent to Vietnam.*
>
> *There are present goods, future goods*
> *Consumer goods and capital*
> *Wholesale goods and wholesome goods*
> *Goods not for children.*

There are stolen goods, hot goods
Used goods and services
Intermediate goods and final goods
Goods made for retail.

Dry goods, Hong Kong goods
Import goods with taxes
Traded goods, home goods
Goods made with axes.

Substitutes, complements
Bread, butter, and cheese
Superior goods, inferior goods
Goods made for deepfreeze.

Outputs, inputs
Goods and factors
Inventions, patents
Plays by actors.

Goodness!

A good is a thing that directly affects enjoyment. However, some things subtract from enjoyment. We could, therefore, distinguish between goods and bads or positive goods and negative goods. But we can equally well make use of the fact that deprivation of a good is the mirror image of it. Instead of saying that clean air is a good and dirty air is a bad, we can say that clean air in some cities is a *scarce* good.

Scarcity is a central concept in economics. A scarce good is one that is not free in the sense that nobody has to pay for it. In an uncrowded world, gifts of nature such as scenery, water, clean air, privacy, and space are free. But as the world fills up with factories, automobiles, and people, these gifts become scarce; they cannot be had in unlimited quantities and are no longer free. Streams and lakes become polluted with sewage, city air absorbs factory smoke and exhaust fumes, virgin mountain slopes become crowded with ski lifts and crowds, and privacy and freedom diminish in the complexity of an indifferent social life.

The economic concept of scarcity has to be kept distinct from the physical fact that resources are limited. The water in the Atlantic Ocean is limited, for example, but it is not scarce, and likewise air in the atmosphere is limited but not scarce. Scarcity is not an attribute of a good, but the reflection of a situation, the interplay between wants and resources. In contrast to a free good, which can be enjoyed without giving up another good, a scarce good is one that can only be enjoyed by sacrificing the enjoyment of another good.

The concept of scarcity would exist even if physical resources were not limited. For there are, inherent in man, limits on his ability to consume and enjoy. Even if a man had all the money he could possibly use, his activity would be conditioned by scarcity. He would still have to allocate his time if only because life is limited. In choosing a meal, a man has to take account of the fact that his stomach is limited even if he is rich enough to ignore the expense of buying the meal. Life is always conditioned by the fact that time is irreversible and scarce and by limitations on the number of activities that can be pursued at the same time. Scarcity, therefore, gives rise to the act of choice.

Choice is selection from "alternatives." The word itself suggests scarcity. Choice implies two things. It implies a set of things that are available, called *opportunities*. And it implies a criterion of selection called *preferences*. The act of rational choice is the act of selecting the *best*, the most *preferred*, opportunity.

What are preferences? They are a ranking of things according to a criterion of selection. Preferences imply that the enjoyer—the entity making the choice, whether an individual or group—has an interest, but not necessarily a selfish interest, to maximize. An individual may want to maximize "happiness," "utility," "well-being," "enjoyment," or "virtue"; call it what you will. A business firm may want to maximize profits, the capital value of the firm, or the well-being of the managers or owners. A government may want to maximize social welfare or the power of the state or to minimize social tension. On the most general level, preferences imply only that the entity can rank desires in an order according to the degrees of enjoyment their satisfaction would provide.

Rational choice implies more than this, however. It also implies that the entity not only can but *will* select the most desired opportunity and that the ranking of desires into preferences is done in a noncontradictory way. Thus if a man prefers A to B and B to C, then he will be inconsistent if he does not also prefer A to C. If a man prefers a redhead to a blonde and a blonde to a brunette, surely he also prefers the redhead to the brunette. If he said he preferred the brunette to the redhead, he would contradict himself.

In simple choices, rational men and groups do not contradict themselves, but in complex decisions, groups and even individuals can be placed in positions where they do contradict themselves. This possibility is of great importance, not only in analyzing schizophrenic behavior and in formulating appropriate structures for government decision making but also in dealing with quite common contradictions within the human personality. Complex decision-making procedures of any entity may involve contradictions.

The act of choice is the action of making a decision. A chooser is a decision maker. He confronts aspirations with limitations, preferences with opportunities, intentions with resources.

The act of choice integrates the psychological categories of wants, desires, and preferences with the objective categories of resources, goods, and opportunities. Wants (which are passive) produce desires (which are active), and desires are transformed into preferences; resources produce goods, and goods are transformed into opportunities. Preferences are joined with opportunities in the act of choice.

The act of rational choice leads to the law of economy. This law states that a given benefit will be achieved at the lowest cost; of things yielding equal satisfaction, rationality implies choice of the cheapest. The corollary is that at a given cost the best will be chosen; among things costing the same, rationality means choice of that which yields the most satisfaction. You never pay more for a particular thing than you have to. You find the highest market for something you want to sell, the cheapest for something you want to buy.

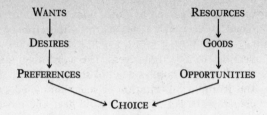

The law of economy is the basic postulate of economics and indeed a basic law of all human activity. It means that of two equal qualities of gasoline you would buy the cheapest. It means that if two colleges charged the same tuition, you would choose to enter that which you thought was better adapted to developing your talents and satisfying your social interests. It means that a government choosing among weapons systems that cost the same will choose the one it believes to be most effective. It means that a composer choosing among notes will select those which produce the greatest effect and that an author choosing a word will select the most effective one in his vocabulary.

Simple, obvious, even trivial though this principle seems, it yields tremendous insight into economic behavior and into fundamental problems of real life. Despite its simplicity—indeed, because of its simplicity—the law of economy gives us invaluable insight into how goods should be produced, distributed, and consumed, how defense strategy should be organized, how a work of art should be arranged, and even how a bride should be chosen!

3

What Is Political Economy?

James O'Connor

> *Political economy, in the widest sense, is the science of the laws governing the production and exchange of the material means of subsistence in human society.* (*Frederick Engels,* Anti-Duhring)

The central social fact in the United States, Western Europe, and Japan is the division of society into two main classes—the handful who own the means of production and control social production knowledge, and the vast majority who are compelled to sell their power to work for wages and salaries. In the Third World, capitalism has also divided the population into classes—landlords, bankers, merchants, and industrialists, on the one side; farm tenants, share-croppers, wage laborers, etc., on the other.

Today, compared with a century ago, there are fewer *independent* tradesmen, artisans, farmers, and men in the professions and a greater number of wage and salary workers in both the economically developed and underdeveloped capitalist societies. In the developed countries, there are fewer (much richer) capitalists, or men who live by buying and exploiting the labor power of others. In the underdeveloped countries, there are relatively fewer independent peasants, workers in cottage industries, craftsmen, and others who own their land and tools and produce objects for their immediate use, or the direct use of others. Everywhere in the world capitalist system, ownership of the means of production and control of production knowledge are increasingly *concentrated in fewer hands*.

The social relations within production and also in political life between those who monopolize the means of production and the vast majority of society which lives by selling labor power are central to the study of the development of capitalist society. Political economy uses the theoretical category "relations of production" to signify the actual social relations between those who buy labor power and those who sell labor power, or between those who organize labor and those who labor.

The social character of production is another central feature of capitalist society. People satisfy their needs by working with each other—whether or not under the same roof—not in isolation. People also work for each other, in the sense that what they produce is used by others. "All these needs are satisfied socially," Ernest Mandel writes, "not by a purely physiological activity, by single combat between the individual and the forces of nature, but by activity which results from mutual relations established between the members of a human group." [1] Again compared with one hundred years ago, workers today are more interdependent, and there exists a greater social division of labor and specialization of function.

There has emerged one single world capitalist system (the laws of development of which are modified by the survival of independent national tariff, fiscal, monetary, and other policies), a single world labor force, and a single world product. Within the developed capitalist countries technical knowledge—a productive force far more social than the traditional "factors of production," land, buildings, machinery, and physical labor power—has become a major form of labor power. And within the large corporations the growth of the "technostructure" replaces individual determination of investment and other decisions with social decision-making.[2] Two centuries ago, the vast majority of mankind lived in comparative economic isolation, and it was possible to calculate more accurately an individual's contribution to production. Today, few people live in societies unintegrated into the world market. The objects people use are made of materials drawn from dozens of countries. No one would be "worth" the equivalent of even a few dollars yearly were his or her labor not "mixed" or combined with the labor of millions of others.

As with production, so with needs; social production creates social

---

[1] Ernest Mandel, *Marxist Economic Theory* (Volume I), (New York: Monthly Review Press, 1968), p. 24.
[2] John Kenneth Galbraith, *The New Industrial State* (Boston: Houghton Mifflin, 1967), Chapter Four.

needs. It is true that the individual consumer decides what commodities to purchase, and in what quantities, but these decisions are rooted in his or her economic and social needs—that is to say, by the relation to the means of production. A day laborer requires food of a certain bulk, protein content, and so on. Nearly all workers in the developed countries today require fast ground transportation, as a result of the separation of places of work, residence, and recreation. It would be impossible for society to reproduce itself in its given material condition were these needs not satisfied.

Political economy uses the theoretical categories "social product" to indicate the actual material product of society and "socially necessary costs" to signify the material and social requirements of workers. In all but some primitive societies, owing to the development of technology and the rise of class society, the social product is more than enough to cover socially necessary costs. The difference between the social product and socially necessary costs, or that part of the social product which is not needed to maintain the producers and their society in their given productive state, is called "economic surplus."

The economic surplus is used in many ways, some of which potentially free people from socially necessary labor, some of which do not. An example of the first is the construction of more and better tools; examples of the second are advertising outlays and military expenditures. Individuals decide the actual uses of the economic surplus, but these decisions are largely predetermined by social relationships. For example, large corporations must invest a certain portion of their net income to protect their markets from their competitors, and the very rich must consume part of their incomes in the form of luxuries in order to maintain their social status.

To summarize, political economy today requires more than ever a theory of social production and social need, in particular, a theory of the actual social relations between people as producers, the development of these relations, and their reconciliation or non-reconciliation.

Historically, society as a whole, at any given time, is subject to a conflict between the economic and social classes that comprise it. In capitalist society the relations between the working class and the capitalist class constitute the basic conflict. Day-to-day relations on the job, labor strikes, lockouts, political agitation around issues such as social insurance, minimum wages, and so on, are normal in or *integral* to capitalist society. These forms of class conflict are the real activity which political economy denotes theoretically as "the contradiction between social production and private ownership of the means of production." It is important to realize that the real social antagonisms *which are specific to capitalism* arise because of the *existence* of a wage earning class engaged in social production for profit, alongside the *existence* of a capitalist class which monopolizes ownership over the means of production.

This conflict can be *contained* politically, by the development of a consensus politics or by the use of force. In the United States, labor unions have the protection of law to the degree that organizational work is confined to narrow constituencies and agitational work to strictly economic demands. In all the developed capitalist countries, rising material standards of life, social legislation, a degree of political influence won by or granted to labor, and the abolition or reduction of gross forms of exploitation in the major industries have resulted from working class struggle and (dialectically) helped to contain class conflict. But the developments which in the past have led to prevailing "consensus" between labor and capital are incomprehensible unless it is understood that they are rooted in class conflict.

Class conflict (as part of the relations of production) is critical in the determination of the use of labor power and economic resources, the size and composition of the social product, the methods used in production, the distribution of the social product between classes, and the disposition of the economic surplus. To cite examples, under certain conditions, militant labor struggles for higher wages and shorter hours of work lead to the substitution of labor-using production techniques by labor-saving techniques. Strikes, lockouts, and political agitation help to determine the distribution of income. And, in the last analysis, the seizure of state power and the means of production by the working class (or a group acting in the name of the working class) leads to profound changes in the composition and distribution of the social product.

The relations of production are also critical in the determination of social, cultural, and political relations. To use one example, the education system in the United States systematically excludes Marxist, anarchist, and other doctrines of social conflict and disharmony as social theory, concentrating instead on doctrines of social harmony and responsibility. Primary and secondary education also structure human personality to the requirements of wage labor; teachers and administrators place a premium on the willingness of students to follow instructions, to compete with fellow students, and to respect private property.[3]

II

Economic theory, the key element of social theory, consists of the ideas people have about themselves in the realm of economic production, distribution, and exchange. Bourgeois economic theory is the theory adopted by the capitalist class, and used to explain the economy to itself, and to other classes. In the universities today, bourgeois economic theory has a clear monopoly, reflecting and reinforcing the monopoly the capitalist class enjoys over the means of production.

There are two main branches of economic theory, micro-economics and macro-economics. The first branch concerns itself with the allocation of scarce economic resources between competing uses; it attempts to "explain" the determination of prices, the composition of production, the production techniques employed, and the distribution of income. In terms of its *aims*, although certainly not its methods, economic theory partly parallels political economy. The second branch deals with the determination of income, production, investment, and employment *as a whole*, including the private *level* (as opposed to the price *structure*, the study of which is

---

[3] Herb Gintis, "Production Functions in the Economics of Education and the Characteristics of Worker Productivity," manuscript.

undertaken by micro-economics). Again, there is a partial correspondence between the aims of macro-economics and political economy.

Both bourgeois micro- and macro-economics at their roots are unscientific, except in the limited sense of providing practical guides to action for the capitalist class. Neither branch of economics, alone or together, affords an understanding of the development of capitalism as a whole, and neither branch has any immediate value for the working class.

The reason that both branches of economic theory are unscientific is that they employ *individual*, as opposed to social, theoretical categories. The basic unit of analysis is the individual, as worker, *rentier*, entrepreneur, or consumer. Micro-economics begins with an analysis of the "economically rational" individual in isolation from other individuals, whose behavior is assumed to be based on his own unique "utility function." Individual behavior is then "aggregated" and the result is labeled "social behavior." Two examples are the aggregation of the demand for a commodity by a number of different individuals and the aggregation of the marginal cost curves of competitive firms to derive total industry supply.

Macro-economics derives its "social" categories by aggregating individual "preferences" and "propensities"—that is, individual psychological motivations and responses—and abstracts from the ever-changing, concrete socio-economic setting which decisively conditions behavior. In particular, "business forecasts" are given undue weight in the analysis of the cyclical movements of the economy, without reference to objective factors such as the rate of profit. The concepts of individual propensities, preferences, and "anticipations and expectations" are very fragile foundations for such an elaborate structure as macro-theory. This approach is not able to identify the various *social* constituents of individual behavior.

The development of micro-economics as a field of study provides one proof of this. During the late 19th and 20th centuries *actual* social production has pressed on micro-economics' basic *theoretical* categories. In place of a thorough revision of these categories, micro-economists have "tacked on" new "social" categories. Examples of new categories invented to comprehend the *fact* of social production and social need are numerous— social costs, social benefits, external economies, spill-over effects, wash effects, and linkage effects are some of the best known. That social categories are introduced merely to modify the basic analysis is reflected in the language of modern micro-economists: "*In addition to* the direct productivity of a skilled man's abilities, conceptualized in the economist's 'marginal productivity,' *we should not overlook his indirect influences upon the productivity of others, and of non-human resources as well* [emphasis added]."[4] The foundations of micro-economics thus remain unchanged, and the "maximizing individual," individual commodity demand, and private production still lie at the center of economic theory.

Another indication of the inability of micro-theory to comprehend actual social activity is the treatment it affords the activity of workers. Micro-economics separates the individual into *consumer* and *worker*. Commodity demand is seen as the "revealed preference" of the individual consumer;

---

[4] Martin Bronfenbrenner, "University Programs and Brain Drains: The Case of Development Economics," manuscript.

the choice of occupation is also seen as an individual choice. But labor strikes are not viewed as the *social* "revealed preference" of workers acting collectively. There is not considered to be any fundamental antagonism between wage labor and capital. On the contrary, strikes are viewed as a special application of the theory of bargaining, or bilateral monopoly, equally applicable to ordinary commodity market situations.

Macro-economics also provides the proof of its own lack of scientific foundation. First, macro-theory has failed to develop a theory of the causes of state spending; in its place there is merely a set of hypotheses of the effects of state spending. Therefore, macro-economic theory is unable to evaluate the relation between private and "public" spending. Thus, "growth models in their present form," Peacock and Wiseman write, "cannot be treated as anything more than exercises in a technique of arrangement." [5] Macro-theory is unscientific because it contains no theory of state expenditures. A well-known macro-economist notes that government expenditures can be dealt with in one of three ways: they can be assumed to be "exogenous" to the system, they can be merged with consumption expenditures, or they can be assumed "away altogether." [6] The latter alternative is completely unsatisfactory, and to assume that government expenditures are determined by "outside" forces is tantamount to admitting that they are beyond the realm of comprehension. Merging all government spending with private consumption merely substitutes fiction for fact.

The reason why macro-economists do not know the actual determinants of state spending is that there are no markets for most goods and services provided by the state, and hence it is not possible to lean on the doctrine of revealed preferences. A theory of state expenditure requires an investigation of the social and political forces influencing and conditioning demand. But micro-economics forbids any such inquiry, putting aside statistical "explanations" such as the age composition of the population, climatic conditions, and so on.

Paradoxically, government spending is increasingly placed in the middle of discussions of growth and stagnation. Most economists view the state as a kind of *deus ex machina* and assume that government spending not only can but should make up the difference between the actual volume of private expenditures and the level of spending which will keep unemployment down to a tolerable minimum. "In our time," Paul Baran writes, "faith in the manipulative omnipotence of the state has all but displaced analysis of its social structure and understanding of its political and economic functions." [7] State expenditures in this way are incorporated into models of fluctuations and growth. What is considered, however, is not what actually determines government spending, but rather the volume of spending and taxation necessary to achieve certain goals given certain assumptions about and characteristics of the model.

---

[5] Alan T. Peacock and Jack Wiseman, *The Growth of Public Expenditures in the United Kingdom* (Princeton, N.J.: Princeton University Press, 1961), p. 10.

[6] Evsey Domar, *Essays in the Theory of Economic Growth* (New York: Oxford University Press, 1957), p. 20.

[7] Paul Baran, "On the Political Economy of Backwardness," A. N. Agarwala and S. P. Singh, editors, *The Economics of Underdevelopment* (London: Oxford University Press, 1958), p. 86.

Secondly, macro-economic theory is essentially *reified* theory—for example, it poses the question "what causes inflation?" when the real question is *"who* causes inflation?" Thus, it cannot comprehend the totality of production relations which leads to inflation. This can be illustrated in the form of a hypothesis: suppose that inflation is caused by the classes or social strata which benefit from inflation, and, further, that anti-inflation policy is in the hands of those who caused the inflation. Anti-inflation policy will leave some classes or strata better off and some worse off, and among those who are better off will be the strata which were the prime movers of the inflation, the original beneficiaries. Next, suppose that the capitalist class employs economists to study inflation; indeed, not only to study inflation, but to find acceptable ways to cause inflation. In this case, it is clear that a political economy of inflation would require that economists study not only their employers, but also themselves. Macro-economists adamantly refuse to do either, they refuse to consider themselves a part of the experimental field. Yet it is obvious that economics is a social phenomenon, and because of its technical character it may be true that only economists are equipped to comprehend their own social role.

Thirdly, macro-economics fails to disaggregate the economy and is not able to deal with the question of the effects of government spending on the structure of the economy. To take an example, disaggregation of Federal government expenditures in the United States in recent years would demonstrate that compensatory spending leads to an expansion of the corporate sector at the expense of small business, and to the further concentration of capital as a result of urban renewal, transportation investments, and military spending. One of the hypotheses of political economy is that the concentration of capital is the *intention*, as well as the result, of corporate-inspired government policies. In French economic planning, this fact is not concealed.[8]

The ultimate proof of the class character of economic theory consists of the *uses* to which it is put. In point of fact, the owners of the large corporations constitute the dominant stratum of the capitalist class, and they use economic theory in a number of important ways.

The corporate owners long ago accepted the inevitability and desirability of self-regulation and control,[9] or government intervention in the economy. Macro-economics has been adopted as a major instrument of national and international economic planning, as it has proven in the past to have practical value in helping the state to underwrite business investments and business losses, or, to use a euphemism, in helping to stabilize the economy and encourage it to grow. What is more, its practical value to the corporations has been greatly enhanced by the fact that business in general, as well as the corporate leaders, have in the past taken it for granted that macro-theory *is* an accurate description of the mechanics of operation of the United States economy.

In its general outlines, the process of corporate policy formation is

---

[8] Andrew Shonfield, *Modern Capitalism: The Changing Balance of Public and Private Power* (New York: Oxford University Press, 1965), pp. 138–140, 149–150.
[9] Gabriel Kolko, *The Triumph of Conservatism* (Chicago: Quadrangle Press, 1967); James Weinstein, *The Corporate Ideal in the Liberal State* (Boston: Beacon Press, 1968).

simple and straightforward. Studies of inflation, the balance of payments, foreign aid, wage/productivity relations, and other pressing corporate problems are conducted under the auspices of corporation-dominated institutions —Harvard University, Committee for Economic Development, Brookings Institution, Foreign Policy Association, Stanford Research Institute, and other key corporate policy-planning organizations.[10] In turn, these studies become guidelines for Federal government economic policy, and set the framework within which debates take place on specific issues. The interests of the corporate owners dominate the Executive branch of the Federal government and their political deputies are in a strategic position to translate the plans of their policy planners into practice.[11] The health of modern capitalism depends almost exclusively on the health of the hundred or so dominant corporations, and thus fiscal and other policies must of necessity be formulated in their interests.

Micro-economics has also been adopted as a tool of the intra-corporate and micro-economic planning. This branch of economic theory still provides opportunities for esoteric exercises in various branches of mathematics, yet even in this great warehouse of "empty economic boxes" there is a dominant pragmatic tendency. Micro-theory is important in cost-benefit analyses of infra-structure projects required by the corporations. Micro-theory is also used by financial analysts to judge future corporate rates of return by estimating the effects of changes in the outputs of substitute and complementary products on prices and costs. Micro-economics is also used to introduce "efficiency" into Federal government departments and agencies. Perhaps of greater long-run importance, the corporate owners have adapted micro-theory to its immediate operational needs by emphasizing the practical component—linear programming. Thus, even in the traditional home of "pure theory" the pragmatists in the service of the corporate ruling class exercise dominant influence.

III

At this point, we may summarize the differences in scope and method of political economy and bourgeois economic theory. First, political economy concerns itself with the social relations between individuals, employs real, historical causes, and its causal variables are not abstractions such as the interest rate, the supply of money, and the level of prices, but rather *human agents*. Economic theory is concerned with the relations between individuals and *things*, for example, the "utility" of a commodity to its owners. It also deals with the relations between abstract conceptions; an illustration is "quantity theory of money," which hypothesizes that under certain conditions an expansion of the supply of money "causes" an increase in prices. Economic theory by and large ignores the social relations between individuals and classes, and, strictly speaking, is not a social science.

---

[10] David Eakins, Ph.D. dissertation, University of Wisconsin, 1964.
[11] G. William Domhoff, *Who Rules America?* (Englewood Cliffs, N.J.: Prentice-Hall, 1967); Gabriel Kolko, *The Roots of American Foreign Policy* (Boston: Beacon Press, 1969), Chapter One.

Second, political economy attempts to comprehend society as a whole, its total development, in terms of the relations between its constituent parts —the relations of production, social, and political relations. Economic theory confines itself to exchange or market relations and deliberately separates itself from "sociology," "social psychology," and "political science."

Third, and related to the first two differences, political economy is a *critical* science in the sense that it views the capitalist mode of production (including private property, wage labor, profits, and so on) as a historical phenomenon. Economic theory takes the foundations of capitalism for granted, fails to subject these foundations to analysis, and is concerned exclusively with the specific malfunctions of the system. Capitalism functions less and less rationally as time goes on, and hence both micro- and macro-elements become more and more policy-oriented, "purely pragmatic . . . technique(s) for the practical consolidation of capitalism." [12] In short, bourgeois economic theory is an *instrumental* science, specifically, the instrument of the owning class. Economic theorists do not seek to remove the extremes of society—capital and labor, rich and poor, privileged and underprivileged, rulers and ruled—but rather attempt to, in Marx's words, "weaken their antagonisms and transform them into a harmonious whole." Consequently, in the last analysis, economic theory is used to manipulate human beings, and for this reason thwarts our free development.[13]

Is Economics Obsolete? No, Underemployed

Charles L. Schultze

The current disenchantment, particularly among the young, with the optimistic, problem-solving approach to social issues that characterized the 1960s not surprisingly has rubbed off on economics. As a number of other articles in this symposium demonstrate, many members of the economics profession now question the relevance and meaning of the fundamental

---

[12] Mandel, *op. cit.*, p. 15.

[13] A well-known economist writes: "In 1960 I went on record in opposition to an immediate enactment of the [Truth in Lending Bill]. At that time I was concerned about an impending recession—which did set in toward the end of the year—and feared that the bill would have a deflationary effect over the short run. Some people upon learning that installment credit costs were, say, 16% per annum, rather than 6% as they had thought, might be shocked and postpone their purchases. Because of the possibility of such an 'announcement effect,' *the time at which new information on interest rates is given to consumers is of importance* [emphasis added]." George Katona, *The Mass Consumption Society* (New York: McGraw-Hill, 1964), p. 241, note 6.

assumptions underlying the economics that is currently taught and practiced. Some of the critics have been saying these things for several years but have only lately found someone to listen. A few are recent converts from orthodoxy. And among the younger members of the profession, these critical views are becoming fairly widespread.

There is merit in some of the criticism, but little in the general notion that economics has grown obsolete or irrelevant. The indictment against it should read not that economics is irrelevant but that its very relevant tools have been too sparingly applied to the kinds of problems now confronting us. In some instances, economics is a victim of its own highly relevant successes.

One of the major counts in the indictment is that Keynesian economics is incapable of handling the central policy issue of the era: how to make full employment compatible with reasonable price stability. Yet, in the twenty-five years since the Second World War, a period during which Keynesian fiscal policy emerged from advanced theory courses to become the conventional wisdom of Presidents, unemployment in no year averaged more than 7 per cent, compared with the 1930s, during which unemployment never fell below 14 per cent. The major depressions and massive financial panics that sporadically afflicted industrial economies for the century-and-a-half before 1940 are no longer even a dim threat. And aside from the brief aftermath of World War II, the inflations that quite rightly gave Americans cause for worry have not exceeded 5 or 6 per cent per year at their worst, a far cry from the persistent rates of 10 and 20 per cent per year with which some nations of the world have been living for decades.

Modern economics can and has successfully prescribed the means of preventing large-scale unemployment without bringing on major inflation. It can devise, and has devised, ways of preventing major inflation without precipitating serious depressions. Although the prescriptions of economists are not solely responsible for the sharply improved postwar performance of the Western economies, they surely played a major role. What we now label a failure of theory and policy has been a roaring success by pre-Keynesian standards.

The puzzle economics has not yet solved, and which critics quite properly point to, is the worrisome, but far from catastrophic, inflation that appears when overall demand and supply come into balance during periods of high, but not excessive, prosperity. Yet this failure may stem not so much from shortcomings of the basic theoretical apparatus as from the difficulty of making precise measurements. Economics has little difficulty in prescribing counterbalances to large swings in prices and employment. But in recent years we have been dealing with variations in the employment rate between 3.5 and 6 per cent and with differences of 2 to 3 per cent in the rate of inflation. And within these ranges the analysis of how wages and prices interact and the prescribing of policy require more precise and complex measurements than we have yet devised. Still, a good carpenter can make a perfectly satisfactory joint with instruments that would be useless for calibrating the tolerances in an Apollo guidance mechanism. Which is by no means to say that the carpenter should throw away his tools as being irrelevant to modern society.

A better understanding of the inflation that accompanies high (even though not excessively high) employment may not ultimately rest on some radical new breakthrough in economic theory. Rather it may well result from gradual improvement in our knowledge about labor markets, about the role of people's expectations during inflation, and about how the market power of unions and business is translated into specific wage and price decisions. Policy instruments to deal with the problem may correspondingly be found in improvements in manpower training programs and antitrust policy, and in the gradual development of wage-price standards sufficiently flexible to avoid smothering the economy in regulation, yet tough enough to influence a key decision when it counts.

Whatever the outcome, any successful prescription for jointly achieving full employment and price stability will undoubtedly contain a large dose of what I may loosely call Keynesian economics—extended, modified, and supplemented, but not abandoned.

Another major indictment against contemporary economics runs approximately like this: Because economics ignores the substantial economic power now concentrated in large firms and unions, and because on a larger scale it accepts the fundamental status quo of current power relationships in society and ignores the relationship between the distribution of power and the distribution of income, it either has no policy prescriptions for pressing social problems or offers ameliorative remedies that only scratch the surface.

To some extent, the charge that modern economics has produced little in the way of remedies for the current siege of social problems is valid, but paradoxically this is so for reasons precisely opposite to those advanced by economics' critics. Economics may be faulted, not because it possesses a theoretical apparatus of no relevance to current social problems, but because in many cases it has failed to apply, or only recently begun to apply, an apparatus that is particularly well suited to dealing with a large segment of those problems.

Much of economics deals with the problem of how a decentralized decision-making system can be made to provide proper incentives so that individual decision-makers, apparently pursuing their own ends, nevertheless tend to act in a way consistent with the public good—the "invisible hand" of Adam Smith. Since time immemorial it has been too often assumed that the apparatus of analysis which dealt with this problem applied only to the private market and that the public sector of the economy must operate by a completely different set of rules. Yet, a little reflection will demonstrate that many of the major social problems with which government is now seized require solutions under which the decisions of thousands of communities and millions of individuals are somehow channeled toward nationally desired objectives.

Cleaning up environmental pollution, changing the delivery structure of an ineffective and inequitable medical-care system, providing compensatory educational programs, and offering training and labor market opportunities to the previously disadvantaged depend for their success or failure on day-to-day decisions made by particular communities, business firms, and individuals throughout the nation. No program that merely seeks to transfer these hundreds of thousands, indeed millions, of decisions to a few officials in Washington can hope to be effective. Nor, conversely, can any program that simply shovels federal revenues to state and local governments, and then hopes for the best. Somehow institutional frameworks and incentives that guide a multitude of particular decisions toward national ends have to be developed.

And here, traditional economics and its incentive-oriented apparatus suggest a number of approaches. The major problems of environmental pollution, for instance, stem from the fact that air and water are given free to all comers, and like any good that is given away these commodities will be over-used; with no incentives to conserve them, neither individuals nor business firms will lend their talents toward developing and using new conservation technology. But old-fashioned economic analysis suggests that placing a stiff charge on the dumping of pollutants into the air or water will marvelously stimulate the discovery of production methods that reduce pollution, just as the rising cost of labor has promoted a steady growth in techniques to increase output per man-hour, at a rate that roughly doubles the efficiency of labor every twenty-five years. Economics also brings into question whether it makes any more sense to rely solely on detailed regulation and court decision for minimizing pollution than it would to use these devices for minimizing other industrial costs.

As for health care, conventional economics indicates that the nation can hardly hope to have an efficient use of scarce medical resources when the current health care system provides a powerful set of incentives to waste and misdirect those resources: insurance plans that cover hospitalization but not office visits, thereby encouraging excessive use of hospitals; private and governmental insurance that reimburses hospitals on a cost-plus basis, penalizing the efficient and rewarding the inefficient; financial rewards keyed to dramatic intervention (the cardiac surgeon) but quite niggardly for the practice of preventive medicine; etc.

In the area of public education, economic analysis points to the difficulty of getting superior performances from a monopoly with a captive market (the public school system of the inner city) and can help design means of introducing incentives for improvement and innovations. It also emphasizes the impossibility of designing and enforcing urban land-use plans in an economic environment where many aspects of the tax laws and land laws provide large positive incentives for urban sprawl. It provides insights into the problem of urban congestion by showing how most auto users are not now required to pay the real social costs that their ride imposes on other citizens and how this fact provides incentives for socially excessive use of crowded highways.

As these examples indicate, many of our social problems arise because the current system of markets, laws, and customs provides positive incentives for individuals, business firms, and local communities to engage in what can objectively be called antisocial conduct. Correspondingly, substantial improvement in these areas is most unlikely to come from governmental programs that rely principally on traditional, centralized decision-making, but must rest in part on a restructuring of incentives and institutions—a task for which economics, far from being obsolete, has been too little used.

In terms of social problems, economic analysis also has a relevant role to play as a bearer of unpleasant truths—that in some areas of social policy the nation is seeking to pursue conflicting goals. It is literally impossible, for example, to design a welfare program that simultaneously meets four often-sought goals: providing a generous minimum income to the poor; preserving incentives for productive work by avoiding a rapid reduction in welfare benefits as recipients begin to earn outside money; instituting welfare reform in a way that does not reduce the income of any beneficiaries under the current system; and preventing such large budgetary costs that those not far above the poverty line have to be taxed heavily to support those just below it. No program can do all of these things simultaneously.

In the same vein, a public service job program must seek a compromise between two conflicting objectives: to provide wages and working conditions sufficiently attractive to appeal to the unemployed and the low-paid casual worker and to avoid drawing workers away from productive jobs elsewhere. A national medical program cannot at one and the same time guarantee virtually all the medical care private citizens can demand regardless of income, provide a financial mechanism and a set of incentives that hold down escalation of costs, and avoid comprehensive detailed regulation of medical care by Washington bureaucrats.

Pointing out relevant truths of this sort, however, appears to be one of the factors underlying the charges of irrelevancy leveled against economics. Such observations about conflicting objectives imply the need for compromise. But to those for whom compromise is inherently evil, and for whom most problems fundamentally trace back to the greed of the power structure, calling attention to the technical difficulties that would face even a liberated world seems to be irrelevant at best and obstructionist at worst.

A similar reaction, perhaps, will greet the assertion that there are many social issues in which economics should not be expected to play a central role. Economists can seek to ferret out the economic consequences of racial discrimination and help in devising means to expand opportunities for racial minorities. But the eradication of discrimination itself will necessarily depend heavily on a combination of legal steps, education, and political leadership. Economists can trace many of the causes of financial crisis now afflicting large central cities. But the job of rationalizing the archaic jumble of local government in metropolitan areas, thereby providing a viable economic base for large cities, is a task beyond what should be expected of economists. While many of our social ills have major economic consequences, there are some that will yield only to political solutions.

One area in which the economics profession has a decidedly mixed record is the field of income distribution. The problem is not so much a deficiency in economic theory as it relates to income distribution but rather a tendency on the part of the profession to exhibit an excessive concern for efficiency as compared with equity in dealing with situations where the two are in conflict.

An economic system can be very efficient in providing private and public goods to meet the demands generated by a very lopsided income distribution —fine mansions, good public protection, and rapid mass transit for affluent suburbanites while the poor live in hovels, are victimized by crime, and spend inordinate amounts of time getting to work. The formal structure of economics recognizes that its rules for an efficient allocation of resources are blind with respect to the distribution of income; that efficiency considerations alone cannot justify policies which have significant effects on that distribution; and, conversely, that policies which redistribute income in a direction society thinks more just may be warranted even when those policies reduce efficiency. Most economists working in the field of taxation have paid close attention to matters of distribution, and the large majority have raised their voices in favor of strengthening the redistributive features of the tax system. On the other hand, in many areas of public policy, economists as a body have had a bias toward letting efficiency considerations rule.

Higher efficiency, however, is often secured at the expense of particular groups of workers and individual communities. It is not so much that the remedies for these problems need be sought in protectionism, subsidies to dying industries, or rigid featherbedding work rules. Rather, an affluent society might well be expected to provide better income guarantees to workers then ours now does, particularly to older workers, whose skills have been rendered obsolete by economic change and growth. Economists have generally been much more active in pointing to the efficiency gains of unimpeded economic change than in devising means of minimizing its impact on particular workers and communities. In a similar vein, it is only recently that economists and statisticians have begun to look deeply into the often perverse income distribution consequences of many public programs—farm subsidies, low tuition at state universities, urban highway building, irrigation and flood control projects, and the like.

Paying more attention to the problems of income distribution, however, would not rescue conventional economics from attack. To the Western economist, income distribution problems can be approached through such pragmatic measures as reforming the tax system, restructuring welfare programs, and providing more equal educational opportunities. But to radical critics, these are Band-Aid measures. The basic cause of maldistribution of income, they say, is the maldistribution of power that inevitably accompanies a market-oriented free enterprise system. Any pragmatic measures will eventually be perverted by the holders of economic power to their own ends. Only the demise of the market system itself will make it possible to provide a just distribution of the fruits of man's productive activity.

Here indeed is a fundamental difference in approach. An evaluation of the merits of the case would go far beyond the scope of this article, and, in any event, logical argument seldom makes converts in this controversy. I cannot resist pointing out, however, that in any complex society, whatever its original structure, there is a tendency for power, influence, and wealth to become concentrated in relatively few hands, and this is particularly true whenever societies seek to provide incentives for abundant production. Eternal vigilance is the price of an egalitarian distribution of income. Even in the "post-revolutionary state," the old pragmatic measures of progressive taxation, transfer payments such as welfare benefits, and equal educational opportunities would still be important tools for securing a just distribution of income.

There remain two major areas in which even the most sympathetic view of modern economics would have to concede that charges against the state of the art do strike home. One involves the behavior of producers, the other, that of consumers.

The panoply of tools with which economics seeks to explain how resources are allocated in the private market relies quite heavily on the premise of profit-maximizing firms, each responding to but not controlling the market in which it operates and making decisions subject to reasonably good knowledge about the future consequences of those decisions. For purposes of analyzing the long-run effects of economic policy actions, this "model" of the world is quite serviceable. In the long run, firms do seek to maximize profits; they cannot control basic changes in their economic environment; and there is sufficient feedback from their decisions to provide reasonably accurate information. But in the short run, the behavior of firms with respect to modest changes in prices, wages, and investment policy is much less predictable. They can insulate their own markets against moderate threats; their search for long-run profits is roughly consistent with a number of alternative short-term strategies; and before the feedback from their decisions reaches them, they are faced with great uncertainty.

The inability of economic theory to predict the short-run behavior of firms might not be so important except for the problem of inflation. The long-run allocation of resources, and the shift in price relationships that brings it about, probably does proceed much in the manner explained by economic theory. But it may take place around a generally rising price trend. And unlike market shares, inflation is generally irreversible. A series of short-term decisions on the part of many firms and unions can lead to continuing inflation. The ·weakness of current economics in predicting the short-run behavior of modern firms and unions thus turns into a serious deficiency in terms of the ability of economists to explain today's inflation *cum* unemployment.

The second charge hits home in the sensitive area of consumer preference theory. Traditional economics takes consumer tastes and preferences as given. It neither looks behind them nor seeks to weigh their relative merits. This approach has two consequences. First, the economist has little to say about the social implications of advertising practices that create and destroy preferences, or about the social waste represented by the resources devoted to the satisfaction of manipulated tastes. Nor does he have anything to contribute to the deeper problem of the way in which basic preferences themselves respond to economic development, except to note that "yes, this does indeed happen, and the sociologists better get to work."

Second, and perhaps more important, the economist, by taking individual preferences as given and absolute, sharply limits the field of his analysis when it comes to many matters of public policy. The tools of economics are designed to show how resources can best be deployed to meet society's wants. By its assumption that the relevant social wants are based on the existing preferences of individuals, and that those preferences cannot be questioned, economics has erected a barrier against the use of its analysis in some of the most important matters of public policy. The economist can give advice on the efficiency of the policy instruments chosen to meet an objective. But when it comes to choosing among different objectives, the economist qua economist must be silent. Personal tax cuts that increase society's consumption of beer and whitewall tires hold equal status with increased public expenditures for education. Choice between the two is a "value judgment," which he must eschew.

One promising line of research has been suggested as a means of breaking this impasse. Individual tastes and preferences are themselves hierarchical. Many of our wants are means to a higher set of goals. The demand for the services of physicians and hospitals is itself a means of attaining a higher end, the maintenance of health. The demand for automobiles is (in part, at least) a demand for transportation. To the extent that preferences are considered means to an end, rather than ends themselves, they can be judged in terms of their efficiency—how well does the satisfaction of a particular "lower-order" preference contribute to the attainment of the "higher-order" goal. At least some preferences can be looked at critically and not accepted unquestionably. Once the question of efficiency is introduced, economics is back on familiar ground. It is peculiarly suited to analyze matters of efficiency.

No one has pursued this line of approach at any great length. Whether it will pay off, in terms of providing a more solid footing for economic theory than the shifting sands of "absolute preferences," cannot be foretold. Barring some progress in this area, economics must stand guilty on part of one count of the indictment against it.

Reflection on the nature of radical criticism of economics leads to one further comment. Economics is fundamentally a discipline that deals with man as he is. At its best, economics seeks to harness man's very human motivations to the public interest. Much of the New Left is interested in changing man, elevating his motives, reducing his greed, and intensifying his love for his fellow man. Economics is a social science, but love is a religion. They are both relevant, but they are not on the same plane of discourse. The economist, for example, generally thinks it naïve to hope that pollution will somehow be conquered by bringing public pressure on corporations to exercise "social responsibility." But he does advocate changes in the structure of incentives and the network of contract laws to create a situation in which it becomes a corporation's own self-interest to act "responsibly."

To the young radical, such technical solutions, which accept and play upon man's drive for material advancement, seem shabby and mean. The evangelism of love and understanding mingle curiously with an intolerant hate for institutions built on the search for money and wealth. But they mingle no more curiously than in the Epistles of St. Paul. There is need for both the pragmatist who would harness in the public service man's drive for worldly goods and the idealist who would lift man's drive to more lofty goals. Neither is irrelevant.

5

The Challenge of Radical Political Economics

Raymond S. Franklin and William K. Tabb

This article is an interim summary of the major tenets and general orientation of radical political economy by two authors who are themselves radical economists. What is it? Why is it emerging now? What characterizes its political and ideological perspective?

The second and third questions are perhaps easier to answer than the first. The emergence of a new radical political economy is related to a number of factors: the radicalization of the university campus in the 1960s, the persistence of deeply rooted social and economic problems which appear to transcend the purview of mainstream economics, and, finally, the shrinking confidence of establishment economists themselves. These latter are losing faith in their ability to manage the economy and to cope with such problem areas as the twin processes of inflation and unemployment, imperialist involvements, racism in the marketplace, the fiscal crisis confronting our central cities, and the political barriers obstructing the achievements of modest economic reforms.

The immediate intellectual progenitors of the current crop of radical political economists are a handful of older Marxists. Among the Americans there are Paul Baran, Paul Sweezy, and Harry Magdoff; the main influences from abroad are Maurice Dobb, Joan Robinson, and Ernest Mandel. In addition, Herbert Marcuse (philosopher), William Appleman Williams (historian), and C. Wright Mills (sociologist), all rooted in the Marxian tradition, have had an important influence on many young radical economists. Thus, the current character of radical political economy has been shaped by young and old scholars from a variety of disciplines writing from within and without the orthodox Marxian framework.

It is also important to note that there are many differences among radicals and within the mainstream. We purposely have bypassed some of these differences. We also have omitted discussing areas in which mainstream and radical positions overlap. We do this for the purpose of clarity and realize that these simplifications are in need of modification in many instances.

THE SCOPE OF RADICAL ECONOMICS

Defining the *scope* of radical economics is more complex, but five major elements should be noted. These involve the structural transformation of society, centralized planning, the relationship between political and private economic power, wealth and income distribution, and participation in decision making.

Transforming Society

Unlike their welfarist, liberal mainstream counterparts who accept the broad institutional constraints of the existing system, radical economists are interested in the structural transformation of society. They see themselves as working toward ending, not stabilizing, monopoly capitalism, as working for the establishment of a socialist society which involves participatory planning, public ownership, the elimination of production for profit, and a genuinely egalitarian redistribution of income and wealth. They view theorizing not as an end in itself nor as an aesthetic ritual involving rigorous elegance, however irrelevant; rather, they see it as being linked to their advocacy of fundamental change or to their analysis of the barriers which obstruct such change. Economic analysis must deal with problems concerning political and economic power; rarely are solutions only technical in nature, unrelated to the ends or goals established by the given institutional arrangements. Radical economists, therefore, are devoted to providing the theoretical base for a social transformation; their politics are concerned with producing a political and ideological climate that would stimulate institutional changes.

Centralized Planning

While mainstream economists tend to view planning, especially centralized planning, as authoritarian and antidemocratic, radicals believe such a view is a gross oversimplification. They argue that we already have a great deal of such planning and regimentation in the economy, but it is mainly corporate planning for private ends done by a corporate oligarchy that is hierarchical, self-perpetuating, and largely invisible. Public planning with public ownership would broaden participation and widen the arena of public control over the economy. With respect to socialist planning, most radicals favor decentralized forms; decisions should be made as much as possible at the local level, and citizen-consumer and worker-producer planning groups should decide what and how to produce. Many radicals fear centralized control, whether by large corporations, a powerful Council of Economic Advisers, a Wage-Price Control Board, or a GOSPLAN. Decentralization is a critical element because many radical political economists believe "production" should be concerned not only with the goods and services produced but also, and equally, with the work process itself.

Political and Private Economic Power

Radicals see an intimate relationship between the political apparatus that governs society and the economic concentration of private power. Except for periods of widespread mass agitation, the typical state of affairs is one in which the government does not direct but instead reflects or facilitates the interests of wealth and concentrated economic power. In general, the acquisition of political position and power is seen as something akin to the buying of commodities by the highest bidders.

Income and Wealth Distribution

Because the connection of economic with political power is regarded as so crucial, radical economists assert that any basic understanding of the U.S. social order requires a careful analysis of the distribution of wealth and income and of its generation and transmission over time and between generations. They point to gross inequities in the distribution of wealth. Witness the well-known statistics reported not only in professional journals but also in the more popular business publications:

In almost every year since 1947, the poorest fifth of American families has received only about 5% of the country's total family income while the top fifth got 42%—an 8:1 ratio. . . . From 1949 to 1969 . . . the gap between average real incomes of the poorest and richest fifths of the population widened from less than $11,000 to more than $19,000 in constant 1969 dollars. . . . According to the latest available survey, the top 20% of consumer units . . . owned 77% of all wealth. . . . The richest 2.5% of U.S. families own 44% of all private assets, while the poorest 25% have, on the average, no net worth at all . . . their total debts just equal their assets.[1]

From facts of this kind, which have been more or less permanent features of our system for the past fifty years, radical economists argue that the unequal distribution of income associated with an unequal distribution of wealth begets an unequal distribution of political power. This imbalance influences the political values, objectives, and policies of the government in ways which curtail social and economic justice and obstruct the economic system's ability to recognize and solve its plaguing problems. In other words, the system is flawed intrinsically by the nature of its hierarchical structure, not simply by the absence of "good" people in Congress or the presence of a "bad" president who did "wrong" things. Because mainstream economists either ignore or casually treat the relationship between political power and economic concentration, they do not understand the nature of the system's policy failures. The conscious overlooking of such interconnections, radicals believe, is *poor* not *pure* social science.

Mass Participation

The normative goals that guide the thinking of most radical economists are mass participation in decision making and the equal sharing of society's income and wealth. In practical terms, this implies that economic differences are to be kept to a minimum within a framework which gives cognizance to the variability in aptitudes, tastes, and psychological temperaments among individuals. This vision of society involves the rejection of the idea of individual gain without respect to the general gain or loss experienced by the group; it stresses the importance of moral over economic incentives.

The conception here is probably best expressed in terms of a "solidarity" principle, that is, one works for the benefit of group interests which need to be *consciously* understood by the individual. In the radical vision, group

---

[1] *Business Week*, April 1, 1972, p. 56.

competition is not to be eliminated completely; it is assumed that political and social restraints can be devised which prevent such competition from either turning into anarchy or resulting in the expansion and domination of some group clusters over others.

Community solidarity under capitalism is impossible, according to most radicals, because the life conditions of those who own and control the means of production are almost totally different from those of the people employed in the work places of the society. The use of private rationality by the owners of capital, given the maturation of our economic system, perpetuates an ever-widening gap between the technical means of providing a healthy and sane life for everyone and the alienating social relations of production which thwart the qualitatively more humane use of technical capacities.

This solidarity principle, moreover, leads radicals to reject the mainstream's concept of *efficiency*, which is defined in purely economic and technical terms and which necessitates inequality as a work stimulant. In contemporary U.S. capitalism, the important motivating force that keeps the system functioning "efficiently" is the maintenance of inequities which generate a fear of falling behind Smith and a desire to get ahead of Jones. In a good society, radical economists assert, *efficiency* should have far more than an economic meaning. In its profoundest sense it must involve self-realization through the work process, the worker's control over his own workspace, and a belief that the consumer goods being produced are needed and are important to a good life. These beliefs stem from the more encompassing view among radicals of the human condition: how man is socialized, what motivates him, what defines his welfare and well-being, what constitutes his potential for development and growth. Simply put, the rock upon which almost all mainstream economic thinking rests is that man is "naturally" acquisitive and is primarily motivated by his narrowly defined economic interests; absent is a recognition of the extent to which each man's emotions and values are socially rather than uniquely determined. Because of these beliefs, according to the radical, the mainstream economists obscure both the true potential of man and the social nature of the economic problems of our society.

Man's nature, in the sense that most radicals talk about it, is derived from his social relations in production and consumption. Imbuing man with a false vision which negates his social nature can only lead to alienation and breakdown. Radicals typically argue that the collective nature of production, which is ideologically "privatized" in the form of private ownership and self-interest motivation, is destructive to human development.

In a market-dominated society, cars are produced with built-in obsolescence in order to keep the wheels of profit rolling; the environment is polluted without consideration of its value to those who yearn for clean air and relish the beauty of a natural terrain; the "mere" sentimental value attached to an old landmark building and the security associated with stable neighborhoods are destroyed for the construction of an "efficient" superhighway needed by industry. Furthermore, man's morality, sexuality, and sensibility are manipulated for the purpose of the sale of commodities. In sum and substance, U.S. capitalism destroys human relations in order to maintain purely economic ones involving gain, getting ahead, and the private accumulation of things. To allow the market so much importance in the determination of a person's life-style is to attempt to make of man a one-dimensional creature.

These five general propositions and values which relate to the scope of radical economics will be employed below in the analysis of specific areas and problems. For illustrative purposes, we have selected five topics: imperialism [abbreviated], market stratification, urban malaise, waste and the GNP mania [omitted], and inflation [abbreviated]. Needless to say, there are other important areas with which radicals are deeply concerned, for example, the relationship among value, price, and wages, racial and sexual discrimination, and the origin and nature of "backwardness" in underdeveloped countries.

IMPERIALISM

Capitalism, in the radical view, has an expansionary impulse and a momentum which are driven by the logic of the profit motive. The effect on the economy is to enrich the colonizers and warp indigenous development of the colonized. Dominant members of the corporate hierarchy desire the whole world as a market and wish to control as much of it as possible. Their search for investment opportunities and their need to protect established markets have pushed our economic interests far beyond our geopolitical boundaries. Thus, our government periodically is called into action to protect economic interests (however small they may be relative to the general economy of the United States), to control foreign territories, to subordinate areas, to manipulate weaker foreign ruling oligarchies, and to establish economic dependencies and appendages in ways which have very little to do with the security and sovereignty of the United States.

Latin America is a case in point. There, as in the case of other Third World areas, both liberals and conservatives seek to preserve U.S. ownership claims and to maintain valuable terms of trade advantages. Conservatives favor creating and strengthening military juntas; liberals prefer strengthening a local middle class as a buffer group. The latter policy, under the Alliance for Progress, failed because in the majority of cases it was difficult to create even the facade of bourgeois democracy against the entrenched local oligarchies. Faced with the choice of real reform or military rule, corporate interests accepted "friendly" dictatorships. Business views about Latin America are not based on abstract considerations; they are derived from corporate earnings of profit and interest from Latin America, currently exceeding investments by $1 billion annually.

All this does not mean that the radical economists ignore the chauvinism of the Soviet Union, its bureaucratic styles, and the big-power game it plays in the context of the international nation-state system. But for the most part the Soviet Union's "expansionism" (not to exclude China's) is viewed as border oriented. It is, in other words, perimeter "imperialism" concerned with border security, perhaps pathologically so; it is not one that involves domination entanglements far beyond its frontiers. More often than not, the mainstream assertion that Russia or China is also guilty of imperialism is used as an excuse for ignoring or obscuring the nature of U.S. imperialism; it is rationalized that imperialism appears to be a "way of life" characteristic of all big powers.

In essence, the main area of imperialist penetration is in the underdeveloped world, and it manifests itself primarily in economic terms. It is here that the greatest danger comes from the United States, whose preoccupation with overthrowing "unfriendly" governments, even mildly democratic ones, has been well documented. And while imperialism may be a more general problem which transcends capitalism, to U.S. radicals who live in the United States it is U.S. imperialism against which they are most capable of taking action; therefore, it is U.S. imperialism to which radicals direct their analytic attention.

MARKET STRUCTURE AND STRATIFICATION

Mainstream economists tend to argue that the individual's income and his position in society are directly related to his ability, that altering income and social position is simply a function of acquiring a better education or more skills through work experience. Radical economists believe this is a gross oversimplification—so gross as to be erroneous. Far more goes into the determination of income and social position in the economy than education and work experience. A worker sweeping the floors of an automobile plant in Detroit earns much more than an identical worker sweeping the floor in a New York bank. Contrary to typical mainstream thinking on this matter, this difference has nothing to do with variations in education, work experience, native endowment, or I.Q.; it has little to do with the human capital explanation of the mainstream economists. This difference is a function of industry, location, unionism, and industrial structure.

In addition to institutional considerations, a basic part of the radical argument revolves about the role played by a stratified labor market. Because of the need to put people in various kinds of jobs that are undesirable, the system wittingly or unwittingly generates rules (based on race, sex, ethnic and class origin, and so forth) for allocating people to jobs.

At the bottom of the labor market are those who do the dirty work of the society—the lettuce pickers, chambermaids, dishwashers, janitors, messengers, car washers. For the most part these jobs are low paying, dead-end, and alienating. Such secondary jobs have an extremely high turnover rate; people work for awhile, quit or are fired, and then look for other similar jobs. These workers are mostly blacks, Puerto Ricans, Chicanos, women, or teenagers.

On the next rung up are workers who do routine primary work—tedious manual labor such as assembly-line work, construction work, menial sales or clerical work. Some of these jobs offer a chance for promotion, union protection, and better pay; these are mostly held by white ethnics.

The line between primary and secondary jobs is not always distinct; thus a typist in a typing pool or a keypunch operator is generally in the secondary job market, whereas a personal secretary would be in the primary one.

Below the secondary work force is the welfare population. Above the routine primary jobs are the creative workers, for example, professionals, media people, managers and executives. At the very top are those who receive their income from ownership rather than from participation in the labor market.

While not immutable, such stratification has a strong propensity to maintain itself; it will not be altered without profound change in the rules of the game. If, for example, welfare payments rise to levels that people could live on, then the poorly paid low status job loses its stranglehold. Welfare payments (or any income maintenance or minimum income scheme) must not be too adequate, otherwise secondary workers will lose the incentive to work in those jobs. Nor is it clear that a family assistance or negative income tax plan would overcome this incentive problem. If adequate income or decent housing is offered the very poor, then the working poor—who perceive themselves as bearing the tax burden of paying these costs—become upset. Therefore, the basic line for a negative income tax could not be set at livable levels. Again, when the unionized primary workers see government programs aimed at training secondary workers to compete for their jobs, they often turn to demagogues such as George Wallace. A real educational reform which would enable the sons and daughters of the poor and the working class to gain access in proportion to their numbers into Harvard, Yale, and Berkeley would, radicals believe, bring cries of outrage from upper-middle and high income groups.

The perspective of radical economists in examining institutions such as the educational system is that our economy needs stratification; therefore, it needs inequitable rules to maintain the economic privileges and social equilibrium of the existing order. Segmentation in the economy leads to the "freezing" of social distinctions. Job career ladders are superficially contrived in order to nurture intra- and intervocational status preoccupations among workers who have neither job satisfaction nor control over work. Occupational divisions of the kind we have been discussing are structured for control. In the absence of more intrinsic work motivation, control is the route to efficiency and profit in a capitalist system.

Mainstream economists, who tend to analyze the economy on the assumption that the structure of preferences and the distribution of income and wealth are exogenously determined, generally bypass the needs of those on the bottom of the economic and social ladder. This is not to argue that the class system is immutable, that its socializing institutions conform perfectly to its structure. To the contrary, a real source of pressure for change derives from the contradictions and dichotomies between the noneconomic and the economic components of the system. Unfortunately, because they lack "tidiness" for the use of "pure" economic tools and methods of measurement, the dynamics of such processes frequently are ignored by mainstream economists. When they make policy recommendations for upward occupational mobility, suggestions are linked closely to the changing economic requirements of the *given* system. This is illustrated by the efforts made over the past few years by human capital economists to justify modest improvements in the educational opportunities for minority groups; such changes are not aimed at eliminating an underclass or menial work. Mainstream economists simply do not think in such terms.

The radical solution to the "necessity" of menial work lies in two directions. As long as such work is required, a good society would undertake a more equitable sharing of it and would provide it with the social recognition which it deserves. It might be argued that a street cleaning job never could be respected or made meaningful. Perhaps this is true; however, in a society which takes pride in its public living space, in the beauty of its streets and roads and parks, workers devoted to the maintenance of the environment might not feel that their tasks are demeaning. The elimination of alienation might be even more possible if work roles were either to include a variety of activities or periodically were interchanged.

Radicals hope that technology ultimately will sweep away all remnants of menial work routines. Furthermore, radicals believe that work can be structured under a different system to make it meaningful and intrinsically satisfying; pride in one's work or its purposes can replace the present state of affairs where most individuals work only because it is necessary for survival or to enhance consumption. To mainstream economists the radical view of work is sheer utopian nonsense; as they see it, it violates human nature. The radical reply is that it is no trick to advocate that which already exists. As John Kenneth Galbraith cleverly pointed out with respect to the "virtues" of practical wisdom: "People who are concerned with being practical never urge anything that is new. . . . If you want to be practical, you should vehemently support what has already happened."

URBAN MALAISE

Consider next the urban scene. Whatever might be said about the condition of U.S. cities today as compared with that of fifty or one hundred years ago, few would disagree with the statement that the gap between "what could be" and "what is" has widened. Why has this happened?

The radical answer starts with the generally recognized fact that those higher up on the stratified pyramid have moved to the suburbs, leaving the poor and their problems in the central cities. Rural and suburban controlled legislatures have aggravated matters by their unwillingness to offer effective help. The advice the urban economist has offered for remedying these circumstances often has been harmful to the powerless. Urban renewal frequently has meant tearing down the homes of the poor and building for those who add to the tax base of the city—the nonpoor. In fact, the most sophisticated computer models often offer as policy the destruction of poor neighborhoods, forcing residents to relocate elsewhere. Such a policy enables average per capita income in the city to rise.

The highway program, if it follows standard economic efficiency criteria, builds highways to and for upper income suburbanites, not for the benefit of low income city dwellers. This is because most of the benefit from highway construction is in the commuting time saved, and time saved for the rich is worth more than the same amount of time saved for the poor. This policy usually is followed because of technical calculations and, more important, because of the relative power of the two groups in influencing decision making.

It is reasoned that the best highway route is the one which costs less; this usually means constructing the highway through the black ghetto, where property values allegedly are lower. The new mass transit systems planned for or presently under way in San Francisco, Atlanta, and Washington, D.C., are being built on the basis of economically efficient criteria. They will give best service to the relatively upper income suburbanites who will gain easier access to the central business district. The logic of economic efficiency is the same logic which perpetuates the inequality of the system. Cities need good mass transit systems, but the system likely to be built will be one that meets the requirements of a stratified society. To build a system which meets the needs of lower income families and individuals, or one which might dramatically upset the automobile industry, would require that social and political struggles be waged against the class biases inherent in the system and against those interests which perpetuate a need for the given distribution of activities.

Mainstream's answer to many of these problems is governmental subsidies. When the radical looks at the nature of these subsidies, he finds that they frequently aid the rich rather than the poor. Contrary to official rhetoric, subsidy payments reflect biases similar to those discussed in relation to mass transit systems. It is not surprising to radicals that the largest single "welfare recipient" in recent times has been Lockheed Aircraft, which received a prize of $250 million for not being an efficient business; or that most farm subsidies go to agribusiness, very few to small farmers, and none to those in most need—the agricultural workers; or that the current methods of financing higher education lead to a redistribution of income from the bottom echelons to the middle and upper ones; or that obsolescence in owning oil is given special tax consideration, but not obsolescence in owning a particular skill. Nor is it surprising that the largest single federal housing program is the tax write-off to middle and upper-income homeowners.

The radical sees giveaway programs such as Telstar or the space buggy as a continuation of a long-standing tradition. He sees these subsidies as a logical continuation of a 130-million acre gift to the railroads in the last century (a land area as large as all of the New England states, New York, and Pennsylvania). He sees the defense corporation profiteers as the descendants of Commodore Vanderbilt, who sold leaky ships to the Union Army, or of Gustavus Swift, who sold rotten meat to the Union Army. In the radical view this is the way the state *normally* facilitates capitalist development. Such matters are ignored by mainstream economists, or they are viewed as deviations exposed by liberal muckrakers striving to make capitalism more honest.

INFLATION

Mainstream economists have no general explanation for the culmination of this process [simultaneous inflation and unemployment]. At best, their views are *ad hoc* and fragmented. In contrast, the radical economist would point to the historical and structural context that defines the relations between the monopolistic, competitive, and public sectors. The lead sector in this triad is the monopolistic one, with its ability to maintain or increase profits because of its market power even in the face of restricted demand.

Wage patterns established in the more productive monopolistic sector to some extent spill over into less productive public and competitive sectors. The politics of the public sector have led to accelerated increases in costs without corresponding increases in output or improvement in services by the public sector. The rising costs experienced in the competitive sector tend to lower its profits since businessmen in this sector are unable to pass on cost increases in the form of higher prices. Workers in this sector find it difficult to make a decent living; many appropriately have been identified as "the working poor."

In the postwar period large amounts of government funds have been funneled into the defense and other concentrated sectors of the economy, but the main benefits of such public expenditure have been appropriated by those least in need. Even though the profits in the monopolistic sector have been large at various intervals, they have not stimulated the absorption of the unemployed or the movement of workers from low wage to high wage sectors. This condition has not led to a revolt against corporate privilege; rather, it has stimulated the middle layers of society to focus their anger downward against the lower class. For social class reasons, the middle class erroneously has come to believe that the bulk of its hard-earned taxable income is funneled into wasteful governmental programs to help "ungrateful" blacks. As a result, the government has found it increasingly difficult to justify its expenditures and tax collections and therefore has had to pursue excessive deficit spending in a context of high-level stagnation. The outcome, despite all the governmental hustling and bustling, has been unemployment and inflation.

The public's seemingly misallocated distrust of the public sector, at a time when more and more of our problems appear to require an increase in the public sector's direct involvement, may be perfectly reasonable. The government simply is not delivering the goods. What the public does not understand sufficiently is why this is the case and how the government's deficiencies are related to the needs, power, and policies of the giant corporations. On this question mainstream economists with their neoclassical focus have little to say.

Radicals believe that a simplified Marxian macro model which divides the economy into its class components (for example, workers and capitalists) in the context of a specified structure explains more than the Keynesian groupings of the economy into consumers, investors, and government. In the radical view the mainstream's glib dismissal of a class analysis represents a basic conceptual deficiency in their mode of analysis of both developed and underdeveloped societies. The radical response to mainstream's more "functional" categories is to ask: Should we treat both Jim Bass and David Rockefeller as consumers? Is the corner gas station owner an investor in the same sense as the committee that runs Texaco or General Motors?

The unfamiliarity with radical concepts and general categories on the one hand, and the almost unanimous acceptance of mainstream vocabulary and tools of analysis on the other, put radicals in a competitive disadvantage in many discussions about methodology. The mainstreamists draw on a widely known and axiomatically accepted structure of beliefs. The radical is granted none of his or her premises *a priori*. In a debate with mainstream

professionals who have been nodding in agreement for years, radical statements that originate from outside the "monastery" appear clearly "foreign"
and "invalid." However, outside the monastery there is a real and changing
reality which will, in the radical view, eventually break up the monastic
chanting of mainstream monks. This will happen because, among other
reasons, what is now labeled as radical critical sniping sooner or later will
blossom into an integrated, formal alternative to mainstream's orientation
to the world. This is why radical economists have been so involved in
Thomas Kuhn's basic paradigm idea.

SUMMARY

Radical economists see the U.S. economy as primarily dominated by the
monopolistic sector, consisting of corporate giants. While the government
may not be simply the "committee" of this sector, the government certainly
has and exhibits strong protective biases in its direction. More generally,
the government acts to support class privilege and recreate it intergenera-
tionally through the workings of its major institutions, for example, education, health, police, and the judiciary. This class bias on the part of the
government does not necessarily eliminate the possibility of achieving modest reforms through the political process. But, from the radical perspective,
reforms conceived within the *modus vivendi* of existing institutions cannot
be consequential.

An example is the Nixon freeze of wages and prices, which has been
criticized by the welfare-liberal economists as working better in controlling
wages than prices. From a radical viewpoint, even if liberal democrats were
elected and seriously tried to limit profits, such a policy ultimately would
fail. As Salvador Allende's government found in Chile, capital too can go on
strike. If U.S. corporations actually were to feel the effect of higher taxes,
the response might be "loss of confidence" and a slowdown in the economy,
with the resultant demand for "stimulation" of the corporate sector. With
an economic slowdown jobs are lost, tax revenues decline, and the pressures on politicians to "do something" intensify. In the short run, the only
thing to do is to stimulate the economy. The right-wing Keynesian solution
which has been followed in the United States consists of corporate tax
credits and decreases in personal income taxes, or government work projects
which, because they are poorly conceived, debase the image of government
as producer and innovator and therefore accentuate the already noted problem of the government's justification of its social welfare expenditures.

The difficulty for those who would like to follow a more egalitarian
economic policy, as George McGovern learned, is that such changes would
take time and would require struggle against entrenched interests. At the
same time, politicians need quick results if they wish to remain in office.
Basic reforms which would restructure established patterns would meet
tremendous resistance from those who stand to lose from such restructuring. A full-blown struggle against the maintenance of privilege means that
during such a transformation economic conditions might get worse before
getting better. Time would be needed before new power relations were
established and new leadership groups not wedded to old ways emerged,

until new methods and incentives operated well and people gained confidence. Few or no leaders operating in the U.S. political context of short-run political expediency would survive this kind of transition unless he or she were the representative and spokesman of a movement whose members had a long-term commitment, were aware of the cost of fundamental change, and understood the dimensions of an effort to overhaul the U.S. economy.

Most liberals and conservatives argue within a common framework. Both tend to accept as a premise that the key goal is economic growth, although they sometimes argue about how the benefits of this growth are to be distributed. For both, the key is how to use resources more efficiently. Since the basic instruments of economic growth in a capitalist economy lie within private corporations, the key to growth is to aid these corporations, a view concisely expressed by Nixon on 7 October 1971 when he said: "All Americans will benefit from more profits."

Mainstream economists begin with the question of how, given the existing market structure, legal framework, and so forth, we can best stabilize capitalism (prevent economic crises, help it grow, and so forth). Radicals ask how society can be restructured to fulfill different goals and needs, those which relate to cultivating a different national style of life: a different work process, a different sense of community and neighborhood, different social relations, and a different mode of solving society's problems. To radical economists, such changes cannot occur until commerce, private property and its corresponding privileges, and profit cease to dominate the main aspects of U.S. society. Their politics revolve around class agitation and advocacy programs aimed at nurturing new centers of power among the less privileged members of society. Their intellectual labor is devoted to criticizing mainstream arguments, ideas, theories, and policy recommendations and to exposing the class biases of mainstream recommendations.

While part of what ails U.S. society may be related to industrialism per se, a significant part of the malaise is related to the characteristics of U.S. capitalism itself. It is the radical claim that many of these specific characteristics are not being seriously analyzed by mainstream economists. The persistence of grave economic and social problems capable of breeding social unrest is the basis for the belief that the growth of a new group of radical economists is permanent.

Galbraith, Hymer, and the Development of Capitalism

After World War I America sought a "return to normalcy." Those who yearned for the stability of the past, however, failed to comprehend that the United States was never a traditional society based on status but a capitalist one based on profit. The need for profit-ability necessitates investment, which in turn creates growth. Change is therefore inherent in a capitalist society. The new "normalcy" of the Republican twenties was fated to be short-lived, an illusion of stability soon belied by the depression of the 1930s.

World War II succeeded not only in transforming a stagnant economy into one characterized by boom, but also in laying the foundation for a new era that found its political symbol in President Dwight D. Eisenhower. It is difficult to say precisely when it happened—no parallel exists to the dramatic crash of 1929—but America has gone irrevocably beyond the Eisenhower era of "peace and prosperity," the Cold War parallel to the decade of the twenties. The depression of the mid-seventies currently represents, on the one hand, a crisis and, on the other, a consolidating prelude to the future.

But what form will this new stage of capitalism take? According to John Kenneth Galbraith, the United States has developed a "new industrial state" in which power resides in an elite he calls the *techno-structure*. Galbraith, a world-renowned Harvard economist, has written four best-selling treatises on economics (*American Capitalism: The Theory of Countervailing Power, The Affluent Society, The New Industrial State,* and *Economics and the Public Purpose*). He has also been the Ambassador to India, an adviser to President Kennedy, the chairman of the Americans for Democratic Action, and the author of a variety of other books, including a novel.

In *The New Industrial State*, Galbraith suggests that the picture presented in orthodox economics texts—as well as in most of the sophisticated works of theory on which they are based—is grossly misleading, if not completely irrelevant. Among the special merits of this book are its focus on the decisive business units of the economy (the two or three hundred largest industrial corporations) instead of on the mythical competitive markets that are emphasized by the orthodox text; its rejection of the apologetic thesis that production is geared to enhance the welfare of the consumer; its awareness of the dangers arising out of the power of institutions dedicated to the production of military implements (the so-called military-industrial complex); and its acceptance of the need to analyze economic phenomena within a political and social context.

M.I.T. Professor Robert M. Solow provides an excellent summary of *The New Industrial State* but vigorously criticizes it in Reading 6. This critique, however sharp, originates from a liberal perspective similar to Galbraith's.

In Reading 7 Galbraith's latest effort, *Economics and the Public Purpose,* is subjected to a penetrating analysis from a socialist perspective. The reviewer is Dr. Paul M. Sweezy, known internationally for his theoretical contributions to our understanding of capitalism and socialism. For over twenty-five years he has been coeditor of *Monthly Review,* the highly influential Marxist periodical. Since Sweezy, like Solow, ably summarizes Galbraith's point of view, it was not necessary to include in this section an overview written by Galbraith himself. (A selection from *Economics and the Public Purpose,* which develops an issue peripheral to the book's main theme, is included in this anthology as Reading 58 in section *c* of Part 4.)

For a radical conception of where capitalism is going, we turn to a brilliant, insightful essay of enormous scope (see Reading 8) by the late Professor Stephen Hymer of the New School for Social Research. Hymer's article focuses on the multinational corporation (MNC) and shows that it "creates hierarchy rather than equality." The MNC "erodes [for better or for worse] the cohesiveness of national states," and "in proportion to its success, it creates tensions and difficulties." In short, the multinational corporation is a vehicle for change, and with change comes the possibility that concentrated power may be effectively challenged.

The New Industrial State or Son of Affluence

Robert M. Solow

There is . . . an outside possibility that the profession will ignore *The New Industrial State* because it finds the ideas more or less unhelpful. The world can be divided into big-thinkers and little-thinkers. The difference is illustrated by the old story of the couple who had achieved an agreeable division of labor. She made the unimportant decisions: what job he should take, where they should live, how to bring up the children. He made the important decisions: what to do about Jerusalem, whether China should be admitted to the United Nations, how to deal with crime in the streets. Economists are determined little-thinkers. They want to know what will happen to the production of houses and automobiles in 1968 if Congress votes a 10 percent surcharge on personal and corporate tax bills, and what will happen if Congress does not. They would like to be able to predict the course of the Wholesale Price Index and its components, and the total of corporate profits by industry. They are not likely to be much helped or hindered in these activities by Professor Galbraith's view of Whither We are Trending.

Professor Galbraith makes an eloquent case for big-thinking, and he has a point. Little-thinking can easily degenerate into mini-thinking or even into hardly thinking at all. Even if it does not, too single-minded a focus on how the parts of the machine work may lead to a careful failure ever to ask whether the machine itself is pointed in the right direction. On the other side, Professor Galbraith gingerly pays tribute to the little-thinkers whose work he has used, but it is evident that he has been exposed only very selectively to the relevant literature. There is no point squabbling over this: big-think and little-think are different styles, and the difference between them explains why this book will have more currency outside the economics profession than in it. It is a book for the dinner table not for the desk.

I shall try to summarize the main steps in Galbraith's argument, and shall then return to discuss them, one by one.

1. The characteristic form of organization in any modern industrial society is not the petty firm but the giant corporation, usually producing many different things, and dominating the market for most of them. Nor is this mere accident. The complicated nature of modern technology and the accompanying need for the commitment of huge sums of capital practically demand that industry be organized in large firms.

2. With few exceptions, the giant corporation is in no sense run by its owners, the common stockholders. The important decisions are made—have to be made—by a bureaucracy, organized in a series of overlapping and interlocking committees. The board of directors is only the tip of an iceberg that extends down as far as technicians and department managers. The members of the bureaucracy are all experts in something, possibly in

management itself. Galbraith calls them the "technostructure," but that awkward word is probably a loser.

3. It is the nature of the highly capitalized bureaucratically controlled corporation to avoid risk. The modern business firm is simply not willing to throw itself on the mercy of the market. Instead, it achieves certainty and continuity in the supply of materials by integrating backward to produce its own, in the supply of capital by financing itself out of retained earnings, in the supply of labor by bringing the unions into the act. It eliminates uncertainty on the selling side by managing the consumer, by inducing him, through advertising and more subtle methods of salesmanship, to buy what the corporation wants to sell at the price it wants to charge. The major risk of general economic fluctuations is averted by encouraging the government in programs of economic stabilization.

4. It would be asking much too much of human nature to expect that the bureaucracy should manage the firm simply in the interests of the stockholders. There is, therefore, no presumption that the modern firm seeks the largest possible profit. Nor does it. The firm's overriding goals is its own survival and autonomy; for security it requires a certain minimum of profit and this it will try to achieve. Security thus assured, the firm's next most urgent goal is the fastest possible growth of sales. (Since firms grow by reinvesting their earnings, this goal is not independent of profits; nevertheless, once the minimum target in profits is achieved, the modern firm will expand its sales even at the expense of its profits.) There are two lesser goals: a rising dividend rate, presumably to keep the animals from getting restless, and the exercise of technological virtuosity.

5. Modern industry produces mainly things, and it wishes to grow. Everyone will be happier if everyone believes that a growing production of things is the main object of the national life. People will be happier because that is what they in fact get, and the bureaucracy will be happier because they can feel that they serve the national purpose. This belief has been widely inculcated, but it takes effort really to believe it, because American society already has more things than it knows what to do with.

6. The key resource in the modern industrial state is organized intelligence, especially scientific and managerial intelligence. One of the important things the government does to support the system is the extension of education to provide a supply of recruits for the bureaucracy, and the subsidization of scientific and technological research to provide something interesting for them to do. What Galbraith calls the "scientific and educational estate" therefore acquires a certain moral authority and even mundane power in the society. This is an important circumstance, because the scientific and educational estate—at least its youngest members—can see through the cult of the GNP and observe that it slights the claims of leisure, art, culture, architectural design, and even the innocent enjoyment of nature. Here is the most promising source of social change and of a rather more attractive national style of life.

There is a lot more in the book, much of it full of insight and merriment, but the main logic of the argument seems to be roughly as I have stated it.

. . . [A]t the risk of judging big-think by the standards of little-think, I proceed [to judge the truth of Galbraith's big picture].

1. Professor Galbraith is right that modern economics has not really come to terms with the large corporation. . . . Professor Galbraith is not the first person to have discovered General Motors. Most close students of industrial investment or pricing do make room in their statistical behavior equations for behavior that is neither perfectly competitive nor simply monopolistic. (The long debate over the incidence of the corporate profits tax hardly suggests universal reliance on any simple model.)

There is, after all, a moderate amount of economic activity that is not carried on by General Motors, or by the 100 largest or 500 largest corporations. In fact, only about 55 percent of the Gross National Product originates in nonfinancial corporations at all. Not nearly all of that is generated by the giant corporations (of course, some financial corporations are among the giants). Nor is it entirely clear which way the wind is blowing. The giant corporation is preeminently a phenomenon of manufacturing industry and public utilities; it plays a much less important role in trade and services. If, as seems to be in the cards, the trade and service sectors grow relative to the total, the scope of the large corporation may be limited. Alternatively, big firms may come to play a larger role in industries that have so far been carried on at small scale.

Enough has been said to suggest that it is unlikely that the economic system can usefully be described either as General Motors writ larger or as the family farm writ everywhere. This offers at least a hint that it will behave like neither extreme. . . . What is to the point is a "model"—a simplified description—of the economy that will yield valid predictions about behavior.

2. The "separation of ownership from control" of the modern corporation is not a brand new idea. . . . It is possible to argue—and many economists probably would argue—that many management-controlled firms are constrained by market forces to behave in much the same way that an owner-controlled firm would behave, and many others acquire owners who like the policy followed by the management. I think it may be a fair complaint that this proposition has not received all the research attention it deserves. It is an error to suppose it has received none at all. Such evidence as there is does not give a very clear-cut answer, but it does not suggest that the orthodox presupposition is terribly wrong. Galbraith does not present any convincing evidence the other way, as I think he is aware. . . .

3. The modern corporation—and not only the modern corporation—is adverse to risk. Many economic institutions and practices are understandable only as devices for shifting or spreading risk. But Galbraith's story that the industrial firm has "planned" itself into complete insulation from the vagaries of the market is an exaggeration, so much an exaggeration that it smacks of the put-on.

Consider the supply of capital. There is a lot of internal financing of corporations; it might perhaps be better if companies were forced more often into the capital markets. But external finance is hardly trivial. In 1966 the total flow of funds to nonfarm nonfinancial corporate business was about $96 billion. Internal sources accounted for $59 billion and external sources for the remaining $37 billion. Besides, depreciation allowances amounted to $38 billion of the internal funds generated by business, and much of this sum is not a source of net finance for growth. External sources provided about one-half of net new funds. In 1966, bond issues and bank loans alone added up to about two-thirds of undistributed profits. Trade credit is another important source of external funds, but it is complicated because industrial corporations are both lenders and borrowers in this market. . . .

Consider the consumer. In the folklore, he (she?) is sovereign; the economic machinery holds its breath while the consumer decides, in view of market prices, how much bread to buy, and how many apples. In Galbraith's counterfable, no top-heavy modern corporation can afford to let success or failure depend on the uninstructed whim of a woman with incipient migraine. So the consumer is managed by Madison Avenue into buying what the system requires him to buy. Now I, too, don't like billboards or toothpaste advertising or lottery tickets of unknown—but probably negligible—actuarial value with my gasoline. (Though I put it to Professor Galbraith that, in his town and mine, the Narragansett beer commercial may be the best thing going on TV.) But that is not the issue; the issue is whether the art of salesmanship has succeeded in freeing the large corporation from the need to meet a market test, giving it "decisive influence over the revenue it receives."

That is not an easy question to answer, at least not if you insist on evidence. Professor Galbraith offers none; perhaps that is why he states his conclusion so confidently and so often. I have no great confidence in my own casual observations either. But I should think a case could be made that much advertising serves only to cancel other advertising, and is therefore merely wasteful.

. . . Suppose that all advertising were reduced near the minimum necessary to inform consumers of the commodities available and their elementary objective properties? Galbraith believes that in absence of persuasion, reduced to their already satiated biological needs for guidance, consumers would be at a loss; total consumer spending would fall and savings would simply pile up by default.

Is there anything to this? I know it is not true of me, and I do not fancy myself any cleverer than the next man in this regard. No research that I know of has detected a wrinkle in aggregate consumer spending behavior that can be traced to the beginning of television. Perhaps no one has tried. Pending some evidence, I am not inclined to take this popular doctrine very seriously. . . .

Consider the attitude of the large corporation to the economic stabilization activities of the Federal Government. It is surely true that big business has an important stake in the maintenance of general prosperity. How, then, to account for the hostility of big business to discretionary fiscal policy, a hostility only lately ended, if indeed traces do not still persist? Here I think Professor Galbraith is carried away by his own virtuosity; he proposes to convince the reader that the hostility has not come from the big business bureaucracy but from the old-style entrepreneurial remnants of small and medium-sized firms. Their fortunes are not so dependent on general prosperity, so they can afford the old-time religion. Professor Galbraith is probably wrong about that last point; large firms are better able than small ones to withstand a recession. He is right that the more Paleolithic among the opponents of stabilization policy have come from smaller and middle-sized business.

. . . There is a much simpler explanation for the earlier, now dwindling, hostility that would do no harm to the argument of the book: mere obtuseness.

4. Does the modern industrial corporation maximize profits? Probably not rigorously and singlemindedly, and for much the same reason that Dr. Johnson did not become a philosopher—because cheerfulness keeps breaking in. Most large corporations are free enough from competitive pressure to afford a donation to the Community Chest or a fancy office building without a close calculation of its incremental contribution to profit. But that is not a fundamental objection to the received doctrine, which can survive if businesses merely *almost* maximize profits. The real question is whether there is some other goal that businesses pursue systematically at the expense of profits.

The notion of some minimum required yield on capital is an attractive one. It can be built into nearly any model of the behavior of the corporation. I suppose the most commonly held view among economists goes something like this (I am oversimplifying): for any given amount of invested capital, a corporation will seek the largest possible profits in some appropriately long-run sense, and with due allowance for cheerfulness. If the return on capital thus achieved exceeds the minimum required yield or target rate of return, the corporation will expand by adding to its capital, whether from internal or external sources. If the return on equity actually achieved (after corporation tax) is any guide, the target rate of return is not trivial. The main influence on profits in manufacturing is obviously the business cycle; for fairly good years one would have to name a figure like 12 percent, slightly higher in the durable-goods industries, slightly lower in nondurables. In recession years like 1954, 1958, 1961, the figure is more like 9 percent.

Alternatives to this view have been proposed. Professor Galbraith mentions William Baumol and Robin Marris as predecessors. Baumol has argued that the corporation seeks to maximize its sales revenue, provided that it earns at least a certain required rate of return on capital. This is rather different from Galbraith's proposal that corporations seek growth rather than size. These are intrinsically difficult theories to test against observation. Some attempts have been made to test the Baumol model; the results are not terribly decisive, but for what they are worth they tend to conclude against it. Marris's theory is very much like Galbraith's, only much more closely reasoned. He does propose that corporate management seeks growth, subject to a minimum requirement for profit. But Marris is more careful, and comes closer to the conventional view, because he is fully aware, as Galbraith apparently is not, of an important discipline in the capital market. The management that too freely sacrifices profit for growth will find that the stock market puts a relatively low valuation on its assets. This may offer an aggressive management elsewhere a tempting opportunity to acquire assets cheap, and the result may be a merger offer or a takeover bid, a definite threat to the autonomy of the management taken over. Naturally, the very largest corporations are not subject to this threat, but quite good-sized ones are.

There is, on the other hand, a certain amount of positive evidence that supports the hypothesis of rough profit-maximization. It has been found, for instance, that industries which are difficult for outsiders to enter are more profitable than those which are easily entered and therefore, presumably, more competitive. It has been found, also, that there is a detectable tendency for capital to flow where profits are highest. Serious attempts to account for industrial investment and prices find that the profit-supply-demand mechanism provides a substantial part of the explanation, though there is room for less classical factors, and for quite a lot of "noise" besides.

5. Professor Galbraith does not have a high opinion of the private consumption of goods and services. "What is called a high standard of living consists in considerable measure, in arrangements for avoiding muscular energy, increasing sensual pleasure and for enhancing caloric intake above any conceivable nutritional requirement. . . . No society has ever before provided such a high standard of living as ours, hence none is as good. The occasional query, however logically grounded, is unheard." One wonders if that paragraph were written in Gstaad where, we are told, Professor Galbraith occasionally entertains his muse.

It is hard to disagree without appearing boorish. Nevertheless, it is worth remembering that in 1965 the median family income in the United States was just under $7000. One of the more persistent statistical properties of the median income is that half the families must have less. It does not seem like an excessive sum to spend. No doubt one could name an excessive sum, but in any case the reduction of inequality and the alleviation of poverty play negligible roles in Galbraith's system of thought. His attitude toward ordinary consumption reminds one of the Duchess who, upon acquiring a full appreciation of sex, asked the Duke if it were not perhaps too good for the common people.

6. I have no particular comment on Professor Galbraith's view of the role of the scientific and educational estate as an agent of social and cultural improvement. . . .

7

Utopian Reformism

Paul M. Sweezy

It would be interesting to trace the development of John Kenneth Galbraith's ideas, beginning with *American Capitalism* (1952) and culminating (so far at any rate) with *Economics and the Public Purpose*, which has just been published. Such a survey would show, I think, that Professor Galbraith is very sensitive to the moods of the moment, moving with but little resistance and even less acknowledgment from a kind of Panglossian optimism in *American Capitalism* (and the same year's famous *New York Times Magazine* article "We Can Prosper Without War Orders") through increasing skepticism in the middle books (*The Affluent Society* and *The New Industrial State*) to something which now displays what is at times ill-concealed alarm. That all this goes along with, and in Galbraith's mind no doubt stems from, a basically not much changed vision of the American economy and American society, is a noteworthy fact which may tend to suggest that the correspondence between this vision and the reality is not altogether perfect. It is this aspect which I should like to direct attention to.

To begin with, Galbraith's newest critique of neoclassical (or orthodox or received) economics contains little that is new. It has been repeated, with variations and changing emphases, in all his works. And for the most part it is entirely justified. Economics as the subject is taught in establishment educational institutions has little relevance to reality and is thoroughly apologetic, in effect if not in intent. I will not dwell on this: those who are not already familiar with the Galbraithian critique will find it well presented, with some new angles (Galbraith emerges this time as something of a middle-class women's liberationist), in *Economics and the Public Purpose*. What I wish to focus attention on is the "model" (the term is almost *de rigueur* these days) which he puts in the place of his version of the neoclassical picture of a consumer-dominated and producer-powerless self-adjusting market system which fails to perform satisfactorily only when deluded intellectuals and ignorant politicians meddle with it.

Galbraith's present model differs from his earlier versions in that he now divides the economy into two parts which he calls the "planning system" and the "market system." The planning system, as he acknowledges on page 217, is merely a new name for what is traditionally called the "monopolistic or oligopolistic sector": it comprises a thousand or so giant corporations which produce three quarters or more of the country's industrial output. The market system is the rest of the private economy, with agriculture, services, and retailing as its principal subdivisions. Having identified these two "systems," Galbraith proceeds to analyze the functioning of the economy as a whole in terms of their interaction with each other and with the state or public sector.

According to this analysis, the dominant role is played by the planning system. It is here that the driving force of the economy (the savings-and-investment process) is centered. Given its overwhelming monopoly power, the planning system is able to exploit the largely competitive market system, enforcing on it unfavorable terms of trade in the manner of a metropolis and its colonies. This disparity in power is also reflected in the relations of the two systems to the state: the planning system has easy access to all branches of government and establishes effective control over most of them, while the market system is for the most part left out in the cold. "The modern state," he tells us on page 172, "is not the executive committee of the bourgeoisie, but it *is* more nearly the executive committee of the technostructure." (The "technostructure" is Galbraith's term for the controllers of the large corporation: we shall return to this presently.) The result of this lopsided distribution of power is that the planning system gets what it wants, especially money, from the state, while the market system is starved. This sets up a process of growing inequality between the two systems. Here we may note the striking change in Galbraith's views as compared to the earlier books, most notably *The Affluent Society*. In that work he contrasted private affluence with public squalor, and treated inequality as a problem of diminishing importance no longer worth seriously worrying about. Now the argument is not that the public sector as such is starved (armaments and highways do very well for themselves), but that the allocation of resources going to the public sector is contrary to the "public purpose." And inequality is now seen as one of the greatest and most pervasive evils of the society. It would have been gracious of the author to acknowledge that those who have been saying so all along were right and he was wrong. But that would have required a modicum of humility, which is not exactly Galbraith's specialty.

Compared to neoclassical theory, this two-systems model is undoubtedly an improvement. It integrates monopoly and state power, the dominant forces in the U.S. economy today, into the analysis of the system as a whole (neoclassical theory is artfully designed to avoid doing precisely this), and it succeeds quite well in offering plausible diagnoses of some of the system's major problems. One of these is the already-mentioned allocation of resources to and within the public sector. Another is inflation, which Galbraith recognizes to be endemic to the system, impervious to control through fiscal and monetary policies, and compatible with persistent high levels of unemployment.

I believe, however, that in many respects the Galbraithian model is seriously flawed and ends up as a kind of new, streamlined apologetic for monopoly capitalism. Since to develop this theme satisfactorily would require much more than a brief review, I will confine what follows to highlighting what seem to me to be some of the gravest weaknesses of his analysis.

THE PLANNING SYSTEM

Every economic enterprise, from the smallest to the largest, of course has to do a certain amount of planning. But as a group the large corporations do not do any planning together, and do not constitute a system in the usual sense of a collection of entities strongly interrelated among themselves and more weakly related to their environment. Galbraith as much as admits all this in numerous passages, as for example when he speaks of the need for measures "to ensure the interindustry coordination of which the planning system is incapable" (p. 251), or treats the energy "crisis" as precisely a symptom of the planning system's inability to plan. (chap. 31) Apart from in-firm planning, which is real enough but not peculiar to Galbraith's planning system, what he seems generally to mean by "planning" is the power of the big corporations to throw their weight around in their relations with consumers and government, something which of course is emphasized by all theories of monopoly capitalism without any need to invoke the language of planning.

Why, then, is Galbraith so wedded to the notion of the planning system? The reason, I think, is that it gives him one of the tools he needs for conceptualizing the U.S. power structure in a manner convenient to his own predilections and reform program. To explain this, we need first to understand another of Galbraith's key concepts.

THE TECHNOSTRUCTURE

It is pretty generally accepted by now that the typical big corporation is not controlled by majority vote of its shareholders or even by its board of directors, but by what it is usual to call its management, i.e., its top officers who (except in time of financial trouble) are normally a self-perpetuating group which selects the board of directors rather than vice versa. It is important to recognize that this does not mean what it is often taken to mean, that ownership and control are separated in the large corporation. Quite apart from cases in which management is picked by and represents large stockholders (majority or minority), executives of large corporations are, with few exceptions, wealthy men, owners of substantial amounts of stock in their own and other corporations. Far from being separated from ownership, they are simply the most active echelon of what C. Wright Mills called the corporate rich, who own a large part of the country's wealth. This being the case, one would naturally expect them to run their corporations with an eye single to maximum profit and the most rapid feasible accumulation of capital.

For reasons which will become clear as we proceed, however, this conclusion does not suit Galbraith's purposes at all. He would like to abolish the capitalist altogether, but since this is impossible, the next best thing is to transform him into a functionless (and relatively powerless) *rentier*. But this, as we have already seen, is not accomplished by the theory of managerial control: the managers are in fact capitalists in the fullest sense of the term. So Galbraith is driven to invent a new theory, the theory of the technostructure. The gist of the argument is that corporate managements, in the sense defined above, are not really in control at all. They lack the necessary knowledge, and knowledge is the basis of power. This knowledge is possessed by a large group of specialists, and "to perfect and guide the organization in which the specialists serve also requires specialists. Eventually not an individual but a complex of scientists, engineers and technicians; of sales, advertising and marketing men; of public relations experts, lobbyists, lawyers and men with a specialized knowledge of the Washington bureaucracy and its manipulation; and of coordinators, managers and executives becomes the guiding intelligence of the business firm. This is the technostructure. Not any single individual but the technostructure becomes the commanding power." (p. 82) In this way management is buried in, and subordinated to, the much larger technostructure, which derives its power from specialized knowledge and is in no way beholden to ownership.

The next step is to endow the technostructure with a set of purposes, which Galbraith divides into "protective" and "affirmative." The protective purposes are security and freedom from outside interference by such as creditors or trade unions; the affirmative purposes boil down to the aggrandizement of the technostructure as such. To achieve these goals the technostructure strives for (1) "a certain minimum (though not necessarily a low) level of earnings" (p. 94), sufficient to pay "reasonable" dividends to stockholders, avoid pressure from creditors, and finance growth; and (2) a maximum rate of growth measured in sales, resulting in steady expansion of the power base and job opportunities for the technostructure. Galbraith is emphatic and repetitive that profit maximization in the manner of what at one point he calls the "original capitalist" (p. 247) is *not* an aim of the technostructure. We shall return to this.

It is only necessary to add that the technostructure is in charge of the planning system to control prices, manipulate the consumer, and dominate the state. Since, as we already know, the planning system also dominates and exploits the market system, it appears that we have here a complete picture of the power structure of American society. The technostructure sits at the center and runs the whole show.

In Galbraith's view, however, this is a pretty shaky arrangement. The technostructure doesn't really represent anyone but itself, and its power derives largely from its ability to hoodwink or brainwash most other people into believing that its purposes are identical with the public purpose. (It is in this connection that Galbraith attributes great, and sometimes it even seems decisive, importance to the role of neoclassical economics in persuading people that the greatest of all sins is interference with the natural workings of the economy.) If the public, or sufficiently large segments of it, could be disabused of this way of looking at things, it should be relatively easy to break the society's thralldom to the technostructure. The state could then be "emancipated" and transformed into a "public state," and a whole series of reforms adding up to a "new socialism," or maybe several new socialisms, could be enacted and carried through.

Everyone is of course entitled to his or her utopia, and many are worth discussing for their intrinsic interest as well as for what they reveal about their authors. I confess that Galbraith's does not attract me, though it does undoubtedly contain improvements over what we have, which to be sure is not saying much. Though he talks about socialism, there is little in Galbraith's proposals that resembles what I suppose most people understand by the term. He would nationalize a few sectors of the private economy, most notably the armament industries, but he is not naive enough to imagine that this by itself would change very much. For the rest, the ownership and organization of economic activity would be left as they are, with one exception. Every group would be encouraged, assisted, and in some cases perhaps even forced to organize to pursue its own economic interest. Since we can't have universal competition, he seems to be saying, let us universalize monopoly. And if one were to object that, judging from past experience, this seems a somewhat dubious method of achieving the "public purpose," Galbraith would probably reply that we have never had a "public state" presiding over the whole economy and imposing its benevolent dictates on all the conflicting but (in the new dispensation) relatively powerless groups and interests that make up the economy. The public state presumably embodies the public purpose, and Galbraith is the prophet of both.

But why call this a utopia rather than what Galbraith doubtless believes it to be, i.e., a hard-headed, realistic, and realizable program of social reform? The reason quite simply is that his conceptualization of the power structure is light years away from the reality of monopoly capitalist society.

The technostructure does not dominate the planning system, or anything else for that matter. Galbraith's contrary opinion is based on a confusion between making decisions within a given framework and deciding what goals are imposed by this framework on those operating within it. I do not think he is correct in maintaining that the technostructure rather than the management makes all the operating decisions—whether to build a new factory, how next year's model will differ from this year's, etc., etc. —but even if he were correct it would have no bearing on the ultimate purpose of the enterprise. This is determined not by any individual or group but by the very nature of the business system, or as Marxists would say the nature of capital as self-expanding value.[1] In concrete terms, this purpose is and has to be twofold: to make as much profit as possible and to grow as rapidly as possible. Objectively determined, this becomes the subjective aim of management; and it suffuses the entire ideology and value system of the business world. Personnel (technostructure) are hired accordingly, and any who take it into their heads to pursue some other aim are promptly fired. *Real power in the enterprise is held by those who have the power to hire and fire, and it is precisely this power which inheres in management.* In exercising it, management acts as capitalists and on behalf of capitalists.

It might seem that this argument is really not so different from Galbraith's position. To be sure, he denies that profit maximizing is any part of the corporate purpose; but insofar as he insists that growth *is* central to that purpose, this might seem to be a distinction without a difference. For after all, as any businessman will tell you, profits are the key to growth, whether it is financed by internal savings or by resort to the money markets. The more profitable a corporation, the faster it can grow. So Galbraith's rejection of profit maximizing might be brushed aside as a mere quibble without any real significance. It is important to understand why Galbraith could not admit that this is so. Profit maximizing is unequivocally in the interest of the owners of industry. If it is also a central aim of corporate managements, then there is an identity of interests between owners and managers. But if corporations are not controlled by their managers but by their technostructures which in turn are more interested in self-aggrandizement than in increasing profits, then corporations are not being run in the interests of owners. In that case, control over the key sector of the economy has slipped out of the grip of the owning or capitalist class and into the relatively weak hands of a new technocratic stratum. And, as noted above, this same stratum is also supposed to have gained control over the state. According to this view, the task of the reformer has been vastly simplified and eased, compared to what it used to be. No more need for class struggle or related unpleasantness. Just enlighten the public, emancipate the state, and downgrade the technostructure to its proper subordinate role.

Once we realize that this is all an illusion, that the capitalists dominate the giant corporations of today as completely as they did the smaller enterprises of a hundred years ago, we can hardly help wondering if Galbraith's

---

[1] The concept of capital as self-expanding value is crucial to the entire structure of Marxian economics. It is lucidly explained in the short (34 pages) part 2 of volume 1 of *Capital*.

theory is any more reliable in other respects. And the answer, not surprisingly (to use one of his favorite expressions), is that it is not.

For one thing, the picture of a more or less homogeneous "market system" confronting a handful of giant corporations is fanciful in the extreme. Not that the small exploited and self-exploiting enterprise doesn't exist in such areas of the economy as agriculture, retail trade, and services: it does exist and it is victimized by the system, just as Galbraith says. But there are also plenty of winners who are by no stretch of the imagination in Galbraith's planning system. To name only a few of the more important categories is to reveal how extensive and significant the phenomenon is: small and medium-sized corporations in manufacturing and trade, locally based construction firms (nearly the whole construction industry), large farmers and ranchers, real estate owners and operators, owners of radio and TV stations, local bankers, professionals (especially doctors and lawyers). Not all of those included in these categories are winners, of course. But literally millions of them are in no sense victims of the system: on the contrary, many are among its chief beneficiaries. To put them in the same bag with the owner of the corner grocery store makes so little sense that one must assume it has an ulterior motive. And in Galbraith's case, I believe the ulterior motive, probably unconscious on the part of the author, is further to confuse the picture of the power structure in U.S. society. Many of the people in the categories listed (and others not listed) are wealthy in their own right, with incomes and capital assets well above the average of the technostructure, and they are intertwined in many ways (e.g., through stock ownership) with the corporate rich. Politically, they dominate the communities and the electoral districts, often right up to the state level, in which they live and operate. Socially, they belong to the same class as the corporate rich, sharing the same life-style, the same values, the same ideology. They thus constitute what is, in terms of numbers and geographical spread, by far the largest part of a relatively homogeneous class which derives its enormous wealth and privileges from the economic status quo.

But is this also a ruling class in the sense of dominating the state? According to Galbraith's theory, the answer would have to be no. He makes a rather sharp distinction between the bureaucratic and elective branches of the government. The bureaucracies are similar in composition and outlook to the technostructure, with which they have a strong tendency to develop what he calls a symbiotic relationship: this indeed is the source of the technostructure's power over the state. The elective branches, congress and the presidency, on the other hand, are not necessarily tied to any power group. To be sure, the Republican Party and up to now a large part of the Democratic Party have bought the technostructure's line that what is good for it is good for the country. But these alliances are not unbreakable. As we have already seen, Galbraith believes that beginning with the elective branches, the state can be emancipated from the technostructure and turned into the instrument of the "public purpose."

From the standpoint of class analysis, things look rather different. The higher reaches of the government bureaucracies (including the judiciary) are overwhelmingly staffed by members of the dominant economic class and/or people dependent on them; and the political party organizations are controlled at every level by the vested interests which stand to gain most from the protection and favors which the local, state, and federal governments are in a position to hand out. These are facts which have been confirmed by innumerable empirical studies of cities, towns, and political institutions, though it is true that not all of the authors of these studies draw the logical conclusion that government in the United States is owned lock, stock, and barrel by exactly the same interests that own most of the country's wealth and control its economic life. These interests, taken together, constitute a ruling class in the fullest sense of the term, the richest and most powerful ruling class in the history of the world.

The implications of this for Galbraith's strategy of reform are of course devastating. If the enemy is a rootless, upstart technostructure which maintains itself in power mainly by selling a phony ideological bill of goods, then it makes sense to rely on an ideological counterattack followed by an effort to win over the Democratic Party to Galbraith's new brand of populism. But if the enemy is in fact an enormously powerful bourgeoisie with two centuries of experience in ruling behind it and absolutely no scruples about using every and any available means to achieve its ends,[2] then a rather different strategy seems called for. Above all, one had better look around for possible allies who could enter upon a struggle to unseat the class now in power with a reasonable prospect of success. And I challenge Galbraith, or anyone else, to say where such allies might conceivably be found except in the working class, using the term in a broad sense to include the great majority of those who must work for a living regardless of the color of their collars. Workers have potential power not because they are in the majority—when the chips are down no ruling class cares for the arithmetic of minorities and majorities—but because they are indispensable to the process of production and hence to the very life of society.

Like most liberals, Galbraith sees little hope in the workers. If he is right, things will continue to deteriorate, as Galbraith now recognizes they have been deteriorating for a long time. But it might be more constructive to work on the assumption that at some stage in this process American workers will experience a political awakening, similar to that of the 1930s, only next time on a scale appropriate to the seriousness of the developing crisis of world capitalism. I would like to pay Galbraith the compliment of believing that, should this happen, he will be flexible enough to write another book explaining how and why he expected it all along.

---

[2] So far as I can recall, Vietnam is mentioned only once in a footnote and it does not occur at all in the index. Before he writes another book, Galbraith would do well to ponder what U.S. conduct in Vietnam implies about the lengths to which the American ruling class will go when what it considers to be its vital interests are threatened. A full review of *Economics and the Public Purpose* would have to deal with the author's treatment of imperialism and America's overall role in the world. I will only say here that this treatment is so brief, superficial, and unenlightening as to suggest that Galbraith is unfamiliar with recent work in this area, especially by a younger generation of social scientists in the Third World. This is not surprising since most of this work is either Marxist or strongly Marxist-influenced, and in his references to Marxism Galbraith shows that he is following in a well-established tradition of bourgeois social science: he simply refuses to take it seriously.

The Multinational Corporation and the Law of Uneven Development

Stephen Hymer

PART I. THE EVOLUTION OF THE MULTINATIONAL CORPORATION

The Marshallian Firm and the Market Economy

The hallmarks of the new system [of capitalism] were *the market* and *the factory*, representing the two different methods of coordinating the division of labor. In the factory entrepreneurs consciously plan and organize cooperation, and the relationships are hierarchical and authoritarian; in the market coordination is achieved through a decentralized, unconscious, competitive process.

To understand the significance of this distinction, the new system should be compared to the structure it replaced. In the pre-capitalist system of production, the division of labor was hierarchically structured at the *macro* level, i.e., for society as a whole, but unconsciously structured at the *micro* level, i.e., the actual process of production. Society as a whole was partitioned into various castes, classes, and guilds, on a rigid and authoritarian basis so that political and social stability could be maintained and adequate numbers assured for each industry and occupation. Within each sphere of production, however, individuals by and large were independent and their activities only loosely coordinated, if at all. In essence, a guild was composed of a large number of similar individuals, each performing the same task in roughly the same way with little cooperation or division of labor. This type of organization could produce high standards of quality and workmanship but was limited quantitatively to low levels of output per head.

The capitalist system of production turned this structure on its head. The macro system became unconsciously structured, while the micro system became hierarchically structured. The market emerged as a self-regulating coordinator of business units as restrictions on capital markets and labor mobility were removed. (Of course the State remained above the market as a conscious coordinator to maintain the system and ensure the growth of capital.) At the micro level, that is the level of production, labor was gathered under the authority of the entrepreneur capitalist.

Marshall, like Marx, stressed that the internal division of labor within the factory, between those who planned and those who worked (between "undertakers" and laborers), was the "chief fact in the form of modern civilization, the 'kernel' of the modern economic problem." Marx, however, stressed the authoritarian and unequal nature of this relationship based on the coercive power of property and its anti-social characteristics. He focused on the irony that concentration of wealth in the hands of a few and its ruthless use were necessary historically to demonstrate the value of cooperation and the social nature of production.

Marshall, in trying to answer Marx, argued for the voluntary cooperative nature of the relationship between capital and labor. In his view, the *market* reconciled individual freedom and collective production. He argued that those on top achieved their position because of their superior organizational ability, and that their relation to the workers below them was essentially harmonious and not exploitative. "Undertakers" were not captains of industry because they had capital; they could obtain capital because they had the ability to be captains of industry. They retained their authority by merit, not by coercion; for according to Marshall, natural selection, operating through the market, constantly destroyed inferior organizers and gave everyone who had the ability—including workers—a chance to rise to managerial positions. Capitalists earned more than workers because they contributed more, while the system as a whole provided all its members, and especially the workers, with improved standards of living and an ever-expanding field of choice of consumption.

The Corporate Economy

The evolution of business enterprise from the small workshop (Adam Smith's pin factory) to the Marshallian family firm represented only the first step in the development of business organization. As total capital accumulated, the size of the individual concentrations composing it increased continuously, and the vertical division of labor grew accordingly.

By the early twentieth century, the rapid growth of the economy and the great merger movement had consolidated many small enterprises into large national corporations engaged in many functions over many regions. To meet this new strategy of continent-wide, vertically integrated production and marketing, a new administrative structure evolved. The family firm, tightly controlled by a few men in close touch with all its aspects, gave way to the administrative pyramid of the corporation. Capital acquired new powers and new horizons. The domain of conscious coordination widened and that of market-directed division of labor contracted.

Business developed an organ system of administration, and the modern corporation was born. The functions of business administration were subdivided into *departments* (organs)—finance, personnel, purchasing, engineering, and sales—to deal with capital, labor, purchasing, manufacturing, etc. This horizontal division of labor opened up new possibilities for rationalizing production and for incorporating the advances of physical and social sciences into economic activity on a systematic basis. At the same time a "brain and nervous system," i.e., a vertical system of control, had to be devised to connect and coordinate departments. This was a major advance in decision-making capabilities. It meant that a special group, the Head Office, was created whose particular function was to coordinate, appraise, and plan for the survival and growth of the organism as a whole. The organization became conscious of itself as organization and gained a certain measure of control over its own evolution and development.

The corporation soon underwent further evolution. To understand this next step we must briefly discuss the development of the United States market. At the risk of great oversimplification, we might say that by the first decade of the twentieth century, the problem of production had essentially been solved.

The question was which direction growth would take. One possibility was to expand mass production systems very widely and to make basic consumer goods available on a broad basis throughout the world. The other possibility was to concentrate on continuous innovation for a small number of people and on the introduction of new consumption goods even before the old ones had been fully spread. The latter course was in fact chosen, and we now have the paradox that 500 million people can receive a live TV broadcast from the moon while there is still a shortage of telephones in many advanced countries, to say nothing of the fact that so many people suffer from inadequate food and lack of simple medical help.

This path was associated with a choice of capital-deepening instead of capital-widening in the productive sector of the economy. As capital accumulated, business had to choose the degree to which it would expand labor proportionately to the growth of capital or, conversely, the degree to which they would substitute capital for labor. At one extreme business could have kept the capital-labor ratio constant and accumulated labor at the same rate they accumulated capital. This horizontal accumulation would soon have exhausted the labor force of any particular country and then either capital would have had to migrate to foreign countries or labor would have had to move into the industrial centers. Under this system, earnings per employed worker would have remained steady and the composition of output would have tended to remain constant as similar basic goods were produced on a wider and wider basis.

However, this path was not chosen, and instead capital per worker was raised, the rate of expansion of the industrial labor force was slowed down, and a dualism was created between a small, high wage, high productivity sector in advanced countries, and a large, low wage, low productivity sector in the less advanced.

The uneven growth of per capita income implied unbalanced growth and the need on the part of business to adapt to a constantly changing composition of output. Firms in the producers' goods sectors had continuously to innovate labor-saving machinery because the capital output ratio was increasing steadily. In the consumption goods sector, firms had continuously to introduce new products since, according to Engels' Law, people do not generally consume proportionately more of the same things as they get richer, but rather reallocate their consumption away from old goods and towards new goods. This non-proportional growth of demand implied that goods would tend to go through a life-cycle, growing rapidly when they were first introduced and more slowly later. If a particular firm were tied to only one product, its growth rate would follow this same life-cycle pattern and would eventually slow down and perhaps even come to a halt. If the corporation was to grow steadily at a rapid rate, it had continuously to introduce new products.

Thus, product development and marketing replaced production as a dominant problem of business enterprise. To meet the challenge of a constantly changing market, business enterprise evolved the multidivisional structure. The new form was originated by General Motors and DuPont shortly after World War I, followed by a few others during the 1920s and 1930s, and was widely adopted by most of the giant U.S. corporations in the great boom following World War II. As with the previous stages, evolution involved a process of both differentiation and integration. Corporations were decentralized into several *divisions*, each concerned with one product line and organized with its own head office. At a higher level, a *general office* was created to coordinate the division and to plan for the enterprise as a whole.

U.S. corporations began to move to foreign countries almost as soon as they had completed their continent-wide integration. For one thing, their new administrative structure and great financial strength gave them the power to go abroad. In becoming national firms, U.S. corporations learned how to become international. Also, their large size and oligopolistic position gave them an incentive. Direct investment became a new weapon in their arsenal of oligopolistic rivalry. Instead of joining a cartel (prohibited under U.S. law), they invested in foreign customers, suppliers, and competitors. For example, some firms found they were oligopolistic buyers of raw materials produced in foreign countries and feared a monopolization of the sources of supply. By investing directly in foreign producing enterprises, they could gain the security implicit in control over their raw material requirements. Other firms invested abroad to control marketing outlets and thus maximize quasi-rents on their technological discoveries and differentiated products. Some went abroad simply to forestall competition.

The first wave of U.S. direct foreign capital investment occurred around the turn of the century followed by a second wave during the 1920s. The outward migration slowed down during the depression but resumed after World War II and soon accelerated rapidly. Between 1950 and 1969, direct foreign investment by U.S. firms expanded at a rate of about 10 percent per annum. At this rate it would double in less than ten years, and even at a much slower rate of growth, foreign operations will reach enormous proportions over the next 30 years.

Several important factors account for this rush of foreign investment in the 1950s and the 1960s. First, the large size of the U.S. corporations and their new multidivisional structure gave them wider horizons and a global outlook. Secondly, technological developments in communications created a new awareness of the global challenge and threatened established institutions by opening up new sources of competition. For reasons noted above, business enterprises were among the first to recognize the potentialities and dangers of the new environment and to take active steps to cope with it.

A third factor in the outward migration of U.S. capital was the rapid growth of Europe and Japan. This, combined with the slow growth of the United States economy in the 1950s, altered world market shares as firms confined to the U.S. market found themselves falling behind in the competitive race and losing ground to European and Japanese firms, which were growing rapidly because of the expansion of their markets. Thus, in the late 1950s, United States corporations faced a serious "non-American" challenge. Their answer was an outward thrust to establish sales production and bases in foreign territories. This strategy was possible in Europe, since government there provided an open door for United States investment, but was blocked in Japan, where the government adopted a highly restrictive policy. To a large extent, United States business was thus able to redress the imbalances caused by the Common Market, but Japan remained a source of tension to oligopoly equilibrium.

What about the future? The present trend indicates further multi-nationalization of all giant firms, European as well as American. In the first place, European firms, partly as a reaction to the United States penetration of their markets, and partly as a natural result of their own growth, have begun to invest abroad on an expanded scale and will probably continue to do so in the future, and even enter into the United States market. This process is already well underway and may be expected to accelerate as time goes on. The reaction of United States business will most likely be to meet foreign investment at home with more foreign investment abroad. They, too, will scramble for market positions in underdeveloped countries and attempt to get an even larger share of the European market, as a reaction to European investment in the United States. Since they are large and powerful, they will on balance succeed in maintaining their relative standing in the world as a whole—as their losses in some markets are offset by gains in others.

A period of rivalry will prevail until a new equilibrium between giant U.S. firms and giant European and Japanese firms is reached, based on a strategy of multinational operations and cross-penetration. We turn now to the implications of this pattern of industrial organization for international trade and the law of uneven development.

PART II. UNEVEN DEVELOPMENT

Suppose giant multinational corporations (say 300 from the U.S. and 200 from Europe and Japan) succeed in establishing themselves as the dominant form of international enterprise and come to control a significant share of industry (especially modern industry) in each country. The world economy will resemble more and more the United States economy, where each of the large corporations tends to spread over the entire continent and to penetrate almost every nook and cranny. What would be the effect of a world industrial organization of this type on international specialization, exchange and income distribution? The purpose of this section is to analyze the spatial dimension of the corporate hierarchy.

A useful starting point is Chandler and Redlich's scheme for analyzing the evolution of corporate structure. They distinguish "three levels of business administration, three horizons, three levels of task, and three levels of decision making . . . and three levels of policies." Level III, the lowest level, is concerned with managing the day-to-day operations of the enterprise, that is, with keeping it going within the established framework. Level II, which first made its appearance with the separation of head office from field office, is responsible for coordinating the managers at Level III. The functions of Level I—top management—are goal-determination and planning. This level sets the framework in which the lower levels operate.

Location theory suggests that Level III activities would spread themselves over the globe according to the pull of manpower, markets, and raw materials. The multinational corporation, because of its power to command capital and technology and its ability to rationalize their use on a global scale, will probably spread production more evenly over the world's surface than is now the case. Thus, in the first instance, it may well be a force for diffusing industrialization to the less developed countries and creating new centers of production. (We postpone for a moment a discussion of the fact that location depends upon transportation, which in turn depends upon the government, which in turn is influenced by the structure of business enterprise.)

Level II activities, because of their need for white-collar workers, communications systems, and information, tend to concentrate in large cities. Since their demands are similar, corporations from different industries tend to place their coordinating offices in the same city, and Level II activities are consequently far more geographically concentrated than Level III activities.

Level I activities, the general offices, tend to be even more concentrated than Level II activities, for they must be located close to the capital market, the media, and the government. Nearly every major corporation in the United States, for example, must have its general office (or a large proportion of its high-level personnel) in or near the city of New York because of the need for face-to-face contact at higher levels of decision making.

Applying this scheme to the world economy, one would expect to find the highest offices of the multinational corporations concentrated in the world's major cities—New York, London, Paris, Bonn, Tokyo. These, along with Moscow and perhaps Peking, will be the major centers of high-level strategic planning. Lesser cities throughout the world will deal with the day-to-day operations of specific local problems. These in turn will be arranged in a hierarchical fashion: the larger and more important ones will contain regional corporate headquarters, while the smaller ones will be confined to lower level activities. Since business is usually the core of the city, geographical specialization will come to reflect the hierarchy of corporate decision making, and the occupational distribution of labor in a city or region will depend upon its function in the international economic system. The "best" and most highly paid administrators, doctors, lawyers, scientists, educators, government officials, actors, servants and hairdressers, will tend to concentrate in or near the major centers.

The structure of income and consumption will tend to parallel the structure of status and authority. The citizens of capital cities will have the best jobs—allocating men and money at the highest level and planning growth and development—and will receive the highest rates of remuneration. (Executives' salaries tend to be a function of the wage bill of people under them. The larger the empire of the multinational corporation, the greater the earnings of top executives, to a large extent independent of their performance. Thus, growth in the hinterland subsidiaries implies growth in the income of capital cities, but not vice versa.

The citizens of capital cities will also be the first to innovate new products in the cycle which is known in the marketing literature as trickle-down or two-stage marketing. A new product is usually first introduced to a select group of people who have "discretionary" income and are willing to experiment in their consumption patterns. Once it is accepted by this group, it spreads, or trickles down to other groups via the demonstration effect.

In this process, the rich and the powerful get more votes than everyone else; first, because they have more money to spend, second, because they have more ability to experiment, and third, because they have high status and are likely to be copied. This special group may have something approaching a choice in consumption patterns; the rest have only the choice between conforming or being isolated.

The trickle-down system also has the advantage—from the center's point of view—of reinforcing patterns of authority and control. According to Fallers, it helps keep workers on the treadmill by creating an illusion of upward mobility even though relative status remains unchanged. In each period subordinates achieve (in part) the consumption standards of their superiors in a previous period and are thus torn in two directions: if they look backward and compare their standards of living through time, things seem to be getting better; if they look upward they see that their relative position has not changed. They receive a consolation prize, as it were, which may serve to keep them going by softening the reality that in a competitive system, few succeed and many fail. It is little wonder, then, that those at the top stress growth rather than equality as the welfare criterion for human relations.

In the international economy trickle-down marketing takes the form of an international demonstration effect spreading outward from the metropolis to the hinterland. Multinational corporations help speed up this process, often the key motive for direct investment, through their control of marketing channels and communications media.

The development of a new product is a fixed cost; once the expenditure needed for invention or innovation has been made, it is forever a bygone. The actual cost of production is thus typically well below selling price and the limit on output is not rising costs but falling demand due to saturated markets. The marginal profit on new foreign markets is thus high, and corporations have a strong interest in maintaining a system which spreads their products widely. Thus, the interest of multinational corporations in underdeveloped countries is larger than the size of the market would suggest.

It must be stressed that the dependency relationship between major and minor cities should not be attributed to technology. The new technology, because it increases interaction, implies greater interdependence but not necessarily a hierarchical structure. Communications linkages could be arranged in the form of a grid in which each point was directly connected to many other points, permitting lateral as well as vertical communication. This system would be polycentric since messages from one point to another would go directly rather than through the center; each point would become a center on its own; and the distinction between center and periphery would disappear.

Such a grid is made *more* feasible by aeronautical and electronic revolutions which greatly reduce costs of communications. It is not technology which creates inequality; rather, it is *organization* that imposes a ritual judicial asymmetry on the use of intrinsically symmetrical means of communications and arbitrarily creates unequal capacities to initiate and terminate exchange, to store and retrieve information, and to determine the extent of the exchange and terms of the discussion. Just as colonial powers in the past linked each point in the hinterland to the metropolis and inhibited lateral communications, preventing the growth of independent centers of decision making and creativity, multinational corporations (backed by state powers) centralize control by imposing a hierarchical system.

This suggests the possibility of an alternative system of organization in the form of national planning. Multinational corporations are private institutions which organize one or a few industries across many countries. Their polar opposite (the antimultinational corporation, perhaps) is a public institution which organizes many industries across one region. This would permit the centralization of capital, i.e., the coordinator of many enterprises by one decision-making center, but would substitute regionalization for internationalization. The span of control would be confined to the boundaries of a single polity and society and not spread over many countries. The advantage of the multinational corporation is its global perspective. The advantage of national planning is its ability to remove the wastes of oligopolistic anarchy, i.e., meaningless product differentiation and an imbalance between different industries within a geographical area. It concentrates *all* levels of decision making in one locale and thus provides each region with a full complement of skills and occupations. This opens up new horizons for local development by making possible the social and political control of economic decision making. Multinational corporations, in contrast, weaken political control because they span many countries and can escape national regulation.

A few examples might help to illustrate how multinational corporations reduce options for development. Consider an underdeveloped country wishing to invest heavily in education in order to increase its stock of human capital and raise standards of living. In a market system it would be able to find gainful employment for its citizens within its *national boundaries* by specializing in education-intensive activities and selling its surplus production to foreigners. In the multinational corporate system, however, the demand for high-level education in low-ranking areas is limited, and a country does not become a world center simply by having a better educational system. An outward shift in the supply of educated people in a country, therefore, will not create its own demand but will create an excess supply and lead to emigration. Even then, the employment opportunities for citizens of low-ranking countries are restricted by discriminatory practices in the center. It is well known that ethnic homogeneity increases as one goes up the corporate hierarchy; the lower levels contain a wide variety of nationalities, the higher levels become successively purer and purer. In part this stems from the skill differences of different nationalities, but more important is the fact that the higher up one goes in the decision-making process, the more important mutual understanding and ease of communications become; a common background becomes all-important.

A similar type of specialization by nationality can be expected within the multinational corporation hierarchy. Multinational corporations are torn in two directions. On the one hand, they must adapt to local circumstances in each country. This calls for decentralized decision making. On the other hand, they must coordinate their activities in various parts of the world and stimulate the flow of ideas from one part of their empire to another. This calls for centralized control. They must, therefore, develop an organizational structure to balance the need for coordination with the need for adaptation to a patch-work quilt of languages, laws and customs. One solution to this problem is a division of labor based on nationality. Day-to-day management in each country is left to the nationals of that country who, because they are intimately familiar with local conditions and practices, are able to deal with local problems and local government. These nationals remain rooted in one spot, while above them is a layer of people who move around from country to country, as bees among flowers, transmitting information from one subsidiary to another and from the lower levels to the general office at the apex of the corporate structure. In the nature of things, these people (reticulators) for the most part will be citizens of the country of the parent corporation (and will be drawn from a small, culturally homogeneous group within the advanced world), since they will need to have the confidence of their superiors and be able to move easily in the higher management circles. Latin Americans, Asians and Africans will at best be able to aspire to a management position in the intermediate coordinating centers at the continental level. Very few will be able to get much higher than this, for the closer one gets to the top, the more important is "a common cultural heritage."

Another way in which the multinational corporations inhibit economic development in the hinterland is through their effect on tax capacity. An important government instrument for promoting growth is expenditure on infrastructure and support services. By providing transportation and communications, education and health, a government can create a productive labor force and increase the growth potential of its economy. The extent to which it can afford to finance these intermediate outlays depends upon its tax revenue.

However, a government's ability to tax multinational corporations is limited by the ability of these corporations to manipulate transfer prices and to move their productive facilities to another country. This means that they will only be attracted to countries where superior infrastructure offsets higher taxes. The government of an underdeveloped country will find it difficult to extract a surplus (revenue from the multinational corporations, less cost of services provided to them) from multinational corporations to use for long-run development programs and for stimulating growth in other industries. In contrast, governments of the advanced countries, where the home office and financial center of the multinational corporation are located, can tax the profits of the corporation as a whole, as well as the high incomes of its management. Government in the metropolis can, therefore, capture some of the surplus generated by the multinational corporations and use it to further improve their infrastructure and growth.

In other words, the relationship between multinational corporations and underdeveloped countries will be somewhat like the relationship between the national corporations in the United States and state and municipal governments. These lower-level governments tend always to be short of funds compared to the federal government which can tax a corporation as a whole. Their competition to attract corporate investment eats up their surplus, and they find it difficult to finance extensive investments in human and physical capital even where such investment would be productive. This has a crucial effect on the pattern of government expenditure. For example, suppose taxes were first paid to state government and then passed on to the federal government. What chance is there that these lower level legislatures would approve the phenomenal expenditures on space research that now go on? A similar discrepancy can be expected in the international economy with overspending and waste by metropolitan governments and a shortage of public funds in the less advanced countries.

In conclusion, it seems that a regime of multinational corporations would offer underdeveloped countries neither national independence nor equality. It would tend instead to inhibit the attainment of these goals. It would turn the underdeveloped countries into branch-plant countries, not only with reference to their economic functions but throughout the whole gamut of social, political and cultural roles. The subsidiaries of multinational corporations are typically amongst the largest corporations in the country of operations, and their top executives play an influential role in the political, social and cultural life of the host country. Yet these people, whatever their title, occupy at best a medium position in the corporate structure and are restricted in authority and horizons to a lower level of decision making. The governments with whom they deal tend to take on the same middle management outlook, since this is the only range of information and ideas to which they are exposed. In this sense, one can hardly expect such a country to bring forth the creative imagination needed to apply science and technology to the problems of degrading poverty.

PART III. THE POLITICAL ECONOMY OF THE MULTINATIONAL CORPORATION

The viability of the multinational corporate system depends upon the degree to which people will tolerate the unevenness it creates. The new Mercantilism (as the multinational corporate system of special alliances and privileges, aid and tariff concessions is sometimes called) faces similar problems of internal and external division. The center is troubled: excluded groups revolt and even some of the affluent are dissatisfied with their roles. (The much talked about "generation gap" may indicate the failure of the system to reproduce itself.) Nationalistic rivalry between major capitalist countries (especially the challenge of Japan and Germany) remains an important divisive factor, while the economic challenge from the socialist bloc may prove to be of the utmost significance in the next thirty years. Russia has its own form of large-scale economic organizations, also in command of modern technology, and its own conception of how the world should develop. So does China to an increasing degree. Finally, there is the threat presented by the middle classes and the excluded groups of the underdeveloped countries.

The national middle classes in the underdeveloped countries came to power when the center weakened but could not, through their policy of import substitution manufacturing, establish a viable basis for sustained growth. They now face a foreign exchange crisis and an unemployment (or population) crisis—the first indicating their inability to function in the international economy, and the second indicating their alienation from the people they are supposed to lead. In the immediate future, these national middle classes will gain a new lease on life as they take advantage of the spaces created by the rivalry between American and non-American oligopolists striving to establish global market positions. The native capitalists will again become the champions of national independence as they bargain with multinational corporations. But the conflict at this level is more apparent than real, for in the end the fervent nationalism of the middle class asks only for promotion within the corporate structure and not for a break with that structure. In the last analysis their power derives from the metropolis and they cannot easily afford to challenge the international system. They do not command the loyalty of their own population and cannot really compete with the large, powerful, aggregate capitals from the center. They are prisoners of the taste patterns and consumption standards set at the center, and depend on outsiders for technical advice, capital, and when necessary, for military support of their position.

The main threat comes from the excluded groups. It is not unusual in underdeveloped countries for the top 5 percent to obtain between 30 and 40 percent of the total national income, and for the top one-third to obtain anywhere from 60 to 70 percent. At most, one-third of the population can be said to benefit in some sense from the dualistic growth that characterizes development in the hinterland. The remaining two-thirds, who together get only one-third of the income, are outsiders, not because they do not contribute to the economy, but because they do not share in the benefits. They provide a source of cheap labor which helps keep exports to the developed world at a low price and which has financed the urban-biased growth of recent years. Because their wages are low, they spend a moderate amount of time in menial services and are sometimes referred to as underemployed as if to imply they were not needed. In fact, it is difficult to see how the system in most underdeveloped countries could survive without cheap labor, since removing it (e.g., diverting it to public works projects as is done in socialist countries) would raise consumption costs to capitalists and professional elites. Economic development under the multinational corporation does not offer much promise for this large segment of society and their antagonism continuously threatens the system.

The survival of the multinational corporate system depends on how fast it can grow and how much trickles down. Plans now being formulated in government offices, corporate headquarters and international organizations sometimes suggest that a growth rate of about 6 percent per year in national income (3 percent per capita) is needed. (Such a target is, of course, far below what would be possible if a serious effort were made to solve basic problems of health, education and clothing.) To what extent is it possible?

The multinational corporation must solve four critical problems for the underdeveloped countries, if it is to foster the continued growth and survival of a "modern" sector. First, it must break the foreign-exchange constraint and provide the underdeveloped countries with imported goods for capital formation and modernization. Second, it must finance an expanded program of government expenditure to train labor and provide support services for urbanization and industrialization. Third, it must solve the urban food problem created by growth. Finally, it must keep the excluded two-thirds of the population under control.

The solution now being suggested for the first is to restructure the world economy allowing the periphery to export certain manufactured goods to the center. Part of this program involves regional common markets to rationalize the existing structure of industry. These plans typically do not involve the rationalization and restructuring of the entire economy of the underdeveloped countries but mainly serve the small manufacturing sector which caters to higher income groups and which, therefore, faces a very limited market in any particular country. The solution suggested for the second problem is an expanded aid program and a reformed government bureaucracy (perhaps along the lines of the Alliance for Progress). The solution for the third is agri-business and the green revolution, a program with only limited benefits to the rural poor. Finally, the solution offered for the fourth problem is population control, either through family planning or counterinsurgency.

It is doubtful whether the center has sufficient political stability to finance and organize the program outlined above. It is not clear, for example, that the West has the technology to rationalize manufacturing abroad or modernize agriculture, or the willingness to open up marketing channels for the underdeveloped world. Nor is it evident that the center has the political power to embark on a large aid program or to readjust its own structure of production and allow for the importation of manufactured goods from the periphery. It is difficult to imagine labor accepting such a re-allocation (a new repeal of the Corn Laws as it were), and it is equally hard to see how the advanced countries could create a system of planning to make these extra hardships unnecessary.

The present crisis may well be more profound than most of us imagine, and the West may find it impossible to restructure the international economy on a workable basis. One could easily argue that the age of the multinational corporation is at its end rather than at its beginning. For all we know, books on the global partnership may be the epitaph of the American attempt to take over the old international economy, and not the herald of a new era of international cooperation.

Conclusion

The multinational corporation, because of its great power to plan economic activity, represents an important step forward over previous methods of organizing international exchange. It demonstrates the social nature of production on a global scale. As it eliminates the anarchy of international markets and brings about a more extensive and productive international division of labor, it releases great sources of latent energy.

However, as it crosses international boundaries, it pulls and tears at the social and political fabric and erodes the cohesiveness of national states. Whether one likes this or not, it is probably a tendency that cannot be stopped.

Through its propensity to nestle everywhere, settle everywhere, and establish connections everywhere, the multinational corporation destroys the possibility of national seclusion and self-sufficiency and creates a universal interdependence. But the multinational corporation is still a private institution with a partial outlook and represents only an imperfect solution to the problem of international cooperation. It creates hierarchy rather than equality, and it spreads its benefits unequally.

In proportion to its success, it creates tensions and difficulties. It will lead other institutions, particularly labor organizations and government, to take an international outlook and thus unwittingly create an environment less favorable to its own survival. It will demonstrate the possibilities of material progress at a faster rate than it can realize them, and will create a worldwide demand for change that it cannot satisfy.

The next round may be marked by great crises due to the conflict between national planning by governments and international planning by corporations. For example, if each country loses its power over fiscal and monetary policy due to the growth of multinational corporations (as some observers believe Canada has), how will aggregate demand be stabilized? Will it be possible to construct super-states? Or does multinationalism do away with Keynesian problems? Similarly, will it be possible to fulfill a host of other government functions at the supra-national level in the near future? During the past twenty-five years many political problems were put aside as the West recovered from the depression and the war. By the late sixties the bloom of this long upswing had begun to fade. In the seventies, power conflicts are likely to come to the fore.

Whether underdeveloped countries will use the opportunities arising from this crisis to build viable local decision-making institutions is difficult to predict. The national middle class failed when it had the opportunity and instead merely reproduced internally the economic dualism of the international economy as it squeezed agriculture to finance urban industry. What is needed is a complete change of direction. The starting point must be the needs of the bottom two-thirds, and not the demands of the top third. The primary goal of such a strategy would be to provide minimum standards of health, education, food and clothing to the entire population, removing the more obvious forms of human suffering. This requires a system which can mobilize the entire population and which can search the local environment for information, resources and needs. It must be able to absorb modern technology, but it cannot be mesmerized by the form it takes in the advanced countries; it must go to the roots. This is not the path the upper one-third chooses when it has control.

The wealth of a nation, wrote Adam Smith two hundred years ago, is determined by "first, the skill, dexterity and judgement with which labor is generally applied; and, secondly by the proportion between the number of those who are employed in useful labor, and that of those who are not so employed." Capitalist enterprise has come a long way from his day, but it has never been able to bring more than a small fraction of the world's population into useful or highly productive employment. The latest stage reveals once more the power of social cooperation and division of labor which so fascinated Adam Smith in his description of pin manufacturing. It also shows the shortcomings of concentrating this power in private hands.

Epilogue

Many readers of this essay in draft form have asked: Is there an alternative? Can anything be done? The problem simply stated is to go beyond the multinational corporation. Scholarship can perhaps make the task easier by showing how the forms of international social production devised by capital as it expanded to global proportions can be used to build a better society benefiting all men. I have tried to open up one avenue for explanation by suggesting a system of regional planning as a positive negation of the multinational corporation. Much more work is needed to construct alternative methods of organizing the international economy. Fortunately businessmen in attacking the problem of applying technology on a world level have developed many of the tools and conditions needed for a socialist solution, if we can but stand them on their head. But one must keep in mind that the problem is not one of ideas alone.

A major question is how far those in power will allow the necessary metamorphosis to happen, and how far they will try to resist it by violent means. I do not believe the present structure of uneven development can long be maintained in the light of the increased potential for world development demonstrated by corporate capital itself. But power at the center is great, and the choice of weapons belongs in the first instance to those who have them.

Theodor Mommsen summed up his history of the Roman Republic with patient sadness.

It was indeed an old world, and even the richly gifted patriotism of Caesar could not make it young again. The dawn does not return till after the night has run its course.

I myself do not view the present with such pessimism. History moves more quickly now, the forces for positive change are much stronger, and the center seems to be losing its will and self-confidence. It is becoming increasingly evident to all that in contrast to corporate capitalism we must be somewhat less "efficient" within the microcosm of the enterprise and far more "efficient" in the macrocosm of world society. The dysutopia of the multinational corporate system shows us both what is to be avoided and what is possible.

part 2

Issues in Micro- and Macroeconomics

Microeconomics! Macroeconomics! Beginning economics students encounter these formidable terms, and a textbook filled with intricate diagrams only increases their apprehensions. The real difficulty faced by students with a genuine interest in understanding contemporary economic problems, however, is not the strangeness of a new terminology or even the mathematical rigor applied to the subject matter. These are ultimately questions of style. Rather, the difficulty lies in the failure of orthodox micro- and macroeconomics to integrate their theoretical structure with institutional realities. The result is not science but a pseudoscience biased in favor of the status quo, one that fails to shed much light on the problems that currently plague America.

The readings in this section are designed to clarify the economic issues so often omitted or mistreated in orthodox accounts. Considerations of space have limited the number of subdivisions to three. (The section that follows is devoted to the macroeconomic crisis.) The majority of the topics treated here—monopoly, consumerism, war, imperialism, urban decay— are discussed in most elementary texts, but with a considerable difference in emphasis. For example, in this volume, war expenditures are treated as central to macroeconomic discussion, not as a topic left hanging on the periphery. Urban problems have also been highlighted, since the cities are clearly undergoing as deep a crisis as the macrocrisis associated with unemployment, inflation, and declines in the GNP. Micro- and macroeconomics, as these readings show, need not be reduced to the apolitical abstractions of the orthodox textbook.

Competition, Monopoly, Consumerism, and the State

The revolution in *macro-*economics touched off in 1936 by the publication of John Maynard Keynes' magnum opus, *The General Theory of Employment, Interest, and Money,* has over-shadowed a second "revolution" set off by the Great Depression—one that transformed *micro-*economics. Monopoly and imperfections in competition were among the foremost con-cerns of professional economists during the 1930s. It was not un-usual to read that the venerated ideal of competition was dead. By the 1950s, the social climate had changed. McCarthyism ruled such doctrine "subversive." Either monopoly was not so bad after all (otherwise, how could the economy perform so well?), or apparent monopoly masked the reality of fiercely competitive behavior.

According to postwar apolo-gists for big business, monopoly only characterizes a quarter of the economy, and this share has not increased since the turn of the century. These conclusions are based on statistical studies that define monopoly as existing

whenever the leading four firms of an industry produce 50 percent of total output. Since quantitative studies of this variety often ignore important qualitative factors, the result is misplaced precision.

For example, much of the gross national product (GNP) of the United States is contrib-uted by the retailing, whole-saling, and service industries. To equate their contribution to the GNP with that made by such primary industries as mining, agriculture, transportation, manufacturing, and communica-tions is plainly unwarranted. These primary industries are the foundation upon which the wealth of this nation has been built; to control them is to dominate the entire American economy. Moreover, small suppliers and distributors are often simply satellites of the corporate giants. Nor do the previously mentioned studies take into account the informal links between allegedly inde-pendent competitors, such as trade and employer associations, interlocking directorates, and so forth. Because bourgeois studies overlook mechanisms of this kind, they overstate the degree of competition and tend to ignore the pervasive collusion within many industries. Further, the argument that monopoly has not increased over time depends upon the use of data from a base period that occurred *after* the turn-of-the-century merger movement. Use of earlier dates, such as 1865 or even 1895, would unquestionably show a trend toward pronounced monopolization. Finally, the share of assets, or profits, held by the leading one or two hundred corporations is considerably higher than in the twenties when it was first measured. These considerations lead to the conclusion that orthodox economists have systematically understated the prevalence of monopoly.

Since the sixties, big business has again been under sharp attack. Recent assaults have been directed against the most powerful giants of all—the international petroleum corporations. In Reading 9 Randall Meyer, president of Exxon, defends these corporations and spells out the limited role he believes government should play in a capitalist economy. Meyer alludes to a number of studies that "prove" competition is still alive and well in contemporary America. As indicated above, other authorities can be cited to the contrary. Reading 10, in contrast, was written by Andreas Papandreou, an eminent economic theorist, most widely known in this country for his progressive role in Greek politics. Papandreou first explains how a market economy is supposed to work and then goes on to argue that the orthodox model of the competitive market is ideologically biased and of no relevance to understanding the monopolistic capitalism of the twentieth century.

Another approach to the role of monopoly, competition, and the state is provided in Reading 11 by David Gold, currently affiliated with the Center for Economic Studies in Palo Alto, California. Gold's article summarizes James O'Connor's *The Fiscal Crisis of the State*, a book written from a Marxist perspective. A selection from this work is reprinted in this volume as Reading 16.

It is worth noting the importance O'Connor gives to the competitive sector, since radicals are often accused of denying its existence. As Marxists Paul Sweezy and Harry Magdoff have pointed out elsewhere, the economy may be dominated by the banking and industrial giants, but the dwarfs still play an important role (1) as producers of needed but unprofitable products and services; (2) as supplementary producers when demand is high; and (3) as risk-takers and developers of new products and processes, later imitated or taken over by the corporate giants.

If monopoly capital is the problem, what is the solution? For Ralph Nader and his "raider" associates, it is good government and a restoration of competition. Nader documents well the costs of monopoly in Reading 12, but he does not show the political and economic feasibility of his alternative. Nader's shortcomings are examined from a radical perspective by Alan Stone, a political science professor at Rutgers University (see Reading 13).

While Nader is willing to utilize the authority of government to curb the power of big business, others call for a return to the "free market." Interestingly, the leading proponents of laissez-faire capitalism rarely suggest that government stop its production of war goods. What is euphemistically known as "defense" spending is considered by most conservative economists to be a justifiable departure from the free market. If this major source of governmental intervention is thus left untouched by free market economists, what validity remains in their analysis of government's legitimate economic role? Very little, I would suggest.

Individuals are considered by orthodox economics to be maximizers of what gives them pleasure—such things as income and leisure. Significantly, we are never told how a society that rewards self-interest and mocks good-heartedness can avoid producing selfish people, who do not consider the harm done to others through *their* actions.

This lack of social conscience is further encouraged by the fact that the harm is created through the impersonal market mechanism.

The free market economist is caught in a logical inconsistency. He must assume that people who are programed to achieve personal gain in the economic sphere refrain from similar pursuits in the political arena. It will not do to argue that institutional barriers should be erected to prevent individuals from employing the state to accumulate more wealth. Our Constitution, designed to permit private accumulation, encourages acquisitive "instincts" that, once unleashed, obviously cannot be kept in check by a legal structure created by the wealthy. American history shows that the state has repeatedly intervened to protect special interests. Could it have been otherwise? Until free market economists demonstrate why and how the motivational assumptions they endorse for *economic* behavior are somehow inoperative in *politics*—an endeavor, I suggest, doomed to failure—free market economics remains curiously utopian. Its rhetoric calls for a society of independent maximizers (a rather soulless utopia, at that!); its reality is mainly confined to vigorous attacks on a variety of social reforms, such as rent control and minimum wage laws. Its proponents fail to mention the central government intervention of our time—war spending, profiteering, and their associated evils. The social function of free market economics, therefore, is to buttress the status quo.

The real choice is not between more government and less. It lies in determining what kind of government and what kind of institutions best serve the general welfare. The rhetoric of the conservative advocates of the free market is hollow, but the rhetoric of liberalism has also cloaked a host of social horrors.

The discrepancy between rhetoric and reality has led to disenchantment with the "welfare state" of American liberalism, and has reawakened interest in socialism, a long-standing alternative approach to solving social problems. Debate and struggle over these alternatives—capitalism and socialism—will likely dominate the remaining decades of the twentieth century.

The Role of Big Business in Achieving National Goals

Randall Meyer

In recent years, one of the most disturbing trends in American attitudes has been the decline of public confidence in virtually all the major institutions of society.

When analyzing the evidence of deterioration in public confidence, those of us who work within large organizations in the private sector have been deeply concerned and—to an extent—puzzled. Businessmen naturally wonder why people feel so negatively about the performance of the business community in view of the nation's historical economic record. Consider, for a moment, what has been accomplished under the private enterprise system. During the last century, the United States has gained approximately a 40-fold rise in annual output. Material levels of living have been doubling every generation. Moreover, the fruits of economic progress are widely shared. Broadly based economic growth has done more toward elimination of poverty in this country than any or all of the income distribution programs our government has ever conceived. Even our acknowledged national problems, such as environmental pollution, energy supply, and traffic jams, are essentially byproducts of national economic success. And the national affluence will provide the means for correction of such problems.

AMERICANS BELIEVE "BIG" IS "BAD"

Why do people distrust big companies even more than some other institutions? I believe there are two fundamental reasons:

First, there is a widespread lack of understanding of the *relative* importance and influence of big business in the total economy. People simply do not know enough about how big companies fit into the total economic system, nor do they understand the manner in which big firms are managed.

Second, there is a similar lack of understanding of the essential role and contributions of large business enterprises in achieving national goals.

The attitude of many toward big companies can be understood more readily if it is viewed as a traditional reaction to "bigness" in general. Americans equate size with power, whether economic or political, and have always viewed the growth of large institutions with apprehension. When people think of business, they like to think of the corner grocer, the town druggist, or the service station at the neighborhood shopping center. *Small* business, which is perceived as being accessible, personalized, and understandable, has been the national ideal. As academician Irving Kristol has pointed out, the large corporation is to an extent an "accidental" institution, anticipated by none of the theorists of capitalism and for the most part not welcomed by them. According to Mr. Kristol, "It was always assumed, both by economic theorists from Adam Smith onwards and by public opinion, that large aggregations of capital would be a temporary phenomenon, and would not coalesce into permanent institutions. The reason that the laws of incorporation were made so simple and easy in the United States was because it was assumed that corporate competition would make the large corporation, such as we know it today, impossible."

The perception that "big" is "bad" is reinforced in our schools, which tend to emphasize the past excesses of the business system—such as attempts to create monopolies and efforts by some businessmen to control political affairs. As the nation has grown to maturity, it has learned to control the potential excesses of the business system—and the human beings in it—through powerful deterrents such as the antitrust laws. As a result, business and businessmen today are as a rule quite unlike some of their historical counterparts.

Yet the historical perception of big business continues to permeate the thinking of many Americans. Today the critics of business contend—and many Americans apparently believe—that a handful of the largest corporations increasingly dominate U.S. economic and social life. It is said that U.S. business is becoming highly concentrated in a few giant enterprises. It is generally assumed that big business is steadily squeezing out small business, and that the large companies are progressively accumulating a greater share of the national wealth. Moreover, large corporations are perceived as being largely unresponsive to national goals.

However, this widespread *perception* is simply not in accord with the economic and social realities.

BIG BUSINESS AND SMALL BUSINESS

The facts are that the United States neither is, nor is becoming, a "big business" economy. The dean of writers on American business, Peter Drucker, has pointed out that the period in which big business grew faster than the economy probably came to an end around World War I. Since then, the growth has been roughly parallel. But in *relative* size and power, big business has been declining. Economist Victor Fuchs, who has studied the nation's journey toward a "post-industrial" society, has said: "Most people do not work and have never worked for large corporations; most production does not take place and never has taken place in large corporations. In the future, the large corporation is likely to be overshadowed by the hospitals, universities, research institutes, government agencies, and professional organizations that are the hallmarks of a service economy."

Economist Neil Jacoby of UCLA, former member of the President's Council of Economic Advisers, has done a significant study of U.S. business since World War II. During this period the number of incorporated enterprises has grown four times as fast as the human population. And the scale of corporate operations has increased in response to the scaling up of the economy—just as government, labor, and other institutions have also increased in size. Therefore, many of the bigger U.S. companies have grown much larger—but not *relatively* larger in the context of the total economy. The size distribution of corporations has not changed significantly in a generation. The numbers of companies in each group—large, medium, and small—have expanded at approximately equal rates.

By far the vast majority of corporations are *small* businesses. In fact, the dominant change in business since World War II has been a great infusion of new and small companies. According to Dr. Jacoby: "Small companies hold an important and enduring position in the U.S. economy. It is a serious error to assert that giant corporations 'characterize' or serve as 'prototypes' for American business and that medium and small companies are transient institutions that will ultimately vanish." Small businesses can and do thrive side by side with larger enterprises, each utilizing comparative advantages.

Neither is the American spirit of individual enterprise disappearing under competitive pressures from big business. On the contrary, as large a proportion of working Americans now work for themselves as did in 1945.

CONCENTRATION AND COMPETITION

Nor does there appear to have been any important change in market concentration or in the effectiveness of competition in the economy. After correction for price inflation, the average real volume of business done per American corporation was less in 1968 than it was in 1950. Economist M. A. Adelman of MIT concluded as recently as 1970 that in spite of the growth in size of individual companies and the many mergers and acquisitions, there is little or no evidence of greater concentration in our economy in the last two generations. And Peter Drucker, in an extensive analysis of recent structural developments in U.S. business, concluded that in spite of the growth of large corporations and the development of multinational enterprises and conglomerates, our economy has in fact become *more* competitive.

This can be demonstrated by examining the great historical period of business consolidations which occurred about the turn of the century and contrasting it to the present. In 1899, Standard Oil Company (New Jersey) controlled 82 percent of the nation's refining capacity. In 1900, American Sugar Refining made virtually all the sugar in the country, and International Harvester produced 85 percent of the nation's harvesting machines. In 1902, National Biscuit controlled 70 percent of the biscuit output, U.S. Leather accounted for more than 60 percent of leather products, and International Paper produced 60 percent of all newsprint.

In contrast, these and virtually all other industries are much less concentrated today. For example, although the U.S. petroleum industry has been charged frequently with being monopolistic in character, in fact no single oil company controls more than 10 percent of any segment of the industry. Exxon USA, the largest domestic petroleum company, holds less than 10 percent of total crude oil production, less than 9 percent of domestic refining capacity, and supplies less than 8 percent of the total gasoline sold in the U.S.

Critics contend that big businesses are not subject to normal economic forces. Yet the big corporations are in reality a changing group. Of the 100 largest industrial corporations in 1909, only 36 remained on the list in 1948.

Of the top 100 corporations in 1948, only 65 continued to hold that ranking in 1968. In every generation, substantial changes have occurred among the big companies. For example, the period from 1948 to 1968 saw the emergence of large aerospace and conglomerate companies—and the disappearance from top ranking of many tobacco, motion picture, and merchandising firms. Great size or market position do not guarantee immortality. Carl Kaysen and Donald F. Turner, writing on antitrust in 1958, complained about the "monopoly power" in the publishing business of *Life*, *Look*, and *The Saturday Evening Post*. They failed to anticipate the effects of network television on general magazine publishing.

BIG BUSINESS' SHARE OF NATIONAL WEALTH

Although many believe that big companies are accumulating too great a share of the nation's wealth, studies have shown that over the past 20 years or so the rewards going to the corporate sector in the form of before-tax profits have declined from 16 percent to 11 percent of the national income, while rewards to corporate employees in wages and salaries have gone up. Corporate business holds only about 28 percent of U.S. tangible wealth, and its share has not changed much during the past 50 years. The bulk of the nation's tangible wealth is held by the household and government sectors. And government's share has been expanding at the expense of the other sectors.

In brief, then, the United States is not a "corporate state" as some critics have charged—nor will it become so. The U.S. economy today is a pluralistic economy in which the nonprofit sector has been growing faster than the profit sector.

THE ROLE OF BIG BUSINESS

It is not my intention to seem to minimize the role of big business in the U.S. economy—only to put it in its proper perspective. For I do believe that large enterprises have an essential role to perform for the nation.

There are sound reasons why large business enterprises do develop in certain industries in modern industrial economies. Many studies show that the same industries which generate large industrial organizations in the United States also do so in Canada, Great Britain, West Germany, France, and Japan.

Basically, the tasks to be done dictate the size of companies. Large tasks require the accumulation of large aggregations of capital, physical, and human resources. One efficient way to bring together these resources is to build a large company, thus gaining the advantage of economies of scale. It is important that the nation have such enterprises to undertake big projects in a socially responsible manner. Although small companies are essential, and always will be, our country is far beyond the point where small companies alone can accomplish the major tasks involved in meeting the needs and aspirations of people.

Some projects are so big that no single company, however large, can undertake them. For example, only a consortium of companies could possibly afford to build the Trans-Alaska pipeline at a cost of some $6 billion. Only they—or the government. Although the government could undertake such a project, private enterprise can do the job much more efficiently.

Size is a requirement in certain other aspects of petroleum operations as well. For example, to use a floating drilling rig to explore offshore for oil for one year costs about $15 million. To construct a production platform to operate in 850 feet of water costs from $50 to $60 million. And to construct a new 250,000-barrels-per-day oil refinery in the U.S. costs upwards of $500 million.

Yet while big organizations are needed to finance and accomplish the largest jobs, the U.S. petroleum industry is at the same time characterized by literally tens of thousands of smaller companies engaged in exploration, production, refining, service, supply, and marketing activities—about 40,000 individual companies all told. Small and medium-sized companies are just as essential to the health of the oil business as big ones; each performs different combinations of tasks or the same tasks on a different scale.

The national tasks ahead—such as the Project Independence drive toward energy self-sufficiency—will require tremendous accumulations of resources. The large corporation will be one of the principal vehicles—but certainly not the only one—through which the nation's energy and other goals can be reached. This is true for several reasons.

WHY BIG BUSINESS IS RESPONSIVE TO SOCIAL GOALS

First of all, today's large corporation is responsive to broad social goals because it is managed for the long run. Because businessmen ordinarily speak in economic terms, it is somehow perceived that they look *only* at short-term profits. The public believes—and rightfully—that in a democratic society such a narrow objective for any institution is unacceptable. But the realities of the business system are quite different. The lingering presumption of great and unbridled power exercised by corporate management rests on out-of-date concepts. The day of the tycoon is past. We are in the era of the professional manager. Managements of large companies must harmonize a wide span of obligations to investors, customers, suppliers, employees, communities, and the national interest. As a result, a large corporation may actually have a narrower range for its decision-making than a small business. Elie Abel, Dean of the Graduate School of Journalism at Columbia University, recently told a gathering of oilmen: "I do not myself believe that the major oil companies invented the energy crisis, even if many Americans apparently do . . . I cannot see any long-term advantage for your industry in the present situation. Rational men could not have devised a plot in which they would cast themselves as short-term profiteers and long-term candidates for expropriation."

On the contrary, successful capitalism means that business must profit from others' well-being, rather than from taking advantage of people. Business must conduct its affairs in a way that adds to the general good, making a mutually rewarding contribution to the achievement of worthwhile human goals. The measure of business' success in doing this is profitability over time. *Profit-making* and not *profiteering* is the only basis for the continued existence of business. Thus, large business enterprises are managed so as to respond to broad social goals, thereby helping assure the growth and long-term viability of the business. That is the standard by which the performance of corporate management is judged.

Corporations must act in a manner that will stand the light of examination over a considerable period of time. Large businesses in particular are subject to constant scrutiny by various levels of government. Also, they are subject to the powerful force of public opinion. The actions of a large business are highly visible to concerned citizens, both locally and nationally, in this age of instant communications. Constant exposure serves as a powerful built-in incentive for big business to conduct its affairs in a manner that will stand up to public scrutiny.

In summary, the large enterprise has the means, capabilities, and experience to perform large-scale economic tasks in a socially responsive manner when given the opportunity and flexibility to do so. Unfortunately, private companies currently find it more and more difficult to utilize their full capabilities because of excessive government intervention.

THE ROLE OF GOVERNMENT

The petroleum industry is a prime example of this process. The oil industry today is subject to the most stringent regulation ever imposed on a U.S. industry in peacetime. From the wellhead to the gasoline pump, the industry is involved with more than 60 regulatory and licensing agencies. The federal government controls the price of most domestic crude oil, mandates sales of crude to certain refiners, and determines to whom products can be sold and the price that can be charged for them. The most recent new level of controls, including the creation of a new government body, the Federal Energy Administration, was conceived in the midst of the Mid East oil embargoes and shortages. But today supply and demand have struck a new balance; in fact, world supplies are once again more than adequate at today's price levels. And yet the controls and the bureaucratic apparatus remain and the regulations grow ever more complex. The government has distorted supply patterns, is stifling competition, and is impeding the very thing it proposes to increase—the free flow of trade.

This is characteristic of many of government's attempts to improve on basic economic forces. Well-conceived, well-administered government regulation has a place in the business system, but too much regulation inhibits through the effect of the regulations and through the negative climate thus created. There are two primary kinds of poor regulation. One is *poorly conceived* regulation, intended to achieve a relatively narrow objective without a clear understanding of its broader effects. A prime example of this is Federal Power Commission control of wellhead prices of natural gas over the past 20 years, a policy which has led directly to today's natural gas shortage. The second kind of poor regulation is soundly conceived but *poorly administered* regulation. An example of this was the now-defunct

Mandatory Oil Import Control Program, which in its latter years became so riddled by exceptions granted for reasons of political expediency that it largely defeated the national purposes it was created to serve.

Government's essential role is this: to establish basic ground rules for society, including business—and then to have the wisdom and restraint to leave those ground rules in place so that competition can occur. Government should function as an arbiter through its vested authority and the powerful tools given it, such as the anti-trust laws, which assure that big and small participants alike have a chance to compete on even terms.

In establishing ground rules, government must recognize that the competitive enterprise system should include the freedom to *fail*.

Government persistently tends to over-regulate, yet it cannot react as quickly or as effectively as the competitive market. Government should rely more confidently on the collective wisdom of the people and their enormous innovative talents applied through productive industry.

After all, the market system has meant a great deal to us. As economist George Stigler of the University of Chicago has said: "The immense proliferation of general education, of scientific progress, and of democracy are all coincidental in time and place with the emergence of the free enterprise system of organizing the market place." Surely that is something worth remembering.

10

The Myth of Market Capitalism

Andreas G. Papandreou

ECONOMIC EFFICIENCY

In an introductory book Robert Dorfman neatly sums up what impresses economists as being the signal contribution of the market economy to social organization. "In spite of its intricacy, the basic idea of a free market economy is very simple. It is the idea of *decentralizing control* of the economy down to units of manageable proportions, coupled with a stupendously efficient method for conveying information among the decentralized units, and a highly effective method of motivating the units to perform their appropriate tasks efficiently."

The truly central characteristic of a market economy is the information system which is identified with the parametric role of prices in a decentralized economic process. For any one unit (whether household or business firm) the prices of the commodities it buys or sells are beyond its control. They are given, universal bits of information for all the participants in the grand game. But though no unit is capable of affecting any of the prices through its purchases or sales, prices do respond to the independent, combined action of the multitude of participants in the markets. All prices are responsive to pressure: If aggregate demand for any commodity exceeds its aggregate supply in the market, the price is forced upward. The opposite is true when aggregate supply exceeds aggregate demand. The price of a commodity has no tendency to change, or is in equilibrium if aggregate demand for the commodity is just equal to its aggregate supply. Thus, equilibrium prices just clear the markets.

If this model is to be of interest as a piece of analytical apparatus, one must show that under certain conditions there exists a set of prices that equate aggregate supply to aggregate demand simultaneously in all markets. To state these conditions unambiguously, to establish that a general market equilibrium is theoretically possible, economists must spell out the required features of the underlying or supporting social organization. Specifically, they must state the manner in which information becomes available to the participants in the economic process; they must define in general terms the structure of authority or control; they must make some commitment as to the motivation of the participants; and, finally, they must describe the set of permissible moves (the legal framework) of the game. The specification of these conditions can be done in a fairly abstract manner and in alternative ways. In fact, the organizational requirements for a general market equilibrium have been spelled out for quite a few distinct models of market economies: for a crafts market economy, for the capitalist market economy, for a socialist market economy, for a labor-managed market economy, and so forth. We restrict our attention to the capitalist model.

Not surprisingly, the model of the capitalist market economy, of market capitalism, was and is the central theme of economics in the West. Hence, taking a look at its principal features is worthwhile. To begin with, the role of the state is restricted to the task of providing the legal framework and ensuring that it is not violated. The basic features of the legal framework are private property and contract. Ownership or control of the economy's wealth is lodged in the hands of private persons. The government itself, of course, must own or control some property, if it is to perform its functions; but public ownership is commensurate to these functions, which are limited to the enactment and enforcement of the rules of the game.

The basic legitimate social process in such an economy is exchange. In fact, exchange is the dominant social process in all market economies because production of goods and services is not for one's own use but for the market. In market capitalism three conditions must be met in order that exchange take place. First, each of the parties to the exchange must own the commodity he intends to exchange. Second, he must be legally capable of transferring ownership to someone else. The law of property and contract establishes rules for identifying the owner of a commodity and the conditions under which a transfer may be carried out in a valid manner. Third, both parties must find it advantageous to complete the exchange. This is an essential feature of the total scheme, which is thus characterized as voluntaristic. In a well-developed market economy commodities are exchanged, not against other commodities, but against money. All commodities are for sale. The only complication worth mentioning affects the sale of labor. In a capitalist economy one may sell his labor time, but he may not sell himself;

labor time is a commodity, but the owner of labor time is not. In a crafts market economy, composed exclusively of artisans or craftsmen, no one sells his labor time but only the product of his labor. In contrast, in a slave market economy, the workers themselves are bought and sold in the market.

In market capitalism, firms are controlled by an entrepreneur, who is either the owner or assumed to represent the owners of the net assets (assets minus liabilities) of the firm. The firm's task is conceived as the production of commodities through the (productive) consumption of other commodities. A firm engages, then, both in production and in exchange processes. Households are the ultimate owners of the productive services made available to the firms through the market. They use the proceeds from the sale of these services to buy the commodities produced by the firms. Households, therefore, are both the ultimate sellers of productive services to the firms, and the ultimate buyers of the firm's products. Households, in contrast with firms, engage only in exchange processes.

Informationally, each firm is supposed to be familiar with its own technology and with the prices ruling in the market. Each household is supposed to be familiar with its own wants, tastes, or preferences; its own resources; and, of course, market prices. The system of prices may be viewed as the list of all the rates of transformation of commodities into money.

The scheme is completed by identifying the position or the state of rest of the participating units (households and firms) with an optimal state—that is, with a state in which some index (utility for the households, profit for the firms) is maximized subject to certain constraints. These indexes of well-being for the participating units incorporate a system of rewards motivating the units to perform their tasks efficiently.

It is worthwhile to take a more careful look at these indexes of well-being for the participating units. Given production technology and the prices of commodities, the entrepreneur is confronted with (infinitely) many feasible combinations of inputs and outputs of commodities. To each combination corresponds a profit (the difference between receipts and outlays). The model requires the firm to prefer *more* profits to *less* profits. Thus, the entrepreneur should select that combination which yields the maximum profit. Similarly for the household: given the prices of all commodities and the factors of production (productive services), the household is confronted with (infinitely) many feasible combinations of quantities of factors of production it might dispose of on the market with quantities of consumer goods it might acquire. To each such combination corresponds a level of satisfaction or utility, depending on the household's preferences or tastes. The model requires the household to prefer *more* to *less* utility. Thus, the household should select that combination of factor sales and consumer goods purchases which yields the maximum utility.

It follows, therefore, that in general equilibrium all markets are cleared, each household is in a position of maximum (feasible) utility, and each firm in a position of maximum (feasible) profits. Is it really surprising that, given this model, one can prove that competitive equilibrium (equilibrium in the kind of economy just described) is in some sense a socially optimal state of affairs? All one needs, in fact, is a nominalist view of society. Thus, we may agree that "society" is made "better off" if someone is made "better off" without somebody else being "worse off." And, in turn, a society could be said to be in an optimal position if no one can be made "better off" without somebody else being made "worse off." All this sounds terribly innocuous, but does have rather far-reaching implications, as we shall see later on in the argument.

We may ask, Who is to be the judge of whether some individual is "better off" or "worse off"? The natural (but not the only) extension of the model is to assume that he himself is to be the judge. This is the orthodox approach to the problem of social or economic welfare, identified with the Italian economist Vilfredo Pareto. Economists have proved that (under certain conditions) competitive equilibrium is Pareto-optimal (and vice versa). We must be careful in interpreting this proof. To begin with, it should be clear by the very meaning of the term *proof* that the Pareto-optimal character of competitive equilibrium is contained in its very definition. The equivalence between competitive equilibrium and Pareto-optimality is purely formal; the equivalence does not have the character of an empirical revelation. Second, it must be stressed that this type of social optimality refers *only* to efficiency, to the absence of waste in the economic process. Thus, when we say that a certain kind of equilibrium is Pareto-optimal, we mean that (given the resource-endowment of the economy, the prevalent technology, and the preferences of the individuals that make it up) no change is capable of making some individual "better off" without making some other individual "worse off." Thus, in fact, the key claim that can be made for this kind of economy is simply that it *eliminates waste in the allocation of resources*. To put it somewhat differently, resources are allocated according to the preferences of the households—which, in this sense, are sovereign—in an informationally economical fashion without any kind of central management or control.

The extension of this claim to the workings of some historically given market economy is legitimate only to the extent that the basic assumptions of the model are in fact satisfied historically. But before I turn to this question, I shall examine what the model has to say about the distribution of income and wealth.

THE DISTRIBUTION OF INCOME AND WEALTH

The uninitiated in the intricacies of the model of a market economy might easily be led to believe that it implies a unique equilibrium collection of goods or commodities produced and traded, associated with a unique distribution of income (of claims on the flow of the aggregate social product). Nothing could be further from the truth.

True enough, the factors of production are bought and sold as commodities in the market, and their prices are determined along with the prices of all other commodities. But the equilibrium solution of the system (which yields the equilibrium set of prices and the equilibrium collection of goods produced and traded) cannot be determined without a specification of the initial distribution of claims on the economy's resources. The reason is that the quantities of factors of production supplied in the market by a household, as well as the quantities of products demanded by it, depend on its initial wealth. And the pattern of household demands for final products along with the pattern of factor supplies is directly dependent upon the initial distribution of wealth.

One must begin, therefore, by positing some initial distribution of wealth. Then, and only then, the model will grind out a solution—a set of equilibrium prices and a collection of commodities produced and traded in the market. Indeed, to each initial distribution of wealth there corresponds, in general, a different equilibrium set of prices and a different collection of commodities. It also follows from the very properties of our model, that each of the alternative general equilibria (corresponding to alternative initial distributions of wealth) is Pareto-optimal.

This formulation of the problem of distribution makes it possible for economists to be neutral vis-à-vis distribution questions. The orthodox line takes the following form: "If we ensure a Pareto-optimal solution, that is to say, an unbiased general equilibrium, we make sure that there is no waste in the economy, that we can make no one 'better off' without making someone 'worse off.' Once this is guaranteed, the question of distribution of income (wealth) can be considered, independently, on moral or on political grounds. We can leave such questions to the preacher or to the politician." But this will not do. On strictly technical grounds, any change in the distribution of income (wealth) by the politician implies a shift from one state of general equilibrium to another. The final outcome of the economic process (as depicted by the economist's model) is *not* separable from ethical-political decisions on income (wealth) distribution.

But there is a far more important consideration whose neglect by the main-line economists has been a source of significant bias in their policy recommendations. Social institutions, which form the basis for and the framework of economic activity, are intimately linked to patterns of distribution of wealth. There exists, in general, an organic relationship between social institutions (social structure) and the distribution of wealth. Although in each type of society there may exist some flexibility in this respect—that is, narrower or wider margins for tampering with the distribution of wealth—the general qualitative properties of wealth distribution are set. Sweden is an interesting case in point. While maintaining a capitalist social structure, it has pursued for decades income and wealth redistributive policies of socialist character. There is cumulative evidence that the limits of this process have been reached, that capitalist institutions there cannot be stretched any farther to accommodate an expansion of socialist policies.

No government in the West can underestimate with impunity the capability of the Establishment to strike back when its interests are at stake. There is much the Establishment can do on its own. It can easily create a climate of fear and instability, with far-reaching effects on the rate of annual investment. It can redirect its investment to foreign opportunities in ways that may undermine the country's balance of payments. More than that, the home-based Establishment can claim the support of the international financial community, with a network of political and economic influence, in its struggle to undermine the policies of a government it deems hostile to its interests.

Economists, in describing a market economy, assume in general, implicitly or explicitly, a set of social institutions which are identified with market capitalism. It goes without saying that radical redistribution policies would tend to come in conflict with the very institutional basis of market capitalism. (At the extreme, 100 per cent taxation amounts to expropriation.) Thus, it is obvious that market capitalism cannot accommodate all patterns of distribution of wealth. The silence of economists on these matters, side by side with their assertion of neutrality vis-à-vis "ethical" problems, is a striking example of ideological bias.

In fact, the institutional framework of each society places distinct limitations on the manner in which wealth and income distribution policies can be pursued. And in view of these limitations, the adoption of an income redistribution policy may lead to inefficiency in terms of the requirements of and the assumptions implicit in the model. But this way of thinking ignores the fact that *efficiency* refers to the manner in which a set of goals are achieved. If they are achieved in a nonwasteful way, the process is efficient. If there exists a social preference for a particular pattern of income distribution, which can be achieved, say, only through a particular kind of social intervention, it is not legitimate to characterize the resulting resource allocation as inefficient.

But it is time to raise another question: Is the market economy, as historically experienced, so free of efficiency-distortions, that we are justified, when it comes to public policy decisions, in insisting on efficiency being assigned a primary, prepotent role?

MONOPOLISTIC DEVIATIONS AND PIECEMEAL ANTITRUST

A monopolistic deviation from the model of a market economy takes the form of a violation of the parametric role of prices. A seller who is aware that through his sales he can affect the price of a commodity will take account of his influence on it in maximizing his profit. Such a seller is said to possess monopoly power. The price of the commodity is no longer a given bit of information for that seller, and the price system no longer plays the role attributed to it.

It can be proved easily that in a market economy with no monopolistic deviations every (firm) seller produces that quantity of a commodity which equates the market-given price of the commodity to his marginal cost. This is a straightforward result of maximizing profits. Not surprisingly, it can also be shown that in a Pareto-optimal equilibrium, the prices of all commodities are equal to their marginal costs.

But a firm wielding monopoly power will have no interest in carrying production to the point where marginal cost equals the price of the commodity. The higher the quantity it produces, the lower the price. Price is no longer a measure of the incremental revenue to be gained by producing one more unit of the commodity. The rule of profit maximization now leads to the production of a lesser quantity than that which would equate marginal cost to price. Thus monopoly power leads to an underutilization of resources in the production of the relevant commodity.

No economist doubts the almost universal presence of this type of monopoly power in the market economies of the West. Suffice it to say that the presence of any differentiation among products of the same technological type—be it on the basis of trademark, tradename and related advertising, or on the basis of location of retail outlets—constitutes a source of such monopoly power, the power to raise the price without losing all the customers. Therefore, no economist who accepts the standard model of the market economy and its intimate relation to an optimal or efficient state of affairs, can doubt that the contemporary capitalist economies are imperfectly competitive and incorporate inefficiencies of unknown magnitude.

It is fair to ask, How do economists deal with the policy implications of this generally recognized divergence between the requirements of the abstract model of a market economy and the ubiquitous presence of monopoly power?

We shall not be concerned here with the policy recommendations of economists who *reject* the competitive market economy model as a basis for their analysis and policy recommendations—concepts such as that of workable competition belong to a different ball game. For an economist who sincerely accepts the full implications of the standard model of the market economy, three policy options are available. The first is a do-nothing policy. He might argue that such deviations from the model as exist are of secondary importance. Naturally, this constitutes an act of faith for, admittedly, it is exceedingly hard to obtain a measure of the inefficiency resulting from the ubiquitous presence of monopoly power in the economy. The second policy option is to call for an aggressive antitrust or antimonopoly activity on the part of the government. The objective in this case ought to be not only to break up the monopolies, but indeed to eliminate every vestige of monopoly power. Such a frontal attack on monopoly, however, is sure to destroy the institutional basis of capitalism. For it would be necessary, first, to eliminate all trademarks, tradenames, and advertising; and second, to break up all firms whose share of market is large enough to give them some influence over the product's price. It is certain, of course, that in many cases the large size of the firms would be justifiable on grounds of technological efficiency. To break them up would amount to destroying the technological basis of the economy as well. Thus this option, the option of "atomizing" the economy, can be rejected out of hand.

The third policy option is suggested by Oskar Lange's proposal for market socialism. In the Lange type of market socialism a Central Planning Board establishes a set of prices, searching for their equilibrium values through trial and error. Every firm manager is instructed to equate his marginal cost to the price ruling in the market—that is to say, he is instructed to act as if he were in a (competitive) market economy. This model of socialism, or alternatively, some model of a capitalist economy with centrally determined prices, is the logical terminal point for any economist who is sincerely committed to the efficiency-generating properties of the economy in the context of contemporary technology.

An objection could easily be raised against this Procrustean solution: Rather than acting as if monopoly power does not really matter or going all the way to an economy with centrally determined prices, why not attack the more flagrant violations of competitive behavior, such as cartel agreements? Why not regulate or indeed take over only firms for which it is technologically natural to be monopolies, as in the case of public utilities? After all, can it not be claimed that piecemeal corrections of monopolistic deviations improve the state of affairs? But that is exactly the point. Surprisingly, the opposite can be proved; namely, the correction of isolated monopolistic situations is most likely to make matters worse in terms of the kind of analysis that supports the model of a competitive market economy and the associated concept of a Pareto-optimum.

This is so because, as we know already, a Pareto-optimal equilibrium implies the proportionality of prices to marginal costs across the economy. In the case of a perfectly competitive economy prices are equal to marginal costs, and the ratio of prices to marginal costs is equal to unity everywhere. In the presence of monopoly power prices exceed marginal costs, the ratio of price to marginal cost being a measure of the degree of monopoly power exercised by the firm. If by some accident all the firms in the economy happen to exercise the same degree of monopoly power, prices being proportional to marginal costs, then it would be true that no improvement in the allocation of resources could be brought about by intervention. Characteristically, in any contemporary capitalist economy, monopoly power is unevenly spread, and intervention is called for. But piecemeal intervention —intervention, say, intended to reduce the monopoly power of some particular firm by bringing the price of its product closer to its marginal cost —would be certain to constitute an improvement in the allocation of resources only if no other firm in the economy exercised monopoly power. In the presence of ubiquitous and unevenly spread monopoly power, it is possible that the reduction of the monopoly power of the firm in question would lead to a worsening of the situation. Indeed no intervention can be evaluated by itself, but only in reference to its overall impact on the spread of the ratios of prices to marginal costs in the economy.

Thus, for those who are committed to the model of the market economy only two policy options are truly open: either to wave the problem away or to adopt market socialism. (Or, alternatively, to adopt some model of a capitalist economy with prices determined by a central authority—in the Lange fashion.) To argue that monopolistic deviations can be ignored because of their minor importance is to exhibit ideological bias. To argue that piecemeal antitrust leads to improvements is false. The only bias-free option is the option that leads to a centrally controlled economy. But how many "believers" in fact are prepared to accept this conclusion?

[*Editor's Note:* At this point, Papandreou discusses the social costs that are entailed in the production of certain commodities but are not accounted for in their market prices. For instance, he points out that "the price of a product produced . . . in a process that pollutes the air . . . does not, in general, reflect the damages inflicted on innocent bystanders." He concludes that when such "damaging externalities" are associated with the production of a commodity, the "effective confrontation of the problem leads either to large-scale regulation or to the *internalization* of externalities through reliance on some form of social planning."]

PUBLIC GOODS AND THE ROLE ASSIGNED TO THE STATE

The model of the market capitalism faces one of its severest tests when it becomes necessary to rationalize the role of the contemporary state, and along with it the institutional structure that provides the necessary framework for the carrying on of economic activity. For the orthodox it is an onerous and unpleasant task to explain why anything more is needed than a simple legal-institutional framework with provisions concerning property rights and the rules governing exchange. This is not surprising. The nominalist view of society that provides the philosophical underpinnings of market capitalism relegates the state to the status of a necessary evil, an unfortunate but inescapable afterthought.

The concept of public goods is the economist's entrance ticket to the theory of the state. Unwilling to grant emergent properties to society—and insisting through thick and thin on viewing it as an aggregation of individuals —he seeks the raison d'être of the state in the inherent properties of certain types of goods.

Robert Dorfman, representing a widely held view, states that, "there are certain goods that have the peculiarity that once they are available no one can be precluded from enjoying them whether he contributed to their provision or not. These are the public goods. Law and order is an example, and there are many others too familiar to make further exemplification worth while. Their essential characteristic is that they are enjoyed but not consumed (and that their benefits are derived) without any act of appropriation."[1] But this definition can be rephrased: public goods are goods that must be provided publicly (by the state) because the market mechanism is incapable of performing its allocative functions. Is this really more than an apologetic admission of defeat?

But Dorfman's definition of public goods is limited to what have come to be called "perfect collective consumption goods." These are goods (such as law and order and national defense) associated with a complete breakdown of the allocative capabilities of the private property–market–exchange apparatus. It is known, of course, that there exists an impressive array of goods and services provided by the state which do not meet Dorfman's definition of public goods: public education, public power, irrigation, and so on. In all these instances, it is possible to exclude classes of individuals from participation in their enjoyment, since it is possible to make them available at a charge. And clearly, in at least some of these instances, such goods may be provided privately through the operation of the market mechanism. Thus, the decision to provide them publicly, rather than privately through the market mechanism, must be based on grounds other than their inherent properties.

There seems to be no escape from the conclusion that goods are provided publicly—and thus become public goods—whenever the market is incapable of providing them privately or when it provides them in a manner that is deemed unsatisfactory. (The unsatisfactory aspect of their private provision may relate to monopolistic deviations, to external effects, or to income distribution.) Notwithstanding the fact that this conclusion assigns a residual role to public activity, it contains a recognition of the possibility

---

[1] "General Equilibrium with Public Goods," *Economic Publique*, a conference at Biarritz, September 2–9, 1966 (Paris: Centre National de la Recherche Scientifique, 1968), pp. 49–79.

of large-scale failure of the market economy in providing certain types of goods or in providing other types of goods satisfactorily.

We come up against the inescapable question, Satisfactory or unsatisfactory to whom? Obviously, to the state, which engages in the provision of the public goods. But in whose interest does the state decide? And through what mechanism are its decisions affected by those whose interest it is intended to serve?

At this stage of the argument it is enough to point to the great cleavage of thought between the nominalist and the organicist points of view. The orthodox economist is clearly nominalist. According to this position public goods are provided when markets fail to satisfy individual demands. There is no place here for social as against private demands. Every social demand is decomposable into private demands. This approach creates no problem when the provision of a public good takes the form of an intervention of the state to correct market performance in the case of monopolistic deviations or of external effects because in both cases the intervention is intended to satisfy individual demands. Furthermore, it is distribution-neutral. But what about the provision of public goods in the Dorfman sense (law and order, national defense, the provision of an adequate resource base for future generations)? Are such demands *private?* To treat them as if they were, to include quantities of defense, law and order, and so on as arguments in the preference functions or preference rankings of individuals would stretch the term *private* beyond the breaking point. And what about the provision of a public good which carries with it a redistribution of income or wealth via the financing of its cost or via the allocation of its benefits? Most public goods (including law and order and national defense) clearly have distributive impacts. Some individuals become better off and others become worse off following their provision by the state. Who is to judge whether or not they should be provided? And on what grounds?

It seems inescapable that such decisions must be based on explicit social priorities. Recognition of the need for the articulation of social priorities in the domain of public action unavoidably leads to consideration of the emergent properties of society—to a view of society which stresses its organic or systemic character.

It is difficult to avoid the conclusion that the state must be viewed as an "organic chooser of ends" in the context of a political process whose nature, though different from case to case, makes it much more than a passive receiver of signals from a voting constituency or a mediating instrumentality that aggregates private into public demands. The traditional nominalist view of public goods and of the role of the state does not fit the experience of any society, much less that of our own. It springs from a healthy concern over the arbitrary authority of an ever-expanding state. But, by ignoring the role of the political process—which constitutes an integral part of the mechanism of resource allocation—it lends support to the convenient rationalization that in "democratic" societies, the state does exactly what is wanted by the people. Thus, the attempts by the orthodox nominalists to minimize the role of the state in their models is grist for the mill of the vested interests that employ the machinery of the state to their own advantage, in absentia of the liberal intellectual. Once again ideological bias, unwittingly, becomes the servant of the status quo.

CREATIVE DESTRUCTION VERSUS ADMINISTRATION

Whether one reads Schumpeter or Marx, and whether one is led to view capitalism as an innovative process of creative destruction or as a process of capital accumulation, one is necessarily forced to view it as an evolutionary process. Not a trace of this evolutionary—one could say, revolutionary—dynamic of capitalism remains in the standard model of market capitalism. For clearly, neoclassical economics is an elaborate but expurgated version of the economics of the great thinkers of the nineteenth century.

To use Schumpeter's felicitous distinction, neoclassical economics is concerned with the *administrative* rather than the *creative* aspects of the economic process. The fundamental problem to be solved is how best to allocate known scarce resources among competing independently articulated individual ends, in the light of a known technology. This is fundamentally a managerial problem—even though, of course, no manager is in evidence. Thus the emphasis here is on the allocative properties of a market economy in a static, nondynamic, nonevolutionary context. Certainly economists have been increasingly concerned with the dynamic, intertemporal allocation of resources. The difficulty encountered in extending the efficiency properties of the market economy in the static context to the dynamic, intertemporal context is the absence of futures markets side by side with spot markets, for all but a few commodities (such as foreign exchange and a few internationally traded standardized commodities). But this is only part of the problem because the intertemporal resource allocation process is an integral part of change in the underlying structure. Everything is in flux. The individuals that make up society, their tastes, the known resources, the shopping list of products, the technology to be employed, the supporting institutions, all are in a state of flux. Although this evolutionary process is enormously difficult to comprehend, let alone formalize, one is quite irresponsible to ignore it or to push it out of the social scientist's field of vision. But this is exactly what economists do by restricting their attention to problems of resource management in a nonevolutionary context.

What in fact is truly impressive about the capitalist evolutionary process is its directional interdeterminacy. E. J. Mishan has written an entertaining parable [*Editor's Note:* An excerpt from Mishan's essay has been omitted here; the essay is reprinted in this book as Reading 15.] which brings out forcefully this indeterminacy in the direction of the process. It also suggests the extent to which the limited or "marginal" social vision so characteristic of capitalist economies, buttressed by strongly entrenched vested interests, creates an ironclad bondage for society.

The parable should have made it quite clear that the study of the capitalist market economy, when restricted to the nonevolutionary aspects of the capitalist process, ceases to be relevant to it. Expurgated and anemic, it throws more light on the performance of an ideal society of shopkeepers than on contemporary capitalism. To extend, unwittingly or not, the analytical conclusions of a model best fitted for the study of a shopkeeper society to present-day capitalism is probably the supreme form of ideological bias.

11

James O'Connor's *The Fiscal Crisis of the State:* An Overview

David Gold

One of the most widely noted facts about capitalist economies today is the large and apparently expanding role of the state. Whether measured by the size of spending and taxation, the amount of regulation, or the involvement in price and wage decisions, state activity is huge. In addition, this same activity is the subject of a substantial amount of political conflict. Struggles over who will gain from expenditures and regulations, and struggles over who will pay, or avoid, the necessary taxes, have become commonplace.

Despite the many manifestations of the state's important role in the economy, social scientists have been slow in developing a coherent explanation of the phenomenon. James O'Connor's *The Fiscal Crisis of the State* (St. Martin's Press, 1973) is an ambitious and provocative attempt to fill that gap. In formulating a theory of the state budget, O'Connor has contributed to a rethinking both of the relation between the state and the economy and of the dynamics of accumulation and economic growth.

THE STRUCTURE OF THE ECONOMY

Governments throughout the capitalist world and at all levels in the United States have been experiencing a crisis in their ability to finance the activities that they are being called on to perform. The fiscal crisis is the tendency for government expenditures to grow faster than revenues. This is a phenomenon which is directly observed and which can be explained as the logical outcome of economic growth under capitalism. To find out what this logic is, O'Connor argues, a theory of the government budget is needed. But the budget itself represents only part of the fiscal crisis of the state. The fiscal crisis "reflect[s] and [is] structurally determined by social and economic conflicts between classes and groups" (p. 2). The theory of the budget must explain these conflicts and must, therefore, articulate the links between the budget and the economy and society.

O'Connor begins with a model of capital accumulation and economic growth. He divides the economy into three producing sectors: the monopoly sector, the competitive sector and the state sector.

The monopoly sector is composed of firms whose scale of production is very large and who have substantial control over the markets on which they buy and sell. (Economists call such firms oligopolies.) Firms in the monopoly sector grow primarily through increases in the quantity and quality of their plant and equipment; that is, via growth in capital and improvements in technology.

The way in which the monopoly sector grows has two important implications for the economy. One is that there is a tendency for capital-based growth to utilize less and less labor. As capital-labor ratios rise in production, there is a tendency for labor to be "freed," in the sense of there being a slower growth in job opportunities over time. Thus, capital-based growth tends to create surplus labor.

The second important implication is that the growth process in the monopoly sector tends to create productive capacity, the potential for producing goods and services, faster than can be absorbed by the private economy. If this gap between potential output and realizable demand is not filled, and existing capacity is not utilized, profits will fall. Firms will attempt to cut costs, reduce their use of labor and limit their future expansion. There will be a slower rate of capital accumulation and economic growth, and the economy will be more subject to periodic, long-lasting depressions. Thus, the inability to sell what can be currently produced leads to a decline in productive capacity over time. In a sense, the economy's potential expands too fast, which creates the exact opposite tendency, one toward stagnation.

The problem of surplus capacity is exacerbated by the fact that productivity growth is slowest outside of the monopoly sector. As the competitive and state sectors grow, there has been a tendency for their costs of production to rise rapidly. With production labor-intensive in these sectors, it is extremely difficult to gain cost advantages with the systematic use of capital and technology. Thus, the amount spent in these sectors grows both because the sectors are being called on to do more, particularly in the case of the state, and because what they do costs more.

In summary, surplus capacity is a problem because total demand does not grow as fast as monopoly-sector productive potential, and because the pattern of expenditures shifts away from the monopoly sector.

The monopoly sector, then, is the source of two problems, surplus labor and surplus capacity, which are derived from a single process, capital accumulation. The state has more and more frequently been called upon to deal with these problems, and this has been a major determinant of the growth of state expenditures.

But there is a second, parallel process at work. While monopoly-sector growth creates the problems that lead to the expansion of some key items of the budget, at the same time budgetary expansion is an increasingly important determinant of monopoly-sector growth. The state has taken over more and more of the costs of investment and of the costs of creating and maintaining a skilled labor force—it subsidizes basic research, builds highways and industrial parks, and pays for higher education, to give three examples of state expenditures that promote accumulation and growth. Thus, the relation between the monopoly sector and the state runs both ways. "In other words, the growth of the state is both a cause and effect of the expansion of monopoly capital" (p. 8).

The competitive sector is composed of firms which produce on a small scale and which have little control over the markets on which they buy and sell. Production tends to be unstable, since with little market power these firms are subject to fluctuations from competition, seasonality and changing tastes. Firms in the competitive sector grow primarily through the expansion of low-wage labor.

Because production is less predictable, employment in the competitive sector tends to be unstable, with a more rapid turnover of jobs and a higher average rate of unemployment than in the monopoly sector. Productivity growth tends to be low, and that which occurs is more likely to be passed on to consumers in the form of lower prices than in the monopoly sector. Wages and fringe benefits are lower and unions weaker. Many workers in the competitive sector are members of the working poor—they have jobs, sometimes more than one in a family, but they are still in need of some kind of income supplement.

Competitive-sector workers form the core of the marginal work force, and the problem of surplus labor surfaces as a competitive-sector problem. Some of these marginal workers have, for all intents and purposes, been driven out of the labor force and become a "permanent" welfare population. Others are in and out of the labor force, but when they are in, they work intermittently and receive the lowest wages. Competitive-sector workers increasingly turn to the state for economic support. Sometimes they must also struggle against the state, as they are among the first victims of the fiscal crisis.

With entry relatively easy, competitive-sector industries tend to be crowded and the return on capital tends to be lower than in the monopoly sector. There is a high failure rate, and competitive-sector capitalists feel continuously threatened. They, too, will often turn to the state, seeking protection from unions, from rising costs and from the incursion of monopoly-sector firms, as, for example, in agriculture. Fair-trade laws, right-to-work laws, small-business-loan subsidies and the like have been some of the results. However, many of these state activities benefit monopoly-sector firms far more, and the competitive sector has been far less successful than the monopoly sector in gaining support from the state.

The state sector contains two types of production activities: production which is organized by the state itself, such as the post office, public education and welfare, and production which the state contracts out to private firms, such as military equipment, and research and development. Within this categorization, some production is considered as being completely within the state sector, while, in other instances, firms produce both for the state and for sale on markets. An example is the General Electric Corporation, a producer of military equipment as well as capital and consumer goods for private markets. GE is part of both the state and the monopoly sectors. This empirical overlap is a potential source of confusion in applying the concepts, but the reason for such a definition is a powerful one. Production for the state is undertaken under a different set of criteria than production for markets. There is less competition, the constraint on demand is from the state budget and is more explicitly a political one, and there is less pressure for cost efficiency in production. State production and state contract production have an important characteristic in common—neither is subject to the kind of discipline that is imposed by the market. Instead, if there is a logic to the production process, it is one derived more from the politics of the budget.

THE STATE BUDGET

O'Connor next turns to an analysis of the budget. His "first premise is that the capitalistic state must try to fulfill two basic and often mutually contradictory functions—*accumulation* and *legitimization*" (p. 6). Not only does the state get deeply involved in aiding private investment but it also attempts to create or preserve social harmony. The state's support of accumulation is often in conflict with its desire for peace and harmony. The accumulation process under capitalism is inherently unequal, as some groups and classes reap more of the benefits than others. The state must try to find some justification for its intervention, or it will undermine the basis of its support. (Thus Nixon, in justifying his New Economic Policy in 1971, declared that: "All Americans will benefit from more profits.") Yet successful support of accumulation leads to surplus capacity and surplus labor power, which threatens social and economic stability.

O'Connor's second premise is that the budget, the sum of spending and revenue-raising actions, can best be understood by relating these actions to accumulation and legitimization. The two main categories of expenditures are social capital, which corresponds to the accumulation function, and social expenses, which correspond to the legitimization function. Social capital is those expenditures that contribute to private accumulation, either by improving the productivity of the labor force or by reducing the labor costs that the firm must meet. Examples of the first type of social capital expenditures are physical investments, such as highways, utilities, office buildings, and sports and convention centers, and investments in the skills of individuals, such as public education and research and development performed directly by the government or subsidized out of state funds. These expenditures increase productivity by adding to the amount of capital and improving the level of technology that members of the labor force work with. They clearly increase the ability of firms to accumulate capital and reap profits, but the costs are borne by the state. Examples of the second type of social capital expenditures are items in the budget which provide goods and services that the working class can consume collectively, such as hospital and medical facilities, and items that provide some insurance against economic insecurity, such as social security or unemployment compensation. These are items that would probably have to come out of wage payments, and therefore be subject to higher wage demands by workers, if the state had not absorbed the costs.

Social expenses are those expenditures which attempt to maintain social stability both in the United States and wherever U.S. interests are present throughout the world. They do not contribute to capital accumulation but become necessary because of the results of accumulation. Examples include the police and military on the one hand, and the welfare system on the other. O'Connor argues that the dual problems of surplus capacity and surplus labor have led to an attempted solution in the form of a warfare-welfare state. Military expenditures try to raise demand directly, via purchases of equipment, and are necessary to protect foreign activities of U.S. business. Welfare and other income supplement and social control expenditures represent the strategy employed to deal with a surplus population.

Many items of expenditure perform more than one function. The military budget, in addition to being an example of social expenses, also includes items of social capital. Much research and development is subsidized by the Pentagon, and there are a number of examples of skilled labor, such as airline pilots, where substantial training is obtained in the military. The interstate-highway system was designed with both social capital (moving goods and people) and social expenses (moving troops) in mind. Similarly, the same public-education system will attempt to train and control, though it is often different social classes that are trained and controlled.

The state has three main methods of raising the revenue needed to finance expenditures: it can produce and sell goods and services and use the net proceeds for other endeavors; it can borrow from individuals, firms and banks, and from abroad; and, of course, it can tax.

Nationalized industries and state-run enterprises are much more common in Europe than in the United States. Neither in Europe nor in the United States, however, has the state been able to use this form of activity as a revenue raiser. In fact, since state enterprises draw on the government's borrowing capacity for their expansion, and since capitalists have successfully resisted the incursion of state enterprise into areas that are profitable for private ownership, state enterprises tend to worsen the fiscal crisis. They provide services for private capital, such as running unprofitable but important activities like railroads and the postal service, do not earn profits and draw on the state for financing.

Since World War II, government borrowing has grown as a source of state financing. But this, too, is limited. Bonds must have buyers, and governments have been forced to raise the interest rates they pay in order to find the necessary market. This raises interest costs, which must come out of budget revenues. Government bonds compete with private bonds for scarce funds, and this is frequently viewed as a limitation on the state's ability to expand its debt. Government borrowing also contributes to inflationary pressures, particularly when the federal debt is used as the basis for expanding the money supply at a rapid rate. Inflation not only worsens the fiscal crisis, by making government activity more expensive, but also imposes limits on the ability of the state to finance its expenditures via issuance of debt.

Taxation is the remaining revenue source. Taxes have always been a way for one group to exploit another. In the United States, this is clear when data on tax incidence is examined. Income from labor is taxed at a much higher rate than income from property, and people with very high incomes, most of which is from property, pay a smaller percentage of their income in taxes than middle-income individuals. The state is continually faced with the problem of trying to explain or hide this unevenness, a product of its attempts to aid accumulation, or else run the risk of losing much popular support; that is, losing its legitimacy. It is very difficult to expand the tax base or raise tax rates without clear justification. Thus, taxation is also limited as a means to obviate the fiscal crisis, partly because the main fruits of accumulation, profits, are largely exempt from taxation, and partly because the expansion of existing tax sources are resisted by those who would pay. Taxpayers' revolts threaten both legitimacy and accumulation.

THE STATE'S OPTIONS

The fiscal crisis of the state is a result both of the increased demands on the state which arise from the process of accumulation and growth that characterize contemporary capitalism, and of the inability of the state to expand the sources of revenue fast enough to meet these increased demands. In addition, the fiscal crisis and its effects come back to haunt the firms in the monopoly sector. Inflation and heavy taxation tend to encourage militancy among labor leaders and rank-and-file workers. As O'Connor argues:

Sooner or later, the fiscal crisis begins to threaten the traditional conditions for "labor peace" in the monopoly industries. The fiscal crisis is at root a social crisis: Economic and political antagonisms divide not only labor and capital but also the working class. This social crisis and the fiscal crisis, which mirrors and enlarges it, finally work their way back into the arena where the decisive conflicts and compromises between labor and capital occur—the monopoly sector industries (p. 44).

The warfare-welfare "solution" is incomplete and the state searches for other options. One is to run a managed recession in order to reduce wage and price rises, and to bring interest rates down. This may ameliorate some of the backlash from the fiscal crisis but does nothing to fill in the structural gap between state expenditures and revenues. In addition, a recession that is too long or deep may seriously cut into capital expansion and plunge the economy toward depression, exactly the situation that state intervention is supposed to prevent. Thus, the managed recession strategy is a temporary one.

A second strategy, which has been attempted extensively in Europe and the United States, is to institute wage and price controls in those sectors where wage demands are the greatest. Thus, monopoly- and state-sector wages would be hit the hardest. The experience of the wage-control mechanism in the United States indicates that the problems of legitimacy which they raise are immense. They are extremely difficult to enforce, particularly when unions no longer accept the rationale for their use.

A third strategy is to search for ways of reducing the costs of state activities. O'Connor envisions the possibility of a social-industrial complex, a link between the state and the monopoly sector with the aim of increasing productivity in order to lower costs and relieve the fiscal crisis. A favorite of liberals, the strategy of the social-industrial complex would attempt to stimulate demand through spending on social rather than on military projects, and care for the surplus population through expanded welfare and income-supplement programs. Greater productivity would reduce the costs of budgetary items in the state sector. The problem here is that state-sector productivity gains are extremely difficult to realize. Also, substantial segments of capital benefit from the military program and fight hard to retain their privileges. For the time being, the social-industrial complex seems to have died with the McGovern campaign, but that does not rule out the possibility of a resurrection.

A fourth strategy was attempted during the 1960's nationally, in the early days of the first Nixon Administration, and at state and local levels, most prominently by Governors Reagan in California and Rockefeller in New York. This was an attempt to reduce the costs of welfare and other agencies that deal with the surplus population. This was both an attack on the living standards of those who have been forced out of the labor force and an attempt at increasing the available pool of cheap labor, particularly for competitive-sector firms. This strategy was essentially defeated by a coalition that included many monopoly-sector capitalists, who feared the resulting social unrest. Many states and localities, however, still operate from this perspective.

The lack of a clear alternative strategy implies a continuation of the past: inflation and fiscal crisis, warfare and welfare, recession and attack on the living standards of the working class. What O'Connor's analysis indicates is that the ability of the state to "solve" the current economic crisis is limited by the contradictory nature of the system as a whole. The issue is not just one of tinkering with budgetary devices but one of restructuring the productive apparatus itself. Until that happens, economic crisis and fiscal crisis will continue to be part of our way of life.

12

A Citizen's Guide to the American Economy

Ralph Nader

. . . Most formal inquiries into a more just and efficient use of national wealth have failed to measure how the citizen's dollars are being wasted and depreciated in the market place and his taxes converted into corporate property and income. . . .

What are needed now are analyses of the corporate economy that will do what economists for the most part have failed to do: show how corporations, by their control of both the market and government, have been able to divert scarce resources to uses that have little human benefit or are positively harmful. . . .

To encourage more inquiry into the institutionalized abuses of unchecked corporate power, I would like to outline some of the major categories in which the abuses fall and to give a few of the many possible examples of how they work. I call these categories "sub-economies." In each case, the consumer's dollars are inexcusably wasted or his taxes misused. To some extent these categories have been arranged so that they overlap or converge in order to avoid isolating phenomena artificially and to emphasize the economic realities underlying policy questions. As economic measurements become more precise, new categories will evolve, and these in turn will be replaced by others.

1. *The involuntary sub-economy.* By this I mean the billions that consumers would not have paid if they knew or could control what they were getting, or if corporations observed elementary standards of honesty, safety, and utility in producing and selling the things that are bought. Consumers are now spending billions of dollars for products sold under false pretenses: meat and poultry that are adulterated with fat and water; patent medicines, mouthwashes, and "aids" to beauty and diet that do far less than they are said to do or nothing at all. Both the Food and Drug Administration and the National Academy of Sciences have compiled lists of drugs, patent medicines, and mouthwashes that are valueless for the purposes they advertise and often harmful as well, as in the case of certain antibiotics.

Worthless drugs alone cost consumers one billion dollars a year. The Federal Trade Commission estimates that another billion is wasted on fraudulently sold home improvements or repairs. Last February, Senator Philip Hart of Michigan had this to say about worthless auto repairs:

American consumers spend 25 to 30 billion dollars a year on auto repair. Various studies on the quality of the work were presented to us. They rated the poor, unneeded, or not done work at amounts ranging from 36 per cent to 99 per cent. Even taking the low figure, that means consumers are wasting 8 to 10 billion dollars that they lay out for auto repair yearly.

Equally flagrant is the short-weighting, short-counting, and short-measuring of consumer purchases that were the subject of a report in the *Wall Street Journal* . . . "The pennies add up fast enough," the *Journal* said, "that estimates by state officials of the total US loss from short-weighting start at $1.5 billion a year and rise to as high as $10 billion a year."

All these expenses—and I could list many more—were clearly involuntary: the consumers did not get what they thought they were paying for.

Quite as serious are what might be called "secondary consumer expenditures": the consumer may get something he wants, such as a car, but its defects are such as to force him to incur more costs. The fragile recessed bumpers of most automobiles are a case in point. Collisions at under ten miles per hour have been costing $2 billion a year for damages that could easily have been avoided if these cars had had effective bumpers.

What might be called the "accident-injury industry," composed of companies and professionals providing insurance and medical, legal, and repair services, is now being paid about $12 billion a year. When emergencies occur these services are of course needed; but in fact many of them would not have to be paid for at all if cars were sensibly and safely designed, as could be done without increasing the over-all cost of making cars. Nor would a large proportion of auto repair costs be as expensive or even necessary if key parts were not so inaccessible and fragile, or so constructed that a small defect requires replacement of an entire large unit of the car.

By now some of these involuntary expenditures imposed by the auto industry have become fairly familiar. Less well understood is the way in which many different products, including packaged food, soft drinks, and gasoline, are sold through incredibly expensive advertising of their brand names for which the consumer must bear the cost, but for which he receives nothing of additional value. The staff of Senator Hart's anti-trust committee estimates, moreover, that deceptive packaging and promotion in the food industry alone are causing consumers to lose $14 billion a year, for example, by pushing the large "economy" sized boxes of food that in fact cost more per unit than medium sized boxes. Of course such expenses would not be involuntary for consumers who could set up their own experimental kitchens and prowl the supermarkets with scales and slide rules. But most families are simply duped.

2. It is in the *transfer sub-economy*, for example, that the prices for goods and services may rise unconscionably as they move from the supplier of raw materials to the manufacturer, and then to the wholesaler, the retailer, and the consumer. . . .

Sometimes pressures can be mounted to stop transfers of costs to the consumer. For years the insurance industry failed to encourage programs for fire and auto safety, preventive medicine, and pollution control, which would have helped to prevent huge losses from taking place. It preferred to pass on these costs to its unorganized and generally uncomplaining policy holders in the form of higher premiums.

Recently, however, premiums for car insurance have become so high that many people cannot pay them, and those who can are becoming angry. At the same time, the public generally has been made more aware of auto safety. The insurance companies, more eager now to lower the damage claims for minor crashes, have decided at last to change their policies. They have lately been sharply critical of the auto industry for making over-powered engines and useless bumpers and the auto manufacturers are beginning to respond. It now looks as if more functional bumpers may soon be replacing the ones I mentioned earlier; and by adding a surcharge to the insurance rates for high-powered "muscle cars," the insurance companies are driving down the sales of these absurd machines.

The lesson of this story is that we can no longer depend, as classical market theory held, on consumer response alone to encourage efficiency and competition that will result in higher quality. In a complex multi-layered economy it is necessary that countervailing economic power be brought to bear at each level of the buying and selling process, however remote from the consumer. This is the only way to prevent excessive transfers of costs and to encourage efficiency and innovation.

We are very far from such a situation now. When railroad and trucking groups obtain rate increases from the all too compliant ICC, the large supermarkets and other retail chains rarely say a word; they calmly transfer the new costs on to the consumers. Since most of the railroads and truckers raise their rates uniformly, the supermarkets have no choice among competing transport services, and so the consumer is forced to pay the bill.

3. Both sub-economies I have mentioned so far are facilitated by the *controlled market sub-economy*. By this I mean the thousands of arrangements that make it possible for corporations to avoid competition over the price, quantity, and quality of things made and sold, so that the value of

what buyers receive is often outrageously distorted, by comparison with what the value would be if the market was not controlled.

Many of the practices in this sub-economy are violations of the anti-trust laws that have become both familiar and tolerated: price fixing, product fixing—for example the auto industry's entrenchment of the internal combustion engine—shared monopolies, etc. They also include other barriers to entry into the market such as excessive restrictions on occupational licenses, oil import quotas, the tying up of patents, and other devices that blatantly serve special economic interests while causing consumers and workers to suffer losses.

How much do they lose? The Federal Trade Commission has estimated that if highly concentrated industries were broken up by the anti-trust laws into more competitive companies so that the four largest firms in any industry would not control more than 40 percent of that industry's sales, prices would fall *by 25 percent or more*. This estimate applies to such major industries as autos, steel, copper, aluminum, containers, chemicals, detergents, canned soups, cereals. Nevertheless the figure represents only a small proportion of the unjustifiable costs to the consumer that result from the controlled market.

It is not just a question of price fixing. Concentrated industries can for years resist the innovations that would make them more efficient. The basic oxygen furnace was not used by the big steel firms until 1963, thirteen years after it was developed by a small Austrian steel company. The controlled market, moreover, blocks the individual or small business inventors who are still the source of so many of the really new techniques in our society.

Such inventors find that their chances of entering the market or selling their work to established companies are dim when their ideas would not only serve the consumer but also disturb existing capital commitments or ways of doing business: thus we cannot have a humane and efficient transportation system, nor can we buy engines that cause less pollution, can openers that prevent tiny metal fragments from falling into the can's contents, safer power lawn mowers, and countless other inventions that exist but are not produced. Think of the benefits to the consumer if the computer industry vigorously developed a computerized consumer information system to make more intelligent choices possible in the market place. Or of the uses to which Comsat might be put if it were freed from the heavy hands of the AT&T monopoly complex that controls it.

4. . . . [This] brings us to the *corporate socialism sub-economy* which includes both a) corporate pressure on government to unjustifiably transfer public funds and privileges to corporate control and b) withholding of proper payments and other obligations from the government by the corporations that owe them.

The tax system has become, to a disgraceful degree, an indirect subsidy to corporations and other privileged groups. Many of the glaring tax loopholes that slip through Congress each year are in effect huge payments by the government of money it would otherwise have received: for example the depletion allowances for oil and minerals, the tax dodges allowed to the real estate, timber, and cattle industries, the uses of the capital gains tax that favor the very rich. Thanks to the oil depletion allowance, among other loopholes, the Atlantic Richfield Oil Company, to take an extreme example, had a net income of $797 million, while paying no federal tax whatever, from 1962 until 1968, when it paid at the rate of 1.2 percent.

These "tax expenditures" by the federal government have their local counterparts in the gross underpayment of property taxes by mineral companies, real estate developers, and commercial and industrial property owners. A preliminary estimate shows that local taxpayers are paying a subsidy of at least $7 billion a year to such interests when they allow them to evade property taxes. Of course municipal and county services such as schools, roads, hospitals, and garbage disposal also suffer as a result.

As we might expect, Texas provides excellent examples of such underpayment of property taxes. A recent survey by University of Texas Law School students shows that underassessment of the value of oil and gas properties belonging to Texaco, Shell, and Atlantic Richfield in one part of west Texas caused county taxes for homeowners and small businessmen to be 33 percent higher than they should have been. Over a period of seven years, a county school board in the region lost $7 million in taxes that it should have collected. Another inquiry by law students showed that in Houston, Texas, industrial and commercial properties are assessed at about 1 percent of fair market value, while residential property is assessed at 31.94 percent.

In Gary, Indiana, the tax situation is shocking. Mayor Hatcher, in an attempt to meet the city's financial crisis, has ordered all city agencies to cut their budgets, including the budget for education. The big company in Gary is US Steel. Between 1961 and 1971 its property assessment only rose from $107 million to $117 million, although during that period the company installed $1.2 billion worth of capital improvements. US Steel refuses to allow the city authorities to examine its books and it refuses to apply for building permits, as required by city law, because this would reveal the size of its taxable investment.

US Steel is able to get away with all this because it exerts raw corporate power in a company town. It is not in any way unusual. Timber companies in Maine, mine owners in Appalachia, paper mills and chemical plants in cities and towns that depend on them for employment—all flagrantly evade the constitutional provisions in their states for equal treatment under property taxes.

Before national priorities can even be determined, it is crucial that Congress and the public know how much money is being spent by the government through the tax system. Tax expenditures now amount to roughly $45 billion a year but there is no systematic way of knowing precisely how much is being spent for what purposes. Some tax expenditures have worthy aims, such as the deduction for contribution to pensions, but it is rarely considered whether such deductions are the most desirable or easy ways to achieve these aims. Others, such as deductions for medical expenses, seem useful but are in fact regressive, allowing the same percentage of deduction to rich and poor alike. Others, as we have seen, are merely subsidies for the rich, particularly the capital gains tax and the allowances for accelerated depreciation of property.

What is needed, first of all, is an annual federal tax expenditure budget which will show exactly how much money the government loses for each tax privilege that is granted and just where that money goes instead. . . .

. . . Recently, the Treasury Department without any Congressional authorization issued its new proposals—the "ADR system"—for allowing depreciation for tax purposes. This system would allow fast write-offs of business equipment without any relation to the useful life of such equipment—the traditionally accepted measure of depreciation for tax purposes.

ADR would mean a tax subsidy to business of over $3 billion a year—more than Nixon's welfare reform proposals (which would cost $2.1 billion). More than a dozen tax authorities, including the former Commissioner of Internal Revenue and experts from the Harvard, Yale, and Pennsylvania law schools, have stated that this multi-billion-dollar tax break is an illegal use of Presidential power. It remains to be seen whether the Congress or the courts will declare it invalid.

The direct subsidies paid for agriculture, shipping, business promotion, and "research" are quite as important—and as much neglected by Congress —as the indirect subsidies paid by the tax system. The Department of Agriculture, for example, is now spending over $4 billion each year for its subsidy programs. Who evaluates these payments and the reasons for making them? As it happens, big corporate farms receive the lion's share and Congress does not question the inequities that result.

Agriculture is only one sector of this sub-economy where hard questions must be asked if the public usefulness of *existing* tax dollars is to be improved. The inflated contract and procurement practices of the government are another. Thanks to Senator Proxmire and others, the public has at least begun to learn of the waste and mismanagement in defense contracting, and the consequent multi-billion-dollar "cost-overruns" that have become commonplace—e.g., the $2 billion overrun paid Lockheed for the C5A. But who is looking into the waste in other government contracting—from the leasing of buildings at inordinate cost to the billions of dollars paid for research in "think tanks" and advice from private consulting firms such as A. D. Little, Booz Allen, and hundreds of lesser known outfits, not to mention the hundreds of studies done for HUD, HEW, DOT? Many of these studies are worthless, expensive, used mainly to delay policy decisions and to get the agencies who commission them off the hook. Others are wholly ignored.

If only the grossest forms of waste and corruption in federal, state, and local procurement practices were investigated and eliminated, many billions of dollars would be saved. . . .

Some idea of how much money is being wasted in local procurement can be gained from a recommendation made to the states two years ago by the General Services Administration, the purchasing and housekeeping agency of the federal government. The GSA suggested that state and local governments cooperate in setting up systems of centralized purchasing direct from manufacturers, thus bypassing the 20 to 30 percent mark-up of the wholesalers. If they did this, they would save between $6 and $7 billion a year.

This recommendation was not followed, nor did the GSA pursue it. The wholesalers' trade association immediately launched a campaign against it in Congress, and the Bureau of the Budget suppressed this somewhat unexpected display of good sense by the GSA. The wholesalers' association has plenty of political muscle and uses it on all levels of government.

The great illusion of the public is that it is protected by the conscience of public officials, when in fact aggressive monitoring of these officials and those they deal with is constantly needed. Even tax funds used directly for medical care are funneled unscrupulously to prosperous doctors and drug companies, or to hospitals that use them for unauthorized purposes. Herbert S. Dennenberg, the Insurance Commissioner of Pennsylvania, stated recently that the "Medicare Program is resulting in the American people being overcharged billions of dollars a year"—a conclusion that has been confirmed by Congressional inquiries and independent studies.

5. Unlike the other aspects of the economy that have been discussed here, the *compulsory consumption sub-economy* is not part of any recognized system of economic exchange—but it has grave economic effects. I am referring to the compulsory consumption of environmental pollution and compulsory exposure to occupational health and safety hazards. These reduce the *quality* of the gross national product and thus diminish the value of the citizen's dollar, even when they do not directly compel people to pay for medical treatment, for example. We are just beginning to calculate the billions of dollars that pollution costs in damages to health, in cleaning costs, and in damage to property, resources, and agricultural crops. Air and water pollution are each costing at least $44 billion a year. (The yearly damage to California crops alone from air pollution runs to $45 million a year.) The costs to the unborn, or to the environment in the future, have not even been estimated.

The power of corporations to pollute, in short, is far too great for them to exercise responsibly. General Motors, by virtue of the engines it designs and the plants it operates, has been responsible for over 30 percent of the estimated tonnage of US air pollution. Is there any city street where the citizen can escape the pollution of GM engineering when he breathes? Between 1967 and 1969 GM spent $250 million to change its slogan on billboards, dealers' signs, and other promotional material to read "GM Mark of Excellence." With the same funds it could have easily developed a workable nonpolluting engine.

6. The *expendable sub-economy* is composed mostly of poor people who are being excluded from the services of the economy at large. It is not simply that the poor pay more: they are not being allowed to buy. In Washington, Baltimore, New York, in fact in every large city, insurance and banking firms commonly "red line"—or refuse to do business with—people in the poor districts. What has happened is that *Fortune*'s Five Hundred largest corporations have decided that they have less and less need for the business of the poor. But by cutting off the funds needed for housing, for financing small business, and for municipal bonds in the low income areas

of the cities, the banks and other lenders are causing the deterioration of the urban economy and injuring the well-being of millions of people.

The government, moveover, has become a willing partner in such discrimination. It provides fast tax write-offs for airplanes, computers, bulldozers, and trucks, causing loan money to flow in these directions and not toward loans to the poor and those who have more urgent needs. It provides tax inducements for slum landlords who are allowed to depreciate slum property at an accelerated rate and to pay capital gains taxes on profits from sales— a process which is quickly repeated by the next slum landlord.

The federal government artificially restricts the money supply in order to control inflation. It should ensure that all segments of the borrowing public be given equitable treatment so far as restrictions on borrowing are concerned. Several methods are available to accomplish this. One is to provide for different Federal Reserve Board requirements for different kinds of loans. . . .

Another method would be to link certain kinds of deposits to certain kinds of loans. For example, savings and loan association deposits are now required by law to be used heavily for housing loans. Banks have similar deposits—so-called "time deposits" by individuals. In return for the benefits they receive from the federal ceilings on interest rates, as well as from other government programs, the banks could be required to make time deposits available when there is a shortage of funds for home mortgages and home construction.

. . . For most of this century there has been declared a national consensus in favor of competition, as well as numerous laws designed to encourage it, but both have been for the most part betrayed. When they have not, the benefits for the citizen have been dramatic.[1] Indeed each of the sub-economies I have described subverts values that are deeply rooted in American life.

What has been tragic is the general failure to understand how this has occurred. Fundamentally new ways must be found to make both government and corporations accountable. We should pursue the suggestion already made by some social critics for a "social accounts system" which would enable government and citizens to evaluate whether programs of education, medicine, and transportation, for example, were improving or deteriorating in quality. (The current inclusion of such activities in the gross national product has nothing whatever to say about their quality.)

Similarly computers should be made directly available to the citizen, and should be accessible both at shopping centers and by telephone. Such a cheap and simple source of information, which would give advice on the quality of products and of government and private services, could do much to squeeze the waste and deception out of the economy and give value to the dollar.

---

[1] Last year a new supermarket chain broke into the complacent food market of Washington, D.C., long dominated by three major chains. This episode and a detailed FIC report on monopolization of food prices in the Washington, D.C., area, according to an FIC report, saved Washington consumers $40 million in reduced prices in one year.

Senator Philip Hart has estimated that of the $780 billion spent by consumers in 1969, about $200 billion purchased *nothing* of value. By nothing of value he meant just that: over $45 billion was drained away by monopolistic pricing, for example, and over $6 billion by oil import quotas which drive up the prices of fuel oil and gasoline. His estimate, and it is only a preliminary one, shows how crucial is the need to evaluate how corporate and government wealth is being used—or misused—for individual and social purposes.

Such evaluations simply have not been made in our corporate political economy—not by our blinkered economists, certainly, and not by the government or the corporations themselves. Indeed the corporations have effectively blocked both the government and independent researchers from collecting and analyzing such information. Even the data on pollution must be fought for if it is to be extracted from corporations by government agencies and individuals bringing law suits. The task of the consumer movement now is to gather and analyze and disseminate this type of information by demanding it from the three branches of government and by mounting private actions by consumer groups to publicize it. Such information is the currency of economic democracy, the first tool for changing the perception of citizens, and society itself.

The Soul of Mammon: Corporate Responsibility and Capitalism

Alan Stone

It is sometimes forgotten that Adam Smith's *Wealth of Nations* not only purported to describe the functioning of an economic system based largely on government nonintervention in economic affairs, but in addition provided a moral justification for this system. While occasionally inveighing against the selfishness and rapacity of merchants and manufacturers and certainly not their apologist, Smith, on balance, concluded that political interference in the economic process would be disastrous. "The statesman, who should

Editor's Note: This reading originally appeared in the *International Socialist Review* (December 1974) as a review of the following books:

Chamberlain, Neil. *The Limits of Corporate Responsibility.* New York: Basic Books, 1973.

Heilbroner, Robert, et al. *In the Name of Profits.* New York: Doubleday, 1972.

Nader, Ralph, ed. *The Consumer and Corporate Accountability.* New York: Harcourt, Brace, Jovanovich, 1973.

Nader, Ralph, and Green, Mark. *Corporate Power in America.* New York: Grossman, 1973.

attempt to direct private people in what manner they ought to employ their capitals would . . . assume an authority which could safely be trusted, not only to no single person, but to no council or senate whatever. . . ." (Modern Library edition, p. 423). Adam Smith's conclusion has become a part of the folklore of capitalism, reinforced continually by the paeans of politicians, businessmen, and their apologists subject only to the reservation that when performance in some single industry or group is defective, governmental regulation shall be imposed to remedy the defect.

While Adam Smith's conclusion has become part of the American folklore, the premises upon which it was founded and the specific results which it was to bring have been largely ignored. In the famous "invisible hand" passage (p. 423), he strenuously argued that each individual pursuing his own selfish interest would most effectually promote society's interest. Further, allocation of resources should therefore be left to individual merchants and manufacturers and should not be directed by a public authority (p. 343).

Thus, Smith urged that the system of free competition (a critical premise) was self-regulating and would render the entrepreneur accountable to the consumer interest and responsible to public goals.

Critical attacks on capitalism's human costs and irresponsibility began before Marx and received their most crystalline exposition in *Capital* (see, for example, Volume I, Part III, Chapter X, "The Working Day," which recounts in great detail both capitalist exploitation and irresponsibility). Since then, American muckrakers of both the radical and liberal persuasions researched and wrote on these themes, providing numerous case studies over the years. We will only mention Upton Sinclair's *The Jungle* and J. B. Matthews and R. E. Shallcross' 1935 *Partners in Plunder* as American twentieth century examples. But, like so much else that was progressive in America, critical literature received almost no public attention during the long period of political quiescence from the late 1940s through the early 1960s.

In recent years, probably beginning with the publication of Ralph Nader's *Unsafe at Any Speed* in 1965, the folklore of business responsibility has come continuously under challenge with an accompanying public awareness that the private enterprise system is satisfying neither the interest of the individual consumer nor public economic goals. The businessman, in a word, was becoming perceived increasingly as both not responsible and not accountable. Manipulation of consumers and the failure of regulation to remedy the defects of the business system were the compelling conclusions as the cascade of reports by "Nader's Raiders" and other "public interest" investigators began to be issued. Virtually every major industry was shown to have failed the public in crucial ways: dangerous cars from the automobile industry, pollution from the paper and pulp industry, questionable additives from the food industry, inadequate refining capacity from the petroleum industry, excessive profits and incredible executive compensation across the board, price gouging of especially vulnerable consumers such as the aged by the pharmaceutical and nursing-home industries, etc., etc.

Taken as a whole what these specific instances of corporate action and inaction ineluctably demonstrate is that crucial decisions affecting the public are made by individuals whose policies and decision-making processes are effectively beyond our control. Put another way, a few powerful and wealthy persons make public decisions, often to our detriment, which have the force of law over our lives even though we are never given the opportunity to debate or vote on them. Moreover, the palliative of regulation has been shown by many of the Nader reports and other materials to have been a resounding failure in obtaining appropriate performance from industry.

We are led then to a series of interrelated questions: (1) What are the flaws in the premises of Adam Smith's conclusion? (2) What should be done about corporate responsibility and accountability? (3) Can the problem be effectively solved within the framework of the capitalist system? In the books under review, the third question is not even seriously considered, although it is discussed briefly and superficially in an essay by Heilbroner. The first question is discussed in some of the essays, most notably by Galbraith (Nader and Green, pp. 3–10), but never systematically related to the second and third questions. Instead, except for the Chamberlain volume —by far the most penetrating of them—the focus is on the second question which is variously answered by trotting out in half-hearted fashion a host of familiar liberal panaceas such as breaking up large corporations into smaller units, federal chartering of corporations, criminal sanctions against corporate officials, and the vigorous use of muckraking and public-interest law firms. Indeed, one's overall impression of these books is of a parade of corporate horrors followed by either throwing up one's hands or advocating a shallow "solution."

Let us first examine the question of why the "invisible hand" solution advanced by Adam Smith is no longer appropriate—if it ever was. The most important structural change since 1776 when the *Wealth of Nations* was published is the prevalence of oligopoly as the standard in capitalist countries in place of atomistic competition. Skipping several intermediate steps in the reasoning, competition in price has largely come to an end and been replaced by oligopolistic coordination in price setting, often in the form of an implicit system of price leadership. Serious competition has been restricted largely to the international plane, where the rivalry for markets and areas for investment still carries the threat of trade wars and an international recession. At home, however, the oligopolies have acquired immense power to resist price cuts in response to market dips, so that we are presented with the unpalatable choice between permanent inflation or withdrawal of goods from the market until the monopoly price can be met.

Competition shifts to cost-cutting and the sales effort. With the demise of price competition and the significant increase in scale and importance of the sales effort, firms find a substitute for price attractiveness in the drive for profit in consumer manipulation. Differentiation of largely similar products becomes a way of life, and aided by product complexity, concealment of pertinent information, puffing and irrelevant information, the consumer's capability to judge product quality or to distinguish rationally between competing brands on rational grounds comes to a virtual end. Moreover, as the automobile safety device history shows, firms are loathe to add cost-adding devices unless their competitors will do the same contemporaneously.

This is especially the case where devices or features which will enhance the life of the product—and thus harm repeat sales—are involved. Indeed, oligopolies adopt an unwritten law that they will "live-and-let-live" in a world of diminished standards subject only to the extraordinary situation in which one can gain a decisive long-standing advantage through a truly useful innovation.

Adam Smith imagined that full-scale competition and consumer choice would provide all the regulation needed to make unnecessary a formal system of accountability for private production. That this was never so need not be argued here. But what should be recognized is that even these dubious checks on the power of private industry have largely disappeared. We are left in modern capitalism with a severely limited range of choices made by the few men who made business decisions, unchecked by the two principal instruments of accountability—competitors and consumers—considered by the early ideologists of capitalism themselves as absolutely indispensable if the system were to serve social needs. Moreover, under conditions of oligopoly, the informally coordinated—and in many cases individual—decisions they make, as, for example, the petroleum companies' failure to build new domestic refineries, have an enormous impact on the public.

But can the situation be corrected within the framework of the capitalist system? This breaks down into two further questions: (1) whether capitalists themselves will or can develop a sense of public consciousness—or will they resist this, and (2) whether governmental action can compel such reform. One needn't impute malevolence to capitalists in order to reject the notion that they will suddenly see the light. Unfortunately, many of the Naderite writers adopt this tone; here Marxism, which seeks explanations in systemic terms rather than in a search for individual motivations, shows its superiority. And it is the great virtue of the Chamberlain book that he seeks his answer to the problem of corporate responsibility in realistic (although hardly Marxist) terms, instead of adopting a tone of righteous indignation.

Chamberlain, it should be pointed out, is a professor of corporations at the Columbia Graduate School of Business—hardly a citadel of radicalism. Yet, as is so often the case, there is a great deal more sense to the sober conservative assessment than in the liberal panacea. He bases his thesis that corporations cannot be expected to be attentive to public goals except in marginal ways on the centrality of the profit motive. Citing considerable support for his view from important business leaders, he states:

Even in these limited exercises in social responsibility the individual corporation must recognize two constraints. First, it must show a profit that compares favorably with the profit positions of other major corporations. This is necessary for several reasons. The legal framework vests ultimate corporate authority in a board of directors nominally elected by the stockholders, and incumbent managements must perform well enough to forestall a challenge to their position. . . . Further, although internally generated funds provide much of the capital needed by large corporations, it is occasionally necessary to resort to the capital markets for new financing, whether in the form of equity issues or long-term loans, the terms on which that capital can be secured depend on the price at which the corporation's stock is selling, which in turn reflects its present and prospective profit position. Moreover, a strong profit position is necessary to discourage an attempted takeover by a less socially conscious corporate raider who sees a return on assets that is not being fully realized by a management that may have followed its "corporate conscience" with excessive zeal.

Second, a corporation must maintain a size (preferably a rate of growth) that permits it to continue those facilitating activities—advertising, research and development, personnel policies, public relations—on at least the scale that has brought it to its present position. A decline in size, even a declining rate of growth, creates problems of holding onto and recruiting high-quality talent and of finding places for or dismissing older employees. . . .

Such a fixation on profit and size does not arise because these are necessarily the most desirable objectives that can be imagined . . . but because the company is driven to them by the requirements of its position (pp. 5, 6).

There we have it! Corporations must follow the path of profit and growth to the virtual exclusion of all other values—no matter how this might adversely affect us—not because of the venality of the corporate elite, but because it is endemic to the nature of capitalism. Moreover, it follows from this conclusion that corporate executives will do everything in their power within both the corporate and political arenas to enhance or at least maintain their profit and growth positions.

Thus, in the face of a critical need for investment in new energy sources, we learn that the major petroleum firms are investing heavily in the lucrative debt market.

But if we cannot expect corporate responsibility from corporate officials, can governmental or other action do something about it? Here the Heilbroner, Nader, and Nader and Green volumes are replete with solutions all stated in a political vacuum as if corporations wielded little power in a capitalist society to resist actions perceived as inimical to their interests. Most of the authors offer their pet solutions which come under critical attack from other authors. Thus, Ralph Nader suggests a new form of regulation—federal chartering of corporations with attendant power in a new federal regulatory agency to oversee corporate activities (Nader and Green, pp. 87–94). Yet, why this form of regulation should work in the face of the universally conceded failure of federal regulation in the past is not made clear. Numerous Nader task force studies as well as a large body of political science case studies make eminently clear that the regulated invariably regulate the regulators. One is therefore led to conclude with attorney Simon Lazarus that "A federal corporation agency would be more a captive of industry than its master" (Nader and Green, p. 228).

What accounts for the persistent failure of regulation to control corporate America? Here, again, Chamberlain supplies realism in place of the naive zeal of Nader and his followers. In the first place there is usually a limitation of resources—both staff and money—to effectively carry out the designated task. Second, there is the difficulty in obtaining compliance with administrative orders which require virtual perpetual policing. Third, there is the great difficulty of discovering transgressions; only occasionally, for example, do price-fixers leave uncovered tracks. Fourth, when one considers the large number of activities undertaken by corporations in connection with a multitude of products, the task of supervision seems well-nigh impossible. Fifth, regulators usually depend on the regulated firms to supply necessary information which we can assume will be done most selectively. Sixth, inherent in the bureaucratic-administrative system is the capacity for enormous delay, which transgressors, we may be sure, take advantage of (Chamberlain, pp. 17–20).

All of the above may be described as the administrative reasons why regulation is doomed to failure. We have not yet examined the more imposing political ones which result from the fact that the setting in which regulation takes place is a capitalist society. First, we note the well-known fact that the principal resource in American elections is money and that wealthy contributors with obvious interests in regulatory and other governmental decisions make a very large proportion of the contributions to most campaigns for the presidency and the Senate. The persons selected by elected officials to appointive posts will obviously be safe. But as the experienced Senator Fred Harris, among others, has shown, political influence of corporations doesn't end there. Day-by-day lobbying activities for which only corporations have the requisite resources, the promise of future lucrative jobs in industry to public officials—and sometimes outright bribery—greatly aid the corporate elite in obtaining public policies to their advantage (Nader and Green, pp. 25–42). While Senator Harris and the various Naderites readily concede on the basis of their empirical studies that corporations enjoy overwhelming political advantages, they do not draw the obvious conclusion that such overwhelming advantages are inherent in the nature of capitalist society. Sure, the "people" may win a victory here and there, but the dice are loaded against them.

But this is not all. As we noted earlier many of the statutes which purported to be popular reforms were actually enacted at the behest of business interests to solve problems which required political intercession. Thus, that such statutes favor corporate interests should not surprise us, notwithstanding rhetoric to the contrary. Finally, we should note a pervasive fact of capitalist political culture: To all but socialists there is a congruity between the well-being of capitalist economic institutions, principally corporations, and national well-being. Public policies must therefore be arranged so as to encourage corporate investment, and to assure the "well-being" of such enterprises, the definitions of which are supplied by corporate officials. Thus, attitudes favoring big business in public officials—which are usually there in the first place—become ingrained and reinforced.

If one, then, is led to conclude that political solutions to corporate reform on the scale needed are impossible within the economic structure of contemporary capitalism and if the corporate elite cannot be expected to reform themselves, what are the other possible solutions? One is, of course, socialism, to which we will return in a moment. The other, a great favorite among many of the Naderites and allied liberal reformers, is to restructure American industry by breaking up large corporations into smaller ones through antitrust action. They wistfully wish to re-create a supposed era in which small business units were presumably responsible to the public (see, for example, Nader, pp. 314–24). Yet as Robert Heilbroner persuasively points out, highly competitive industries characterized by small units

> . . . have also been the models of industrial backwardness, characterized by low research and development, low wages and long hours, antiunionism, company towns, etc. I see no reason to believe that an IBM cut down to size would spend its fragmented profits in a more socially beneficial manner than its master company. . . . The power of the corporation to work social good or evil would not be lessened by fragmenting it. It would only be made less visible and hence, in the end, less accountable or controllable than by bringing it out into the open at the top (Heilbroner, p. 210).

One need only add that the large number of FTC orders entered against small firms for false advertising confirms Heilbroner's observation. Finally, one should add that even if it were politically possible to break up, say, General Motors, who but extremely wealthy capitalists could acquire the constituent parts, given the concentration of wealth in this country? Breaking up the Standard Oil Company in 1911 did not exactly result in small-scale enterprises.

So finally we reach the solution of socialism, mentioned by only a few of the contributors to these volumes, rather ambiguously approved by Galbraith (Nader and Green, p. 9), and discussed, at least somewhat seriously, by Heilbroner. Yet he rejects socialism for the bizarre reason that socialism "must use as its main weapon against the irrationalities of corporate capitalism the irrationalities of the nation-state" (Heilbroner, p. 222).

There is no reason to deny that Stalinist Russia and other bureaucratized countries that have established socialized property forms have followed narrowly nationalist policies. But this kind of chauvinism is still not based on the export of capital and merchandise in the search for profits, as under capitalism. In any case it is a gross distortion to equate the predatory nationalism of American capitalism, or the provincial nationalism of the Stalinist bureaucracy, with the nationalist and socialist appeals of oppressed peoples to build and improve societies for the benefit of exploited classes. Such nationalist struggles in the underdeveloped nations do not tie socialism to the "nation-state" but are stepping stones on the road to the creation of a humane internationalist society, which is the motivation of socialists. Moreover, there is no logical reason to assume, as Heilbroner does, that the phenomenon of Stalinist Russia, generated by a revolution under conditions of extreme poverty and underdevelopment, would be repeated in modern capitalist societies.

But beyond that, and without downgrading the serious problems of bureaucracy and potential for repressive abuse that socialist societies have manifested, only socialism is capable of solving the problems of responsibility in the economic realm. Only in a socialist society can economic priorities be set democratically so that investment is directed toward human needs and not into profitable junk that consumers are manipulated into buying. Under socialism motives to undertake economic acts in conflict with the public interest in order to improve profits and sales disappear. Similarly such absurdities as badly needed social services being cut back and working people excessively taxed in order to pay the interest on bonds held by the wealthiest segment of the population will disappear. Indeed, socialism offers the only prospect for responsibility and accountability.

Why then have the decent, well-meaning contributors to these volumes largely disregarded socialism as an answer? The apparent reason is that it is not viewed as a "practical" solution. As the costs of preserving capitalism become heavier and more intolerable it is precisely these practical realists who will discover themselves to be the true utopians. Masses of people in other advanced countries have committed themselves to fight for socialism. The socialist demon will not be vanquished by some general agreement not to mention it. It is the only answer to the horrors of capitalism, some of which are so graphically depicted by the reformers.

Cities, the Automobile, Work, and Alienation

No one has to be reminded that our cities are disaster zones. Residents are afraid to walk the streets. Services deteriorate: streets are strewn with litter; libraries, virtually insolvent, operate part-time; entire school systems close down for lack of funds. Urban decay has its origins in various social phenomena, each an outcome of the unplanned capitalist market. The automobile's rise to a position of dominance led to an inefficient dispersal of population, suburban exploitation of the city, and erosion of the urban tax base. Further, as rural blacks, who were left jobless by the application of technology to Southern agriculture following World War II, moved to the cities, middle-class whites and tax-producing businesses fled to the suburbs. Unskilled and often illiterate, rural people of any land invariably find conditions difficult in the cities or adopted countries to which they migrate. If they are black Americans, they meet special obstacles that make progress even tougher. Included in this section are readings that systematically develop these themes.

Only recently have we come to appreciate the mounting social costs of our automobile culture. The triumph of this four-wheeled way of life was made possible by an extensive system of arterial highways. In the planning and realizing of this network of highways through New York City, no one was more instrumental than Robert Moses, the subject of Robert Caro's fascinating biography, *The Power Broker*. Reading 14, an excerpt from Caro's book, shows how a poor, powerless, but vibrant Bronx community was destroyed for the convenience of commuters and well-off Catskill vacationers. Such "progress" contributes to the ruination of cities, as Caro makes clear in his description of the destructive social aftermath of the construction of the Cross-Bronx Expressway. Caro's devastating picture of what happens to the not-so-well-off is all the more revealing of the nature of power in America as we learn what happens to the rich when *their* property is threatened by the relentless bulldozer.

So accustomed are we to the automobile that we take its noise, noxious emissions, and other harmful accompaniments almost for granted. The orthodox but maverick economist E. J. Mishan, of the London School of Economics, tries to bring these problems to our attention by presenting a parable about crime (see Reading 15). He shows in passing that one of the treasured conclusions of bourgeois economics makes little sense. Organizing production according to individual choice in the marketplace does not maximize human welfare; to the contrary. As orthodox economists are well aware, A's purchase can negatively affect B's satisfaction, and they even have a number of technical terms—such as "externalities," "spillovers," and "neighborhood effects"—to describe this condition. Once one acknowledges, however, that neighborhood effects are of central importance, much of mainstream economics stands discredited; beneficial effects can no longer be imputed to the unregulated workings of a market economy. As a solution to problems of excessive noise and traffic, Mishan calls for the gradual elimination of the privately owned automobile. He and others attempt elsewhere in their writings to redress the effects of pollutants by calling for tax levies that compensate for the harm inflicted on innocent bystanders. (See also,

section 5a on ecological problems.) Alternatively, they propose restricted traffic zones, similar to no-smoking sections in theaters and restaurants. But ecological solutions in the form of effluent taxes and restricted zones are not likely to achieve success within a capitalist context. If taken seriously— that is, if a thoroughgoing attempt is made to ensure that the full costs of production and consumption are borne by the appropriate parties—solutions of this kind would challenge, or at least undermine, the hegemony of capital itself. It would call for an extension of social planning that would appear to be incompatible with capital's needs, wishes, and privileges.

Mishan, an Englishman, appears to hanker for an old-fashioned, quiet life in a peaceful cottage, a desire neither uncommon nor surprising in view of what contemporary city life actually offers. But why, one might ask, have cities become so unlivable? In a selection from his important work, *The Fiscal Crisis of the State* (see Reading 16) radical professor James O'Connor of San Jose State College demonstrates how the city is exploited by the suburbs. Moreover, he shows that this exploitation "is rooted in the nature of monopoly-sector production relations" and has helped to impoverish further the less affluent members of the work force.

Other explanations of urban

decay are offered in Reading 17 by Frances Fox Piven, Columbia University professor and author in the field of welfare. Her article explains why, in a country as wealthy as ours, there is a financial crisis in virtually every city. Piven's insightful analysis makes interdisciplinary use of history, sociology, political science, and economics as they apply to the contemporary urban crisis. Her essay is must reading for those who erroneously think (or used to, before the current downturn) that black people were getting for free what others had to earn.

Our next reading is closely related to what precedes it but is more a discussion of the role of automobiles in modern capitalist society than a discussion of urban problems per se (see Reading 18). Written by Professor Matthew Edel of Queens College (CUNY), it originally appeared as a review of Barry Weisberg's *Beyond Repair: The Ecology of Capitalism*. From Edel's review, it is but a short trip to the Vega plant at Lordstown (see Reading 19, by Emma Rothschild). While the automobile itself has caused general devastation and upheavals in American life, producing it has left an equally deep scar on those who work the line. It is no surprise that corporate production, built on a concept of efficiency that does *not* take into consideration the physical (and emotional) wear and tear on the worker, has been plagued by a rising rate of absenteeism. Until inflation and recession took their toll, workers were apparently using their increases in real earnings to escape at least momentarily the boring or brutalizing experience of their jobs.

But perhaps jobs need not be that way. A number of corporations, perhaps more out of desperation than humanity, are attempting to modify working conditions to cope with worker alienation. In fact, it can be persuasively demonstrated that the abolition of autocratic forms of organization and the introduction of "industrial democracy"—increased decision-making power for employees— leads to more efficiency, not less. A leading advocate of industrial democracy is David Jenkins. He ends his book *Job Power: Blue and White Collar Democracy* (a selection from which is included as Reading 20) with these words: "Freedom is within reach."

But is it? Why do corporations persist in resisting what people like Jenkins tell them— specifically, that industrial democracy can *increase* their efficiency and their profits as well? One answer is that those at the top of the corporate heap may fear the long-term consequences of democratizing the work place. For, once the process starts in earnest, what is to prevent the workers from demanding power *in toto*? In the last reading of this section (21), Professor Herb Gintis of the University of Massachusetts, Amherst, discusses these questions. By placing work within its capitalist context of unequal wealth and a hierarchical system of power, Gintis shows alienation to be an unavoidable feature of the capitalistic mode of production.

This section shows that almost everywhere, whether in the city, in the suburb, or on the job, problems are growing in spite of (or because of) our increasing GNP. Radicals suggest that the ultimate source of the problems is the system of unplanned production known as capitalism. Until this system is replaced, we can only expect more of the same.

14

The Northern State Parkway and the Cross-Bronx Expressway: A Revealing Contrast

Robert A. Caro

I. THE NORTHERN STATE PARKWAY

. . . Moses was playing by the rules of power now and one of the first of those rules is that when power meets greater power, it does not oppose but attempts to compromise. He had met power invulnerable to him—or even to his champion in the Governor's chair—in the barons of Long Island's North Shore [Mrs. Henry Phipps, Payne Whitney, Claus Spreckels, Clarence Hungerford Mackay, Henry Carnegie Phipps, Henry Payne Whitney, Francis P. Garvan, E. D. Morgan, Mrs. William K. Vanderbilt II, Bronson Winthrop, Henry Rogers Winthrop and Otto Kahn]. And where once, in laying out the original route of the Northern State Parkway exactly where he believed it should ideally go, laying it out without compromise, running it right past the massive porticos of the barons' castles, he had spat in the eye of power, now he hastily administered eyewash.

He would not move the parkway route down out of the hills the barons held and onto the plains in the Island's center. This would mean that the parkway could never be truly beautiful. But, within the hills, there were many possible routes, and he was willing to compromise with the barons on which route would finally be chosen. He made deals: with at least a dozen barons he covenanted that he would move the parkway away from the homes to the edges of their property, out of sight of their castles, if they would in return donate the right-of-way so that he would not need a legislative appropriation for it; with a dozen more, where moving it to their estates' borders was impractical, he agreed to move it as far as was practical —and, so the estate would not be sliced in half by the parkway, so that equestrians could proceed unchecked on their rides and hunts, to build, at state expense, bridges, one for each estate, over the parkway for the exclusive use of the baron in residence and his retainers and guests.

The compromising did not stop there. Were the barons afraid that the alien hordes brought to Long Island on the parkway might encroach on their lands? Precautions against this could be arranged. Specifically, he would covenant with the concerned barons that there would be no exits from the parkway within their borders. And he gave his solemn oath that state troopers patrolling the parkway would be under orders to keep automobiles from the city moving, not allowing their occupants to picnic, or even to stop, by the side of the parkway within their borders. Publicly, Moses never stopped excoriating the Long Island millionaires. But in private, many of them were coming to consider him quite a reasonable fellow to deal with.

None found him more reasonable than financier Otto Kahn. In dealing with Kahn, Moses, in his excursions beyond the limits of the spirit of the law, went further than he had ever gone before. The Legislature, subservient to the will of the barons, refused all through 1924, 1925, 1926 and 1927 to give Moses a cent for the Northern State Parkway. Funds were refused even for the surveying of proposed routes—a refusal which made it almost impossible for Moses to work out deals with the barons because he could not be sure whether routes proposed were engineeringly feasible. But in 1926, Kahn learned that Moses intended to run the parkway right through the middle of the eighteen-hole private golf course he had constructed for his pleasure on his Cold Spring Harbor estate.

Kahn, who happened to be a relative of Moses—he was married to the daughter of one of Bella's sisters—offered to secretly donate $10,000 to the Park Commission for surveys, if some of the surveys found a new route for the parkway in the Cold Spring Harbor area, a route which would not cross his estate at all. And Moses accepted the money.

Regard for power implies disregard for those without power as is demonstrated by what happened after Moses shifted the route of the Northern State Parkway away from Otto Kahn's golf course. The map of the Northern State Parkway in Cold Spring Harbor is a map not only of a road but of power—and of what happens to whose who, unwittingly, are caught in the path of power.

The parkway was originally supposed to run through Otto Kahn's estate. Since Otto Kahn had power—the power that went with money—he was able to get the route shifted to the south. South of Otto Kahn's estate lay the estates of two other men of wealth and of influence with the Legislature—Congressman Ogden Livingston Mills and Colonel Henry Rogers Winthrop. The Congressman and the Colonel were able to get the route shifted farther south, far enough so it would not touch their estates either. But shifting the route south of the Mills and Winthrop estates meant that it would run through the estates of two other men of wealth and influence, Colonel Henry L. Stimson and Robert W. De Forest. So the route was shifted south again. And south of the Stimson and De Forest estates lay a row of farms, and farmers had neither wealth nor influence.

James Roth was one of those farmers. When he had purchased his forty-nine acres in 1922, much of it had been woodland and all of it had been rocky. Roth had hauled away the rocks and cut down the trees. He owned a team of horses, but they could not budge many of the stumps. As the horses pulled at them, Roth pulled beside them. So did his wife, Helen. So that both would be freed for the pulling, their son, Jimmy, at the age of five, had to learn how to handle the team. As his parents sweated at the ropes, he sat on one of the horses, kicking him forward.

After the farm was cleared, the Roths found that the southern fifteen acres were no good for planting. But the rest of the land was rich and fertile. In the afternoons, during harvest season, James Roth, who had been up since before dawn working in the fields, would load up one of his two wagons and drive to market. While he was gone, his wife and son, who in 1927 was six, would load the other. When Roth returned he would—without pause, since every minute was important to a farmer trying to work thirty-four acres without a hired man—unharness the team, hitch it to the loaded wagon and begin the trip again—while Helen and Jimmy would reload the first wagon. But by 1927 the farm had begun paying. "We felt pretty secure," Jimmy recalls. "We had a nice farm. In those days, a farm wasn't just real estate, like it is now. In those days, a farm was your living. It was your home. And we had a nice farm."

Then, in 1927, a representative of the Long Island State Park Commission—of Robert Moses—drove up to the Roths' farm and told them the state was condemning fourteen acres out of the farm's center for the Northern State Parkway. James Roth argued with Moses' representative. He pleaded with him. All he wanted the commission to do, Roth said, was to move the parkway route about four hundred feet south, less than a tenth of a mile. That would put it in the barren part of the farm. Taking fourteen acres from the center meant that a substantial part of the fertile acreage would be gone. Even more important, it meant that the farm would be sliced in two. How would he get from one side to the other? How would he be able to work it? But Moses' representative refused to listen to the Roths. The route had been decided on the basis of engineering considerations, he said. It could not possibly be changed.

Robert Moses had shifted the parkway south of Otto Kahn's estate, south of Winthrop's and Mills's estates, south of Stimson's and De Forest's. For men of wealth and influence, he had moved it more than three miles south of its original location. But James Roth possessed neither money nor influence. And for James Roth, Robert Moses would not move the parkway south even one tenth of a mile farther. For James Roth, Robert Moses would not move the parkway one foot. Robert Moses had offered men of wealth and influence bridges across the parkway so that there would be no interference with their pleasures. But he wouldn't offer James Roth a bridge so that there would be no interference with his planting.

In years to come, James Roth would talk often about the injustice that had been done him. "My father was really rocked by this; he talked about it until the end of his life," says his son, Jimmy, who had watched his father and mother sweating side by side over their land. "And I don't know that I blame him. I'll tell you—my father and mother worked very hard on that place, and made something out of it, and then someone just cut it in two. To have someone take away something you have . . ." The farm never really paid again. There just wasn't enough fertile acreage left. And the Roths found that it took fully twenty-five minutes to drive their team to the nearest road that crossed the parkway and then to get back to plow the other side of the farm. Each round trip took about fifty minutes, and these were fifty-minute segments slashed out of the life of a man to whom every minute was necessary. "It was quite a ways," Mrs. Roth recalls. "It was quite a ways for a man who was working hard already." The condemnation award "never came to much," Mrs. Roth says. And because there were two separate, rather small pieces of property instead of a single big one, she says, they couldn't even sell the farm.

The situation was the same for the other Cold Spring Harbor farmers whose farms were ruined by the Northern State Parkway. To the end of their lives most of them would remember the day on which they heard that "the road was coming" as a day of tragedy. There was only one aspect of the tragedy that alleviated their bitterness. That was their belief that it was unavoidable, that the route of the parkway had indeed been determined by engineering considerations, and therefore really could not be changed. Forty years later, when the author asked them about the possibility of the parkway being built through the big estates to the north, not one of those farmers thought that such a possibility had ever existed. . . .

The great piece of [Moses'] business left unstarted at the close of [Governor] Smith's regime was the Northern State Parkway. In the North Hills, the name given to the terminal moraine near the New York City line, Moses had found a line of small farms that could make a right-of-way —twisting, turning, but still a right-of-way between the holdings of the North Hills barons. Where there was not the slightest crevice between estates, he had introduced into the parkway's route still more curves, so

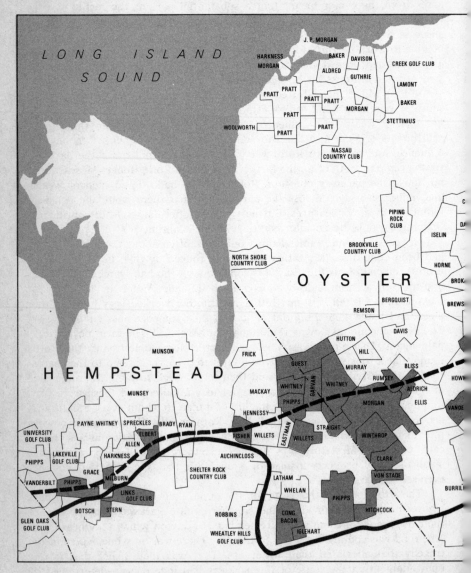

that it would run along the very edges of the barons' estates and not disturb the serenity of their manor houses. He had threaded the route along that portion of the rough at the Links Country Club that could most easily be spared without spoiling the barons' favorite golf course. And by paying them tribute in the form of private bridges and personal entrances, he had persuaded them to donate the right-of-way he needed. The barons of the Dix Hills in the western portion of Suffolk County—Otto Kahn, Stimson, Mills, Winthrop and De Forest—had thrown back with contemptuous ease his attempt to penetrate the fastnesses they controlled, but Kahn's $10,000 had enabled him to snatch from James Roth and other meek farmers of the plains to the south thirteen more miles of right-of-way.

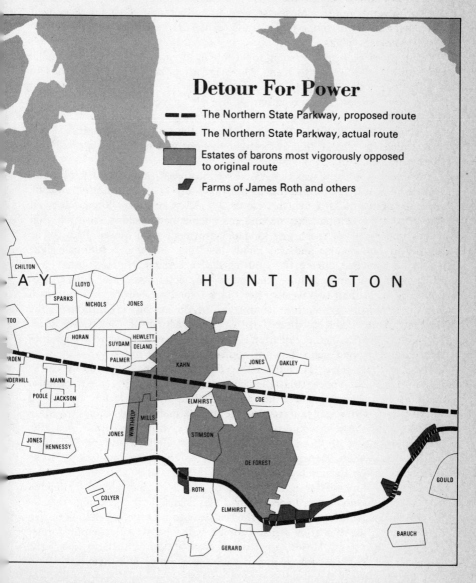

But between the North Hills and Dix Hills stood the Wheatley Hills, the meeting place of the two moraines, the bolt of the scissors that made Long Island beautiful. And in the Wheatley Hills, the estates—identified by black-and-gold signs bearing such names as Morgan, Whitney, Winthrop, Grace, Garvan and Phipps—clustered around the little village of Old Westbury so thickly that there was no path, no matter how tortuous, that could be picked out without running through their holdings. These barons therefore refused to parley and instead hired champions to fight Moses—and the champions included Grenville Clark, whose brilliance as an attorney was not at all dimmed in their eyes by the fact that he had been a Harvard classmate of Franklin D. Roosevelt.

For several months, Moses seemed to be winning the fight. Roosevelt drove over the two routes himself and wrote Clark that he saw no reason to change Moses' plans.

But those plans were soon to be changed nonetheless. For Grenville Clark discovered how Otto Kahn, Moses' relative, had persuaded Moses to shift the parkway route off his private golf course.

At first, Moses' new executive [Roosevelt] gave him support, backing the Wheatley Hills route. But Clark began hinting that any attempt to push that route would result in the disclosure to the public of the Moses-Kahn deal, which, he said, if "finally brought to light will not make a creditable chapter in the history of this State."

Whether Roosevelt was motivated by the threat of public disclosure to prevail on Moses to compromise is not definitely known. But the following sequence of events is clear. On October 23, 1929, Clark gave Roosevelt what amounted to an ultimatum: he and his clients had decided, he said, that it was impossible to reach any kind of agreement with Moses, because he refused to compromise and was highly insulting, and that a full-scale fight would be launched during the 1930 legislative session. Nineteen-thirty was an election year; among those running for re-election would be Franklin D. Roosevelt. Less than two weeks after Clark issued the barons' ultimatum to Roosevelt, Moses agreed to a "compromise." Under the "compromise," the Northern State suddenly altered its eastward course at Glen Cove Road, the western border of the Wheatley Hills, just as it was about to plunge into the estate area, and instead swung south for two full miles, far enough so that when it resumed its course, it would never come near the Wheatley Hills. To make it appear that the "compromise" was really a compromise and that both sides, instead of just the state, had given in, Moses announced to the public with great fanfare that the barons had agreed to pay the state $175,000, which he said would pay for the entire cost of the detour. Actually, however, the cost of the additional right-of-way alone would be $2,250,000, so that more than 90 percent of the bill for the accommodation Moses reached with the barons had to be footed by the state's taxpayers.

The long-term costs to the public of Moses' accommodation include figures that cannot be prefaced with dollar signs. For one thing, the accommodation condemned users of the parkway to a perpetual detour of five miles around the Wheatley Hills. Coupled with the six-mile detour forced on parkway users by Moses' previous accommodation with Otto Kahn and the other Dix Hills barons, it meant that a commuter who lived anywhere east of Dix Hills and who used the parkway to get to his job in New York City was condemned to drive, every working day of his life, twenty-two extra and unnecessary miles. He had to drive 110 unnecessary miles per week, 5,500 per year—all because of Moses' "compromise." By the 1960's there were about 21,500 such commuters, and the cost to them alone of Moses' accommodation totaled tens of millions of wasted hours of human lives.

More important, Moses' great accommodation deprived the public forever of parks in the loveliest part of Long Island. He had once wanted parks on the wooded hills of the North Shore, and his original concept of the Northern State Parkway was therefore of a road leading to parks, as the Southern State Parkway led to parks. But, as part of his "compromise," he had to promise the barons that there would not be a single state park anywhere along the parkway, or anywhere in the section of the North Shore that they controlled—and with a single exception, acquired in 1967 and still undeveloped in 1974, there are no state parks anywhere in that part of Nassau County or western Suffolk that was known as the "North Shore" or the "Gold Coast." Robert Moses' "compromise" with the North Shore barons amounted to unconditional surrender. In later years, most of the barons would have disappeared from the Long Island scene. The names of most of them would be unfamiliar to the new generations using the Northern State Parkway. But every twist and curve in that parkway—and, in particular, the two great southward detours it makes around the Wheatley and Dix Hills—is a tribute to their power, and to the use to which they put it after they discovered the chink in Moses' armor. Farmer James Roth was not the only person who paid for Moses' deal with Otto Kahn.

II. ONE MILE OF THE CROSS-BRONX EXPRESSWAY

Robert Moses built 627 miles of roads in and around New York City. This is the story of one of those miles.

There is something strange about that mile. It is one of seven that make up the great highway known as the Cross-Bronx Expressway, but the other six, like most of the other miles of Moses' expressways, are—roughly—straight, on a road map a heavy red line slashing inexorably across the delicate crosshatch of streets in the borough's central expanse. There is logic—the ruthless, single-minded logic of the engineer, perhaps, but logic —in that line. When it curves the curves are shallow, the road hastening to resume its former course. But during that one mile, the road swerves, bulging abruptly and substantially toward the north.

If the bulge in the expressway was puzzling to anyone studying it, it was tragic to those who didn't have to study it, to the people who lived in or near that right-of-way. For to these people, the fifty-four apartment buildings that would have to be destroyed were not just buildings but homes. That mile of buildings was the very heart of the neighborhood in which they lived, a section of the Bronx known as "East Tremont."

The people of East Tremont did not have much. The Jews of East Tremont were luckier than those who had to stay behind on the Lower East Side, but not so lucky as the Grand Concourse Jews. They were not the milliners or the cloak-and-suiters but the pressers, finishers and cutters who worked in the bare workrooms behind the ornate showrooms of the garment district. They were a long way from being rich, and their neighborhood proved it.

But the neighborhood provided its residents with things that were important to them.

Transportation was important to the fathers who worked downtown, and the neighborhood had good transportation. With the Third Avenue El and the IRT White Plains Road line running right through it, it was only a few easy blocks from anywhere in East Tremont to a subway that took you right down to the garment district.

Jobs were important to the fathers who didn't work downtown, and the neighborhood had jobs available—good jobs by East Tremont standards—in a miniature garment and upholstery manufacturing district that had sprung up around Park Avenue, just ten minutes away.

Shopping was important to the mothers who stayed home and took care of the kids, and the neighborhood had good shopping. East Tremont Avenue, which ran conveniently right across its center, was a bright, bustling mile of bakeries which didn't bother advertising that they baked only with butter because all of them did, of groceries where your order was sliced and measured out and weighed ("You didn't get everything in packages like you do now"), of kosher butcher shops ("We weren't, but I bought kosher for my mother's sake. And it's the kind of meat you know in the pot"), of mama-and-papa candy stores, of delicatessens, filled always with the pungent aroma from the pickel barrels, whose owners got up before dawn to mix olives and pimentos and chives—or dates or caviar—into manufactured cream cheese to create individualized loaves they named "Paradise" or "Dark Jewel."

And the southwestern border of the neighborhood was Crotona Park. "Beautiful. Lovely. Playgrounds. There was a lake—Indian Lake. Nice. We used to sit there—under the trees. We raised our children in Crotona Park." Social scientists, who had never lived on the Lower East Side, might consider East Tremont "crowded." The people of East Tremont, who had, considered it open and airy, wonderfully open and airy.

Schools were terribly important to the people of East Tremont (a quarter of a century after their kids had graduated, some parents could still remember the precise student-teacher ratio in their classes), and East Tremont had good schools. They were old—PS 44, at 176th and Prospect, the neighborhood's junior high school, had been built in 1901, and the city said there was simply no money to replace it—but there were no double sessions and standards were high. PS 67, off Southern Boulevard, was the first elementary school in New York to offer lessons—and supply instruments—for any child who wanted to learn to play the violin. And all the schools were close, close enough for kids to walk to.

To the people of East Tremont, East Tremont was family. East Tremont was friends—real friends, not just acquaintances you happened to meet because they took their children to the same playground to which you took your children, or because they belonged to the same PTA as you, but friends whom you had grown up with and were going to grow old with, boys and girls—turned men and women—who knew and understood you and whom you knew and understood.

Robert Moses didn't think much of the apartments of East Tremont. The buildings were old, the plumbing was bad, most of them didn't even have elevators—he referred to them as "tenements," as "walkups" or, if those nouns didn't seem to be eliciting the desired horror from his listeners, as "slums." But Moses had never lived on the Lower East Side.

"Tenements?" says Mrs. Silverman. "Listen, I *lived* in tenements. These were not tenements at all." If the apartments' plumbing was not modern, neither—happily—was the size of their rooms, large—huge by postwar standards—and high-ceilinged. They had foyers—real foyers, L-shaped some of them—as big as rooms themselves. "I served dinner for eighteen in my foyer, that's how big it was," Mrs. Silverman says. They had dining rooms, not dining areas. The apartment houses might not have had elevators, but they had—almost all of them—courtyards, and there were enough small frame houses interspersed among them to let sunlight in. "Those apartments were light and airy and cheerful," Mrs. Roberts says.

They loved them—and they could afford them. If the water pressure was low, so was the rent, scaled originally to their ability to pay by landlords who could afford to do so because they had bought land in East Tremont for as little as two dollars per square foot, and kept at that scale by city-instituted rent control. Mrs. Silverman was paying $100 per month for her four rooms, and that was high. Lillian Roberts was paying $62 for her four rooms. Cele Sherman had a six-room apartment—three bedrooms, a living room, kitchen with large dining area, and a foyer with a recess large enough to be a full-scale dining room—and for that apartment Mrs. Sherman was paying $69.

The letters came on December 4, 1952.

. . . [I]n hundreds of mailboxes, letters signed by "Robert Moses, City Construction Coordinator" inform[ed] each recipient that the building in which he or she lived was in the right-of-way of the Cross-Bronx Expressway, that it would be condemned by the city and torn down—and that they had ninety days to move.

The ninety-day figure was meaningless, of course. At the time Moses sent out his letter the money to build the East Tremont stretch of the expressway was nowhere in sight; months, if not years, would be required to obtain it. The city had not even acquired title to the property yet, and there were months of procedures necessary before it could do so—and before demolition could begin. Privately, Moses was figuring not on three but eighteen months to clear the area. The use of the ninety-day figure was a scare tactic—"to shake 'em up a little and get 'em moving," a Moses aide explains.

But East Tremont's panic was soon replaced by hope. The hope was based on faith in Robert Moses, or, more accurately, in the Moses mystique. East Tremont's pious Jews still held the campaign of 1934 against him—"I hated him since the time he said he wasn't Jewish," one says—but they still believed in his image as a man above politics and bureaucrats. Believing in that image, the people of East Tremont were sure that if they could only present Moses with an alternate route through their neighborhood that was truly better than the route he had chosen, he would accept it. And it did not take them very long to find out that such a route was indeed available.

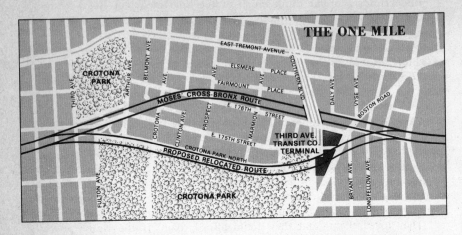

The arguments in favor of the park route were clear. By making only a gentle alteration in the road's route—swinging it just two blocks (one block in some places) to the south, 1,530 apartments would be saved at no cost to anyone: the road would not be made longer, its curves would not be made sharper—its efficiency as a traffic-moving device would not be harmed in the least. "We were happy then," recalls Lillian Edelstein. "We had been worried, but when we found there was a feasible alternate route, we figured we were in business." The arguments in favor of the alternate route were so clear. Believing in the myth of Moses, the housewives of East Tremont were sure he would accept them. And it wasn't until they tried to present them to him that panic set in again. For neither he nor any of his aides would even listen to those arguments. There would be no point in any meeting, Moses' office told Mrs. Edelstein when she telephoned after letters and telegrams had gone unanswered. The Coordinator had already decided on the route. It would not be changed.

Nonetheless, a small band fought. Most of its members were business-men who knew the mass evictions of their customers would destroy their businesses, but it was more than businessmen. Among the men and women of East Tremont were the sons and daughters of the revolutionaries who had preached socialism and Zionism in the Pale of Settlement, and on the Lower East Side, and some of them hadn't lost their faith in justice. "At that time there were a lot of lefts around here," recalls Saul Janowitz.

But mostly, it was Lillian Edelstein who fought.

Finding engineers willing to defy Moses, the housewife put them to work drawing maps detailed enough to prove from every engineering standpoint that their route was technically feasible. Then she put them to work obtain-ing hard figures: exactly how much more Moses' mile would cost than theirs. When they came up with those figures—Moses' route would require the demolition of fifty-four apartment houses, ninety one- or two-family homes and fifteen one-story "taxpayers" housing sixty stores, for a total of 159 separate buildings; condemning and demolishing them would cost more than $10,000,000 more than would be required if the road ran where they wanted it to, even without the cost of relocating 1,530 families and the loss of the real estate taxes (close to $200,000 per year at current rates) from the demolished buildings, income the city would be losing year after year forever—she undertook the harder fight of bringing those maps and figures to the attention of the public and of public officials.

The press didn't help much. She took the maps to every daily newspaper in the city; exactly two—the *World-Telegram* and, of course, the *Post*— printed them. Only the *Post* displayed the figures with any prominence. She always found a sympathetic ear at the *Post;* Joe Kahn and Abel Silver dramatically documented the conditions in Section 3. But no other paper portrayed those conditions in any detail. The three papers that counted most in the city—the *Times,* the *Herald Tribune* and the *Daily News*—never mentioned them, and gave the whole Cross-Bronx Expressway fight scanty —and slanted—coverage.

But she fought anyway. Teaching herself to type, she typed onto stencils and cranked out on the Y's mimeograph machine tens of thousands of hand-bills, as well as postcards and form letters to public officials. She persuaded the seven neighborhood movie theaters to show slides advertising the next rally or City Hall hearing. "They let us stand outside their lobbies for days with petitions and trying to raise money—we were grateful for that." She organized card parties—"Subscription $1." Learning that local radio stations such as WBNX were habitually in need of programs to fill up air time, she filled up that time with programs whose scripts she wrote herself.

It was Lillian Edelstein who arranged the rallies and mass meetings to pressure public officials, who chartered buses to take East Tremont house-wives down to City Hall for every official hearing on the expressway. Most difficult of all, it was she who persuaded the housewives to take those buses. The people of East Tremont, who believed as gospel that "you can't fight City Hall," had made one trip down to City Hall on the assurance that, if they went, they would win—and their loss had convinced them that the gospel was gospel. Trying to keep up enthusiasm, Lillian Edelstein sched-uled weekly meetings at the Y but found that now, "if you got twelve tenants coming every week, you were lucky." As for spending more days traveling down to City Hall and sitting there for hours waiting for the Board of Estimate to get to the Cross-Bronx Expressway item, "that was torture," she says. "If the bus left at ten o'clock, at nine-thirty you had to go around and kick in the doors," Janowitz says. But, time after time, she kicked them. In an era in which picket lines in front of City Hall were not yet commonplace she even managed to have picket lines of middle-aged Jewish housewives marching outside City Hall, carrying signs she lettered herself at night. . . .

The tenants sent a telegram to [Mayor] Wagner appealing for an engineering discussion under "proper circumstances." There was no reply —and of the showdown Board of Estimate meeting, Katz was to write:

Dr. Swarthe reported the results of the fiasco in the City Engineer's office. The Board was silent. They made no comment. They permitted all to talk. They made no interruptions or comments, asked no questions. The Mayor set a time limit for public debate and, at the end of it, called for the question . . . for acquisition of funds to acquire property and for building demolition.

Lyons moved the question, saying, "This is an engineer's problem, not a layman's problem, and all the engineers unanimously support this route." One by one the Board members voted—in the affirmative. The last man to vote was Robert F. Wagner, Jr. He voted in the affirmative, too. . . .

Why *wouldn't* Moses shift the route of the Cross-Bronx Expressway slightly, thereby saving 1,530 apartments, millions in state and city money, months of aggravation and delay—and making his expressway straighter as well?

"I asked George Spargo that," says Joseph Ingraham, the *Times* reporter who was occasionally on Moses' payroll and who spent so much time socializing with the Moses team that he sometimes seemed to be one of its members. "On the day of the ribbon cutting they were opening a whole bunch of sections of different expressways, and it was raining, really pouring. George said, 'Let's sit this out, and we'll catch up to them at the next stop.' We went into a small bar in the Bronx and I asked him there. He said, 'Oh, one of Jimmy Lyons' relatives owns a piece of property up there and we would have had to take it if we used that other route, and Jimmy didn't want it taken, and RM had promised him we wouldn't.' At the time, George even told me the piece of property involved, but I've forgotten."

The people of East Tremont also wondered why Moses wouldn't shift the route. "I mean, we heard lots of rumors about the bus terminal," Lillian Edelstein recalls. "The politicians were always trying to tell us that was the reason. But we could never find out anything about it. And, I mean, I never believed that. I could never believe that even Robert Moses would take fifteen hundred homes just to save a bus terminal."

Spargo's statement may have been untrue. So may the rumors. If any relative of Bronx Borough President James J. Lyons owned property along either the alternate or actual expressway route, the author was unable to find evidence of that fact—although, since, in the Bronx, politicians' ownership of property was habitually concealed through a many-layered network of intermediaries and bag men, a network baffling even to contemporary investigators and all but impenetrable twenty years later, his failure is not conclusive. Moses' refusal to alter the route—unexplainable on the basis of his given reasons, all of which are demonstrably false—may have had nothing to do with the fact that the "bus terminal" of which Lillian Edelstein speaks—actually the "Tremont Depot" of the Third Avenue Transit Company, at the northeast corner of Crotona Park—lies in the path of the alternate route and would have had to be condemned if that route was adopted. It is possible that Moses' selection of the original route—it was he, not any engineer, who selected it—was based on no more than whim, and that his subsequent refusal to alter it was due to nothing more than stubbornness, although if so it was a whim quite inconsistent with Moses' customary whims: almost invariably over a period of forty years, whenever he had a choice of routes, he selected the one that would keep his road straight, not the one that would make the road curve.

However, in attempting to find an explanation for Moses' refusal to change the route, the Third Avenue Transit depot stands out. With the exception of six old, small, dilapidated brownstone tenements, housing a total of nineteen families, it was the only structure of any type that would have had to be condemned if the alternate route was used. (See map, page

128.) In effect, for whatever reason, Robert Moses elected to tear down 159 buildings housing 1,530 families instead of tearing down six buildings housing nineteen families—and the terminal. It is a fact that the Third Avenue Transit Company secretly told Moses it was very anxious not to have the terminal condemned, for its location was strategic for its buses. And it is also a fact that for twenty years it was considered an open secret in Bronx political circles that key borough politicians held large but carefully hidden interests in Third Avenue Transit. And it is also a fact that, in Bronx politics of the period, what Third Avenue Transit wanted, Third Avenue Transit got.

But the unfortunate element in searching for the explanation of Moses' refusal is that in the perspective of the history of New York City it is unimportant. Whether Moses refused to change the route for a personal or political reason, the point is that his reason was the only one that counted. Neighborhood feelings, urban planning considerations, cost, aesthetics, common humanity, common sense—none of these mattered in laying out the routes of New York's great roads. The only consideration that mattered was Robert Moses' will. He had the power to impose it on New York.

Five thousand people had been removed from East Tremont, but that was 5,000 out of 60,000. There were still 55,000 left. Chance, moreover, had spared East Tremont the fate of other communities disemboweled by a Moses highway operation—the heart of this community, bustling East Tremont Avenue, had escaped the Coordinator's scalpel.

But the thuds of the "skullcracker," the huge swinging wrecking ball, the crash of crumbling walls and the rumble of trucks carrying the walls away had been merely a prelude, the rattle of rifle fire from a skirmishers' picket line before the battle is fully joined and the big guns come into play. For Moses' Cross-Bronx Expressway had been designed by a single criterion: its efficiency as a traffic-moving device. This meant keeping the expressway as level as possible, and East Tremont was a neighborhood of hills. "To keep the grade down, we had to go down," Ernie Clark explains. Going down meant going under the surface of East Tremont. And under that surface was solid rock, and there is only one way to get rid of solid rock.

The blasting was only intermittent, and it went on no more than a year. But from the huge pit came also the harsh, staccato, machine-gun-like yammer of the jackhammers, the deep rat-tat-tat of the drills cutting holes for the dynamite, the clank and grind of the treads of the bulldozers, the hoarse bellow of the huge earth-moving equipment, and the heavy, jarring pound of the pile drivers driving down the shafts of steel called "long rock anchors" to strengthen unstable formations and, where the ground was soft, piles that would last for centuries—all combining in a roar that made the air shudder. The blasting was bad enough but the roar was unbearable. "It was the drilling, the constant drilling. You just heard it constantly through the day hours. You never got used to it."

Worst of all, to these people for whom cleanliness was so important, was not the noise or the danger but the dirt. One of the by-products of blasting or drilling in solid bedrock is rock dust, an extremely fine-grained, abrasive grit. The grit—East Tremonters called it "fallout"—arose from the excavation in a continual fine mist. "It just filled the air," [tenant Barney] Lambert recalls. "If you closed your windows and put towels in to seal them up, it was there anyway. I don't know how. You got up in the morning, and you felt like you had slept in dust. When you came home from work, you couldn't sit down without sweeping it out of the chair. It was impossible to live cleanly—you felt like you were covered with silt. All the time."

And, worst of all, there was the uncertainty about when the construction work would be over. "It went on year after year, you know," explains Lambert. "Sometimes it would stop for a month or two or three months without any explanation being given, and then it would start up again. After a while, it seemed to have been going on forever." There were perhaps 10,000 people living right next to the excavation. They began to move out.

Some of East Tremont's landlords, trapped for years in the squeeze between rising costs and rents that could be raised only when a tenant moved out, and cursed with tenants who seemed never to move out, welcomed the opportunity of replacing them with tenants whose poverty and lack of family stability insured a higher turnover and more 15 percent increases, and whose lack of big-city sophistication in dealing with landlords made it easier for landlords to skimp on services. The people moving into the vacant apartments were mostly Negroes—not the middle-class or lower-middle-class Negroes with whom East Tremont's middle-class and lower-middle-class Jews had found it easy to be compatible, but impoverished Negroes—many on welfare, many newly fled to New York from the rural slums of the Deep South—to whom the Jews found it impossible to relate, even had they wanted to. Frightened because the newcomers seemed the advance guard of the ravaging army that had previously been kept at bay on the far side of Crotona Park, they didn't want to.

"The vandalism started then all over the neighborhood," one housewife recalls. Furniture in apartment-house lobbies was slashed, urinated on and finally simply lugged boldly out, to be replaced perhaps once, perhaps twice, but finally not to be replaced, so that the lobbies stood empty and bare. The walls of the elevators were marked by things sharp, were painted, were marked again—and finally not painted any more. Break-ins began. New, stronger locks appeared in apartment doors, and then strips of steel to keep intruders from prying under the door jamb. The break-ins increased. Then there began to be the first, terrifying, reports of muggings.

Still, most of East Tremont's people stayed; their apartments were simply too precious to them for even fear to scare them away. In 1960, the year the expressway's East Tremont section opened, there were still—four years after demolition in the area had begun—an estimated 25,000 Jews in that neighborhood.

More people moved out of the buildings bordering the expressway. Some of the vacancies were filled by the type of family that would have filled them in the days before there was an expressway, for there were still tens of thousands of Jewish families in New York struggling to get out of the Lower East Side and other slums. But, with the noise, most moved out again—as fast as they could. And the families that replaced them were the families from the other side of the park. Muggings increased, and there began to be reports of robberies, thieves breaking right into your home. Before long, the old residents of the 3,000 apartments bordering the expressway were gone, moved away. Then the residents of the apartments next to those began to move, and then the residents of the apartments next to *those*.

The one mile of the Cross-Bronx Expressway through East Tremont was completed in 1960. By 1965, the community's "very good, solid housing stock," the apartment buildings that had been so precious to the people who had lived in them, were ravaged hulks. Windows, glassless except for the jagged edges around their frames, stared out on the street like sightless eyes. The entrances to those buildings were carpeted with shards of glass from what had been the doors to their lobbies. In those lobbies, what remained of the walls was covered with obscenities. And not much remained. Plaster from the walls lay in heaps in corners; the bare wood which had been exposed was shattered and broken. The pipes which had been behind the wood were gone, ripped out, melted down and sold for the few dollars that would buy the next fix. Elevators no longer worked. Staircases were broken and shattered. Banisters had been ripped from their sockets, for scrap and a fix if they were iron, for malice, an expression of hatred and revenge on an uncaring world, if they were wood. Raw garbage spilled out of broken bags across the floor. The stench of stale urine and vomit filled the nostrils. One tried to look down only enough to avoid stepping on the piles of feces, whether mercifully dried or reeking fresh—animal and human. There was no heat in those buildings; if they were homes, they were homes as the cave of the savage was a home. And yet they *were* homes—homes for tens of thousands of people. They were homes for welfare tenants and for the poorest of the working poor, for families that drift from one apartment to another without, seemingly, ever paying a month's rent in full—urban gypsies —for mothers who say desperately to the stranger, when they can be induced to talk to the stranger: "I got to get my kids out of here," and for children who come to the door long after the knock is heard and peer around and ask the stranger, with fear in eyes and voice: "Are you the man from the welfare?"

After seven o'clock, the residential streets of East Tremont are deserted, roamed by narcotics addicts in gangs like packs of wolves. Even on East Tremont Avenue, by nine o'clock most of the stores are closed, the lights out, huddled behind steel gates and iron bars.

The streets of East Tremont are carpeted so thickly with pieces of shattered glass that they shine in the sun. Garbage, soaked mattresses, bits of broken furniture and, everywhere, small pieces of jagged steel fill the gutters. The sidewalks are full of holes, the streets—particularly the streets overlooking the expressway, for the expressway has made them dead-end, reducing traffic on them to a minimum—with the hulks of stripped automobiles. Once East Tremont, while the expressway was being built, had had the look of blitzkrieged London; now it looked as London might have looked if, after the bombs, troops had fought their way through it from house to house. It had the look of a jungle.

Of the people who had lived in East Tremont, who had found in that neighborhood security, roots, friendship, a community that provided an anchor—friends and synagogue and Y—a place where you knew the people and they knew you, where you could make a stand against the swirling, fearsome tides of the sea of life, only the very old, too poor to move, still lived, almost barricaded in their freezing apartments. As for the rest of the people who had lived there, they were gone.

15

Crime and Traffic: A Parable and a Proposal

E. J. Mishan

I

The social significance of both the market and the engineering criteria
involved, as well as that of the alternative solution proposed here, may
be better understood if, for a while, we skirt direct controversy and approach these issues by a sort of parable. Thus, without straining his
credulity perhaps, the reader may be able to picture to himself a region
of some continent, say, on the other side of the Atlantic [*Editor's Note:*
Professor Mishan teaches in London.] in which the traditional right to carry
firearms is never questioned. Indeed, on the initiative of the manufacturers,
who spend colossal sums in advertising their new wares, more than one
pistol is to be seen in a man's belt. The young men in particular are anxious
to be seen with the latest de-luxe "extra hard-hitting" model. Obviously the
manufacture of holsters and other accessories flourishes as also does the
manufacture of bullet-proof vests, leggings and helmets. There are not the
only growth industries, however, for notwithstanding the purchase of bullet-
proof items, the members of the undertakers association do a flourishing
trade. The windows of all but the poorer houses are fitted with shatter-proof
glass, while the bullet-proofing of rooms and offices in the more dangerous
districts is a matter of ordinary precaution. No family is foolish enough
to neglect the training of their sons, and even their daughters, in the art
of the quick draw. In any case, a number of hours each week is devoted
to target practice and dodgery in all the best schools. Life insurance is,
of course, big business despite the exorbitant premia, and expenditure
on medical attention continues to soar. For in addition to such normal
ailments, as bullets embedded in various parts of the anatomy, there is
widespread suffering from a variety of chafed skin diseases, the result of
wearing the unavoidably heavy bullet-proof apparel. Moreover, owing
to nervous diseases and anxiety, about every other adult is addicted
either to strong liquor or to tranquillizing drugs. Taxes are burdensome
for obvious reasons: a swollen police force employed mainly in trying
to keep down the number of victims of the perennial feuds, extensive
prisons and prison hospitals, to say nothing of the public funds devoted
to guarding offices, banks, schools, and to the construction of special
vans for transporting the children to and from schools.

In such an environment the most peace-loving man would be foolish
to venture abroad unarmed. And since it is observed by the *laisser-faire*
economist that men freely choose to buy guns, it would be regarded as
an infringement of liberty to attempt to curb their manufacture. Moreover, since the market is working smoothly, the supply of firearms being

such that no one need wait if he is able to pay the market price, no government intervention to match industrial supplies to rising demand is called for. Provided there is enough competition in the production of firearms so that over the long period prices just cover costs (and tend also to equal marginal costs of production) the allocation economist is well satisfied. Looking at the promising signs of growth in the chief industries, firearms and accessories, the business economist pronounces the economy "sound." If, however, for any reason the Government begins to have misgivings about some of the more blatant social repercussions, it consults with the pistol economist, a highly paid and highly regarded expert. The pistol economist constructs models and, with the help of high-powered statisticians, amasses pistological data of all kinds, from which he calculates the optimal set of taxes on the sale of pistols and ammunition in recognition of those external diseconomies, such as occasional corpse-congestion on the better streets whose monetary costs can, he believes, be estimated.

Notwithstanding all his scientific advice, matters eventually come to a head, and amid much government fanfare a committee of inquiry is set up under the chairmanship of a highly competent engineer, Mr B. If there ever was a realist, Mr B. is one, and he soon satisfies himself that the economy is heavily dependent upon pistol production and all the auxiliary industries and services connected therewith. Besides, the evidence is incontrovertible: the demand for guns continues to grow year by year. It must, therefore, be accepted as a datum. Undaunted, Mr B. faces "the challenge" by proposing a radical remodelling of the chief towns and cities, at an unmentionable cost, in the endeavour to create an environment in which people can have both their guns and a peaceful life as well. The chief features of his plan are based on what he aptly calls "pistol architecture," and includes provision for no-shooting precincts fenced high with steel, the construction of circular and wavy road design to increase the difficulties of gun-duelling, the erection of high shatter-proof glass screens running down the centres of roads to prevent effective cross-firing, and the setting up of heavily protected television cameras at all strategic positions in the towns in order to relay information twenty-four hours a day to a vast new centralized police force equipped with fleets of helicopters. Every progressive journalist pays tribute to the foresight and realism of the B-plan and makes much of the virtues of "pistol architecture," the architecture of the future. Alas, the Government begins to realize that any attempt to raise the taxes necessary to implement the B-plan would start a revolution. So the plan is quietly shelved, new committees of inquiry are formed, masses of agenda are produced, and things continue much as before.

II

We need not continue save to press home a few parallels. Over the last fifty years we have witnessed a transposition of ends and means. Originally the motor vehicle was designed for the roads. Today roads are designed for vehicles. Originally the motor vehicle was to be fitted into the pace of life.

Today the pace of life is adapted to the speed of the vehicle, the saddest casualty of all being an irretrievable loss of the sense of ease, space and leisure.

The dominance exerted over our lives by this one invention is without precedent in history. So pervasive is its influence and so inextricably is it bound up with our way of life and habits of thought that the extent of its intrusion in our civilization is barely noticed. To insist on seeing it as no more than one of several alternative schemes of travel, and to propose a careful assessment of its benefits and costs smacks almost of the quixotic. Imagine a modern sceptic returning on a Wellsian time-machine to the second half of the eighteenth century and presenting the following conundrum to Dr Johnson: What gift to mankind is of such worth as to warrant an annual sacrifice of two hundred thousand lives, an annual list of five million people crippled, the transformation of the world's towns and cities into a concrete wasteland made hideous with noise, filth and danger, the dissipation of the countryside, the slow poisoning of the air in town and suburb, the enfeeblement of the health and the corruption of the character of peoples, and the creation of conditions favourable to the generation and execution of crimes of robbery and violence? What reply could the sage give, but that it must be of a nature, sir, that is beyond the bounds of man's imagination.

And what, in fact, may we count as benefits? They are certainly not to be linked with the more salient features that have developed in response to the private automobile:

(1) The creation of a *physical* environment in which, while time spent commuting has grown, the motor-car appears increasingly indispensable. For the very existence of a universal private means of transport encourages the geographical dispersion of housing, shopping, entertainment, and consumer services generally. The distinction between suburb and countryside is blurred. Population begins to spread everywhere in a vain bid to "get away from it all," which further increases the need for the private motor-car.

(2) The growth of an *economic* environment that has become closely dependent on the continued popularity of the private motor-car. So large a part of the modern economy is geared to automobile production that it is officially recognized as a barometer for industry as a whole and, indeed, as a fiscal lever in regulating aggregate demand. Worse, the size of the complex of industries involved in producing and maintaining automobiles, to say nothing of the army of car-owners, have given rise to entrenched interests that bar the road to consideration of all radical proposals that appear to threaten their immediate gains.

(3) The growth, finally, of a *psychological* environment, one of almost abject dependence on the automobile; one that has indeed transformed it into a fetish, a sex symbol, a status symbol, and a power symbol.

There is left, then, only the most illusory of all claims, the alleged "freedom to go where one likes, at any time one likes, and in privacy and comfort." As though the highways are uncongested! As though driving is a known specific for sweetening the temper and improving the digestion! As though the locust horde of private cars does not destroy, surely and rapidly, the very pleasure, variety and amenity that each is seeking! And when men, knowing all this, can do no more than shrug in resignation one must seriously wonder whether free-will is not, after all, also illusory.

III

Be that as it may, the clear alternative to the Buchanan Plan emerging from the parable is inescapable. We must begin to think in terms of abandoning all engineering schemes for *accommodating* the mounting road traffic. Instead, we must start evolving schemes for *containing* it. Indeed, the one radical alternative we should take a long look at before contemplating the range of compromise solutions that are feasible is that of a plan for the gradual abolition of all privately owned automobiles.

For a fraction of the money the nation is currently spending on the maintenance of private cars and on the Government services necessary to keep the traffic moving—to say nothing of the cost of all the spillover effects already described—we could simultaneously achieve three desirable objectives:

(1) provide a comfortable, frequent and highly efficient public transport service, bus, train, or tube, in all the major population areas (and, in the interest of quiet and clean air, preferably electrically-powered transport),

(2) through government control of public transport, to restrain and gradually reverse the spread of population that has followed in the wake of post-war speculative building and is in the process of transforming the south-east into an uninterrupted suburban region, and

(3) to restore quiet and dignity to our cities, and to enable people to wander unobstructed by traffic and enjoy once more the charm of historic towns and villages.

Further radical changes would, of course, have to be made in the organization of freight delivery if we are successfully to avoid massive investment in refashioning our cities to cater for the growing commercial traffic. The movement of such freight should be minimized: (*a*) by substituting as far as possible existing railways in the built-up areas during off-peak hours; (*b*) similarly, by adapting and extending London's Underground to carry freight, initially during the night; and (*c*) removing freight deliveries from a multitude of small and large firms and placing them instead under a single authority in order, like the post office, to avail ourselves of the economies of co-ordination. Finally, in order to maintain the environment of the city, the possibilities of organizing shop deliveries at times when people are off the streets, say between three and seven in the mornings, deserves careful study.

At any rate—if we are to have a single solution for the country at large —here is one alternative solution towards which we might advance, a radical one to be sure, but technically practicable, and one providing a relatively inexpensive way, in terms of money and lives, of establishing a more civilized pattern of living.

It is not a solution that will be presented to us by the market, however, and understandably, not one that will be proposed to us by the technocrats, yet it is one that is worthy of consideration by a nation that prides itself on its social awareness and political maturity. In the meantime, local plans to prohibit motor-cars, during certain hours at least, from designated special areas in resorts, historic towns, and city centres— in London, certainly the area about Soho, including Piccadilly Circus and Leicester Square, so that, as in times gone by, people may stroll freely through the city streets enjoying once more the hubbub and gaiety of human voices, and recapturing perhaps a lost sense of community and citizenship—will make some modest contribution towards making the physical environment more enjoyable.

The only alternatives to this radical solution, that are both feasible and inexpensive, are those based on the principle of "separate facilities," already discussed; in other words the provision of large viable areas for those citizens who want, with varying degrees of intensity, to opt out of the environment of mounting disamenity and disaster created by the private automobile and air travel.

But within the city, at least, there can be no socially acceptable solution to the traffic problem that aims to accommodate the private automobile. Continuation of the present policy of attempting to do so by piecemeal alterations leads ultimately to the crucifixion of the city by its traffic—an epithet that just about describes what has happened in Los Angeles.

16

Suburban Exploitation of the City

James O'Connor

Social consumption outlays can be classified into two subgroups: goods and services consumed collectively by the working class and social insurance against economic insecurity. The first group includes (1) suburban development projects (e.g., roads, elementary and secondary schools, and recreation facilities, together with home mortgage subsidies and guarantees); (2) urban renewal projects (e.g., high rises for white-collar, technical, and professional workers, mass transit, parking garage, and other commuter facilities); and (3) related projects such as some child care and hospital and medical facilities. The second group includes workmen's compensation, old age and survivors insurance, unemployment insurance, and (in the near future) medical and health insurance. In general the greater the socialization of the costs of variable capital [i.e., the public bearing the costs of labor], the lower will be the level of money wages, and (*ceteris paribus*), the higher the rate of profit in the monopoly sector. For this reason, monopoly capital often actively supports the expansion of social consumption expenditures.

Modern capitalist societies are compelled to allocate an increasing share of the social product to social consumption spending, particularly for workers in the monopoly sector. The general reason is that nineteenth-century rural and farm families typically provided their own water supply, waste disposal systems, transportation and communications, housing, and recreational and cultural facilities. And the cities extended family systems, ethnic organizations and groupings, and private philanthropy constituted a kind of social insurance against sickness and old age, unemployment, and other catastrophic events. By contrast, modern capitalism requires mounting social consumption outlays because of growing interdependencies in industrial, commercial, transportation, housing, and recreational patterns. With the increased proletarianization of the general population, intensified specialization of functions and division of labor, and rampant suburbanization, it has become more and more difficult for the typical working-class family to supply its own amenities. And because of private ownership of the means of production and the absence of overall social planning there is considerable duplication and overlapping of facilities and economic waste; hence social consumption outlays are especially burdensome.

Two related questions are at issue in an analysis of social consumption: first, the determinants of the total volume of social consumption, and second, the distribution of outlays on social consumption within the working class. In this and the following sections we will discuss the growth of social consumption in the cities and suburbs, which requires analysis of the political-economic relations within the modern metropolitan area. As will be seen, the political relations between city and suburb reflect the social relations between working class and capitalist class, as well as social relations between monopoly sector and competitive sector workers.

Until the late nineteenth century "native" Protestant industrialists and businessmen ran most American cities, which ensured that the forces of capitalist production would develop relatively unchecked and unhampered. Land itself began to be seen mainly as a marketable asset, and not (as in Europe) as a place or home. Indeed, the rectangular gridiron characteristic of nearly all North American cities was established to widen the market and facilitate speculation in urban land.

By the last half of the century immigration and industrialization had decreed the central political fact in the growing urban centers: the elementary division of classes under capitalism—capitalists and workers. But men of property were relatively few in number and divided among themselves. Scandalized by rampant corruption and unable to control their environment, the upper classes sought refuge in the villages on the periphery of the city, where market forces were pushing out the farmers. Public transportation systems and the automobile, which vastly increased the accessibility of the peripheral area, were drafted into the service of the fleeing upper and middle classes. Class relations soon manifested themselves in a new form: city-suburb relationships. At the same time businessmen shifted the focus of their political activities and attempted to run the city from the State House.

For the great majority in the middle classes—commercial property owners and businessmen, independent professionals, and the new corporate retinue—the city became a wasteland which they could not control and therefore could not enjoy. Hence they became suburbanites—to control their environment (in particular to get more space), acquire political autonomy, and escape from big-city politics. Only the near-rich and very rich could afford nonresidential land-use and thus create livable enclaves within the core city. Some remained.

Class conflict, which in an earlier period sharply divided the city, finally was placed on a metropolitan basis. The result was the 1400 governments of the New York metropolitan area, the 457 tax-levying bodies in Illinois' Cooks County, and the proliferation elsewhere of state organs—municipalities, trusteeships, school, sewer, and other special districts. The fundamental class issues of state finance—the relative burden of taxes and the division of state expenditures between the different social classes—reemerged, but in a new form. The new suburban political units were compelled to defend themselves against city programs—tax redistribution, central-city income taxes, consolidation or merger of the entire metropolitan area.

These struggles have become more complicated and diffuse with the exodus of the more prosperous sections of the working class, particularly monopoly sector workers. The automobile and freeway and federal mortgage insurance programs opened up hundreds of thousands of subdivisions in the new suburbs. Federally subsidized suburban development began in earnest in 1932, when the Federal Home Loan Bank Act put the credit of the state behind financial institutions chartered by state and federal governments. And the creation of the Federal Savings and Loan Insurance Corporation in the same year protected small savers and thus helped savings and loan associations mobilize capital for suburban housing mortgages and development. Partly as a result, savings and loan capital rose twentyfold (to $120 billion) between 1945 and 1967. Mortgage debt on nonfarm residential properties increased from about $25 billion during World War II to roughly $250 billion in 1968, when there was an outstanding $50 billion in FHA-insured mortgages and another $34 billion in VA-guaranteed mortgages. In recent years 80 percent of all new private homes have been built in the suburbs. *Business Week* has written,

on the record the government's program to promote the construction of middle-class housing has been enormously successful. Mortgage insurance . . . has made it possible for middle-income earners [i.e., monopoly and state sector workers] to become home owners, and in doing so it has created and maintained a huge market for modern, well-equipped, medium-priced houses, especially in the suburbs.

While the proportion of the suburban work force employed in business and professional occupations continues to increase, the number of semiskilled and skilled workers living in the suburbs also rises. Traditional class divisions are being reproduced outside the city limits, generating political struggles between, and within the suburbs as well as between suburb and city.

The suburb and the city have evolved a relationship very similar to the one that developed between the imperial powers and their colonies which produced and exported primary commodities. Just as the export economy offers a natural resource, the city provides at no cost its central location and hence enormous advantages to economic activities in communications, trade, and exchange. (If communications, trade, and exchange are the city's raison d'être, centrality is its most valuable resource.) Central-city services (banks and other financial houses, law offices, research, advertising and public relations services, and central office administration for the giant corporations), which are essential to monopoly capital, expand rapidly. Meanwhile, with the development of modern one-story plants (which cannot be located in the city because land values are too high) and the rise of trucking and air freight (which have made locations along the freeways and near airports more desirable), manufacturing and warehouse and other facilities—and the better-paid monopoly sector working-class jobs —move to the periphery. What is left is small-scale manufacturing, retail trade, and food and other competitive sector services where productivity and wages are relatively low. In effect, except for downtown bank and corporate activity, the city becomes the competitive sector—a reservoir of cheap labor.

One difference between the export economy and the city is that a natural resource sooner or later is exhausted, whereas a central location increases in value with more intensive use. This simple fact accounts in large part for the simultaneous dynamism and decay of the central city. The export sector in the colonies was partly or wholly owned by foreign capital, and sometimes even the working force was of foreign extraction. Key downtown economic activities are owned mainly by suburbanites. The wage share generated by these sectors is small and the share going to salaries (and therefore suburbanites) is correspondingly large. "The central cities [i.e., downtown areas] are becoming more and more specialized in functions which require chiefly professional, technical and clerical workers," one economist has written, "but the skilled and literate groups are precisely those segments of the population which are increasingly choosing to live outside the urban center." When the export economy expanded the largest part of the rise in income was channeled abroad as repatriated profits. When the city's economy expands, profits and salaries are "repatriated" to the suburbs. To be sure, suburbanites patronize central-city stores, thus contributing to sales-tax revenues, and bear some of the burden of property taxes on suburbanite-owned real assets. Moreover, income taxes siphon off some of the flow, and grants-in-aid from state and federal governments return it to the city. Nevertheless, the only study available indicates that the income-employment multiplier is lower in the central city than in outlying districts. Incomes earned in the central city thus tend to be "exported" to the suburbs. From the standpoint of both the imperial power and the suburb, the system is partly self-financing: Resources are transferred from the colony and the city and paid for with the increased income (repatriated earnings and profits) generated by the expansion of demand for central-city services. This one-way transfer of resources tends to pauperize colony and city alike.

Extending the analogy further, commodities and services not available locally to the colonists were imported. For the "new colonists" suburban living itself takes the place of luxury and other goods not available locally. Foreigners utilized the colonial social and community services at little or no cost. Suburbanites similarly exploit transport, hospital, police, fire, and other services. Thus the suburbanite appropriates two sets of social consumption facilities and services. Meanwhile, the central city must widen its highways to accommodate peak rush-hour traffic, invest in more parking and police services and traffic control systems, and bear the burden of generally increased costs of congestion, including air pollution. The flight of industry erodes the value of the existing tax base, and, at the same time, the removal of land from the tax base reduces the tax base itself. In Roy Bahl's words,

The flight of higher income families and some industries to the suburbs has eroded the fiscal capacity of the central city. At the same time, the suburban residents, through an interaction with the core city, draw heavily on public services and multiply such city problems as traffic congestion and air pollution. This charge of fiscal mercantilism—the exporting of the tax base from the central city and the importing of service costs—finds much support in empirical research.

The argument that central-city voters will rebel against meeting the needs of the suburbanites (and thus that city expenditures may be less than "optimum") ignores the fact that the city bureaucracy has little choice in the matter, and that the voters have little or nothing to say about either the volume or composition of the city budget. A study of fifty-five city governments in the San Francisco–Oakland area revealed that the property tax rate and level of per capita expenditures were higher in the central city than in the dormitory, industrial, or balanced suburbs. The dormitory suburb enjoyed the lowest tax rate and its per capita expenditures were only 58 percent of those in the central city. Suburban parasitism is suggested by another analysis which showed that the expanding suburban population was correlated with all categories of city expenditure except outlays for recreation facilities, whereas the central-city population did not appear to influence the level of per capita expenditures. And a third study demonstrated that the ratio of central-city public payrolls to payrolls in the entire metropolitan area increases with the proportion of the population living in the suburbs.

The exploitation of the predominantly working-class city by monopoly sector workers and middle-class and capitalist-class suburbanites probably has intensified since World War II. There has been a historic shift in the terms of trade between suburb and city—to the advantage of the former. Salaries tend to advance more rapidly than wage payments and wages tend to expand more rapidly in the monopoly sector than in the competitive sector. The shift is reflected also in the increasing number of residential and mixed suburbs (compared with industrial suburbs). And although the typical metropolitan area has become more economically self-sufficient, or autarkic, the central city increasingly specializes in "export" services. Thus the city experiences a certain amount of economic growth but little economic development. Finally, it should be stressed that to the degree that the evolution of city-suburb relationships is attributable to the ability of monopoly sector workers and capital to escape the city, suburban exploitation of the city is rooted in the nature of monopoly sector production relations. In other words, the city-suburb relation is one (of many) specific mechanisms that have created the impoverishment of one-third of the working class—the competitive sector work force.

17

The Urban Crisis: Who Got What, and Why

Frances Fox Piven

For quite a while, complaints about the urban fiscal crisis have been droning on, becoming as familiar as complaints about big government, or big bureaucracy, or high taxes—and almost as boring as well. Now suddenly the crisis seems indeed to be upon us: school closings are threatened, library services are curtailed, subway trains go unrepaired, welfare grants are cut, all because big city costs have escalated to the point where local governments can no longer foot the bill. Yet for all the talk, and all the complaints, there has been no convincing explanation of just how it happened that, quite suddenly in the 1960s, the whole municipal housekeeping system seemed to become virtually unmanageable. This is especially odd because, not long ago, the study of city politics and city services was a favorite among American political scientists, and one subject they had gone far to illuminate. Now, with everything knocked askew, they seem to have very little to say that could stand as political analysis.

To be sure, there is a widely accepted explanation. The big cities are said to be in trouble because of the "needs" of blacks for services—a view given authority by the professionals who man the service agencies and echoed by the politicians who depend upon these agencies. Service "needs," the argument goes, have been increasing at a much faster rate than local revenues. The alleged reason is demographic: The large number of impoverished black Southern migrants to the cities presumably requires far greater investments in services, including more elaborate educational programs, more frequent garbage collection, more intensive policing, if the city is to be maintained at accustomed levels of civil decency and order. Thus, city agencies have been forced to expand and elaborate their activities. However, the necessary expansion is presumably constricted for lack of local revenues, particularly since the better off taxpaying residents and businesses have been leaving the city (hastened on their way by the black migration).[1] To this standard explanation of the crisis, there is also a standard remedy: namely, to increase municipal revenues, whether by enlarging federal and state aid to the cities or by redrawing jurisdictional boundaries to recapture suburban taxpayers.[2]

It is true, of course, that black children who receive little in the way of skills or motivation at home may require more effort from the schools; that densely packed slums require more garbage collection; that disorganized neighborhoods require more policing. For instance, the New York City Fire Department reports a 300 percent increase in fires the last twenty years. But fires and similar calamities that threaten a wide public are one thing; welfare, education, and health services, which account for by far the largest portion of big city budgets, quite another. And while by any objective measure the new residents of the city have greater needs for such services, there are several reasons to doubt that the urban crisis is the simple result of rising needs and declining revenues.

For one thing, the trend in service budgets suggests otherwise. Blacks began to pour into the cities in very large numbers after World War II,

---

[1] This view of the urban problem was given official status by the "Riot Commission." According to the commission:

> [The] fourfold dilemma of the American city [is:] Fewer tax dollars come in, as large numbers of middle-income tax payers move out of central cities and property values and business decline; More tax dollars are required, to provide essential public services and facilities, and to meet the needs of expanding lower-income groups; Each tax dollar buys less, because of increasing costs. Citizen dissatisfaction with municipal services grows as needs, expectations and standards of living increase throughout the community [*Report of the National Advisory Commission on Civil Disorders* (New York: Bantam, 1968), p. 389].

Similarly, Alan K. Campbell and Donna E. Shalala write: "Most of the substantive problems flow, at least in part, from . . . the fact that the central cities have been left with segments of the population most in need of expensive services, and the redistribution of economic activities has reduced the relative ability of these areas to support such services" ["Problems Unsolved, Solutions Untried: The Urban Crisis," in *The States and the Urban Crisis* (Englewood Cliffs, N.J.: Prentice-Hall, 1970, p. 7]. The conventional wisdom is again echoed by the U.S. Advisory Commission on Intergovernmental Relations:

> The large central cities are in the throes of a deepening fiscal crisis. On the one hand, they are confronted with the need to satisfy rapidly growing expenditure requirements triggered by the rising number of "high cost" citizens. On the other hand, their tax resources are growing at a decreasing rate (and in some cases actually declining), a reflection of the *exodus of middle and high income families and business firms from the central city to suburbia* [italics in original] [*Fiscal Balance in the American Federal System: Metropolitan Fiscal Disparities* (Washington, D.C.: Government Printing Office, 1967). Vol. II, p. 5].

Politicians share this view. "In the last 10 years, 200,000 middle-class whites have moved out of St. Louis," said Mayor A. J. Cervantes, "and 100,000 blacks, many of them poor, have moved in. It costs us *eight times as much* to provide city services to the poor as to the middle-class" [italics in original] [*The New York Times*, May 22, 1970].

[2] As a matter of fact, city revenues have not declined at all, but have risen astronomically, although not as astronomically as costs. Presumably if the city had been able to hold or attract better off residents and businesses, revenues would have risen even faster, and the fiscal aspect of the urban crisis would not have developed.

but costs did not rise precipitously until the mid-1960s.[3] *In other words, the needs of the black poor were not recognized for two decades.* For another, any scrutiny of agency budgets shows that, except for public welfare, *the expansion of services to the poor, as such, does not account for a very large proportion of increased expenditures.* It was other groups, *mainly organized provider groups,* who reaped the lion's share of the swollen budgets. The notion that services are being strained to respond to the needs of the new urban poor, in short, takes little account either of when the strains occurred or of the groups who actually benefited from increased expenditures.

These two facts should lead us to look beyond the "rising needs–declining revenues" theory for an explanation of urban troubles. And once we do, perhaps some political common sense can emerge. School administrators and sanitation commissioners may describe their agencies as ruled by professional standards and as shaped by disinterested commitments to the public good, and thus define rising costs as a direct and proper response to the needs of people. But schools and sanitation departments are, after all, agencies of local government, substructures of the local political apparatus, and are managed in response to local political forces. The mere fact that people are poor or that the poor need special services has never led government to respond. Service agencies are political agencies, administered to deal with political problems, not service problems.

Now this view is not especially novel. Indeed, if there is any aspect of the American political system that was persuasively analyzed in the past, it was the political uses of municipal services in promoting allegiance and muting conflict. Public jobs, contracts, and services were dispensed by city bosses to maintain loyal cadres and loyal followers among the heterogeneous groups of the city. Somehow political analysts have forgotten this in their accounts of the contemporary urban crisis, testimony perhaps to the extent to which the doublethink of professional bureaucrats has befogged the common sense of us all. That is, we are confused by changes in the style of urban service politics, failing to see that although the style has changed, the function has not. In the era of the big city machine, municipal authorities managed to maintain a degree of consensus and allegiance among diverse groups by distributing public goods in the form of private favors. Today public goods are distributed through the service bureaucracies. With that change, the process of dispensing public goods has become more formalized, the struggles between groups more public, and the language of city politics more professional. As I will try to explain a little later, these changes were in some ways crucial in the development of what we call the urban crisis. My main point for now, however, is that while we may refer to the schools

---

[3] It should be made clear at the outset that the costs of government generally rose steadily in the years after World War II. This is the subject of James O'Connor's analysis in "The Fiscal Crisis of the State," *Socialist Revolution,* 1, 1 (January/February 1970), 12–54; 1, 2 (March/April 1970), 34–94. But while all government budgets expanded, state and local costs rose much faster, and costs in the central cities rose the most rapidly of all, especially after 1965. Thus, according to the Citizen's Budget Commission, New York City's budget increased almost eight times as fast in the five fiscal years between 1964 and 1969 as during the postwar years 1949 to 1954. From an average annual increase of 5.5 percent in 1954, budget costs jumped to 9.1 percent in 1964 and to 14.2 percent in 1969 (*The New York Times,* January 11, 1960). It is with this exceptional rise that this article is concerned.

or the sanitation department as if they are politically neutral, these agencies yield up a whole variety of benefits, and it is by distributing, redistributing, and adapting these payoffs of the city agencies that urban political leaders manage to keep peace and build allegiances among the diverse groups in the city. In other words, the jobs, contracts, perquisites, as well as the actual services of the municipal housekeeping agencies, are just as much the grist of urban politics as they ever were.

All of which is to say that when there is a severe disturbance in the administration and financing of municipal services, the underlying cause is likely to be a fundamental disturbance in political relations. To account for the service "crisis," we should look at the changing relationship between political forces—at rising group conflict and weakening allegiances—and the way in which these disturbances set off an avalanche of new demands. To cope with these strains, political leaders expanded and proliferated the benefits of the city agencies. What I shall argue, in sum, is that the urban crisis is not a crisis of rising needs, but a crisis of rising demands.

THE POLITICAL DISTURBANCES THAT LED TO RISING DEMANDS

If the service needs of the black poor do not account for the troubles in the cities, the political impact of the black migration probably does. Massive shifts of population are almost always disturbing to a political system, for new relations have to be formed between a political leadership and constituent groups. The migration of large numbers of blacks from the rural South to a few core cities during and after World War II, leading many middle-class white constituents to leave for the suburbs, posed just this challenge to the existing political organization of the cities. But for a long time, local governments resisted responding to the newcomers with the services, symbols, and benefits that might have won the allegiance of these newcomers, just as the allegiance of other groups had previously been won.

The task of political integration was made difficult by at least four circumstances. One was the very magnitude of the influx. Between 1940 and 1960, nearly 4 million blacks left the land and, for the most part, settled in big Northern cities. Consequently, by 1960, at least one in five residents of our fifty largest cities was a black, and in the biggest cities the proportions were much greater. It is no exaggeration to say that the cities were innundated by sheer numbers.

Second, these large numbers were mainly lower-class blacks, whose presence aroused ferocious race and class hatreds, especially among the white ethnics who lived in neighborhoods bordering the ghettos and who felt their homes and schools endangered. As ghetto numbers enlarged, race and class polarities worsened, and political leaders, still firmly tied to the traditional inhabitants of the cities, were in no position to give concessions to the black poor.

Not only was race pitted against race, class against class, but the changing style of urban politics made concessions to conflicting groups a very treacherous matter. Just because the jobs, services, and contracts that fueled the urban political organization were no longer dispensed covertly, in the form of private favors, but rather as matters of public policy, each concession was destined to become a subject of open political conflict. As a result, mayors found it very difficult to finesse their traditional constituents: New public housing for blacks, for example, could not be concealed, and every project threatened to arouse a storm of controversy. Despite their growing numbers and their obvious needs, therefore, blacks got very little in the way of municipal benefits throughout the 1940s and 1950s. Chicago, where the machine style was still entrenched, gave a little more; the Cook County AFDC rolls, for example, rose by 80 percent in the 1950s, and blacks were given some political jobs. But in most cities, the local service agencies resisted the newcomers. In New York City and Los Angeles, for example, the AFDC rolls remained virtually unchanged in the 1950s. In many places public housing was brought to a halt; urban renewal generally became the instrument of black removal; and half the major Southern cities (which also received large numbers of black migrants from rural areas) actually managed to reduce their welfare rolls, often by as much as half.[4]

Finally, when blacks entered the cities, they were confronted by a relatively new development in city politics: namely, the existence of large associations of public employees, whether teachers, policemen, sanitation men, or the like. The provider groups not only had a very large stake in the design and operation of public programs—for there is hardly any aspect of public policy that does not impinge on matters of working conditions, job security, or fringe benefits—but they had become numerous enough, organized enough, and independent enough to wield substantial influence in matters affecting their interests.

The result was that, over time, many groups of public employees managed to win substantial control over numerous matters affecting their jobs and their agencies: entrance requirements, tenure guarantees, working conditions, job prerogatives, promotion criteria, retirement benefits. Except where wages were concerned, other groups in the cities rarely became sufficiently aroused to block efforts by public employees to advance their interests. But all of this also meant that when blacks arrived in the cities, local political leaders did not control the jobs—and in cases where job prerogatives had been precisely specified by regulation, did not even control the services—that might have been given as concessions to the black newcomers.

Under the best of circumstances, of course, the task of integrating a new and uprooted rural population into local political structures would have taken time and would have been difficult. But for all of the reasons given, local government was showing little taste for the task. As a result, a large population that had been set loose from Southern feudal institutions was not absorbed into the regulating political institutions (or economic institutions, for they were also resisted there) of the city. Eventually that dislocated population became volatile, both in the streets and at the polls. And by 1960, that volatility was beginning to disrupt national political alignments, forcing the federal government to take an unprecedented role in urban politics.

---

[4] For a discussion of the uses of welfare in resisting black migrants, see Frances Fox Piven and Richard A. Cloward, *Regulating the Poor: The Functions of Public Welfare* (New York: Pantheon, 1971), Chapters 7 and 8.

Accordingly, [Kennedy] administration analysts began to explore strategies to cement the allegiance of the urban black vote to the national party. What emerged, not all at once, but gropingly, was a series of federal service programs directed to the ghetto. The first appropriations were small, as with the Juvenile Delinquency and Youth Offenses Control Act of 1961, but each program enlarged upon the other, up until the Model Cities legislation of 1966. Some of the new programs—in manpower development, in education, in health—were relatively straightforward. All they did was give new funds to local agencies to be used to provide jobs or services for the poor. Thus, funds appropriated under Title I of the Elementary and Secondary Education Act of 1965 were earmarked for educational facilities for poor children; the medicaid program enacted in 1965 reimbursed health agencies and physicians for treating the poor; and manpower agencies were funded specifically to provide jobs or job training for the poor.

Other of the new federal programs were neither so simple nor so straightforward, and these were the ones that became the hallmark of the Great Society. The federal memoranda describing them were studded with terms like "inner city," "institutional change," and "maximum feasible participation." But if this language was often confusing, the programs themselves ought not to have been. The "inner city," after all, was a euphemism for the ghetto, and activities funded under such titles as delinquency prevention, mental health, antipoverty, or model cities turned out, in the streets of the cities, to look very much alike. What they looked like was nothing less than the old political machine.

Federal funds were used to create new storefront-style agencies in the ghettos, staffed with professionals who helped local people find jobs, obtain welfare, or deal with school officials. Neighborhood leaders were also hired, named community workers, neighborhood aides, or whatever, but in fact close kin to the old ward heelers, for they drew larger numbers of people into the new programs, spreading the federal spoils.

But federal spoils were not enough, for there were not many of them. What the new ghetto agencies had to offer was small and impermanent compared to ongoing municipal programs in education, housing, or health. If blacks were to be wrapped into the political organization of the cities, the traditional agencies of local government, which controlled the bulk of federal, state, and local appropriations, had to be reoriented. Municipal agencies had to be made to respond to blacks.

Various tactics to produce such reform were tried, at first under the guise of experiments in "institutional change." This meant that the Washington officials who administered the juvenile delinquency program (under Robert Kennedy's direction) required as a condition of granting funds that local governments submit "comprehensive plans" for their own reform (that is, for giving blacks something). But the mere existence of such paper plans did not turn out to be very compelling to the local bureaucrats who implemented programs. Therefore, as turbulence spread in the Northern ghettos, the federal officials began to try another way to promote institutional change—"maximum feasible participation of residents of the areas and members of the groups served." Under that slogan, the Great Society programs gave money to ghetto organizations, which then used the money to harass city agencies. Community workers were hired to badger housing inspectors and to pry loose welfare payments. Lawyers on the federal pay-roll took municipal agencies to court on behalf of ghetto clients. Later the new programs helped organize the ghetto poor to picket the welfare depart-ment or to boycott the school system.

In these various ways, then, the federal government intervened in local politics, and forced local government to do what it had earlier failed to do. Federal dollars and federal authority were used to resuscitate the functions of the political machine, on the one hand *by spurring local service agencies to respond to the black newcomers,* and on the other *by spurring blacks to make demands upon city services.*

As it turned out, blacks made their largest tangible gains from this process through the public welfare system. Total national welfare costs rose from about $4 billion in 1960 to nearly $15 billion in 1970. Big cities that received the largest numbers of black and Spanish-speaking migrants and that were most shaken by the political reverberations of that migration also experienced the largest welfare budget rises. In New York, Los Angeles, and Baltimore, for example, the AFDC rolls quadrupled, and costs rose even faster. In some cities, moreover, welfare costs were absorbing an ever-larger share of the local budget, a bigger piece of the public pie. In New York City, for example, welfare costs absorbed about 12 percent of the city's budget in the 1950s; but by 1970 the share going to welfare had grown to about 25 percent (of a much larger budget), mainly because the proportion of the city's population on Aid to Families of Dependent Children increased from 2.6 percent in 1960 to 11.0 percent in 1970.[5] In other words, the blacks who triggered the disturbances received their biggest payoffs from welfare,[6] mainly because other groups were not competing within the wel-fare system for a share of relief benefits.[7]

But if blacks got welfare, that was just about all they got. Less obvious than the emergence of black demands—but much more important in ac-counting for increasing service costs—was the reaction of organized whites to these political developments, particularly the groups who had direct material stakes in the running of the local services. If the new upthrust of black claims threatened and jostled many groups in the city, none were so alert or so shrill as those who had traditionally gotten the main benefits of the municipal services. These were the people who depended, directly or indirectly, on the city treasury for their livelihood: They worked in the municipal agencies, in agencies that were publicly funded (e.g., voluntary

---

[5] *Changing Patterns of Prices, Pay, Workers, and Work on the New York Scene,* U.S. Department of Labor, Bureau of Labor Statistics (New York: Middle Atlan-tic Regional Office, May 1971), Regional Reports No. 20, p. 36.

[6] The dole, needless to say, is a very different sort of concession from the higher salaries, pensions, and on-the-job prerogatives won by other groups. For one thing, the dole means continued poverty and low status. For another, it is easier to take away, for recipients remain relatively weak and unorganized.

[7] That poor minorities made large gains through the welfare "crisis" and other groups did not is important to understanding the furious opposition that soaring welfare budgets arouse. Organized welfare-agency workers were competing for the welfare dollar, of course, but were not nearly so successful as the workers in other services, for they were not in a position to take much advantage of polit-ical turmoil. They were not nearly so numerous or well organized as teachers, policemen, or firemen, and they could not use the threat of withholding services to exact concessions nearly so effectively. Unlike school teachers or garbage men, their services were of importance only to the very poor.

hospitals), in professional services that were publicly reimbursed (e.g., doctors), or in businesses that depended on city contracts (e.g., contractors and construction workers). Partly they were incited by black claims that seemed to threaten their traditional preserves. Partly they were no longer held in check by stable relationships with political leaders, for these relations had weakened or become uncertain or even turned to enmity: Indeed, in some cases, the leaders themselves had been toppled, shaken loose by the conflict and instability of the times. In effect, the groups who worked for or profited from city government had become unleashed, at the same time that newcomers were snapping at their heels.

The result was that the provider groups reacted with a rush of new demands. And these groups had considerable muscle to back up their claims. Not only were they unusually numerous and well organized, but they were allied to broader constituencies by their class and ethnic ties and by their union affiliations. Moreover, their demands for increased benefits, whether higher salaries or lower work load or greater autonomy, were always couched in terms of protecting the professional standards of the city services, a posture that helped win them broad public support. As a result, even when the organized providers backed up their demands by closing the schools, or stopping the subways, or letting the garbage pile up, many people were ready to blame the inconveniences on political officials.

The result was a virtual run upon the city treasury by a host of organized groups in the city, each competing with the other for a larger share of municipal benefits. Benefits multiplied and budgets soared—and so did the discontent of various groups with the schools, or police, or housing, or welfare, or health. To illustrate, we need to examine the fiscal impact of mounting political claims in greater detail.

RISING DEMANDS AND THE FISCAL CRISIS

Education is a good example, for it is the single largest service run by localities, accounting for 40 percent of the outlays of state and local government in 1968, up from 30 percent in 1948.[8] The huge expenditures involved in running the schools are also potential benefits—jobs for teachers, contracts for maintenance and construction, and educational services for children—all things to be gained by different groups in the local community. Accordingly, the educational system became a leading target of black demands,[9] at first mainly in the form of the struggle for integrated schools.

---

[8] See *State and Local Finances: Significant Features 1967–1970*, U. S. Advisory Commission on Intergovernmental Relations (Washington, D.C.: Government Printing Office, 1969), Figure 6, p. 39.

[9] Conflict and competition over the schools have been further heightened because the proportion of blacks in the schools has increased even more rapidly than the proportion of blacks in the population, owing to the youthfulness of blacks and the flight of whites to private schools. In Washington, blacks constituted 54 percent of the local population in 1965, but 90 percent of the school children; in St. Louis blacks were 27 percent of the population, but 63 percent of the school population; in Chicago, they were 23 percent of the general population, but 53 percent of the school population; in New York City, where blacks and Puerto Ricans make up about 27 percent of the population, 52 percent of the children in the schools were black or Puerto Rican. Of the twenty-eight largest cities in the na-

Later, worn down by local resistance to integration and guided by the Great Society programs that provided staff, meeting rooms, mimeograph machines, and lawyers to ghetto groups,[10] the difficult demands for integration were transformed into demands for "citizen participation," which meant a share of the jobs, contracts, and status positions that the school system yields up.[11]

Blacks made some gains. Boards of education began hiring more black teachers, and some cities instituted schemes for "community control" that ensconced local black leaders in the lower echelons of the school hierarchy.[12] But the organized producer groups, whose salaries account for an estimated 80 percent of rising school costs,[13] made far larger gains. Incited by black claims that seemed to challenge their traditional preserves and emboldened by a weak and conciliatory city government, the groups who depend on school budgets began rapidly to enlarge and entrench their stakes. Most evident in the scramble were teaching and supervisory personnel, who were numerous and well organized and became ever more strident—so much so that the opening of each school year is now signaled by news of teacher strikes in cities throughout the country. And threatened city officials strained to respond by expanding the salaries, jobs, programs, and privileges they had to offer. One result was that average salaries in New York City, Chicago, Los Angeles, Philadelphia, Washington, D.C., and San Francisco topped the $10,000 mark by 1969, *in most instances having doubled* in the decade. Nationally, teachers' salaries have risen about 8 percent each year since 1965.[14] Not only did the teachers win rapid increases in salaries but, often prompted by new black demands, they exploited contract negotiations and intensive lobbying to win new guarantees of job security, increased pensions, and "improvements" in educational policy that have had the effect of increasing their own ranks—all of which drove up school budgets,

---

tion, seventeen had black majorities in the school system by 1965. See *Racial Isolation in the Public Schools*, U.S. Commission on Civil Rights (Washington, D.C.: Government Printing Office, February 20, 1967), Table II-2.

[10] The federal government was also providing direct funds to improve the education of the "disadvantaged" under Title I of the Elementary and Secondary Education Act of 1965. However, although in four years following the passage of the Act, $4.3 billion was appropriated for Title I, it was widely charged that these funds were misused and diverted from the poor by many local school boards.

[11] A series of training guides to such efforts, prepared with federal funds by a local poverty program known as United Bronx Parents, included a kit on "How to Evaluate Your School" and a series of leaflets on such matters as "The Expense Budget—Where Does All the Money Go?" "The Construction Budget— When the Community Controls Construction We Will Have the Schools We Need," as well as an all-purpose handbook on parents rights vis-à-vis the schools. Not surprisingly, Albert Shanker, president of the teachers union in New York City, charged there was "an organized effort to bring about rule in the schools by violence," involving the use of flying squads of disrupters who went from school to school and who, he said, had been trained with government (i.e., poverty program) funds (*The New York Times*, November 16, 1970, p. 2).

[12] See Urban America, Inc., and the Urban Coalition, *One Year Later: An Assessment of the Nation's Response to the Crisis Described by the National Advisory Commission on Civil Disorders* (New York: Praeger, 1969), pp. 34–35. See also, Naomi Levine with Richard Cohen, *Oceanhill-Brownsville: A Case History of Schools in Crisis* (New York: Popular Library, 1969), pp. 127–128.

[13] This estimate was reported by Fred Hechinger, *The New York Times*, August 29, 1971.

[14] Averaging $9,200 in 1970–1971, according to the National Education Association.

especially in the big cities where blacks were concentrated.[15] In Baltimore, where the black population has reached 47 percent, the school budget increased from $57 million in 1961 to $184 million in 1971; in New Orleans from $28.5 million to $73.9 million in 1971; in Boston, school costs rose from $35.4 million in 1961 to $95.7 million in 1971.[16] Total national educational costs, which in 1957 amounted to $12 billion, topped $40 billion by 1968,[17] and the U.S. Office of Education expects costs to continue to rise, by at least 37 percent by 1975. In this process, blacks may have triggered the flood of new demands on the schools, but organized whites turned out to be the main beneficiaries.

What happened in education happened in other services as well. Costs rose precipitously across the board as mayors tried to extend the benefits of the service agencies to quiet the discordant and clamoring groups in the city. One way was to expand the number of jobs, often by creating new agencies, so that there was more to go around. Hence, in New York City, the municipal payroll expanded by over 145,000 jobs in the 1960s, and the rate of increase doubled after Mayor John V. Lindsay took office in 1965.[18] By 1971, 381,000 people were on the municipal payroll. Some 34,000 of these new employees were black and Puerto Rican "paraprofessionals," according to the city's personnel director. Others were Lindsay supporters, put on the payroll as part of his effort to build a new political organization out of the turmoil.[19] Most of the rest were new teachers, policemen, and social workers, some hired to compensate for reduced work loads won by existing employees (teachers won reduced class sizes, patrolmen the right to work in pairs), others hired to staff an actual expansion that had taken place in some services to appease claimant groups who were demanding more welfare, safer streets, or better snow removal.[20] As a result, total state and local governmental employment in the city rose from 8.2 percent of the total labor force in 1960 to 14 percent in 1970. A similar trend of expanded

[15] State averages reflect the political troubles in big cities. Thus, in an urban state like New York, $1,251 was spent per pupil in 1969–1970 and New Jersey, California, Connecticut, and Massachusetts were not far behind. This represented an increase of about 80 percent in per pupil expenditures since 1965–1966.

[16] Educational costs have also risen sharply outside the central cities, particularly in the adjacent suburban school districts. These rises are a direct reverberation of troubles in the cities. Suburban school boards must remain competitive with the rising salary levels of educational personnel in the central cities, particularly considering the high priority placed on education by the middle-class suburbs. For example, between 1968 and 1969, enrollment in the Westchester, New York, schools increased by 1.5 percent, and the operating budget by 12 percent. In Fairfield, Connecticut, enrollment increased by 5.2 percent, the budget by 13.2 percent. In Suffolk County, New York, enrollment increased by 6.6 percent, the budget by 11.6 percent. In Monmouth, New Jersey, enrollment increased by 4.4 percent, the budget by 19 percent. Moreover, there are also increasing numbers of blacks in some of the older suburbs, with the result that these towns are experiencing political disturbances very similar to those of the big cities.

[17] *State and Local Finances, op. cit.*, p. 39.

[18] *Changing Patterns of Prices, Pay, Workers, and Work, op. cit.*, pp. 7–8.

[19] Some 25,000 of the new jobs were noncompetitive (*The New York Times*, May 28, 1971). Not surprisingly, the governor suggested that the mayor economize by cutting these, instead of always talking about cutting the number of policemen and firemen.

[20] Welfare is the main example of an actual expansion of services, for the number of welfare employees increased largely as a reflection of increasing caseloads. But so were new policemen hired to appease a broad constituency concerned about rising crime, sanitation men to answer demands for cleaner streets, and so forth.

public employment took place in other big cities. In Detroit state and local employment rose from 9 percent of the labor force in 1960 to 12.2 percent in 1970; in Philadelphia from 6.9 percent to 9.8 percent; in Los Angeles from 9.8 percent to 12.0 percent; in San Francisco, from 12.2 percent in 1960 to 15.2 percent in 1970.[21]

Another way to try to deal with the clamor was to concede larger and larger salaries and more liberal pensions to existing employees who were pressing new demands, and pressing hard, with transit, or garbage, or police strikes (or sick-outs or slowdowns) that paralyzed whole cities.[22] In Detroit, garbage collectors allowed refuse to accumulate in the streets when the city offered them only a 6 percent wage increase, after the police won an 11 percent increase.[23] In Cincinnati, municipal laborers and garbage collectors threatened a "massive civil disobedience campaign" when they were offered less than the $945 annual raise won by policemen and firemen.[24] In Philadelphia garbage collectors engaged in a slowdown when a policeman was appointed to head their department.[25] A San Francisco strike by 7,500 city workers shut down the schools and the transit system and disrupted several other services simultaneously.[26] An unprecedented wildcat strike by New York City's policemen, already the highest paid police force in the world, would have cost the city an estimated $56,936 a year for every policeman (and $56,214 for every fireman), if demands for salaries, pensions, fringe benefits, and reduced work time had been conceded.[27] If these demands were perhaps a bit theatrical, the pay raises for city employees in New York City did average 12 percent each year in 1967, 1968, and 1969. Meanwhile, the U.S. Bureau of Labor Statistics reported that the earnings of health professionals in the city rose by 80 percent in the decade, at least

---

[21] *Changing Patterns of Prices, Pay, Workers, and Work, op. cit.*, p. 9. Moreover, big payrolls were a big city phenomenon. A study showed that, in three states studied in detail, the ratio of public employment per 100 population varied sharply by city size, more so in New Jersey and Ohio, less markedly in Texas. See *Urban and Rural America: Policies for Future Growth*, U.S. Advisory Commission on Intergovernmental Relations (Washington, D.C.: Government Printing Office, April 1968), pp. 47–49.

[22] According to Harold Rubin:
Time lost by state and local government employees due to work stoppages climbed from 7,510 man-days in 1958 to 2,535,000 man-days in 1968, according to the U.S. Bureau of Labor Statistics. Such strikes have not been limited to those performing "nonessential duties." For example, during the first half of 1970 there have been strikes by prison guards (New Jersey), sanitation men (Cincinnati, Ohio; Phoenix, Arizona; Atlanta, Georgia; Seattle, Washington; and Charlotte, North Carolina), teachers (Youngstown, Ohio; Minneapolis, Minnesota; Butte, Montana; Tulsa, Oklahoma; Boston, Massachusetts; Newark and Jersey City, New Jersey; and Los Angeles, California, to list only some of the larger school systems involved), bus drivers (Cleveland, Ohio; Tacoma, Washington; and San Diego, California), hospital employees (State of New Jersey; Detroit, Michigan), policemen (Newport, Kentucky; Livonia, Michigan; and Winthrop, Massachusetts), and firemen (Newark, Ohio, and Racine, Wisconsin) ["Labor Relations in State and Local Governments," in Robert A. Connery and William V. Farr (eds.), *Unionization of Municipal Employees* (New York: Columbia University, The Academy of Political Science, 1971), pp. 20–21.]

[23] *The New York Times*, June 13, 1971.

[24] *The New York Times*, January 31, 1970.

[25] *The New York Times*, February 26, 1970.

[26] *The New York Times*, March 17, 1970.

[27] *The New York Times*, March 15, 1971. These estimates were given to the press by the city's Budget Director.

double the increase in factory wages. In other cities across the country similar groups were making similar gains; municipal salaries rose by 7–10 percent in both 1968 and 1969, or about twice as fast as the Consumer Price Index.[28]

To deal with these troubles, city officials made concessions, with the result that the municipal budget almost quadrupled in the last decade. And as the turmoil rose, so did city costs: an annual budget rise of 6 percent in the 1950s and 8.5 percent in the early 1960s became an annual rise of 15 percent after 1965.[29] New York now spends half again as much per capita as other cities over a million (excluding educational costs), twice as much per capita as cities between 500 thousand and a million, and three times as much as the other 288 cities.[30]

A few cities where the existing political organization was firmly entrenched and machine-style politics still strong were spared. Chicago is the notable example, and Chicago's political organization shows in lower welfare costs, in per pupil expenditures that are half that of New York City, in garbage collection costs of $22 a ton compared to $49 in New York City. Mayor Daley never lost his grip. With the white wards firmly in tow, he made modest concessions to blacks earlier and without fear of setting off a chain reaction of demands by other groups. And so he never gave as much, either to blacks or to organized whites. But most other large cities show a pattern of escalating discontent and escalating service budgets more like New York City than Chicago.[31] By 1970, the total costs of local government had risen about 350 percent over 1950.

---

[28] Rising wages and pensions benefits among municipal employees are frequently attributed to unionization, which has indeed spread in the 1960s, rather than to changes in city politics. Membership in the American Federation of State, County, and Municipal Employees increased from 180,000 to 425,000 in one decade; The American Federation of Teachers enlarged its ranks from 60,000 members in 1961 to 175,000 in 1969. But to point to unionization as a cause simply diverts the argument, since the spread and militancy of unionism among city employees in the 1960s must itself be explained. In any case, a Brookings Institution study of nineteen local governments showed no conclusive differences between unionized and nonunionized wages; both had risen substantially. See David Stanley, "The Effect of Unions on Local Governments," Connery and Farr (eds.), *op. cit.*, p. 47.

[29] Put another way, the average annual increase in New York City's expense budget during the last five years was $582 million, or eight times as high as the $71 million annual average increase from fiscal 1949 to fiscal 1954.

[30] "Report on Financing Our Urban Needs," *Our Nation's Cities* (Washington, D.C.: Government Printing Office, March 1969), p. 21.

[31] According to *Fiscal Balance in the American Federal System:*

> National aggregates for 1957 and 1962 and more restricted data for 1964–65 indicate that local government in the metropolitan areas spends more and taxes more per person than in the remainder of the country . . . there is a striking contrast in non-educational expenditures—which include all the public welfare, health, hospital, public safety and other public services essential to the well-being of citizens. These general government costs are two-thirds higher in the metropolitan areas than they are in the rest of the country [*op. cit.*, Vol. II, p. 59].

Specifically, per capita expenditures during 1964–1965 averaged $301.20 in the thirty-seven largest metropolitan areas, compared to $218.31 in small or non-metropolitan areas (*ibid.*, Table 16, p. 60). As for the central cities themselves, "central cities contained 18.6 percent of the population (in 1964–65), but accounted for almost 25 percent of all local expenditure." In per capita terms, local government expenditure in the large central cities "was 21 percent higher than in their outside regions, and almost two-thirds above that for the rest of the

The cities are unable to raise revenues commensurate with these expenditures; and they are unable to resist the claims that underlie rising expenditures. And that is what the fiscal crisis is all about. Cities exist only by state decree, and depend entirely on the state governments for their taxing powers.[32] Concretely this has meant that the states have taken for themselves the preferred taxes [33] leaving the localities to depend primarily on the property tax (which accounts for 70 percent of revenues raised by local governments),[34] supplemented by a local sales tax in many places, user charges (e.g., sewer and water fees), and, in some places, a local income tax.[35] The big cities have had little choice but to drive up these local taxes to which they are limited, but at serious costs.[36] New York City, for

---

nation" (*ibid.*, p. 62). Moreover, when educational costs are omitted (suburban communities spend a great deal on education), the thirty-seven largest central cities "had an outlay of $232 per capita in 1965—$100 greater than their suburban counterparts" (*ibid.*, p. 6). By 1966–1967, the disparity had become more dramatic in many cities. Per capita general expenditures, *including* education costs, was $475 in Washington, D.C., compared to $224 in the Washington suburban ring; $324 in Baltimore, compared to $210 in the suburban ring; $441 in Newark, compared to $271 in the suburban ring; $335 in Boston, compared to $224 in the suburban ring; $267 in St. Louis, and $187 in the suburbs (*State and Local Finances, op. cit.*, p. 70). Similarly, a study of fifty-five local governments in the San Francisco–Oakland metropolitan area showed that both the property tax rate and the level of per capita expenditures were higher in the central city. In dormitory suburbs, per capita expenditures were only 58 percent of those in the central city. See Julius Margolis, "Municipal Fiscal Structure in a Metropolitan Region," *Journal of Political Economy*, 65 (June 1957), p. 232.

[32] The New York State Constitution, for example, specifies that:

> It shall be the duty of the Legislature, subject to the provisions of this Constitution, to restrict the power of taxation, assessment, borrowing money, contracting indebtedness, and loaning the credit of counties, cities, towns and villages, so as to prevent abuses in taxation and assessments and in contracting of indebtedness by them. Nothing in this article shall be construed to prevent the Legislature from further restricting the powers herein specified [Article VIII, Section 12].

Traditionally the states have granted powers of taxation to the localities only very reluctantly.

[33] Not only do states limit the taxing powers of localities, but they have the authority to mandate local expenditures—e.g., salary increases for police and firemen—with or without adjusting local taxing powers to pay for them. They also have the authority to vote tax exemptions at local expense for favored groups. State legislatures are given to doing exactly that, exacerbating the financial plight of local governments.

[34] This was $27 billion out of $40 billion that localities raised in revenues from their own sources in 1967–1968 (*State and Local Finances, op. cit.*, Table 8, p. 31). It should be noted that property taxes are declining relative to other sources of local revenue. At the turn of the century about 80 percent of state and local budgets were financed by the property tax. Today, the states hardly rely on it at all. Nevertheless, local governments still finance about half their budgets with property taxes.

[35] The first city income tax was levied in Philadelphia, in 1939, when the city was on the verge of bankruptcy. The use of the income tax by big cities spread in the 1960s, with Akron and Detroit adopting it in 1962, Kansas City in 1964, Baltimore and New York City in 1966, and Cleveland in 1967. See *City Income Taxes* (New York: Tax Foundation, Inc., 1967), Research Publication No. 12, pp. 7–9. City income taxes must, of course, also be approved by the state, an approval that is not always forthcoming.

[36] By 1964–1965, per capita local taxes in the central cities of the thirty-seven largest metropolitan areas had risen to $200 per capita. In Washington, D.C., taxes were $291 per capita; in New York City $279; and in Newark $273. Overall, central city residents were paying 7 percent of their income in local taxes and in the biggest cities 10 percent (*Fiscal Balance in the American Federal System, op. cit.*, Vol. II, pp. 75–79).

example, taxes property at rates twice the national average, yielding a property tax roll three times as large as any other city. New York City also has an income tax, which is rising rapidly. Newark, plagued by racial conflict, ranks second in the nation in its rate of property tax.[37]

The exploitation of any of these taxes is fraught with dilemmas for localities. By raising either property or sales taxes excessively, they risk driving out the business and industry on which their tax rolls eventually depend, and risk also the political ire of their constituents. For instance, it was estimated that a 1 percent increase in the New York City sales tax had the effect of driving 6 percent of all clothing and household furnishing sales out beyond the city line, along with thousands of jobs.[38] A New York property tax rate of 4 percent of true value on new improvements is thought by many to have acted as a brake on most new construction, excepting the very high yielding office buildings and luxury apartments. Boston's 6 percent of true value property tax brought private construction to a halt until the law was changed so that new improvements were taxed only half as heavily as existing buildings.[39] Increases in either sales or property tax rates thus entail the serious danger of diminishing revenues by eroding the tax base. To make matters worse, with the beginning of recession in 1969, revenues from sales and income taxes began to fall off, while the interest the cities had to pay for borrowing rose, at a time that local governments were going more and more into hock.[40]

FISCAL CONSTRAINTS AND POLITICAL TURMOIL

In the face of fiscal constraints, demands on city halls do not simply stop. The political instability, which escalating demands both signify and exacerbate, rocked one city government after another. Indeed, many big city mayors simply quit the job, something that does not happen very often in politics.

---

[37] By 1968, official statistics for the nation as a whole showed local property taxes totaling $27.8 billion. The annual rise since then is estimated at between $1 and $3 billion.

[38] *Our Nation's Cities, op. cit.,* p. 24.

[39] *Our Nation's Cities, op. cit.,* pp. 36–37. To understand the full impact of property taxes, one must remember that these are taxes on capital value, and not on income yielded. Thus, a 3 percent of true value tax on improvements can easily tax away 75 percent of the net income that a new building would otherwise earn —a loss, economists generally agree, that tends to be passed on to consumers. See, for example, Dick Netzer, *Economics of the Property Tax* (Washington, D.C.: The Brookings Institute, 1966), pp. 40–62.

[40] Local tax collections increased by 500 percent between World War II and 1967, but costs have risen 10 percent faster, and the bigger the city, the tighter the squeeze. If the process were to continue, and today's growth rate of city spending vs. city revenues to continue, a recent study commissioned by the National League of Cities estimates a gap of $262 billion by 1980 (*Our Nation's Cities, op. cit.,* p. 22). Measured another way, state and local indebtedness combined rose by 400 percent since 1948, while the federal debt rose by only 26 percent (*U.S. Fiscal Balance in the American Federal System, op. cit.,* Vol. I, p. 55). In the thirty-six large central cities alone, the cumulative tax gap could reach $25 to $30 billion by 1975 (*Ibid.,* Vol. II, p. 91). A special Commission on the Cities in the Seventies, established by the National Urban Coalition, concluded that by 1980 most cities will be "totally bankrupt" (*The New York Times,* September 24, 1971).

Those who for the time survived the turmoil were even shriller in sounding the alarm. Mayor Joseph Alioto of San Francisco said simply: "The sky's falling in on the cities; it really is. We've had six cops killed in San Francisco since I took office. We need jobs and money for the poor and haven't money for either . . . We can't go on like this. Even the capitalistic system's not going to survive the way we're going." Kenneth Gibson, the black Mayor of Newark: "Wherever the cities are going, Newark's going to get there first . . . If we had a bubonic plague in Newark everybody would try to help, but we really have a worse plague and nobody notices." Mayor Wesley Uhlman of Seattle said he was so busy putting out fires, he had no time to think about anything else. Moon Candrieu, the Mayor of New Orleans: "We've taxed everything that moves and everything that stands still, and if anything moves again, we tax that too . . . The cities are going down the pipe and if we're going to save them we'd better do it now; three years from now will be too late." "Boston," said Mayor Kevin White, "is a tinderbox . . . The fact is, it's an armed camp. One out of every five people in Boston is on welfare. Look, we raise 70 percent of our money with the property tax, but half our property is untaxable and 20 percent of our people are bankrupt. Could you run a business that way?" And Mayor Lindsay of New York proclaimed: "The cities of America are in a battle of survival . . . Frankly, even with help in Washington, I'm not sure we can pull out of the urban crisis in time." [41] (Not long afterwards, Governor Rockefeller suggested that perhaps New York City's government, at least, ought not to survive, that it might be a good idea to abolish the present city structure, and begin all over).[42]

The mayors speak of the twin troubles of scarce revenues and racial confrontation. And it is no accident that the troubles occur together and are most severe in the biggest cities. It was the biggest cities that experienced the most serious disturbance of traditional political relations as a result of the influx of blacks and the outflux of many whites. In this context, demands by black newcomers triggered a rush of new demands by whites, especially the large and well-organized provider groups that flourished in the big cities. The weakened and vulnerable mayors responded; they gave more and more of the jobs, salaries, contracts, and services that had always worked to win and hold the allegiance of diverse groups. The eventual inability of the cities to garner the vastly increased revenues needed to fuel this process helped bring the urban political process to a point of crisis. The fiscal crisis is indeed real—not because of mounting "needs" for services, but because of mounting demands for the benefits associated with the municipal bureaucracies. To block the responses of the

---

[41] James Reston, "The President and the Mayors," *The New York Times*, March 24, 1971. In another column on April 21, 1971, Reston summarized the reports of the big city mayors as: "First, they felt the crisis of the cities was the major threat to the security of the nation—more serious than Vietnam or anything else. Second, they felt that the bankruptcy and anarchy were underestimated. . . . They sound like communiques from a battlefield. . . . They have got beyond all the questions of race or party and are looking for power and leadership to deal with the urban problem."

[42] The Governor said he had in mind a new structure like the London County Council. City political leaders, for their part, had been proposing to abolish city-state relations by declaring New York City a separate state.

bureaucracies to these demands for lack of revenues is to block a process of political accommodation in the largest population centers of the nation. The defection of the mayors was another sign of how deep the disturbances were, not in health agencies or welfare agencies, but in the urban political structure.

FEDERALISM AS A CONSTRAINING INFLUENCE

If mayors cannot resist the demands of contending groups in the cities, there are signs that the state and federal governments can, and will. The fiscal interrelations that undergird the federal system and leave the cities dependent on state and federal grants for an increasing portion of their funds are also a mechanism by which state and federal politics come to intervene in and control city politics. This is happening most clearly and directly through changes in state expenditures for the cities.

With their own taxing powers constricted from the outset, the mayors had little recourse but to turn to the states for enlarged grants-in-aid, trying to pass upward the political pressures they felt, usually summoning the press and the urban pressure groups for help. Since governors and legislators were not entirely immune to pressures from the city constituencies, the urban states increased their aid to the big cities.[43] Metropolises like New York City and Los Angeles now get roughly a quarter of their revenues from the state.

Accordingly, state budgets also escalated, and state taxes rose.[44] All in all, at least twenty-one states imposed new taxes or increased old taxes in 1968, and thirty-seven states in 1969, usually as a result of protracted struggle.[45] North Carolina enacted the largest program of new or increased taxes

---

[43] By 1966–1967, per capita intergovernmental aid was substantially higher for the central cities than suburban localities (contrary to popular impression). Per capita aid to Washington, D.C., was $181, compared to $81 in the outlying suburbs; $174 to Baltimore, and $101 to the suburbs; $179 to Boston, and $74 to the suburbs; $220 to New York City, and $163 to the suburbs; $144 to Newark, and $53 to the suburbs; $70 to Philadelphia, and $61 to the suburbs; $88 to Chicago, and $55 to the suburbs; $126 to Detroit, and $115 to the suburbs (*State and Local Finances, op. cit.*, Table 29, p. 69).

[44] Arthur Levitt, Controller of the State of New York, recently released figures showing that state spending had increased from $1.3 billion in 1956 to $3.9 billion in 1964, to an approximately $8 billion in 1968. In the four years ending in 1968, state spending rose by an annual average of $875 million, or 18.7 percent. In 1968 the spending increase was $1.4 billion, or 22.1 percent over the previous year (*The New York Times*, April 2, 1969–July 7, 1969). During this same five year period, state revenues from taxes and federal aid increased from $3.7 billion to $7.2 billion. In other words, spending exceeded revenues and by greater margins in each of the successive years. The total deficit for the five year period amounted to $2.5 billion, which, of course, had to be borrowed. A large part of this rise in New York State's budget reflects aid to localities, which increased from $622 million in fiscal 1955 to $1.04 billion in fiscal 1960, to $1.67 billion in 1965, and $3.23 billion in fiscal year 1969. State spending for aid to education has doubled in the last six years, and the state share of welfare and medicaid costs doubled in only four years.

[45] By 1971 the estimated difference between revenues and outlays was in excess of $500 million in New York, California, and Texas. Florida was short $120 million; New Jersey $100 million; Connecticut $200 million (*The New York Times*, January 3, 1971). A handful of rural states, however, were considering tax cuts.

in its history; Illinois and Maine introduced an income tax, bringing to thirty-eight the number of states imposing some form of income tax; South Carolina passed its first major tax increase in a decade. Even Ohio moved to change its tradition of low tax and low service policies that had forced thirteen school districts in the state to close. Overall, state and local taxes rose from 5 percent of the Gross National Product in 1946 to more than 8 percent of the GNP in 1969. Americans paid an average of $380 in state and local taxes in the fiscal year 1968, $42 more per person than the previous year, and more than double the fiscal year 1967. The rate tended to be highest in urban states: In New York the per person tax burden was $576; in California, $540; in Massachusetts, $453. The low was in Arkansas, with a tax rate of $221.[46]

But raising taxes in Albany or Sacramento to pay for politics in New York City or Los Angeles is no simple matter, for the state capitals are not nearly as vulnerable as city halls to urban pressure groups, but are very vulnerable indeed to the suburbs and small towns that are antagonized by both higher taxes and city troubles. Besides, the mass of urban voters also resent taxes, especially when taxes are used to pay off the organized interests in the service systems, without yielding visibly better services.[47] Accordingly, even while taxes are raised, state grants to the cities are cut anyway. Thus, the New York State legislature reduced grant-in-aid formulas in welfare and medicaid (programs that go mainly to the central cities and mainly to blacks in those cities) in 1969 [48] and again in 1971 (1970 was an election year and so the governor proposed increased aid to the cities without tax increases). Each time, the cuts were effected in all-night marathon sessions of the legislature, replete with dramatic denouncements by Democratic legislators from the cities and cries of betrayal from the mayors. Despite the cuts, anticipated state spending still rose by $878 million in 1969, the highest for any single year excepting the previous fiscal year in which the rise had been $890 million. By 1970 when the proposed budget

---

[46] Data provided by the Commerce Clearing House, as reported in *The New York Times*, September 27, 1970.

[47] A Gallup poll in 1969 showed that 49 percent would not vote for more money to pay for schools if additional taxes were sought, against 45 percent who would (*The New York Times*, August 17, 1969). Another key fact in understanding the populist character of the tax revolt is that state and local taxes consist mainly in sales and property taxes, and various user charges, all of which tend to be relatively regressive. Even the state income tax, when it is used, is usually imposed as a fixed percentage of income (unlike the graduated federal income tax, which takes more from those who have more, at least in principle). In any case, fully two-thirds of state revenues were raised from sales and gross receipt taxes. [*State and Government Finances in 1967*, U.S. Bureau of the Census (Washington, D.C.: Government Printing Office, 1968), Table I, p. 7]. Consequently the new taxes have had a severe impact on the working and middle classes, who are paying a larger and larger percentage of personal income to state and local government. In New York, state and local taxes now absorb over 13 percent of personal income; in California, over 12 percent; in Illinois and Ohio over 8 percent. As a result of rising state and local taxes (and price inflation), per capita real disposable personal income fell considerably between 1965 and 1969. See Paul M. Schwab, "Two Measures of Purchasing Power Contrasted," *Monthly Labor Review* (April 1971). By contrast, federal taxes declined as a percent of Gross National Product between 1948–1968, during which period state and local taxes rose from about 5 percent to 8 percent of GNP (*State and Local Finances, op. cit.*, Figure 5, p. 29). The "tax revolt" in the states should be no surprise.

[48] Most of the 1969 welfare cuts were restored within a short time, but the 1971 cuts were not.

had reached $8.45 billion, requiring $1.1 billion in new taxes, the outcry was so terrific that the governor reversed his proposals and led the legislature in a budget-slashing session, with welfare and medicaid programs the main targets.

When Governor Ronald Reagan, a self-proclaimed fiscal conservative, nevertheless submitted a record-breaking $6.37 billion budget for the 1969–1970 fiscal year, he met a storm of political protest that threatened a legislative impasse, leaving California without a budget. The next year Reagan proposed to solve the state's "fiscal crisis" by cutting welfare and medicaid expenditures by $800 million; even so, he submitted another record budget of $6.7 billion. When the long legislative battle that ensued was over, the governor signed an unbalanced budget of $7.3 billion, with substantial cuts in welfare and medicaid nevertheless.

Pennsylvania's former Republican Governor Raymond P. Shafer, in his short two years in office, managed to win the opposition of all but 23 percent of Pennsylvania voters as he and the legislature fought about how to raise $500 million in new revenues. At the beginning of his term in 1967, the governor was forced to raise state sales taxes to 6 percent, despite his campaign pledge of no new taxes, and early in 1969, with the budget $200 million short, he proposed that state's first income tax. When Shafer left office the income tax was enacted by his successor, Democratic Governor Milton Shapp, only to be voided by the Pennsylvania Supreme Court in 1971. A modified income tax law was finally passed, but by that time the state legislature was also making spending reductions, including a 50 percent cut in state education appropriations for ghetto districts.[49]

Other state governments are locked in similar fiscal and political battles. Michigan began the 1972 fiscal year without authorization to spend money after the legislature had been virtually paralyzed by a six-months struggle over the $2 billion budget, which the governor had proposed to finance with a 38 percent increase in the state income tax. Wisconsin cut welfare and urban aid expenditures over Governor Ody J. Fish's protest and, having enacted a new and broadened sales tax, precipitated a march on the capital by Milwaukee poor. Not long afterward, Governor Fish resigned, imperiling the Wisconsin Republican party. In Rhode Island, Democratic Governor Frank E. Licht promised no new taxes in his reelection campaign in 1970 and two months later recommended an income tax, amidst loud voter protest. When Texas, having passed the largest tax bill in its history in 1969, faced a deficit of $400 million in 1971, Governor Preston E. Smith vetoed the entire second year of a two-year budget, which totaled $7.1 billion.

In brief, pressures from the big cities were channeled upward to the state capitals, with some response. At least in the big urbanized states, governors and legislatures moved toward bailing out the cities, with the result that state expenditures and state taxes skyrocketed. But the reaction is setting in; the taxpayers' revolt is being felt in state legislatures across the country. And as raucous legislative battles continue, a trend is emerging:

---

[49] *The New York Times*, February 16, 1971; June 9, 17, 19, 25, 1971; and July 2, 1971.

The states are turning out to be a restraining influence on city politics, and especially on ghetto politics.

While in the main, grants-in-aid were not actually reduced, they were not increased enough to cover rising city costs either, and the toll is being taken. Some municipalities began to cut payroll and services. By 1971, vacancies were going unfilled in New York City, Baltimore, Denver, and Kansas City. San Diego and Cleveland reduced rubbish collection; Dallas cut capital improvements; Kansas City let its elm trees die.[50] Detroit started closing park toilets. And some city employees were actually being dismissed in Los Angeles, Cleveland, Detroit, Kansas City, Cincinnati, Indianapolis, Pittsburgh, and New York City. "This is the first time since the Depression that I have participated in this kind of cutback of education," said Cincinnati's Superintendent of Schools.[51] "You run as far as you can, but when you run out of gas you've got to stop," said Baltimore's Mayor Thomas J. D'Alesandro.

But the biggest cuts imposed by the states were in the programs from which blacks had gained the most as a result of their emergence as a force in the cities. Special state appropriations for health and education in ghetto districts were being cut; nine states cut back their medicaid programs;[52] and most important, at least nineteen states reduced welfare benefits by mid-1971, according to a *New York Times* survey. Moreover, new state measures to root out "welfare fraud," or to reinstitute residence restrictions, or to force recipients into work programs threatened far more drastic erosion of black gains in the near future.

There are signs that the federal government has also become a restraining influence on city politics. In the early 1960s, the national Democratic administration had used its grants to the cities to intervene in city politics, encouraging ghetto groups to demand more from city halls and forcing recalcitrant mayors to be more responsive to the enlarging and volatile ghettos, whose allegiance had become critical to the national Democratic party. But a Republican administration was not nearly so oriented to the big cities, least of all to the ghettos of the big cities. Accordingly, the directions of the Great Society programs that the Nixon administration had inherited were shifted; bit by bit the new federal poverty agencies were scattered among the old-line federal bureaucracies, and the local agencies that had been set up in the ghettos were given to understand that confrontation tactics had to be halted. By now the Great Society looks much like traditional grant-in-aid programs; the federal fuel for ghetto agitation has been cut off. And new administration proposals for revenue sharing would give state and local governments firm control of the use of federal grants, unhampered by the "maximum feasible participation" provisions that helped to stir ghetto demands in the 1960s.

---

[50] *The New York Times*, August 30, 1970; November 27, 1970; and May 25, 1971.
[51] Nationally the annual rise in teacher salaries slumped to only 5.5 percent, after rising by about 8 percent each year for several years.
[52] Usually by limiting eligibility, or limiting the types of services covered, or requiring co-payments by patients. See *Health Law Newsletter* (Los Angeles: National Legal Program on Health Problems of the Poor, June 1971), p. 2.

There are other signs as well. The wage freeze stopped, at least temporarily, the escalation of municipal salaries, and this despite the outcry of teachers across the country. Finally, and perhaps most portentous for blacks, the administration's proposal for "welfare reform" would give the federal government a much larger role in welfare policy, lifting the struggle for who gets what outside of the arena of city politics where blacks had developed some power and had gotten some welfare.

To be sure, a Democratic administration might be readier than a Republican one to refuel local services, to fund a grand new cornucopia of social programs. The pressures are mounting, and they come from several sources. One is the cities themselves, for to say that the cities are no longer as important as they once were is not to say Democratic leaders will want the cities to go under. Moreover, the inflated costs of the city are spreading to the suburbs and beyond, and these communities are also pressing for federal aid. Finally there is the force of the organized producers themselves, who have become very significant indeed in national politics; the education lobby and the health lobby already wield substantial influence in Washington, and they are growing rapidly. But while these pressures suggest that new federal funds will be forthcoming, the rise of the suburbs and the parallel rise of the professional lobbies indicate that it is these groups who are likely to be the main beneficiaries.

The future expansion of the federal role in local services has another, perhaps more profound, significance. It means that the decline of the local political unit in the American political structure, already far advanced, will continue. No matter how much talk we may hear about a "new American revolution," through which the federal government will return revenues and power to the people, enlarged federal grants mean enlarged federal power, for grants are a means of influencing local political developments, not only by benefiting some groups and not others, but through federally imposed conditions that come with the new monies. These conditions, by curbing the discretion of local political leaders, also erode the power of local pressure groups. As localities lose their political autonomy, the forces that remain viable will be those capable of exerting national political influence. Some may view this change as an advance, for in the past local communities have been notoriously oligarchical. But for blacks it is not an advance; it is in the local politics of the big cities that they have gained what influence they have.

The general truths to be drawn from this tale of the cities seem clear enough and familiar enough, for what happened in the 1960s has happened before in history. The lower classes made the trouble, and other groups made the gains. In the United States in the 1960s, it was urban blacks who made the trouble, and it was the organized producer groups in the cities who made the largest gains. Those of the working and middle classes who were not among the organized producers got little enough themselves, and they were made to pay with their tax monies for gains granted to others. Their resentments grew. Now, to appease them, the small gains that blacks did make in the course of the disturbances are being whittled away.

There is, I think, an even more important truth, though one perhaps not so quickly recognized. These were the events of a political struggle, of groups pitted against each other and against officialdom. But every stage of that struggle was shaped and limited by the structures in which these groups were enmeshed. A local service apparatus, which at the outset benefited some and not others, set the stage for group struggle. Service structures that offered only certain kinds of benefits determined the agenda of group struggle. And a fiscal structure that limited the contest mainly to benefits paid for by state and local taxes largely succeeded in keeping the struggle confined within the lower and middle strata of American society. School teachers turned against the ghetto, taxpayers against both, but no one turned against the concentrations of individual and corporate wealth in America. Local government, in short, is important, less for the issues it decides, than for the issues it keeps submerged. Of the issues submerged by the events of the urban crisis, not the least is the more equitable distribution of wealth in America.

18

Pogo Is Wrong
(Pogo: "We have met the enemy, and he is us")

Matthew Edel

Both sides in the environmental battle had their day last month. The New England International Auto Show was held at the Hynes Auditorium, and Beacon Press published Barry Weisberg's *Beyond Repair: The Ecology of Capitalism*.

Weisberg is a co-director of the Bay Area Institute in San Francisco, one of several radical think-tanks around the country. His new book discusses the role of auto and petroleum interests, and the war industry in ecological destruction. He also explores the structure of the capitalist institutions that bear responsibility for ecological damage. If you believe, as Pogo says, that "We have met the enemy and he is us," then you should read this book. Although Weisberg falls short in outlining an alternative, he has written the best book yet to emerge from the ecology movement.

While agreeing with Weisberg, I thought it only fair to hear out the opposition—so I went to the auto show. To guard against my own jaundiced vision, I invited an eight year old friend to accompany me. When I was his age, I used to cut out pictures of Hudsons and Studebakers from the *Saturday Evening Post*. Kids today seem less impressed, even if they still recognize all of the models. The racing and skill games at the show were still fun, but as for the automobile as a form of transportation, my friend found it no more exciting than I. As we neared the Prudential Center, I said that all we had to do was find a parking lot. "I always get worried," he said, "when somebody says that all we have to do is find a parking place."

Lack of parking spaces isn't the only problem with the automobile. The car will get you where you want to go, when you want, as long as a road is going there, and not too many other drivers are. But we rarely find those neat conditions.

Automobile use accounts for 80 percent of intracity commuting trips, and 86 percent of intercity trips. The roads get crowded, and the alternative means of transportation have been allowed to decay in this country. Meanwhile, the automobile is fouling the air: In 1965, the government estimated the car produced 66 million tons of carbon monoxide, out of 72 million produced by all forms of combustion. Motor vehicles also accounted for 6 million tons of nitrogen oxides (out of 13 million), and 12 million tons of hydrocarbons (of 19 million), as well as adding a million tons each of sulfur oxides and particulates to the air. Individual use of gasoline for driving took up about one-third of the petroleum produced, while automobiles accounted for 95 percent of the installed horse power in the country.

This represents tremendous inefficiency. Autos can rarely operate at full power. Weisberg cites a study showing that only 5 percent of the energy used in refining and supplying petroleum and driving the car actually moves the motorist. Spillage of oil in transit is fouling the waters of the world, while the cars themselves fill our cities with noise as well as smog. Automobiles kill more people than the Vietnam War or industrial accidents.

The automobile companies don't even deny these facts any more. Apart from a few new bumpers, designed to reduce the cost of repairs after minor collisions, nothing at the auto show promised any improvement. The only huckster even to put on a lab coat at Hynes auditorium was juggling lightbeams and ultrasonic detectors to demonstrate that Volkswagens were somehow pretested before sale to the public. But even he did not claim the car was really clean or safe, much less that the automobile is a good form of transportation for the public.

The cars and highways of the future that used to be a central attraction of auto shows were not there. The issue of the Motor Club News which arrived unsolicited in my mailbox to advertise the show still talked about the threat by "nature purists" to the highwaymen, or as they put it, "the more practical devotees of economic survival." But none of the exhibitors at the show wasted their time on generalities. They just presented their new models, with emphasis on small cars.

But if the car isn't defensible, how did we get stuck with it?

First, there is the power of the automobile companies and those firms producing fuel and auto parts. Of the twenty largest industrial corporations, three produce autos, and seven are petroleum companies; another makes tires, while most of the others sell some of their ware to Detroit. The automobile-petroleum nexus, says Weisberg, "may constitute as much as 40 percent of the entire GNP." This may be slightly overestimated, but at least according to the government, 20 percent of Gross National Cost (a better term than national product) is devoted to auto-related expenditures—and these figures don't include the value of time spent on the road as a cost.

There's gold in all that combustion, but how is that translated into power, and how is that power translated back into automobile use?

A few years ago, commentators talked about advertising, or hidden persuaders, as manipulating people to love their cars. At the auto show, there were a few appeals to the prurient interests of male consumers. Underdressed models were draped over Ford's and Fiat's "latest models" in obviously suggestive poses. Weisberg says Chevrolet spends 45 dollars on advertising for each car sold. But psychological manipulation does not explain most car sales. The road hog may be a male chauvinist pig, but that is not the only reason he drives. The U.S. male's "love affair" with his car has been a shotgun marriage. Men and women alike must drive to get to work and home again. This is due, in part, to the oil and auto company monopolies.

For example, lead got into gasoline when GM, DuPont and Standard Oil jointly patented ethyl lead additives, and forced other companies to go along. If the biggest gas company sold the stuff, auto companies had to build cars to burn it. Since the biggest auto maker built cars that way, most gas companies had to pay the patent royalty or lose customers. A similar monopoly removed the trolley cars from the streets in some cities, making them "safe" for the car. Several auto, tire and oil companies bought up trolley lines in the 1920's through a front, and replaced them with buses.

Still, monopoly alone does not explain the prevalence of cars—and it is unlikely that anti-trust action would help the environment. Weisberg cites the AFL-CIO as claiming that if GM had been satisfied with profit rates similar to those smaller corporations make (13 percent instead of 20 percent in 1965) it could have cut its wholesale prices by 300 dollars per vehicle. Oil companies pressure the US to impose quotas, which also keeps prices up. But if this use of monopoly were ended, and prices lowered, the result would be more automobile use and pollution. (It would transfer some wealth to the poor, so it isn't a bad idea to attack monopoly, but the air wouldn't improve.)

Similarly, outbreaks of competition among oil producers can be ecologically damaging. The competitive rush of companies to exploit new oil fields, where gas pressure keeps costs low, accounts for the haste with which offshore and Arctic fields are opened. A rational policy would involve completing extraction from existing fields before new ones opened, allowing time to develop safe methods of undersea extraction and Arctic transport.

Size and power do help the auto and petroleum companies to influence political decisions to avoid development of serious competitors to the automobile. The devotion of the "highway lobby" to preserving the Highway Trust Fund, which allocates gasoline taxes to cementing over the country, and preventing the rescue of rail lines or public transit is well known. "In 1969, the Federal Government spent approximately 50 dollars on highways for every dollar spent on mass transit," Weisberg points out. "To date the interstate highway system has cost the American taxpayer $32 billion."

Special tax breaks are showered on oil, from depletion allowances, to tax credits for foreign royalty payments in lieu of leases. Nixon's recent proposal of an auto-excise tax reduction instead of other personal tax cuts are part of the package, while his "job development" investment tax credit will give benefits to the auto industry. Since GM invests annually in new plants to be able to change its models, it can now reduce tax payments as a reward.

"Four of the last five secretaries of state were Rockefeller employees. . . . In the 1968 campaign, of the top five corporate contributors, two were auto and one petroleum," writes Weisberg, "the chairman of the board of Atlantic-Richfield was the last man seen to leave President-elect Richard Nixon's suite before Nixon announced the appointment of Walter Hickel as Secretary of the Interior." ARCO is one of the companies involved in Alaskan oil development, and its president (like ex-secretary Hickel) supports ecology causes as long as they don't interfere with the petroleum business.

Interlocking directorates can be cited from now to doomsday, however, without really detailing all of these power machinations. Weisberg scratches a few other surfaces, like the links between petroleum companies and companies producing coal, uranium, or other forms of energy. But these revelations are nothing new. We've all guessed them, if not known them (as was true with the Pentagon papers).

The important question is: Why do individuals simply go out and buy cars (and pollute) rather than changing the system that prevents alternatives?

It is by raising this question that Weisberg goes beyond Pogo. Once the question is asked, some of the answers follow. People have to defend their individual positions in life; the alternative is often to be destroyed. When you must drive to get to work, and you must work to eat, it follows you must drive to eat. When the highway cuts through the inner city, destroying its neighborhoods, you must protect your own family by moving to a suburb and becoming a commuter. When a polluting oil refinery is the only business that will offer you a job and when lack of a job will drive you to an already-polluted city, you support the refinery.

The kind of self-defense required to survive in America pits groups outside of corporations against each other. Subway riders against taxpayers; commuters against air cleanliness advocates; people against people.

Engaged in the business of daily life, it is hard to make the big changes that are needed. Barrington Moore, in an essay entitled "The Society Nobody Wants," argued that revolutions that virtually everyone desires are unlikely, because of the risks involved in starting them. The lack of a shared vision of an alternative; the lack of time away from the business of subsistence to ponder the problem; and the divisions engendered by the system lessen the odds for change. So we are stuck with the ecology that almost nobody wants.

The widespread emphasis on individual cleanup of litter, Weisberg argues, "mirrors the capitalist organization of society itself. Rather than emphasizing the social character of the problem, and thus the social character of the solution, we are told that we are to blame." (At the auto show, several companies gave away litter bags.)

Guilt cannot be the basis for a successful revolution. Only consciousness of a better alternative, and the possibility that it can be achieved will inspire people to make needed changed. Weisberg tries to outline a vision, and a strategy, in his final chapter "The Conditions of Liberation." His answers —decentralization of industry, community control, etc.—pull together some of the themes that have been prevalent in the New Left over the past decade. To some of us, they have been inspiring, but they have not inspired enough people.

At the auto show a man was selling sew-on patches for jackets. My companion glanced at the offerings, and immediately selected not the ones with the symbols of different cars, but one with a gas mask. "That's a good one for an automobile show," said the salesman. "A lot of people buy it."

"Doesn't the management of the show object to it?" I wondered. It turned out they didn't care. "People aren't being attracted by big cars this year," said another salesman. "The people who are buying are the ones who have to buy a car. They need it; their old one broke down."

He was right. But there are a lot of such people. In September, said the auto show program, the American automobile industry sold more cars than in any previous month. That's why the auto show wasn't trying to answer critics like Weisberg, and at least part of the reason why even the old pitches to status and sexism were toned down.

My young friend told me, as we left the show, that he would like to invent a steam car. That might help reduce pollution. But we will need a more complete vision if we are to free ourselves from our destructive economy.

19

G.M. in Trouble: The Vega Plant at Lordstown

Emma Rothschild

During the present disturbances, GM executives have restrained their public enthusiasm for Vega technology. They have suggested that the discontent at Lordstown is a consequence of exceptional worker emotions: Lordstown workers are undisciplined or too young (their average age is twenty-four) or have a mysterious modern attitude toward work. . . . GM management has now introduced "sensitivity sessions" at Lordstown, occasional small group therapy meetings for assembly line workers. . . .

GM's sudden interest in worker psychology has been successful in diverting attention from the actual working conditions at Lordstown. Yet the corporation's own statements in the last two years make it clear that production work on the Vega is exceptionally arduous and that the Lordstown organization of production follows predictably from corporate strategy to increase productivity.

The Vega was introduced in 1970 as GM's major project to fight declining profits and the growing sales of imported cars: the new car would be built (at Lordstown) with the latest methods of intensive marketing. . . .

Since the launching of the Vega, the US auto industry has been the most depressed sector of a depressed economy. Nineteen seventy was a disastrous year for the auto manufacturers. US car production was less than it had been since 1961: a third lower than in the record year 1965, a fifth lower than in 1955, and a twentieth lower than in 1950. Nine hundred and fifty-five domestic new car dealers went broke, or one dealer in twenty-eight. The dealers' journal *Automotive News* commented that "it was the fifteenth consecutive year that the domestic dealer total has declined, and one need to look no further than the lack of profits to find the principal reason."

The most serious of all the auto industry's present troubles is the problem of productivity—the problem to which the Lordstown project is addressed. Each senior auto executive has commented publicly on the crisis of national and local efficiency. According to a Ford spokesman, automotive productivity increased 4.5 percent a year between 1960 and 1965, and only 1.5 per cent a year between 1965 and 1970. The auto corporations have operated recently with 20 per cent capacity unused, and they are estimated to have enough capacity to meet all future auto demands between now and 1980. Because sales are growing only slowly, the auto corporations are reluctant to build new factories and buy new machines.

One consequence of the auto industry's low level of profits and high excess capacity has been that the auto corporations have invested comparatively little in capital equipment. Throughout the 1960's, the motor vehicle and parts industry had one of the lowest rates of growth of assets per employee of any manufacturing industry listed in the *Fortune* "500" directory. . . .

The Lordstown factories, which cost more than $100 million to build, contain an unusually high concentration of technological innovations. . . . Yet the Lordstown innovations are based on the same methods of increasing productivity that GM and its competitors use in other auto factories. . . .

The main principle of Lordstown technology is the speed-up, as developed by Henry Ford. One hundred cars can pass along the Lordstown assembly line each hour (a usual speed for assembly lines is sixty cars an hour). Workers face a new Vega every thirty-six seconds—800 Vegas in each eight-hour shift. Jobs have therefore been rearranged to suit a thirty-six-second rhythm of production. Every innovation supports the assembly speed-up: Vegas were designed with comparatively simple parts, so that each part could be added in thirty-six seconds, by a diligent but unskilled worker.

Precise work, for auto engineers, usually means increased work. There is more work to be done in each minute or second. This increase in what the UAW-GM contract calls the "work content" of the "job" has been a major issue at Lordstown. Some workers say that they have to run along the assembly line to keep up with their assigned work. . . .

The Lordstown organization of work depends on traditional principles of time study and speed-ups. . . .

The assembly line, for example, moves up and down, so that workers do not lose time on unnecessary (unproductive) muscular movements. Chevrolet's Lordstown coordinator boasted to *Automotive News* when the factory opened, "Even the conveyor system at Lordstown is unique. It has four elavations and varies in height from fourteen to seventy-two inches, according to assembly sequence, in order to bring the job closer to the operator at each station." The effect of such refinements is to increase the number of times each job can be performed in an hour, and to increase the concentration required.

Before the present disturbances, GM was reluctant to discuss the state of labor relations at Lordstown. The company's most serious attempt to communicate with Lordstown workers apparently consisted of decking the factory with signs in foreign languages: an appropriately cost-conscious way to invoke the menace of German and Japanese competition. Mechanics in charge of maintenance for the Unimate robots were also urged to "think of themselves as doctors."

Corporate spokesmen insist that worker discontent, at Lordstown and elsewhere, has no connection with the nature of assembly line work. . . .

Monotony [answered Joseph E. Godfrey, head of GM Assembly Division] is not quite the right word. There is a great deal of misunderstanding about that, but it seems to me that we have our biggest problems when we disturb that "monotony." The workers may complain about monotony, but years spent in the factories leads me to believe that they like to do their jobs automatically. If you interject new things, you spoil the rhythm of the job, and work gets fouled up. . . .

. . . Too often all we do is listen to the complainers and the growlers and the troublemakers. Hell, I can write a story about my own job that could be a tear-jerker. You know if all I want to do is talk about the problems and the pressures and the monotony and the reading of all the reports you have to go through. . . .

The company executives must also know that the connection between labor unrest and intense, repetitive work has been documented exhaustively. . . .

Meanwhile, the major sociological study of working conditions in the auto industry has found that auto workers quit their jobs twice as often as the average for US industry—and that the rate of quitting is twice as high among people working directly on an assembly line as among other auto workers. Even Chrysler, in Detroit, sponsored a research project on the treatment of industrial accidents. The researchers found that the incidence of industrial accidents was related to how workers felt about their jobs. One doctor in the project wrote of the agreeable aspects for an auto worker of being involved in an accident:

He hears his full name used several times . . . from a number on an assembly line, [the worker in an accident] has suddenly blossomed into a person, a man with a name, and, more significantly, a man with a disease.

Still, if you listen to what management says in Detroit, you might think there are no rational alternatives to the standard US auto assembly line. This is not true. In Sweden, Volvo subsidized a study of the peculiar muscle fatigue caused by repetitive work. The results were so striking that Volvo began to move its workers around from one job to another; it is now attempting to phase the assembly line out of its auto production. One US automotive products manufacturer, Motorola, has experimented with abandoning the assembly line on one of its minor electronics operations. The project proved profitable: more machinery was required, and more workers, but there were fewer rejects, and the company noted a sharp decline in staff turnover with "all the training costs that such turnover implies."

The US auto corporations do not accept the humane findings of doctors and industrial psychologists. . . .

The policy of the US auto industry, led by GM, has been to pursue discipline at the expense of labor relations. As at Lordstown, increasing the productivity has meant increasing the pace and intensity of unskilled work. . . .

As a pioneer of time study technology, the auto industry is badly placed to participate profitably in the anticipated Fordization of US labor. It has already applied the basic techniques of industrial engineering with incomparable rigor. It employs large numbers of unskilled workers whose jobs have been subjected to Fordist regulations for at least fifty years. Tasks and motions cannot be simplified indefinitely: automotive attempts at such simplification become increasingly frenzied, as at Lordstown. Without a fast growth of sales and without great scope for cutting labor costs, the US auto corporations face a grave and worsening crisis of productivity.

Yet the corporations continue to make huge profits by mass producing cars, and although these profits are growing less and less fast, corporate distaste for innovation is certain to prevent any immediate transformation of production policy. The US auto industry has been famously unwilling to abandon the tactics responsible for its early successes, even when those tactics yield diminishing returns. . . .

. . . Fordist industrial engineering is increasingly troublesome for the auto business, but its future seems assured: there will be more cars, more productivity, more inspections, more speed-ups, more layoffs, more Lordstowns.

20

Industrial Democracy

David Jenkins

The problems—which have remained essentially unchanged since the very invention of industrial capitalism—are clear. For most of this book, we have been discussing various attempted solutions; how does this accumulation of experience provide us with clues to the future of industrial democracy?

Most importantly, it indicates that workers do very much want more influence over their work. Whether we look at opinion polls, studies by behavioral scientists, spontaneous comments by workers themselves, experience under virtually any democratic system that has been tried, or some of the more explosive manifestations of worker attitudes, the conclusion is much the same: The desire for democracy is overwhelmingly strong. A common occurrence in democratization procedures is a strong expression of worker hostility to the new methods and an agreement to cooperate only on condition that the old methods will be reinstated when the workers so demand. But when democratic methods are put into effect, employees are almost invariably enthusiastic, and a frequently voiced opinion is that "there is no road back." Sociologist Paul Blumberg notes: "There is hardly a study in the entire literature which fails to demonstrate that satisfaction in work is enhanced or that other generally acknowledged beneficial consequences accrue from a genuine increase in workers' decision-making power. Such consistency of findings, I submit, is rare in social research."

The democratic spirit is not only virtually universally liked, but it also works. In surveying the variety of approaches, and despite the serious defects that afflict many of them, we see in almost every case the advantages outweigh the disadvantages. In the Israeli kibbutzim, the deep, direct involvement of each individual in the affairs of the group works out well in terms of both hard economic results and satisfaction for members. The Yugoslav self-management system suggests that even a rather poorly designed system, slowly improved by trial and error over the years, can result in rapid economic growth for the country and attract the widespread support of the populace. Both Yugoslav self-management and West German codetermination indicate that the direct transfer of power to worker representatives on top-level bodies in a company (although that may not be the best place to start a democratization process) does have its merits. Workers do have an interest in the matters that are discussed at these levels, and they do manage to acquire the competence to make contributions of value. The scientific studies of organizations carried out in Britain and the United States show not only that possession of decision-making power, autonomy, and control over a wide work span is a prime demand of individuals but that, when organizations find ways to meet these demands, one result is higher quality and better productivity. The experience of Scandinavia provides dramatic evidence that sound scientific methods can be used for the promotion of industrial democracy, in a clearly political context, with significant benefits for all concerned. Though the manifestations of the democratic spirit we have been examining display great differences, they are all part of the same basic picture. They show that the need for freedom, control, and opportunities for self-actualization is virtually universal in advanced societies; that democratization of work organizations can meet this need; and that this process is in the best interests of employees, organizations, and society as a whole.

As I know from many conversations on this subject, it will be objected that the evidence is meager, scattered, and inconclusive, and that where democratic methods do work, it is only because the organization in question is a "special case." I have had it pointed out to me that the kibbutzim in Israel are special because of ideology (or poverty, or because the country is at war); that Yugoslavia is special because it is Communist (or underdeveloped, or in conflict with the Soviet Union); that West Germany is special because of the unusual conditions under which codetermination was introduced; that Texas Instruments is special because it is a technologically advanced company; that Orrefors Glass is special because it is in a craft industry and thus technologically backward; that Procter & Gamble is special because it is a large company; that Nobø is special because it is a small company; that anyway the whole Scandinavian experience is special because everybody knows Scandinavians are "different"; that Monsanto is special because it is capital-intensive; that R. G. Barry is special because it is labor-intensive; and so on. To an extent, of course, any company is special, but such objections seem rather difficult to justify; managers in capital goods companies, say, do not ordinarily refuse to engage in marketing activities with the excuse that marketing is "special" and only of interest to consumer goods companies.

The fact is that democratic methods have worked under an astonishing variety of conditions—and with such varied groups as salesmen, scientists, ordinary production workers in process industries, ordinary production workers in mechanical, assemblyline plants, office workers, and people across the spectrum of education and skills. One of the most successful projects at Texas Instruments involved maintenance personnel with average below-fifth-grade education.

The very fact that uncannily similar situations have been worked out in widely varying contexts indicates that the underlying ideas are of wide validity. The "community" decision-making arrangement that has evolved at Procter & Gamble's Lima, Ohio, plant is strangely similar to the direct democracy practiced at kibbutzim in Israel. Rensis Likert's "linking-pin" concept—where interlocking circles of influence cut through the entire organization—bears a remarkable resemblance to the network of workers' councils and economic units in Yugoslavia, which, as Tito explains, comprise a basic "unity and interconnection of relationships, from the worker at his job, who is the first link in the chain, through the work organizations. . . ." The basic ideas in either of these systems might be described as follows: "In the company, there is a hierarchisation, a restriction of information at every level. It can only be remedied by establishing a kind of pyramid of committees which would have the job of coordinating information coming from the bottom and the top and working out solutions to submit to workers at the bottom." But this statement was actually made by a French worker during the events of May 1968, giving a "revolutionary" view of how companies should be managed. Take this description of work organization: "Nobody has one exclusive sphere of activity but each can become accomplished in any branch he wishes . . . to do one thing today and another tomorrow, to hunt in the morning, fish in the afternoon, rear cattle in the evening, criticize after dinner. . . ." Despite the bucolic context, this is essentially a kind of job-enrichment program, and it is specifically aimed at combating work alienation, in principle much the same approach as that used by Frederick Herzberg—but this quotation is from Marx's description of life under communism. Another kind of job enrichment, though of an unusual kind, is represented in Communist China by the "May 7 Cadre" schools—where upper-level bureaucrats and executives get their lives enriched by carrying out menial jobs alongside peasants and workers. (Some observers feel that Western managers might derive great benefit from similar experiences; Ralph Nader, for example, has suggested, to "sensitize managers to real worker problems, they could usefully spend two or three weeks annually 'on the line.'") This description of how workers in China solved a tough technical problem in drilling a new oilfield might be a description of the merits of participative management (with a few key alterations): "The Taching workers . . . broke the assertion of capitalist technical authorities that when the oil-bearing structure is irregular it is impossible to get a clear picture. The workers' new theories provided a solid scientific ground for opening Taching. The Taching workers applied a principle from Chairman Mao. . . . The approach led to a whole set of new technologies in oilfield exploitation." Now that America has taken steps toward solving its problems with China, observers have been increasingly intrigued with the Chinese theories of worker participation. One U.S. journalistic survey of life in China asserted: "China has made remarkable strides toward eliminating one of the major social ills faced by Western societies since the Industrial Revolution: the alienation of the worker."

To be sure, it is not possible to manufacture one rigid recipe to precisely fit the needs of all countries. Some examples can be instructive. In West Germany, virtually all companies are required to include a quota of one-third worker representatives on company supervisory boards. But labor leaders insist that if they cannot get full equality of representation with capital, the system is decidedly unsatisfactory. In Norway, however, the unions are perfectly content with the third of the places allotted to workers on the newly created "company assembly," which is very similar to the German board. The moral is that Norwegians and Germans are different and that perhaps different solutions are suitable in different places. Cultural variances also show up in other ways. When the Harwood firm set up a plant in Puerto Rico and tried to introduce participative methods there, it was soon discovered that turnover was alarmingly high. Alfred Marrow wrote: "The workers had decided that if management were so 'ignorant' that it had to consult its employees, the company was badly managed and would soon fail. So they quit to look for jobs with 'well-managed' companies that did not consult their employees but told them what to do." Syntex encountered somewhat similar problems in Mexico and other countries with strong "authority" traditions. Nevertheless, the company finds there is a "subculture" of receptivity to participative methods. Dale Miller of Syntex told me: "We have been able to export our methods because we have found that the 'subculture' is more powerful than the surface culture." Scott Myers of Texas Instruments, who has lived and worked in Iran and other countries, concurs. Though he cautions that "intercultural conflict" can cause problems, he nevertheless emphasizes that "principles of autonomy and delegation apply in the developing countries . . . no less than they do in America."

Therefore, even though not every detail of every democratic arrangement is universally valid, there are common threads that point to the industrial democracy of the future. It has been amply demonstrated that industrial democracy works; the problem is to develop methodologies for puting the principles into practice.

21

Alienation From Work-Process and -Product

Herbert Gintis

Work is of utmost importance for one's personal life. Work directly engages nearly half of one's waking daily activity and is potentially the single major outlet for initiative, creativity, and craft. Moreover, work-roles are basic and formative in individual personality development. But are these considerations reflected in the actual social decisions determining the structure of work-roles? For instance, is the factory worker's welfare considered when the capitalist decides to produce automobiles by routine and monotonous assembly line operations? Are the secretary's needs considered when she (or he?) is reduced to the full-time subservient role of typing, stenography, and stamp-licking? NO! The structure of work-roles is essentially determined by a set of basic economic institutions which operate on quite different criteria. The most important of these is the market in labor, which, by depriving the worker of control over his services, leaves the determination of work-roles to those who control capital and technology.

In rudimentary and small scale capitalist production, the control passes directly from capitalist to the mass of workers, with perhaps a few foremen as middle-men. But in firms of greater complexity, the requirements of secure control for the top dictates an increasing number of levels in the hierarchical ladder of authority. Thus the modern form of *bureaucratic order in production* is born. Bureaucratic order protects the firm against decentralized, participatory, and "bottom-up" decision-making, all of which threaten the determination of technologies and work-roles according to profit criteria. Because of its flexibility in promoting control from the top, this form of work organization has been taken over intact by most of the state-socialist countries in the Soviet Union and Eastern Europe.

The fact that the institutions controlling work are alienated has both subjective and objective implications. Subjectively, workers for the most part experience their work-activities as "alien"—as opposing rather than contributing to their personal well-being and psychic growth. This is understandable in that their own needs were peripheral in the decision-process determining the nature of work-roles—their work-activities have been snatched from them.

Defenders of capitalist production have argued that it is *not* an alienated decision-process because, although the worker has no control once he accepts a working position, he does have choice over which position to accept. Thus the desirability of various jobs is reflected in the supply-price of labor, and capitalists have an incentive to organize work as relevant to the worker as possible, in order to lower his labor costs. Indeed, this aspect of the market in labor is operative to some extent. An individual can decide to be a postman rather than an assembly-line worker, because the former position allows him or her more control of his or her activities. Since the greater desirability of the job leads to an increased supply of postman-labor, its wage-level may be lower than that of assembly-line work. The individual then chooses between more pay and a little more control. Similarly an electrician can work in unionized construction with higher pay, or in independent contracting, with more individual control at lower pay. The university professor is in a similar position.

Indeed all of us, in deciding our life's work make some trade-offs between income and job desirability. The capitalist does have some incentive to make work attractive, hence lowering his labor costs. That this aspect of the market in labor is not operative to any major extent should be clear, however, from the fact that wages and salaries are in general *higher* for more desirable jobs, not lower. This is because the labor force is *stratified*, so that only a restricted number of alternatives are open to a given individual. An assembly-line worker does not have the choice to become an electrician, a salesman, or a university professor because of his or her social class background and level of education (contrary to common opinion, intelligence is *not* an important factor in determining job-status and income). Hence capitalists have no incentive to improve working conditions beyond the few real alternatives available to the workers in a given occupational stratum. This is one reason why there is no tendency for all jobs to approach the most unalienated work-roles in desirability.

But there are other reasons as well. First, the cultural ideology of alienated labor is involved. This ideology tells us that work is *inherently* bad, and that all we can expect from our jobs is income and status. So long as workers value their jobs mainly in terms of relative wage and status, the capitalist has free rein to organize production along lines of profit-rationality, job fragmentation, and secure control from the top. Second, in the sphere of corporate production and state administration, secure control from the top is a *pre-condition* to profit-making and so-called "decision-making flexibility." Beyond a certain minimal point, no lowering of labor costs through providing less alienated work-roles is warranted, as any extensive worker control threatens the very basis of bureaucratic order.

Work is what it is because of the alienated decision-mechanisms which govern the structure of work-roles. In the early stages of the Industrial Revolution, this took the form of brutalizing, unhealthy, boring, and repetitive tasks, and long hours. In recent times, in bureaucratic organization, individual work-roles are so fragmented and formalized that the worker finds his initiative and autonomy totally muffled by and subordinated to a mass of regulations and "operating procedures." Also, hierarchical stratification of workers along lines of status and authority subjugates some workers to the control of managers and capitalists, and precludes cooperation and equality as a condition of production. Hence bureaucratic organization and hierarchical control are the concrete modern manifestations of the worker's alienation from his work-activities.

But in capitalist society the worker is not only alienated from the *process* of his work. He is also alienated from its *product*—the good or service he produces. When the good or service the worker helps produce neither reflects his personal contribution through its properties and attributes, nor contributes to his welfare either personally or through those with whom he has bonds of community, the *goal* of his work-activities becomes meaningless and absurd. He is alienated from his product. In an integrated society, workers control their activities, and hence the attributes of their product, as skilled craftsmen. The worker's attachment to his product results not only from his pride in the object of his labor, but also in the personal regard he holds for the community it serves. But in capitalist society, both disappear. Since the market in labor and capitalist control of production eliminate worker's control of resources, fragment and impersonalize community, his product becomes impersonal and external. Moreover, since the attributes of products are determined on the basis of profit, in a decision-process out of workers' hands, intrinsic craft is sacrificed to superficial saleability, enforced obsolescence, stylistic frills, shoddiness, and irrational waste foisted upon the consumer either unwilling, or ignorant of the craft involved.

Of course, there is a standard objection to the above analysis. Whereas we have attributed alienation from work-activities to the set of economic institutions—free market in labor and capital, hierarchical control over production decisions—some argue that bureaucratic organization and hierarchical control are simply immutable aspects of "industrial technology"; that, in effect, any "advanced" society must experience alienated labor. This view is essentially incorrect. It is not true that bureaucratic organization is chosen by capitalists only because it is "efficient" and "modern." It is chosen because it is the only means of maintaining and stabilizing control over the profit generated in production, and of avoiding workers' gaining enough general expertise and initiative to embark on cooperative production on their own, or to challenge the hegemony of capitalists in the factory or office. Technologies which potentially increase the breadth of collective and individual control of workers, however productive and efficient, must be avoided if the "stability" of the corporate enterprise is to be secured. The loss of control, even in minor areas, might get out of hand: workers-collectives might voice "wild" and "unrealistic" demands in a sort of free-for-all; union and management alike might lose control over workers.

Proof that task fragmentation, job specialization, and hierarchical control in the modern factory system are not technologically determined is not immediate. Both the social relations of modern production and their underlying material technologies in fact developed concurrently, making causal arguments quite difficult. The arguments presented above are only *logical*, urging that we not embrace technological determinism by superficial appearance. The fact that modern science is applied to production in an alienated manner does not mean that technology is *itself* inherently alienating. For other applications of science may be available but undeveloped because they conflict with the bureaucratic order of production that the capitalist deems desirable in itself. Modern communications instruments like two-way television and tape recorders, the information systems of computer technology, and cybernetic automation could all lead to the abolition of the most alienating jobs and an extensive decentralization of production, although such applications are scarcely compatible with present social relations of production, just as programmed and computerized learning could free classroom time for democratic participation by all, if this were not incompatible with the present social relations of education.

We have also presented the *logical* argument that from the fact that capitalists both maximize profits and choose hierarchical and job-fragmented work-roles, it does not follow that bureaucratic order in production is itself technically efficient. A system of worker control, job rotation, equal participation, decentralization, and job enlargement cannot be ruled out as impractical and inefficient merely because they are not embraced by bosses.

But we should like to present some *empirical* evidence supporting this view. First, we shall argue that in the first Industrial Revolution, which occurred in England late in the eighteenth century, the minute division of labor of the putting-out and factory systems, as well as the centralized control of the factory system, derived not from their technical efficiency—from more output per unit of factor inputs. Rather, capitalists saw both as necessary to preserve their lucrative position between the actual producers and the consumers of his product, to enforce a longer work-week and more strenuous pace of work, and to tap a low-wage labor market of women and children.

Thus the factory system was not even *historically* a product of new technologies. Independent peasant and guild production used much the same technologies as the early capitalist organization. This situation maintained, with rapid growth of the factory sector and vast capital accumulation, until a firmly ensconced factory system began to utilize modern sources of power.

In addition to historical material, we shall argue that recent experiments in worker control and investigations in industrial social psychology show fairly conclusively that bureaucratic order is *not* efficient from the point of view of cost-minimization, worker performance, or job satisfaction. Thus the social relations of production under capitalism are far from technologically determined.

Let us begin with the division of labor.[1] Before the Industrial Revolution in England, the fragmentation of work was not a major problem. Most families were rural, practiced farming on individual plots of land, and supervised agricultural production from beginning to end. What little non-agricultural production there was took place either in the family or in the system of craft-guilds. The apprentice in a particular trade could expect to become competent in all aspects of his trade, and pass to the level of journeyman and eventually, with some luck, of a master craftsman in his own right.

The Industrial Revolution changed all that. Small individual farms were appropriated by large capitalist landowners, and the rural population was freed for fragmented farm labor, or upon emigrating to the larger urban areas, for equivalent factory jobs. The craft-guilds were destroyed and replaced by fragmented capitalist production.

It is generally acknowledged that the triumph of capitalist over guild production was due to the lower production costs of the former. Just as

---

[1] The following material draws heavily on an unpublished report of a friend and colleague, Steve Marglin, *What Do Bosses Do?*, Harvard University, February 1971.

today many attribute the success of the giant corporation to its bureaucratic order, so many attribute the success of the early capitalist entrepreneur to his implementation of a minute division of labor. Adam Smith, the first of the great proponents of capitalism among economists, gave three reasons for the increased technical superiority of job fragmentation. First, said Smith, specialization to a narrow task increases the dexterity and speed of operation of each worker. Second, the minute division of labor saves time otherwise lost in passing from one task to another. Third, job specialization allows the introduction of machinery rigidly engineered to specific operations.

While Smith's reasoning is appealing, it is probably incorrect. The argument concerning time-saving in passage from task to task is correct, but implies only that the worker must process a large amount of material at each stage. Instead of spinning a few yards of thread, then weaving it, then fulling and dyeing, spinning more yarn, etc., the efficient worker will spin a great deal, thus minimizing time loss. In continuous process industries, where excessive standing time between stages is impossible (e.g., in steel production, where the product must be treated while it is still at the proper temperature), Smith's argument implies a work-group of equals—each performing all operations at different times. But this is exactly how a group of guild-journeymen operated! This argument cannot explain the hegemony of capitalist production.

For similar reasons, Smith's third argument is not relevant. The use of specialized machinery will increase the number of separate steps in the production process and perhaps require a larger work-group in a continuous process industry, but requires neither hierarchy, inequality, or job specialization. Also, the early putting-out and factory system did *not* use technologies very different from direct peasant and guild production![2]

Thus we are left with Smith's first argument: job fragmentation leads to increased dexterity on the part of each worker. However, Marglin's evidence suggests that all the various skills in early factory and putting-out production were quickly learned—even by children. For instance, it required only six weeks for an average fourteen year old boy to learn the art of weaving cotton. When the Napoleonic Wars erupted, enlisting all able-bodied men, women quickly learned wool weaving and took their place.[3] Much the same occurred in the United States during World War II. Moreover, workers seem to perform more satisfactorily and with fervor when they rotate jobs. Even today it is likely that most jobs can be rotated—within blue-collar and white-collar jobs and between the two. The exceptions are mainly in areas of specialized technical expertise (e.g., computer, chemical, and electronic technologies).

Why then the historical emergence of capitalist production? The answer seems to be that it was an efficacious means of social control. First, if all workers could perform all tasks, their knowledge of the production process would allow them to band together and go into production for themselves. In the guild system this was prevented by legal restrictions—the guild-masters had control over the number of new masters admitted, and all

---

[2] See Marglin, *op. cit.*, for a detailed argument of this proposition.
[3] See Marglin, *op. cit.*

production had to be under the direction of a legal guild-approved master. In "free enterprise" this form of control was interdicted.

Second, even within the capitalist firm, the boss's control depended on the *lack* of control of each worker. To allow all workers the capacity to deal knowledgeably and powerfully with all parts of the production process both increases their sense of control and autonomy, and undercuts the boss's legitimacy as the coordinator of production. Yet it is this legitimacy which maintains his position of financial control and intermediary between direct producers and consumers. Job rotation and job enlargement would soon threaten the political stability of the firm. That this policy of "divide and conquer" through task-fragmentation was central in the minds of bosses is amply illustrated in Marglin's cited essay.

But if early factories used apparently similar technologies as the contemporary worker-controlled operations, and if the division of labor did not increase efficiency, why were the former able to undersell and eventually displace their more traditional competitors? To what was the increase in per capita productivity in the early Industrial Revolution due? The answer seems to lie in the system of hierarchical control. Having all workers under one roof allowed the capitalist to increase drastically the length of the work week. Instead of making his or her own work-leisure choice, the capitalist worker is forced to accept a 15- or 18-hour work-day, or have no work at all. Since all workers were paid more or less subsistence wages *independent* of length of work-day, the factory system drastically reduced labor costs. Moreover the system of direct supervision in the factory allowed the capitalist to increase the pace of work and the exertion of the worker. Lastly, the factory system used pools of pauper, female and child labor at much lower cost than able-bodied men.

As a result, the capitalist was able to pay generally higher weekly wages to the male labor force, while reducing the cost of output and accruing huge profits. But this was due to increased exertion of labor, not the technical efficiency of the factory system. This situation forced the independent producers to increase their own work-day to meet falling prices of their product, but these producers maintained their position alongside the factory for over a quarter century.

Eventually, however, the factory system did win out on technical grounds. The reasons are interesting in light of our discussion of technological determinism. First, because only the capitalist producer had the financial resources to invest heavily in new machinery, inventors geared their innovations to types compatible with the social relations of factory production. Second, because of the large number of independent producers, it would have been impossible to protect patent rights, whereas the large size of the capitalist firm provided a stable and conspicuous market for the inventor. Third, most inventors aimed at allying with a capitalist partner and going into production for himself.

All these reasons led the direction of innovation toward the hierarchical, fragmented capitalist firm. Rather than technology dictating the social form of production, the reverse was preponderantly the case. The same is likely true today. Some modern empirical proof of this possibility follows.

First, bureaucratized and routinized tasks do not flow from the nature of "technology" but from the needs of centralized control. As Vroom notes in his masterful survey of experimental literature in industrial social psychology:

> . . . [the evidence indicates that] decentralized structures have an advantage for tasks which are difficult, complex, or unusual, while centralized structures are more effective for those which are simple and routinized.[4]

That is, given that the corporate unit is based on centralized control, the most efficient technologies will be those involving routinized, dull, and repetitive tasks. In a decentralized environment, the exact reverse would be true.

Second, workers do not like fragmented jobs. The experimental literature shows that job enlargement and decision-making control on the part of workers increases their satisfaction, while lowering absenteeism and turnover (Vroom, pp. 199–201). Nevertheless, managers have organized the normal bureaucratic division of tasks so that actual worker performance is *substantially independent of the worker's attitudes and satisfactions*. This startling, counter-intuitive fact is one of the major results of fifty years of investigation by industrial psychologists (Vroom, p. 199).

Third, bureaucratic organization of production, while insuring managerial control and corporate security against the vagaries of workers' morale, is by no means efficient in the wider sense. For even *moderate* worker participation in decisions and goal-setting increases productivity (Vroom, p. 228). The mean quality of decisions made by a group is moreover greater than the mean quality of individual decisions (Vroom, p. 230), and the best results are obtained when individuals *think up* solutions individually, and *evaluate and choose* among them as a solidary team (Vroom, pp. 232–233).

Let us give some examples. The MIT-generated Scanlon Plan of "participatory management" has been tried in some ten U.S. plants. This plan gives workers unlimited power to organize and improve the work process and working conditions, guaranteeing them a share in the proceeds of cost-reduction. In these ten plants the average yearly increase in productivity amounted to 23.1 percent, and in one company 408 out of the 513 innovative ideas were successfully implemented because they led to real improvements in the productive process. Clearly, a stable dialogue between workers, technicians, and planners would even increase this fertile activity.

These results are reproduced in many other individual studies: when workers are given control over decisions and goal-setting, productivity rises dramatically (Vroom, pp. 234–236). As Blumberg concludes:

> There is scarcely a study in the entire literature which fails to demonstrate that satisfaction in work is enhanced or . . . productivity increases accrue from a genuine increase in worker's decision-making power. Findings of such consistency, I submit, are rare in social research . . . the participative worker is an involved worker, for his job becomes an extension of himself and by his decisions he is creating his work, modifying and regulating it.[5]

---

[4] Victor H. Vroom, "Industrial Social Psychology," Gardner Lindzey and Elliot Aronsen (eds.), *The Handbook of Social Psychology*, Vol. V, 2nd ed. (Reading, Mass.: Addison-Wesley, 1969).
[5] Paul Blumberg, *Industrial Democracy* (Constable, 1969).

But such instances of even moderate worker control are instituted only in marginal areas and in isolated firms fighting for survival. When the crisis is over, there is a return to "normal operating procedure." The threat of workers escalating their demand for control is simply too great, and the usurpation of the prerogatives of hierarchical authority is quickly quashed. Hence, efficiency in the broader sense is subordinated to the needs of bureaucratic control.

Moreover, it is wrong to think of "technology" as a single unidimensional force of which an economy can only have "more" or "less," but whose substance and form are essentially independent of social decision. What "technology" is at a point in time is the sum total of the past decisions made as to what *forms of research* are undertaken, and which *results of research* are embodied in actual production in factory and office. Technology is "alienating" in capitalist society (and its state-socialist imitators) in the first instance because it is developed and diffused on the sole criterion of profit, and it is "locked into" bureaucratic organization only because capitalist and managerial representatives will introduce no new technology which is incompatible with their maintenance of power. Thus liberated, integrated, and anti-hierarchical technologies can develop only when we replace capitalist economic institutions by a system of direct worker and community control. Workers are alienated from their work-activities because they are powerless to determine, or even significantly affect, the nature of work-roles which hold sway over their lives. Even when workers are organized into unions, they are able to affect only the wage scale and the grossest aspects of work-process—health conditions, coffee-breaks, line-speeds, etc. The white-collar unions are no exception to this rule.

Work is for the most part "meaningless" not because of the nature of technology and the division of labor, but because the institutions determining them are alienated—the criteria according to which they make decisions (i.e., produce outcomes) are independent from workers' needs.

Military Spending and Imperialism

Beware the military-industrial complex! This prophetic warning was issued more than a decade ago by President Dwight D. Eisenhower in his 1961 farewell address. One major war later, the question may be raised whether armament production can be reduced within the framework of a capitalist society. For Nobel laureate Paul Samuelson, the most influential American economist, the answer is a simple one: the only barrier is a conservative political obstinancy (see Reading 22). Samuelson's argument is standard liberal fare, although the liberal litany of peaceful alternatives has changed under the impact of urban decay. What used to be touted a decade ago—schools, hospitals, housing, and roads—has been replaced by "pollution control, poverty relief, and urban blight."

Two questions should immediately be asked those who adhere to Samuelson's thesis. First, when he speaks of the *"temporary* increase in unemployment that would result from massive cutbacks in military expenditures" [emphasis added], does he mean by "temporary" the quarter-century of unemployment that characterized much of West Virginia after the coal mines shut down or merely the decade of unemployment in New England when its textile mills moved south? And second, why is there no mention of the monumental loss in profits—even to the extent of bankruptcy—some corporations might suffer?

What is most revealing, however, about this passage from Samuelson's best-selling text—apart from the fact that it does not even appear until page 803—is that less than two pages are devoted to the economics of armaments! But readers who think there is no more to say will be disabused of any such notion in Reading 23, by Michael Reich and David Finkelhor. Reich and Finkelhor make a damning critique of a society that has become heavily dependent on the making of weapons for its limited prosperity.

Other than its ostensible purpose of ensuring national security, military spending performs two decisive functions for a capitalist economy. First, it provides a spending base on which jobs, profits, and prosperity can be created. Second, it builds material strength capable of supporting an imperialist empire. After Vietnam and Chile, few serious students of contemporary history would deny that America is an imperialist power. The question is whether the taproot of imperialism is to be found in the "game of power politics," as Professor Benjamin Cohen of Tufts University asserts (see Reading 24), or whether it is to be traced to the capitalist character of American society. The latter formulation comes from Reading 25, by Professor Thomas Weisskopf of the University of Michigan.

An overview of American imperialism is provided by Dr. Paul M. Sweezy, coeditor of *Monthly Review* magazine and author of *The Theory of Capitalist Development* (see Reading 26). Orthodox economists often try to downgrade the importance of economic motivation in the workings of American foreign policy. But foreign investment is not merely of marginal interest. Sweezy quotes extensively from the *Wall Street Journal* to show that precisely the opposite is true: foreign investment is increasingly the lifeblood upon which corporate profits depend. This point is further confirmed in a recent article in *Fortune* magazine, which publicly revealed—apparently for the first time—that the First National City

Bank of New York makes as much as 40 percent of its total profits in the Third World, that is, the underdeveloped countries. Finally, a brief description of the destructive impact of U.S. imperialism on Puerto Rico is provided by the Committee for Puerto Rican Decolonization (see Reading 27). As this article makes clear, the intensification of North American corporate efforts to exploit Puerto Rican mineral lands, shorelines, and labor makes all but inevitable a breakdown in relations between the United States government and the Puerto Rican people.

Foreign operations being what they are, it is not surprising that there is fear in capitalist circles that other producers of raw materials might form cartels similar to the one created by the petroleum exporting countries (OPEC). A mainstream economist, Professor Raymond Mikesell of the University of Oregon, assesses the situation on a resource-by-resource basis (see Reading 28). He concludes that, except for bauxite, there is little likelihood of any successful cartels being formed. Rather than suggest squashing such attempts militarily, Mikesell recommends the stockpiling of commodities as a deterrent to collusion. But if "collusion" conjures up an image of sinister behavior, it is noteworthy that at a special session the U.N. General Assembly passed a resolution calling for cooperation (or collusion, if you prefer) among resource-producing nations as a means of combating under-development (see Reading 29).

The United States, if the past is any indication, is likely to use its power to sabotage such efforts. As Harry Magdoff demonstrated in his influential treatise *The Age of Imperialism*, imperialism in a capitalist economy is not a matter of choice but a way of life. Increasingly, it is a way of life that enriches the few at the expense of the many. "The many," as readings elsewhere in this volume show, have recently come to include most of the American work force, whose real wages have been sharply eroded (when not completely cut off by loss of employment). Presumably, this state of affairs will continue as long as foreign policy reflects the imperial exigencies of American capitalism.

22

Defense Expenditure and Prosperity: An Important Digression

Paul A. Samuelson

Before leaving the problem of achieving and keeping full employment, we should examine what would happen if the Vietnam war (and the cold war generally) were to give way to a period of relaxed international tension. If America were to cut down drastically on her defense expenditures, would that confront her with a depression problem that has merely been suppressed by reliance on armament production?

The answer here is much like that given [previously] to the problem of some future acceleration of automation.

If there is a political will, our mixed economy can rather easily keep $C + I + G$ [Consumption + Investment + Government] spending up to the level needed for full employment without armament spending.

There is nothing special about G spending on jet bombers, intercontinental missiles, and moon rockets [1] that leads to a larger multiplier support of the economy than would other kinds of G expenditure (as on pollution control, poverty relief, and urban blight). And the temporary increase in unemployment that would result from massive cutbacks in military expenditures could be offset by substantial tax reductions that would increase disposable incomes and lead to enhanced C to meet family demands. With cold-war expenditure no longer needed, our gigantic government expenditures abroad could be reduced and our international deficit would probably disappear almost overnight. With the dollar no longer overvalued, militant expansion of monetary and credit policy could stimulate capital formation (i.e., I) to utilize the resources released from armament production.

---

[1] Actually, expenditures on aerospace probably lead to fewer valuable research findings applicable to industry in general than did earlier military expenditure. It may cost $10 million to find a reliable control device that can be put into a match box; but to produce ordinary civilian products, there is no need to keep parts as light, small, and dependable as in traveling to the moon. Recent defense programs may have *used up* as much high-powered scientific and engineering resources as they have contributed to fruitful civilian uses.

If the cutback in military use of resources were not matched by an equivalent expansion in government programs for urban renewal, conservation, education, and medical care, the alternative pattern to full employment might require a larger budgetary deficit (or a smaller surplus) than now prevails. Such a deficit would *not* be inflationary, since it comes into being only to offset the deflationary impact of the military cutback. But it might exacerbate the ideological problem of those congressmen and citizens who simply do not believe in any of the macroeconomic mechanisms that economic science has expounded.

America's potential and actual growth rate, far from depending upon war preparations, would be markedly increased by an end to the cold war.

Is the story fully as optimistic as this? Yes. A laissez faire economy might face a crisis of some duration; but a mixed economy that has been using the tools of macroeconomics developed in the last 30 years need fear no such debacle.

There is but one possible flaw in the story. It lies inside the realm of politics, not economics. An economically illiterate electorate may less reluctantly use the tools of the new economics for war than for peace purposes. Any citizenry, any time and any place, that cannot *ideologically* stomach the political moves necessary to maintain healthy growth and high-capacity economic activity, can create *for itself* a problem of mass unemployment. But this is a quite different matter from that which critics of laissez faire (like Lenin and Rosa Luxemburg) faced at the turn of the century prior to the mixed economy.

23

Capitalism and the "Military-Industrial Complex": The Obstacles to "Conversion"

Michael Reich and David Finkelhor

Why does the United States spend eighty billion dollars each year on military expenditures? . . .

THE LIBERAL OPTIMISM

The liberal analysis can be outlined as follows:

1. Liberals like to lay the blame for the growth of the military budget on the doorstep of an unchecked troika. In their demonology a) a scheming set of restless militarists in the Pentagon combined with b) a few large military contractors and enlisted the help of c) some "neanderthal" congressmen (mostly Southerners) to get the ball rolling. The Pentagon militarists used their privileged access to security to scare other congressmen and the general public into support of massive defense expenditures. The contractors used the prospects of bringing the pork back to the home constituency to win over more legislators, while the Neanderthal Congressmen wheeled and dealt from their powerful positions of seniority in the important congressional committees.

[Liberals, then,] emphasize the politics of bureaucracy and characterize militarism as essentially a political aberration.

2. The liberal conversion strategy is based on a second assumption that minimizes the dangers of the withdrawal of military spending from the economy. Keynesianism, as expounded by liberal economists, says that any form of government spending is just as good as any other for the purposes of stimulating the economy, i.e., maintaining aggregate demand and keeping down the level of unemployment. Thus spending for needed social services could easily replace military spending without the economy falling into depression. There are no purely economic obstacles to military expenditures; it is just a question of using the political process to change the particular mix of goods and services purchased by the government each year.

3. Finally, [while] conversion is sure to hurt some important companies, these contractors constitute an economic enclave. [A] few large but isolated corporations who do most of the government work . . . will, of course, kick and scream, but the other segments of the corporate community can be brought to see the wisdom of demilitarization and will provide more than adequate counter-pressure. These are the three cornerstones of liberal optimism.

The radical analysis challenges the liberal approach at every step. Militarism was not the creation of simple conspiracy of subversion of the normal institutions. Military spending was the American system's only workable solution to the dangerous and profound crisis created by the Depression of the 1930's. No other solution is available which could adequately stem an inherent tendency towards economic crisis.

Although particular interests do benefit more than others, this military spending solution has generally had the tacit support of all the elements of the American ruling circles. The military sector is not an enclave. Its tentacles are implanted deep in the heart of the capitalist economy, and it is entirely fused with it. The vast majority of politicians, corporate executives, and military officials have all contributed to its growth and each has benefited. Today they all stand to lose some degree from the dismantling of the military-industrial establishment.

The liberals' faith that equivalent forms of non-military spending can be found to substitute for military spending is a completely abstract one. . . . Such spending is neither economically feasible nor politically possible. It disrupts work incentives, profitability in the private sector, and other key aspects of a capitalist economy. It also jeopardizes the existing structure of privilege, thus mobilizing the opposition of powerful vested interests.

Radicals argue that the militarization of foreign policy and extensions of worldwide commitments are here to stay. The American role in the Cold War was not a response to Soviet aggression, but part of a strategy of capitalist encirclement of the Communist countries. American foreign policy is an outgrowth of the need to protect overseas economic expansion, to integrate the entire globe into the international capitalist system, and to maintain the dollar as the world's key currency. It also requires the containment of socialism and of national liberation movements. These goals imply a huge military machine. The United States could not fundamentally dismantle its international military operations without fatal harm to the process of capitalist development and growth.

THE IMPACT OF MILITARY SPENDING ON THE ECONOMY

Before World War II, military spending never exceeded 1% of the Gross National Product. Over a trillion dollars have been spent on the military since 1951, consuming each year at least 9% of the GNP. In 1969, the United States spent about eighty billion dollars on the military, about 10% of the total GNP. In 1967, 4.08 million civilian employees worked on defense-related jobs; add to this the 3.5 million soldiers in uniform, and we have well over 10% of the entire labor force engaged in military-related employment.

The military sector of the economy is huge. Yet the image of the weapons industry often projected by liberals is of a small, albeit powerful, coterie of contractors, many of whom owe their existence solely to defense work. Producing exotic military hardware, these corporations form an economic *enclave* somehow separated from the remainder of the economy.

According to the enclave view, most corporations in the country are not affected one way or another by the military budget (except, of course, insofar as aggregate incomes and demands are stimulated). There is some superficial evidence for this image. After all, only one hundred corporations receive over two-thirds of all prime contract awards each year and 50 corporations receive 60%, and the list of the top one hundred contractors has exhibited very little turnover in the last twenty years. Prime contract awards are concentrated among just four industries: aircraft (43%), electronics and telecommunications (19.3%), shipbuilding and repairing (10.3%), and ammunition (5%). Moreover, subcontracts appear to be just as concentrated among the big firms.

But this enclave image is highly misleading. First, a list of the top military contractors is virtually a list of all the largest and most powerful industrial corporations in America. Nathanson estimates that of the 500 largest manufacturing corporations in 1964, *at least* 205 were significantly involved in military contracts, either in production or in research and development. Among the top 100 firms, 65 are significantly involved in the military market. All but five of the largest twenty-five industrial corporations in 1968 were among the 100 largest contractors for the Defense Department. Of these five, one—Union Carbide—is the largest Atomic Energy Commission contractor, two are oil companies indirectly involved in military sales, and one is a steel company also indirectly involved. It is difficult to think of these top corporations as constituting an "enclave."

Second, there are no self-contained enclaves in the American economy. As the study of input-output economics has revealed, the structure of American industry is highly interdependent. Focusing only on the prime contractors is like looking at only the visible part of an iceberg. This is only the direct impact of the military budget; the indirect impact on subcontractors, on producers of intermediate goods and parts, and on suppliers of raw mate-

TABLE I □ SECTORAL DISTRIBUTION OF PRIVATE EMPLOYMENT ATTRIBUTABLE TO MILITARY EXPENDITURES IN 1967

Sector	Per Cent of Total Military-Related Employment in Sector
1. Agriculture, forestry, and fisheries	2.5
2. Mining	1.3
3. Construction	2.3
4. Ordnance and accessories	6.2
5. Textile and apparel products	3.4
6. Chemicals and allied products	2.1
7. Petroleum and refining	0.5
8. Rubber and plastic products	1.1
9. Other non-durable goods manufacturing *	3.5
10. Primary metals	4.5
11. Fabricated metals	2.9
12. Machinery, not electrical	5.9
13. Electrical equipment and supplies	13.3
14. Aircraft and parts	16.0
15. Other transportation equipment	3.2
16. Instruments	1.9
17. Other durable goods manufacturing **	2.6
18. Miscellaneous manufacturing	0.3
19. Transportation and warehousing	6.9
20. Communications and public utilities	2.1
21. Wholesale and retail trade	5.6
22. Finance, insurance, and real estate	2.1
23. Business services	4.3
24. Medical, educational services, and non-profit organizations	3.2
25. Other services	1.7
Total, manufacturing	68.0
Total, all private employment	100.0

Source: R. Oliver, "The Employment Effect of Defense Expenditures," Monthly Labor Review, September, 1967, Table I, pp. 10–11.
* Food and kindred products, tobacco, paper and related products, printing and publishing, leather and leather products.
** Lumber and wood products, furniture and fixtures, stone, clay, and glass products.

rials ties military spending into the heart of the economy. For evidence, look at Table I, which indicates the wide range of industries over which direct and indirect effects of military spending were distributed in 1967. With the exception of the aircraft and electrical equipment industries, no one industry accounted for more than 7% of total private military-related employment. Aircraft and parts accounted for 15%, and electrical equipment and supplies accounted for 13%. This industrial profile shows that despite the enclave image, a broad spectrum of the domestic corporate economy is involved in military production.

Third, corporations in the civilian market have been racing to get a piece of the military action. Between 1959 and 1962, years for which a study was done, "manufacturing firms outside the defense sector purchased 137 companies in the defense sector (i.e., aircraft and parts, ships and boats, ordnance, electrical machinery, scientific instruments and computers)." By 1966, 93 of the top 500 manufacturing firms had diversified into the defense sector from a traditional non-defense base.

Military spending is very important for a large number of industries within manufacturing. About 11.5% of all manufacturing output as early as

1958 is attributable to military-related expenditures; the corresponding figure is 20% for the metalworking production sector, comprised of metals and metal products, non-electrical machinery, electrical equipment and supplies, transportation equipment, ordnance, and instruments. The percentage of profits attributable to military spending is probably even higher, given that profit rates are higher on military contracts—as is shown below.

Within the key metalworking sector, a broad range of industries are dependent on military sales. The importance of the metalworking sector in the domestic economy can be seen from the following statistics cited by Nathanson: in 1962, metalworking industries accounted for more than 47% of all manufacturing employment, 41% of total expenditures for plant and equipment, and 40% of the total value added in manufacturing. Table IV [omitted], indicates that military-related demand accounted for at least 10% of 1958 sales for every detailed industry in the sector. A 1964 *Steel* magazine survey of 5,000 metalworking plants found that 2,000 were producing directly for the Pentagon; of these, 1,400 reported that at least 31% of their output was for the military.

HOW GREAT A STAKE IN THE MILITARY

Military spending has been a key force behind the trend toward increasing concentration of economic power. We have already observed that prime contract awards are concentrated among a small number of corporations; fifty firms in an average year get 60% of the procurement contract dollar, about 94% of the research, development, and testing contract dollar. This makes the war industry much more concentrated than the economy as a whole, where the top one hundred firms usually account for only 35% of the manufacturing sales. The business of the war industry goes to the biggest firms and is used by them as a base from which to expand their area of control. So it is not surprising that between 1947 and 1963 the top two hundred industrial corporations boosted by defense business increased their share of total value added in the economy from 30% to 41%.

. . . Almost all of military spending goes to the most concentrated industries in the economy. . . . Industries in which four firms monopolized over 50% of the sales accounted for about one-quarter of all sales by manufacturing industries in 1958. But 90% of all military contracts go to these most concentrated industries. The most powerful elements in the economy have a large stake in the military production because of the opportunities it provides them to increase the concentration of their economic control. Military expenditures have a political base far stronger than the magnitudes involved would suggest.

Military spending has also created privileged interest groups within the occupational structure; . . . For example, nearly half of all engineers and scientists employed in private industry are at work on military or space-related projects. Many of the scientists and engineers pursuing research in the universities receive money from the Pentagon.

The military industries generally employ a highly skilled work force. A 1962 Department of Labor study of the electronics industry showed that at military-space-oriented plants 59.2% of employees were highly paid engineers, executives, or skilled blue-collar craftsmen. In the consumer-oriented plants of the same electronics industry, in contrast, 70.2% of the employees were semi-skilled and unskilled blue- and white-collar workers. . . .

Military spending has a regressive impact on the distribution of income within the United States, i.e., benefits the rich and hurts the poor. This is suggested by the higher proportion of professional and skilled workers in defense-related work. Computations by economist Wassily Leontief show that one dollar of military spending generates half as many jobs, but 20% more in salaries, than does one dollar of civilian spending. This means that tax money extracted from the whole population is paid out in such a way as to benefit high earners much more than low earners. Perhaps by accident, or perhaps by design, military spending is one of the mechanisms by which higher income groups use the government to prevent redistribution of income from taking place.

ATTRACTIVENESS OF THE MILITARY MARKET

The attractiveness of the military market to big corporations—the opportunities for growth and fantastic profits—has been described by a number of journalists and muckrakers. . . . Where these studies fall short, however, is in failing to emphasize that the waste and profiteering have a systematic basis in the structure of the military "market." This market differs in several important respects from markets in the civilian economy.

Unlike other industries, military contract work is not determined in a "market" at all, in any usually understood sense of the word. Contracts are arrived at through negotiations between a company and Pentagon contracting officers. The arrangement is rife with opportunities for the companies. Government as purchaser is alleged to have the same interest as a private consumer in cutting costs and buying only what is needed. In fact, this is not the case. First of all, procurement officers—who represent the government in these affairs—have an interest as military men in expanding the arsenal of weapons and thus the power and prestige of their branch of service. And so long as there is slack in the economy, higher-ups don't pressure them to hold down costs. Secondly, if they are on the lookout for their future in the business world, and they are, they have the most appealing reasons for currying the favor of the corporations with whom they are supposed to "bargain." When they retire, many military men involved in procurement regulation go directly to jobs in one of the defense companies. In 1967, 2,072 retired regular military officers were employed by the ninety-five top contractors. The top ten contractors had an average of 106 former officers apiece on their payrolls.

Contracting is supposed to take place competitively. In fact, it almost never does. Any one of the catalogue full of excuses can be reason for bypassing the competitive bidding procedure, e.g., if the item is critical, if delivery is urgent, if security considerations preclude it, etc.; 90% of the Pentagon's contract dollars are negotiated under such "exceptions."

The exotic technologies involved in weapons provide a perfect opportunity for boondoggles. . . . Subcontracting creates the opportunity for pyramiding profits on multiple tiers of subcontracts. Moreover, once a contractor has done some work on a weapons system—whether in another contract or in a research and development study—he obtains a virtual monopoly over the area. Since he is the only one with relevant experts and the relevant experience, the government is stuck with giving him the business. . . .

. . . Final costs average 320% of original cost estimates. That is, the average contractor ends up charging the government over three times the cost estimate he initially submitted to "win" the contract. Since most contracts are on a cost-plus basis, his profits go up three times also.

Companies do not lose their privileged status if their weapons do not meet up to specifications or perform properly. A recent study of thirteen major aircraft and missile programs since 1955 which cost in total forty billion, revealed that only four of these (costing five billion) performed at as much as 75% of the design specifications. Yet the companies with the poorest performance records reported the highest profits.

What this all amounts to, of course, is that profits for defense work are higher than those in every industry except pharmaceuticals. This is obscured by the Defense Department, which sometimes releases profits computed as a percentage of sales or costs. But, in the normal business world, profits are figured as a percentage of *investment*. Defense contractors invest very little of their own money because in most cases the government provides most of the investment and working capital needed by contractors to set up plants and machinery and to buy the necessary materials and parts. The profits when measured against investment are often huge.

A study by Murray Weidenbaum, formerly an economist for the Boeing Company and now Assistant Secretary of the Treasury, of a sample of large defense contractors showed that between 1962 and 1965 they earned 17.5% on investment, compared to average civilian market earnings of 10.6%. And this probably understates the case. Many military contractors also sell in the civilian market. The machinery provided free by the Pentagon, the allocation of all overhead costs to military contracts, and the technological edge gained in cost-plus military contracts can be of enormous importance in increasing profits on *civilian* sales for firms doing some business with the Pentagon. In one of the most outrageous cases that has come to light, a tax count showed in 1962 that North American Aviation Company had realized profits of 612% and 802% on its investment on "military" contracts in two successive years.

The waste and profiteering . . . are not aberrations or mistakes. . . .
. . . Massive, wasteful military spending is allowed to exist because it fulfills a need of the system as a whole. The waste is what helps military spending fulfill its function: providing a cushion to ward off stagnation and economic crisis.

MILITARY SPENDING AND STAGNATION

In the post-war period, . . . military spending has been responsible for a large part of the economic growth that has taken place. The fluctuation of military spending has virtually determined the cyclical pattern of the economy. Declines in military spending have been followed by declines in overall economic growth. Sectors highly involved with the military, including the aerospace, communications, and electronics industries, have been among the fastest-growing industries in the economy in the post-war period. This is easy to understand, since the Pentagon has underwritten much of the technological development that has occurred in the economy: 75% of all research and development activity in the country is paid for by the government, and of this 50% is disbursed directly by the Defense Department, and another 38% by the defense-related NASA and AEC.

Liberals do not deny that arms spending has served the necessary function of averting stagnation. But they argue that other forms of public sector spending are equally feasible. Instead of weapons, the Federal government could sponsor vast projects to improve health, education, housing, transportation, etc., etc.—some even envisage a "domestic Marshall plan."

But in order to provide an equivalent aggregate economic stimulus, social welfare spending like that called for by liberals would have to be roughly the same magnitude as the present level of military spending. It would have to be just as expandable to keep pace with the growth of the economy. Can social welfare spending do this? The answer historically seems to be no.

Massive civilian government spending was tried as a stimulus in the 1930's, and failed. . . . Between 1929 and 1939 government expenditures on non-defense purchases and transfer payments nearly doubled from $9.1 billion in 1929 to $17.8 billion in 1939. . . . The GNP in the same period slumped from 104.4 billion to 91.1 billion and unemployment rose from 3.2 to 17.2%. . . . But government spending on arms, once the war mobilization had begun, was enough—exactly what the disease called for.[1] Between 1939 and 1944 military spending increased from 1 billion to 77 billion; GNP shot up in the same years to 211.4 billion.

Spending on arms succeeded where social services spending had failed, because only government spending on arms can be enormous and expandable almost without limit. Why is this so? For one, only military spending is so amenable to waste that it can be made publicly and politically acceptable. Secondly, only military spending can expand so freely without damaging the basic framework of the economy. Massive social spending would compete with the private sector; it would damage the labor market; it would clash head on with hundreds of powerful vested interests at every level of the economy. Given such opposition, social spending could never expand adequately to fill the economic gap. Consider the factors that allow the enormous size, rapid expandability, and wastefulness of the military budget.

First, a convenient rationalization of the need for massive armaments expenditure exists. The ideology of anti-communism and the Cold War has

[1] The decline in military spending after World War II from 40% to 5% of GNP with only a 1.7% increase in unemployment was accomplished only because of unique historical conditions. In particular, savings of $160 billion, accumulated during wartime, fueled a consumer goods boom, and 10 million servicemen went to school under the G.I. Bill. By contrast, the decline in military spending following the Korean War was accompanied by a sharp recession; the unemployment rate in the United States has never fallen below 4% during peacetime. See B. Nossiter, *The Mythmakers* (Beacon, 1964), pp. 171–173.

been drummed into politicians and public alike for over twenty years. This is a powerful force behind defense spending as well as a general legitimizer of capitalism.

Second, armaments are rapidly consumed or become obsolete very quickly. Bombers get shot down over Vietnam, ammunition gets used up or captured, etc. More important, the technology of advanced weapons systems becomes obsolete as fast as defense experts can think of "improvements" over existing weapons systems (or as soon as Soviet experts do). Thus many weapons systems have proved obsolete even before production on them was completed. The demand for weaponry is a bottomless pit.

Third, the kind of machinery required for armament production is highly specific to particular armaments. So each time a new weapon is needed or a new process created, all existing production machinery must be scrapped. Extensive retooling at very great new outlays is required.

Fourth, there is no generally-agreed-upon yardsticks for measuring how much defense we have. . . . Since few people are willing to gamble with national defense, the expertise of the Managers is readily accepted. Politicians and the general public have little way of adequately questioning their judgment.

These factors combine so that defense expenditures can be enormous and expandable probably without limit. But the same is not the case for social services spending. The above factors are all highly specific to the military sector.

No readily available rationalization yet exists behind massive social service spending. Of course, everyone has to admit health care, hospitals, and schools are not good, but that does not mean they are prepared to see masses of federal tax dollars funneled into these areas.

Investments in social facilities are usually durable—they do not become obsolete very quickly and are not rapidly consumed. Right now, of course, there are plenty of unmet needs in these areas. But once everyone is provided with a decent house, once there are new schools and health clinics stocked with materials, then what? They cannot be immediately torn down and built all over again.

The technology of social welfare facilities is not particularly exotic. Very conventional standards exist to tell us how much a house should cost and how much a hospital should cost. There is no possibility for enormous padding here to absorb funds.

Furthermore, there are generally accessible yardsticks to ascertain how well social needs have been met. The public knows when adequate and convenient public transportation is available. No one would want to extend it out to a suburb that did not exist.

In general, social spending beyond a certain point cannot be rapidly and wastefully expanded. The difference here is that investment in social services deals with people, not objects like weapons. People are much more resistant to allowing their lives to be dominated by the priorities of waste . . . even if it does help to keep the economy running.

For example, what would happen if a housing project were built in the same way as a new missile? If a missile doesn't work, the company is excused and the planners go back to their drawing boards armed with another huge contract. Since it already has the expertise, the same company is more than likely to get a new missile contract. Imagine the political repercussions of a lousy, but expensive housing project? The tenants complain, a public scandal is declared, and all contracts are cancelled. The housing bill has a rough going the next time it comes up in the legislature.

So social spending can never provide the opportunities for waste that are provided by military spending. But this is not the most important reason why social spending is impossible. For massive social spending inevitably interferes with the basic operations of a capitalist system. How does this occur?

First, many kinds of social spending put the government in direct competition with particular industries and with the private sector as a whole. This is taboo in a capitalist economy. For example, if the government built low-cost housing in large amounts, it would cut heavily into profits of private builders and landlords who own the existing housing stock. It would add to the supply of housing and take land away from private developers who want to use it for commercial purposes. Similarly, building *effective* public transportation would compete with the automobile interests. . . . Furthermore, the capitalist system as a whole is threatened by massive governmental social spending because the very necessity of private ownership and control over production is thereby called into question. The basic assumption in any capitalist society that goods and services should be produced by private enterprise according to criteria of market profitability thus also fuels the general ideology limiting social spending.

Second, social spending upsets the labor market, one of the essential institutions of a capitalist economy. Public expenditures on an adequate welfare program would make it difficult for employers to get workers. If the government provided adequate non-wage income without social stigma to recipients, many workers would drop out of the labor force rather than take low-paying and unpleasant jobs. Those who stayed at jobs would be less likely to put up with demeaning working conditions. The whole basis of the capitalist labor market is that workers have no income source other than the sale of their labor power. Capitalist ideology has long made a cardinal rule that government must not interfere with this incentive to work. Powerful political forces thus operate to insure that direct income subsidization at adequate levels can never come into being.

Third, social service spending is opposed because it threatens the class structure. Education, for example, is a crucial stratification mechanism, determining who gets to the top and legitimizing their position there. Good universal education, extending through college, would put the whole system of inequality into question. Moreover, having the possibility to get an advanced education undermines the labor market as well. Few workers would settle so willingly for the miserable, low-paying jobs they now do.

Finally, good social services, since they give people security, comfort, and satisfaction, i.e., fulfill real needs, interfere with the market in consumer goods. Corporations can only sell people goods in an economy of abundance by playing on their unsatisfied needs and yearnings. In an era when most basic necessities have been provided, these new needs are mostly artificially created; the need for status, sex appeal, etc. They are based on fears and anxieties and dissatisfactions that people have and that are continually pandered to by the commercial world. But if people's needs were being fulfilled by the public sector, that is, if they had access to adequate housing, effective transportation, good schools, and good health care, they would be much less prey to the appeals of the commercial hucksters. These forms of collective consumption would have interfered with the demand for consumer products in the private market.

In addition, massive social services spending runs up against the obstacles of the existing vested interests in the social services sector itself. The AMA opposes the extension of federal aid to medical education and is thereby able—in part with corporate assistance from the drug companies —to limit the supply of doctors produced each year. Entrenched civil service bureaucracies find grave threats in extensive Federal intervention in local programs. The list could be prolonged indefinitely.

. . . Military spending is acceptable to all corporate interests. It does not compete with already existing industries, it does not undermine the labor market, it does not challenge the class structure. Social spending does all these things, and thus faces insurmountable obstacles for its own expansion. . . .

The facile liberal response to this argument—one that views the problem in an abstract fashion—is that "anything can be made appealing" to corporations just by making the incentive sufficiently large. With enough promised profit, defense corporations can be lured away from defense to just about anything. Even assuming that a total giveaway to corporations could be somehow made politically palatable—a dubious assumption—this view lacks plausibility.

Corporations do not make large-scale investment decisions just in terms of short-term profit from a particular project. Their minimum horizon is much greater, and a substantial element of inertia operates. First, what is to convince corporations that there are long-term growth opportunities in the social services sector? Corporate executives are well aware that social service spending has in the past been very capricious. Since the impetus behind a conversion program might well dry up after a few years, corporations are reluctant to make large long-term commitments for fear of becoming shipwrecked. . . .

There have been attempts by major defense contractors in the last twenty-five years to initiate large-scale conversion. But almost without exception, these have been failures. Murray Weidenbaum . . . concludes his survey of early diversification efforts as follows:

> Most of the diversification activities by the major, specialized defense contractors which were begun at the end of World War II were abandoned as unsuccessful or marginal or sold to firms, traditionally oriented to industrial or consumer markets. The expansion of the military budget brought on by the Korean War soon turned the primary attention of these firms back to the military market. When faced with the alternative, few aircraft companies preferred to manufacture powered wheelbarrows or busses rather than bomber or fighter airplanes.

Efforts at diversification after the Korean War were equally unsuccessful:

> Most of these industrial diversification efforts outside of aerospace fields have since been abandoned. The surviving diversification programs continue generally

at marginal levels—either actually losing money, barely breaking even, or at best showing profit results below typical military business returns.

The explanation of these failures is offered by Weidenbaum; many top corporate executives were convinced that military spending would continue to expand, perhaps a self-fulfilling prophecy:

. . . the belief of the top managements [is] that there are adequate sales opportunities in government work and that the profit rates are, if anything, higher than on risky commercial ventures. *Interviews with chief executives of the defense industry repeatedly brought out their firm belief in the long-term nature and rising trend of the military market.* Also, their many prior unsuccessful diversification attempts have engendered a strong conviction that inadequate commercial opportunities exist for companies which have become oriented primarily to government work. [italics added]

The corporate elite is not going to sponsor a move away from military expenditures on its own. If they continue to oppose conversion, and we have every reason to believe they will, there is little reason to believe their opposition can be overcome within the existing political and economic framework.[2] The conclusion which emerges: the military sector is just too crucial to capitalist stability and to capitalist profits.

We have tried to show in this article that the military-industrial complex is thoroughly integral to American capitalism. The only possibility for uprooting it, it would seem, is to challenge the legitimacy and structure of basic capitalist institutions and overthrow them. Furthermore, militarism is only one of many social problems resulting from capitalism. The problem with America has not been merely that too little money goes into social spending. Rather, the problem is that the whole society has been dominated by capitalist priorities. The priority of production for profit and corporate aggrandizement takes precedence over the satisfaction of the real needs of the people in the society. These priorities would continue to predominate, even if corporations were making money by building more schools instead of more missiles.[3] It is facile to believe that dollars alone are what is needed to build a decent society. For liberalism, the myth that we can dismantle the military-industrial complex is just one myth among many.

---

[2] Not surprisingly, the few senators and congressmen who have consistently opposed militaristic priorities have failed to make any appreciable dent in the military budget. An occasional budget item may be delayed or modified, as in the case of the Anti-Ballistic Missile Program, but the general sanctity of the military budget survives intact.

[3] Social services spending in some categories has increased rapidly in the postwar years; for example, public expenditures on education at all levels rose from about $5 billion in 1948 to about $50 billion in 1968. But these increases do not contradict our argument. For one thing, the increases in educational expenditures, a response to changing manpower needs in the economy, have occurred in such a way as to *preserve* the overall degree of inequality. In general, as the U.S. economy becomes increasingly urbanized and technologically complex, a more extensive social infrastructure is required for the smooth operation of the economy. Thus, the rise in social services spending may reflect *increasing needs*, rather than a reversal of militaristic priorities. . . .

24

Toward a General Theory of Imperialism

Benjamin J. Cohen

WHAT THE TAPROOT IS NOT

Marxists and radicals have no doubt that there is indeed a common taproot to the various forms of imperialism, and it is to be found in the presumed material needs of international capitalism. However, as the present study demonstrates, there is remarkably little evidence to support this point of view. The strictly economic interpretation of imperialism is substantiated neither by logic nor by the facts.

At the level of logic, there is little validity to any of the economic theories that have been developed by marxist or radical writers. Chapter 2 showed the intellectual weaknesses of the original underconsumption hypothesis as well as of Marx's alternative concept of the rising organic composition of capital. Chapters 4–6 showed the parallel weaknesses of the several contemporary lines of argument derived from these early approaches. None of the theories considered in these chapters can prove that economic imperialism is necessary or inevitable as part of mature capitalist development, or that poor countries are necessarily retarded or exploited. The theories are all much too highly deterministic.

Neither is there much validity to any of these theories at the level of empirical observation. These weaknesses were also shown in Chapters 2 and 4–6. The nations of the periphery have rarely assumed the importance ascribed to them as markets or investment outlets, or even as sources of raw materials. This was true during the era of the new imperialism; it is equally true during the modern era of decolonization and the multinational corporation. In fact, for many LDCs [less developed countries] economic relations with the metropolitan center have actually proved to be enormously beneficial in economic terms. The gains of the international capitalist economy do not all necessarily go to the rich.

All through history there have been innumerable examples of imperialism having nothing to do with the international capitalist economy or the presumed needs of its most advanced constituents. Chapter 2 pointed out that some of the most aggressive imperial powers of the late nineteenth century could in no way be described as mature capitalist societies. (It was also pointed out that some of the most mature capitalist societies could in no way be described as aggressive imperial powers.) Chapter 3 indicated that the political form of imperialism both antedates and postdates the development of modern capitalism. Empires were known long before the industrial revolution began; empires still persist even where capitalism has been swept away. The behavior of the Soviet Union today in eastern Europe and elsewhere certainly qualifies for description as imperialistic.

In short, marxist and radical theories of economic imperialism do not stand up to close analytical scrutiny. All that needs to be said about them has by now been said. As intellectual constructs, they are like elaborate sand castles—a few waves of the incoming tide, and much of their substance gradually dissolves and washes away.

WHAT THE TAPROOT IS

Does this mean that there is no common taproot of imperialism—that it is impossible to account for all of its various forms within a single analytical framework? On the contrary, evidence is strong that a single theme does effectively explain each major variation. That theme is "the good old game of power politics."

Power Politics

Power politics figured prominently in Chapter 2 as a guide to explaining imperial behavior in the nineteenth century, before as well as after the revival of formal empire-building around 1870. It also appeared in Chapter 3 as a principal motive for more contemporary forms of political imperialism, and in Chapters 4 and 6 as the basic force behind modern economic imperialism. In all these variations, major emphasis was laid on considerations of politics, power, and national prestige. I suggested that the condition of international inequality has been actively affirmed by dominant nations because of the strategic needs of the state, not the commercial or financial needs of private business.

The real question is *why* people and groups have been ready to take advantage of a disparity of power. Why do nations exercise a will to power? Why do they yield to the temptations to domination? Here is where we approach the real nub of the matter.

In essence, this is the same question that has intrigued students of international relations at least since the days of Aristotle and Plato. It is the central problem of all international political theory, the problem of the cause of war and conflict among nations. Many different answers have been offered, perhaps more than could be fully comprehended by any single scholar in a lifetime. In his classic *Man, the State and War*, Kenneth Waltz comprehended as many as any scholar might, and suggested that all causes could usefully be ordered under three broad headings: (1) within man; (2) within the structure of the separate nation-states; or (3) within the structure of the system of nation-states. The first of these three images of international relations stresses defects in the nature and behavior of man; the second, defects in the internal organization of states; and the third, defects in the external organization of states (the state system). Together they exhaust all possible explanations (unless, of course, one cares to entertain metaphysical or extraterrestrial hypotheses).

Marxist and radical theories of imperialism clearly fall under the second of Waltz's headings. They are all variations on the same image of international relations; indeed, as Waltz himself notes, they "represent the fullest development of the second image." Nations exercise a will to power be-cause they are organized internally along capitalist lines. Domination and conflict among nations are the direct result of the defects in social and economic structures within nations. The alternative theme I have sug-gested, by contrast, falls under the third of Waltz's headings. The "good old game of power politics" focuses deliberately on the state system itself, rather than on systems within states. The logic of dominion, I wish to argue, derives directly from the defects in the external organization of states.

National Security

As we know it, the state system consists of a relatively small number of separate national constituents—150 or so social collectivities, each or-ganized within a particular constitutional order prevailing over some specific geographical terrain. The principal consequence of the system is that no constituent can claim the right to exercise even partial sovereignty over the external affairs of nations. No body of law, no rules, can be enforced in the realm of international relations. There is no automatic harmony, no auto-matic adjustment of interests. Each state is the final judge of its own ambitions and grievances. The system as whole, though interdependent, is formally in a condition of anarchy.

What is significant about this condition, from our point of view, is that in anarchy there can be no such thing as absolute security. No state can afford, without risk, to take its own national survival for granted. Preoc-cupation with national security is the logical corollary of the state system as we know it.

At a more immediate level, the practical problem facing each state is to translate the basic objective of national security into an operational strategy of foreign policy. This is no easy matter, for two reasons. First, the state itself is not a unitary policy-maker. To the extent that interest is institu-tionalized, particular interest expresses itself with political power, and out of governmental processes of tension and conflict the foreign policy of the state emerges—a consensus of purposes and actions that are essentially the end products of a system of domestic power relationships.

Marxists and radicals have always shown the keenest awareness of this domestic background of foreign policy. Indeed, the very idea is inherent in the traditional marxist theory of class, which takes for granted that the purposes and actions of the state abroad will reflect directly the system of power relationships at home. The only difference is that in the marxist scheme of things the power system is monopolized by a monolithic capitalist class, with the result that foreign policy equates the conception of overall national interest with the particular interest of the bourgeoisie.

The weaknesses of the traditional marxist theory of class have already been discussed in Chapters 2 and 4. It is enough simply to repeat here that, in advanced capitalist countries at least, political rule in practice has been a good deal more pluralistic than the theory would have us believe. Govern-mental processes have operated to reconcile the conflicting interests of all groups with bargaining power within the system. Consequently, state action abroad usually turns out to be less monolithic than marxists and radicals generally allege. Often, in fact, it seems to be random, haphazard, or even irrational. Foreign policy will frequently take the form of an uneasy compromise as a result of deadlocked judgments. Sometimes a nation will adopt no foreign policy at all, but will instead, owing to indecision, or unwillingness or inability to act, simply drift with the force of events.

The second reason why translation of the basic security objective into an operational strategy is not easy is that the concept of national security is not a precise or well-defined guide for action. In fact, it is highly ambiguous. The presence or absence of external threats to a state's independence and territory can never be measured objectively.

The Role of Power

Despite all these difficulties, the nation must at least *try* to develop an operational strategy of foreign policy. It must attempt to define, for the purpose of guiding its own actions, a set of proximate foreign-policy goals and objectives. To see how this is done, it will be useful to draw an analogy between the behavior of states in the international arena and that of competing firms in an oligopolistic market. Both situations are particularly apt examples of a nonzero-sum game in operation [omitted].

Firms in the marketplace tend to be much more rational in their behavior than states in the international arena. I have already emphasized that foreign policy, being largely the product of an internal political process, often seems anything but rational. All kinds of variables enter into its determination. Nevertheless, as trustee of the interests of the national community, the government must steer the state away from destruction; national survival is its first responsibility. Therefore, even though there is a wide latitude for irrational elements in foreign policy, that latitude is not without limits. Small, poor states cannot rationally aspire to dominate the world; large, rich states cannot effectively isolate themselves. The proximate goals of foreign policy must fit the resources available, however tenuously. Ultimately, national power sets the limits to the state's choice of a strategy of foreign policy, just as market power sets the limits to the oligopolist's choice of a strategy of competition.

The key word is choice. In a situation of competition, interdependence, and uncertainty, the survival of any one unit is a function of the range of alternative strategies available to it. The oligopolistic firm with only one strategic option leads a precarious existence: if that strategy fails to result in profit, the firm will disappear. Likewise, the state with only one strategic option can never feel truly secure: if that strategy fails, the state will disappear, be absorbed by others, or, more likely, be compelled to abandon certain of its national core values. For both the firm and the state, the rational solution is to broaden its range of options—*to maximize its power position*, since power sets the limits to the choice of strategy. . . .

This does not mean that more power must be accumulated than is available to any of one's rivals, or that this power must be used coercively. It only implies that power must be accumulated *to the extent possible* in order to maximize the range of available strategies. In a nonzero-sum game, the crucial imperative is always to make the most of one's relative bargaining strength. This is the conduct we observe of firms in an oligopolistic market. To the extent that governmental processes are rational, it is also the conduct we observe of states in the international arena.

Dominance and Dependence

We are nearing the end of the argument. It remains only to ask what constitutes national power, and what determines the extent to which it can be accumulated.

Essentially, power represents the ability to control or at least influence the behavior of other nations. Such an ability need not actually be exercised; it need only be acknowledged by one's rivals to be effective. The ability derives from the interdependence which is inherent in the international state system.

It follows that if a state is to enhance its national security, it must, to the extent possible, try to use its foreign policy to *reduce* its dependence on others. At the same time, in order to counterbalance forms of dependence that cannot be avoided, it must try to enhance its *net* power position by *increasing* its own influence on others—that is to say, its *dominance* over them. This means that *imperialistic behavior is a perfectly rational strategy of foreign policy.* It is a wholly legitimate and logical response to the uncertainty surrounding the survival of the nation.

But, of course, there is a limit to the extent to which a state can behave in this way. This is determined by the entire range of resources available or potential, particularly those resources that have been or could be placed at the disposal of the nation's foreign-policy makers.

In short, resources available or potential determine the cost of alternative foreign policies. Imperialism may be a rational strategy for behavior, but only as far as costs permit.

For example, I emphasized above that the definition of what constitutes a nation's "core values," being subjective, is often apt to prove elastic over time, particularly if the nation's available resource base is growing at all rapidly. Again quoting Tucker, "the interests of states expand roughly with their power." It is a familiar phenomenon that military bases, security zones, foreign investments, commercial concessions, and so on, which may be sought and acquired by a state to protect basic national values, themselves become new national values requiring protection. The process works very much like the imperialism of the "turbulent frontier" described in Chapter 2. The dynamic of expansion acquires its own internal source of generation. Pushed to its logical conclusion, such an expansion of the range of national interests to include more and more marginal values would not stop short of the goal of total world domination. Yet in practice, at any single moment in history, world domination has rarely figured in the operational foreign-policy strategies of nations. The reason is, simply, that the cost was far too high.

When the cost is not too high (in relation to benefits), superiority over dependent nations will be actively affirmed. Then it is perfectly logical to behave in an imperialistic fashion—to subordinate, influence, and control others. Tucker said that "dominion is its own reward." We now see that this means that dominion is prized because it maximizes the collectivity's range of choice in the international arena. It makes both territorial integrity and political independence more secure in an insecure and uncertain world. Above all, it enables a country to preserve the entire range of values that it has come to consider basic. As Tucker also remarks, one of the main reasons for imperialism

must be sought in the variety of motives that have always led preponderant powers to identify their preponderance with their security and, above all, perhaps, in the fear arising simply from the loss of preponderance itself. The belief that the loss of preponderance must result in a threat to the well-being of the collective, and this irrespective of the material benefits preponderance confers, is so constant a characteristic of imperial states that it may almost be considered to form part of their natural history.

The Taproot of Imperialism

Tucker is perhaps putting it a bit strongly when he speaks in terms of "natural history." This smacks of the determinism of marxism and its "iron laws." But there can be no doubt that this and his other remarks point in the right direction.

It is not only the division of humanity into the rich and the poor that gives rise to the various forms of unequal relationships the radical equates with imperialism. It is also the division of humanity into discrete collectives.

In short, the answer [of what lies behind a nation's will to power] must be found in the character of the international political system.
Historian E. M. Winslow . . . also argued that "imperialism is a political phenomenon":

[T]he organization of peoples into regionally segregated political groups is the most potent cause of modern war.

Here is the real taproot of imperialism—*the anarchic organization of the international system of states.* Nations yield to the temptations to domination because they are driven to maximize their individual power position. They are driven to maximize their individual power position because they are overwhelmingly preoccupied with the problem of national security. And they are overwhelmingly preoccupied with the problem of national security because the system is formally in a condition of anarchy. *The logic of dominion derives directly from the existence of competing national sovereignties.* Imperialism derives directly from this crucial defect in the external organization of states.

SOME POSSIBLE OBJECTIONS

Too Narrow

One possible objection might be that the theme depends too much on a single explanatory variable. [We have] emphasized that most social theories which attempt to reduce reality to a single causative factor can be seriously faulted on grounds of excessive consistency and limited applicability. Some readers might argue that the same seems true of the political interpretation of imperialism. The explanation seems *too narrow*.

However, this would not be a valid objection. Although the explanation depends ultimately on a single causative factor, this does not mean that the theme thereby does serious violence to the complexity of reality. While I have argued that the key to understanding the behavior of nations is their preoccupation with national security, I have also argued that what actually guides the actions of governments is their operational strategy of foreign policy—and this comprises a whole set of proximate goals and objectives. Therefore, imperialism can arise for any number of practical reasons, not just for a single one (such as, for instance, material need). At a more immediate level, the explanation depends on a multiplicity of operationally causative factors. In this sense, the political interpretation is not at all limited in analytical applicability. It is sufficiently comprehensive to encompass virtually all possible subtypes or special cases. Viner put the point best (read *imperialism* for *war*):

In my view, therefore, war is essentially a political phenomenon, a way of dealing with disputes between groups. Every kind of human interest which looks to the state for its satisfaction and which involves real or supposed conflict with the interests of other peoples or states is thus a possible source of contribution to war. Every kind of interest which can conceivably be served by successful war will be in the minds of statesmen or will be brought to their attention. Given the existence of nation-states, the factors which can contribute to war can be as varied as the activities, the hopes and fears, the passions and generosities and jealousies, of mankind, in so far as they are susceptible of being shared by groups and of being given mass expression.

Too Broad

This suggests an alternative objection. Perhaps, rather than being too narrow, the explanation is really *too broad*. This objection, converse to the first, is frequently stressed by marxist and radical writers. By allowing for such a multiplicity of causative factors, they say, the political theme gets so lost in ambiguity and vague generalities that it is devoid of any genuine analytical value. As one young radical argues: "By associating imperialism with a phenomenon that has characterized international political relations since the beginning of time, this conception is so broad as to deprive the term 'imperialism' of any specific meaning." Or as Magdoff puts it: "This interpretation, correct or incorrect, is at so high a level of abstraction that it contributes nothing to an understanding of historical differences in types and purposes of aggression and expansion. It is entirely irrelevant. . . ."

The best answer to this objection has been suggested by Tucker:

That a general interpretation of expansion may contribute little to an understanding of historical differences in types of expansion is no doubt true. It does not follow, however, that general explanations are therefore irrelevant. All that follows is that specific cases cannot be understood in their specificity merely by applying to them otherwise valid general explanations.

In other words, a general theme does not relieve the analyst of responsibility for identifying the specific causes of particular historical variations. But it does give him a common thread with which to sew them all together in the "seamless web of history." The proper test of a social theory is not whether it is at a higher or lower level of abstraction, but whether the theory offers a useful insight into a variety of historical experiences. On the evidence of the present study, the political interpretation of imperialism does just that. The economic interpretation favored by marxists and radicals, on the other hand, fails to pass the test.

Too Shallow: I

A third possible objection might fault the political interpretation for being not too narrow or too broad, but *too shallow*. Marxists and radicals frequently stress this objection. The problem is not in attributing imperialism to the anarchy of the international state system, but in not going deeper, to ask what lies behind that anarchic organization of relations. As one young marxist writes, "it is necessary to ask more fundamental questions—about why nations struggle for power or come into conflict with one another, why they seek to increase their rank in the international system."

As we shall see below, there may be some validity to this objection, but *not* for the reasons that marxists and radicals typically suggest. What these writers see lurking behind the anarchy of international relations is, of course, the omnipresent hand of business. Nations come into conflict, and seek to increase their rank in the system, because of the selfish desires of private enterprise. To quote the same marxist: "The struggle for power is now seen for what it is—the ideological mask of monopoly capital." These writers are suggesting, in effect, a return to Waltz's second image of international relations: the objection merely paraphrases the traditional marxist theory of class. However, by now the flaws of this discredited theory of politics should be more than clear. In fact, the approach makes the error of inverting ends and means. Governments do not play "the good old game of power politics" for the sake of corporate interests. All the evidence of the previous chapters indicates that the situation is, rather, the reverse— corporations being influenced to play the international power game, whenever possible, in ways that will serve government interests. If governments come into conflict over economic issues, it is because they are concerned about the security of the nation, not because they are trying to protect the security of corporate profits.

The question of the connection between economics and politics in the behavior of nations is an old one in the study of international relations. It would be rash to try to provide a definitive answer here. For the purposes of this study, it is enough to emphasize two particular points. First, there can be no doubt of the *importance* of strictly economic factors to any conception of what constitutes national security. Security depends on power, and power depends on resources. Consequently, it is only natural that nations would define their minimum core values to include at least some values that are obviously economic in nature, such as investments, commercial and financial concessions, and so on. To this extent, there is little point in distinguishing at all between economics and politics in a discussion of international relations, since both are essential elements in the perpetual struggle for survival.

However, this does not mean that economic factors are therefore the ultimate *driving force* in the struggle for survival. This is the second point to be emphasized. To assume that economics is the end rather than the means of international politics, it is necessary to make one of two key assumptions. One must assume either that governments exist exclusively to serve the interests of the bourgeoisie, a view which is now discredited, or that national security is sought for no other reason than to enhance the nation's income and material possessions, a view which is equally indefensible. Greed is hardly the sole motivation of state action in the international arena. Nations, and the people in them, appreciate many objects of value for their own sake, apart from their transferability into current consumption or future wealth. These include international rank and prestige, and even the nation's domestic culture and religion, its "way of life" and language. (Consider, for instance, France's determined efforts to promote use of the French language in international organizations and around the globe.) They even include the exercise of power itself. All go into the conception of what constitutes national security.

This suggests why marxists and radicals are so misleading when they try to explain, for example, U.S. policy in Vietnam. Some writers, as indicated in Chapter 4, have tried to find a specific economic motivation for our prolonged military involvement (so reminiscent of the bloody "sporting wars" of Bismarck's day). However, even many marxists and radicals concede that such "scandal" or "devil" theories are hardly persuasive. For someone like Magdoff or MacEwan, the real explanation is much more subtle, having to do with concern over the system as a whole, rather than with a particular set of interests. As MacEwan puts it:

In terms of particular interests, there is simply not much at stake for U.S. business in Vietnam.
However, in terms of the general interest of maintaining South Vietnam as part of the international capitalist system, there is very much at stake. . . . *What is at stake in Vietnam is not just a geographic area but a set of rules, a system.*

I could not agree more with MacEwan's concluding sentiment. What is at stake in Vietnam *is* a set of rules, a system in which the United States enjoys an exceptional position of preponderance. But does this mean that the capitalist system is the ultimate driving force of policy, as MacEwan and others like him consequently argue? Not at all; with that sentiment I could not be more in disagreement. It means that the system is viewed as the necessary means to achieve other ends—specifically, to protect the whole range of national values that America, in its preponderance of power, had come to consider "basic." Defeat for our clients in Vietnam, it was somehow decided, would threaten our national security "in the greater than physical sense." As Tucker summarized:

The threat held out by Vietnam was real. It was not America's physical security that was threatened, but the security of an economic and social system dependent upon the fruits conferred by America's hegemonial position. A world in which others controlled the course of their own development, and America's hegemonial position was broken, would be a world in which the American system itself would be seriously endangered. To prevent this prospect from materializing, to reveal to others what they can expect if they seek to control the course of their own development, the United States intervened in Vietnam.

Too Shallow: II

This brings us to a fourth possible objection to the political interpretation of imperialism, which can perhaps be best phrased in the form of a question: Would a socialist (or communist) America have done the same thing? Marxists and radicals argue that it would not have. More generally, they argue that no socialist state would have done the same thing. Imperialistic behavior would be impossible, *by definition*, in a world of socialist states. The argument is implicit in the modern economic theory of imperialism. As one young radical has written: "Imperialism is capitalism which has burst the boundaries of the nation-state. . . . [The] two phenomena are inseparable: there can be no end to imperialism without an end to capitalism and to capitalist relations of production."

In effect, this line of argument simply repeats the third objection above, that the political interpretation is *too shallow*. The question still involves what lies behind the anarchy of the international state system, with the answer still framed in terms of Waltz's second image of relations. The only difference is that in this instance the logic is reversed. Instead of insisting on the reasons why survival of capitalism must necessarily mean perpetuation of imperialism, the converse is implied—that the demise of capitalism must mean the end of imperialism. Socialism would correct the basic defects in the internal organization of states. Accordingly, in a socialist world there could be no serious problems of war or international conflict. No state would have reason to fear for its territorial integrity or political independence. No nation's security, physical or otherwise, would be threatened by any of its neighbors.

The fallacy of this sort of logic should be clear. As Waltz puts it: "To say that capitalist states cause war may, in some sense, be true; but the causal analysis cannot simply be reversed, as it is in the assertion that socialist states mean peace." It is necessary to supply some sort of proof, at the level either of logic or of empirical observation. Unfortunately, marxists and radicals can do neither.

At the level of empirical observation, it is difficult to prove that socialist states mean peace, especially since the record shows very much the opposite. The Soviet Union in particular, as I have already emphasized, has obviously been guilty of imperialistic and warlike behavior—not only in relation to its sphere of influence in eastern Europe through the years since World War II, but especially, in more recent years, in relation to its Chinese neighbor in the Far East. Marxists and radicals retort that this demonstrates nothing. If the record shows "social imperialism," it is for one of two reasons—either because no socialist state in a predominantly capitalist world is free to realize its true nature, or because the "social imperialists" are no longer truly socialist. Magdoff has written that in his opinion the imperialism of the Soviet Union is simply a symptom of the degree to which the Russians have departed from socialism and adopted some form of sociocapitalism. For Magdoff, as for most marxists and radicals, it is impossible to conceive of imperialism persisting in a world of *genuine* socialism.

This suggests that the proof must be sought at the level of logic. However, here, too, marxists and radicals have a difficult time. If conflict and war are to be ended, it must be because there is some automatic harmony, some automatic adjustment of interests. Where would this come from in a world of *genuine* socialism? The usual answer is from the change in the attitudes of men and institutions. With all states becoming socialist, the elements of competition in the system would be eliminated. Cooperation, harmony, and mutual collaboration would become the hallmark of international relations. The minimum interest of each state in its own self-preservation would become the maximum interest of them all. The strategical game, in a sense, would be finished forever.

Merely to state the answer is to make obvious the utopian quality of the marxist and radical argument. It assumes a possibility of the existential perfection of all players in the game that goes far beyond anything the evidence of history would lead us to believe is feasible. In effect, it simply assumes the past to be irrelevant in projecting into the future: men and institutions are viewed as they might become, rather than as they have been. Ultimately, as Tucker notes, it "rests on the assertion—a tautology—that if men are transformed they will then behave differently."

But would socialist states behave all that differently? Such a leap of faith is courageous, even touching, but it is hardly a persuasive tool of intellectual debate. In fact, a strong case in logic can be made that socialist states would not behave differently; indeed, they might behave in even a worse fashion. Once sovereign states become socialist and take over the means of production within their borders, all distinctions between territorial jurisdiction and property ownership disappear. As a result, the inherent inequality of nations becomes a permanent source of potential disharmony in the system. A political element is injected into all important forms of international economic relations. Any dispute over commercial or financial interests automatically implies a measure of friction between states; if disputes are serious enough, they might even achieve the status of *casus belli*. Within a single nation, economic conflicts are ultimately resolvable through the fiscal mechanisms of the state or through legislative or judicial processes. Between nations, however, these same conflicts are ultimately resolvable (in the absence of world government) only through force or the threat of force.

The situation just described bears a striking resemblance to classic laissez-faire capitalism as outlined in traditional marxist analysis. Like a nation organized along capitalist lines, a world system of socialist states would consist of a number of "sovereign" property owners, all formally "equal" partners in a network of "free" exchange relationships. According to marxist analysis, at the national level these conditions necessarily lead to dominance for capitalists (who own the means of production), dependence for workers (who have correspondingly less control over resources other than their own labor power), and exploitation of the latter by the former. By analogy, it may be argued that the same outcome would obtain at the international level—dominance for large, rich countries, dependence for small, poor ones, and exploitation of the latter by the former. Of course, it is possible that cooperation among socialist states would act to moderate and limit the antagonisms generated by international differences of wealth and development; socialism is intended to be a humane system, after all. But it is improbable that mutual collaboration would succeed in eliminating tensions entirely. As one scholar has pointed out:

> [T]he "fraternal assistance" and "mutual aid" allegedly informing the relations among Socialist states do not essentially change the character of these relations, but leave them, in Marxian terms, fairly and squarely at the level of typical capitalist relations. . . . The point is that nations *cannot help but be* self-regarding, as long as their position is that of owners of property in a wider community characterized by economic interdependence.

Too Shallow: III

This leads us to a fifth, and final, possible objection, which can also be phrased in the form of a question: *Why is it* that nations cannot help but be self-regarding? Why must the world community be divided into distinct, and potentially antagonistic, national units? In effect, this objection also faults the political interpretation of imperialism for being *too shallow*. The existence of separate national collectivities is simply assumed. The deeper question is: Why do these horizontal distinctions persist?

Marxists and radicals are unable to give a truly satisfactory answer to this question, since the focus of their analysis is generally directed toward a different kind of distinction—not the horizontal division of mankind into nations, but vertical division into classes. Here, they insist, is the true source of conflict. If horizontal group diversity tends to persist, it is only because of the antagonisms generated by the warfare between classes, between capitalists and workers; the idea is inherent in the marxist class theory of politics. Conversely, if class warfare is ended by the coming of socialism, all conflicts and tensions will be eliminated in the international arena as well. As Marx himself put the point: "Is the whole inner organization of nations, are all their international relations anything else than the expression of a particular division of labor? And must not these change when the division of labor changes?" In other words, nations are self-regarding only because they are capitalist. Will they not stop being self-regarding as soon as they stop being capitalist?

Once again, merely to state the argument is to make obvious its utopian quality. All the evidence of history argues to the contrary. Horizontal distinctions in human society have prevailed since long before capitalism came into existence, in fact since the birth of time; they have persisted long after capitalism has been overthrown. As even Soviet spokesmen now willingly admit, national differences seem every bit as enduring in this world as class distinctions, if not more so. Certainly the experience of communism in more than a dozen nations since World War II has demonstrated that the centrifugal pull of national identity is at least as strong as the centripetal attraction of socialist fraternity. The leap of faith implied in the marxist and radical analysis is simply not justified by the facts.

What accounts for the persistence of national differences in this world? Unfortunately, *no* satisfactory answer is possible here. To account fully for the phenomenon would require at least another entire volume, drawing at a minimum on the combined insights of sociology, anthropology, and psychology. All that is possible here is to note that for whatever reasons one might conceivably imagine, men have always preferred to group themselves into distinct national units, and seem content to continue doing so. Separate nations are *a given fact,* and what characterizes them, as I pointed out in Chapter 1, is a feeling of homogeneity. This means not only that the members of a nation feel a sense of belonging to one another; more significantly, they feel little or no sense of obligation to others. Accordingly, as members of national collectivities, men find it most convenient to reconcile their own internal conflicts and tensions, whenever possible, mainly at the expense of outsiders. This is the meaning of "self-regarding." Foreigners don't vote, but nationals do. Even the most genuine socialist nation, maintaining the highest standards of justice and equity at home, is apt to act with less justice and equity in most of its relations abroad. The best definition of a nation I have ever seen is: "A people with a common confusion as to their origins and a common antipathy to their neighbors."

This implies that there is some validity to the objection that the political interpretation of imperialism is too shallow. In this sense, it is too shallow. By concentrating on Waltz's third image of international relations, it takes the persistence of self-regarding nations for granted, and therefore takes the nature and behavior of man for granted. But what is suggested now is that it is precisely with the nature and behavior of man that we ought to be most concerned—in other words, Waltz's first image. In the end, it is a question of the defects in ourselves, not in our national or international systems—our selfishness, our aggressiveness, our prejudices. We cannot relieve ourselves of the blame merely by blaming "society." Real solutions are never as simple as that.

25

Theories of American Imperialism: A Critical Evaluation

Thomas Weisskopf

INTRODUCTION

Almost a decade of overt war in Indochina; military interventions in Greece, Iran, Lebanon, the Congo, Cuba, the Dominican Republic, Colombia, Guatemala, Panama, Bolivia, China, Korea and Thailand; military missions throughout most of the "free world"; and American economic dominance of countless Third World countries have combined to impress upon all but the most recalcitrant observer the truth in the assertion that in the postwar period the United States has been a formidable imperialist power. That the United States is now and has long been an imperialist power is a proposition that is no longer subject to serious debate. Very much a matter of dispute, however, are the sources of American imperialism.

I believe that what fundamentally unites radical theorists is an insistence on analyzing societies as integrated social systems in concrete historical circumstances. The radical approach differs from the orthodox approach to the social sciences in the Western world (1) by emphasizing the interdependence of different spheres of a society rather than compartmentalizing these spheres and treating them independently, and (2) by analyzing a society in terms of its specific institutional structure rather than in terms of abstract universal propositions.

The prevailing orthodox view attributes American imperialism primarily to the existence of a system of geographically distinct societies claiming independent political sovereignty. Orthodox theorists hold that the internal socioeconomic organization of a society has relatively little to do with the propensity for imperialist behavior. Rather, it is the externally imposed competition among sovereign states that generates imperialism in general and American imperialism in particular.[1]

Against this orthodoxy there is arrayed a variety of revisionist radical theories, inspired largely by the Marxist tradition.[2] The unifying distinctive feature of the radical theories is the assertion that American imperialism results to a significant extent from the fact that the United States is a capitalist society.

In this essay I will use the term imperialism in a non-Marxist sense according to the following definition: imperialism is activity on the part of a national government which involves the use of power (or the threat of its use) to establish or maintain a relationship of domination or control over the government or (some of) the people of another nation or territory over which the imperialist government has no traditional claim to sovereignty.[3]

In analyzing alternative interests in imperialism I will distinguish carefully between a "national interest" and a "class interest." I will say that there is a national interest in an imperialist activity when the activity is expected to benefit the imperialist nation as a whole, in the sense that the aggregate benefits to citizens of the imperialist nation are expected to exceed the aggregate costs. I will say that there is a class interest in an imperialist activity when it is expected to result in net benefits for a particular class of people from among the citizens of the imperialist nation. If there is a national interest in an imperialist activity, there is bound to be also at least one class interest, although there may be other classes for whom the

---

[1] Thus Cohen (1973), p. 245, states that "the real taproot of imperialism" is "the anarchic organization of the international system of states. . . . The logic of dominion derives directly from the existence of competing national sovereignties"; and Tucker (1971), p. 73, asks: "Why may we not say simply that the interests of states expand roughly with their power and that America has been no exception to this experience?"

[2] Not all radical theorists of imperialism would describe themselves as Marxists, but they do share the Marxist methodological emphasis on analyzing the internal socioeconomic structure of a society in order to understand its behavior.

[3] My definition of imperialism is not equivalent simply to intervention abroad, for it excludes instances of economic or military aid to foreign friends and allies which do not entail any relationship of domination and control.

anticipated net benefits are negative. On the other hand, if there is a class interest in an imperialist activity, there may or may not also be a national interest.

If one can identify a national interest in an imperialist activity, there is a *prima facie* motivation for the government to undertake it. The government will refrain from the imperialist activity only if (1) there is some class which stands to lose by the activity, *and* (2) that class has disproportionate power to prevent the government from undertaking the activity even though other classes stand to gain more than the particular class expects to lose by it. If one can find no national interest in a potential imperialist activity, there may nonetheless be a motivation for the government to undertake it if (1) there is a class interest in the activity, *and* (2) the interested class has the disproportionate power to induce the government to undertake the activity even though other classes stand to lose more than the particular class expects to gain by it.

1. A major national motivation for imperialism that is always cited and most strongly emphasized by orthodox theorists is to enhance *national security*. It is argued that every nation has a collective interest in defending its territory against possible attack by other nations that may be or may become hostile and aggressive. Nations that are sufficiently powerful to engage in imperialist activity will find that efforts to control other nations can contribute significantly to national security by improving the military posture of the imperialist nation vis-à-vis its actual or potential enemies.

2. A second possible national motivation for imperialism is one that is suggested in the work of many radical theorists: to maintain *macroeconomic prosperity*, i.e., to avoid economic crises that threaten the viability of the whole economy.[4] [Five variants of this argument have been omitted.]

3. The desire to maintain macroeconomic prosperity and to avoid major crises is not the only possible national economic motivation for imperialism. Most writers would agree that imperialism may be motivated on national economic grounds simply in order to increase the *aggregate economic gains* accruing to the imperialist nation from its economic relations with other nations.

4. A fourth kind of national motivation for imperialism that has been suggested by some writers is based on a generalized *missionary spirit*. It is argued that the people of a nation can be so imbued with a belief in the desirability of their own institutions and values that they feel morally

---

[4] The desire to maintain macroeconomic prosperity is often presented by radical theorists in the context of a capitalist society as a class-based rather than a national motivation for imperialism. The reasoning is that only the dominant classes have a real interest in maintaining prosperity because it is primarily they who benefit from the existing economic system, while most of the people would be better off under another system which might replace a crisis-stricken capitalism. But this long-run outcome is problematic: in the short run everyone stands to lose if the economy is in crisis. Thus there is at least a short-run national interest —and possibly also a long-run national interest—in maintaining economic prosperity. This kind of national interest is quite distinct from the kind of class interests in which the short-run and the long-run benefits accrue only to particular classes.

justified—indeed morally obliged—to extend their system to other parts of the world, even where this requires the use of power to impose the system on recalcitrant foreigners.

5. A final national motivation for imperialism resembles the missionary spirit in that it involves psychic rather than military-strategic or economic gains: this arises simply from a generalized *urge to dominate.* Proponents of this view often contend that there is inherent in human nature an aggressive instinct that applies both on an individual and a group or national level.

A. Among possible class-based motivations for imperialism one can identify first a motivation based on the interest of the dominant classes of any unequal society in promoting their own *social legitimacy.* There are several ways in which imperialist actions might serve to legitimate the dominance of some classes over others within a nation. By generating or accentuating antagonisms between the nation and other nations on an international level, imperialism can deflect attention and concern away from internal conflicts between dominant and subordinate classes and rally all people behind the leadership of the dominant classes. By maintaining or extending the geographical spread of institutions and values characteristic of the imperialist nation, and by limiting the spread of alternative institutions and values, imperialism can discourage the notion that there are any real alternatives to the existing system with its particular class relations. For such reasons a national "missionary spirit," and indeed excessive concern over "national security," may actually result from the efforts of dominant classes to promote their own social legitimacy on an ideological plane.

B. A second possible class-based motivation for imperialism may arise from the interest of civilian or military government bureaucracies in *organizational expansion.*

C. One last major class-based motivation for imperialism, most frequently stressed by radical writers, arises from opportunities for particular firms, agencies or classes to increase their *particular economic gains* from international economic relations. Such opportunities are as varied as the opportunities cited earlier for increasing the aggregate economic gains from international economic relations, the only difference being that in this case there may be losses to other groups within the society which outweigh the gains from imperialism.

MOTIVATIONS FOR AMERICAN IMPERIALISM

To demonstrate the plausibility of a motivation for imperialism one must first identify an interest in imperialism and then show that the structure of power is such that the interest in imperialism will be reflected in government policy. In the case of a national interest one need only show that there is no class opposed to imperialist activity which has sufficient power to prevent it. In the case of a class interest one must show that the interested class has sufficient power to promote imperialist activity.

1. Explanations for American imperialism based on a *national security* interest have a ring of plausibility. American political leaders have not hesitated in the postwar period to brand the Soviet Union or China as an aggressive hostile power and to justify military interventions and military bases around the world as necessary to protect the United States against enemy attack. Yet it is difficult to see how any rational calculus based on national security considerations could explain many instances of American intervention that have taken place in small and/or distant countries such as Vietnam, the Dominican Republic, Guatemala, etc., which pose no visible threat to American security no matter with whom they might be allied. Nor is it plausible that national security considerations could require American economic dominance of many countries in the world with little economic or military potential. Of course, an irrational calculus might give rise to exaggerated notions of what is required for American national security, but to appeal to irrationality to explain such a persistent pattern of behavior is to place much too heavy a burden on a thin reed. Granted that a national security interest probably plays some role in motivating American imperialism, it cannot by any stretch of the imagination be regarded as the primary tap-root.

2. The possibility that American imperialism has been motivated by a national interest in promoting *macroeconomic prosperity* is one which has given rise to a great deal of controversy. Several orthodox theorists have undertaken detailed analyses which purport to demonstrate that the American economy is not structurally dependent upon imperialism for its prosperity, i.e., that it could maintain its prosperity without resorting to any imperialist activity. This proposition may well be true. But even if imperialist activity was not absolutely necessary to maintain prosperity, it remains perfectly possible that imperialist activity has been—and will continue to be—motivated by an interest in promoting prosperity. One need only show that imperialism *can* contribute to prosperity, and that it is plausible to attribute some American imperialist activity to this motivation.

The first two variants of the macroeconomic prosperity motivation for imperialism are based on the presumed need to maintain a high level of aggregate demand. There can be little question that the maintenance of an adequate level of aggregate demand has been an important economic policy problem of the U.S. government. Several postwar recessions attest to the persistence and the difficulty of the problem. It is also undeniable that increases in net exports (exports minus imports) and/or military expenditures contribute to higher levels of aggregate demand. And one can envision circumstances in which imperialist activity could promote both of these sources of demand. Hence, these arguments for a macroeconomic prosperity interest in imperialism are logically valid; the only question is whether they are empirically plausible in the context of the postwar United States.

A glance at the relevant macroeconomic statistics casts great doubt on the significance of net capital exports in maintaining aggregate demand. Throughout the postwar period net exports from the United States have rarely exceeded 1% of the gross national product (GNP), and in recent years they have actually become negative. One might argue that in the absence of imperialist activity the net export figures would have been even lower, but the quantities involved are so small in relation to total GNP that it is quite implausible to suggest that American imperialism has been motivated to any significant extent by a national interest in promoting macroeconomic prosperity through higher net exports.

The case that military expenditures have been undertaken to bolster aggregate demand is much stronger. The rate of military spending as a proportion of GNP has varied between 7% and 13% since 1950, and military spending has been by far the largest single component of aggregate demand under government control. Moreover, there has been an unmistakable correlation between periods of relatively high military expenditures and periods of relatively high levels of aggregate demand. Such observations are suggestive, although by no means conclusive. Even granting a significant role to military spending in maintaining aggregate demand, one must still consider whether it is plausible that imperialist activity has been motivated by an interest in keeping up military spending. Certainly many kinds of imperialist activity—from the maintenance of military bases abroad to actual military interventions abroad—serve to increase the demand for military expenditures. Moreover, by antagonizing other nations imperialist activities can increase the threat of military action against the imperialist nation or its nationals abroad and thereby indirectly contribute to a greater demand for military expenditures. But the fact that imperialism often results in higher military expenditures does not prove that it is undertaken even in part for that purpose. There are many ways in which an increase in military spending can be and has been justified by the American government (e.g., in terms of national security), and it seems rather implausible to suggest that imperialist activity has been intended to legitimize military spending.

The three remaining motivations for imperialism based on a national interest in macroeconomic prosperity focus on the need for foreign investment, exports and imports, respectively.

Turning first to foreign investment, there is no doubt that the magnitude and rate of growth of U.S. direct private investment abroad in the postwar period has been formidable. The total value of U.S. direct private foreign investment rose from $11 billion in 1950 to $86 billion by 1971. As a proportion of the corresponding total value of U.S. corporate assets at home and abroad, direct private foreign assets represented approximately 5% in 1950 and 10% in 1971. The relative importance of after-tax profits from this foreign investment appears to have been even greater, rising from less than 10% of total after-tax corporate profits to approach 20% two decades later.

Should the U.S. economy suddenly be deprived of access to these foreign investment assets, it is likely that macroeconomic prosperity would be threatened. At the very least there would be a very difficult period of economic readjustment. Yet it does not follow that U.S. imperialist activity can plausibly be ascribed to an interest in assuring sufficient investment opportunities abroad to preserve macroeconomic prosperity. For many of these opportunities are available and will remain available whether or not the United States undertakes any imperialist activity. More than two-thirds of the total investment assets and more than one-half of the profits therefrom result from investment undertaken in the "developed" capitalist countries whose borders are generally open to foreign investors without serious hindrance.[5] Of the remaining U.S. assets and profits generated in the "under-developed" countries, some might well be dependent on the pursuit of an imperialist policy while others would not. But it is difficult to argue that the overall prosperity of the American economy would be seriously affected by the loss of investment opportunities that accounted for substantially less than 5% of total corporate assets and substantially less than 10% of total after-tax corporate profits. The U.S. economy—and certain particular firms —would suffer some economic losses, but there is every reason to believe that the economy would remain buoyant with a somewhat lower level of direct private investment abroad.

The case of exports is similar to the case of foreign investment: the magnitude of exports dependent upon the pursuit of an imperialist foreign policy appears too low to render plausible the hypothesis that American imperialism has been motivated to some extent by an interest in maintaining macroeconomic prosperity through export promotion.

At first glance it might appear that a similar case could be made for imports, whose total value as a proportion of GNP in the United States is virtually the same as that of exports, but imports can have a significance far greater than their nominal value if they consist of raw materials required as imports into some production process. For unless the flow of raw materials is maintained, the production of an entire industry may have to be cut back, and this in time can have significant repercussions throughout an interdependent industrialized economy.

The extent to which the American economy has come to make use of imported raw materials has been extensively documented in a variety of sources.

Granted that the United States currently imports significant quantities of key raw materials from "underdeveloped" countries, it remains to be determined whether imperialist activity may plausibly be motivated by an interest in keeping up the flow of such imports. Critics of this view have argued (1) that possibilities for substitution in the process of production or in the composition of end-products consumed are plentiful enough to provide alternatives to the import of any particular raw material, and/or (2) that imperialism is not necessary to assure access to needed imports because the exporters of key raw materials have nothing to gain (and much to lose) by denying their products to the huge American market. These arguments may hold in some long-run sense, and they may well support the proposition that the American economy is not critically dependent upon imperialism for its ultimate survival. But they do not rule out the possibility that imperialist activity may have been intended to contribute to macroeconomic prosperity within a shorter time horizon by preventing critical raw material shortages from arising. For in the short run it is very difficult to change production processes or consumption patterns, and in the short run it is quite possible that a raw material exporting country (or several such countries acting together) might withhold their exports from the United States for economic or political reasons. In conclusion, it appears

---

[5] Among the "developed" capitalist countries only Japan places strict limitations on foreign investment in the domestic economy.

that the only plausible argument that some American imperialist activity has been motivated by an interest in maintaining macroeconomic prosperity is one which is based on the importance of ensuring regular and dependable access to foreign sources of key raw materials.

3. Quite apart from any incentive for imperialism based on considerations of macroeconomic prosperity, there can be little doubt that an interest in *aggregate economic gains* has played some role in motivating American imperialism. American domination of many poor countries in the world has increased the share of the gains from trade and investment accruing to Americans rather than to citizens of the dominated countries or to citizens of rival industrialized capitalist countries. It would be quite implausible to suggest that the U.S. government would refrain from taking advantage of potential aggregate economic gains made possible by imperialist activity.

4. Turning now to national interests in imperialism based on psychic gains, one must consider the plausibility of the *missionary spirit* and the *urge to dominate* as contributing elements in motivating American imperialism. Certainly the U.S. government has often cast its imperialist activities in the light of a modern "white man's burden," and this has made imperialism more palatable for those involved in carrying it out. Without yet inquiring into the roots of the missionary spirit itself, one can plausibly attribute to it a role in encouraging American imperialism.

5. Like the missionary spirit, the urge to dominate would seem to be applicable to a significant extent to contemporary American society. It is trite but no less true to point out that most Americans are steeped in a competitive ethic that places a tremendous premium on winning. That there are always winners and losers, that some must be dominant and others subordinate—these are propositions that generally go unquestioned. It follows that there is a great urge to dominate, if only to avoid being dominated. And this individual urge is easily translated into a national urge to dominate other nations, whether or not there is a serious danger of being dominated. Again, without inquiring into the origins of the urge to dominate, it seems quite plausible to ascribe to it a role in motivating American imperialism.

Class interests in imperialist activity are almost invariably cloaked in an ideological cover that emphasizes alleged national interests. Sometimes a national interest is actually involved, but often the rhetoric of national interest merely serves to obscure situations in which only a class interest is really at stake.

A. One can quite plausibly ascribe to the dominant classes in the postwar United States a class interest in imperialism based on the desire to promote their own *social legitimacy*. By encouraging imperialist activity against actual or potential socialist societies in various parts of the world, the dominant classes in American society could hope to restrain the territorial spread or the success of institutions and values that might ultimately undermine the legitimacy—and hence threaten the viability—of the American capitalist system in which they dominate. Indeed, it is plausible to suggest that the ideology of anti-communism so prevalent in the United States and so often used to justify American imperialism has been promoted by the same interest of the dominant American classes in preserving

American capitalism against competing alternatives identified with socialism or communism.

B. The interest in *organizational expansion* of the civilian and especially
the military bureaucracies involved in American imperialist activity has
surely also been a force favoring postwar American imperialism.

C. Probably the most significant class interest in imperialism in the
postwar United States has been based on the opportunity for *particular
economic gains* by private enterprises. There can be no doubt that in the
postwar period many—if not all—American firms have had an economic
interest in some kind of imperialist activity. First of all, those firms that
have invested abroad, that export to foreign markets, or that import from
foreign sources have stood to gain by having the power of the American
government exercised on their behalf in shaping the terms and conditions
of foreign economic relations. Secondly, private firms without any past
involvement in foreign economic relations may nevertheless have looked
forward to future opportunities made possible by imperialist actions that
help to preserve or to extend the areas open to American private enterprise. Finally, even those firms that never trade or invest abroad have stood
to gain to the extent that imperialism promotes an increasing internationalization of the division of labor, for this places relatively scarce American
labor in increasing competition with relatively abundant foreign labor. For
all of these reasons it is no exaggeration to suggest that there exists a
substantial class interest in imperialism on the part of the American capitalist class.

It remains now to consider whether the distribution of power in the
United States has been such as to permit the interests in imperialism
identified above to be translated into imperialist government policy. To
answer this question one must first seek to identify those groups within
American society who have something to lose by imperialist activity and
might therefore possibly oppose it. First of all, there are all the taxpaying
citizens and firms who ultimately bear the financial burden of imperialism.
In the case of military action there are the soldiers who suffer injury or
death. There may also be particular groups whose interests are adversely
affected by the results of an imperialist activity: for example, the consumers of oil who pay higher prices when the monopolistic position of the
oil companies is protected; or the workers who lose their jobs because a
firm shifts its operations to a more profitable foreign location; or the
businesses which find themselves at a competitive disadvantage because a
rival firm secured a privileged position abroad.

In the case of a national interest in imperialism the losses to such
groups are by definition outweighed by the aggregate gains to whole population. There may even be offsetting gains to groups that have something
to lose. Only if a group that suffers net losses has also a vastly disproportionate power to influence government decisions on imperialism can it be
expected to prevent imperialist activity that is in the national interest. A
glance at the categories of possible losers listed above reveals little political
strength. The financial costs of imperialism are diffused widely among the
taxpaying public and may be offset by diffused aggregate gains. Soldiers
are disproportionately drawn from the poorest and politically weakest
strata of society. Consumers, workers and businesses who lose from a

particular imperialist activity tend to be isolated and organizationally weak. In sum, there is every reason to believe that in the postwar United States, a national interest in imperialism is sufficient to motivate government policy without serious opposition.

To demonstrate that a class interest in imperialism is sufficient to motivate government policy, even in the absence of a national interest, one must make a stronger case. It must be shown not only that the potentially anti-imperialist opposition tends to be weak, but also that the pro-imperialist class is disproportionately strong.

There are several factors that work to favor the beneficiaries of imperialist activity over the losers in the determination of American foreign policy. First, although the beneficiaries may be much fewer in number, they typically command much greater wealth and power than the losers and therefore have a vastly disproportionate influence on decision-making even in the most democratic of political frameworks. The dominant classes with an interest in promoting their own social legitimacy have by definition a dominant position and correspondingly disproportionate power to shape foreign policy. The civilian and military bureaucracies interested in organizational expansion can count on the potent political force represented by the Pentagon and its allies in the military-industrial complex in contemporary American society. And the capitalist class with its interest in particular economic gains is obviously much stronger economically and politically than the rest of American society. Moreover, within the capitalist class, the firms most directly involved in foreign economic operations include many of the most powerful corporations in the United States. In 1965, 9 of the largest 10 and at least 18 of the largest 25 corporations (ranked by sales) were significantly involved in foreign operations. These 18 corporations alone accounted for almost 20% of the total sales and almost 30% of the after-tax profits of all American industrial corporations. Hence even when there are conflicts of interest within the capitalist class over particular imperialist activities, the balance of power often tilts in favor of the pro-imperialists.

A second factor that enhances the effective power of the beneficiaries of imperialism is that the gains from an imperialist action tend to be large for the immediate beneficiaries while the losses tend to be spread widely and therefore thinly over the much larger number of losers.

Finally, the gainers from imperialism can often generate support—or at least consent—from among the objective losers by playing upon compelling ideological themes that suggest a national rather than a class interest.

In sum, the balance of power seems likely to tilt in favor of imperialism in contemporary American society unless the costs of a given activity become so high as to weigh heavily and obviously on large segments of the population, or unless the activity involves a sharp conflict of interest among powerful classes themselves. Such situations do arise from time to time (e.g., the war in Vietnam), and they set limits on the extent to which—or the manner in which—the U.S. government is motivated to pursue imperialist policies. But it is clear that long before such a point is reached there is a great deal of scope for American imperialism based on class interests without any national interest necessarily at stake.

One final point deserves mention here. The analysis in this essay has been developed in a framework of assumed rationality. To attribute a major role to misperceptions and irrationality in explaining American foreign policy is to subscribe to a fundamental cynicism about human behavior that would make social studies difficult and meaningful action virtually impossible.

CAPITALISM AND AMERICAN IMPERIALISM

Capitalism is a form of socioeconomic organization (or a "mode of production," to use the Marxist term) which is characterized by *all* of the following conditions.

(1) *Private ownership of the means of production:* a significant share of the productive wealth of the society is owned by private individuals pursuing private profits.

(2) *Proletarianization of the work force:* a large proportion of the population has virtually no claim to ownership of the means of production and is obliged to sell its labor services in the labor market in order to receive any income. Conversely, a small proportion of the population owns most of the means of production.

(3) *Hierarchical control of the production process:* economic activity is carried out by units of enterprise in which decision-making control is vested in (at most) a few top owners and managers while the great majority of workers have no such control.

(4) *Individual material gain incentives:* labor is allocated and work is motivated by a system of differential economic rewards in the form of money wages and profits received by individual workers and owners of the means of production.

There can be no doubt that the form of socioeconomic organization prevailing in the contemporary United States as well as in Canada, most of Western Europe, Japan, Australia and New Zealand, conforms to each aspect of the above definition of capitalism. Not so obvious, perhaps, is the fact that there is nothing inevitable or universal about the capitalist form of socioeconomic organization. Not only have earlier historical eras displayed examples of societies that are characterized by few or none of the conditions associated with capitalism, but contemporary "socialist" societies show evidence of varying degrees of departure from the four basic features of a capitalist society listed above.[6]

Certain consequences of the capitalist form of socioeconomic organization deserve emphasis here. The viability of any social system requires that there be a prevailing set of institutionalized values which encourage patterns of behavior consistent with the smooth functioning of the system. These values are an essential complement to the basic socioeconomic

---

[6] China appears to have moved farthest from a capitalist mode of production; Cuba to a lesser degree; and the Soviet Union only to the extent of abolishing private ownership of the means of production. For useful discussions of the contemporary Chinese mode of production, see Gurley (1971) and Riskin (1973).

institutions that define the system. In the case of capitalism, the successful operation of individual material gain incentives requires that people behave as "homo economicus," the economically rational man.

A second important consequence of capitalism concerns the process and the outcome of income distribution. Private ownership of the means of production and reliance on individual material gain incentives imply that in a capitalist society income distribution is linked directly to the process of production. This process of income distribution is bound to create great inequalities of income. Not only does the small proportion of the population that owns most of the means of production receive the lion's share of property income, but also labor income is very unequally distributed because of the need to allocate and motivate work through differential economic rewards. Hence, a capitalist society is inherently an economically unequal society.

A final important consequence of the capitalist form of socioeconomic organization stems from its inherent economic inequality and from the inherent social inequality that results from hierarchical control of the production process. Economic and social inequality (which are bound to be highly correlated) imply political inequality. A society that is predicated upon significant economic and social differentials is a society in which there cannot be a genuine democracy, in the sense of equal participation in political decision-making by those affected by the decision. So long as some people have much greater access to economic resources than others, they can have much greater influence on political decision-making; and so long as the structure of decision-making at the workplace is highly authoritarian, one cannot expect the structure of decision-making at the community or national level to be egalitarian. Thus capitalism is fundamentally incompatible with democracy.

The question to be considered now is whether the sources of American imperialism identified [earlier in this essay] are related in any significant manner to the capitalist institutions that characterize the contemporary United States, or—alternately—whether they have little to do with the specifically capitalistic character of American socioeconomic organization. In the following paragraphs, I will examine each plausible source of American imperialism to evaluate its relationship to capitalism.

1. The first motivation for imperialism that appeared applicable to the contemporary United States was based on a national interest in *national security*. So long as the world is divided into nation-states without an accepted and respected superior authority to maintain world peace, each individual nation-state will have some justifiable concern about its national security. Hence the national security motivation for imperialism is one which would not seem to be attributable in any significant sense to capitalism, or to any other specific form of socioeconomic organization.

2. Among various motivations for imperialism arising from a national interest in *macroeconomic prosperity*, the only one that appeared plausible in the context of the contemporary United States was based on a need to secure access to foreign sources of key raw materials. At first glance such a need does not seem to be peculiar to capitalism. If the American economy is critically dependent upon key raw materials, it is hard to see why this

dependence should be any less significant under some form of socioeconomic organization other than capitalism. Yet closer examination of the question suggests a line of reasoning which might well link raw-material oriented imperialism in some degree to capitalism.

The demand for raw materials in an economy depends upon both the aggregate level and the sectoral composition of output. The higher the level of output, and the more heavily the sectoral composition of output is weighted toward industries requiring imported raw materials, the greater will be the demand for such imports. Given the emphasis placed on economic growth in a capitalist society, one can argue that capitalism is likely to generate a more rapid rate of growth of output and correspondingly higher levels of demand for imported raw materials than might an alternative form of socioeconomic organization. Moreover, the very unequal distribution of income associated with capitalism may lead to a sectoral composition of output that is oriented more heavily toward products requiring imported raw material inputs than would be the case under conditions of greater equality. For the kind of products whose production is most dependent upon the import of key raw materials tend to be industrial and technologically sophisticated (e.g., jet engines), and such products cater disproportionately to the demand of rich consumers. The demand of the poor and middle-income classes is more heavily concentrated on agricultural and simpler industrial products whose production is less dependent on scarce raw materials. Assuming that the composition of output reflects to some extent the structure of demand,[7] inequality in the distribution of income will be associated with greater dependence on key raw material imports.

Obviously a non-capitalist society could also generate a motivation for imperialist activity designed to secure access to foreign sources of raw materials. But there are nonetheless grounds for believing that under otherwise similar circumstances such a motivation would be especially strong under capitalism because of its emphasis on economic growth and its inherent economic inequality.

3. A national interest in *aggregate economic gains*—like a national interest in macroeconomic prosperity—could serve to motivate imperialist activity both in capitalist and in non-capitalist societies. But again there is good reason to believe that such a motivation would be particularly forceful under capitalism. First of all, the emphasis placed on the desirability of increasing the available supply of goods and services in a capitalist society puts a great premium on the ability of a government to promote economic growth. In a society where there is such pressure to "deliver the goods," the government will be more highly motivated to seek out and exploit opportunities for economic gain through imperialism than it would in a society where other social goals were relatively more important.

One alternative social goal that is notably de-emphasized under capitalism is economic self-sufficiency. Capitalism encourages a relatively high degree of economic specialization in order to reap the economic gains

---

[7] In principle foreign trade can break the link between the composition of domestic output and the structure of domestic demand, but in practice trade is never carried out so extensively as to divorce the two entirely.

made possible by a wide division of labor. Hence a capitalist society is likely to be more heavily involved in international economic relations than an alternative society with greater orientation to self-sufficiency and a capitalist government would have correspondingly greater opportunities as well as a greater incentive to secure economic gains from imperialism.

4. The existence of a national *missionary spirit* that motivates imperialism requires that two conditions be satisfied. On the one hand, there must be a strong belief by the people of a society that their own way of life is a superior one. On the other hand, there must be a belief in the acceptability of imposing a way of life on others through the use of dominant power. The first of these conditions cannot be identified more strongly with one form of socioeconomic organization than another. For good or bad reasons, people in both capitalist and non-capitalist societies may well come to believe in the superiority of their own system. But whether people will find acceptable the use of power to spread a system depends upon the extent to which concern about outcomes overrides concern about the processes whereby outcomes are achieved. The more highly the values of a society stress genuine democracy—participation in decision-making by those affected by the decisions—the less acceptable will be the imposition of a system on others no matter how "good" for them it may appear to be. Hence the more truly democratic the form of socioeconomic organization, the less will be the motivation for imperialism based upon a *missionary spirit*. And because capitalism precludes true democracy, a capitalist society will be more susceptible to undertake missionary imperialism than an alternative society more compatible with democracy.

5. The *urge to dominate* as a source of imperialism is often described as an innate human drive, an element of human nature impervious to the social environment. Yet it seems quite unreasonable to insist that the form of socioeconomic organization and the values that complement it have no influence on the attitude of people toward one another. The more competitive a society, the more an individual is likely to be motivated to dominate others, and the more the society as a whole may be motivated to dominate other societies. Without question capitalism is a highly competitive form of social organization, and the urge to dominate is therefore more likely to motivate imperialism in a capitalist society than in many other less competitive social systems.

For a class interest alone to motivate imperialism, there must be a class with both the interest and the power to influence the government to undertake an activity that is not in any national interest. In studying the relationship between capitalism and class-based imperialism, one must therefore examine both the nature of class interests and the distribution of class power. Turning first to the question of power, it is clear that there can be no class-based motivation for imperialism in a genuine democracy. For if everyone in a society participated equally in the political process, the government could not undertake imperialist activities whose anticipated costs to the society as a whole were greater than the anticipated benefits to a particular class. Since capitalism is incompatible with true democracy, a capitalist society offers a potential for class-based imperialism of various kinds which would not be possible in an alternative democratic society.

It can also be argued, however, that capitalism generates certain class interests in imperialism that would either be absent or be less forceful under other possible forms of socioeconomic organization. This appears to be true of at least two of the three types of class interest that [have already been cited] as applicable to the contemporary United States.

A. A class interest in promoting *social legitimacy* through imperialism becomes significant whenever dominant classes in a society have reason to be concerned about the acceptance of their dominance by the rest of the people. As a very unequal form of socioeconomic organization, capitalism obviously generates some dominant classes, and these classes have a potentially greater concern about their social legitimacy than would (less) dominant classes in a more equal society. But while its basic economic institutions imply profound inequalities, the value system associated with capitalism—with its emphasis on the right (and obligation) of individuals to compete wth one another in striving for personal advancement—suggests an ideal of free and fair competition. As people within a capitalist society come to recognize how unfree and unfair the competition often is (because of the inequality inherent in the underlying institutions), they are unlikely to accept the domination of the dominant classes. Thus under capitalism a contradiction between the socioeconomic base and certain aspects of the ideological superstructure will increase the interest of dominant classes in providing some kind of legitimacy for their dominance. For the reasons suggested [previously], imperialism can help to serve this purpose.

B. A class interest in promoting *organizational expansion* through imperialism would not appear to be more or less likely under capitalism than under any other form of socioeconomic organization.

C. Of the three types of class interest in imperialism discussed in this paper, it is the class interest in *particular economic gains* that is most clearly linked to capitalism as a form of socioeconomic organization.

To see this, one must recognize that an imperialist activity motivated by a class interest in economic gain involves in effect an anticipated redistribution of economic benefits from the rest of the population to the particular interested class. This redistribution does not involve any direct transfer, but it results indirectly from (1) taxing (or otherwise burdening) the society as a whole for the cost of the activity, and (2) benefitting the particular class by bringing about changes in the international economic situation which increase its income-earning opportunities.

It is precisely the *indirect* character of the distribution that makes it attractive to particular classes in a capitalist society. For under capitalism income is supposed to be distributed to individuals in accordance with their market-valued contribution to production. Hence any significant redistribution in favor of the rich and powerful can be brought about only indirectly by government activity which affects the *process* by which the market distributes incomes.

In a society where income were distributed according to explicitly political criteria rather than according to an apparently apolitical economic mechanism, it would make no difference whether redistribution of income were brought about directly or indirectly. The outcome of the income distribution process would be the object of concern rather than the process itself. In such a situation a powerful group would find it no easier to get income redistributed by an activity that might reduce the size of the aggregate economic pie. But under capitalism redistribution in favor of powerful groups can be brought about only indirectly. Hence in any government activity which indirectly redistributes income in favor of particular classes, even if the activity involves aggregate economic losses. There are a variety of ways in which a government can indirectly redistribute income, through domestic as well as foreign programs. But imperialist activity clearly offers many such opportunities, and a class interest in achieving particular economic gains through imperialism is therefore significantly linked to the capitalist form of socioeconomic organization.

CONCLUSION

The [preceding] analysis leaves no doubt that postwar American imperialism can be traced in significant respects to the capitalist character of American society. The only relevant source of imperialism that appears to be quite unrelated to the internal socioeconomic organization of the United States is the one based upon a national interest in national security. Not surprisingly, this is the source that is given the greatest (if not the sole) attention by orthodox theorists. But every other relevant source of American imperialism based upon a national interest, as well as every source based upon a class interest,[8] is conditioned by certain aspects of the (capitalist) internal socioeconomic organization of the United States. The radical view that American imperialism cannot be adequately explained without reference to American capitalism is therefore fully confirmed.

It cannot be argued that capitalism is the only form of socioeconomic organization that leads to imperialism, nor even that capitalism is more likely than any other form of socioeconomic organization to lead to imperialism. What does follow from the analysis of this paper is that capitalism leads to substantially more imperialist activity than would result from at least some alternative forms of internal socioeconomic organization under similar external circumstances.

The analysis also lends no support to the proposition that a capitalist society requires imperialism in order to survive. This proposition may be asserted by some radicals, but it is more often attributed to radicals by orthodox theorists who find it convenient to present radical views in simplistic and therefore vulnerable form. It is virtually impossible to prove that imperialism is necessary for the survival of a capitalist society, for there are many means by which a capitalist society could conceivably remain viable. Yet the fact that a capitalist society may in theory be able to survive without imperialism in no way diminishes the extent to which capitalist institutions can and do in practice stimulate imperialist activity.

Within the context of a capitalist society, the motivations for the government to undertake imperialist activity may be lessened to the extent (1) that the primacy of economic gain as a social objective can be dimin-

---

[8] All class-based motivations for imperialism are conditioned by capitalism because they depend for their force on the absence of genuine democracy, and capitalism precludes genuine democracy.

ished; (2) that the distribution of income can be made a more explicitly political issue; and (3) that income inequality can be reduced and democracy can be made more effective.

But one must recognize that the very nature of capitalist society places significant limits on the extent to which political reform movements can expect to curtail imperialism under capitalism. An egalitarian society in which economic activity was based upon collective rather than individual incentives and cooperative rather than competitive behavior would encourage a set of institutionalized values in which social goals other than economic gain were paramount and would facilitate the functioning of a truly effective democracy. Utopian as such a system may appear to contemporary observers, it represents the kind of long-run goal toward which an anti-imperialist movement must be directed if it is to achieve any significant and lasting progress.

26

Growing Wealth, Declining Power

Paul M. Sweezy

I

I shall be talking about the U.S. empire as it has taken shape in the period since the Second World War, and I should explain at the outset that by "empire" I mean not only a mother country and its colonies, nor even only a metropolis and the whole collection of its clients and dependents regardless of their juridical status. I mean a metropolis and the ensemble of its international economic and political interests. As used here, therefore, "empire" and "imperialism" are terms which refer to the international aspects of monopoly capitalism in the advanced industrial countries.

One other preliminary: the driving force of imperialism, as of capitalism generally, is the inherent self-expansionism of capital. This idea does not exist for bourgeois economics, but it is central to Marxian economics. Those to whom it is unfamiliar should read Part 2 of Volume 1 of *Capital*, which is only 34 pages long and amply repays careful study. In its incessant drive to expand, capital pushes aside or leaps over all barriers such as industry boundaries and national frontiers. This explains why the typical and dominant units of capital in the period of monopoly capitalism are both conglomerate and multinational—giant corporations operating in many industries and many countries. The global expansion of these giant corporations has been the core phenomenon of U.S. imperialism in the last quarter century.

II

An empire is a structured system with the metropolis at its head and a hierarchy of subordinate units under it. It operates according to certain rules and norms which are enforced by an appropriate mechanism of rewards, sanctions, and, in the final analysis, force. These rules and norms are both national and international in character, and so also must be the enforcement machinery. Each unit in a capitalist empire must obviously enable capital to function more or less freely within its jurisdiction, which means there must be reasonable security for private property and an exploitable labor force. (In Marxian theory an exploitable labor force means a labor force which is obliged to sell itself to capital in order to make a living.) As between the units of an empire there must be relatively unimpeded mobility of commodities and money and to a certain extent labor (at least particular kinds of labor). Flows of capital and profit of course take the form of money flows. It follows that for the international structure of a capitalist empire the trading and monetary systems are crucially important. The enforcement of the appropriate conditions with respect to property and labor is in the first instance the responsibility of national (or colonial) governments, while the shaping and enforcement of the trading and monetary system is basically a function of the metropolis. According to this view a capitalist empire is essentially a collection of countries practicing or open to the capitalist mode of production and accepting the lead of the most powerful among them in trade and monetary matters. We would then have to say that a country leaves the empire if it either (1) changes its social system internally in such a way as to exclude capitalism, or (2) goes its own way in trade and monetary matters. The leading metropolis is naturally always on the lookout for tendencies of either kind and does its best to counteract them. This could be said to be the art of holding together and managing an empire.

III

Turning now to the American empire, let us look at the arrangements and mechanisms which were worked out during and after the Second World War to ensure its cohesion and functioning. Most American leaders of course do not think in terms of empire and imperialism; but there is no doubt that these terms, if understood in the sense just indicated, accurately describe their intentions and actions. Their language runs in terms of the free world and its leadership. By "free world" they of course mean a world open to capitalist enterprise; and by "leadership"—which they never doubted could belong only to the United States—they mean the right to determine the operating rules of the free world and the possession of the necessary military strength to see that these rules are adhered to.

U.S. policies during and after the war therefore had three main purposes: (1) keeping as many countries as possible in the American empire, alias the free world, which means preventing revolutions and promoting counter-revolutions; (2) devising an appropriate set of international rules and institutions; and (3) building up predominant military strength. Let us examine these in turn.

The free world suffered the loss of Eastern Europe in the war itself, as the Red Army moved into the middle of the continent. To prevent further loss after the war required massive U.S. aid for the reconstruction of Western European capitalism (loans to Britain, Marshall Plan, etc.). This effort succeeded. In Asia another massive effort (much bigger than most people in this country recognize) failed to block the Chinese Revolution or to prevent the "loss" of North Korea and North Vietnam. Since then, the United States has had to fight two major wars to prevent further losses in Asia—in Korea in the 1950s and in Vietnam in the 1960s. One further loss, however, was suffered, in Cuba. And a series of counter-revolutions instigated or backed by the United States has been necessary to prevent further defections—in Greece, Iran, Guatemala, the Dominican Republic, and most recently Chile. (Other cases, e.g., Lebanon and Indonesia, might plausibly be included in the list.) One can say without any fear of exaggeration that this problem of preventing more losses has never been absent in the last quarter century and at all times has been one of the dominant concerns of American policy-makers. It is this aspect which accounts for anti-communism's becoming the ideological keystone of American imperialism, playing somewhat the same role as the "white man's burden" in nineteenth-century British imperialism.

Next we come to the devising of appropriate international rules and institutions for the system as a whole. A dominant economic power naturally favors two things: free trade (at least for everyone else) and the universal acceptance of its money as a standard of value and means of international payment. Thus Britain was the champion of free trade in its imperial heyday, and London's pre-eminence in finance and banking was such as to enthrone the pound sterling as the world's premier currency. The United States set out to pursue similar policies and achieve a similar position long before the end of the Second World War. Lend-lease assistance to allies during the war was as far as possible coupled with the requirement that recipient countries liberalize their trade policies after the war; and an attempt to universalize the liberalization of trade policies was undertaken with the creation in 1947 of the General Agreement on Tariffs and Trade (GATT). Meanwhile, the system's most important new international institutions had been created at the famous Bretton Woods conference in 1944. Bretton Woods established gold and the dollar as co-equal in international monetary matters: the value of gold was fixed at $35 to the ounce, and all other countries were obligated to treat them as the same in their reserve and payments activities. As subsequent experience was to show, this amounted to presenting the United States with a free gold mine. It was a wonderful system—while it lasted. Bretton Woods also set up the International Monetary Fund (IMF) and the World Bank, a kind of stick-and-carrot arrangement for keeping lesser countries in line.

Finally we come to the military aspect of the American empire. Washington's original intention was to keep an effective monopoly over the system's military power in its own hands. Other countries were to have enough military strength to combat internal subversion, but not much more; and the various national military establishments were to be kept tied as closely as possible to the Pentagon. Any large-scale fighting against the "enemy" would be done by the United States using its own forces and calling on its allies for no more than token support. (The enemy, of course, was called communism and consisted of two parts, which as time went on had less and less to do with each other: on the one hand, the socialist countries, and, on the other, revolutionary national liberation movements in the Third World.) This policy involved the necessity for the United States to build a huge military machine costing tens of billions of dollars annually. From the point of view of U.S. monopoly capitalism, paradoxically, this was all to the good: during the whole postwar period it has been this astronomical military budget which has maintained relative prosperity in the United States and thereby prevented the entire capitalist system from sinking once again into a new great depression like that of the 1930s. As we shall see, however, the possibility of maintaining a near monopoly of military power (though not the policy of huge military budgets) gradually eroded and now, like almost everything else related to the U.S. empire, faces a highly uncertain future.

IV

But before we get to this aspect of the problem, it is necessary to record some of the successes achieved by the American metropolis during the period of its greatest power, roughly the 1950s and the first half of the 1960s. One was negative, the holding of losses after the victory of the Chinese Revolution to one small country, Cuba. On the positive side, by far the greatest success was the enormous expansion on a global scale— throughout the entire free world/empire—of giant U.S. multinational corporations.

At the end of the Second World War the direct foreign investments of U.S. corporations were about the same as they had been at the beginning of the great depression of the 1930s. By 1950 when official figures began to be published, direct foreign investment stood at about $12 billion, which was still a relatively unimportant fraction of the total assets of U.S. corporations. By the end of 1972, 23 years later, the total had increased to $94 billion or by nearly 700 percent. It should be added that this is book value, which everyone knows is much less than market value. The head of the European bureau of the *Wall Street Journal* has estimated that on the average the market value of foreign investments is around three times book value. It is thus obvious that official figures understate rather than overstate the magnitude of the expansion which has taken place in the postwar period.

According to the logic of orthodox economics, this is in no sense a manifestation of American imperialism, let alone of exploitation of other countries. On the contrary, the economists argue, it must be obvious to anyone with eyes to see that by investing tens of billions of dollars in other countries the American corporations have been conferring enormous benefits on the recipients. But let us look a bit more closely. First, where did all that capital for foreign investment come from? If we look at figures for capital actually exported from the United States, we find that of the $82 billion increase in foreign holdings between 1950 and 1972, about $50 billion represented actual capital exports. The remainder was furnished by the recipient countries themselves, either in the form of reinvested earnings of foreign subsidiaries of American corporations or of borrowing by these subsidiaries in local money markets. In other words, during this period U.S. corporations, in addition to sending abroad $50 billion, absorbed more than $30 billion of savings generated in the foreign countries themselves.

Well, you may say, that does cut down on the size of the net benefit conferred on the recipient countries, but isn't it still pretty big? But again we must take a closer look. We have been taking account of only one side of the ledger. Investment is a two-way street: in one direction flows capital, in the other, income. And when we examine this other flow, i.e., of income from the recipient countries to the metropolis, we find a truly startling picture. While the capital outflow was $50 billion, the income inflow was $99 billion, almost exactly twice as much! The upshot is that giant U.S. corporations have been draining enormous amounts out of the rest of the free world while at the same time acquiring control over a larger and larger share of the rest of the free world's assets. This, I submit, is what U.S. imperialism is all about.

V

It is a commonplace that in the last two years U.S. imperialism has been in a period of crisis. The institutions established at the end of the Second World War are in a shambles: the Bretton Woods system collapsed during the later 1960s and was officially buried by Nixon's speech of August 15, 1971; the trade liberalization principles underlying GATT are flouted more openly every day, not least by the United States itself; the once almighty dollar had to be devalued twice in two years, and no one knows whether its recent recovery is more than a flash in the pan. At the same time the supposed military omnipotence of the United States has been exposed as a lie by the Vietnamese: after nearly ten years of fighting in Indochina—at one time with an army of more than half a million and more airpower than was deployed in the whole of the Second World War—the United States finally had to withdraw, leaving large parts of South Vietnam in the hands of the Provisional Revolutionary Government. Moreover, and this may be the hardest blow of all, Vietnam has shown that the people of the United States are simply not prepared to support counter-revolutionary wars, nor are conscripted armies willing to fight them.

Most of the assumptions on which the American empire was based have either crumbled or been called into serious question. And yet the underlying expansionist drive of U.S. corporate capital has not been checked or even slowed down. On the contrary, it has been accelerating and gathering momentum just when the institutions which nurtured and protected it were foundering. Let me adduce a few facts in support of this statement.

According to official figures (*Survey of Current Business*, September 1973), additions to U.S. direct investments abroad in 1972 were slightly less than the record amount of the previous year ($7.9 billion as against $8.0 billion), but the financing of the increase differed markedly. Reinvested earnings accounted for $3.2 billion in 1971 and $4.5 billion in 1972; while capital outflow from the United States dropped from $4.9 billion in 1971 to $3.4 billion in 1972. In other words, the so-called recipient countries are paying for more and more of the U.S. corporations' investments within their borders. On the income side, too, the corporations never had it so good. The take in dividends and interest (not including royalties, fees, and funds transferred through phony pricing of intra-firm shipments) was $10.4 billion in 1972 as against $9.5 billion in 1971. And, in the words of the *Survey of Current Business:* "Identifiable U.S. corporate transactions had a net favorable impact of $8.9 billion on the 1972 U.S. balance of payments, up $4.0 billion from 1971." No signs of crisis in *that* quarter!

Leaving aggregate statistics for a moment, let us note how the business world itself sees the situation. A leading article in the *Wall Street Journal* of November 1, 1973, is headlined as follows: FOREIGN VENTURES FETCH MORE PROFIT FOR FIRMS BASED IN UNITED STATES—DEVALUATION IS A HELP: GAINS IN SALES KEEP EARNINGS UP FOR REINVESTMENT ABROAD—"OPPORTUNITIES ARE UNLIMITED." And here are some excerpts from the story which follows:

U.S. corporations have created real money-making machines by investing in operations abroad.

The pounds—and the francs, marks, lire, pesetas, and yen—are flowing in this year.

On top of a profitable 1972 for foreign operations, many U.S.-based companies expect 1973 to wind up even better. Some are looking for profit increases of 30 percent, 40 percent, and 50 percent on their already lucrative foreign operations. In some cases, profits from abroad will offset lackluster domestic trends. . . .

You can run your finger down the list of the 500 biggest industrial firms in the United States, stop at most any one of them, and find an international success story this year. Union Carbide earned $44.7 million abroad in 1971 and $62.9 million in 1972; this year, the company says, should prove another winner. Hercules Inc., a big Delaware chemicals concern, says it is "doing just fabulously abroad." All three big automobile makers report sharply rising foreign earnings. Though International Business Machines Corporation won't talk publicly about this year's foreign earnings, analysts think they are partly responsible for what looks like a rich year for IBM. "IBM is very, very healthy overseas," says one analyst.

Polaroid, for the third straight year, expects its foreign sales to rise by more than 30 percent from prior-year sales. Profits? They're "increasing at rates exceeding the sales gains," says Thomas H. Wyman, senior vice president.

International Harvester's foreign profits nearly doubled in 1972 to $86.6 million from $45.2 million in 1971. . . . International Telephone and Telegraph Co., with 32 percent of its assets abroad, got 45 percent of its net income overseas last year, up from 35 to 40 percent in the previous four years. . . .

Demand abroad is so great, says Harvester's Mr. Voss, that "neither we nor our competitors have had enough production to take advantage of it." "The opportunities for Proctor & Gamble's products overseas seem almost unlimited," says a P&G spokesman; the company's foreign earnings have more than doubled over three years. . . .

"The potential for expansion of the soft-drink business is greater outside the United States simply because of the maturity of the business in this country," says a Coca-Cola spokesman. Coca-Cola got 55 percent of its total profits overseas last year, up from 53 percent in 1971.

And still there are people who will tell you that the American economy is only marginally involved in international affairs!

VI

Let us pause and try to fit together some of the parts of the total picture. We have seen that at the end of the Second World War the United States in effect turned the whole free world into an empire under its military and economic hegemony. In these circumstances, U.S. monopoly capital in the form of giant multinational corporations exploded throughout the parts of the globe open to it, and this is continuing at an accelerating rate. In the meantime, however, the Vietnam war and the collapse of the Bretton Woods monetary system have gravely impaired the structures which organized, stabilized, and guaranteed U.S. hegemony. In other words, while the U.S. empire is growing more rapidly than ever before in terms of wealth, it is becoming steadily weaker in terms of financial and military power. One cannot help wondering whether this is not an absolute contradiction. How long can growing wealth and declining power continue to coexist? Historical experience over many centuries and even millennia suggest that they cannot coexist for very long.

The U.S. ruling class will of course do its utmost to arrest and reverse the decline in the nation's financial and military power. For my part, I do not believe there is any prospect of being able to restore the kind of trade and financial dominance which characterized the period of hegemony. There is no longer anything that can be called an international monetary system in the sense that the old gold standard and the dollar/gold standard of the Bretton Woods arrangements were international monetary systems. The currencies of the advanced capitalist countries float against each other and will probably continue to do so. This is always a situation which invites fragmentation, competitive devaluations, controls on money and capital flows, etc. Weaker countries tend to tie their currencies and hence their whole economies to those of stronger countries. Out of this situation there are likely to arise rival blocs having increasingly the character of rival empires. The world has had a good deal of experience with rival empires, and so far the rivalry has always ended in major wars. No one can predict that this will happen again, but neither is there any guarantee that it will not. In any case the freedom of U.S. corporations to go on expanding inside other countries and/or empires is hardly likely to remain what it has been. And as economic warfare heats up, the temptation for developed capitalist countries harboring large U.S. investments to nationalize American-owned branches and subsidiaries will steadily mount.*

---

* There may even come a time when the United States too will fall under such temptation. Reporting on the testimony of John J. McCloy before a Senate committee inquiring into the background of the energy crisis, the *New York Times* reporter included the following tidbit: "As an aside, Senator Case asked if the Shah [of Iran] should be allowed to use Iran's new oil profits 'to buy a controlling share in General Motors.' Mr. McCloy answered, 'Let them come in, then nationalize them. The Arabs learned that.'" (February 7) McCloy, it should be remembered, is one of the most powerful elders of the American business establishment.

27

U.S. Capital in Puerto Rico: The Dollar Brings Destruction

The Committee for Puerto Rican Decolonization

The penetration of the Puerto Rican economy by the United States began with the U.S. military invasion and occupation of the island in 1898. In the course of three years, 1899–1902, the sugar and tobacco industries were developed, protected by U.S. tariffs. These industries thus became the fountainhead for U.S. domination of Puerto Rico, preventing the development of Puerto Rican national control over its own economy.

During the late 1930's, fifty-one corporations, predominately U.S. owned, controlled a total of 249,000 acres of the island. Six-tenths of 1% of the farms owned 31% of all farm land and controlled 44% of the total value of the land, structures and agricultural equipment in Puerto Rico. The campesino, or jibaro, as he is called in Puerto Rico, who used to live off his own plot, no longer owned any land.

In 1942, the Economic Development Administration, or FOMENTO, started the first phase of "Operation Bootstrap." Backed by American interests and set into motion by the colonial governor of Puerto Rico, Rexford Tugwell, this plan was continued by the Commonwealth Government, established in 1952. Operation Bootstrap is supposedly a plan for the industrial development of Puerto Rico. Its answer to Puerto Rican underdevelopment is two-pronged: (1) encourage industrial developers with tax incentives and cheap labor; (2) develop a plan which the Commonwealth Government, the managing agency for United States capital in Puerto Rico, could follow to complete the development program.

Basically, industrial development was to consist of three stages. The first involved light government-owned industry, more of a trial balloon to prove to United States capitalists that industry was possible in Puerto Rico. The second stage was light privately owned industry and the third, the current stage, heavy industry.

The government, of course, explained that this development would result in an integrated, independently productive economy. Just the opposite has happened.

Through offers of 100% tax exemption for 10–17 year periods (guaranteeing U.S. corporations approximately 50% higher rates of return on their investments in Puerto Rico) and the incentive of a cheap and largely unorganized labor force, the Economic Development Administration of the Commonwealth Government has succeeded in establishing 2,000 factories. They represent a total investment of $3.2 billion, 85% of which is controlled by U.S. capital.

The profits, in general, do not get plowed back into the Puerto Rican economy. A deficit in the Puerto Rican balance of payment has been a constant phenomenon since 1940, reaching $656 million in 1969 and almost doubling to $1,153 million by 1972. U.S. economic control of Puerto Rico has forced the Puerto Rican economy to import far more than it exports so that its trade deficit, $15 million in 1940, rose to $995 million in 1973. The tiny island of Puerto Rico is the fourth largest market in the world for U.S. produced goods. From 1950–1969 the colonial government paid $700 million in principal and interest on money loaned to it by the financial houses of Wall Street. During this same period private industry contracted outside debts, almost all in the United States, of more than $3.1 billion.

During the third phase of Operation Bootstrap, from the mid-1960's on, the most powerful American corporations established affiliates or subsidiaries in Puerto Rico. Investments passed from light industries to enterprises of large capital investment, particularly in petroleum refineries, petrochemical and chemical industries. These "heavy" industries are characterized by a high level of mechanization, requiring a small labor force in proportion to the investment of capital they represent.

In 1955, two petroleum refineries started operations, the Caribbean Gulf Refining Corporation and the American-owned Commonwealth Oil Refining Company (CORCO). A third, Sun Oil, started in 1969. Today, with the added establishment of petrochemicals and pharmaceuticals, these industries represent over one-third, or $1.3 billion, of the total investment in Puerto Rico; 83% (or 43 out of 52 plants in operation) are subsidiaries of U.S. firms.

The petroleum and petrochemical industries are taking on even greater significance today with the development of plans put forward by the Commonwealth Government of Puerto Rico for the establishment of a giant petroleum "Superport" in Puerto Rico. All of the studies conducted by the EDA claim that the petroleum and petrochemical industries are the answer to Puerto Rico's main economic problem: a non-integrated economy and staggering chronic unemployment. What the studies do not reveal are the following:

☐ Several states in the United States rejected construction of a superport within their borders because of the environmental problems it would create.
☐ The Superport would actually *create* unemployment by accelerating the destruction of jobs caused by the existing petroleum industries, through pollution and the takeover of valuable land.

In Guayanilla, Union Carbide, CORCO and Pittsburgh Plate Glass are slowly killing off marine life by dumping wastes containing mercury and caustic soda directly into the Bay. In Barceloneta, fishermen are finding their livelihoods destroyed by pharmaceutical companies such as Merck, Sharp and Dohme, which are polluting the river. Thermo-electric plants in Cataño destroy marine life by returning to the sea waters used by the plants at temperatures 10 to 20 degrees hotter than the ocean. Air pollution, mainly sulphur oxides, grew from 13,563 tons in 1970 to 27,050 tons in 1972 from the Union Carbide plant in Peñuelas (Environmental Quality Board). The sugar-cane tonnage in the area surrounding the Phtalic Anhydrous petrochemical plant in Arecibo, Puerto Rico, was reduced from 40 tons to 13 tons per acre.

The agriculture and fishing industries currently employ approximately

40,000 people. Over the last 18 years the petroleum and petrochemical industries have provided only 8% of the jobs promised at their inception.

☐ By the year 2000, with the establishment of a superport, the U.S. corporations and the U.S. military would directly occupy over 30% of the land of Puerto Rico.

☐ Behind the superport plan are such companies as Exxon and Gulf; this plan is essential to their oil importation and refining needs and would represent a doubling or tripling of present U.S. investment on the island.

Although these factors have been hidden from the public by the Commonwealth Government, sectors of the growing movement for the independence of Puerto Rico are publicly opposing the operation and expansion of U.S. industry on the island, which they consider to be actively against the interests of the Puerto Rican people. Through their investigations and education, tens of thousands of Puerto Ricans, from all sectors of the nation, are joining in massive protest. No definite step has been taken to begin construction of the superport, but expansion of the refining and petrochemical industries, particularly CORCO and Union Carbide, is going ahead at a rapid pace.

Another prospective focus of U.S. development in the area of heavy industry is the exploitation of Puerto Rican copper by the U.S. mining firms, American Metal Climax and Kennecott Copper. These corporations have been attempting since 1969 to obtain the rights to mine large deposits of copper in 36,000 acres of the central-western part of the island. Again, massive opposition to these plans has arisen from the exposure (by the independence movement) of various deals between AMAX, Kennecott and the Commonwealth Government which would allow these companies to gain total control of mineral exploitation at tremendous environmental cost. The most recent draft contract submitted in April 1974 to the Commonwealth Government by Kennecott and AMAX proposes a "joint venture" of all three entities for extraction and refining over a 30-year period, each putting up one-third of the initial $240 million investment, with government responsible for infrastructure costs. Recently, however, a memorandum from the mining companies was made public by the President of the Commission of Natural Resources which showed that half of the percentage to be given to the Commonwealth was not from profits but from taxes, royalties and token payments for electric power.

Aside from this there is the question of whether the U.S. mining companies will pay for gold and the valuable mineral, molybdenum, which they can extract from the copper, as well as the fact that the copper extracted will be paid for at U.S. prices, which are lower than world market prices. Governor Hernandez Colon has recently announced that he will sign this latest contract with the mining companies although no date has yet been set. Meanwhile, the most militant elements of the movement for independence on the island have raised the slogan, "not one pound of copper will leave Puerto Rico."

The militance of that slogan is based on the increasing consciousness among the Puerto Rican people of what U.S. economic penetration has meant for their country. With the monopolization of the sugar industry, hundreds of thousands of Puerto Ricans lost their land. Through Operation Bootstrap, one million Puerto Ricans were forced to leave their homeland to look for work in the United States. In Puerto Rico today, the situation is intolerable. Unemployment is 30%; wages are half those in the United States, and prices in Puerto Rico, according to a document presented to the United Nations by the Puerto Rican Independence Party and the Puerto Rican Socialist Party in 1972, are 25% higher than in the United States.

The physical condition of the island is rapidly deteriorating. Whole towns, living under the sickening pall from nearby petrochemical plants, have lost their livelihood from the contamination of the ocean. The land has been encroached upon not only by the spread of the petrochemical and pharmaceutical industries, but also by the military—including atomic installations—necessary to protect the massive U.S. investment in Puerto Rico. Hundreds of people have been poisoned by chlorine and mercury and the numbers are growing.

To the U.S. interests it is a different story: in the first years of the decade of the 1950's the profits of "American" capital in Puerto Rico did not surpass $22 million annually. Its yield however increased as the inflow of capital increased until in 1959 it reached $83.6 million. The decade of 1960 began with annual profits amounting to $115 million; by 1966, dividends and interest rose to $281 million; and by 1970 this figure rose to $583 million.

Clearly the interests of the Puerto Rican people and U.S. capital are at opposite poles. The very expansion and concentration which the United States sees as profitable means to the Puerto Rican people their own destruction. The Puerto Rican nation cannot afford the migration of another million of their people to the United States, which a leader of the Commonwealth Government has predicted. They cannot stand by while their island is being physically ripped apart by strip-mining and polluted by petroleum. For their own survival, they must take a stand *now* against the further exploitation of even *one pound* of copper.

The crisis between the survival of the Puerto Rican people and the interests of U.S. capital grows sharper each day. By learning what the U.S. occupation of Puerto Rico means, North American people can understand why they must take a stand for the decolonization of Puerto Rico.

28

More Third World Cartels Ahead?

Raymond F. Mikesell

The fourfold price increase achieved by the Organization of Petroleum-Exporting Countries (OPEC) quickly led the industrialized nations to assess their vulnerability on other raw materials imports. At the same time,

OPEC's highly visible success spurred many countries exporting primary commodities to examine their existing terms of trade and pricing mechanisms.

Even without collusion among governments, U.S. dollar prices of many primary commodities exported by developing countries have more than doubled over the past year. Between January 1973 and April 1974, dollar prices of metals exported by the less developed countries increased by about 120 percent, while food prices rose by about 75 percent. In particular, the price of copper on the London Metal Exchange nearly tripled between January 1973 and May 1974 (although copper prices have fallen by half since then). The question now is whether collusion can maintain or increase these already high prices.

In international trade, collusion is difficult. The success of any attempt to control the world market price will depend on how big the association's combined share of the market is, how easily nonmembers and producers of substitutes can increase their production, and how competitive the world market structure is. Each member's financial position, the political and economic orientations of the participating countries, and the cohesiveness and discipline of the members in carrying out joint policies are also important factors.

COMPETITION FROM SUBSTITUTES

A producers' association controlling no more than, say, one-fourth of the world's supply of a mineral may hike prices in the short run, but in the longer run nonmember suppliers will increase output, thereby dampening prices.

There is a parallel in the case of substitute products, since increased production of a close substitute will also tend to erode artificially high prices. How much a rise in prices curtails demand for a mineral is partly a function of the time consumers require to adjust to substitutes. Once a consumer adopts a substitute for a certain use of a mineral, his switch is often permanent. For most minerals, demand is likely to be insensitive to higher prices in the short run, but highly responsive in the longer run. Producers are usually concerned about the relationship between the prices of their products and those of substitutes, particularly when the supply of a substitute commodity can be readily increased. CIPEC [French acronym for the copper council] members, for example, are certainly aware that high copper prices may mean a permanent loss of market to aluminum. The association even charts the ratio between world copper and aluminum prices in its quarterly and annual reports.

Price increases could still occur. CIPEC and the bauxite producers could combine efforts and raise prices of both copper and bauxite. But bauxite prices would need to be raised substantially in order to have a significant direct effect on the price of aluminum. In a world of growing materials shortages, there is always the chance that an increase in the price of one commodity might induce a rise in the price of a close substitute, even without collusion between two producers' associations.

Scrap metal also provides an important substance for primary produc-

TABLE I □ SELECTED COMMODITIES OF WHICH 20 PERCENT OR MORE OF U.S. REQUIREMENTS ARE CURRENTLY SUPPLIED BY IMPORTS OR LIKELY TO BE SUPPLIED BY IMPORTS BY 1980

Commodity	Major Sources of U.S. Imports in 1972	Over One-third U.S. Imports from Developing Countries	Over One-half U.S. Imports from Developing Countries	Projected Rate of Growth of U.S. Demand (Percent)	Net Imports as Percent of Domestic Use in 1970
Bauxite-alumina	Jamaica, Surinam, Canada, Australia	X	X	7	86
Chromium	South Africa, USSR, Turkey	X		5	100
Cobalt	Zaïre, Zambia, Norway, Finland	X	X	2	96
Copper	Canada, Peru, Chile	X	X	4–5	8
Iron ore	Canada, Venezuela	X		1.5–2.5	30
Lead	Canada, Australia, Peru, Mexico	X		1.6	40
Manganese	Brazil, Gabon, South Africa, Zaïre	X	X	3	94
Nickel	Canada, Norway			3	91
Potash	Canada			4	42
Sulfur	Canada, Mexico			4	0
Tin	Malaysia, Thailand, Bolivia	X	X	4	71
Tungsten	Canada, Bolivia, Peru, Australia, Thailand	X		8	50
Zinc	Canada, Mexico, Peru			3	59

Source: Mining and Minerals Policy (Second Annual Report of the Secretary of the Interior Under the Mining and Minerals Policy Act of 1970), 1973; and Material Needs and the Environment, Today and Tomorrow, National Commission on Materials Policy, 1973.

tion in several minerals, and in the case of copper, scrap sometimes constitutes a third or more of the raw material. The potential supply of scrap
and of recycled material is very large for many commodities and supply is
sensitive to price even in the relatively short run.

Unless the responsiveness of demand to price changes for a raw material
is low, a rise in its price will not increase producers' export revenues and
may even reduce them. According to a World Bank study, short-run world
demand for CIPEC copper is so responsive to price changes that CIPEC
could barely improve the export earnings of its members through an increase in price. And in the longer run, higher prices would actually reduce
export earnings.

SOME POLITICAL CONSIDERATIONS

Needless to say, along with the economic forces underlying market actions
there are the political ones. One of the strengths of OPEC has been the
broad area of common interest among its members. But this community
of interests is rare. The USSR, South Africa, Rhodesia, and Turkey produce
the bulk of the world's chromium, but these nations would make strange
bedfellows. Moreover, given South Africa's political and economic orientation, that country would be unlikely to force up the world chromium price
by taxing chromium producers. Nor is South Africa likely to join with
Gabon, Zaïre, and Brazil to raise the price of manganese. CIPEC members
are currently in strong disagreement regarding the desirability of collusive
action to raise copper prices.

ASSESSING THE CHANCES

Given the conditions necessary for a successful cartel among nations, what
is the outlook for supplies and prices of those nonfuel minerals directly
or indirectly important to U.S. interests? Let us review them one by one.

Copper

In 1972 CIPEC members accounted for 38 percent of the copper produced in the noncommunist world (including concentrates, blister, and
refined). CIPEC's share of exports is even larger—amounting to 53 percent
in 1971. If other Third World producers, such as Papua New Guinea and
the Philippines, joined CIPEC, the association's share of exports would
climb to almost two-thirds.

Clearly the CIPEC members could exercise a strong influence on the
world price of copper. However, the OPEC tax formula would not be effective, since only a small portion of their output is taken by the affiliates
of firms with substantial investment in CIPEC members. Among current
members of CIPEC, well over half of the production—and almost all of the
marketing—is in government hands. Contract prices are tied to those on the
London Metal Exchange. No CIPEC member dominates the world market

enough to negotiate contracts at a price significantly above that on the exchange.

CIPEC could gain market control through production and export quotas or a buffer stock arrangement. But each of the association's four members would apparently like to expand domestic production and capacity. Peru, the nation with the largest undeveloped reserves, is producing only about one-fourth as much as Chile or Zambia. Peru's policy makers are anxious to double or triple its productive capacity, and Chile is planning to double its output by 1980. These ambitions make any long-term agreement on production or export quotas unlikely. The CIPEC members have discussed establishing a buffer stock for controlling the London price. And there is the possibility that members could agree to a minimum contract price above that on the London exchange when the latter declined below a certain level. But that sort of an arrangement would be difficult to police.

CIPEC members, already concerned with the relationship between the price of copper and that of aluminum, copper's main substitute, would undoubtedly welcome the formation of an association among aluminum producers strong enough to raise prices of that commodity. We could even envisage short-term agreements for maintaining a certain ratio between the prices of the two commodities. In the longer term, however, such a ratio would be difficult to sustain, since the price of bauxite is only a small part of the total cost of producing aluminum.

Bauxite

Approximately 75 percent of the world's exports of bauxite and alumina is shipped from the seven countries in the recently formed International Bauxite-Producers' Association. Excluding Australia (which accounts for 15 percent of world exports), all the members of the association are developing countries: Guinea, Guyana, Jamaica, Sierra Leone, Surinam, and Yugoslavia. Production of bauxite and alumina is largely controlled by vertically integrated international firms, except in Guyana, where Alcan properties were recently nationalized. While the vast share of bauxite reserves and production is in the developing countries plus Australia, nearly all of the aluminum metal is produced in the developed countries. The rate of growth in U.S. demand is relatively high (7 percent), and the growth rate for the rest of the world has been considerably higher.

This is perhaps the closest parallel to the OPEC situation, and member governments may be able to raise taxes, which companies would pass on to consumers in the form of higher prices. In May 1974 Jamaica, which accounts for 30 percent of world exports, proposed to raise taxes on the foreign companies by nearly eightfold. If similar tax demands are made by other producing countries, Jamaica may achieve a severalfold rise in tax revenues without a significant loss of output.

There are, of course, important differences between bauxite and petroleum. There is a range of substitutes for aluminum, and most producing countries are sorely in need of foreign exchange. The crucial difference in terms of final price is that four tons of bauxite costing a total of $36 to $60 are needed to produce one ton of aluminum ingots worth over $600. Doubling the price of bauxite would increase the price of aluminum by less than 10 percent. (By comparison, the value of refined petroleum products is ordinarily less than double the value of the crude input.)

Tin

Just four countries—Bolivia, Indonesia, Malaysia, and Thailand—account for 80 percent of the noncommunist world's production of tin and claim a somewhat larger share of world exports. Because of the high concentration of production in a few developing countries, there is some chance of an agreement on production or export quotas. However, there is a wide range of substitutes available for the important uses of tin. Moreover, the United States has a stockpile of the metal. Thus, producers are likely to continue using the buffer stock established under the International Tin Agreement as a mechanism for stabilizing prices. That arrangement, by the way, has the support of the IMF and all major consuming countries except the United States.

Chromium

Chromium is an essential ingredient for many metal products, and, in the short term, demand is probably insensitive to price changes. Since most ferroalloys are substitutes for one another, however, demand is likely to respond to price increases over the longer run.

South Africa, Rhodesia, Turkey, the Philippines, and the USSR account for nearly 80 percent of world mine production of chromium and an even larger share of world exports. The structure of the industry and the differing political-economic orientations of the major exporters make the probability of collusion small. Nevertheless, if one of the major producers, say South Africa, should take the initiative to raise prices (by putting a special tax on exporters, for example), other producing countries might very well follow. The United States is wholly dependent upon foreign sources for chromium, importing approximately equal amounts from the USSR, South Africa, and Turkey. U.S. demand is growing at about 5 percent per year.

Manganese

The principal use of manganese is in steelmaking, where there is no satisfactory substitute. Even though demand has been growing by only 3 percent per year, the lack of a substitute probably means that demand would not be much dampened by a price increase. The Soviet Union, South Africa, Brazil, Gabon, and India account for over 80 percent of world output but a somewhat smaller share of world exports, since the Soviet Union consumes a large portion of its own output. The United States imports about 90 percent of its needs—chiefly from Gabon, Brazil, South Africa, and Zaïre. The bulk of these imports comes from subsidiaries of U.S. steel firms, making increased taxation which would be passed on to U.S. consumers of steel a possibility. But a producers' association would have difficulty maintaining production controls, since much manganese is a co-product of the production of iron and other metals. Moreover, the diverse political orientations of the major producers would make effective collusion difficult.

Cobalt

Cobalt, like manganese and chromium, is used in the production of steel, as well as in certain chemical processes. Nickel is often a substitute for cobalt. World production and export of cobalt are dominated by Zaïre, but because the mineral is a by-product of copper production, its supply is insensitive to price movements. Moreover, there are very large reserves in Canada, New Caledonia, and Australia, so that any attempt to maintain very high prices would probably result in substantial expansion of sources outside of Zaïre.

Iron Ore

Iron ore production and reserves are widely distributed around the world among both developed and developing countries. Although some of the production is controlled by vertically integrated international firms, as in Canada, Brazil, Liberia, and Venezuela, much of the world's output in the developing countries has been nationalized. The Venezuelan government has recently announced its intention to nationalize the Venezuelan iron ore industry currently controlled by U.S. Steel and Bethlehem.

The absence of concentration in reserves, production, or exports, and the wide differences in the political orientations of the major exporting countries would make effective collusion quite unlikely. The United States is currently dependent on foreign sources for about 30 percent of its iron ore requirements, and this dependence will increase over the coming decades. However, the United States could supply its own requirements with lower grade ores.

Lead, Zinc, and Other Minerals

On the whole, the world market structure does not appear conducive to collusion by either lead or zinc producers. The United States has the world's largest output of lead and the largest reserves; it also has large reserves of zinc and is the world's second largest producer. Although the United States is expected to be increasingly dependent upon foreign supplies for both minerals, most imports will probably continue to come from Canada, with smaller amounts from Australia and the Latin American countries. Vertical integration in the industry outside the United States is not substantial.

The United States is now heavily dependent upon foreign sources of nickel, potash, tungsten, and mercury, and in the future will become increasingly dependent on foreign sources of sulfur. Currently Canada is the major source of U.S. imports for all of these minerals, and in most cases collusive action among world producers would probably require that country's cooperation.

WHAT THE UNITED STATES CAN DO

The best candidate for world market control by means of OPEC-type action is bauxite; however, even a severalfold rise in taxes on bauxite producers would not have a major impact on the price of aluminum. Collusive action for raising copper prices seems remote given the divergent policies of the CIPEC members. Moreover, the financial position of the CIPEC countries precludes their being able to restrict exports over long periods or to accumulate large stocks. Collusion between bauxite and copper producers is likely to be of little help in raising or maintaining copper prices because of the minor impact on the price of aluminum. There is some potential for a sharp rise in prices of chromium and manganese through joint action, since output of both is heavily concentrated in a few countries and there are no readily available substitutes for their most important uses. Nevertheless, there appear to be political barriers to effective collusion on either of these metals. For most other minerals, either production and reserves are widely distributed or substitutes are readily available, or both. For a few commodities such as nickel, Canada would have to be included in any collusive association by developing countries.

We conclude with a recommendation. For every case of possible collusion, significant harm to the U.S. economy could be avoided by a stockpile of each commodity equivalent to one or two years' import requirements. Successful market control by producers' associations for periods longer than that simply does not appear feasible.

A New International Economic Order

The General Assembly of the United Nations

We, the Members of the United Nations, having convened a special session of the General Assembly to study for the first time the problems of raw materials and development, devoted to the consideration of the most important economic problems facing the world community, bearing in mind the spirit, purposes and principles of the Charter of the United Nations to promote the economic advancement and social progress of all peoples, solemnly proclaim our united determination to work urgently for the establishment of a new international economic order based on equity, sovereign equality, interdependence, common interest and co-operation among all States, irrespective of their economic and social systems which shall correct inequalities and redress existing injustices, make it possible to eliminate the widening gap between the developed and the developing countries and ensure steadily accelerating economic and social development and peace and justice for present and future generations, and, to that end, declare:

1. The greatest and most significant achievement during the last decades has been the independence from colonial and alien domination of a large number of peoples and nations which has enabled them to become members

of the community of free peoples. Technological progress has also been made in all spheres of economic activities in the last three decades, thus providing a solid potential for improving the well-being of all peoples. However, the remaining vestiges of alien and colonial domination, foreign occupation, racial discrimination, *apartheid* and neo-colonialism in all its forms continue to be among the greatest obstacles to the full emancipation and progress of the developing countries and all the peoples involved. The benefits of technological progress are not shared equitably by all members of the international community. The developing countries, which constitute 70 per cent of the world's population, account for only 30 per cent of the world's income. It has proved impossible to achieve an even and balanced development of the international community under the existing international economic order. The gap between the developed and the developing countries continues to widen in a system which was established at a time when most of the developing countries did not even exist as independent States and which perpetuates inequality.

2. The present international economic order is in direct conflict with current developments in international political and economic relations. Since 1970, the world economy has experienced a series of grave crises which have had severe repercussions, especially on the developing countries because of their generally greater vulnerability to external economic impulses. The developing world has become a powerful factor that makes its influence felt in all fields of international activity. These irreversible changes in the relationship of forces in the world necessitate the active, full and equal participation of the developing countries in the formulation and application of all decisions that concern the international community.

· · ·

I. FUNDAMENTAL PROBLEMS OF RAW MATERIALS AND PRIMARY COMMODITIES AS RELATED TO TRADE AND DEVELOPMENT

1. Raw Materials

All efforts should be made:

(*a*) To put an end to all forms of foreign occupation, racial discrimination, *apartheid*, colonial, neo-colonial and alien domination and exploitation through the exercise of permanent sovereignty over natural resources;

(*b*) To take measures for the recovery, exploitation, development, marketing and distribution of natural resources, particularly of developing countries, to serve their national interests, to promote collective self-reliance among them and to strengthen mutually beneficial international economic co-operation with a view to bringing about the accelerated development of developing countries;

(*c*) To facilitate the functioning and to further the aims of producers' associations, including their joint marketing arrangements, orderly commodity trading, improvement in the export income of producing developing countries and in their terms of trade, and sustained growth of the world economy for the benefit of all;

(*d*) To evolve a just and equitable relationship between the prices of raw materials, primary commodities, manufactured and semi-manufactured goods exported by developing countries and the prices of raw materials, primary commodities, food, manufactured and semi-manufactured goods and capital equipment imported by them, and to work for a link between the prices of exports of developing countries and the prices of their imports from developed countries;

(*e*) To take measures to reverse the continued trend of stagnation or decline in the real price of several commodities exported by developing countries, despite a general rise in commodity prices, resulting in a decline in the export earnings of these developing countries;

(*f*) To take measures to expand the markets for natural products in relation to synthetics, taking into account the interests of the developing countries, and to utilize fully the ecological advantages of these products;

(*g*) To take measures to promote the processing of raw materials in the producer developing countries.

. . .

V. REGULATION AND CONTROL OVER THE ACTIVITIES OF TRANSNATIONAL CORPORATIONS

All efforts should be made to formulate, adopt and implement an international code of conduct for transnational corporations:

(*a*) To prevent interference in the internal affairs of the countries where they operate and their collaboration with racist régimes and colonial administrations;

(*b*) To regulate their activities in host countries, to eliminate restrictive business practices and to conform to the national development plans and objectives of developing countries, and in this context facilitate, as necessary, the review and revision of previously concluded arrangements;

(*c*) To bring about assistance, transfer of technology and management skills to developing countries on equitable and favourable terms;

(*d*) To regulate the repatriation of the profits accruing from their operations, taking into account the legitimate interests of all parties concerned;

(*e*) To promote reinvestment of their profits in developing countries.

. . .

VII. PROMOTION OF CO-OPERATION AMONG DEVELOPING COUNTRIES

And growing co-operation among developing countries will further strengthen their role in the new international economic order. Developing countries, with a view to expanding co-operation at the regional, subregional and interregional levels, should take further steps, *inter alia:*

(*a*) To support the establishment and/or improvement of an appropriate mechanism to defend the prices of their exportable commodities and to improve access to and stabilize markets for them. In this context the increasingly effective mobilization by the whole group of oil-exporting countries of their natural resources for the benefit of their economic development is to be welcomed. At the same time there is the paramount need for co-operation among the developing countries in evolving urgently and in a spirit of solidarity all possible means to assist developing countries to cope with the immediate problems resulting from this legitimate and perfectly justified action. The measures already taken in this regard are a positive indication of the evolving co-operation between developing countries;

(*b*) To protect their inalienable rights to permanent sovereignty over their natural resources;

(*c*) To promote, establish or strengthen economic integration at the regional and subregional levels;

(*d*) To increase considerably their imports from other developing countries;

(*e*) To ensure that no developing country accords to imports from developed countries more favourable treatment than that accorded to imports from developing countries. Taking into account the existing international agreements, current limitations and possibilities and also their future evolution, preferential treatment should be given to the procurement of import requirements from other developing countries. Wherever possible, preferential treatment should be given to imports from developing countries and the exports to those countries;

. . .

VIII. ASSISTANCE IN THE EXERCISE OF PERMANENT SOVEREIGNTY OF STATES OVER NATURAL RESOURCES

All efforts should be made:

(*a*) To defeat attempts to prevent the free and effective exercise of the rights of every State to full and permanent sovereignty over its natural resources;

(*b*) To ensure that competent agencies of the United Nations system meet requests for assistance from developing countries in connexion with the operation of nationalized means of production.

part

3

The Crisis of Depression

Depression! Orthodox economists—at least those within the Keynes-Samuelson tradition—never thought we would see unemployment rates at or near double digits with inflation rates appropriate to banana republics. Establishment economists repeatedly assured us that our system was basically sound, that prosperity was permanent. Constantly refined, their esoteric models made it appear that resolutions of social and economic problems depended solely on technique and should therefore be left to the administration of experts.

In reality, though, capitalism at the three-quarters point of this strife-ridden century is as crisis-prone as ever. Moreover, the economic issues before us are quintessentially political: the "solutions" of government benefit some classes at the expense of others. This is most obvious when economic programs are put forth by political figures such as President Gerald Ford. But politics and class interests also join forces in the secret decisions of the "nonpolitical" Federal Reserve Board, although this agency is headed by Dr. Arthur F. Burns, a professional economist. "The Fed," as it is known, is not primarily engaged in technical decision making. Instead it functions as an economic agency making policy of a fundamental nature. Nor does it do this on the basis of a representative spectrum of American opinion. If this were the case, the board would include large numbers of spokespersons for workers and their allies. To the contrary, its membership and ties to the financial community, particularly the giant international banks of New York, make it one of the most important coordinating institutions serving the interests of the capitalist class, especially during the present economic crisis. This, at least, is the reality as seen by those who consider themselves radical.

This Part attempts to probe the nature of the current crisis. It is divided into three sections: (a) an overview of the causes and background of the crisis, (b) the special situation in oil and food, and (c) the prospects for planning.

Readers have before them two general orientations. One is that blunders, accidents, and foreign powers (i.e., the Arabs) are responsible for the crisis, from which we can extricate ourselves only by pulling in our belts and perhaps accepting a temporary form of national planning in the public interest. In contrast, the radical view is that depressions perform a necessary function for capitalist society and so are inevitable. All "solutions" to the crisis tend to benefit disproportionately the wealthy, since they aim to strengthen the long-term ability of the capitalist class to extract profits from their workers. Students should keep these alternative approaches in mind as they read the articles that follow.

An Analysis of the Crisis

For years, the gray eminences of the economic academy have assured us that we had nothing to fear from that old bugaboo of the past, economic depression. Tax cuts, government expenditures, and easy money, they told us, would readily reinstate prosperity should the economy display signs of weakness. Basically, orthodox economists were saying that spending creates jobs. Any doubts about orthodox solutions lay not in the economics of the situation but in its politics. Whether out of ignorance or ideological obstinancy, conservative mossbacks, for instance, might create roadblocks to stall or delay Keynesian solutions. In recent years, this threat from the right virtually disappeared, bolstering the faith of Keynesian economists that capitalism could be made to work. The unbearable hardships of the system were thought to be part of history. Unfortunately, events have begun to refute this assumption, much as the great depression of the thirties invalidated the orthodox theory of its day. The orthodoxy of that era had be-

come irrelevant (and was eventually replaced by the Keynesian paradigm) because it theoretically ruled out the possibility of depression, and did so at a time when a quarter of the work force was unemployed! This historical analogy suggests the possibility that the orthodoxy of our day— neo-Keynesian economics— might suffer the same fate.

Keynesian economists are not about to relinquish their long-labored-over analytical framework without a struggle. Instead, quite naturally, they seek modifications that will once again make their analysis appropriate to conditions as they unfold. The first entry in this section (Reading 30), written on the eve of the downturn, is by M.I.T.'s Paul Samuelson, Nobel laureate and author of an economics textbook whose editions are soon to match in digits the inflation of 1974. A leader of the "liberal" forces in the profession, Samuelson, in his thoughtful overview, reaches a revealing conclusion— inflation might best be solved by slow growth and a two- or three-year dose of 5 1/2 percent unemployment. Is this "solution" so fundamentally different from the 7–8 percent conservative game plan of Gerald Ford? (One wonders what kind of policies would emerge from the Samuelsons of our day if the unemployed were chosen by lot rather than in the "rigged" marketplace that inevitably ensures a disproportionate contingent of blacks and blue-collar workers.) Writing in the midst of the decline, Wilfred Lewis, Jr., chief economist of the mainstream National Planning Association, surveys recent economic history and concludes that the "free enterprise system" can only or best be redeemed by the imposition of wage, price, and other government controls. In Reading 31, Lewis points to modifications that Keynesian economics must make if it is to survive as an ideological force. It will have to integrate into a government-planned macromodel all the key microelements that it currently omits: profit and wage rates, productivity, monopoly, indebtedness, and so forth. But to do so is to acknowledge that capitalism divides society into conflicting classes, with the interests of capital in diametrical opposition to those of labor. A state-capitalist neo-Keynesian model of this sort, should it develop, moves orthodox economics one step closer to being the official theory of the capitalist class, in the sense that its dual purposes are to guide the economy on its behalf and to make such

policies appear respectable and responsible to the public at large. The alternative to this kind of theory is Marxism, which is first represented in this section (in Reading 32) by Professors James Crotty of the University of Massachusetts (Amherst) and Raford Boddy of American University.

A central point in their article is that "recessions are inevitable in the unplanned economy of the United States because they perform an essential function for which no adequate substitute has thus far been available." This function is to "correct the imbalances of the previous expansion," especially the problem (from the capitalist point of view) of rising labor costs. In short, periodic unemployment (and inflation, should we postpone the unemployment) is the price we must pay for preserving the capitalist system. The planning that Lewis and others call for will, according to Crotty and Boddy, be used to expand profits at the expense of wages. (See also section c of Part 3.)

Bad as economic conditions are, they could easily get worse, eventually degenerating into financial panic. Economist Charles Kindleberger of M.I.T., author of *The World in Depression 1929–1939*, explains from a mainstream point of view why bankers are worried (see Reading 33). Similarly, Harry Magdoff and Paul Sweezy, the Marxist editors of *Monthly Review*, specify some causes, mechanisms, and consequences of the fact that our banks, especially the biggest among them, are involved in highly speculative endeavors. The evidence cited by Magdoff and Sweezy supports the radical contention that the capitalist system (which, during most of the postwar period, was not confronted with the consequences of its basic contradictions) is once again increasingly unstable (see Reading 34). Finally, the nature of some of these contradictions is explained in Reading 35, by Professor Roger Alcaly of John Jay College, CUNY. Writing from a Marxist point of view, Alcaly presents the reasons why depressions in a capitalist society are inescapable.

As a consequence of these contradictions, we are in for an extended period of hard times. A recent article in *Business Week* has caught the essence of the contemporary situation:

Finally, and most distressing of all, it is not at all certain how graciously Americans, or any other people for that matter, will accept what is plainly today's (and history's) economic reality: that there is no such thing as perpetual plenty and no party that does not eventually end. . . . [I]t will be a hard pill for many Americans to swallow—the idea of doing with less so that big business can have more.

Worldwide Stagflation: An Overview on the Eve of the Downturn

Paul A. Samuelson

The international economy has seen in recent years a reacceleration of inflation in virtually every region. Creeping inflation that had earlier displayed a 3% or 4% or 5% average yearly trend has generally more than doubled that rate.

The current inflation, to be sure, has not represented hyperinflation or galloping inflation of the 1920–23 German experience or the Hungarian and Chinese experiences after World War II; nor is it akin to the 300% rate of inflation reached in Chile at the end of the Allende regime, or (as yet) akin to the chronic Latin American inflation that has averaged out to more than 20% per year for decades and even generations.

Compounding the economic problem of inflation is the fact that, often and in many countries, there persists a simultaneous problem of unemployment and stagnant growth. "Stagflation" is a new name for a new disease: stagflation involves inflationary rises in prices and wages at the same time that people are unable to find jobs and firms are unable to find customers for what their plants can produce.

FALLACIOUS SINGLE-CAUSE EXPLANATIONS

A variety of monistic explanations have been offered for the current inflation. The monetarists, of course, identify excessive growth of the money supply as the sole or prime cause. Other economists trace the global speedup of inflation principally to the long string of balance-of-payments deficits experienced by the U.S. in the 1960s. And for still others, wage-push is the villain, with the wage explosion that has occurred so widely in recent years attributed to various structural changes in the labor market that are said to have worsened the so-called Phillips-Curve trade-off between movements in unemployment and wages. Other monistic explanations of current inflation relate to forces disturbing individual commodity or labor markets: to droughts, floods, strikes, cartel behavior, and so on. And a great number of people are convinced, of course, that our inflationary troubles trace to the rise in both the official and unofficial prices of gold—that is, to the general devaluation of currencies vis-à-vis gold that has occurred in the last several years. A related explanation runs in terms of the additional depreciation of particular currencies—such as the dollar—against other major currencies, a phenomenon that links domestic cost and price increases to exogenous forces abroad.

As we apply the best tools of modern economic analysis to the pattern of available evidence, I believe that no monistic theory can be validly maintained. One is forced by the facts of experience into an eclectic position. It is not a case where intellectual indecision or uncertainty leads to a hedged position of eclecticism. It is rather that explanation of the varied pattern of ongoing experience calls for bold combination of causations.

I certainly have no doubt that the Asian and African droughts and Soviet crop shortfalls have been one critical element in the international run-up of food prices. Sudden supply shifts combined with sudden demand shifts obviously tend to produce dramatic price fluctuations, particularly in an area such as agriculture, where changes in prices do not quickly induce either enlarged supply or reduced demand. Microeconomic commodity inflation—whether in food, in fuels, or indeed in any important sector of the domestic or international economy—refuses to remain microeconomic. It is true that a family which spends more on beef or electricity than it has been spending previously may spend less for other things, tending thereby to depress their prices. And one could conceive of money wage rates falling when bad harvests or dear Near-East oil induces a lower real wage rate. But this sort of offsetting occurrence seems to happen only in history books. In the world in which we actually live, strong upside price pressures originating in a particular sector tend to disturb the whole price structure and raise its average level. This is partly because fiscal and monetary policies—for reasons I explore in the paragraphs that follow—generally work in a way that prevents compensatory price declines from occurring. It is also because existing institutional arrangements (such as escalator clauses in collective-bargaining contracts) tend to set in motion a phase of price-wage leapfrogging whenever a major instance of microeconomic inflation erupts. If one focuses narrowly on some especially visible part of the complicated transmission process—on explosive wage behavior or rapid monetary growth—it may well seem that the critical causal element has been identified. But that is illusory. Monetary expansion, for instance, is typically more the result than the cause of sustained general inflation, simply because in the end central bankers—like governments—must be responsive to public opinion of populist electorates. They must be accommodative and avoid policies that would acutely worsen short-run unemployment and stagnation problems. The whole explanation of the inflation we are experiencing is something more than the sum of its separate parts. But it is not something other than the combination of those analytically distinguishable separate strands of causation.

OVERVIEW OF GLOBAL INFLATION

I believe that the present inflation is rooted deep in the nature of the mixed economy. And it is the mixed economy—which is not laissez-faire capitalism any more than it is centrally-controlled state socialism—that characterizes most of the world today: North America, Western Europe and Australasia, Japan, and much of the developing world outside of Eastern Europe and mainland Asia.

For one thing, we live in the Age After Keynes. High employment or full employment is everywhere a goal insisted upon by the electorate of all politi-

cal persuasions. A half century ago there was no comparable political sentiment effective against incurring prolonged depression or even stagnation;
rather there was often a preoccupation with the perils of inflation, of budget
and foreign-trade deficits. This shift in populist attitudes of governments
necessarily shifts the odds against stable prices (and of course against falling prices). No longer can one expect half the peace-time years to experience
falling prices. If general price levels rarely stand still and often rise, then
the secular trend of prices must be upward on the average.

The present diagnosis is in some ways *not* a pessimistic one. The microeconomic laws of supply and demand that have pulled the prices of major
staples to high levels can be expected at least in some instances to pull those
same prices downward. Indeed, the prices of many key farm products are
now well below earlier peaks, and outside the U.S. a number of metal prices
have recently come down appreciably. Microeconomic commodity inflation
—except perhaps for OPEC oil—does not have the irreversible character that
we properly associate with cost-push inflation in the mixed economy. Moreover, the pre-World War II pattern of a common synchronous business cycle
has to a considerable extent reappeared. The coincidence of business cycle
exuberance widely throughout the world in 1972–73 was a prime reason for
the intensity of inflationary pressure. Now, we seem to be witnessing a
widespread relaxation of demand in many countries at the same time. The
old-fashioned business cycle has been tamed in the Age After Keynes, but it
is by no means yet dead.

A PESSIMISTIC DIAGNOSIS?

But in a deeper sense, for anyone who is nostalgic for an era in which prices
are reasonably stable and in which the purchasing power of money might
even rise under the impact of cost-reducing technical change and innovation, the present general diagnosis may be profoundly pessimistic. The
modern mixed economy simply will not tolerate that large numbers of people starve or suffer. The old dictum, "He who will not take any kind of
work that is offered him, however disagreeable and low-paid it may be, must
be starved into doing so," just does not hold any more. But it is a corollary
of this deep-seated structural change in both attitudes and institutions that
prices and wages are increasingly rigid against downward movement. Thus,
during the U.S. recession of 1969–70, the rate of unemployment went from
3 1/3% of the labor force up to 6% without doing very much even to slow
down the positive rate of increase of money wage rates; and it never did
slow the rate of wage increase down to the level of average labor-productivity improvement in the American economy. Looking beyond 1974, one must
expect that union wage settlements will lose their "moderate" character and
move from the 5%-to-7% annual range up toward the 10%-to-12% range.

SPECIFIC FACTORS IN RECENT INFLATION

The mechanisms through which the overvaluation of the dollar contributed
to global inflation are multivarious but are not in doubt. The swelling of

U.S. imports of goods and services provided strong export markets for the surplus countries such as Germany and Japan. Export orders, microeconomically, raised the prices German firms could charge; they also reduced the excess capacity in the export sectors, raising real marginal costs there and hence the mark prices charged to either Germans or non-Germans. The enhanced incomes enjoyed in the export sectors were, in turn, respent on local goods and services, putting upward price and wage pressures in those sectors. Thus, whether we use the language of microeconomics or the Keynesian multiplier language of macroeconomics, one understands how the international U.S. payments deficit contributed to inflation in other countries. (In the U.S., the ability to get goods from abroad did—but in an inadequate degree—do something to lessen upward pressure on the U.S. wage and price level.)

The tendency for the rest of the world to import some inflation from the United States was reinforced, moreover, by the workings of the Bretton Woods system. Prior to 1971, the surplus countries generally supported the official parity of the U.S. dollar. This meant that firms and persons in Western Europe were, in the end, given local currencies by their own central banks. This added to their local supplies of money. And one does not have to be an over-simple monetarist to recognize that the effect of such an increase in money is to strengthen the direct stimulative multiplier effect that flows from an export surplus. Inevitably, of course, the policy of "benign neglect" in the U.S. with regard to the payments deficit was bound to create apprehension and to induce a speculative flight out of the dollar and into the undervalued currencies of the surplus countries. When that happened, a further bulge occurred in local money supplies outside the U.S., thereby intensifying the multiplier process.

TRADE AND PAYMENTS CONSIDERATIONS

For the future, there is reason to think that the American dollar is no longer overvalued from a long-run point of view. This has to be a tentative judgment, especially because of the difficulties involved in assessing the outlook for food exports and oil imports over a several year span. But with the dollar now showing a cumulative trade-weighted average depreciation of about 18% from June 1970 parities vis-à-vis 14 other major currencies, it is not unreasonable to think that the period of chronic balance-of-payments disequilibrium for the U.S. is over, at least in relation to other oil-consuming industrialized countries. (Germany may still be an exception to this: she still runs a surprisingly strong payments surplus in mid-1974.) If this is so, the stimulative multiplier process described above that prodded global inflation rates higher may have run its course. Countries no longer with chronic surpluses thus could get some relief from "imported" inflationary pressures. This would be decidedly the case if the overhang of dollars accumulated prior to the Spring of 1973 was gradually to be reduced by U.S. payments strength. However, it's a bit premature as yet to count on such a relative surplus trend.

There is another facet of international economic relations that must be analyzed if we are to understand the recent worldwide speeding up of the

rate of inflation. Ten years ago the need to compete for world export business served effectively to hold down many prices in the European and
Japanese economies. Professor Erik Lindahl of Sweden and others have described the dual-price system that emerged: a domestic price index of commodities sheltered from international competition rose steadily in the early
1960s at 4% per annum or more; at the same time a price index of standardized goods moving in international trade was held down to virtual stability
by the need to compete with exporters abroad. What was true for Sweden
was also true for other countries: Italy and Japan provide good examples
of the dual-price system at work; a striking contrast exists between them
and the United States, which because of its continental size and tradition
of domestic orientation lacked such a dual-price system.

What needs emphasis is the fact that for many years this element of international competition did serve to restrain price increases for industrial
goods and to moderate the over-all rate of inflation. It is a nice analytical
question as to how equilibrium could be maintained for long in a common
labor market between two such disparate sectors—one with selling prices
rising several percent more per year than the other. Undoubtedly, a
squeezing of profit margins in the competitive international sector provides
part of the explanation. The influence of keen competition in that sector
also may have done much to induce more rapid technical productivity
advances and rationalizations than occurred in the domestic sector. Gradually, however, it clearly became more and more difficult to insulate the two
sectors from one another. *And some part of the explanation for the recent
worldwide quickening of inflation of industrial prices must be found in the
fact that, at long last, stability in the price levels of internationally traded
goods did come to an end.*

ON THE BRIGHTER SIDE

Precise forecasting of global price trends during the next several years is
beyond my ability. For the relatively near-term, I am encouraged chiefly by
two considerations: first, by the incipient evidence that high prices recently
for food and fibers may well be inducing a significantly enlarged flow of
goods onto markets; second, by the indications that simultaneity in busi-
ness-cycle situations in different countries—characteristic of the century
before World War II—is reconstituting itself. In 1974, this second consideration carries disinflationary implications because we seem to be witnessing
a rather general easing of demand pressures. Indeed, some concern is being
voiced (e.g., an article in *The Economist* of June 1 titled, "The Approaching
Depression") that we have entered into an oil-affected period of sluggishness
internationally that will cumulate into very serious unemployment. While
the extreme view strikes me as unjustifiably alarmist, I do believe that the
fact that the present circumstance of economies tending to be in step together heightens prospects that price increases will moderate for a while.
Parenthetically, I would note that I see no compelling reason why in the
Age After Keynes this coming of business cycles into goose step should have
to prevail in the future. As in the 1950s and 1960s, America can still have its

minirecessions when other countries are having their booms—and vice versa.

THE LONGER-RUN OUTLOOK

Apart from the relatively near-term, however, I do not think anyone ought to count strongly on persistent improvement in price performance. Certainly, it seems only realistic to perceive the outlook for the mixed economies not as an outlook for stable prices but rather for a series of compromises which will make for creeping or trotting inflation. The problem is how to keep the creep or trot from accelerating. This includes the challenge of finding new macroeconomic policies beyond conventional fiscal and monetary policies that will enable a happier compromise between the evils of unemployment and of price inflation. The rhetoric of John Kenneth Galbraith notwithstanding, direct wage and price controls are not an incomes policy that, in my assessment of experience, modern mixed economies know how to use effectively in other than the short run. Periodically, for short periods, price-wage freezes and phases of price-wage regulation for large-scale economic units can be used to advantage. Presidential or Ministerial wage-price guidelines and guideposts also have a limited function; but experience does not make one optimistic that these can be relied on much in the longer run.

Manpower and labor market programs to reduce the structural elements of unemployment certainly need to be explored further; but it is not clear from experience in the United States or in Europe that they have anywhere been able to solve the problem of giving a much-improved Phillips Curve to any economy.

Since I have been stressing that, even with creeping inflation, we are left with stagflation imperfections and trade-offs as people increasingly come to anticipate any maintained rate of inflation and to become habituated to that unchanging rate—then why do I not recommend a Draconian policy of insisting upon absolutely stable prices at whatever cost to current unemployment and short-run growth, always in the hope that after this original costly investment in fighting inflation has been made the economy can live happily ever afterwards with stable prices and nothing worse than moderate amounts of unemployment? I think making any such recommendation is academic, since in any modern mixed economy—featured politically by very limited tolerance of policies of constraint—it will assuredly never be followed. But more than that: I am not persuaded by the force of theoretical argument, or by the statistical and historical data so far available for different mixed economies, that even in the longest run the benefits to be derived from militant anti-inflationary policies don't carry excessive costs as far as average levels of unemployment and growth are concerned. And even if the benefits did decisively outweigh the costs in the longest run, history is a onetime thing and mankind at this stage of the game can ill afford to make irreversible academic experiments whose outcomes are necessarily doubtful and whose execution could put strains on the already-strained political consensus of modern nations.

What is not academic is the more relevant debate going on behind the scenes of official life: Would it not be desirable, in the interests of keeping inflation from accelerating, to countenance and even contrive slow U.S. growth for two or three years, so that unemployment will remain above the 5 1/2% level? Even if desirable, is such austerity feasible in the present American political environment?

The Economics of Restraint

Wilfred Lewis, Jr.

President Nixon's economists, faced in 1974 with possibly the most severe and stubborn inflation this country has ever experienced, and after five years of a bewildering array of other approaches in rapid succession, wound up preaching "old time religion" as our only hope for salvation. By their own explanation, old time religion describes a policy of controlled gradual economic recession brought about by holding down the federal budget and having the Federal Reserve hold down the money supply and credit extension through the banking system. Fiscal and monetary restraint are indeed the traditional approaches to managing the economy to combat inflation, at least compared to such newer heresies as price and wage controls, which the Nixon economists felt were sinful even while they were tempted periodically to use them, or at least to go through the motions, and which they said had been proven not to work. However, no administration prior to Nixon's applied fiscal and monetary restraint during a period of rising unemployment—perhaps because we have never before faced rising prices and rising unemployment at the same time.

In his first address to Congress on August 12, 1974, three days after taking office, President Ford asked for a restoration of the Cost of Living Council, which was allowed to expire last spring, but he indicated only a monitoring role for the council and made it clear that he too would place primary reliance on old time religion, starting with significant cuts in the federal budget already submitted for fiscal 1975.

That the agony will be bitter in terms of high unemployment for a long period of time is increasingly obvious. Otto Eckstein, respected head of a well-known economic forecasting firm and a former member of President Johnson's Council of Economic Advisers, recently estimated that we would have to let unemployment rise to 8 percent of the labor force (compared to the present 5 1/4 percent, and more than double the 3 1/2 to 4 percent rate considered to represent full employment) and keep it at this high level for two years in order to get inflation down as *low* as 4 percent per year. Four percent inflation would admittedly be a big improvement over the recent rate. But it is still a lot higher than what used to be considered normal and acceptable inflation for the U.S. economy, and much higher than the inflation rates we have had for more than brief infrequent periods any time in our history prior to 1973.

All told, an economy with 8 percent unemployment compared to a full employment economy with only 4 percent unemployment will have perhaps as many as 6 or 7 percent fewer people employed, and they will be producing as much as 10 percent fewer goods and services. At 1976 levels of the economy, the restraint scenario would entail a loss—conservatively estimated—of more than $150 billion of gross national product.

Moreover, these financial costs do not include the psychic and social costs associated with 3 million or so additional men and women looking unsuccessfully for work; another 2 or 3 million people so discouraged in their job search that they drop out of the labor force; a substantial worsening of the already bleak outlook for teen-agers and college graduates looking for their first jobs; and a major setback to the hopes of Black, brown, and red Americans of all ages and of women of all races who have been striving for equality of opportunity within our economic system.

Heavy as these economic and social costs are, a majority of the opinion that counts in such matters—that is to say the bankers, the business executives, the professional economists inside and outside government, the policy makers in both the executive and legislative branches of government, and the leaders of both major parties—appears likely to conclude that, if suffering these costs is the only way to curb inflation, then we will have to screw up our courage and accept the necessary costs, since we simply *must* bring inflation under control. To their credit, many of those recommending the policy of restraint are relatively honest about the attendant costs and have been recommending liberalized unemployment compensation and public sector jobs programs to alleviate some of the more obvious hardships.

But the trade-off described above, conventional wisdom to the contrary notwithstanding, is an incomplete and incorrect way to view the problems facing the U.S. economy at the present time. First, the financial and social costs listed above are only part, and perhaps the smaller part, of the total costs of the restraint scenario. In fact, the restraint policy threatens permanent severe damage to the productivity and productive capacity of the U.S. economy. After two years of controlled recession brought about by such a policy, we would be left with a permanent inability to reduce unemployment below 7 or 8 percent of the labor force without running into essentially the same capacity constraints and excess demand inflation that were encountered in 1973 at 5 percent unemployment and in 1966 at 4 percent unemployment. Just as last January's *Economic Report of the President* [1974] undertook to explain why full employment should be taken as 5 percent of the labor force unemployed, rather than the 4 percent definition used by the Kennedy and Johnson administration economists, or the 3 percent target proposed by the AFL-CIO (attained in 1950–53 and attainable again, I believe, with the right mix of policies), we will be reading two years from now that 7 percent or 8 percent is really the true definition of full employment.

Moreover, since we will not really have cured inflation in any lasting or fundamental way, it will be only a matter of time before renewed inflationary tendencies emerge again, whether from the effects of bad weather on food prices, world raw material shortages, a slight slip-up in managing federal budget or monetary policy, or whatever.

Lest 8 percent unemployment and excess demand inflation seem a farfetched combination, we can observe that a number of countries around the world—mostly developing countries which are short on stocks of productive capital—are quite accustomed to the side-by-side occurrence of runaway rates of excess demand inflation and unemployment rates that are astronomical by U.S. standards. Some analysts explain this phenomenon, which has been observed in both developed and developing countries, in terms of "dual labor markets"—a theory which says that some groups in society are condemned to high unemployment even when other sectors of the economy are prosperous, because the former don't have the education, training, habits, information, acceptability, or physical access which allows them to compete successfully for available jobs. An alternative explanation more consistent with available evidence is that an economy can simply have too little plant and equipment to allow full employment of the labor force at prevailing wage rates and with existing technology.

The simple fact, glossed over in both Keynesian and Friedmanesque economics as well as in recent public debate, is that the size of the capital stock can set a separate limit on an economy's productive capacity lower than the limit set by the supply of labor, such that excess demand inflation sets in while there is still massive unemployment.

A basic imbalance of this sort had already begun to emerge in the United States in the early 1970s and continues in 1974. In 1969, the economists of the incoming Nixon administration self-confidently announced an end to the price-wage guideposts with which the Kennedy and Johnson administrations had attempted to moderate inflationary price and wage pressures during the 1960s. The new approach to combatting inflation was to be fiscal and monetary restraint, which had its initial manifestation in the controlled recession of 1969–70.

Recession was not an altogether new phenomenon in the modern U.S. economy. In previous years since World War II, there were four full-fledged recessions—in 1948–49, in 1953–54, in 1957–58, and in 1960–61—and a "minicession" in 1967. However, the 1970 recession was different from its predecessors in one important respect: it was the only recession up to that time that was brought about by deliberate, rather than accidental, fiscal and monetary restraint. It had the unprecedented character of being officially tolerated, indeed, advertised and bragged about in advance. The advertised character of the 1970 recession allowed private decision makers to plan accordingly. In previous unplanned recessions, the business community had been caught unprepared, with excess inventories and excess plant and equipment capacity on their hands, and had been forced to mark down prices in an effort to get rid of excess stocks. In the 1970 recession, by contrast, which was both gradual and predictable, the business community was able to hold back on plant and equipment capacity expansion and had much less unwanted inventory on hand that had to be disposed of at cut-rate prices. As a result, the rate of inflation, which had moderated significantly in previous recessions, actually accelerated during 1969 and 1970.

By 1971, with both unemployment and inflation getting worse rather than better, and with the presidential elections little more than a year away, the Nixon administration realized the sterility and futility of its policy of restraint, and abruptly changed course. Monetary and fiscal policy became sharply stimulatory, and the economy responded accordingly. After more than two years of virtually no growth, the real gross national product (adjusted for price changes) grew about 5 percent during 1971 and another 7 1/2 percent during 1972. Unemployment, which reached 6 percent of the labor force by the beginning of 1971, at first responded hardly at all, but in 1972 started to decline slowly.

By mid-1973, the extent of the lasting damage that had been done to the economy during the controlled recession of 1969–70 began to surface. Although unemployment was still 5 percent of the labor force, which is high by historical standards, capacity bottlenecks became evident in industry after industry. Because of the slow, deliberate way in which the economy was depressed, businesses were able to adjust capacity and inventories to depressed market conditions, so that when policy signals were changed and the economy asked to expand, they simply didn't have the capital stock wherewithal.

The [current] policy of restraint is doomed to failure because it fails to recognize that a predictable and predicted recession will allow the business sector to adjust its investment plans accordingly, bringing about structural changes in the economy which condemn it to permanently high unemployment without remedying the problem of excess demand inflation. Business plans for plant and equipment spending, which last fall and winter represented one of the few bright spots on the economic horizon for 1974, have been cut back sharply in the last few months, and will remain depressed as long as aggregate demand is held down by fiscal and monetary policy restraint.

Advocates of the policy of demand restraint do not make clear the mechanism by which they expect that policy to reduce inflationary pressures. The alleged mechanism is inside a kind of black box, and we are expected to take it on faith that it works. If we think about it a little bit, however, it becomes increasingly dubious that there can be any effective mechanism there! From a logical viewpoint, holding down aggregate demand, if it is to have an anti-inflationary effect, must work in one or another of two ways: either the creation of redundant supply in labor markets by letting unemployment increase will serve to moderate wage demands and thereby hold down business costs, or the holding down of demand for goods and services will cause producers and raw material suppliers to mark down their prices (or increase them less than they otherwise would). Unless one or the other of these things can be expected to happen, demand restraint is clearly a bankrupt policy as a means of curbing inflation.

It is exceedingly difficult to see why the rate of increase of either wage rates or product prices can be expected to be moderated during a gradual, controlled economic recession. Most wage rates that count for anything in our system are set through collective bargaining between employers and employees, and while the recent rate of consumer price inflation weighs heavily in these bargaining sessions, the rate of unemployment has little obvious relevance. Product and raw material sellers can be expected to mark down prices, or to moderate the rate of increase in their prices, if they are selling in competitive markets and productivity gains are large enough to reduce unit costs of production, or if there emerges a condition of excess supply. But restraining demand on a gradual and predictable schedule is likely to be met by adjustments to production schedules and capacity expansion programs that are carefully tailored to *avoid* excess supply situations, which no prudent business person wishes to have happen if there is any way to avoid it, and productivity is always lower during recession periods than during expansions. It must be remembered that the great bulk of goods and services supplied by the U.S. economy are produced by modern sophisticated firms which spend a great deal of time and effort and apply considerable expertise in demand forecasting as an integral part of their production scheduling and capacity expansion planning. In short, the policy of demand restraint as an anti-inflationary strategy rests on a wholly unwarranted extrapolation of a theory that works decently well in explaining price behavior during unplanned cyclical contractions in the economy to a quite different situation in which the government arranges, and advertises for all to see, a gradual and predictable reduction in demand.

If demand restraint is a bankrupt policy, what then are the alternatives? Are we condemned to accept inflation as a necessary price of prosperity? The answer to that is no. We must not, indeed, we cannot afford to accept inflation of the current magnitude. Even to contemplate such a course would be foolhardy, for we would shortly be faced by still higher rates of inflation and hasten the day when the whole system is likely to collapse with a loud bang.

A successful anti-inflationary strategy must take account of several factors simultaneously.

1. There can be no return to full employment, with or without inflation, without an expansion of the capital stock relative to the employed labor force.

2. While the encouragement of needed investment requires expanding demand and markets, we are currently up against capacity constraints in many industries because of past mismanagement of the economy, so that the expansion must be at a moderate and deliberate pace. Overly rapid stimulus of the economy just now would touch off a new round of excess demand inflation.

3. Improving the productivity of the U.S. economy must be an integral part of any effective strategy to combat inflation.

4. The concern to get private investment moving again has been translated by some analysts into recommendations for tax gimmicks favorable to investment, such as accelerated depreciation or a step-up in the investment tax credit. There is not a good case for such actions. If demand is gradually expanded, and business becomes convinced that the expansion will continue, private investment will revive satisfactorily without the need for special tax relief. If aggregate demand does *not* expand, tax relief for investment would tend to stimulate labor-saving investment rather than investment in expanded capacity. In the jargon of economists, it would encourage capital "deepening" rather than capital "widening," which would worsen rather than improve the already serious imbalance between productive capacity and labor supply.

5. Because of the need at this time to redress a capital-labor imbalance, the required expansion in the economy should feature, as much as possible, private fixed investment in plant and equipment, as distinct from personal consumption expenditures or government spending. For this reason, the need for mild stimulus rather than continued restraint should be executed through monetary policy rather than fiscal policy.

6. The principal requirement for Congress and the executive, aside from leaning heavily on the Federal Reserve to begin pursuing more constructive monetary and credit policies, is the establishment of effective price-control machinery. The correct word is "establishment" rather than "re-establishment," since the various phases applied by the Nixon administration, aside from the 3-month freeze during Phase 1, were public relations exercises aimed at proving controls can't work. A much more relevant piece of evidence on the question of whether controls can be effective is to observe that for more than two years during the Korean War, from the beginning of 1951 to the spring of 1953, price and wage controls allowed us to maintain an inflation rate of under 2 1/2 percent per year while unemployment was kept below 3 percent of the labor force!

Unwinding an inflation as stubborn as the present one, in which expectations of more inflation to come have been allowed to develop a strong independent inflationary force of their own, will not be easy. It is not likely to be accomplished on the price side by monitoring and "jawboning," although a voluntary guidepost approach is probably all that is required on the wage side. Effective price controls require sanctions or penalties of some kind, perhaps graduated profit taxes similar to those requested at the beginning of the year for the oil companies (and so far ignored by the Congress). On the other hand, an effective system probably requires policing only large firms in a few key industries.

A policy of controlled gradual recession which the Ford administration and the Federal Reserve are promising to intensify and prolong is a completely unworkable strategy which cannot succeed in controlling inflation even if continued for 100 years, for the simple reason that the business sector, by being able to anticipate the intended results, can frustrate their achievement by holding back on plant and equipment spending. The off-again on-again application of this policy over the past five years has already done serious lasting damage to the U.S. economy by shrinking the productive base required to keep the labor force fully employed, and the longer this policy is continued, the more our economy will grow to resemble the economies of the developing countries, many of which experience excess demand inflation along with 15, 20, or even 25 percent of the labor force unemployed. If the authorities lose control of the recession and plunge us into a genuine crisis (which admittedly could happen one of these days), then inflation *might* be arrested, but at a price no one is recommending and no responsible official could seriously contemplate.

A workable anti-inflation strategy requires gradual expansion of the economy rather than gradual recession. It should be accompanied by price controls, wage guideposts, and flexible industry-specific monetary and credit policies targeted toward capacity expansion in bottleneck industries.

The strategy proposed here will perhaps strike some as smacking of socialism and economic planning since it calls for greater government attention to investment and price behavior in specific industries than has heretofore been considered desirable or necessary during peacetime. But if these policies are unusual, so too are the economic problems we face.

One is tempted to recall that when President Roosevelt began applying the then unorthodox principles of Keynesian economics to the unprecedented economic situation of the 1930s, he was criticized by many bankers and business executives as threatening the free enterprise system. By the late 1930s, however, it became clear that Roosevelt's policies had rescued the capitalist system from dilemmas the old orthodoxies were incompetent to deal with.

President Ford faces a comparable situation. If he persists in old policies in the face of an economic situation which is different from any we have faced before, the continuity of our economy and society will be increasingly threatened. The free enterprise system can be redeemed once again from the new problems it has gotten into, but only if the business and financial communities are willing to accept a closer working partnership with the federal government than has previously been acceptable.

32

Who Will Plan the Planned Economy?

James R. Crotty and Raford Boddy

Four months have passed since President Ford announced his ten-point economic program to a joint session of Congress. The program was dismissed at the time by most commentators as unimaginative, inconsistent, and ineffectual. The *Wall Street Journal* characterized the program as "biting the marshmallow."

This was hardly an appropriate characterization for the *real* program chosen by the Ford Administration to deal with the crisis—a long, deep and potentially disastrous recession. While Ford was unveiling his marshmallow before Congress, the government monetary authorities were continuing the severe restriction of money and credit begun in the spring, while on the fiscal side, the federal high employment budget would have been in surplus for more than a year if high employment had prevailed.

The *real* Ford program is working—with a vengeance. The take-home pay of the average worker, adjusted for inflation, is more than 5% lower than a year ago. The unemployment rate has been rising since October 1973, and recently began a dizzying ascent. It is now generally agreed that it will top 8% sometime this year. The inflation-adjusted value of the gross national product has been declining for over a year. There is no hard evidence of an upturn in sight.

The Administration has made it clear that it intends to take any steps that are necessary to restore order to the economy. If the recessionary policy does not work, even stronger means are available, as we will note later in this article. What may not be as clear is our understanding of how we got into this mess. What is the nature of the crisis which has brought us to this chaotic and dangerous juncture in American and world history?

THE ROOTS OF THE CRISIS: INSTABILITY AND IMPERIALISM

The roots of the current crisis cannot be found in poor world grain harvests, nor in the diabolical machinations of some Harvard-trained sheiks, nor in the profligacy with which Arthur Burns has handled the money supply, though food, oil, and money problems have had their effect. Rather, the crisis has evolved out of the basic institutions of American capitalism and the changing position of the United States in the world capitalist system during the past quarter century. That is, the roots of the current crisis lie in the fundamentally unstable nature of the capitalist growth process— instability which, though relatively dormant at the height of American imperialist power, resurfaced during the past decade when the United States fought to maintain its declining international hegemony.

By its very nature, a capitalist market economy develops through sporadic phases of hectic expansion followed by periods of recession or even depression. The contradictions in our system are such that balanced, full employment growth cannot be sustained. When an economic expansion reaches the stage of relatively full employment, a whole series of distortions and imbalances develop which destroy the basis for the continuation of that expansion. For example, increased worker militance at full employment results in an increase in wage rates and a reduction in the rate of growth of productivity. Inflation accelerates, but not by enough to prevent profit margins from starting to decline. Corporations are forced to turn increasingly to external sources in order to finance investment in plant and equipment and inventories. Debt thus accumulates just as the time when interest rates are highest. Moreover, serious balance-of-trade problems develop as the rising price of U.S. products retards exports, and, aided by strong aggregate U.S. demand, stimulates imports.

Eventually, of course, lower profits lead to cutbacks in production and investment and thus, before long, to the end of the expansion. The government also reacts to these developments, particularly to the decline in profits and the problems in the international sector. With the critical exception of the late 1960s, the government has reinforced the recessionary pressures developing in the private sector by restricting the supply of money and credit, and tightening its own budget. Thus, the expansion turns into its opposite—recession.

It is the economic function of the recession to correct the imbalances of the previous expansion and thereby create the preconditions for a new one. By robbing millions of people of their jobs, and threatening the jobs of millions of others, recessions erode worker militancy and end the rise of labor costs. They eventually rebuild profit margins and stabilize prices. During recessions, inventories are cut, loans are repaid, corporate liquidity positions improve, and the deterioration in the balance-of-payments position turns around. All the statements of Keynesian economists to the contrary notwithstanding, *recessions are inevitable in the unplanned economy of the United States* because they perform an essential function for which no adequate substitute has *thus far* been available.

The adoption in the postwar period of Keynesian approaches to managing the economy has not changed this basic characteristic of the system, nor has the continued monopolization and concentration of market power in the hands of the major corporations lessened the potential for economic instability. Until recently, these factors did moderate the fluctuation of the business cycle, but they managed to do so under what now appear to have been a set of unusually favorable conditions which are no longer operative.

From the end of World War II until the early 1960s, the United States was the unchallenged leader of world capitalism, and the dominant world military, political, and economic power. The economic strength of China and the Soviet Union could not compare with that of the United States, and American foreign policy was built on this fact. Western Europe and Japan, on the other hand, began the period with devastated economies; they were almost completely dependent upon the United States for imports, particularly capital goods.

In the world of the 1950s, the United States could pour hundreds of billions of dollars into its military machine, waste countless billions on consumer gadgetry and planned obsolescence, and still dominate world trade, accumulate a vast corporate empire in the developed world, and maintain control of the vast natural resources of the underdeveloped world.

The world of the 1950s is gone forever. The United States' political power is now constrained by a stronger Soviet Union; its economic supremacy has been challenged by Western Europe and Japan; and its assured supply of cheap raw materials has disappeared. The economic chaos we are now witnessing is the re-emergence of the basic instability of our economic system, a re-emergence triggered by the desperate attempts of the United States to maintain its status as the unchallenged leader of world capitalism in the face of the erosion of its power monopoly.

THE DECLINE OF THE EMPIRE AND THE EMERGENCE OF THE CRISIS

The changing status of American imperialism has had its greatest effect on the economy through the Indochina War, though its impact would eventually have been felt even if that war had not occurred. The outpouring of military expenditures on Vietnam between 1965 and 1968 came on top of an economic expansion which had about run its course.

But American imperialism demanded the pursuit of victory in Vietnam, so the Johnson Administration chose to overheat the economy through 1968 by accelerating military spending while taking no effective steps to reduce private spending. The prolongation of the U.S. expansion in turn created an environment in which the export-oriented economies of Japan and West Germany could sustain expansions.

In other words, in order to protect the world-wide empire of the multinational corporations, the U.S. government, by extending the expansion many years beyond its "natural life," created a situation wherein the distortions, pressures and imbalances in the capitalist economies were magnified to proportions which could only be eliminated by an unusually long and severe recession.

The incoming Nixon Administration did engineer a recession by the end of 1969, but it only lasted five or six quarters—clearly not long enough to restore balance to the economy. The Administration was forced to abandon restrictive policies in 1970 because their continuation would have resulted in an unemployment rate too high to be reduced to a politically acceptable level for the 1972 election; because corporate profits, squeezed first by five years of full-employment wage pressure and then by the initial impact of the recession, were in need of immediate relief; and because the debt and liquidity problems of many corporations and banks were too severe to respond to the usual medicine.

By 1971 the economy was clearly in crisis. Falling U.S. interest rates had triggered huge short-term capital outflows, and our trade surplus had completely eroded, leading to an explosion in the U.S. payments deficit. The international monetary system was drowning in a flood of U.S. dollars. These dollars in turn were bloating the money supplies of Japan and Europe, causing both inflation and demand-induced economic expansions.

The attempt to shore up the failing U.S. empire through the war in Vietnam can thus be said to have had several important repercussions. First, by prolonging the American economic expansion for three or four years, it left the system vulnerable to its fundamental instability. Second, by laying the foundation for a decade-long expansion in the world capitalist system, it led to a world-wide commodity or raw-material inflation. Third, by accelerating the relative decline in U.S. power, it created the preconditions for the political and economic revolt of the Third World raw-material suppliers, most significantly the actions of the exporters of oil. Fourth, it led to the introduction of government economic controls through Nixon's New Economic Policy, thus signaling the end of the postwar "miracle" of the Keynesian revolution.

THE ROLE OF FOOD AND OIL PRICES

The rise in oil and food prices is of relatively recent origin and cannot be held responsible for either domestic inflation or the international financial crisis. But it has seriously exacerbated the existing crisis, and clearly must be taken into account.

The most important cause of the food crisis is the accelerated, worldwide growth in the demand for food which evolved from the sustained world economic boom of the last decade. The food crisis cannot be understood in isolation from the entire set of forces under analysis. There were bad harvests in 1972 but these were more than compensated for by the good harvests of 1973. The average rate of growth of the world's food supply has not declined over this period. It is the growth of demand which has accelerated, leading to higher prices.

The staggering increase in food prices in the United States has the peculiar characteristic of being deliberately supported by the U.S. government. In an attempt to protect its international financial strength, the government embarked on a "great agricultural export drive." One reason the dollar was devalued was to make U.S. food exports more competitive in world markets. Further, the wage-price controls of 1971–74 fostered the export of agricultural commodities. Raw agricultural products were exempt from controls, as were food exports. Profit margins on exported food products were thus higher than profit margins on food sold domestically. And wage controls in the face of skyrocketing food prices meant that American workers could not afford their historic share of agricultural production.

The export drive succeeded. Agricultural exports rose from an average of $5 billion per year in the late 1960s to $9.4 billion in 1972, and $17.5 billion in 1973.

Even in the case of oil prices, the declining world power of the United States has played a role. As long as this country enjoyed a virtual monopoly on economic, political, and military power, it could depend on a supply of cheap raw materials. Because of our weakened international position, however, it was impossible to prevent the oil-producing countries from quadrupling the price of crude oil in the fall of 1973. Despite the saber-rattling rhetoric from Washington recently, the U.S. government has been forced to exercise caution in its attempts to discipline the oil-producing nations and reduce the price of imported crude.

WILL IT TAKE A DEPRESSION TO STOP INFLATION?

What are the likely prospects for the future? There is no easy way out of the current crisis of inflation and falling real wages. In the twisted logic of capitalist development, the current crisis requires a prolonged recession as well as the possible imposition of wage and price controls.

The price of dampening world-wide inflationary pressure will be high, but no one really knows how much unemployment, idle capacity, and other waste it will take to win the fight against inflation. Unfortunately, there is little reason for optimism. The recession of 1969–70 was too short, and thus failed to restore balance to the economy. The Ford Administration certainly does not intend to repeat that mistake. The White House noted recently in a fact sheet distributed with Ford's October 8 speech that "twice within the past decade, in 1967 and in 1971–72, we let an opportunity to regain price stability slip through our grasp." Apparently, then, the present recession will have to be deeper and more widespread than any previous postwar recession if it is to overcome the forces of inflation.

But can the recession be contained within reasonable bounds without deteriorating into a major economic depression? Several considerations indicate that the current crisis is easily the most serious of the post–World War II period. The relative prosperity of the entire postwar era in America has been built on the foundation of U.S. imperialism, and the long expansion of the 1960s and early 1970s was dependent on an incredible accumulation of corporate and family debt.

The declining international position of the United States has received much comment, and now the debt and liquidity position of the U.S. economy is in the spotlight. As *Business Week* put it in their special issue on the Debt Economy:

The U.S. is leveraged as never before. There is nearly $8 of debt per $1 of money supply, more than double the figure of 20 years ago. Corporate debt amounts to more than 15 times after-tax profits, compared with under 8 times in 1955. Household debt amounts to 93% of disposable income, compared with 65% in 1955. U.S. banks have lent billions overseas through Euro-currency markets that did not even exist in 1955. (October 12, 1974)

Faced with profits levels which have probably peaked and will surely decline as the recession rolls into high gear, debt-ridden corporations will find it increasingly difficult to meet their fixed-interest obligations. A snowballing of bankruptcies could follow the failure of a few giant corporations. The inability of unemployed workers to maintain payment on their debt would only exacerbate the problem.

Astounding as it may seem, even some *countries* appear to be in danger of bankruptcy under the tremendous pressure of mounting bills for oil imports. At the moment, Italy is the most likely candidate. In addition to its debt to the International Monetary Fund and the central banks of other countries, Italy has borrowed $10 billion in the past few years from private international sources. Default on these massive debts would reverberate throughout the capitalist system—to what eventual effect no one is sure. Nor is it possible to forecast with any accuracy the political, economic, and financial impact of the massive accumulation of petrodollars by the oil-producing countries.

Moreover, Western Europe and Japan can no longer serve as a buffer to mitigate the impacts of a U.S. recession. They too are experiencing rising unemployment and falling output, bringing pressure on U.S. export markets just as our recession is pressuring their exports. To make matters worse, this recession-induced decline in world exports is occurring at a time when most capitalist countries have huge balance-of-payments deficits toward the oil-producing countries. These deficits, coupled with declining exports, might lead to export-import controls, controls on long-term capital movements, or competitive devaluations.

With the weakening of U.S. hegemony, it is no longer certain that the United States can organize and discipline their competitors in order to generate an orderly treatment of the deficit problem. The American defeat in Vietnam and the breakdown of international monetary arrangements in August of 1971 have had serious consequences for the world capitalist economic order. And the political strains emerging in Greece, Great Britain, Italy, Portugal, Japan, and France—not to mention the United States—make it even more difficult to count on economic cooperation as opposed to competition in dealing with mounting economic and political dislocations. This growing economic instability is fostering political instability which threatens capitalist governments throughout the Western world.

Because American capitalists no longer have the political and economic strength to control their allies, they may turn to a strategy of exploiting the existing economic and political instability. Although the decline in the power of the United States and the coming of age of Germany and Japan were the factors that permitted the oil-producing nations to impose dramatic price increases, the most damaging effects of higher oil prices have not been felt by the United States. Rather, the economies of Japan and Western Europe were, at least temporarily, most severely pummeled.

Furthermore, since Japan and Western Europe are much more immediately dependent on their export sectors than the United States, the prospect of severe world-wide recession poses a more direct threat to them than it does to the United States.

Paradoxically, then, the combination of high oil prices and world recession constitutes the situation in which the strength of the United States relative to its allies is greatest, because of their dependence on oil imports and world markets. It has become possible for a U.S. recession needed for domestic purposes to be turned into a weapon to be used against both the oil producers and our economic rivals.

If, as recent statements by high-level American officials seem to indicate, the U.S. oil strategy is to "break" OPEC and eventually reduce energy prices, then a huge reduction in the world demand for oil is essential. One way to guarantee such a decline in world oil demand is to have a long, deep, world-wide recession. Indeed, the mere threat of such an event may be enough to pressure Germany, Japan, and even France into participating in a subservient way in U.S.-designed and -dominated international economic and political tactics in the oil conflict. Maximizing the threat of world recession may therefore be attractive to those concerned with the maintenance of the American empire.

But this would be a dangerous gambit because the American corporate elite clearly has fewer means at its disposal for controlling the dynamics of a world-wide recession than it has with respect to a domestic one. And the political implications of an out-of-control world depression must be sobering indeed to corporate and government leaders.

PLANNING ON THE HORIZON

All of these strains and uncertainties make it increasingly likely that the managers of the American system will seek new tools and policies for coping with their economic and political crisis. The contradictions inherent in the attempt to "solve" the current multidimensional economic crisis through the exclusive use of orthodox monetary and fiscal tools seem overwhelming.

If the government is unwilling to risk a depression, it could choose to postpone the day of reckoning by imposing mandatory wage and price controls. Although wage-price controls are generally thought of as a mechanism used to control inflation during an economic expansion, they have attracted increased interest in the face of projections of an 8% unemployment rate *and* a 10% rise in the hourly wage rate this year. Wage controls might handle part of the job of the recession by reducing the rate of wage increase.

But these controls are themselves contradictory. The experience in Western Europe and the United States with temporary or on-off aggregate wage-price controls indicates that a repetition of such controls as Nixon's Phases I through IV can only promote increased instability in the system. For one thing, wage and price decisions are themselves affected by the removal of controls or the anticipation of their introduction. Under these conditions, temporary controls simply reallocate inflation over time, they do not eliminate it. Moreover, controls eventually lead to surpluses and shortages because they suppress market forces which, however socially irrational, have their own internal coherence in our system. This is perhaps best seen in the confused decision to freeze the price of meats and poultry in the summer of 1973, a decision that led to the withdrawal of these foods from the market, followed by a mammoth increase in food prices in August of 1973.

In light of these considerations, more permanent and extensive controls than we had in 1971–74 appear to be required. The Democratic party at its mini-convention in Kansas City in December called for "an across-the-board system of economic controls, including prices, wages, executive compensation, profits and rents." Leonard Silk reported in the *New York Times* that some leading Democrats were "moving to support a program that would put far more stress on economic planning as a means of directing industrial investment to meet critical needs. . . ." We assume that there has been serious private discussion among the corporate elite on the same topic. And since it is recognized that the use of planning by Japan, Germany, Sweden, and France contributed heavily to their superior economic performance in the 1960s and early 1970s, there are long-run as well as short-run forces pressuring the United States toward a planning imperative.

A move toward planning, it should be clear, would have profound economic and political implications. Government policy will directly determine the share of total income going to capital as opposed to labor, and perhaps the distribution of labor income among workers as well. This alone might produce considerable conflict because organized labor could be expected to fight for its share of production. But there would be more to permanent controls than the setting of wages and prices. They could require government-directed allocation of raw materials and credit, a detailed system of tax credits and subsidies, anti-strike or even anti-collective-bargaining legislation, and administratively coordinated investment strategies among firms and industries.

The planning process eventually will require detailed management of the economy and of people. This can obviously lead to serious political conflict. In short, controls may not deliver us from our current crisis, but may instead create a new one, overtly political in nature.

The development of detailed economic planning within the present array of political forces in the United States will undoubtedly mean corporate control of the planning process, just as the introduction of federal regulatory agencies has historically meant control by and for the regulated industries. It is therefore more important now than ever before that the present political balance of power be changed, and the power of the corporate elite broken. What we need now is a democratic, socialist, national political organization to defend the interests of the majority of the American people against the fundamentally antagonistic interests of the corporations and the super-rich who own and control them.

Because the problems we face are derivatives of our capitalist institutions, neither the Republican nor the Democratic party offers real hope to the working people of this country. These parties are committed to existing power relations, and dominated by corporate money and capitalist ideology. Democratic-party reformers may wish to return to the corporate liberalism of the 1950s and 1960s, but if the arguments presented here are correct, there can be no turning back.

It seems clear that over the long run the only permanent solution to the economic instability and insecurity which derive from the monopoly, inequality, and imperialism of modern capitalism is to build a democratic, socialist society. A nationwide socialist organization will be necessary to defend ourselves in the short run and to aid us in the task of developing an egalitarian society wherein production is for use rather than profit, and decisions are collectively made by workers, not bosses.

[*Editor's Note:* In a separate article, Professors Boddy and Crotty develop aspects of their analysis more fully. Excerpts from this article follow and may be considered a technical appendix to the above.]

MARX AND MACRO-POLICY

Under the "old-fashioned" business cycle as analyzed by Marx, it was understood that capitalism was incapable of balanced, full-employment growth. The hallmark of the modern Keynesian has been the presumption that such growth is at least a technical possibility, given the appropriate macro-policy, and is assuredly a primary policy goal (albeit one that must occasionally be sacrificed to the pursuit of price stability). In spite of the monopolization of the American economy, the birth of Keynesianism, and the tremendous growth of the government sector, we believe that the key to understanding both macro-economic policy and business cycles in the postwar era is still to be found in Marx's theory of the dynamics of the cycle in competitive capitalism—particularly the behavior of wages and prices.[1]

Marx argued that the reduction in the reserve army of the unemployed which accompanies economic expansions strengthens the bargaining position of the working class in its labor-market confrontation with capital. This allows workers to struggle successfully for higher real wages and a larger share of total income, thus squeezing profits toward the peak of the boom. Relaxation of this profit squeeze requires the termination of the expansionary phase of the cycle and a rebuilding of the reserve army. As Marx explained it:

> If the quantity of unpaid labor supplied by the working class, and accumulated by the capitalist class, increases so rapidly that its conversion into capital requires an extraordinary addition of paid labor, then wages rise, and, all other circumstances remaining equal, the unpaid labor diminishes in proportion. But as soon as the diminution touches the point at which the surplus labor that nourishes capital is no longer supplied in normal quantity, a reaction sets in: a smaller part of revenue is capitalized, accumulation lags, and the movement of rise in wages receives a check. The rise of wages therefore is confined within limits that not only

---

[1] We do not intend to argue that there has been no essential change since Marx's day in the dynamics of the cycle. Rather we want to strongly emphasize that the state, through its monetary and fiscal operations, can and has significantly altered the pattern of economic activity. The business cycle of the postwar period has been determined by the interaction of both private sector and state activities. The postwar cycle is *political* as well as economic.

leave intact the foundations of the capitalist system, but also secure its reproduction on a progressive scale.[2]

Keynesians have largely glossed over the importance of the full-employment profit squeeze. Born in the Great Depression, Keynesian theory has focused almost exclusively on the problem of chronically insufficient aggregate demand. Based on their pluralist theory of the state, Keynesians have assumed that the basic objective of macro-policy in the postwar era has in fact been the pursuit of full employment. And, using the enormous unemployment of the 1930s as a benchmark, they have judged the postwar level of demand to be generally adequate, with exceptions considered to be the result of inefficiencies in policy execution. Even radical critiques of the policy of this period have centered more on the social irrationality of the composition of demand and the dubious long-term viability of the Keynesian solution than on the size of the reserve army. Yet compared to other leading capitalist countries, the United States has experienced significant economic cycles with only brief episodes of relatively full employment.

It was the seminal contribution of Kalecki to point out the contradiction between Keynesian "full employment" policies and the political and social requirements of liberal capitalism. Kalecki predicted that in order to maintain capitalist political and social control, which depends on the power of the "sack" and the role of capitalist as job provider, the state would have to refrain from attempts to maintain continuous full employment. But, unlike Marx, Kalecki saw no contradiction between full employment and high profits. Based on his own theory of monopoly pricing, which assumed that corporations could maintain their profit margins under full employment conditions, Kalecki argued that

the rise in wage rates resulting from the stronger bargaining power of the workers is less likely to reduce profits than to increase prices and thus affects adversely only the rentier interests. But "discipline in the factories" and "political stability" are more appreciated by the business leaders than profits. Their class instinct tells them that lasting full employment is unsound from their point of view.[3]

Several modern radicals have supported Kalecki's position. But, as shown below, a close examination of the relevant data supports the proposition they deny, and reaffirms the crucial Marxian insight. Labor's share typically does rise in the latter half of an expansion. The profit squeeze does occur. Capitalists have more than their class instinct to tell them that sustained full employment is manifestly unsound. The Marxian economic effects of the business cycle mutually reinforce the socio-political aspects stressed by Kalecki. Together they have formed the basic context within which macro-policy has attempted to maximize long-run profits. Their interaction has ensured that the state, in pursuit of maximum profits, could not even *attempt* to use macro-policy in pursuit of balanced, full-employment growth.

---

[2] Karl Marx, *Capital*, vol. 1 (New York: International Publishers, 1967), p. 620.
[3] Michal Kalecki, *Selected Essays on the Dynamics of the Capitalist Economy* (Cambridge: Cambridge University Press, 1971), pp. 138–145.

THE CYCLICAL BEHAVIOR OF FACTOR SHARES

The class conflict inherent in macro-policy emanates from the boom-induced, full-employment profit squeeze. Because the movement of factor shares has been the subject of a great deal of confusion and contradictory claims, we have summarized some basic findings on the cyclical behavior of profits and related variables such as unit labor costs, productivity, and prices. ("Factor shares" is the economists' term for the proportion of total income received by the owners of different kinds of inputs to the production process, i.e., wages, profits, interest, and rent.)

Chart 1 depicts actual variations in factor shares over recent cycles.[4] The chart shows that halfway through the typical expansion, the economy experiences a pronounced decline in the ratio of profits to wages. The level of profits comes under severe pressure at the same cyclical juncture and typically falls thereafter as well. For the capitalists, it becomes increasingly preferable to accept the adverse but temporary profit decline of a recession. A prolongation of the boom would continuously erode their profit position, while a recession would create the foundation for a new period of expanding profits.

In Table 1 we present the data on wages, prices, and productivity that underlie the movements of the shares of capital and labor. To determine the impact of the stage of expansion upon the various series, each expansion is divided into two parts, (1) "through to mid-point" and (2) "mid-point to peak."

Looking first at wage rates, we find that in both of the longer expansions wage rates increased very significantly in the latter phase of the expansion. These variations in wage rates provide some information on the source of the noted profit squeeze, but labor cost per unit of output probably best shows the impact of the cycle on profits, as viewed from the capitalists' position. It is particularly instructive to compare unit labor cost to an index of the wholesale price of industrial commodities, a rough measure of non-labor input cost, and to output price. Output prices increased faster than wholesale prices in the last half of two of the three postwar expansions; unit labor cost increased much faster than both price indices in all three. It is only in the initial phase of the expansion that wholesale prices increase more rapidly than output prices. Thus, we can reject the idea that an increase in the price of non-labor inputs relative to output price is the basis of the profit squeeze. In contrast, we see that unit labor cost declines relative to the output price index in the first part of the expansion, but overtakes it after the mid-point of the expansion. The resultant decline in the profit rate is thus directly attributable to labor "problems" rather than rising non-labor input cost.

Let us now turn to productivity, the other determinant of unit labor cost. Productivity gains in the early expansion are tremendous. In the second part of the expansion there is a noticeable decline in the rate of increase, but generally not in productivity itself. The early increase in

---

[4] Albert E. Burger, "Relative Movements in Wages and Profits," *Federal Reserve Bank of St. Louis Review* (February 1973).

productivity is attributable partly to a return to optimal factor proportions which occurs as output rises toward "desired" levels. The later slowdown in productivity is attributable partly to subsequent technical bottlenecks which develop during the later part of the expansion.[5]

Although technical reasons help to explain the noted slowdown in labor productivity, knowledgeable observers of the labor scene have pointed directly to an increasingly obstreperous labor force as an influence on the decline in productivity during the expansion. Full employment affects not only wage rates, but also quit rates and strikes. It has been a long-standing observation that such favorable conditions for labor imply less effort on the shop floor. For example, a plant superintendent testifying before the Commission on Labor in 1904 had the following to say:

Five years ago men did not restrict their output, union or non-union men, because they wanted to hold their jobs and a man would do anything and all he was told to do. Now a man knows that all he has to do is to walk across the street and get another job at the same pay. During the hard times we took contracts at any price we could get, and in some places and cases men were driven at high speed to get this work out, so as to lose as little money on it as possible. Men will not keep up that speed rate in these days.[6]

After the 1970–1971 recession, the *Wall Street Journal* ran a front-page story under the title "Conciliatory Mood." The story reported that a very large company had just forced the union representing its employees to accept a pay cut of 25 cents an hour, the removal of two cost-of-living increases, and an agreement to forego any raises until 1974. It continued:

Across the country at large and small companies, workers are frequently choosing to be more conciliatory when faced with the threat of losing their jobs. That is in sharp contrast to the labor scene of recent years [i.e., when unemployment was low], both union and corporate officials agree. Not long ago, they say, rank-and-filers . . . would probably have been angered by the thought of concessions. But these days . . . are bringing about a softer approach. . . . Many manufacturing executives have openly complained *in recent years that too much control had passed from management to labor*. With sales sagging and competition mounting, they feel safer in attempting to restore what they call "balance." [7]

One direct measure of labor militancy is the incidence of strikes. Strike activity has generally receded after the beginning of a recession. Corre-

---

[5] As stressed by Marx (*Capital*, vol. 1 [New York: International Publishers, 1967], pp. 630–633), cyclical variations are not free from the pressures of longer-run technological forces. The optimal factor proportions of the current expansion are not those of the previous one. Correspondingly the bottlenecks will have changed too. Investments in the early part of an expansion are concentrated preponderantly in equipment. Equipment typically substitutes directly for labor and therefore increases labor productivity and the reserve army of unemployed. In the later part of the expansion the depletion of building space requires that the composition of investment shift towards structures. Structures have a weaker impact than equipment on labor productivity.

[6] Quoted in Wesley Mitchell, *Business Cycles and Their Causes* (1913) (Berkeley: University of California Press, 1941), p. 33.

[7] *Wall Street Journal* (January 26, 1972, emphasis added).

CHART I □ RATIO OF PROFITS TO WAGES

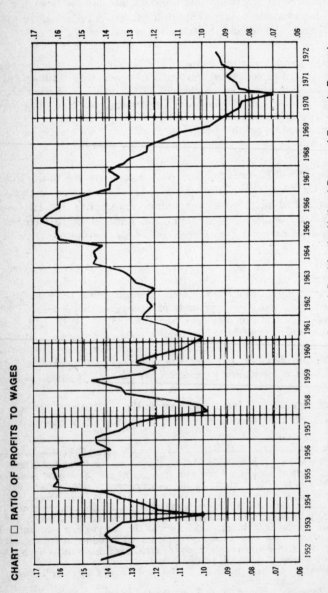

Shaded areas represent periods of business recession as defined by the National Bureau of Economic Research. Profits are measured by profits after taxes for nonfinancial corporations. Wages are measured by total compensation in nonfinancial corporations.

TABLE I □ FACTORS INFLUENCING PROFITS/WAGES RATIO (ANNUAL RATES OF CHANGE)

As seen in three business cycle expansions from the third quarter of 1954 (III/54) to the fourth quarter of 1969 (IV/69). The data are shown separately for two phases of each expansion:

A—The period from the trough to the mid-point of the expansion
B—The period from the mid-point to the peak of the expansion

Three Expansions	Wage Rate[1]	Unit Labor Cost[2]	Wholesale Prices of Industrial Goods	Output Prices[3]	Output Per Person	Capacity Utilization	Output	Profits[4]	Compensation of Employees[5]
A. III/54-I/56	4.6%	2.3%	3.5%	-0.2%	3.5%	5.6%	8.7%	21.6%	11.9%
B. I/56-III/57	6.8	4.1	3.1	2.8	1.4	-4.0	0.9	-4.2	5.7
A. II/58-II/59	4.9	-4.1	2.3	1.3	12.9	16.4	20.8	63.0	13.2
B. II/59-II/60	4.5	4.7	0.0	0.6	-1.7	-3.8	-0.9	-13.9	4.9
A. I/61-III/65	3.9	-1.4	0.4	0.7	6.5	4.5	10.1	25.6	7.8
B. III/65-IV/69	6.5	4.2	2.7	3.3	1.6	-1.3	4.2	-4.0	10.2

Note: Profits and compensation pertain to nonfinancial corporations. All other data pertain to total manufacturing.
[1] Employee compensation divided by manhours
[2] Compensation divided by output
[3] Consumer price index of commodities less food
[4] Corporate profits after tax liability for nonfinancial corporations
[5] Compensation of employees in nonfinancial corporations
Source: Albert E. Burger, Ibid.

spondingly after long expansions such as those of the Second World War and the Indochina War, strike activity has increased.

We conclude on the basis of an examination of these data that the avoidance of sustained full employment is a necessary condition for both the maximization of long-run profits and the maintenance of capitalist-class hegemony.

33

Why World Bankers Are Worried

Charles P. Kindleberger

Q. For the first time in more than a generation, the American public seems to be genuinely concerned about another Great Depression like that of the thirties. Your recent book *The World in Depression* deals with that earlier collapse. Do you see any disturbing parallels between 1974 and 1929?
A. I don't think that we are going to have another Great Depression. But there are some interesting—and disquieting—similarities. As I said in my book, it was not a shock to the system that produced the depression: it was the fact that the system itself was unstable. No one was playing the role of stabilizer. The British had ceased to play that role, and the United States had not taken it on.

There are a number of shocks to the system now—the overhang of dollars, the oil payments problem, and so forth. But the really awkward thing is that there is no leadership. The United States showed in 1971 and 1973 that it is no longer willing to take the heat; and nobody else, including the EEC [European Economic Community] is ready to take its place.

Q. Your book makes a strong point about the unwillingness of U.S. monetary authorities to follow Walter Bagehot's dictum that some institution has to be ready to provide easy credit in a financial crisis. Is that what you have in mind now?
A. Yes. The question is whether we are set up to handle a real liquidity crunch.

In my interpretation of the depression, I paid much more attention to the stock market crash than most people have—more certainly than the Chicago School. Actually, the quantity of money did not begin to go down significantly until the depression was well under way in March of 1931. In my view, what happened is that, after the stock market began to fall, the New York banks began to worry very much about how to replace the call money funds—short-term loans to stockbrokers—that were being withdrawn because of fear that these assets would be frozen if the stock market closed down. So, the New York banks just stopped lending to anyone. People couldn't buy automobiles because nobody would extend automobile credit.

Now, as more than one person has noticed, the stock market has been going down in the United States and elsewhere. This suggests to me the beginning of a race for liquidity. Banks are beginning to worry about whom they will lend to, not because of the quantity of money, which is still growing, but because of the risk that the system will suddenly freeze up. They have long-range commitments to lend to their best customers, but not to anyone else.

This suggests some distressing possibilities. Things appear to be unraveling in Italy right now, and the Eurodollar banks are sitting with $5 billion in loans to Italy. (Eurodollars are dollars on deposit in banks outside the United States.) Suppose the Italians found that they could not pay interest on those loans and a little run on the Eurodollar banks started. That is the type of scenario that makes people uneasy. The governor of the bank of Italy says that the lender of last resort in this case should be the U.S. Federal Reserve System. But will the Federal Reserve respond to that?

Q. So your concern is that when we need a lender of last resort, there might not be one?

A. There isn't a clear designation as to who it is. And it is worrisome that, if a crunch came, Mr. Simon or someone would say, "we don't want to throw good money after bad." Good money after bad is the name of the game. That is the way you keep money from getting worse. It's one of those poker games in which you have a lot at stake and have to keep on betting.

I don't mean to talk panic. But I just think the reasonable position is to have some clear idea as to what would happen if some of the small signs of unraveling that we now see continue to grow.

Q. Is it a political problem—namely, the rather obvious decline in the spirit of international cooperation? Or is it a problem that is centered in the international financial system itself—say, the organization of the Eurodollar market?

A. Both, of course. You can never really separate them. The U.S. renunciation of leadership in a coherent world economy makes the international financial system more vulnerable to the shocks I was talking about earlier.

One concern is that the Eurodollar market is under strain partly because it has been lending Italy funds that it has been getting from the Arabs on a five-day basis. If the Arabs start taking their money out, things might get rather complex. I don't envisage anything like that, but it's the kind of a thing a product man has to think about.

Part of the trouble is related to the foreign exchange speculation of the Franklin National Bank, the Herstadt collapse, Lloyds' losses in Ticino, and a number of things like that. This begins to nibble away at the foundations of trust in the banking community. A number of depositors have taken their money out of little banks and put it into big banks—and sometimes even left it in currency. That has echoes of the past that are not very attractive. So a loss of confidence in the system is not completely out of the realm of possibility—and we've never had that before. I don't look for another Credit-Anstalt—which was a terrible bank to begin with. But that is the kind of thing that people have on their minds. Once the market sees a weak spot, it finds it hard to stop looking for others.

Q. If the dire pessimists turned out to be correct and we had something like a repeat of the 1930s, where do you think that future historians would begin their account?

A. Where the United States made a big mistake was in trying to run an independent monetary policy when the markets were all joined through the Eurodollar system. We tried to put on a big boom for the election of '72. We tried, with great difficulty, to drive down interest rates here; instead we drove down the German rate at the cost of a horrendous outflow of capital. The Germans kept on taking in dollars—until they finally quit in March of 1973 and floated the mark.

What we should have done was to be prepared to run U.S. monetary policy as world monetary policy. Because, you see, when the world is on a dollar standard, U.S. monetary policy *is* world monetary policy. I once proposed that we put Europeans and Japanese on the Federal Reserve Open Market Committee. That's not very practical. But we could run monetary policy through the Bank of International Settlements, taking our credit conditions from the Eurodollar market just the way every other country does.

Our big mistake—and here economists are at fault—has been in not understanding that we can no longer run an independent monetary policy in a world where capital markets are joined so closely.

Q. I am sure that you don't mean that everything was working fine until 1972. The Europeans—particularly the French—have been criticizing U.S. economic policies for years.

A. I don't think that the dollar was in bad shape until 1968.

My thesis has been that the balance-of-payments deficit was required because we had become the banker to the world. Bankers are never loved—populism is not limited to Texas—and it may be that once our role as banker was recognized, it was no longer legitimate. Some Europeans complained that we were printing money to buy their businesses. Anyway, by the end of the 1960s the Europeans began to see our banker role as exploitation, and we began to see it as a burden. What seemed to get the wind up for Mr. Connally and Mr. Nixon was the turn in our trade balance in 1970.

Q. Many economists have attributed that adverse balance to inflation in the United States, but I think that you have talked about it as something more far-reaching.

A. Yes, I think there was a significant change in U.S. comparative advantage about 1970. It used to be that our advantage was in new goods, which other people then took over and imitated. But the speed of imitation has gotten faster and our speed of replacement has been slowing down. It may be that our innovative drive is slowing down like that of the British at the end of the nineteenth century. And it may be that this is one deep-seated reason why we are now backing away from our previous role as world economic leader. Maybe when you begin to slip, in terms of industrial vitality, you are finished as a banker. I don't know. The British continued until 1913.

34

Banks: Skating on Thin Ice

Harry Magdoff and Paul M. Sweezy

The specter haunting today's capitalist world is the possible collapse of its financial institutions and an associated world economic crisis. The miasma of fear is hardly surprising in the light of the coincidence in many capitalist countries of seemingly uncontrollable inflation, declining production, and instability in financial markets. The banking and credit community is showing increasing signs of weakness. Thus, in the span of one year the United States witnessed the two largest bank failures in its history (U.S. National Bank in San Diego and Franklin National Bank in New York). In addition, according to a report in the *Wall Street Journal* of December 18, 1974, more than a dozen European banks reported big losses or failed in 1974.

Superficial apologists are inclined to gloss over these warning signals by dwelling solely on the special and, by implication, unique errors of the banks that collapsed, thereby ignoring the fact that these so-called errors are merely distorted reflections of more basic difficulties besetting the money markets. The more responsible financial leaders of the capitalist class tend to speak more frankly. For example, Robert V. Roosa, a partner in Brown Brothers Harriman and former Undersecretary of the Treasury, observed last August, according to a *Washington Post* dispatch:

"There has been a loss of confidence in the [financial] machinery most of us took for granted. There is a fear, a kind of foreboding." It is "not too much," Roosa added, to say that these concerns are similar to the kind that prevailed in the 1930s. (Published in the *Boston Globe*, August 5, 1974.)

And the chairman of the Federal Reserve Board, Arthur F. Burns, in a major address to the latest convention of the American Bankers Association (October 21, 1974) also went back to the Great Depression as a point of comparison for today's critical conditions. While he did not specifically identify the decade of the 1930s, he could not have meant anything else by his opening sentence: "This year, for the first time in decades, questions have been raised about the strength of the nation's, and indeed the world's, banking system." Rather than sweep this notion under the rug, as one might expect from a conservative government official charged with the responsibility to sustain the public confidence and faith on which banks rely to stay in business, Burns went on to spell out in considerable detail why such fears are justified, tracing the problems to the fact that the "goals of profitability and growth have been receiving more and more attention [by bank managements]." He did, of course, utter the necessary endorsement of faith in the banks, but made it clear that it does not rest on the liquidity and stability of the banks themselves. Instead, he pointed out that "for the first time since the Great Depression, the availability of liquidity from the central bank has become . . . an essential ingredient in maintaining confidence in the commercial banking system. . . . Faith in our banks . . . now rests unduly on the fact that troubled banks can turn to a governmental lender of last resort." (Full text of Burns's speech in *The American Banker*, October 23, 1974.)

Why is it that matters have been permitted to reach such a state—where banks can't stand on their own feet and must hopefully rely on the government to prevent collapse? Why, indeed, when there are long-established laws and regulatory bodies—notably, the Federal Reserve Board itself—designed to prevent precisely the dangerous developments analyzed coldly and competently by Burns in the aforementioned speech? Surely, the reason can't be ignorance. The relevant data about the operations of the large commercial banks are available to the Federal Reserve Board, and are publicly distributed by the Board itself, from week to week. Moreover, the important changes, showing increasing sources of instability, are not new, but, as we shall show below, have been developing since the early 1960s and accelerating since the mid-1960s.

The answers to these questions are not to be found in ignorance, absence of wisdom, or lack of will power. What has to be understood is that the ruling class and government officials could hardly have prevented the present situation from developing no matter how much they may have wanted to. The overextension of debt and the overreach of the banks was exactly what was needed to protect the capitalist system and its profits; to overcome, at least temporarily, its contradictions; and to support the imperialist expansion and wars of the United States. Those who now complain and tremble over excesses are the very same people who helped bring them about, or at the least did nothing to forestall them, for fear of bringing down the whole financial network. This should become clearer as we examine some of the key facts.

Before we get into the workings of the banking system in these years of inflation and credit expansion, we should understand that there are two sides to the debt explosion: (1) capitalists borrow as much as possible not only from necessity but, more importantly, as a way to increase their individual profit rates, and (2) banks and other institutions aggressively increase their lending as a means of maximizing their own profits. The first point can easily be seen with a simple arithmetical illustration.

Investment—First Stage
Let us assume that a capitalist has invested in a manufacturing
process $1,000

Profit
Assume that he makes a gross profit of 20% on this investment . $ 200
Assume further that he pays 50% of profits in taxes .... $ −100
He then makes a net profit of 10% on his investment .... $ 100

Investment—Second Stage
The capitalist decides to double his capacity, but, instead of plowing back his profits, he borrows another $1,000 by issuing bonds. The capital in his business then consists of

Stock investment $1,000
Bonds $1,000
Total capital $2,000

Profit

Gross profit (20%) on total capital .... $ 400
Assume bondholders are paid 6% interest on their $1,000 of bonds $ −60
The capitalist then has, after interest payments .... $ 340
Deduct the 50% he pays in taxes .... $−170

The capitalist now gets a profit rate of 17% on his original $1,000
invested .... $ 170

This arithmetic of profits (in our simplified example, a potential increase in the profit rate from 10 to 17 percent) is what lies behind a good deal of the vast expansion of long-term debt shown in Table 1.

TABLE I □ INVESTMENT IN ALL U.S. CORPORATIONS

Year	Long-Term Debt Bonds and Mortgages	Direct Investment by Owners of the Corporation: Stocks	Long-Term Debt as a Percent of Stock Investment
	BILLIONS OF DOLLARS		
1940	$ 49	$ 89	55.1%
1950	66	94	70.2
1955	98	113	86.7
1960	154	140	110.0
1965	210	161	130.4
1970	363	201	180.6

As can clearly be seen from Table 1, the rapid accumulation of corporate capital since the end of the Great Depression involved both equity investment and debt, but the growth in the use of bonds and mortgages far outpaced that of stocks. Stock investment (equity capital) increased $112 billion (from $89 in 1940 to $201 billion in 1970), while debt capital (bonds and mortgages) grew by $314 billion (from $49 in 1940 to $363 billion in 1970). This shift to much greater use of debt capital has two origins: (1) the drive to increase profit rates, as explained in the foregoing arithmetical example; and (2) the constant pressure to increase the mass of profits, even though, as in Marx's words, this means "driving capitalist production beyond its own limits," and means relying on debt because of the insufficiency of funds capitalists are able to generate internally or through flotation of new stock issues to finance expansion. Note that we are now discussing all corporations (financial and nonfinancial); the impulse to rely on borrowed money for investment capital extends over the entire spectrum of capitalist enterprise.

As much as this long-term debt of corporations has grown, it has nevertheless proven to be insufficient to appease the capitalist appetite for accumulation. And hence corporations, with the collaboration of the banks and other financial institutions, began to depend more and more on short-term borrowing as a means of obtaining capital both for new investment in

TABLE 2 □ SHORT-TERM DEBT OF NONFINANCIAL CORPORATIONS

End of Year	Bank Loans	Other Borrowing [a]	Gross National Product Originating in Nonfinancial Corporations	Bank Loans as Percent of GNP	Other Borrowing as Percent of GNP
		BILLIONS	OF DOLLARS		
1950	$ 18.3	$ 1.4	$151.7	12.1%	0.9%
1955	25.6	3.0	216.3	11.8	1.4
1960	37.7	6.8	273.1	13.8	2.5
1965	60.7	8.8	377.6	16.1	2.3
1970	102.5	24.3	516.1	19.9	4.7
1974 (first half)	183.6	37.6	727.9	25.2	5.2

[a] Includes commercial paper sold by corporations on the open market and loans by finance companies.

plant and equipment and for their everyday operations. Salient facts on these changes for all nonfinancial corporations are shown in Table 2.

Especially noteworthy in the data presented in Table 2 is the marked difference between the years before and after 1960. Bank loans increased in the decade of the 1950s, but pretty much in line with the general expansion of nonfinancial corporate business: bank loans as a percent of nonfinancial corporate GNP were 12.1 in 1950 and 13.8 in 1960—a rise, but not an especially significant one. Other short-term borrowing also grew in this period, but in 1960 it was still small potatoes. Now look at the decisive change that begins with 1960. Between 1960 and 1974 bank loans grew at a much faster rate than nonfinancial business activity, the ratio of the former to the latter almost doubling: from 13.8 percent in 1960 to 25.2 percent in the first half of 1974, while at the same time other forms of short-term borrowing spurted forward.

Still more interesting is the acceleration in the dependence on bank credit. Thus, if we examine the rate of increase of this dependency (as expressed in the column of Table 2 headed "Bank loans as percent of GNP"), we find that reliance on bank credit increases by 17 percent between 1960 and 1965, by 24 percent in the next five-year period, and by 27 percent in only three-and-a-half years from the end of 1970 to the end of June 1974.

While this kind of debt acceleration helps keep the economy going by "driving capitalist production beyond its limits," the dependence on debt produces limits of its own. If we assume for the sake of argument that the sale of bonds and mortgages and the granting of bank loans can keep on increasing endlessly, business borrowers can still absorb this expanding debt only as long as they can make enough profit to meet the rising interest payments. Eventually, if the debt load keeps accelerating, the interest on the debt begins to choke off profits and hence also the incentive, as well as the financial ability, to keep the underlying accumulation process going.

The capitalist answer to this dilemma up to now has been to feed the fires of inflation. As interest burdens increase—the result of larger debt as well as higher interest rates stimulated by the huge demand for money capital—capitalists raise prices to meet these obligations. And as price hikes spread throughout the economy, the need for even more borrowing follows.

Thus debt obligations, interest charges, and prices chase each other in the upward spiral of inflation.

Thus far we have examined only one side of the problem: the demand for money by business, assuming in effect that there is no end to the supply of money. To a certain extent, this is a tenable assumption, but only if one assumes that the government's money-printing presses go mad and end up producing a hyperinflation that destroys the country's currency. Short of such a runaway inflation, we are beginning to see obstacles emerging in the ability of the banks to keep on supplying credit at the accelerated rate of the past. It is true that the banks, in pursuit of ever more profits for themselves, have tried to keep up with the demand for loans. But in doing so they have stretched themselves so thin that their own liquidity is in question, and legitimate fears have been raised about the possible collapse of the financial system.

To understand this aspect of the problem we need to review a few simple fundamentals of how commercial banks operate. The traditional function of such banks has been to act as a depository (safekeeper) of money. Individuals and business firms place their money in these banks in the form of deposits in checking or savings accounts, which the banks should always be able to return on request. The banks in turn accept these deposits because they can make a profit by using the major part of them either to buy bonds or to make loans. Bankers base their operations on the assumption of a certain pattern of withdrawal of deposits by customers, i.e., that only a certain portion will be withdrawn each day. To meet these withdrawals, banks keep a reserve of cash. Since one cannot be too sure that there may not be unexpected surges of deposit withdrawals, an additional part of the deposits is invested in short-term U.S. Treasury bills and notes. The prices of these investments do not fluctuate very much and, more important, they can be sold almost instantaneously in the money market to raise cash, should deposit withdrawals suddenly increase. On top of this, banks invest another part of the deposits in longer-term bonds of the U.S. Treasury, other government bodies, and corporations. On such investments banks make more money than on short-term debt instruments, their disadvantage being that the prices of these bonds fluctuate, which means that the banks can lose money if they are forced to sell when prices are down. Still more profitable for the banks than bonds are loans to businesses and consumers, but these cannot normally be turned into cash until they mature, so they provide little or no protection against a sudden dash by depositors to withdraw funds. Hence, for the sake of safety, banks have traditionally maintained a pattern of investment which consists of retaining a margin of ready cash and then distributing their money-making assets among a variety of notes, bonds, and loans.

Against this background look at Table 3, which shows how banking practices have been changing in recent years and why doubts have been arising about the general viability of the banking system.

The rise in the percent of loans to deposits between 1950 and 1960 is not especially noteworthy. Cash reserves in banks (and in business firms) were still very large, reflecting the cash accumulated during the Second World War. Further, the fact that 56 percent of the deposits of the large commercial banks were loaned out still left the banks in a fairly secure position,

TABLE 3 ☐ LOANS AND DEPOSITS: COMMERCIAL BANKS

End of Year	Loans	Deposits	Loans as Percent of Deposits
LARGE COMMERCIAL BANKS [a]			
Billions of dollars			
1950	$ 31.6	$ 87.7	36.0%
1955	48.4	105.3	46.0
1960	71.6	127.2	56.3
1965	120.3	181.8	66.2
1970	188.8	266.8	70.8
1974	319.3	389.4	82.0
LARGE NEW YORK CITY BANKS			
1950	$ 9.9	$ 25.1	39.4%
1955	14.2	27.9	50.9
1960	18.6	31.0	60.0
1965	31.8	45.7	69.6
1970	45.5	63.2	72.0
1974	78.9	93.5	84.4

[a] Banks that had total deposits of $100 million or more on Dec. 31, 1965.

with comfortable reserves in cash and short-term securities to meet emergencies. It is the inexorable growth of the percentage of loans to deposits since 1960 that cries out for attention. The heating up of the economy under the stimulus of the Vietnam War and the consequent kindling of the flames of inflation induced an expansion of the bank-lending activity beyond any traditional understanding of the so-called fiduciary responsibility of the banks, a process that endangers the safety of the money left for safekeeping and begins to bump against the ultimate ceiling of how much money banks can lend.

Clearly, the banks cannot lend out all of their deposits; some part must be held in reserve to pay depositors who wish to withdraw their money and to cover losses arising from defaulted loans. While there is no trustworthy guide to the "proper" ratio of loans to deposits, the persistent rise in the ratio, especially since 1970, reveals that even apart from their responsibility as safekeepers of other people's money, the banks are fast approaching the absolute limit (100 percent) of the deposits that could be loaned out. Thus, as shown in Table 3, by the end of 1974 the large commercial banks had committed 82 percent of their deposits to loans; the same pattern is seen in the large New York City banks—at the heart of the country's main money market. To see this in perspective, it should be noted that the highest ratio of loans to deposits in U.S. banks between 1900 and 1970 was 79 percent (and that in only one year, 1921); in 1929 the ratio was 73.1 percent.

How the banks were able to reach the extraordinary ratios of the 1970s will be explained below. But for the present it should be noted that a sizable part of the deposits recorded in Table 3 are far from what would be considered "normal" deposits of banks. No less than 40 percent of the deposits of the large New York City banks consists of large certificates of deposit, money borrowed by banks to facilitate the rapid growth of loans beyond otherwise practical limits; and half the increase in these deposits between 1965 and 1974 was generated by the sale of these specially issued short-term certificates of deposit. But more on this later.

This is not yet the whole story. In their search for profits and since they are bumping against limits to their outright lending power, the banks have introduced and are expanding a new technique of lending, called "standby letters of credit." (See *Business Week*, February 16, 1974, p. 120.) For a fee, they guarantee the IOUs issued and sold on the commercial paper market by big corporations. In other words, the banks commit themselves to paying the borrowed money if the corporations default. Since it is the financially weaker corporations that need such bank guarantees in order to sell their IOUs, this type of "indirect loan" is itself of the shakier variety. These letters of credit are not reported on the balance sheets of the banks and are therefore not included in the loan figures shown in Table 3. If they were included, the 1974 percentages of loans to deposits would be even larger than those shown.

Why this mad rush by the banks to expand loans? There are two basic reasons: the lust for profit and the pressure of competition. Banks operate according to the laws of capitalism expounded by Marx. Their dominant motive is the continuous search for ways to expand profits: by accumulating capital and by increasing their rate of profit. They search in every nook and cranny of the economy, using salesmen, newspaper and television advertising, testing new devices—all geared to opening up new opportunities both for lending large amounts to business firms, real estate operators, stock market speculators, finance companies, and also for extending small loans (at even higher rates of interest) to the garden-variety of citizen. This incessant drive for business and profits goes on even as the banks' lending potential (as shown in Table 3) narrows; in this fashion, they are being true to their nature as capitalist entrepreneurs.

The second stimulus for the ballooning of loans is the competition among the banks themselves. Turning down the request for a loan to an established customer always carries with it the threat that the borrower will shift his entire banking business to a competitor. If the customer is a big corporation, there is every reason to expect that another bank will stretch itself to latch on to a new source of business, even if the loan in question does not measure up to "sound" banking practice.

Both of these pressures—the drive for profits and the need to protect one's already existing market—lead to a larger and larger share of relatively unsafe loans in the banks' portfolios. It should be noted that the very ease with which the larger corporations can get loans facilitates their carrying on their own business affairs beyond safe limits, as clearly seen in the steady decline in the ratio of liquid reserves relative to what the corporations owe. (See "The Long-run Decline in Corporate Liquidity," in *Monthly Review*, September 1970.) And the harder it becomes for the corporations to repay their bank loans (because of declining liquidity), the more the banks are obliged to grant further loans to prevent borrowers from going bust and thus defaulting on the backlog of loans. As willing or unwilling collaborators in the process by which the large corporations operate closer and closer to

TABLE 4 □ LIQUIDITY OF LARGE COMMERCIAL BANKS

End of Year	Cash Reserved [a]	U.S. Treasury Bonds [b]	Short-Term U.S. Treasury Notes [c]	Cash + All Treasures as a Percent of Total Deposits [d]	Cash + Short-Term Treasuries as a Percent of Total Deposits [d]
1950	$13.7	$33.7	n.a.	54.0%	n.a.
1955	14.9	30.1	n.a.	42.7	n.a.
1960	14.0	30.2	$ 8.2	34.7	17.5%
1965	16.3	24.3	8.6	22.3	13.7
1970	20.2	28.1	10.3	18.3	11.4
1974	29.5	23.4	7.9	13.6	9.6

n.a.: Not available.
[a] Cash in vault plus reserves with Federal Reserve banks, as required by the Federal Reserve Board.
[b] Bonds here include bills, certificates, notes, as well as bonds.
[c] All treasury securities that mature in less than one year.
[d] The data on deposits used as the denominator are those given in Table 3.

the edge of the precipice, the banks are themselves drawn nearer to the same edge, for they can manage to lend at such a furious rate only by impairing their own liquidity. What has been happening on this score is shown in Table 4.

The last two columns of Table 4 are measures of the liquid position of the banks. In other words, they show what percentage of deposits can be got hold of quickly by bank managements to pay back depositors' money in case of an upsurge of withdrawals. The decline in liquidity shown in the penultimate column of this table (the persistent decline from 54 percent in 1950 to under 14 percent in 1974) should come as no surprise after one has examined Table 3, for this decline has been a necessary complement to the increasing percentage of loans to deposits. (This inverse relation is not precisely complementary because of the growth of bank borrowing, as will be explained presently.) Yet even this meager liquidity ratio exaggerates the reserve position of the large commercial banks. First, in order for a bank to qualify as a depository for U.S. Treasury funds, it must keep a specified reserve of U.S. treasuries to back up the government's deposits. Hence, not all of the treasuries included in this liquidity ratio would be available to meet sudden large drains on deposits. Second, the data shown in the third column represent what the banks originally paid for the bonds. (This is standard accounting practice for bank assets.) The market prices of bonds, however, go up and down: as interest rates rise the prices of bonds go down, and vice versa. For example, if a bank wanted to sell a 20-year, 3-percent Treasury bond which had been bought for $1,000 (and so recorded on the bank's books), all that could be realized on that bond in the market at the end of 1974 would have been about $550. Furthermore, if several big banks began to unload their bond holdings quickly, the market price would drop even further.

It follows that the data in the penultimate column of Table 4 overstate the degree of liquidity, sharp as the drop shown has been. A more realistic picture is given in the last column of the table, where only the short-term treasuries (those with a maturity of less than one year) are counted. And here we see the same pattern: a persistent decline in liquidity, dropping by almost half from 17.5 percent in 1960 to 9.6 percent in 1974. There is an interesting feature here that is worth noting. If you look at the first column, you can see that cash reserves have been rising since 1960, not as much as the growth in deposits but a significant increase nevertheless. The reason that the banks did this was because they were forced to in order to live up to the requirements of the Federal Reserve Board. But for the next most liquid asset—short-term treasuries—there is no such pressure from the Board. What the banks do with respect to short-term treasuries is their own business. So here the investment by the large commercial banks was actually *reduced* somewhat between 1960 and 1974 while their liabilities in the form of deposits were more than tripling during the same period.[1]

Liquidity ratios are not the only way of looking at the safety problem. Traditional theory of good banking practice points out that while loans are a source of risk, banks protect themselves by maintaining special reserves in reasonable anticipation of a certain percentage of defaults, and in the final analysis rely on the bank's equity capital (bank stockholders' original investment plus accumulated profits) to make good on unexpected loan losses (thus preventing loss of deposits). But here too the ratio of equity capital to outstanding loans has been steadily dropping, most noticeably since 1960, as pointed out by Arthur Burns in the speech quoted above:

. . . this enormous upsurge in banking assets [in other words, increase in loans] has far outstripped the growth of bank capital. At the end of 1960, equity capital plus loan and valuation reserves amounted to almost 9 percent of total bank assets. By the end of 1973, this equity capital ratio had fallen to about 6 1/2 percent. Furthermore, the equity capital banks had been leveraged in some cases at the holding company level, as parent holding companies have increased their equity investments in subsidiary banks by using funds raised in the debt markets. Thus, the capital cushion that plays a large role in maintaining confidence in banks has become thinner, particularly in some of our largest banking organizations.

For a better understanding of Burns's argument we should know something about bank holding companies. A "loophole" in the amendments to the 1956 Bank Holding Company Act has been used by most of the big banks to expand their activities into a diverse range of nontraditional financial operations. What happens is that a holding company is set up which owns a bank and at the same time may own, for example, mortgage, finance, and factoring businesses. A number of these bank holding companies have gone to the money market to borrow funds in order to carry on this variety of operations, and in the process have used some of the borrowed money to

---

[1] One of the common illusions concerning this subject is the belief that even if bank liquidity is inadequate the Federal Deposit Insurance Corporation (FDIC) is at hand to protect the savings of depositors. The truth is that the FDIC is only an insurance company and can therefore rescue depositors only to the extent that it has enough assets to cover bank losses. Thus, as an insurance agency the FDIC was designed to deal with occasional breakdowns of one or more banks, and not with a major financial catastrophe. The dimensions of the problem can be seen from the following facts. According to the last annual report of the FDIC, the deposits covered by FDIC insurance amounted to $465.6 billion at the end of 1973. Against this the FDIC had $8.6 billion: $5.6 billion of assets, plus the right to borrow, according to existing law, $3 billion from the U.S. Treasury.

increase their equity investment in their own banks. This is what Burns is referring to: even that small ratio of equity capital to assets is overstated, since some of the equity is really only debt owed by the parent company.

And now we come to where the dog is buried. How do banks manage in practice to keep on extending loans to reach such percentages as shown in Table 3? Normally, banks get resources to meet the demand for loans by increasing their capital, attracting additional deposits, or selling off investments in bonds. As we have just seen, the increase in equity capital was insufficient to support the explosion in loans. Nor have deposits increased sufficiently. Finally, the banks did not want to take the losses that would result from selling off all or a major part of their bond holdings, assuming that they could do so without destroying the market for bonds. So beginning in the 1960s the banks themselves have become major borrowers in order to enable them to indulge in their furious rush to lend. In the process they have created a complex network of borrowing and lending throughout the business world which not only further stimulated the inflationary process, but also resulted in a kind of delicately balanced debt structure that is constantly in danger of breaking down. Now let us look at the facts as shown in Tables 5 and 6.

Before discussing the significance of the facts presented in these tables, let us first explain what some of the headings mean. The first item, money borrowed "From Federal Reserve Banks and others," is a catchall, which includes among other things a usually relatively small amount of money that the Federal Reserve Banks lend for a short period to help banks maintain their required reserves, and money borrowed by banks on their promissory notes and other collateral.

The series on "Federal funds purchased" represents, in large measure,

TABLE 5 □ SHORT-TERM BORROWING BY LARGE COMMERCIAL BANKS

	BORROWED MONEY (BILLIONS OF DOLLARS)					
End of Year	From Federal Reserve Banks and Others	Federal Funds Purchased [a]	Large Negotiable Certificates of Deposit [b]	Euro-dollars [c]	Total	Short-Term Borrowing at a Percent of Total Loans Outstanding [d]
1950	$0.7	—	—	—	$ 0.7	2.2%
1960	1.8	$ 1.4	—	—	3.2	4.5
1965	6.2	2.6	$16.1	—	24.9	20.7
1970	1.5	18.8	26.1	$7.7	54.1	28.7
1974	4.8	54.0	92.2	4.0	155.0	48.5

[a] The data for 1960 and 1965 are from a special series designed by the Federal Reserve Board, based on the 46 most active commercial banks in the federal funds market. The data for these years are not comparable with those for later years, but are given here to indicate the trend. The data for 1970 and 1974 include, in addition to federal funds purchased, securities sold under agreements to repurchase identical or similar securities, and sales of participations in pools of securities.
[b] These are short-term certificates of deposit issued in minimum amounts of $100,000.
[c] These data are the reported "Gross Liabilities of Banks to Their Foreign Branches." According to the Federal Reserve Bank of New York, Glossary: Weekly Federal Reserve Statements, this item is often used as a proxy for Eurodollar borrowings, though these data include some other types of transactions between domestic banks and their foreign branches.
[d] The data on loans used as the denominator are those given in Table 3.

TABLE 6 □ SHORT-TERM BORROWING BY LARGE NEW YORK CITY COMMERCIAL BANKS

BORROWED MONEY (BILLIONS OF DOLLARS)

End of Year	From Federal Reserve Banks and Others	Federal Funds Purchased [a]	Large Negotiable Certificates of Deposit [b]	Euro-dollars [c]	Total	Short-Term Borrowing at a Percent of Total Loans Outstanding [d]
1950	$0.4	—	—	—	$ 0.4	4.0%
1960	1.0	$ 0.8	—	—	1.8	9.7
1965	2.5	1.4	$ 6.9	—	10.8	34.0
1970	0.2	5.5	7.9	$5.2	18.8	41.3
1974	1.7	13.6	31.7	2.8	49.8	63.1

[a] Same as in Table 5, except that the earlier data are based on a series for eight New York City banks.
[b] Same as in Table 5.
[c] Same as Table 5, except that the figure for 1974 is estimated, based on past ratios of Eurodollar borrowing by New York City banks to all commercial banks.
[d] Same as in Table 5.

borrowings for one business day of excess reserves from other banks willing to lend their funds. There are other borrowing devices included in this category, which as in the case of the federal funds were originally designed to cope with temporary adjustment problems of the banks. But these devices became transformed during the 1960s to meet an entirely different purpose: a tool by the biggest banks to mobilize the maximum of money resources, through going extensively into debt, in order to accelerate the pace of lending.

Still another method of borrowing developed by the big banks in the 1960s was the issuance on a large scale of negotiable certificates of deposit (CDs) in minimum amounts of $100,000. These too are short-term debts of the banks. Funds raised in this fashion are used to create new loans by the banks which, in addition to being usually of longer duration than the life of the CDs, do not necessarily mature at the same time. This puts the banks under constant pressure to refinance the CDs when they become due, hopefully by issuing still more CDs.

Finally, there is the resort to Eurodollar borrowing. This in effect means the borrowing by U.S. banks from their branches abroad, and is based on the dollar deposits in these foreign branches. This method began to be used in 1966, but became especially important during the credit crunch of 1969. As can be seen from the data for this item shown in the accompanying tables, this method is used intermittently.

There are various technical aspects to these data which need not be gone into here. The important thing is to understand the speculative nature of the enormous debt expansion by the banks—both as borrowers and lenders. On the one hand, the banks are gambling that businesses will be able to repay their loans despite (1) declining corporate liquidity, and (2) the fact that many firms are borrowing to pay for investment in plant and equipment that will take longer to produce the income needed than is required by the loan repayment schedules. On the other hand, the banks are speculating on being able to support this large and growing lending by having recourse to the mercurial money markets. How rapidly this short-term borrowing has grown and how dependent banks have become on this type of debt to expand their loan load is shown in Tables 5 and 6. From Table 5 we learn that the reliance on short-term borrowing by the large commercial banks reached a point by the end of 1974 such that it represented almost 50 percent of outstanding loans. Even more striking is the case of the large New York City commercial banks, where, as can be seen in Table 6, 63 percent of their outstanding loans is accounted for by short-term borrowing.

It is also important to understand the degree of uncertainty involved in these various forms of borrowing by the banks. They are almost all interest-sensitive, which means that the quantity of such borrowing can fluctuate very widely over relatively short periods, depending on the interest differentials for various types of borrowing. Arthur Burns in the previously quoted speech refers to the "volatile character" of these borrowings. And it is on these foundations that the equally volatile structure of loans, which keep the economy going, is based.

In short, the commercial banking structure, and the entire business world that relies on this structure, is skating on thin ice that is getting progressively thinner.

Why haven't the powers-that-be done something about this? As noted above, there is good reason to believe that all this has been well known for some time by the government agencies set up to prevent such menacing developments. From time to time, these agencies, and in particular the Federal Reserve Board, have taken steps to moderate one or more abuses, only to find that the financial community either found a loophole in the regulations or discovered another avenue to stretch out the debt load. Basically, the regulatory agencies were helpless, despite all their bold stances, because they too were committed to the same ends as the ruling financial and other business circles: to increase profits and to expand business opportunities, with all that these ends entail, including imperialist expansion and the Vietnam War. Rowing in the same boat as the business community, the regulators had to close their eyes to the dangers, trusting in lucky stars. Once the excesses began to reach a critical point it was too late to retreat, for too much disturbance of the intricate and complexly interrelated debt structure could all too easily break the thin ice.

The transformations described here also illuminate how fanciful are the myths of economists, Keynesians and non-Keynesians alike, who insist that they can produce a smoothly running capitalist economy by manipulation of such matters as fiscal policy, interest rates, and the money supply. The point is that all such devices do not get to the heart of what makes the capitalist economy go.[2] At best, they cover up for a while the contradic-

---

[2] In addition, hands of the policy-makers are usually tied. It is impossible to devise consistent policies that can at one and the same time handle the conflicting pressures on a capitalist economy: for example, the need to finance the military budget; to keep the money markets in shape to absorb the debts of federal, state, and local governments; to support the dollar abroad; to improve the balance of payments by attracting foreign funds and stimulating exports; to try to keep inflation from getting completely out of hand; to see that the banks have enough money to rescue tottering corporations; to keep the economy expanding at a rate sufficient to provide jobs for the labor force, etc., etc.

tions of the capitalist system—contradictions that cause eruptions at one time or another—with the credit and banking arrangements being, as Marx long ago explained, at the center of capitalism's vulnerability to crisis.

The advanced thinkers of the ruling class are well aware of the inadequacy of the traditional nostrums as well as of the potential threat of a United States and world-wide depression. They are therefore searching for new and more reliable ways to keep the ship from sinking. It is possible to discern from the business press two important approaches emerging. One is to get the government's finances more actively engaged in salvaging business and banking firms that begin to flounder. This, however, has certain limits, for it entails widening the money and credit stream, and thus reinforcing the inflationary trend. (Over $1 billion, and by some estimates close to $2 billion, was lent by the Federal Reserve to Franklin National, merely the 20th largest commercial bank at one time, to keep the institution's head above water until some sort of reorganization could be effected, and to sustain public faith in the banking system, thus avoiding a possible flood of withdrawals from other banks. Imagine what would be required if one of the real giants began to gasp!)

The second, and more basic, line of thought is to create a firmer financial foundation for business, so that corporations can rely more on equity capital and less on debt. For this, a greater rate of profit would be needed by business. But that alone would not be enough. The government would have to step in more actively: first, to mobilize federal finances to fatten the equity position of industrial and financal firms; and second, to rationalize monopoly capital by weeding out the weaker firms. Within the limits of capitalism, measures of this sort can have only one meaning: to cut into the living standards (wages and welfare) of the working class, the old-age retirees, the petty bourgeoisie, and smaller businessmen. This is the only way that profit rates can be beefed up and finances procured to strengthen the equity capital position of the bigger corporations.

Here lies the challenge to the working class and whatever allies may be available to it. Above all, it is necessary to destroy prevailing illusions about the possibility of regulating capitalism in such a way as to produce prosperity for all classes. The ruling class will soon be sharply drawing the class issues with the hope of stabilizing their own affairs. Only by facing up militantly to the fundamental class nature of the impending struggle, which means challenging capitalism as such, does the working class have a chance to protect its true interests.

35

The Relevance of Marxian Crisis Theory

Roger Alcaly

In the most basic sense, crises can be said to dominate the dynamics of capitalist development because capitalism is a system of production for profit rather than production for use.[1] This means, of course, that anything which endangers profits will eventually lead to cutbacks in production and rising unemployment—in short, to economic crises. Thus, the formal possibility of crises which exists in any economic system in which the acts of purchase and sale are not identical and hence are capable of rupture is vastly enhanced under capitalism, where production will only take place if it expands the value of capital. Moreover, there are several systematic factors which operate in the course of capitalist economic development to depress profits and consequently aggregate economic activity. These elements turn the possibilities of crises into actual crises.

Capitalist economic development is propelled by the continual investment of capitalists' profits in never-ending search of still larger and larger profits. The capitalist, *qua* capitalist, has no choice in this regard. He is compelled to act in this manner by the competitive struggle for survival. As Marx wrote in Volume I of *Capital:*

The capitalist shares with the miser the passion for wealth as wealth. But that which in the miser is a mere idiosyncrasy is, in the capitalist, the effect of the social mechanism of which he is but one of the wheels. Moreover, the development of capitalist production makes it constantly necessary to keep increasing the amount of the capital laid out in a given industrial undertaking, and competition makes immanent laws of capitalist production to be felt by each individual capitalist, as external coercive laws. It compels him to keep constantly extending his capital, in order to preserve it, but extend it he cannot, except by means of progressive accumulation.

The principal strands in Marxian crisis theory revolve around the effects of the reserve army of the unemployed on wages and profits, the

---

[1] More specifically, capitalism is a system of commodity production, or production for market exchange, in which labor power is also a commodity. The emergence of labor power as a commodity presupposes the separation of the means of production from the masses of the population, and the concentration of these resources in the hands of the capitalist class, a "historical condition" which Marx notes "comprises a world's history. Capital therefore announces from its first appearance a new epoch in the process of social production." See *Capital*, Vol. I, International Publishers, p. 170.

Capital employs labor as long as it will produce a surplus or profit, while the laborer is "free" to offer his labor power for sale in the sense that "as a free man he can dispose of his labor power as his own commodity, and that on the other hand he has no other commodity for sale, is short of everything necessary for the realisation of his labor power." *Capital*, p. 169.

ability of capitalists to realize full profits on all they produce or are capable of producing, and the generation of profits themselves.[2] Each will be considered briefly in turn.

As accumulation of capital, or investment, proceeds, additional physical capital and labor power are required in order to expand production. The labor requirements depend on the pace of accumulation and on the relative importance of labor in the production process. The more rapid the rate of capital accumulation, and the more labor-intensive the production process, the greater will be the tendency for the demand for labor power to outrun the supply, eventually exhausting the reserves of cheap labor power provided by the reserve army of the unemployed and the noncapitalist sectors of production like subsistence farmers and the self-employed. The exhaustion of the reserve army of the unemployed, however, weakens a crucial element of capitalist discipline on wages. As a consequence, wages could be expected to rise, profits to fall, and the economic expansion to reverse itself.

The exhaustion of the reserve army, like the other major crisis tendencies of capitalism, can be offset to a certain extent by imperialist expansion. For example, export of capital to areas where labor is in more abundant supply, and cheaper, increases the overall rate of profit in two ways: the capital invested abroad earns a higher rate of profit than it could have earned at home, *and* the investment of capital overseas rather than at home tends to lessen the demand for domestic labor power and lower its price. In effect, the reserve army is simultaneously recruited at home and abroad.[3]

The crisis tendencies of capitalism should properly be viewed as the driving force behind imperialist expansion. This crucial aspect of the development of capitalism as a world-wide economic system cannot be pursued in the following discussion, which is confined essentially to a domestic perspective.

Capitalists might respond to the reduction of profits as a result of the exhaustion of the reserve army by introducing labor-saving technology which replenishes the reserve army by making part of the working population redundant. Wage discipline is thus restored. However, this line of attack opens up two other threats to the rate of profit and continued expansion. On the one hand, the relatively small incomes of the majority of the population limit their ability to consume the output that the economy is increasingly capable of producing. But consumption of all that is produced, or is capable of being produced, is necessary to keep the whole cycle going. In order to "realize" their profits, the major part of which will

---

[2] These crisis tendencies are generally referred to as crises arising from the exhaustion of the reserve army of the unemployed, which is discussed by Marx in *Capital*, Vol. I, ch. 25, entitled "The General Law of Capitalist Accumulation"; realization crises or crises arising from underconsumption (see Paul Sweezy, *The Theory of Capitalist Development* [Monthly Review Press, 1968], ch. 10); and crises arising from the tendency of the rate of profit to fall (see Marx, *Capital*, Vol. III, part III).

[3] Cf. Maurice Dobb, *Political Economy and Capitalism* (London, Routledge and Kegan Paul Ltd., 1940, pp. 231–32), who goes on to note that "this double gain is the reason why, fundamentally, the interest of capital and of labour in this matter are opposed, and why a capitalist economy has a motive for imperialist policy which a socialist economy would not have."

go into further accumulation, capitalists must sell their output at its value. If this can't be done, prices will fall, production will be cut back, workers will be laid off and accumulation will fall off. And once the recessionary sequence has started in any part of the economy, it is very difficult to contain because of the interdependencies among the various sectors. The same thing in effect will result if, in anticipation of their not being able to sell all that their firms are capable of producing, capitalists choose to keep some productive capacity idle and to hire fewer workers.

On the other hand, the increased use of physical capital per worker in the production process tends to restrict the basis from which profits are extracted. Profits arise essentially from the difference between the amount capitalists must pay workers and the amount they receive from the sale of the workers' output. The decreased reliance on labor in the production process thus tends to restrict the rate of profit unless there is a concomitant increase in the profit generated by each worker, a situation which will tend to occur to the extent that productivity rises. Thus, if the increased use of labor-saving technology is not offset by sufficiently rapid technological progress and by increases in productivity, it too can lead to a deterioration in the rate of profit and economic contraction. These interconnected pressures on the rate of profit preclude an uninterrupted expansion. Rather, they tend to produce the crisis-ridden pattern of development characteristic of capitalist economic history.

Moreover, the entire process of capitalist development takes place within the context of the "anarchy" of capitalist production; that is, within an industrial structure whose interrelated parts tend to be coordinated by the "invisible hand" of the market. Such a system is capable of magnifying disruption in any one sector and transmitting it throughout the entire economy, as was the case to a certain extent in the so-called energy crisis. The "anarchy" of capitalist production thus may be considered an independent source of crisis or, more appropriately, an important part of the framework within which the older crisis tendencies operate.

No matter how these tendencies interact to produce a fall in the rate of profit, the falling rate of profit eventually sets off a cumulative process of declining production and employment. Investment will eventually drop in response to a fall in the rate of profit, either because the fall in the rate of profit results in a decline in the funds available for investment or because capitalists have, or expect to have, more profitable alternative uses for their funds. In either case the economic contraction will be reversed only when the basis for profitable production is restored.

The debate between those who believe in the underconsumption argument as the dominant cause of capitalist crises and those who favor the falling rate of profit approach can be reduced theoretically to the question of which investment mechanism is most appropriate. If capitalists mechanically invest all of their unconsumed surplus at the best available rate of return, then underconsumption is not possible because investment will compensate for reduced consumption spending. But while this view is a reasonable approximation of long-run behavior at a very high level of abstraction it seems less appropriate for more concrete discussions of short-run behavior. In such instances investment may well depend on the expected rate of profit (rather than on the absolute amount of profits available for accumulation) with underconsumption a real possibility.[4]

At a concrete level of analysis it is also important to take explicit account of the fact that at any particular moment capital goods are "crystallized in more or less durable forms, and adopted to particular uses and only to those uses." [5] These capital structure rigidities restrict capital's ability to introduce labor saving technology in the short run and tend to make the law of the falling rate of profit a secular rather than cyclical phenomenon. At the same time, greater prominence must be given to the exhaustion of the reserve army and its effect on wages and profits as an explanation of cyclical fluctuations.

A good case can be made that a process similar to the one described above was occurring in the American economy during the last decade. The prosperity of the middle and late 1960's, largely a consequence of the escalation of the Vietnam War, resulted in tightened labor markets, increased wages and a shrunken capital share of national income. Monopolistic corporations were able to pass wage increases on to the rest of the economy in the form of higher prices, thus protecting absolute profits (with the help of weakening labor markets and wage-price controls) despite the fall in profit shares and profit rates. The result, however, was inflation-induced declines in real income, consumption and output. Clearly, investment was not sufficient to compensate for falling consumption indicating that the underconsumptionist element of Marxian crisis theory was also operating. Furthermore, lower levels of capacity utilization have been accompanied by falling productivity, rising unit labor costs and declining levels of profits and investment.

In a very real sense economic crises serve an essentially restorative function for capitalism if they are not accompanied by widespread unrest and the development of movements for social change which threaten capitalism's continued existence. By forcibly, and at great social cost, re-establishing the basis for profitable production, crises set the stage for subsequent expansions. For Marx, "Permanent crises do not exist." Rather, "these contradictions [of capitalism] lead to explosions, cataclysms, crises in which by momentaneous suspension of labor and annihilation of a great portion of capital the latter is violently reduced to the point where it can go on."

The classical way to deal with an economic recession has been to ride

---

[4] See, for example, Joan Robinson, *An Essay on Marxian Economics*, 2nd ed. (Macmillan, 1966), ch. 6; Paul Mattick, *Marx and Keynes* (Porter Sargent, 1969); David S. Yaffe, "The Marxian Theory of Crisis, Capital and the State," *Economy and Society* (May 1973); Paul Sweezy, *op. cit.*, ch. 8–10; and Paul Sweezy, "Some Problems in the Theory of Capital Accumulation," *Monthly Review* (May 1974). In a sense the terms "underconsumption" and "falling rate of profit" are misleading since both occur during a crisis. The real question is whether the fall in the rate of profit is the cause of underconsumption or *vice versa*.

[5] Dobb, *op. cit.*, p. 104. See also Makoto Itoh, "The Formation of Marx's Theory of Crisis," mimeographed, for an argument similar to that suggested below. As Itoh and Marx point out the introduction of new technology, even if available, requires that it be sufficiently profitable so as to compensate for losses on old equipment and, at least by implication, other costs associated with conversion.

it out essentially on the backs of working people. This is the course advocated by more conservative members of the capitalist class and their economic advisers and is the tack being followed by the present Administration. Milton Friedman is reported to have called this the "bang-bang" approach to policy: restrict government spending and growth of the money supply, allowing unemployment to rise and the adjustment process to take place as rapidly as possible. Similarly, Nobel Laureate Friedrich von Hayek has recently argued that the "teachings of Lord Keynes are a seductive doctrine" which merely postpones, and thereby intensifies, the inevitable economic downturn.

The "Keynesian Revolution" was supposed to have eliminated the capitalist business cycle. Balanced growth at full employment, with stable prices, was presumably attainable with the aid of appropriate governmental macroeconomic policy. But the Keynesian doctrines, widely accepted by policy makers in this country since the tax cut of 1964, have not enjoyed a very long run. The root of the problem appears to be the relative lack of attention given to the profit squeeze which tends to accompany economic expansions. For example, Raford Boddy and James Crotty have shown that all the periods of expansion in the American economy between 1954 and 1970 have been characterized by a declining profits/wages ratio during the second half of their duration.[6] Yet this phenomenon and its implications have generally been ignored in the ideological structure generated by the work of Keynes despite the fact that Keynes himself and so-called "neo-Keynesians" or "left Keynesians" like Joan Robinson were well aware of its importance.

People making policy in the interest of capital can ill afford to ignore the behavior of profits over the course of the business cycle because capital is in essence self-expanding value, and a squeeze on profits interferes with this expansion. The paramount importance of profits to a capitalist economy is at least partially reflected in the attention this variable has been receiving from segments of the business press, newsletters of banks, like the Morgan Guaranty Trust Company and First National City, and the papers on economic activity published by the Brookings Institution, a prestigious "think tank" located in Washington, D.C. Capitalism's ideologues, on the other hand, cannot afford to recognize the profits squeeze which eventually accompanies expansion because its implications call into question their neat theories about the harmony of class interests.

In some respects of the Hayekian position, with its recognition of the inevitability of the downturn and the consequences of the "Keynesian" attempt to eliminate this phase of the capitalist business cycle, is similar to the Marxian view outlined above. However, Marxian analysis is far more

---

[6] See Raford Boddy and James Crotty, "Class Conflict, Keynesian Policies and the Business Cycle," *Monthly Review* (October 1974). Their work draws on Michal Kalecki's "The Political Aspects of Full Employment," *Selected Essays on Economic Dynamics* (Cambridge University Press, 1971), pp. 138–45. Boddy and Crotty tend to attribute the fall in the profits/wages ratio solely to the exhaustion of the reserve army in the course of expansion. I prefer to see this development as the result of the interaction of the three crisis tendencies outlined above. More work obviously needs to be done in pinning down the precise nature of this interaction and in applying this set of explanations to a concrete situation such as the present one. [See Reading 32, pp. 272–278, above.]

sophisticated. It recognizes that the capitalist state's stabilization policy must ultimately maintain some form of the business cycle in order to maintain profits. But it is also cognizant of the fact that the restorative effect of cycles on profits must also be balanced against the social unrest which is likely to accompany severe downturns, and full restoration of profits. This balancing act—one which James O'Connor describes more generally as involving the contradictory objectives of maintaining profitable conditions for capital accumulation as well as ensuring the continued legitimacy of a fundamentally exploitative system [7]—constitutes the real problem of "fine tuning" which crops up so often in discussions of government macroeconomic policy.

With this in mind it is somewhat easier to sort out the various perspectives on the economy and economic policy. Conservatives tend to consider Keynesians silly for not understanding how the economy functions, while Keynesians view conservatives as naïve for not taking the political implications of economic policy sufficiently into account. Marxists, on the other hand, understand the tension arising from the relationship between the "economic" and "political" aspects of economic policy, because they view the system in class terms and see its "laws of motion" arising from the contradictions contained in the antagonistic capital-labor relationship.

---

[7] See James O'Connor, *The Fiscal Crisis of the State* (St. Martin's Press, 1973).

Energy and Food

The previous section contained readings on what might be called the *macro*economics of the current crisis. In contrast, this section singles out two of the key *micro*economic elements— energy and food. It has been argued that the crisis stems from the quadrupling of petroleum prices following the Middle Eastern war of October 1973. The readings in section *a* show this to be false. The fourfold rise in the price of oil, as well as the resulting vast sums of petro-dollars (oil-based revenue) in Arab and Iranian hands, complicated and worsened an already difficult and deteriorating situation.

But Arabs should not be made our scapegoats. Nor should we take seriously the pronouncements of government and oil officials, who, when not blaming the Arabs, say that *we*, the greedy American people, are the real culprits. After victimizing us for decades with gas-eating mechanical monsters and a wasteful, inefficient system of transportation designed to maximize petroleum and automobile

profits, they now have the gall to blame the *victims* for the crisis *they* have created!

Reading 36, by Michael Tanzer, author of two books on the political economy of oil, is a welcome antidote to this sort of poisonous propaganda. In his brief history of the energy crisis, he lays the ultimate responsibility on the international petroleum corporations and the U.S. government, which promotes their interests.

The discussion of oil is continued in two additional articles. The first, by mainstream economist and World Bank official Hollis B. Chenery, originally appeared in the influential establishment magazine *Foreign Affairs* (see Reading 37). The second, Reading 38, is by Professor Richard Kronish of the University of Massachusetts (Boston). Chenery's article calls for a cooperative program to restructure and thereby stabilize the capitalist world economy. Kronish focuses on the options open to the oil cartels and projects how they will try to restructure the petroleum industry to ensure the preservation of monopoly profit.

When we turn to the question of food price inflation, we are immediately struck by the contrast between the textbook model of agricultural production, where competition reigns supreme, and the real world of food production and distribution, much pervaded by monopoly. How many of the economists who drone on about supply and demand have ever heard of Iowa Beef, a giant meatpacker, or Cargill, one of a handful of monopolistic grain dealers? Theorists might be more aware of reality if they were to read institutional data like the following testimony from a Senate hearing concerning the source of Thanksgiving food:

The Smithfield ham comes from ITT, the turkey is a product of Greyhound Corporation, the lettuce comes from Dow Chemical Company, the potatoes are provided by the Boeing Company and Tenneco brought the fresh fruits and vegetables. The applesauce is made available by American Brands while both Coca-Cola and Royal Crown Cola have provided the fruit juices. (Quoted in William Robbins, *The American Food Scandal*, pp. 10–11, New York, 1974.)

The eminent agricultural economist D. Gale Johnson, Chairman of the University of Chicago's Department of Economics, presents in Reading 39 a careful assessment of the prospects for future downward movements in farm prices, and does so from the orthodox perspective of supply and demand. But although supply and demand continue to play an important role in determining market prices, especially at the level of the farm, the increased monopolization of the food system as a whole undermines "free" market forces. This is borne out by a statement from Reading 40, an unsigned article that appeared originally in the *New Republic:* "Middlemen now collect about 60¢ out of every dollar spent on food, up from 50¢ in the early 1950s." This selection documents the growing inroads made by monopoly corporations. It is not simply, though, a problem of monopoly, as Reading 41 makes clear. This reading summarizes the findings of a special food project undertaken by PEA (Political Education and Action), a group established by the Union for Radical Political Economics. Its principal conclusion is that "food inflation has flowed directly from the internal structure and dynamics of our capitalist economic system." Radical economists insist that, as long as this system exists, the average American worker will continue to suffer needlessly either through unemployment and downgraded jobs or through persistent inflation, a principal component of which will be rising food and energy prices.

36

The International Oil Crisis: A Tightrope Between Depression and War

Michael Tanzer

Recent events have drastically changed the equilibrium of the international oil industry, with major repercussions for all countries of the world. The industry is still in a state of flux, and the new equilibrium is far from clear at this point. To understand the present situation, it is necessary to review at least the recent historical background.

CHANGING TIMES

Up until the beginning of the 1970s the Big Seven (five American and two British-Dutch international oil companies) dominated the industry through their ownership of the great majority of the world's low-cost oil as well as their vertical integration into the refining, marketing, and transporting of oil. The economic power of the Big Seven was backed in turn by the power of their home governments, of which the Anglo-American overthrow of the Mossadegh government in Iran in the early 1950s was one single visible effect.

In the 1960s, however, the combination of the enormous potential over-supply of cheap oil from the Middle East (with costs at about 10 cents per barrel) and the competition from profit-maximizing newcomers to the international oil industry led to a steady decline in the market price of crude oil. During this period, the Organization of Petroleum Exporting Countries (OPEC), which was born in 1960 in response to the companies' cuts in the posted prices of crude oil, was a relatively weak organization. (The significance of the posted prices was, and is, that producing-country taxes on crude oil are calculated as a fixed percentage [then about 50 percent] of the posted price, regardless of the market price; thus, in 1960 if posted prices had been cut by 20 cents per barrel, the governments would have gotten 10 cents a barrel less from the companies whose profits would have been increased by that same 10 cents per barrel.) However, OPEC generated sufficient pressure to stop the oil companies from cutting the posted prices any further, so that government revenues per barrel remained constant and the declines in market prices were reflected in declining per barrel profits for the companies.

Nevertheless, the per barrel drops in company profits were more than offset by increases in the volume of production, so that company profits on total crude oil sales rose over the 1960s, even if at a much slower rate than OPEC government revenues.

A plausible "static" economic projection at the end of the 1960s would have been more of the same for the 1970s. The reasons for this belief were that the governments were too diverse and disunited by their short-run economic self-interest to agree on a common front against the consumers.

Now, as the reader is quite aware, the 1970s projections based on these assumptions rank with Herbert Hoover's "Prosperity is around the corner" as among the worst in history. Rather than continuing to decline, crude oil prices have jumped as much as tenfold since 1969. Exactly why this dramatic reversal took place in the 1970s is not fully clear even now, but with the benefit of hindsight we can trace some of the forces which led to the change.

WHY THE DESERT WINDS BLEW

An important underlying force was the growing weakness of American imperialism in the mid-1960s and after, culminating in its defeat in Vietnam, which was already apparent and irreversible by the end of the 1960s. The whole Vietnam experience (which had gravely weakened the American economy through inflation and balance of payments problems) had also generated a strong antiwar, anti-interventionist mood in the American people. This made it increasingly unlikely in the late 1960s that the U.S. government, the strongest ally of the Big Seven, could intervene physically in the Middle East as it had before.

A second underlying factor was the smashing Israeli victory in the June 1967 war. In hindsight it can be seen that this abject defeat of the Arabs, combined with continued U.S. support for Israel, made it very difficult for any Arab government, no matter how reactionary, to fail to use the ultimate trump card of the "oil weapon" when war broke out again, as it did in October 1973.

On a more immediate level, one of the most significant changes seems to have been the overthrow of King Idris in Libya and the taking of power by Colonel Muammar el-Qaddafi in September 1969. Today, it is hard to realize that in the period before Qaddafi took power the OPEC governments used to bargain with the international oil companies for months and years in order to gain additional crumbs of the potentially enormous oil pie. In the hands of Qaddafi, who is a fiercely anti-imperialist (and anticommunist), religiously ascetic Arab nationalist, Libya's bargaining position was used to whipsaw the international oil companies. In turn, the achievements of Libya virtually forced the rest of OPEC to use them as a standard for the Teheran Agreement of February 1971, which raised posted prices sharply; Libyan prices were further raised in the Tripoli Agreement of March 1971.

Another factor in Qaddafi's success was that he adopted a policy of ordering the companies to cut production if they would not agree to his demands. This was particularly effective in Libya where newcomer oil companies like Occidental Petroleum were heavily dependent upon Libyan production for their total company profits, and hence were in a much weaker bargaining position than the Big Seven, which had vast worldwide oil supplies.

While due credit should be given to Libya (as well as Algeria, with which it worked closely) for these aggressive tactics, there are strong indications that the "fight" at Teheran was fixed from the start.

According to the testimony of an oil company insider, the critical turning point in the early Libyan negotiations was the refusal of the major international oil companies, particularly Exxon, to help Occidental Petroleum resist Libya's demands. Thus, Occidental had requested the major internationals to agree to provide it with crude oil from their other sources in the event it found its Libyan supplies reduced, but the majors refused. This predictably forced Occidental to cave in to Libya's demands for increased prices and taxes, which demands predictably the majors would then have to meet.

Surely, if the majors really wanted to keep oil prices down they could easily have provided Occidental with some of their low-cost crude from other countries. Their failure to do so suggests one or both of the following. First, that they wanted prices to rise, which would happen if Occidental agreed to Libya's demands in order to save itself from nationalization. Second, that they wanted to eliminate Occidental as a strong competitor, which would happen if Occidental refused the Libyan demands and was nationalized or had its production cut back. In either case, the companies could only gain by refusing support to Occidental.

GOVERNMENT FOR BUSINESS

There is additional evidence that the international majors had the interrelated goals of increasing foreign crude oil prices and eliminating competition. For one thing, raising the prices on foreign crude oil would not only increase the profitability of the majors' U.S. oil, but also the profitability of their other energy sources such as natural gas, coal, and uranium. In particular, since it was already foreseen around this time that the United States in the 1970s would be far more dependent on crude oil imports than in the 1960s, there was increasing pressure to end the United States oil import quota law. This law, which restricted imports of foreign oil, had kept the price of domestic crude oil more than $1 a barrel above that of foreign crude oil.

In fact, in February 1970, President Nixon's own task force studying the law had recommended its abolition and replacement by a steadily declining tariff. This new system would sharply reduce the majors' profits on both foreign and domestic crude oil. While Nixon, who always was favorably disposed to big oil (and vice versa, as evidenced by oil industry contributions of over $5 million for his 1972 campaign), rejected his commission's recommendation, it must nevertheless have been clear to the majors that there was considerable danger in that direction. If the price of foreign crude were increased to the level of U.S. crude, then the oil import quota law could be safely abolished without threatening the majors' profits. Thanks to the rises in foreign crude oil prices triggered by the early 1970–71 negotiations, this was accomplished six months before the 1973 October War.

The necessary piece to complete the picture of a revitalized cartel is the U.S. Justice Department's removal in January 1971 of antitrust restrictions on the American companies negotiating at Teheran. According to U.S. government officials, this was done to give the American oil companies the ability to present a common front at the negotiations. This was purportedly needed because of the administration's concern with "national security" and its fear that, if harmonious agreement was not reached, the United States might lose access to Middle Eastern oil.

Whatever the U.S. government's motivation, the removal of antitrust restrictions on the U.S. oil companies opened the door for them to make comprehensive plans for worldwide cartelization. That the companies took the opportunity to drive a truck through this opening appears to be confirmed by a top Justice Department official. In announcing in mid-1974 the end of the antitrust clearance, an assistant attorney general gave as reasons that the coordinating body of the companies (the London Policy Group) which "was to be an ad hoc organization had become a quasi-permanent institution for oil company cooperation." He noted: "Studies within it tend to approach sensitive competitive areas of supply, cost, demand, control of downstream distribution, and possible exclusion of independents by means of exclusive buying-back arrangements."

At the same time, some of the fruits of such efforts were being uncovered by an investigative body representing the nation's 5,000 prosecuting attorneys, which found that the major oil companies were pursuing "anticompetitive practices and tactics":

The group, a committee of the National District Attorneys Association, said that a five-month probe had uncovered enough preliminary indications to warrant formal antitrust investigations and prosecutions by local district attorneys across the country. . . .

Not only are the oil companies showing monopolistic tendencies in petroleum production and sales, the prosecutors charged, but they are also attempting to gain control over the entire energy industry.

The U.S. government's role in the 1971 negotiations is also quite revealing, in that it reportedly undercut the nominal common front of the oil companies vis-à-vis the producing countries. President Nixon sent Undersecretary of State John Irwin to Teheran in mid-January of 1971, ostensibly to show the U.S. government's support for a common effort by the oil companies to resist higher taxes and prices. In fact, Irwin undercut this effort by advising that the talks be divided into separate discussions with the Gulf countries and Libya and Algeria, thereby leaving the companies open to leapfrog tactics by the OPEC countries.

While many people, such as Professor M. A. Adelman of MIT and Senator Frank Church, have attributed this action of the State Department, which contributed to the future rapid upward spiral of oil prices, to "bungling," another interpretation is quite possible. For one thing, the U.S. government and the State Department in particular have been close to and strongly supportive of the major U.S. international oil companies. Since the major oil companies wanted higher crude oil prices, the State Department's action could be just one more in a long history of service to the companies. Moreover, rising crude oil prices along with increasing oil company profits could well be seen by the American government as helpful to the U.S. economy as a whole. This would be true because the increased cost of importing oil would reduce Western Europe's and Japan's balance of payment surpluses, while the U.S. balance would benefit from the increased oil company profits.

GIVE A LITTLE, TAKE A LITTLE

The Teheran and Tripoli agreements of 1971 and the "participation agreements" of 1972 seem to mark a new era of monopolistic control of oil supplies, this time shared by the companies and the OPEC governments. From these agreements the OPEC governments got a sharp increase in posted prices and in their per barrel revenues, as well as a minority share of the oil companies' production, with the promise of a majority share by the early 1980s. At the same time, however, with the previous oversupply of crude oil now under control, the market prices of crude oil rose even more rapidly than the posted prices and taxes, and the per barrel profits of the companies soared.

From a market low of perhaps $1.25 per barrel in 1969—of which about 10 cents was cost, 95 cents government taxes, and 20 cents company profits—by the middle of 1973 the market price had risen to about $2.50 per barrel, with $1.50 for the government and 80 cents for the companies. Both parties had gained significantly here, but while the government's per barrel revenues had increased by about three-fifths, the companies' had quadrupled.

In addition, the countries had received the right to buy participation in the oil production end. While this was a relatively good deal for the countries, it was not all bad for the companies since it also reduced the pressure for total nationalization. At the same time, "buy back" provisions of the oil agreements allowed the companies to go on selling most of the oil produced in the countries. This was extremely valuable in a world of increasing, artificially created scarcity. The fact that the governments were still largely tax collectors—since they sold back most of the "participation oil" and therefore did not get into the refining and marketing areas—made them much less of a threat to the operations of the major companies.

All this of course was but prelude to the vast changes in the wake of the 1973 October War. The cutback in Arab oil production, as well as the embargo on sales to the United States, created near panic buying which sent market prices of crude oil skyrocketing. In this context the OPEC countries attempted unilaterally to fix the division of crude oil revenues between the governments and the companies at an 84:16 ratio in their own favor. Thus, in two stages, the posted price of Arabian Light was raised from $3 per barrel before the war to over $11 per barrel by December 1973. The governments' per barrel revenues from this Arabian Light thereby leaped from less than $2 per barrel to over $7 per barrel.

This attempt by the OPEC governments to set the level of crude oil profits was undoubtedly a blow to the big oil companies. More direct blows were also sustained from the Iraqi nationalization of all American and Dutch oil interests. In addition, the new climate destroyed the timetable for gradual transfer of majority ownership of the oil fields. Instead of 51 percent for the governments by 1982, it appears that something like 60 percent in 1974, possibly escalating in the future (the deal negotiated by Kuwait in 1974), will be the minimum goal of the OPEC governments.

On the other hand, the developments stemming from the October War have also had their bright side for the international oil companies, and particularly the Big Seven. Thus, even the original OPEC target, now abandoned, of an 84:16 split on profits still would have left a profit for the companies on Arabian Light of $1.20 per barrel, or 50 percent more than the per barrel profit level before the October War. Moreover, the OPEC split was based on setting posted prices at 40 percent above what it considered market prices. But, since most crude oil is sold in integrated channels within the international companies, there was no guarantee that the companies were not selling their crude oil at prices far above OPEC's estimates of what market prices would be in arms-length deals. Certainly with crude oil being auctioned after the October War at prices in the $15–$20 per barrel range, it is highly unlikely that the international oil companies were selling crude at OPEC's estimated $8 per barrel level. Hence, in reality the companies were able to use their control of market prices to increase their crude oil profits well above OPEC's target limit.

In addition, the real impact of the speeded up movement for majority participation and ultimate nationalization is far from clear. As long as the OPEC governments combine these steps with agreements to sell back most of the crude oil to the companies, for them to market, then the effect may be more one of form than substance. What the companies are primarily interested in is the quantities of oil which they can draw and the per barrel profits on each, and if satisfactory arrangements can be made for them on these questions, they are quite willing to accede on formal questions of legal title. Witness the much ballyhooed "nationalization" of the oil industry by the Iranian Shah in 1954, which was the figleaf which imperialism installed in place of the real nationalization by Mossadegh.

The real danger to the international oil companies is nationalization in which the government of the oil-producing country takes command of the crude oil supplies and either uses them internally, by building indigenous refineries, or markets them directly to foreign buyers. This would mean that the oil-exporting countries could deal directly with foreign governments or refiners or marketers in consuming countries, thereby cutting off the oil companies' crude oil and gas profits, and ultimately their refining profits. Little wonder then that the September 1973 Libyan nationalization discussed above brought the State Department into quick action on behalf of the majors, just as fear of real nationalization in the leading oil-exporting countries has pushed the major oil companies to seek concessions for oil and gas exploration all over the world.

THE POOR PAY MORE

Who are the losers from these changes in the international oil industry? Insofar as the price of crude oil has shot up tremendously, all oil-importing countries have been hurt, but obviously some have been hurt more than others. In human terms probably the most badly hurt will be the great majority of underdeveloped countries which rely on imported crude oil for their main energy source. This is because their economies are always in such weak condition that any adverse event can easily topple them; as one third-world representative discussing the impact of the energy crisis on these countries put it, "In an anthill the morning dew is a storm."

Thus, the World Bank has lamented that oil price increases, which have jumped third-world oil imports from $2 billion in 1969 to $15–20 billion in 1974, have completely wiped out all the effects of foreign aid given in recent years. If the World Bank is not simply shedding crocodile tears over this event, then it should hide its head in shame, since its own policy of not only refusing to lend money to governments of underdeveloped countries for use in developing their oil sectors, but actively opposing such activities, has contributed heavily to the drastic plight these countries are now in.

In any event, for a country like India, the increased foreign exchange bill for crude oil imports, to well over $1 billion in 1974, equals more than one-third of its total exports, and undoubtedly means that imports of other vital commodities, including foodstuffs and fertilizers, will have to be cut. The result, in the poor underdeveloped countries, then, is not adequately measured by percentage changes in GNP, but is truly registered in bellies bloated from malnutrition and increased death.[1]

NO CAPITALIST MONOLITH WHEN IT COMES TO PROFIT

The second group of losers are the developed countries of the world, but the relative extent of their losses depends in part on the proportion of their energy supplies made up of imported oil. In this regard Japan is worst off, with Western Europe in the next worst position, while the United States is much better off, particularly because most of the profits of the international oil companies return to the United States. In fact, it has frequently been suggested that the United States has not been averse to certain aspects of the energy crisis, since it has weakened Western Europe and Japan to its own benefit—witness the rapid strengthening of the dollar vis-à-vis other currencies following the October War. This is a point to which I shall return later.

Even within the United States, however, there are winners and losers from the energy crisis. The major winners, of course, have been the oil companies, and to a secondary extent the defense industries, which have been strengthened by the increasing world tension. Major losers have been the giant auto industry and its supplying satellites, the electric and gas utilities, as well as the widespread leisure industries dependent on the automobile and travel, such as motels, resorts, boating, summer homes, etc. One of the things which is likely to come out of this energy crisis is a sharpening of tensions between capital invested in different industries of the economy, particularly insofar as there is suspicion that the crisis has been artificially created by the oil companies and/or that they are not doing and will not do enough to overcome it in the future.

Thus, the recent demands of many members of Congress for a more

---

[1] Given this, it is most heartening that the OPEC countries have expressed their willingness to provide financial assistance to the oil-importing third-world countries to help alleviate this situation. Moreover, an OPEC country, Algeria, took the lead in proposing the historic April 1974 United Nations special session on raw materials in developing nations. At this General Assembly meeting an oil loan fund was established for the poorest countries, and support provided for all third-world countries to raise prices on their own raw materials so as to help change the historically unfair terms of trade between underdeveloped and developed countries.

active government role in the oil industry, ranging from gathering data on energy resources and prices all the way to establishing a government energy corporation, reflect not only pressure from ordinary constituents. They also must be responding to demands from leading sectors of big business that the state move to help restore equilibrium among various industries of the economy.

While the amount of capital invested in the auto and related industries and the utilities is obviously enormous, the oil-military complex has up until now had the dominant say in American government circles. Undoubtedly the struggle between the large sectors of industry which have been hurt by the energy crisis and the oil-military complex will not end quickly. Thus we have the recent lawsuits which have been brought by various utility companies charging the oil companies with illegal restraint of trade which increased the cost of fuel supplies. In the long run, however, what is most likely is that within the United States there will be compromises worked out such that at least American industry as a whole gets adequate energy supplies.

TIGHTROPE BALANCE

Given this general background, we can now turn to the critical question, Whither the international oil industry? Because of the enormous size and influence of this industry, the question is largely synonymous with, Whither the international economy?

The problem reduces to two related questions: How can the importing world continue to pay for the oil it needs; and what might be done with the enormous monetary reserves that the OPEC countries could pile up? (At the 1974 level of revenues, OPEC countries could take in well over $500 billion by 1980, a sum greater than total world foreign exchange reserves.)

Without drastic modifications, the future situation seems untenable for Japan and Western Europe. The latter's oil imports, which amounted to $10 billion in 1969 and $20 billion in 1973, are expected to jump to $50–60 billion in 1974. This means Western Europe's oil imports already amounted to 10 percent of its total export revenues in 1973 and could reach 20–25 percent in 1974. For Japan the situation could be even worse. Oil imports rose from $2 billion in 1969 to $7 billion in 1973, at which point they already amounted to over 20 percent of total exports, and in 1974 the proportion could reach one-third. Clearly, for Western Europe and Japan as a whole such levels of oil imports are not sustainable for very long. Moreover, the gravity of the situation is compounded by the fact that within Western Europe some countries, notably Italy, were in serious financial straits even prior to the recent oil changes.

The United States would also tend to be hard hit in the balance of payments area because not only have prices jumped, but U.S. imports are rising much more rapidly than those of Western Europe or Japan as U.S. production levels off. Thus, U.S. oil imports have risen from $3 billion in 1969 to $8 billion in 1973, and an estimated $25 billion in 1974, which would amount to about one-fourth of total exports.

However, the key to the better position of the United States is the enormously growing foreign profits of its international oil companies. While current data are not readily available, even if the oil companies were making only $1.00–$1.25 a barrel on OPEC crude oil, this would amount to about $10 billion. Moreover, many more billions of dollars are clearly being made from refining and marketing abroad, since foreign product prices have also shot up greatly. With these profit inflows helping to offset the cost of America's oil imports, the share of total exports needed to pay for vital oil supplies for the United States would tend to be relatively low compared to those of Western Europe and Japan. And when one takes into account the fact that much of Western European trade is within the bloc, so that its net exports to the outside world are far lower, then it is even more likely that the changed oil situation would be a relatively greater burden on Western Europe. Furthermore, the United States has more room to maneuver in that it can increase production substantially within its borders by producing from formerly unprofitable shut-in wells, in addition to expanding quick-return development and exploration drilling, an option which is not open to Western Europe or Japan.

Thus, one key effect of the changes in the international oil industry is a drastic shift in economic power from Western Europe and Japan to the United States.

In response to this situation, each developed country has been frantically and unilaterally seeking its own way out. One method has been for each country to seek to increase its exports, but since most of the developed countries' trade is among themselves, this clearly cannot be a solution for all of them. Another route has been to negotiate direct government-to-government barter deals with individual OPEC countries, swapping a range of developed-country goods for crude oil. For example, by early 1974 France had tentative agreements with Saudi Arabia, Abu Dhabi, and Iran to trade Mirage jets and petroleum refining and industrial equipment for crude oil; similar deals were also announced for Britain, West Germany, and Japan. However, there are many barriers to a large number of such deals being finally consummated. Nevertheless, they do pose serious problems for the United States, since presumably in such direct government-to-government deals the oil companies would not get their usual profits. This would then cut into the protective cushion the American companies form for the U.S. balance of payments.

Therefore we are left with the following conclusion. At present prices of oil, in the next few years Western Europe and Japan would be badly hurt while the United States would be greatly strengthened vis-à-vis these countries. However, since the United States has a big stake in investment and trade with Western Europe and Japan, a collapse there is not to U.S. advantage and hence to be avoided. It is quite conceivable, however, that the U.S. strategy is to try to walk the tightrope of benefiting from Western Europe's and Japan's weakened position in the short run while not allowing the latter's situation to deteriorate to complete collapse.

Now, after the October War, the United States is in an even better position to sit back and watch the treasuries of Japan and Western Europe being relatively quickly emptied, figuring to share these riches with the OPEC countries. If and when a point is reached where oil prices threaten to harm the United States, either directly or through a collapse of the other developed countries, then it could use its power to try to pressure the OPEC governments to reduce prices, with the ultimate threat being military intervention.

However, since military intervention would raise the danger of confrontation with the Soviet Union as well as of prolonged guerrilla warfare in the Middle East, it will not be chosen lightly. But it is a very real possibility. Trial balloons were sent up after the October War by everyone from Senators Fulbright and Jackson to Secretary of State Kissinger to Secretary of Defense Schlesinger. But with the American people sick of war and suspicious of the oil companies and the president (according to the polls at that time the majority of people blamed the oil crisis on the oil companies and the government and not the Arabs) intervention may not have been tenable. Instead such warnings may have been directed at preserving the privileged position of U.S. oil companies in the Middle East. That is to say, the saber-rattling may have been a not so subtle way of warning the OPEC governments not to truly nationalize American oil companies in the Middle East nor to set prices so as to reduce the companies' profitability sharply.

In any event, this is a most tricky and dangerous game for the United States, threatening to plunge the world into a war—or a major depression. Ironically, a major economic crash in the Western world would also help "solve" the oil problem by drastically reducing the demand for oil and hence putting strong downward pressure on the price. Indeed, the developed countries have long been teetering on the edge of a financial breakdown which would precipitate a major world depression; the international oil crisis might yet be just the factor necessary to tip the world economy over the precipice. After all, nothing on the world scene indicates the degree of coordination necessary among capitalist powers to prevent the recurrence of a severe depression.[2]

---

[2] The OPEC countries do not have the power to stop this process of decline, because its roots run much deeper and lie in the basic rivalries in the developed capitalist world. Given the likelihood that an economic deluge is in the cards regardless of what OPEC does, the only rational course for its members is to pile up as much money and resources as possible aboard their own Noah's Ark.

Moreover, in a fundamental sense what is involved as a result of increased OPEC crude oil prices is the long overdue need for a sizable shift of real resources from the developed countries to the oil-producing countries. The huge economies of the developed countries are certainly capable of making these resources available, not only to the oil-producing countries but also to all the world's underdeveloped countries.

37

Restructuring the World Economy

Hollis B. Chenery *

The world economy is currently in a state of disequilibrium of a magnitude not seen since the aftermath of World War II. The symptoms of underlying stress have been manifested over the past two years in the form of raw-material shortages, a food and fertilizer crisis, a dramatic rise in petroleum prices, and finally, worldwide inflation and threats of impending financial disaster. . . .

Some of the symptoms of commodity shortages and high prices are purely cyclical and are already disappearing as a result of the current stagnation in world incomes. Others, however, reflect long-term shifts in demand and supply that were merely accelerated by the recent period of rapid growth. This is notably true of the supply of energy and foodstuffs, where the evidence of shifts in the balance of supply and demand was apparent before these markets were disrupted by booming demand, crop failures, and the behavior of the Organization of the Petroleum Exporting Countries (OPEC). Before the world economy can return to a condition of orderly development, substantial redirection of investment and production in these and related sectors is imperative. . . .

II

To define the dimensions of the structural changes that are needed in the world economy, we must first separate out the cyclical effects of the recent boom that are likely to be corrected by market forces over the next several years. The coincidence of shortages and price rises for most commodities during 1972–73 has left the impression of a general "commodity problem" and led to a number of false analogies between petroleum and other commodities. Price reductions since the ending of the boom nearly a year ago confirm the diagnosis that most of these were cyclical phenomena: hence, we can now identify more clearly areas in which longer term adjustments are needed.

The interpretation of movements in international prices is also complicated by the persistence of inflation on a worldwide basis. While the sharp rise in commodity prices in 1972–73 was a significant factor in causing inflation to accelerate, this is no longer the case; the overall effect of trends in commodity prices—including oil—is now deflationary. . . .

Now that the normal cyclical adjustment is under way, there are only a few commodities whose high prices (or short supplies) are likely to have an important continuing effect on the economic welfare of large numbers of people. These are primarily petroleum, some of the major foodstuffs (grains, oilseeds, beef, sugar), and fertilizer. . . .

* I am indebted for advise and comment to Bela Balassa, John Foster, Robert McNamara, Joseph Pechman, Jo Saxe, Ernest Stern, Wouter Tims and Elinor Yudin. However, neither they nor the World Bank with which I am associated bear any responsibility for the opinions expressed.

Although recent events have shown that relatively small changes in the supplies of petroleum and foodstuffs can have a very disruptive effect on world trade and development, in most other respects these two commodities are very different. Petroleum has a dominant impact on world trade because it supplies nearly half of world energy consumption, and resources are concentrated in a small number of countries. Consequently, two-thirds of all petroleum produced moves in international trade. The present and prospective value of petroleum exports (even if present prices were somewhat reduced) roughly equals the value of all other mineral and agricultural exports combined. For this reason the position of the petroleum exporters is unique; it is hard to conceive of any combination of producer cartels that would have as much effect on world trade in the next few years as an increase of even one dollar in the price of oil.

As is now well-known, the actions of the OPEC countries in late 1973 raised the average price of oil in the Persian Gulf from about $2.40 per barrel in the early part of 1973 to about $9.60 per barrel in 1974. (This and all subsequent figures in this article are in 1974 dollars except as specifically noted.) The short-run effect has been to increase the value of OPEC exports in 1974 by over $80 billion, about 10 percent of the value of world exports in that year. Only a fraction of this increase has so far been absorbed by increased OPEC imports, and the resulting surplus of some $60 billion is a measure of the present disequilibrium in world trade.

At first glance the effects of rising food and fertilizer prices on the world economy appear to be of quite a different order of magnitude from the oil impact. Even though the total value of grain produced in the world is considerably greater than that of petroleum, most countries are relatively self-sufficient in grain, and only marginal quantities are traded. While the position of the United States and Canada as grain exporters is as dominant as that of the Persian Gulf countries in oil, the total value of world grain exports is only one-fourth that of petroleum.

Yet the disruptive effect of the rise in food and fertilizer prices on world development is much greater than this comparison would suggest. . . . Although the shortfall in LDC production of foodstuffs in the past several years has been relatively small, the rise in import requirements combined with large price rises have had as damaging an effect on the growth prospects of many developing countries as have rising oil prices. . . .

III

The nature of the present world economic crisis has been aptly characterized by Helmut Schmidt as "The Struggle for the World Product." [1] When viewed in these terms, the rise in oil prices is only the most dramatic of a series of events—some deliberate and some resulting from market forces —that have been operating to change the distribution of world income through the system of international trade and capital flows.

Although the changes in relative prices described above will have a substantial effect on the distribution of the world's income and wealth, their direct impact can easily be exaggerated. To measure this, assume that the OECD [Organization for Economic Cooperation and Development] coun-

---

[1] See *Foreign Affairs*, April 1974.

tries and the non-OPEC members of the Third World had been able to pay for the increase in the cost of imported oil by shifting $80 billion worth of commodities per year from domestic use to increased exports to OPEC. The result of this one-time cost increase would have been to reduce total national income in the OECD countries by two percent and in the non-OPEC Third World by three percent, while nearly doubling the total income of the OPEC countries. Although these are large amounts, the direct losses would amount to giving up six months' worth of growth—with the lively hope of then resuming the pattern of four to six percent average growth thereafter.

In reality the threat to the world economy from the rise in oil prices comes not so much from the need to transfer two percent of world income to the oil-exporting countries as from the uncertainties that are inherent in the policies adopted to effect this transfer. . . .

To put the point differently, the major consequences of the change in OPEC price policy stem more from its suddenness than from its magnitude. If the price of oil had reached its present level by a three percent annual increase in its relative price over the past 25 years, the adjustments needed to accommodate this increase would have had little effect on world growth and indeed some benefit in directing behavior patterns and technological efforts toward more efficient use of energy. Instead, the progressive cheapening of oil for 20 years led to its wasteful use—particularly in the United States—and postponed the development of other energy sources. We are now faced with accelerated changes in consumption patterns and large investments for the development of non-OPEC sources of supply, in addition to financing the cost of the imports that will still be required. And the danger is that in adjusting to these changes the OECD countries may adopt policies that will operate to freeze or reduce their growth so that it does not move back soon to the past pattern of four to six percent growth.

While the food aspect of the world restructuring problem does not loom so large as the oil aspect in global terms, it raises issues that are just as acute for the LDC [Less Developed Countries] countries involved. On optimistic assumptions, it will take at least five years to make up for the lags in fertilizer capacity and in agricultural investment in the developing countries so as to balance supply and demand, restore stocks, and bring food prices down to more normal levels. In the meantime, some restraint will be needed in the high-income countries of the OECD to avoid bidding away the limited supplies of foodstuffs and fertilizer from the poorest countries, whose consumption cannot be compressed further.[2] . . .

There are two great dangers in the present situation, the first involving the relations between the OECD and OPEC countries, and the second involving their common relationship to the LDCs. At present individual OECD nations are acting on their own to protect their balance of payments in ways that are inimical to their collective interest in increasing their trade and their GNP. Moreover, given their uncertainty as to future OPEC oil price policies, OECD governments are also taking steps both to limit oil

---

[2] More complete statements of the nature of these transitional problems and the changes in agricultural production that are needed are given in the United Nations World Food Conference, *Assessment of the World Food Situation*. See also, Lyle P. Schertz, "World Food: Prices and the Poor," *Foreign Affairs*, April 1974; and Lester Brown, *By Bread Alone*, New York: Praeger, 1974.

imports and to invest in high-cost substitute energy sources to an excessive extent that affects their future growth. Thus, the continuation of uncoordinated responses to the oil problem will almost certainly result in a lower rate of OECD growth and make the transition much more costly in the end. . . .

Secondly, the future of the LDCs—and particularly the poorest among them—depends on the ability of the OPEC and OECD countries to work out some agreed basis for financing the 100-percent increase in LDC balance-of-payments deficits that has resulted from the higher prices of oil and food. Although the problem of the most seriously affected is only five percent of a $60 billion global disequilibrium, existing mechanisms for balance-of-payments adjustment and capital transfers are clearly unable to cope with it. . . .

IV

To analyze the possible adjustments to the oil problem more concretely, let us first examine the varying positions of the principal oil exporters. The members of OPEC are all developing countries for whom petroleum is the principal source of foreign exchange and the key to their further development. They differ greatly, however, in their current needs for imports and in the volume of their oil reserves in relation to present levels of production. Assuming that OPEC will continue to set prices cooperatively, countries in different resource positions will have different views as to the best price and output policy for the group.

To indicate the effects of differences in resource positions on the production and price policies that might be followed, the 11 principal oil exporters are grouped in Table I below into three categories having the following characteristics:

☐ *Group I* (Saudi Arabia, Libya, Kuwait, Qatar, Abu Dhabi) has 65 percent of proven reserves and 48 percent of current output, but only 12 million population and limited levels of absorption for economic development. The five countries in this group must take a long-term view of petroleum policy; their reserves have a potential life of 50 years or more, and they have few other natural resources.

☐ *Group II* contains four countries (Iran, Venezuela, Iraq, Algeria) that have already achieved considerable economic development and are depleting their petroleum reserves at higher rates than Group I. They contain 70 million inhabitants and are in a position to make effective use of most of their increased oil revenues for internal development within the next decade, although they will accumulate substantial surpluses for the next several years. This group is more likely to try to secure maximum revenues in the short run because of the greater opportunities for productive investments within their own economies.

☐ *Group III* consists of two large countries (Nigeria and Indonesia) that have only a limited share of OPEC resources and little problem of absorbing all their oil revenues in the near future. They will not accumulate significant financial surpluses.

While maintaining or even increasing the 1974 Persian Gulf price level of approximately $9.60 per barrel (in 1974 prices) might seem to be in the

TABLE I □ OPEC COUNTRIES: 1973 OIL PRODUCTION AND RESERVES

	Population (millions)	Proven Reserves (billion tons)	Output (million barrels per day)	Reserves Years of (at 1973 output rate)
Group I				
Saudi Arabia	8.1	19.3	7.5	51
Libya	2.1	3.4	2.1	32
Kuwait	0.9	10.1	3.0	66
Qatar	0.2	0.9	0.5	31
Abu Dhabi	0.1	2.9	1.2	45
Subtotal	11.5	36.4	14.3	50
Share of OPEC		65%	48%	
Group II				
Iran	31.9	8.2	5.9	28
Venezuela	11.3	2.0	3.5	11
Iraq	10.4	4.3	2.0	44
Algeria	14.7	1.0	1.0	20
Subtotal	68.3	15.5	12.4	25
Share of OPEC		28%	41%	
Group III				
Nigeria	73.4	2.7	2.0	27
Indonesia	125.0	1.4	1.3	22
Subtotal	198.4	4.2	3.3	25
Share of OPEC		7%	11%	
TOTAL	278.2	56.1	30.2	

Sources: Oil and Gas Journal (Reserves), World Bank

interest of countries in the second and third groups, this price is well above the long-term costs of major alternative energy sources. Accordingly, such a policy could be expected to induce a maximum effort by the OECD countries to cut back on consumption and to develop alternative energy sources (such as North Sea and Alaskan oil, coal, oil shale, tar sands, and of course nuclear energy). Studies by the OECD, the Federal Energy Administration, and the World Bank suggest that such a maximum effort, although involving a considerable amount of investment that would be uneconomical at somewhat lower prices, could have the effect of leveling off the demand of the OECD countries for OPEC oil.[3] By 1980 OECD imports from OPEC would be no greater than at present and would be likely to decline thereafter.

However, if the Persian Gulf price were reduced to $7 or $8 per barrel (in 1974 prices), with some assurance that supplies would be forthcoming at this level, the OECD countries would probably forgo the uneconomical forms of investment in higher cost energy sources and would be less likely to limit growth of consumption. Thus, OPEC exports of oil to the OECD countries would continue to rise in 1980 and beyond. The total revenues available to OPEC for the next decade would probably be as great as through maintaining higher prices, and total OPEC production in 1980 and 1985 would correspond roughly to the productive capacity now planned by the OPEC countries.

In this situation the OPEC countries are faced with the classical monopolist's dilemma of trying to estimate the speed with which alternative

[3] OECD, *Long Term Energy Assessment* (forthcoming); Federal Energy Administration, *Project Independent Report*, November 1974.

TABLE 2 □ PROJECTIONS OF OPEC REVENUES AND CAPACITY
(in billions of 1974 dollars and millions of barrels per day)

	Group I	Group II	Group III	Total Revenue	Production Total
Case I:					
Price Remains at $9.60					
1980	$49	$47	$13	$109	33
1985	51	54	16	121	36
1990				88	26
Case II:					
Price Declines to $7.00 by 1980					
1980	$52	$41	$11	$103	42
1985	58	52	12	122	49
1990				135	55
Planned Productive Capacity					
1980	27.8	16.3	4.5		49

Source: Based on estimates of the OECD and the World Bank

supplies will be developed and whether the gains of maximizing short-run profits will exceed the losses from lower volumes (and perhaps lower prices) in the future. Unless a high discount is applied to the future, the OPEC countries—and particularly the Group I countries with large reserves—would benefit in the long run from reducing the price of oil to the cost of major alternative sources in order to maintain their share of future market growth.

This conclusion is illustrated in more concrete terms in Table II above. Case I assumes that the price is maintained at $9.60 (in 1974 dollars) by upward adjustments to offset inflation. Case II assumes that the price declines gradually by some 30 percent to $7.00 (again in 1974 dollars). In both cases, it is assumed that total energy demand in OECD countries would continue to grow, but at a rate of only 3.8 percent in Case I as compared to 4.3 percent in Case II (both, of course, reduced from the recent 5 percent rate for OECD as a whole). As to investment in alternative sources, the underlying assumptions are conservative, not assuming development of domestic or other energy sources that will cost more than imports.

Even so, the table indicates that after 1985 total OPEC revenues would be considerably greater under Case II. . . .

. . . From the standpoint of both the OECD and OPEC countries, the difference between Case I and Case II is particularly great in terms of the decisions on investment in alternative energy sources. In round numbers, if the OECD countries felt compelled to reduce their demand for OPEC oil by 1985 by the 13 million barrels a day difference between Case I and Case II, they would need to make *additional* investments on the order of $100 billion in this period. The expansion of OPEC capacity, on the other hand, would involve much less cost. In short, since decisions on tens of billions of dollars of investment in both OECD and OPEC over the next several years will hinge on the assessment that is made of future OPEC price and production policy, this becomes one of the most critical determinants of the future pattern of world trade and capital flows.

In order to maintain any given price, the oil exporters need to have some form of agreement as to how any needed reduction below capacity production will be allocated. Then, in deciding on its preferred production level, each country must estimate two elements: its current need for foreign

exchange for internal development, and the prospective return on its investment of any surplus revenues in comparison to the prospective appreciation
in value of oil reserves. At current prices there is only a limited prospect for
a further increase in value of oil relative to other commodities over the
next ten years and a greater probability of decline. Even if the real return
on their investment of surplus funds is negligible and only offsets the effects
of inflation, exporting countries are better off producing than keeping their
oil in the ground. Countries with growing needs for foreign exchange for
internal development will have a stronger incentive to increase output than
those producing in excess of current needs.

Weighing the several factors that affect these decisions, it seems to me
likely that oil prices will come down by 1980 to a level approximating the
long-term cost of non-OPEC sources of energy, which is currently estimated
to be the equivalent of $7.00 to $8.00 per barrel (in 1974 prices) in the
Persian Gulf. This reduction would make possible relatively full use of the
presently planned expansion of OPEC capacity to 49 million barrels per day
by 1980. On this assumption oil prices would still be three times as high as
their relative level in 1970 and twice as high as the peak period of the early
1950s.

V

. . . The preceding discussion has already considered three of the actions the
OECD countries are taking in the face of the oil crisis, namely, the reduction
of nonessential energy needs, the development of their own energy sources
and those of other non-OPEC countries, and trying to persuade the OPEC
producers to lower the price of oil. Even with some success in each of these
efforts, the OECD countries confront a substantial financial problem of, in
effect, borrowing from OPEC to finance continuing balance-of-payments
deficits with those same countries. Because of the limited absorptive capacity of the OPEC countries, the OECD countries—even under the Case II
assumption of gradually lowered prices—would have to finance aggregate
annual deficits of $30 to $40 billion (in 1974 prices) until the early 1980s.
(Imports would be lower and the deficits slightly higher under Case I.) Unless the OECD countries further reduce their oil demand through rationing
and economic stagnation, they will have to accept a growth in OPEC claims
on their assets (debt plus direct investment) that will cumulate to a total
of up to $300 billion by 1980 (in constant 1974 dollars).

There is an inclination in many quarters to regard the task of financing
any such amount as both unmanageable and unsound in the light of traditional principles of financial management. But it is hard to sustain either
of these conclusions on economic grounds. Both the postwar experience of
the European Recovery Program and the current management of capital
flows to developing countries demonstrate the adjustment mechanisms that
are needed. The economic desirability of borrowing from the OPEC countries should be judged on the basis of the cost—in terms of lower incomes
and higher unemployment—of *not* borrowing. The feasibility of borrowing
in the amounts indicated depends on the burden of debt service and future
repayment over the next several decades. Because of the large sums in-

volved, there is a tendency to exaggerate these prospective burdens and to ignore the cost of lower rates of growth.

In many respects the economic adjustment now required of the OECD in relation to OPEC is similar to the typical problem of developing countries that have increased their capital inflow in order to accelerate their rates of growth. . . . The desirability of incurring external debt depends on the additional growth that can be secured from greater imports and investment in relation to the real cost of borrowing.

The OECD oil deficit differs from the normal trade gap of less developed countries in one significant respect: its current magnitude is determined primarily by the ability of the lending countries to utilize imports from the borrower rather than by the latter's ability to supply them. . . .

Another way to judge whether this process of adjustment is feasible is, however, to compare it to the last major adjustment involving the European members of what is now OECD. In the wake of World War II, these countries engaged in a program of reconstruction that lasted through the period of the Marshall Plan and extended to about 1955. During this period there was, in effect, a massive transfer of resources from the United States to Europe, while Europe developed the productive capacity to meet what was then called the "dollar gap"—that is, to export sufficient goods and services to pay for their import requirements from the United States. . . .

To make the comparison real, let us assume that in both periods the "debtor" group of nations was required to repay the principal of the total "debt" over a period of six years, beginning in 1952 and 1974 respectively, and that the "interest" (actual interest on debts, plus dividends on investment) was at identical rates of five percent. On this basis, Table III below shows (in 1974 dollars for both cases) the growth of GNP, international

TABLE 3 □ COMPARISON OF ADJUSTMENT PROCESSES: 1947–55 AND 1974–85
(billions of dollars in 1974 prices)

A. 1947 ADJUSTMENT (OECD EUROPE)			
	1947	1950	1955
1. Gross National Product	350	435	578
2. Exports	51	94	134
3. Imports	75	90	116 [a]
4. Net Capital Inflow	31	11	2
5. Total Debt	31	74	92
6. Hypothetical Debt Service [b]	1.4	3.6	17.9
7. Debt Service/GNP	0.4%	0.8%	3.1%
8. Debt Service/Exports	2.8%	4.0%	13.0%
B. 1974 ADJUSTMENT (OECD EUROPE AND JAPAN-OCEANIA)			
	1974	1980	1985
1. Gross National Product	1,921	2,695	3,082
2. Exports	361	524	776
3. Imports	329	460	710
4. Net Capital Inflow	40	45	34
5. Total Debt	40	285	500
6. Hypothetical Debt Service [b]	8	48	51
7. Debt Service/GNP	0.4%	1.8%	1.6%
8. Debt Service/Exports	2.2%	9.2%	6.6%

[a] Actual imports were reduced to take account of the need to service hypothetical debts.
[b] Hypothetical debt service calculated at 5% interest, repayment of each year's borrowing over six years beginning in 1952 or 1974.

trade levels, capital inflows, and debt service requirements for 1947 to 1955, and projections of the same magnitudes for 1974 to 1985.

When put in these terms, the adjustment to higher oil prices that is now required is shown to be of somewhat lesser magnitude than the postwar adjustment process. . . . The important lesson of the postwar period is that such a large restructuring was accomplished with relative ease *because economic growth was sustained at a high rate.*

Even without much fall in OPEC oil prices between now and 1980 the OECD countries of Europe and Japan will reach a maximum indebtedness to OPEC in the early 1980s. . . .

By 1990 almost all of the OPEC countries are likely to have reduced their outstanding investments in the OECD very substantially as their internal absorptive capacity continues to grow. While capital may then flow in the opposite direction to support the continued growth of the oil producers as their oil revenues stagnate or decline, the magnitudes will not be so large as to interfere with the growth of the OECD countries. Therefore, it is difficult to argue on economic grounds that the world economy cannot sustain capital flows of the required magnitude, or that the OECD countries need to suffer heavily in the process.

The other major obstacle to acceptance of borrowing from OPEC countries as a desirable solution to the oil problem is the fear that they will acquire excessive ownership and control of OECD assets. The magnitudes involved up to $300 billion (in 1974 prices) by 1980 must be judged in relation to the total assets of the OECD countries including the United States. The figure of $300 billion would be perhaps five percent of the value of all stocks and bonds in the major OECD countries in 1980 or two percent of their fixed assets. . . .

[VII]

. . . The policy conclusions to this analysis can be summed up in three propositions: (a) once the dimensions of the basic problem are accepted, it should be quite feasible to devise a set of policies to enable the several parts of the world economy to resume satisfactory rates of development; (b) the various elements of the solution are highly interdependent and require a quality and sincerity of international cooperation that has been lacking since the early 1950s; (c) the effects of a failure to make the adjustments in the international system would be considerably more costly to most of the participants than the gains that each country can hope to achieve by acting independently, and the burden of such a failure would fall disproportionately on the poorest countries.

Although it is not my purpose to analyze the various institutional changes that are needed to bring about these results, the principal elements in a cooperative approach to a solution can be sketched out:

1. Reduction of Uncertainty in Oil Marketing

Uncertainty as to OPEC oil policies and the desirable responses to them is the main obstacle to the acceptance of the problem of higher prices by the importing countries. Reduction of this source of uncertainty would greatly aid the adoption of other measures to restore equilibrium in the world economy.

2. Financing Oil Deficits

It is generally agreed that the existing recycling mechanisms—OPEC loans to preferred governments, limited use of the international institutions, direct OPEC investments, and the private banking system—will become increasingly inadequate to the magnitude of the OPEC surplus in the course of 1975. Although a more satisfactory system would expand use of all of these routes, it should also guarantee a volume of lending adequate to finance the oil deficits of the OECD countries and the upper tier of those developing countries which are able to assume additional debt. Such guarantees are needed to avoid "beggar thy neighbor" policies through which importing countries attempt to reduce their individual oil deficits at each other's expense. However, the poorest countries are not able to assume much additional debt other than on concessional terms.

3. Support for OPEC Development

Since the main object of the OPEC governments is the rapid and secure development of their economies, their willingness to cooperate in solving the problems of the rest of the world is likely to be increased by measures that would enable them to reach that goal. Such measures should include a secure return on external investment and assistance in their internal development. In return they might be willing to forgo high short-run profits in favor of a larger and more secure future market for their oil.

4. OECD Growth

Even with adequate recycling mechanisms, some short-term reduction in the growth of the industrial countries is virtually inevitable as part of the worldwide effort to control inflation. However, a restoration of the trend rate of five-percent growth of GNP for the OECD countries by 1976 is quite feasible and would make an important contribution to the solution of the problems of the developing countries.

5. Restoration of LDC Growth

In the present atmosphere of inflation, payments deficits, and economic recession, it seems politically impossible for the industrial countries to give adequate attention and support to the developing countries. This condition is unlikely to be reversed until the OECD countries are on the way to solving their own problems. Until that is achieved, the erosion of aid by inflation is not likely to be offset, and the tendency to restrict LDC imports will be hard to resist.

In quantitative terms, the needs per year of the developing countries for additional support to restore reasonable rates of growth are modest: $3 to $4 billion (in 1974 prices) for the rest of this decade. Depending on the rates of growth of the OECD countries, this would bring total concessional lending back to between 0.3 and 0.4 percent of the gross national products of the OECD and OPEC countries. These were the levels that were maintained by the OECD until recently, when they were reduced by the effects of the inflation. But to achieve them will require substantial increases in current appropriations, in order to offset higher prices.

Without some expansion of aid, restoration of growth in the rest of the world will do relatively little for the most seriously affected countries because they cannot readily shift their exports to take advantage of it. Nor can they make extensive use of recycling facilities on conventional terms. Thus there is no short-run adjustment mechanism available to them except to reduce their growth. Some special assistance—either in the form of reduced prices for oil and food or increases in concessional lending—is needed to avoid inflicting on them the main burden of both the oil and the food adjustments.

[VIII]

Since the series of negotiations and institutional changes required to bring about this rather optimistic scenario will require an appreciable period of time, we will have to improvise temporary solutions. In the short run, there is no alternative to the use of existing institutions for recycling, the reallocation of aid budgets and food stocks to the most affected countries, and an ad hoc sharing among the stronger OECD and OPEC countries of the burdens of adjustment and risks of lending.

In the longer run, the world does have a choice. It lies between mounting a cooperative effort on the model of the postwar period or accepting the much higher costs of an uncoordinated readjustment in which all parties are likely to suffer.

38

Responding to OPEC: An Assessment of Oil Cartel Options

Richard Kronish

The transfer of power at the point of international production thus nears completion. The OPEC [Organization of Petroleum Exporting Countries] countries threaten, certainly within the next decade, to force the oil companies entirely out of crude pricing and crude production. What remains for the companies is the limited and, in the context of the modern structure, far less profitable role as transporters, refiners, and merchandisers of crude petroleum. Phillips Petroleum, for example, recently identified its return on investments in combined refining, distribution, and marketing properties as only 0.17 per cent in 1971 and 1.92 per cent in 1972. The major oil firms have, however, successfully grappled with other serious challenges to their hegemony. There is no reason to expect that they will not make a further attempt to defend their profitability and dominance. In the present setting, four alternative courses of action for the companies stand out. The major firms can attempt to:

1. increase the supply of petroleum available from alternative sources;
2. turn to alternative fuels;
3. prompt military intervention;
4. restructure the industry, making "downstream operations" more profitable.

In examining these options, it is important to keep in mind that they are not mutually exclusive.

A veteran oilman described the first alternative to *Forbes:*

We don't have the oil in the U.S. to meet our future requirements. Either we are going to have our future committed to those crazy Arabs or we are going to develop Southeast Asia, the West Coast of Africa and the West Coast of Latin America as alternative sources—and hopefully, build the Alaskan pipeline.

Oilmen have certainly tried to develop alternative sources of petroleum. After a three-year struggle with conservation groups, the extensive lobbying efforts of the companies to construct an Alaskan pipeline have prevailed. Nevertheless, the Alaskan reserves are inadequate to forestall reliance upon the OPEC members. According to one estimate, the Alaskan reserves, while the "greatest discovery in the history of the U.S. . . . will merely offset declining production in the Lower 48."

The oil companies have also actively sought to discover new foreign sources outside the Middle East. In recent years, fully ninety-five per cent of new exploration efforts have been outside the Persian Gulf. Efforts have particularly centered on the offshore areas of Southeast Asia, where military regimes have not (yet) adopted OPEC's aggressive posture. In Indonesia, for example, the terms between the government and the oil companies are, according to *Fortune*, "exceptionally favorable to the oil companies." In contrast with the division of revenue with the OPEC members (approximately 79:21 against the companies before the 1972–73 price increase), in Indonesia the companies receive sixty per cent of the total output.

The offshore areas of South Vietnam have also attracted considerable American interest. In May of 1973, according to the *New York Times,* oil companies—including Jersey Standard, Mobil, Gulf, and Standard of Indiana —submitted bids for rights to drill for oil off the coast of South Vietnam. Oil officials have, however, interlaced high hopes with concern over the political situation. Indeed, the importance of the political regime in South Vietnam has led *Forbes* to suggest that oil may be "the hidden factor in the Vietnam equation."

While the international oil companies and the Nixon administration appear committed to a politically "satisfactory" government in Saigon, even the achievement of this goal—however unlikely in reality—does not significantly mitigate in the near future the reliance of the advanced capitalist countries upon the OPEC members for crude petroleum. In the first place, it is highly unlikely that Southeast Asia can supplant the Middle East as the primary source of crude imports. In Indonesia, anticipated production for 1975 is no more than the (1972–73) two-million-barrel level of Libya. While it is true that much of the vast archipelago remains unexplored, known reserves account for only about five per cent of the world's total. By contrast, the countries of the Middle East sit on seventy-five per cent of the world's 670 billion barrels of proven reserves, while Saudi Arabia alone accounts for twenty per cent of the total. Secondly, "the long gestation period between planning and actual production in the petroleum industry" means that it may well take until the end of the 1970s before production begins in earnest. Finally, it is quite possible that Indonesia, if not South Vietnam, will follow OPEC's path and perhaps even affiliate itself with OPEC. Alternative petroleum sources thus appear to be inadequate and potentially subject to the same actions that the OPEC members have taken.

The major companies have also responded to the OPEC challenge by turning to alternative sources of energy and transforming themselves into "energy companies." Natural gas, which accounts for approximately twenty-five to thirty per cent of all energy consumed in the United States, has, for example, historically been associated with the search for oil. All the majors now engage in the production of natural gas and account for perhaps sixty per cent of production and reserve ownership. Atomic energy has also come within the control of the petroleum giants: oil companies, headed by Kerr-McGee, Jersey Standard, and Gulf, now control forty-five per cent of the known domestic reserves of uranium. The petroleum companies have also made considerable investments in potential sources of energy such as oil shale, Canadian tar sands, and even underground steam. Finally, beginning in 1963 with Gulf Oil's purchase of Pittsburgh & Midway Coal, the petroleum majors have acquired a number of leading coal companies. At the present time, oil companies own two of the three largest coal producers, five of the largest ten, and seven of the largest fifteen. Peter Barnes has quite correctly predicted the consequences of the majors' concentration of energy resources.

there will be less inter-fuel competition and higher prices, all to the companies' benefit and at the public expense. . . . Some of this has already started to happen. In the last two years (1969–71), for example, coal prices have jumped 79% on the average and more than 100% in some localities though demand and production both rose at about the same 5% rate. . . . The situation has been much the same in natural gas, the one fuel whose interstate price is federally regulated. Oil/gas companies . . . have been pressing the Federal Power Commission for enormous gas rate increases.

While major oil companies' efforts to dominate the entire field of energy have increased both the prices of "competitive" fuel and their own profits, it is unlikely that in the near future the development of alternative sources of energy will significantly reduce the dependence of the advanced capitalist countries upon the OPEC members for crude petroleum. Coal, for example, the most abundant of the fossil fuels, requires either deep or strip mining, both of which "are objectionable because of human hazards or environmental depredation." "Clean" coal with a low sulfur content lies largely in a few western states. Transported to mid-continent markets, it costs twice as much as local coal.

Oil-shale deposits might supply enough oil for a hundred and fifty years. However, there is scant possibility of producing shale oil in large volume before the eighties, because of the huge investment and long lead times required to build the necessary plant and pipelines. At the present time, the extraction of oil from the tar sands is also not profitable.

The use of nuclear energy is also limited in the short run. The twenty-nine "conventional" nuclear fission reactors now operating in the United States employ only uranium-235 as a raw material. U-235 is relatively rare (comprising less than one per cent of all available uranium) and is "in danger of depletion in a few decades." Accordingly, attention has been devoted to the fastbreeder nuclear reactor, which produces more fuel than it consumes. The fastbreeder reactor is, however, extraordinarily dangerous, producing radioactive wastes with lifespans of over two hundred thousand years. In any case, operation of the fastbreeder cannot be expected before 1990. Use of controlled thermonuclear power (fusion), while a "clean, cheap and virtually inexhaustible source of energy," similarly cannot be expected to replace petroleum in the near future. Indeed,

success is decades and billions of dollars away. Estimates of the time when fusion power will be feasible range from 20 to 100 years.

While the major companies have profited, then, from their expansion throughout the energy field, it is unlikely that the development of either alternative sources of petroleum or alternative sources of energy will permit the international oil companies to overthrow their dependence upon the OPEC members for crude petroleum.

Direct United States military intervention, perhaps against the Libyan or Iraqi governments, offers another possible means for breaking OPEC's power. According to the *New York Times*, "the Arab world"—undoubtedly with recollections of Marines landing in Lebanon in 1958 following the overthrow of the pro-Western regime in neighboring Iraq—views the possibility of direct military intervention "as real." Nevertheless, direct United States military intervention at this time appears unlikely in the light of likely Arab resistance, possible Soviet intervention, and an uncertain response at home. Somewhat more likely is clandestine action by the CIA along the lines employed in Iran in 1952. At the present time, however, the United States government seems primarily intent on exploiting the ideological and territorial divisions within OPEC in an effort to splinter its unity. American support coupled with the fear of internal radicalism has drawn the conservative governments of Kuwait, Abu Dhabi, Saudi Arabia, Pakistan, and Iran into a "virtual alliance."

The uncertainty of these efforts to reduce OPEC's bargaining leverage, if not to crack OPEC itself, have not, however, left the major oil firms without an alternative. As profits from production decline, the majors seem to be determined to make downstream operations more profitable. Putting downstream operations on a "moneymaking basis" is, however, no mean task. The majors must restructure downstream operations and production. In the first place, the majors must effect increases in the prices of refined petroleum products, particularly gasoline (which represents sixty-five to seventy per cent of the revenue of refined products) both absolutely and relative to crude prices. Then, in order to maintain prices and profits in marketing at a high level, the majors must significantly reduce the number of gasoline service stations that now operate. In addition to reducing the number of stations, the majors must also reduce the share of the market garnered by independent marketers (or nonbranded stations). Throughout the late sixties, independents continuously increased their share of the total gasoline market, capturing 25.6 per cent of the market in 1972. As long as the majors were primarily interested in realizing the enormous profits locked in the crude barrel, the market losses sustained by their stations were no great concern. The majors' new interest in securing high prices and profits in marketing puts the independents, which have tended to be a source of price competition, in an entirely different light. To secure control over marketing and to put marketing on a "moneymaking basis," the majors must reduce the share of the market held by the independents. Indeed, in order to boost their own profits, rather than the profits of the branded stations, the majors must restructure their relationship with those who operate the majority of service stations. Since the 1930s,

the major oil companies have preferred to lease their stations to dealers who would work long hours on their own (at low pay) rather than have to pay employees who might not have as much incentive to sell extra gasoline.

With marketing far more profitable, the majors may well decide to re-assume direct ownership control of the stations. The total number of stations, for example, peaked in 1968 somewhere between 200,000 and 230,000 (exact figures are not available), remained static in 1969 and 1970, and slowly diminished in 1971 and 1972. This slow decline reflects the majors' gradual reduction in their own stations. In the first five months of 1973, however, the Federal Trade Commission estimates that more than 1200 independent stations closed, while thousands of stations—particularly independent stations—faced gasoline rationing imposed by their suppliers, the major oil companies.

Finally, as gasoline prices have risen and as a consequence made it more attractive for the majors to operate service stations outright, the major companies have raised the rent and cancelled previous rent waivers for leased branded stations, "some of them on unreasonably short notice."

The impetus for these changes has been the so-called "gasoline shortage" of the summer of 1973, which itself followed on the heels of the fuel oil scare of the previous winter (1972–73). Before looking more closely at the shortages, it is worth considering the explanations of the major companies. The majors have rooted the shortages in the controls imposed by Nixon's Phase II over petroleum pricing. The majors have also charged environmental groups with exacerbating the shortages, particularly by blocking construction of new refineries.

The available evidence, however, discounts these charges. While the petroleum price freeze may have increased the attractiveness of gasoline relative to fuel production, a government investigation determined that "in spite of the firms' protestations to the contrary, Humble (Jersey Standard), Texaco, Mobil, Shell, Atlantic Richfield, Cities Service, Phillips and Marathon probably could produce more fuel at present control levels." Similarly, according to General Lincoln, former director of the Office of Emergency Preparedness, the "Cost of Living Council/Price Commission staff have concluded . . . that the oil industry can make a profit on current prices of No. 2 [fuel] oil, and they know it."

The majors' second charge is somewhat more complex. They claim that the shortage of domestic refining capacity developed in the late 1960s as the gap between new construction and increasing demand rose to over one million barrels per day by 1972, and that environmental groups have played a role in this by blocking construction of new refineries, particularly on the Maine coast. Neil Rolde, former executive assistant to the governor of Maine, challenges, however, the assertion that environmental groups were responsible for blocking refinery construction in Maine. Rolde observes that

from our standpoint in Maine . . . [Lichtblau's charge] is a misleading statement. In the recent past, we have had two serious proposals before us for oil refineries. Of these, the more serious was the proposal by Occidental Oil to build a refinery for Libyan crude in the foreign-trade zone at Machiasport, Me.

It is true that there was opposition to this project by environmental groups in Maine. But the lion's share of the opposition came from the major oil companies, which were determined not to let Dr. Armand Hammer's company get a foothold in the United States for importing oil and thus break through the oil import quota barrier.

Had it not been for the unrelenting opposition of the major oil companies, a refinery would have been built at Machiasport because, at the time, both environmental laws were weak in Maine.

The major companies also limited new refining construction in a second way. By restricting refinery profits (through the posting of crude prices at a premium), the majors effectively discouraged independent companies from entering refining. In any case, what engendered the fuel and gasoline shortages was not the price freeze or the impending shortage in refinery capacity. It was, quite simply, a decline in refinery capacity utilization.

The decline in heating oil inventory which left the industry short during the winter of 1972–73, like the decline in gasoline inventory which left the industry short during the summer of 1973, had a simple explanation: the utilization of refinery capacity during the first four months of 1972 averaged 84.2 per cent, 3.0 per cent lower in 1971 and fully 6.5 per cent lower than in 1970, despite an increase in demand. Federal officials entreated the industry to increase refinery output sufficiently.

Notwithstanding government urgings, refineries east of the Rocky Mountains operated at only 89% of capacity in the final quarter of 1972. . . . This was the beginning of the first peacetime petroleum product shortage in the U.S.

The failure of refineries to increase utilization sufficiently continued during the first five months of 1973, despite a 7.4 per cent increase in demand for gasoline, and produced "the gasoline shortage which occurred during the peak summer season."

Responsibility for the decline in refinery output rests heavily on the very largest of the major firms. According to the Senate report, the ten largest refineries—Jersey Standard, Indiana Standard, Texaco, Shell, Gulf, Mobil, ARCO, Sun, Sohio, and Standard of California—"were the major contributors to the drop in refining capacity utilization during the first four months of 1972 below that of 1971 in spite of demand exceeding production." Finally, the available evidence militates against the notion that crude shortages drove the top ten refiners to cut back refinery operations. Standard of New Jersey, Shell, and Gulf refused in fact to avail themselves of any of the additional crude allocated to them.

While a crude shortage did not drive the top ten refiners (with the possible exception of Sohio, a large net crude buyer) to curtail their refining operations during 1972, an inability to obtain sufficient crude-oil feedstocks did force small (and especially independent) refiners to limit their operations. What is more, there is evidence to suggest that the major companies were primarily responsible for the crude shortage experienced by the smaller refiners. In the first place, two Federal Power Commission economists . . . have charged that the major companies are withholding production on nearly one million acres of the nation's richest offshore oil lands. The second piece of evidence requires some explanation. Many smaller American refineries, especially those inland, have traditionally not been "in a position to economically utilize imports." To some extent, this may reflect the shape, direction, and operating rates of the nation's pipeline networks. In any case, most foreign crude has a very high sulfur content that many inland, independent American refineries are not equipped to process. The FTC charges, however, that the major firms have been

preventing many independent refineries, particularly those in the Midwest, from obtaining sufficient supplies of "sweet" crude. Therefore these refineries are running far below capacity.

The major companies have made good use of the fuel shortage of the winter of 1972–73 and the gasoline shortage of the summer of 1973, shortages that they themselves largely created. With independent refiners curtailing their operations and with the majors reducing their sales of gasoline to independent marketers, more than 1200 independent service stations closed their doors during the first five months of 1973. As the FTC observed, "the major integrated oil companies are . . . taking advantage of the present shortage[s] to drive the only viable long-term source of price competition, the independent marketer, out of market after market." At the same time, the shortages were enormously profitable.

The production boycott imposed by the Arab members of OPEC following the October War has provided the major companies with still further opportunity to restructure downstream operations. *Business Week* reports that during 1973, as a whole,

some 10,000 gas stations have gone out of business, nearly 5% of the 218,000 stations that existed when the year began.

And now, the target is no longer just the independent marketer. As a Texaco dealer puts it,

last summer, it was the independent gasoline dealers who were badly hit by gasoline shortages. Now it's the people who lease gasoline stations who are being driven out of business.

The boycott has also permitted the major companies to create an atmosphere where they can override the demands of environmental protection groups. Clean-air standards, for example, have been put to the side throughout the country. The atmosphere of crisis has also permitted further price jumps as the majors have passed on the OPEC increases plus a little something extra.

Despite the majors' success thus far, it is still too early to determine the overall success of the majors' attempt to restructure the industry. Indeed, the drama is merely unfolding. The new strategy, much like the structure imposed upon the industry by the old Standard Trust, contains a highly vulnerable side. Should the OPEC members decide to integrate forward and develop their own refining and marketing operations and/or choose to sell their crude to independent refiners and marketers,

improving those "downstream" profits won't be simple. New competition from Arab-owned companies and independents could depress prices.

Under these circumstances, it is likely that the major companies will again turn to the federal government for assistance. It is important, however, to recognize and not mystify the genesis of the structure that maintained the predominance of the major companies for some thirty-five years. That structure emerged from fierce political struggle between the majors and their opponents. The majors are now engaged in another struggle to structure the industry in accord with their new needs. Public anger against the majors coupled with pressure from petroleum independents struggling to survive could limit the success of the majors' efforts.

Are High Farm Prices Here to Stay?

D. Gale Johnson

A short answer to the question posed by the title of this article is: "Not for very long." This year and next should see the beginning of a significant weakening of some farm prices, though adverse weather in any major grain producing area could postpone the decline for a year or perhaps two years.

Mother Nature has been quite uncooperative in North America so far in 1974. First there was the wet weather during planting time in the Corn Belt and Northern Plains that delayed and decreased planting. Then significant areas of the Corn Belt suffered hot weather and limited rainfall for a month during a critical period of plant growth. From the first of May, when a bumper winter wheat crop and large acreages of feed grains and soybeans were expected, to mid-August the prices of wheat, corn, and soybeans increased by approximately 50%. Thus the prices of wheat and corn approached the peak levels achieved during the last eighteen months.

Even though there are good reasons to believe that prices of grains and most other farm products probably will decline significantly within the next year or two, without question a very precarious situation now exists in agriculture. Of prime importance is the fact that world stocks of grain are very low. At the beginning of the 1974–75 crop year grain stocks in the major exporting countries (the only countries with reliable stock data) were very near the minimal levels required for working stocks. A serious production shortfall in North America in 1974 could result in grain and soybean prices going above their recent peaks and could impose major burdens and hardships upon the peoples of poor countries that find it necessary to import grain.

A more permanent and pervasive problem, in the view of some observers, is a fundamental change that is said to have taken place in the basic demand and supply relationships for food products. It is claimed that a high rate of population growth and rising "real" per capita incomes have resulted in an increased demand for food that has outstripped the capacity to expand production, except at much higher real prices than we have seen in recent decades.

To me, such claims of basic changes in demand-supply relationships are not convincing. I can see no evidence that there has been a significant change in the annual rate of growth of world demand for food. The rate of world population growth during 1962–72 was the same as in 1952–62 and the United Nations medium projection of growth in population from 1970 to 1985 is approximately the same rate as for the past two decades—about 2% annually. Nor does there appear to have been any significant change in the growth rate of per capita income in the 1970s compared with the 1960s.

Why, then, have we seen such substantial increases in farm prices, especially for grains? The reasons are primarily to be found on the supply side, though governmental interventions in major consuming areas that prevented the rationing effects of higher prices were also important.

In the mid-1960s a series of shortfalls in grain production in China, the Soviet Union, and South Asia resulted in a substantial reduction in world grain stocks. Grain production, especially wheat production, expanded rapidly in the major exporting countries—Australia, Canada, and the United States—from 1967 through 1969. Stocks of grain in the three countries increased rapidly and as a consequence grain prices fell. Farmers and governments reacted as one might expect. In the three countries the land devoted to wheat production declined from 45.1 million hectares in 1968 to 35.7 million hectares in 1969 and to 29.1 million hectares in 1970. The production of wheat in 1970 was 53.7 million metric tons, compared with the high level of 75.4 million metric tons in 1968. The attack of corn blight in the United

States in 1970 resulted in a further reduction of grain stocks in the major exporting countries and in the world.

Major shortfalls in grain production were again a problem in South Asia, the Soviet Union, China, and Australia in the 1972–73 period. Grain production in the United States in the 1972–73 crop year was below the previous year, in part in response to low grain prices following the large 1971–72 crop. All told, world grain production in 1972–73 was approximately 5%, or 60 million metric tons, below trend production for that year. This shortfall was nearly as much as the world's grain reserves (excluding the USSR and China) in excess of working stocks. While the 1973–74 world grain crop was a relatively good one, it was not significantly in excess of trend production for that year and world grain stocks were further drawn down. As a consequence, stocks at the beginning of the current crop year (1974–75) were barely above required working stocks.

EFFECTS OF GOVERNMENTAL POLICIES

Demand considerations did play a role in the upsurge in grain prices in 1972–73. One important change in expected demand was the willingness of the Soviet Union to import enormous quantities of grain in 1972–73 to maintain its livestock herds. In 1963–64, following the poor 1963 crop, the Soviet Union imported enough grain to maintain direct human grain consumption. Rather unexpectedly, in 1972 the decision was made that grain was to be imported in sufficient quantities to prevent a significant drop in meat and milk production. Thus grain imports were at least twice as large as would have been called for by the policies of the 1960s.

Another demand-related factor has stemmed from the efforts in many large industrial countries to prevent the rise in world grain prices from pushing up domestic consumer or producer prices. Owing to the combined effects of the devaluation of the dollar and the variable import levies of the European Economic Community (EEC), the increase in U.S. export prices for wheat—from about $60 per ton in 1971–72 to $130 per ton in early 1973—had no effect on the consumer or producer in EEC. When wheat prices increased even further, EEC imposed export taxes and export licensing to discourage sales of domestic wheat in foreign markets. As a result, grain prices in local currencies increased by no more than 10% between 1971 and early 1974 in the Six, except for Italy. During the same period international prices of grain (in dollars) were doubling and trebling. But within EEC (except for the new members) grain became a bargain during a period of real food stringency in the world. The same nationalistic approach has been followed in Japan and the Soviet Union.

Consequently, virtually all required price adjustments have been imposed on a limited part of the world—the major grain exporters and a number of developing countries which rely heavily on food imports. There is no doubt that if there had been something approximating free trade in grains and other foods over the past few years price increases would have been significantly smaller than they have in fact been.

Except for the effect of the devaluation of the dollar, there seems to be no fundamental reason why the long-term decline in real grain prices should not reassert itself. Reflecting major gains in farm productivity, the real farm price of feed grains and hay in the United States between the years 1910–14 and 1971–72 declined by 40%. Similarly, the real price of food grains fell by 37%. In these calculations, the prices received by farmers have been adjusted to reflect the large direct government payments received in 1971–72. If these payments had not been included the declines in real prices would have been approximately 50% for all grains. The dollar devaluation effect is unlikely to increase the real prices of grains, priced in dollars, by more than 10% or 15%.

And yet, predictions are cropping up on all sides that the real costs of producing grains are likely to rise sharply. Why should that be? The reasons cited appear to be the following: first, there is relatively little uncultivated land remaining and all of the diverted acreage in the United States has been returned to production; second, increasing yields will increase costs in part because of diminishing returns from application of fertilizer; third, the prices of farm inputs—especially those based on petroleum products—will be substantially higher in the future than in the past.

On a worldwide basis, the first two reasons for rising real costs of grain can be said to be either incorrect, irrelevant, or both. There are substantial possibilities for expanding the cultivated land area in Africa, South America, South East Asia, North America and Australia. It is true that the potential for expanding cultivated land in parts of Asia is relatively small, but this does not mean that the real costs of producing grains must increase. It is not at all certain that cultivating additional land is generally a significantly lower-cost means of expanding output than increasing yield per acre. The answer for the past several decades in the United States appears to be that it has generally been cheaper to expand output through higher yields than by adding new land; some new land has been brought into cultivation but far more has been retired. It is clearly possible to increase yields in the developing countries, and yields have increased in the developing countries in the past three decades. But yields are still much lower in the developing countries than in the industrial countries.

THE FERTILIZER FACTOR

The second reason cited for higher costs—diminishing returns from fertilizer—is not a valid one. While higher yields may require more fertilizer per unit of output, it does not follow that real costs will increase due to the higher yields because fertilizer is only one of many inputs used in grain production. As yields increase per unit of land, the productivity of other inputs increases and thus contributes to lower costs if the returns to these resources remain constant. In addition, farmers do not continue to operate on a single fertilizer-yield function, but the function changes over time. As farmers use fertilizer for longer periods of time, they learn how to use fertilizer more effectively through a multitude of adjustments such as better adapted seed varieties, greater plant density, timing of application, location of fertilizer in the soil, and more effective types of fertilizer.

There is a possibility that the prices of farm inputs having a significant energy component will be substantially higher in the future than in the past. The cost of energy is an important element in fertilizer production cost. Estimates of the Tennessee Valley Authority indicate that a fivefold increase in the price of natural gas—from $0.20 per thousand cubic feet to $1.00 per thousand cubic feet—would increase the plant-gate price of a ton of urea by $22 or approximately 24%. But there are many other factors that affect the cost of nitrogen fertilizer, including technology, size of plants, and percentage of capacity utilized. In fact, with a natural gas price of $1.00 per thousand cubic feet, the cost of producing nitrogen fertilizer with the 1974 technology would be less than the cost with free natural gas and the 1960 technology.

Another factor affecting the cost of fertilizers in the developing countries is the low ratio of output to capacity. In such countries most of the nitrogen plants operate at 60% to 70% of capacity. If capacity utilization were increased to the level achieved in the industrial countries of approximately 90%, fertilizer costs would decline significantly. Many developing countries protect their fertilizer industries, thus imposing unnecessarily high costs on their farmers. If a durable peace is achieved in the Middle East, enormous quantities of nitrogen fertilizer could be available at costs comparable to those of recent years.

I do not believe that a strong case for significant increases in the real costs of producing grains in the years ahead has been made. It has only been asserted. The improvements in methods of production that we have seen over the past four decades will continue into the future. There is a major potential for relatively low cost increases in output in the developing countries if the appropriate conditions are established and if we consider a dynamic rather than a static framework.

ENERGY INTENSIVENESS—THEN AND NOW

The agriculture of the industrial countries is often accused of being highly energy intensive and increasingly so over time. In many respects the technology associated with the high yielding varieties in the developing countries has similar characteristics. Yet, surprisingly, it is not obvious that the agricultural technology associated with the major U.S. grains was more energy intensive in 1970 than it was a quarter century before. Pimentel and associates have estimated that the ratio of corn output per unit of energy declined from 3.7 in 1945 to 2.82 in 1970. But this calculation does not tell us what the ratio of energy output to energy input would have been if 1970 technology had been used to produce the 1945 output level. The 1945 corn output was less than 60% of the 1970 output. Or put another way, the calculation does not indicate what the energy output/energy input ratio would have been if the 1945 technology had been used to produce the much larger 1970 output. To have produced the 1970 corn output, with the 1945 energy inputs and methods of production, would have required 140 million acres of corn or 80 million acres more than actually was harvested in 1970.

In effect, a 32% increase in energy requirements per bushel of corn "saved" 80 million acres of cropland. If we assume that land had been available to produce the 1970 corn output with the 1945 yield, and all energy requirements are converted into gallons of gasoline, the use of 1.2 billion gallons of gasoline replaced 80 million acres of cropland. Even at today's high prices, 1.2 billion gallons of gasoline has a value at the refinery of about $325 million. Is such an exchange one that we would want to make, assuming it were possible? I think not.

FOOD PROBLEMS IN DEVELOPING COUNTRIES

I am confident that the world has the capacity to increase food production more rapidly than the growth of population, as it has for the past two decades. This is not solely my own view: it is the view expressed in *Preliminary Assessment of the World Food Situation: Present and Future*, which was prepared for the World Food Conference to be held next November and was cited earlier in this discussion. It is also the conclusion of projections that have been made by the Economic Research Service of the U.S. Department of Agriculture. Both of these projections are consistent with relatively low grain and food prices in international markets by the end of this decade.

But cautious optimism about the re-emergence of significantly lower international prices for grains should not be permitted to gloss over a number of important problems that confront the developing countries. Brief note will be made of two of these problems.

While world grain production is capable of expanding somewhat more than world demand over the next decade and at real prices not far above those of the period before the recent high prices, it is probable that grain imports by the developing countries may need to increase significantly unless recent trends are modified. As in the past two decades the growth of demand for food, especially grains, in the developing countries will be twice that of the industrial countries. Based on past trends, grain production is likely to increase at about the same rate in the two groups of countries. The growth of demand in the developing countries must be slowed and special and additional efforts to expand food production must be made. Unless this is done, the dependence on imported foods will increase to very high and perhaps not achievable levels.

For the past two decades the world has depended upon North America to hold its grain reserves. Importing countries, whether high or low income, generally held only working stocks with the expectation that the reserves in North America would be available to meet their needs. These reserves were large enough, until 1973, to provide a remarkable stability of grain prices, around a declining trend. The reserves were not the consequence of deliberate policy decisions by the American and Canadian governments to accumulate reserves but were the results of price and other agricultural policies.

Whereas the reserves accumulated prior to 1972 were inadvertently accumulated, the Agricultural Act of 1973 will require a positive policy decision for the U.S. government to accumulate stocks of grain. The minimum price support levels in the Act are low enough so that the Commodity Credit Corporation would only occasionally accumulate stocks, even if the demand-supply balance for grains eases significantly over the next few years—as it did in the 1967–69 period. And unless the United States holds reserves, Canada will not find it in its interest to do so.

It is now U.S. policy not to have governmentally held stocks of grain, except as a part of an internationally agreed program under which the costs of maintaining reserves would be shared by the importing countries. It is not clear that such an undertaking is possible, but even if it were, the size of reserves is likely to be much smaller than that maintained in the past by the major grain exporters. Consequently the developing countries are likely to be faced by much greater instability of grain prices than in the past. And, if their normal import needs increase substantially, the impact on their economies can be importantly adverse.

The potential for expanding grain and food production in the developing countries is large relative to the expected increase in demand during this century, even if population growth rates do not decline in the near future— as they must in the longer run. But this potential can only be realized if there is a substantial increase in agricultural research, in the supply of modern farm inputs (fertilizer, herbicides, pesticides), and in the harnessing of irrigation water. Above all, the developing countries must provide their farmers with adequate incentives, something that many have not been willing to do.

SUMMING UP

The world has not entered a new agricultural era in the sense that real grain and food prices will be significantly higher in the future than they have been in the past. One depressant on international prices—the overvaluation of the dollar—has been removed and because of this it may not be necessary for the United States to reintroduce subsidy programs such as we have had in the past. But other than this I can see no substantial reason for believing that demand has expanded more rapidly than anticipated or that the basic factors responsible for declining real costs of producing grain have disappeared.

Unless the basic features of the Agricultural Act of 1973 are changed, I do not see the United States once again accumulating large stocks of grain— at least not doing so unilaterally. We may find it in our interest to join with the other exporting countries and the major importers to hold stocks with an equitable sharing of costs in order to achieve a significant degree of trade liberalization. But it is not in the national interest of the United States to once again become, with Canada, the holder of the world's grain reserves.

40

Those Soaring Food Prices

The New Republic

Rising food prices do more than anything else to shrink the average American's take-home dollar. While the Consumer Price Index was climbing 1.3 percent in August, food prices in grocery stores went up 1.7 percent (wholesale prices rose at an annual rate of 91 percent). Poor families have the worst of it. The US Department of Agriculture's low-cost food budget cost 17 percent more in June 1974 than it did the previous June; the higher-price food budget cost "only" 12 percent more.

Can food prices be held where they are, or lowered? It depends upon how much of the upward surge is artificially created and how much is unavoidable. Almost nothing in our economy is as complex as the pricing of food. The shopper's bill at the checkout counter is affected by weather, commodity speculation, exports and imports, middleman profits, government price supports and a host of other factors, many of which defy control. At the moment they are all pushing upward simultaneously. Production costs on the farm—fuel, fertilizer, machinery, baling wire, credit—are on the rise. So are packaging and transportation costs. Foreigners want more of our grain and soybeans and are willing to pay. The Midwest drought has hurt corn, driving up feed prices for livestock and poultry.

But there are elements of artificiality as well in recent price rises, one of which is the inflationary effects of concentrated market power. In the meat packing, cereal, soup, baby food and canned fruit and vegetable industries, among others, three or four firms dominate sales. Campbell sells 90 percent of the soup we buy; Kellogg, General Mills, General Foods and Quaker Oats have cornered 90 percent of the breakfast cereal market. Del Monte is king of the fruit and vegetable canners; Gerber reigns over baby food. According to Russell C. Parker of the Federal Trade Commission, 50 food processing companies account for more than 60 percent of food processing profits, and the trend toward concentration—attributable almost entirely to mergers rather than internal expansion—is continuing. These market giants specialize in highly advertised, artfully packaged, overpriced products. In 1972 the FTC says, the cost to consumers of less-than-competitive pricing in 13 food industry lines exceeded $2 billion. At the retail level 20 large chains made 40 percent of grocery store sales in 1970, up from 30 percent two decades ago. Most cities are at the mercy of two, three or four supermarket chains, which account for the stickiness in retail prices when prices to the farmer go down. When wholesale beef prices in Chicago plummeted 25 percent earlier this year, retail prices dropped 10 percent. A supermarket executive explained the discrepancy by saying the chains were "only trying to make up a little of what we lost—1973 was a bad year." They seem to have succeeded: *Business Week* reports that for the first quarter of 1974, profits of the largest chains were 59 percent higher than a year ago, though sales were up only 14 percent. The largest supermarket chain, Safeway Stores, nearly doubled its net profit in the third quarter of this year ending September 7—$32 million compared to $16.4 million in the same period in 1973.

The growing market power of processors and retailers does as little for farmers as it does for consumers. Middlemen now collect about 60 cents out of every dollar spent on food, up from 50 cents in the early 1950s. A USDA study found that between 1952 and 1971, 94 percent of the rise in consumer food prices resulted from increased marketing costs; 6 percent of the rise got to the farmers.

The lettuce industry is an example of what happens when conglomerates move into food production and marketing. About a third of our lettuce comes from the Salinas Valley in California. A few years ago United Brands (formerly United Fruit) began leasing lettuce farms in the valley. It joined the Central California Lettuce Producers Cooperative, a marketers' association that thwarts competition and is exempt from the antitrust laws under the Capper-Volstead Act of 1922. (The intent of the Capper-Volstead Act was to permit small farmers to market cooperatively, thereby avoiding middlemen; large integrated food companies now use it to increase profits and victimize consumers.) United Brands also launched an advertising campaign to sell lettuce as an expensive brand-name product, as it does with Chiquita bananas. In a recent decision the FTC refused to order United Brands out of the lettuce business, as a hearing officer had recommended. In a concurring opinion, Commissioner Mayo J. Thompson said that he could find "little in the way of redeeming social value . . . in an advertising program designed to make something out of nothing, or as country folks say, 'a silk purse out of a sow's ear.' "

The government's contribution to rising prices, through price supports, quotas, subsidies, reserves, set-asides and marketing orders, has not had the notice it deserves. Most of these special interest gifts came out of the Depression and had the commendable purpose of helping small farmers stay alive. They now help primarily the bigger farmers and food corporations. Take marketing orders, which are devices permitting growers and distributors of a given commodity to collectively set production quotas and quality standards—in effect government-sanctioned cartels. The marketing board for peaches figures out how many peaches can be grown each year without undermining the desired market price. It then allocates production, requiring peach growers to "green drop" a certain percentage of their crop. The percentage is the same for small and large growers alike, though small growers can't afford to lose a portion of their crop as easily as big growers can. Each year millions of peaches rot in the fields so that the price in the supermarket will stay high. There are similar marketing orders for oranges, lemons, apples, pears, grapefruit, plums, avocados, figs, raisins, wine grapes, strawberries, lettuce, potatoes, almonds and other crops. Only one marketing board—the California Egg Board—has a consumer representative on it—one.

The most regulated commodity of all is fluid milk. As we have been reading in the newspapers, the price of milk is set as much by political as by economic pressures. In California where the retail price of milk has risen

33 percent in the past 18 months (and where the California Milk Producers Association dumped 420,000 gallons of raw skim milk into the sewers of Los Angeles last July because it couldn't sell all that milk at prevailing prices) the state director of agriculture sets minimum prices at the processing, wholesale and retail levels. At the processing level, Class 1 milk—which goes into cartons to be sold fresh—gets a substantially higher price than milk used for butter, ice cream, cheese and other dairy products, and each dairyman is assigned a quota for the higher price milk. According to Roy Alper, a lobbyist for the California Citizen Action Group, these quotas—which can be sold—have become quite valuable in recent years. Any dairyman who wishes to increase his sale of Class 1 milk must pay for the right to do so, and sometimes the quota price is the dairyman's single largest expense. "The quota system has not brought us better milk," says Alper. "It has simply made a few dairymen wealthy and raised the price of milk."

Wholesale prices are fixed in such a way that supermarket chains, such as Safeway, which has its own milk processing operation, make a fatter profit than stores that buy from independent creameries. But even nonintegrated retailers fare well, since the minimum retail price set by the director of agriculture includes a 20 percent mark-up for the store. The state auditor general in California conducted a survey of 92 supermarkets and found that the milk mark-up was higher than the mark-up for 11 basic food products whose retail prices are *not* regulated. Some products, such as coffee and sugar, were sold at a loss by a majority of the supermarkets surveyed. Is coffee more nutritious than milk? Should the state require milk drinkers to subsidize coffee drinkers?

One welcome consequence of double-digit inflation is that consumers are more curious than they were about who's picking their pockets, and how. At "mini-summits" and summits, at regulatory commissions and before congressional committees, in local boycott groups, people are asking what portion of recent price hikes represents unavoidable higher costs, what represents high profits and what reflects noncompetitive market power or politically secured favors. When they learn that their food bills are bigger because of government misregulation or government-sanctioned combinations in restraint of trade, consumers may get mad enough to do more than plant victory gardens.

41

The Capitalist Food System: A Framework for Understanding Food Inflation

URPE/PEA National Food Collective

Food prices continue to soar. With every passing month it becomes obvious that we are experiencing a world food crisis. Business and the government tell us that the crisis will go away soon enough, but their reassurances seem increasingly meaningless. Orthodox economists tell us that supply adjustments will soon bring prices back into line, but we've been waiting for those adjustments too long already. What's wrong?

The recent explosion of food prices has not been an "accident," the product of some temporary disturbances in the normal balance between supply and demand. We would argue that food inflation has flowed directly from the internal structure and dynamics of our capitalist economic system. The food crisis is not likely to go away within this economic system, and food prices are not likely to return to their former levels. More generally, food crises of the kind we have recently experienced are themselves natural and necessary outgrowths of the normal development of capitalist economies. In short, we cannot reform our food system to prevent further food crises without fundamentally restructuring the economic system upon which the food economy is based.

In our view, the recent inflation of food prices has been jointly caused by three kinds of developments which interact in complex ways, feeding back upon each other. Nor can the crisis be explained by any one of these developments alone, for the effect of each depends in part on its interaction with the other two. The depth of the roots of these developments and the complexity of their interaction reflect the systemic character of the causes of the crisis and the need for systemic solutions.

These developments are: (a) a series of short-term events, coincidentally acting simultaneously upon supply and demand; (b) the transformation of the food economy in the United States, through which large corporations have been able to achieve an increasingly oligopolistic concentration of power over the production and distribution of food; and (c) a series of economic adjustments flowing from the intensification of the current world economic crisis, itself reflecting the basic instabilities of capitalist economies.

I. SHORT-TERM EVENTS

We reject apologetic arguments that food inflation can be explained entirely by a series of "accidents," blaming the soaring prices on bad weather and shifting currents. We would agree that some short-term events have contributed to this inflation and in some cases may have "triggered" the explosion of longer-term forces, providing the occasion for the manifestation of concentrated corporate power to manipulate prices. We must clearly understand the importance of these short-term events in order to avoid illusions about the temporary character of the crisis.

Four short-term events seem clearly to have had some impact: calamities of nature, the unusual coincidence of hog and beef cycles, the Soviet wheat deal and the sudden increase in fuel prices.

Effects

Calamities of nature—drought in Russia and Africa, inadequate rain in South and Southeast Asia, shifts in the Humboldt current, heavy rains in the United States—coincided in 1972 to reduce world grain output by about 3 per cent from the previous year's level. The hog and beef cycle in this country intensified the effects of rising beef prices because pork supplies, at that moment, were at the bottom of their own cycle. The Soviet wheat deal, *only because of the way it was handled*, intensified the shortage of grains. The rise in fuel prices after 1973 placed increasing pressure on the supply prices of farm inputs *and* on our balance of payments problems.

Insufficient Explanations

These short-term factors triggered such a sharp inflation of food prices precisely because they did not operate in isolation. They occurred in a particular economic context, a context dominated by increasing American control of world grain exports, by the longer-term erosion of world grain stocks, by the increasing corporate power of American agribusiness and by the emerging world economic crisis. It was the dominance of these underlying forces which conditioned the intensity of the impact of these short-term events.

Moreover, we argue that we cannot properly interpret all of these short-term factors as "accidents." While the calamities of nature and the coincidence of meat cycles seem random, our vulnerability to their occurrence reflects the anarchy of capitalist production. Further, the Soviet wheat deal and the increase in fuel prices were not accidents at all; they reflected the symptoms of more fundamental underlying developments in the world economy.

Symptoms of the System

The importance of these short-term factors as triggers reflects the character of our economic system. Two aspects of that argument seem most important.

First, as we noted above, our vulnerability to these kinds of events reflects the general "anarchy" of capitalist production. In an unplanned market economy, no matter how its vicissitudes are "moderated" by government management, proportional growth of basic supplies is unlikely to continue for sustained periods. Almost any accident can throw the system out of whack.

More concretely, the mechanisms through which these short-term events "triggered" inflation reflect the specific forms of post–World War II capitalist development: American hegemony, growing corporate concentration and uneven development between advanced and Third World countries. These developments contributed to the long-run erosion of world grain reserves during the 1960's and to the increasing international economic instability of the current period—themselves some of the aspects of the current situation which left us so vulnerable to the short-term events.

II. CONCENTRATION OF CORPORATE POWER IN THE AMERICAN FOOD ECONOMY

Many of the reassurances offered us by the media, the government and conventional economists rely on the presumptions of competitive economics. For all of us, the food economy has provided the archetype of competitive market economics. Prices could never increase, we're told, because increasing prices would generate, through competitive market adjustments, a rapid increase in food supplies.

This view of the food economy is antiquated. Lagging behind the rest of the economy, the food sector has nonetheless achieved "maturity": that is, it has slowly been transformed over the past fifty years, and particularly since World War II, into a system of production and distribution nearly as concentrated as the rest of the economy. Small farmers remain, but their freedom to adjust "competitively" has been eroded by the squeeze of suppliers of farm inputs on the one hand, and by food processors on the other. Even agriculture itself has fallen more and more under the control of corporate agribusiness. Any analysis which elides this fundamental transformation of the food economy will necessarily obscure some of the major forces effecting the explosion of food prices and the current food crisis.

Effects

The trends toward concentration of the food economy are unmistakable. Corporations now control roughly four fifths of farm output, either through direct control or by control over its distribution. The top twenty food-processing firms made 67 per cent of the profits in food processing in 1972. The twenty-five largest supermarket chains account for half of all retail food sales. This concentration now seems to grow with every year.

Concentrated market power tends to create an upward pressure on prices and we would firmly argue that this transformation of the food economy helps explain the intensity of recent food inflation.

We do not succumb to the simple view that corporations can "fix" prices absolutely. Rather, we argue that corporations create upward pressures by their ability to limit the growth of supplies in response to increasing demand and rising prices on one side, and by their ability to respond to falling demand by contracting production and charging higher prices at the same time. (This latter possibility is illustrated by the auto companies' price hikes when demand for their cars has been collapsing.) Corporations also create upward price pressure through the mechanisms by which they seek to consolidate their concentrated power—through contracting arrangements, through advertising and product differentiation, through increasingly capital-intensive production techniques. The upward pressure on prices results, in short, from an interaction between the means by which corporations increase their power and the consequences of that power.

These effects can be seen at several different levels.

1. In the economy as a whole, concentration has generated increasing prices. During the nineteenth century the wholesale price index, though fluctuating cyclically, revealed no upward tendency over time. During the twentieth century the aggregate wholesale price index, still fluctuating cyclically, reveals a dramatic upward secular rise.

2. Within food itself, the competitive price adjustment becomes less and less evident as corporate power becomes consolidated. After the rapid inflation of farm prices during the Korean War, those prices returned quickly to their previous levels, apparently reflecting the continuing influence of competitive supply adjustments. During the current inflation, even during the recession of 1974–75, there has been no evidence of food prices returning to their previous levels, much less declining at all, and therefore no evidence of that same competitive supply-adjustment effect.

3. The means by which corporations have consolidated their control over the food economy have also held the growth of world food supplies below its potential. Internationally, the American grain companies and the government used foreign-aid programs and surplus commodities to undercut grain production in underdeveloped countries, always keeping the world price of grains low enough—by threatening to dump surplus grains on the world market—that underdeveloped countries were deterred from investing in the expansion of their own domestic agricultural capacity. (In just thirty years, almost all the underdeveloped countries have changed from being substantial exporters of basic food grains to being substantial net importers of basic grains.) Domestically, price-support and acreage-restriction programs, whose subsidies largely benefited large farmers, were used to keep much productive U.S. farming land *out of* production, artificially limiting potential supplies. (As late as 1973, after the shortages of 1972, the government was still paying over $3 billion to keep roughly 50 million productive acres out of farming use.)

4. In the current situation, at the concrete level, we can see the ways in which corporations can limit the competitive supply adjustment characteristic of the earlier food economy. Large meat processors withheld supplies in their freezers, able by their financial strength to weather the temporary loss in revenues. Sugar refiners can continue to raise prices, given relatively inelastic demand, and forestall supply adjustments by their control over sugar production. The power of farm input suppliers to raise their prices keeps farm margins so low that many small farmers, heavily in debt, are unable to borrow enough to increase current production.

Insufficient Explanations

While these consequences are fundamentally important, they cannot explain the explosion of food prices by themselves. First, at one end, the short-term factors did operate as triggers. Second, at another level, the intensification of the current world economic crisis conditioned some of the forces to which corporations in the food economy were responding. While the government was always helping agribusiness with one hand, for instance, it was also desperately pursuing policies which would help ameliorate the declining trade position of the United States; these policies provided an occasion for agribusiness to manifest its power in ways which might not otherwise have become possible.

Symptoms of the System

Many "neo-populists," clearly aware of the effects of corporate concentration on the food economy, call for "trust-busting." They offer the hope that we could prevent recurrence of these kinds of food crises by returning to the "golden days" of competitive agriculture.

We submit that these arguments miss the essential point. Concentration flows inevitably from the rules of capital accumulation in capitalist economies. It did not happen as a result of government neglect; it happened because it was the only way of resolving the contradictions of overproduction in competitive markets. If we could somehow magically break the power of the current "trusts," the laws of capital accumulation would, in our opinion, produce new and equally powerful corporations rising out of the ashes of the old.

Others maintain that concentration in the food economy is "efficient," allowing us to take advantage of "economies of scale." It may conceivably be true, these apologists hold, that corporations create inflationary pressures, but they also permit higher standards of living and more consumer choice.

In reply, we argue that the evidence does not support these claims. "Economies of scale" do not require the current level of concentration—far from it. Moreover, the means by which corporations develop and use their power waste enormous resources on advertising, packaging and food gimmicks while they simultaneously adulterate the quality of the food we eat. A more rational use of our resources, we suggest, could provide us with just as high a "standard of living" without wasting resources and poisoning our food.

III. WORLD ECONOMIC CRISIS

The food crisis, finally, has been both triggered and fundamentally exacerbated by the development of the world economic crisis. It has been influenced especially by the kinds of policies which the U.S. government has desperately pursued in trying to salvage the stability and hegemony of the American economy.

Effects

Two main aspects of the developing world crisis underlay the policies which ultimately helped cause the food inflation. First, the American balance of payments continued to deteriorate during the late 1960's as American corporations faced increasing international competition and as the sustained American boom pushed U.S. prices further out of line. Second, the growth of multinational corporations further exacerbated some of the impact of international competition as multinational corporations rapidly transferred credit and currencies around the advanced countries, amplifying the wild gyrations of monetary movements and speculation.

To correct the increasingly persistent deficit in the balance of payments, the U.S. government pursued two policies, both of which simultaneously created the basis for exploding food prices. First, the government sought to push food exports as fast and as fully as possible; food exports more than tripled between 1969 and 1973. These policies tended not only to create a situation of tight supplies in the United States but also to divert American food surpluses from Third World countries without funds to more affluent advanced countries. (The Soviet wheat deal was only one of many packages encouraged by this export drive.) Second, the government was pushed to devalue the dollar twice. This tended to increase American exports in general and American food exports in particular as U.S. prices became relatively cheaper internationally.

The several aspects of the developing world crisis, by 1971, also combined to produce converging business cycles in all the advanced industrial countries. As the United States tried to pay its way out of the short recession of 1969–70, its expansionist policies tended to exacerbate an unusually amplified world inflation, with every country's prices moving rapidly together. These increasingly *general* price movements obviously reinforced the tendencies in the food sector itself.

The international fuel crisis, finally, also had an important effect on food prices through its effects on food input supply prices and transport costs. This crisis, partly the creature of accident but more fundamentally the product of American oil corporations' strategies and the developing world economic crisis, had causes parallel to those of the food inflation and ended up exacerbating the food crisis itself.

IV. THE SIGNIFICANCE OF THIS ANALYSIS

This analysis provides an essential corrective and counterpoint to the reigning conventional explanations of the food crisis.

Orthodox economists have often applied simple supply-and-demand analysis, based on competitive models. Their apologies almost always imply —though they manage to hold on to this faith less and less—that food prices will somehow eventually come down as supplies expand. We fundamentally oppose this kind of analysis because we don't believe that competitive forces dominate the food economy any longer or that "equilibria" represent the typical situation in capitalist economies.

The government seeks to turn our attention away from the fundamental character of the food crisis by blaming its various coincidental causes. We should all be patient, President Ford says, and we should all eat a little less, Nixon said, while the market weathers the storm. If we get too piggy, we are told, we will merely make things worse. We fundamentally oppose this orientation as well, because we feel that important forces in the development of the economy have caused the current crisis, not our own piggishness. Government policies have been framed by the effort to force the American people to pay the costs of a crisis created by large corporations and by the instabilities of world capitalism.

Critical opposition to these apologists has been dominated, so far, by the collection of "neo-populists" clustered around Ralph Nader and some public interest groups. In the neo-populist view, monopoly pricing and power have uniquely caused the crisis. If we were able to break monopoly power, we could prevent such crises. We should restore, they say explicitly, the protective blanket of market competition in the food economy. Power to the small farmer! We also oppose this orientation, not because we think monopoly power has had no effect, but rather because we believe that we cannot eliminate monopoly power without changing the basic rules of capital accumulation in capitalist economies. Nor could we eliminate the basic instabilities of capitalist economies, manifested through cycles and crises, by simply busting the power of the trusts.

Our analysis bears much more than this simple critical significance, finally, because it clarifies the very limited options we have for dealing with the present crisis and preventing future crises. If the combined causes of this crisis all flow, directly or indirectly, from the nature of the capitalist system, then we must clearly transform that system itself.

Toward a Controlled Economy

The twin afflictions of unemployment and inflation have prompted renewed calls for wage and price controls. Capitalist countries have increasingly resorted to this type of governmental planning, but usually on a stopgap basis only. In this country, controls were dramatically introduced— initially in the form of a "freeze" —by President Richard M. Nixon on August 15, 1971. Created chiefly as a political ploy (the election of '72 was little more than a year away), enforcement was delegated by the Nixon Administration to a group of economists known for their ideological opposition to wage and price controls. Under these circumstances, it was no surprise that controls were soon discredited. This is not to say, however, that they did not work; Nixon was, after all, elected. But what were controls designed to accomplish economically? One answer is provided by the man in charge—Arnold Weber, Executive Director of the Cost of Living Council:

Business had been leaning on [Secretary of the Treasury] Schultz and [Chairman of the Council of Economic Advisers] McCracken to do something about the economy, especially wages. The idea of the freeze and Phase II was to zap labor, and we did. (*Business Week*, April 27, 1974, p. 108.)

However, even when administered by those sympathetic to business, controls disrupted the plans of individual corporations. In Reading 42, journalist Robert Samuelson provides vivid illustrations of how this process worked. C. Jackson Grayson, Jr., Dean of Southern Methodist University School of Business Administration and Chairman of the Price Commission during Phase II, is outspoken in his opposition to reinstating controls of this kind (see Reading 43).

Grayson writes authoritatively as an insider, as well as one who ideologically prefers the "free" workings of the capitalist market. Radical economists, on the other hand, believe corporate capitalists are interested less in the alleged virtues of the free market than they are in making profits; towards that end, they will use virtually any means available. In the distant past they generally favored relatively low levels of government planning. During recent decades, however, they have more often sought the aid of government, at first to safeguard their capital, and then to engineer conditions that enlarge their profits. At this juncture, some of the largest of these corporations can now apparently count on government rescue efforts (through the existing machinery of the Federal Reserve) should they run into liquidity problems or be threatened with bankruptcy. For these reasons, radical economists Stephen W. Welch of Kenyon College (see Reading 44) and David Gordon of the New School for Social Research (see Reading 45) view government as the handmaiden of corporate capital and place wage-price controls and other government policies within that context. Both expect the capitalist class to seek increased profits through controls on labor, to be supplemented, if necessary, by limiting the right to strike.

Like Welch, Gordon shows that the current downturn was preceded by years of declining profits. Capital attempted to redress the situation by imposing on workers the traditional program of speed-up. The response was predictable—the previously falling industrial accident rate rose sharply in the sixties. We need only read *Business Week* (October 12, 1974) to confirm that the game plan of business calls for the continued tightening of working-class belts; according to that publication, profits must be increased so that corporations can invest without going more deeply into debt.

"Yet," comments editor John Carson-Parker,

. . . it will be a hard pill for many Americans to swallow—the idea of doing with less so that big business can have more. It will be particularly hard to swallow because it is quite obvious that if big business and big banks are the most visible victims of what ails the Debt Economy, they are also in large measure the cause of it.

So there we have it! Profits that are not reinvested for capital gains are to be distributed as dividends to the wealthy—to be converted, no doubt, into yachts, diamonds, and mansions—while the working class is to make do by tightening their belts. This is literally a program designed to make the rich richer and the poor poorer. Beyond this, the government stands ready if necessary to step in and preserve the capital of the rich should they invest it unwisely. Such is the private enterprise system to which we are patriotically asked to pledge our allegiance! It is not surprising that radicals like Welch foresee a period of rising class antagonism.

Finally, excerpts from the Equal Opportunity and Full Employment Act of 1976 are included, as Reading 46, for what they reveal about the pressures from organized labor and sympathetic politicians to do something about unemployment. As the bill now reads, the government must provide a job with decent pay to anyone who wants it. If it does not, injured parties are entitled to sue the United States for injunctive relief and other damages. Over sixty members of the House of Representatives have joined Congressmen Reuss and Hawkins in cosponsoring this piece of legislation, and sponsors in the Senate include Humphrey, Hart, and Kennedy, among others. As earlier readings have made clear (see Readings 32 and 35), full employment tends to erode the rate of profits. It is therefore highly unlikely that the bill will become law, or if it does, that it will be enforceable. Its precursor, the Employment Act of 1946, was hailed at the time as a significant advance for working people, calling for government "to promote maximum employment, production, and purchasing power." Devoid of enforcement machinery, qualified by clauses that proscribed actions that did not "foster and promote free competitive enterprise," this section of the act soon became a dead letter. The point is that unemployment cannot be legislated away. Unless the capitalist system is replaced either unemployment or government-enforced wage austerity—or both —are apt to be prominent and permanent features of American society during the final quarter of the twentieth century.

42

Why Price Controls Stopped Working . . .

Robert Samuelson

There are a few essentials to know about fertilizers. Plants need nitrogen. Fertilizer gives them nitrogen. The more fertilizer, generally speaking, the bigger the crop. The bigger the crop, the greater the supply. The greater the supply, the lower the price.

There is a fertilizer shortage in the U.S. now. The process works in reverse, so less fertilizer will probably mean higher food prices. No one disputed this logic. Nor, I found, did many people dispute the fact that economic controls had contributed to the shortage.

The story was simple. In 1972 the world price of key fertilizers rose significantly—50 to 75 per cent—above U.S. prices. A very predictable thing soon happened: with U.S. prices held down by controls, fertilizer firms began shipping their supplies abroad.

There were some complaints, but it wasn't until September, 1973—after the industry, through its trade association, the Fertilizer Institute, officially asked for exemption—that the Cost of Living Council began seriously considering the removal of controls on U.S. fertilizer prices. Removing the price ceilings, of course, would allow U.S. buyers to bid for the scarce supplies on an equal footing with foreign purchasers.

The time lag was no surprise. Bureaucracies habitually react to problems, rather than anticipating them. Institutional sluggishness. You could blame it on stupidity, or ignorance, but, in the case of government bureaucracies, there was a more fundamental reason: a problem has to exist before it can be solved. You couldn't take the price ceilings off fertilizer to avoid the problem. People would accuse the controllers of sabotaging their own program without any good reason. You had to wait for the reason to develop. You had to wait for the fertilizer to be exported.

Even after the industry's appeal, the Cost of Living Council hesitated. Part of the problem was ignorance: the inevitable absence of the answers to today's questions today. A lot of fertilizer was already tied up in long-term export contracts, but the Council didn't know how much. The prospect was troubling. Prices might rise without producing much additional supply for U.S. farmers. There was another problem. Exempting the fertilizer industry would inevitably stimulate exemption requests from other industries. Not all these could be cavalierly ignored. The explosives industry complained that if it weren't exempted, it wouldn't be able to compete with fertilizer manufacturers for ammonia nitrate, which is used in the manufacturing of both fertilizer and explosives. Then there would be a shortage of explosives for coal mines, which would eventually lead to a scarcity of coal. The world was complicated. Ultimately the Council exempted both the fertilizer and explosives industries.

But fertilizer was no freak breakdown of controls. Copper and scrap steel supplies also had flowed abroad because domestic prices were held artificially low. Lumber had been withheld from the market. A shortage of tomato paste had developed, in part because the price had been held too low and encouraged a depletion of stock. The experiment with direct food controls had failed conspicuously. Farmers, faced with rising feed costs—which hadn't been controlled—smothered baby chicks and sent their breeder chickens off to slaughter; hog farmers, confronting the same cost-price squeeze, limited expansion of output.

There were dozens of stories in dozens of industries about how controls had misfired. One newspaper executive claimed, for example, that controls had aggravated the newsprint shortage: you held down advertising rates and people advertised more; the more they advertised, the more paper you needed.

But the stories were prone to exaggeration. Consider fertilizer. Controls or no controls, there would have been a shortage. Demand had risen spectacularly because the government had freed nearly 60 million acres of land for production. The industry hadn't expanded in the last few years, because it was just emerging from the economic slump in the late sixties. All that could be said was that the controls had made a bad situation worse. If controls hadn't been lifted, more fertilizer would have been sold abroad. It was a frustratingly ambiguous conclusion.

The same thing that happened in fertilizer happened in plastics. World prices of petrochemicals (the essential raw ingredient for plastics processing) soared above domestic prices, tempting major petrochemical manufacturers (about 25 giants, including DuPont, Dow Chemical, and Exxon Chemical, supply about half the country's plastic resins) to export their product. The incentives to do so were powerful. To give but one example: the domestic price of polystyrene was effectively frozen at 18 cents per pound, while the world price was more than three times as high.

While the diversion of fertilizer supplies overseas undoubtedly hurt U.S. food production, the escape of petrochemicals abroad had more curious consequences.

First, business success—indeed survival—became a matter of who you knew, not how well you ran your business. Because the petrochemical companies were still selling considerable amounts of supplies in the U.S., you could stay in production if you knew the petrochemical company's marketing vice president better than your competitor did.

Second, competition in the plastics industry became more political and less economic. Many of the small independent companies soon realized that their problems lay in Washington: if they could ease the Phase IV rules, allowing domestic prices to rise to world levels, then some of the chemicals would stay in the U.S., and American firms could bid for supplies. So, the small plastic companies formed a Washington-based trade association. . . .

Finally, people tried to get around the price ceilings. The result was "black markets," "distortions," or whatever label you want to attach to intricate, suspicious transactions designed to beat the government rules.

Consider this situation: a marketing vice president of a large petrochemical firm has a huge supply to sell. He must sell the chemicals at prices fixed by government ceilings. At the free market (world) price, the same stock might be worth three or four times as much. What does he do? The possibilities aren't hard to imagine. Sell to a broker friend and split the profit? (Under Phase IV rules, the broker could probably sell at a free price, because, being a "small businessman," he would have been exempted from price rules.) Take a kickback from a grateful buyer, desperate for petrochemicals to keep his plant running? Act honestly?

All this, of course, undermined competition. The artificiality of prices created enormous gaps between firms. If company A bought its petrochemicals at the fixed price, but company B bought its supply at a free price, three or four times as high, it wasn't hard to figure out which firm would prosper.

But again, I ran into maddening ambiguity. Given the oil shortage, there would have been a scarcity of petrochemicals anyway. Some of the big plastics companies had a natural advantage over the smaller firms because they made their own petrochemicals. Eventually, the Cost of Living Council partially decontrolled petrochemical prices. No one knew quite how many small plastics firms had been forced out of business, whether they had been forced out permanently, or whether they might have gone bust under any circumstances.

The Federal Reserve building is a white-marbled temple on Constitution Avenue that's rarely visited by anyone who doesn't work there. Inside the building is Arthur Burns, chairman of the Federal Reserve Board and also chairman of the Committee on Interest and Dividends. The CID, as it was called, maintained a "voluntary" system of controls over interest rates and dividends. These items hadn't been included in the coverage of the original Economic Stabilization Act, but, to give the appearance of being even-handed with business and labor, the Administration believed it couldn't ignore them. Hence the CID.

The incident which interested me occurred in early 1973. At that time, major commercial banks began to raise their so-called "prime rate"—the rate of interest they charge to their very best business customers (less trustworthy borrowers usually received loans at a fixed level above prime which rose and fell with fluctuations in the prime). Over the years the prime rate had become a media superstar, attracting enormous attention—well beyond its real importance—any time it changed. Its upward movements in early 1973 drew the customary page one stories. All this upset Burns. He decided to stop—or at least slow—the rise of the prime.

As chairman of the CID, he fired off telegrams to big banks, demanding that they justify the higher rates and declaring that the increases threatened the Administration's anti-inflation program.

It was an intriguing picture: Arthur Burns holding the big, greedy banks in line, battling to keep inflation under control, and protecting the interests of the common man. That's the picture the press painted. But it is not, alas, what happened. Burns' primary motivation in standing up to the banks was not so much to hold interest rates down as to head off legislation that might place interest rates under *mandatory* controls.

Worried about rising prices and climbing interest rates, congressmen —particularly Rep. Wright Patman, the formidable chairman of the House Banking and Currency Committee—were agitating to require Burns (or someone) to regulate all rates. Burns apparently thought this impossible to do, disastrous to try. The confrontation with the banks was designed to undercut that campaign by demonstrating that Burns was already fighting to hold down the key rates.

It didn't take much research to turn up a few more examples of politics getting in the way of economics.

Consider rents. Not many economists believed rents could be effectively controlled on a nationwide basis. Housing conditions varied too greatly from city to city. Anyway, housing was generally very competitive; there were lots of landlords and lots of builders. If land costs rose, if labor costs rose, and if local taxes rose, it followed that rents would have to rise. To try to hold them back would, in the long run, probably be self-defeating; landlords would cut back on service and maintenance, and, ultimately, new construction might decline.

But rent is a highly visible and emotional symbol of inflation. So, in Phase II, the Price Commission tried to control rents. It was not a very satisfactory experience. The rules were monstrously complicated. "Lawyers in the Price Commission and the Internal Revenue Service found them difficult to write," C. Jackson Grayson, chairman of the Price Commission, would recall later. "We found them difficult to explain, and the general public couldn't understand them. . . . We tried revision after revision to clarify and simplify, and each time we seemed to generate more confusion."

And what about Burns' dance with the prime rate? Was that simply a harmless exercise in politics and public relations? Well, maybe not. It did succeed in neutralizing pressure for mandatory interest rate controls, but its economic consequences may have been less benign.

While Burns was busy sitting on the prime rate, big businesses were stumbling all over each other to take out new bank loans. They knew that the cost of money—that is, the interest rate—would be higher later, so why not take advantage of a bargain while it lasted. In the first half of 1973, business loans at commercial banks rose at an astounding annual rate of about 30 per cent.

The explosion of loans occurred precisely when economists recognized that the U.S. economy was in the midst of a demand boom and was desperately in need of some restraint. Burns realized this. The Fed was attempting to tighten credit, which normally would raise interest rates, choke off some borrowing, and help slow down the economy. As chairman of the CID and the Fed, Burns was moving in opposite directions simultaneously.

How much damage did it do? No one will ever really know. But, at best, Burns was fighting inflation with press releases. At worst, he was pouring the proverbial oil onto the fire.

Lesson Number One was about political reality and economic reality. Politics demanded instant and simple solutions. Prices were going up. Stop them. Damn the torpedoes, full speed ahead. Economic reality didn't work quite that way. There were choices—unpleasant choices—to be made. It was like chocolate: you could eat a lot of chocolate, but you might get cavities. Years later, of course. Wage-price controllers were constantly being tugged between the two realities, but, with their eyes glued to the monthly price indexes, they were always tempted to do anything that might give them instant success, minimizing the possible ill aftereffects—which might take years to surface.

. . . [T]he Cost of Living Council had commissioned a number of reputable economists to try to figure out the overall impact of controls on prices. The economists fed the statistics into their computers, ran the numbers forward and backward, subjecting them to all sorts of generally incomprehensible, but respectable, forms of analysis. The results were mixed. One analysis concluded that controls had had no impact at all. Another estimated that without controls prices would be 1 per cent higher than they are. The final analysis said that controls had generally kept non-food prices down 2.3 per cent.

So we got [remarks Samuelson's source] a 2-per cent reduction in the cost of living, at best, for the controls, and we got a lot of trouble in a lot of industries. Maybe we're lucky, though, because we avoided the biggest risk. A political smash-up, caused by a confrontation between big labor and government. Something like what happened in Britain. People forget that wage-price controls are fundamentally aimed at labor, not business. The price controls are added to make wage controls politically palatable and give the impression of impartiality.

In effect, the government bargains with big unions. The record of government in bargaining situations isn't too good. There's a lot of press coverage. Issues get publicized, and positions get polarized. We've had enough bitter municipal strikes to prove that. There are a lot of unions that can tie this country up pretty quickly: the Teamsters, the railroad unions, the coal miners. Longshoremen and steelworkers and auto workers can make things pretty messy, too. Controls are a natural target for strike or protest. Look what the independent truckers did to the oil allocations, and they were weak and unorganized. I don't like the idea of a really powerful union trying the same trick.

If you want to be totally cynical about it, imagine the following scenario. It's 18 months before a national election. Unemployment is high. Inflation is unacceptable. The party in power, though it's skeptical about the lasting value of controls, puts controls on the economy. By the next summer, things are looking fine. Unemployment has come down. Prices have been artificially restrained. The party wins big, but, after the elections, the problems of the controls become increasingly apparent. Prices soar.

Of course, that's precisely what had happened in 1972.

The lesson in all of this, he said, is simple: controls involve large risks, but promise small rewards.

43

Controls Are Not the Answer

C. Jackson Grayson, Jr.

I will make one clear assertion at the outset: Wage-price controls are not the answer to inflation.

And yet I will also make the following prediction: We will turn again in the United States, in desperation, to some form of controls over wages and prices—just as people have done over the centuries. And the answer will still be the same—they may make some short-term gains, but at the expense of the long-run welfare.

The lessons of history seem pretty clear. Centralized efforts to fight inflation were started before Christ was born. Rome, for example, fought inflation by various means for centuries. Finally, in A.D. 301, the emperor Diocletian imposed the first extensive price-wage control program. His edict (referred to as "commanded cheapness") set schedules for 76 different wage categories and for 890 different price categories (222 of which were for food!). The penalty for an offense was death. Thirteen years later, the program, in shambles, was abandoned. In the thirteenth century, the great Mongol, Kublai Khan, decreed maximum prices. And Medieval Europe had a "just price" code.

Not many people are aware of it, but the United States began some attempts at wage-price controls during its early years. The American Puritans imposed a code of wage and price limitations in 1636; those who violated the code were classed with "adulterers and whoremongers." The Continental Congress set price ceilings even before the Declaration of Independence. A few states enacted price control laws. Inflation became so severe that General George Washington complained in April 1779 that "a wagonload of money will scarcely purchase a wagonload of provisions." The attempts at control were sporadic, highly controversial, and not comprehensive. All efforts were largely abandoned by 1780.

Most modern nations have instituted wage-price controls during periods of war, but it was in Europe right after World War II that almost every nation tried some form of comprehensive peacetime controls (remembering the inflation that had torn apart European economies after World War I). Some European nations had succeeded with their "incomes policies" for a period of time. Some were started, stopped, and reinstated in another version. But none has lasted continuously.

Though specific "lessons" are difficult to transfer across international boundaries, and even difficult to use in one nation from one time to another, it might be helpful to look at a summary that I have made of European experiences with controls (see Table 1).

These experiences were summarized succinctly by Lloyd Ulman and Robert Flanagan in their book, *Wage Restraint—A Study of Incomes Policies*

TABLE I □ GENERAL LESSONS FROM EUROPEAN INCOMES POLICIES

1. If either labor or business does not cooperate, a wage-price controls program will not work.
2. Incomes policies do not work for long. They erode with time.
3. Getting into controls is easier than getting out
4. Rising profits drive wage demands up.
5. Neither business nor labor is very satisfied with any given distribution of their share of income at any given time. Both will seek to improve their share.
6. Voluntary incomes policies have been limited in success and in time. The tendency is toward mandatory policies.
7. Labor nearly always believes that the government figure for estimated productivity in setting wage guidelines is low. History shows that labor is generally right.
8. A wage "drift" occurs over time as business and labor cooperate to break many of the wage guidelines.
9. Efforts to restrain business and labor through education and exhortation have very limited success.
10. It is increasingly difficult to make incomes policies work as demand increases and unemployment decreases.
11. If prices are to be controlled, then so must wages be. The only exception is France, which has had a limited price control program but no wage control program.
12. Cost of living escalators accelerate inflation.
13. Less productive labor groups eventually demand comparability in wages with the more highly productive labor sectors, thereby eroding the wage guideline.
14. Expectations feed inflation.
15. Increasingly interdependent world trade can intrude upon and upset a nation's incomes policies.

in Western Europe: "Incomes policy, to generalize from the experience of the countries in this account, has not been very successful." My conclusions about the accomplishments of the Price Commission do not vary from that. Perhaps we did obtain some short-range impact on price-wage levels, but they were gained under special conditions (slack in the economy, followed by productivity gains from a highly stimulated economy, and cooperation of business and labor) and at the cost of some long-term negative results.

As a result of my sixteen months as a price controller, I can list seven ways that controls interfere (negatively) with the market system and hasten its metamorphosis into a centralized economy.

First, wage-price controls lead to distortions in the economic system, which can be minimized only in the short run. The longer controls are in effect, the harder it is to discern real from artificial signals. No matter how cleverly any group designs a control system, distortions and inequities will appear. It happened in European control programs: it started to happen in Phase II.

For instance, lumber controls were beginning to lead to artificial middlemen, black markets, and sawmill shutdowns. Companies trapped with low base-period profit margins were beginning to consider selling out to those with higher base-period margins, sending their capital overseas, or reducing their operations. Elsewhere, instances of false job upgrading—actually "raises" in disguise—were reported on a scattered but increasing basis. To keep away from profit-margin controls, some companies were considering dropping products where costs, and thus prices, had increased.

And shortages of certain products (such as molasses and fertilizer) were appearing because artificially suppressed domestic prices had allowed higher world prices to pull domestic supplies abroad.

Exceptions and special regulations can handle some of these distortions, but the task grows more difficult as each correction breeds the need for another.

Second, during a period of controls, the public forgets that not all wage-price increases are inflationary. In a freely competitive economy, wage and price increases occur because of real consumer demand shifts and supply shortages. The resulting wage and price increases signal to businesses, "make more," or to labor, "move here," or to the public, "use less."

Controls interfere with this signaling mechanism. An artificially suppressed price can eventually cause shortages; natural gas is an example. Similar examples can be found in the labor market, where suppressed wages do not attract labor to areas in which there are shortages of skills or workers. But with wage-price controls in place, the public believes that all increases are inflationary—almost antisocial—and the clamor is for no increases, or at least very small ones.

"You can eliminate the middleman, but not his function"—this old business saying applies equally to our economic system. We live in a world of scarce resources, and, as much as some would like to repeal the laws of supply and demand, it cannot be done. Some system must allocate resources, we hope to the most efficient use for society. If wage-price controls, other government regulatory rules, or business-labor monopolies prohibit the price system from performing its natural function, then another rationing system (such as central planning and control) must be used. You can eliminate the price system, but not its function.

Third, during a control period, the public forgets what profits are all about. Even before the recent wage-price controls, the public believed profits were "too high," though they actually declined from 6.2 percent of GNP in 1966 to 3.6 percent in 1970, and increased only to 4.3 percent in the boom year of 1972. And with profit increases raised to the top of the news during the recovery of 1972 and early 1973, the negative public sentiment against profits increased. Why? The control system itself heightened the public's negative attitude toward profits at a time when capital regeneration, the fuel of the capitalist engine, was already alarmingly low.

Fourth, wage-price controls provide a convenient stone for those who have economic or political axes to grind, particularly those interested in promoting a centralized economic system. For example, in 1972 Ralph Nader argued that the control system should be used to prohibit automobile companies from raising their prices to reflect style changes. Others argued that price increases should not be given to companies that employ insufficient numbers of minorities or pollute the environment. Nor should wage increases go to uncooperative unions. And so on.

Fifth, wage-price controls can easily become a security blanket against the cold winds of free-market uncertainties. They tell people what the limits are; they help employers fight unions; and they provide union leaders with excuses to placate demands for "more" from their rank and file. The controlled become dependent on the controllers and want regulations continued in preference to the competition of a dynamic market. At the same time, the controllers themselves can become so enamored of their task that they don't want to let go.

The public begins to fear what will happen when controls are ended and seeks continuance. Witness the fears of moving from Phase II to Phase III, and the public (and congressional) pressure for the freeze to replace Phase III. Even Wall Street seemed terrified at the thought of returning to supply and demand in the market. It is much easier to get into controls than to get out.

Sixth, under controls, business and labor leaders begin to pay more attention to the regulatory body than to the dynamics of the marketplace. They inevitably come to the same conclusion, summed up by one executive: "We know that all of our sophisticated analysis and planning can be wiped out in the blink of a Washington controller's eye."

Seventh, and most dangerous, wage-price controls misguide the public. They draw attention away from the fundamental factors that affect inflation —fiscal and monetary policies, tax rates, import-export policies, productivity, competitive restrictions, and the like. The danger is that attention will become permanently focused on the symptom-treating control mechanism rather than on the underlying problems.

In summary, perhaps the most dramatic way I can underscore my views is to point out the recent example of Britain, where years of successive stop-go economic policies and various types of controls (including guideposts) have led that nation to where it is today, economically and politically in a crisis state with one of the lowest income growth rates of modern nations and raging inflation.

Controls are not the answer.

"Zapping" Labor: A Radical Perspective on Wage-Price Controls

Stephen W. Welch

Announcing that "The time has come for decisive action—action that will break the vicious circle of spiraling prices and costs," President Nixon inaugurated the first peacetime wage and price controls in this country in August of 1971. Although he stated that "We must stop the rise in the cost of living," he more accurately should have revealed that he intended to put a crimp in labor's demand for higher wages in hopes of reversing a significant decline in corporate profits over the previous six years. How do various economists, business and labor leaders view controls? What impact could controls have on corporate profits in the early 1970's? Are controls biased in favor of corporate interests rather than labor? Is there a need for controls in the mid-1970's? If so, how would further controls fit into the overall crisis which the economy now faces?

Economists are far from unanimous in their view of controls: essentially three views may be distinguished. Libertarians from the University of Chicago contend that no form of incomes policies is needed to solve the inflation problem; a decrease in the rate of growth of the money supply, given sufficient time, will cure rapidly rising prices. The imposition of controls will only postpone the inevitable price increases associated with pent-up demand; worse still, they will cause distortions in the allocation of goods and services, leading to inefficient use of resources. Investment will be discouraged, supplies will dry up or shift abroad, and black markets may spring up. Recent examples of such distortions and their allocative impact are numerous. For instance, restricting the price of fertilizer below the world price encouraged fertilizer exports in 1972 and short supplies here at home. U.S. farmers consequently realized less output per acre, with the predictable result to farm prices. Similar movements abroad were seen for polystyrene (an essential petrochemical for the plastics industry), tubular goods (tubing, casings, and pipe used in oil drilling), copper, and scrap steel. Administration profit-margin rules led industries to reallocate their production toward those sectors which returned relatively higher profits in the best two fiscal years from 1969 through 1972. In the steel industry the result was a severe shortage of less profitable steel reinforcing bars in 1973, while in the paper industry heavier-weight paper was produced at the sacrifice of resources which could have produced more lightweight substitutable paper products.

Liberal economists, following the lead of Harvard's John Kenneth Galbraith, maintain that controls on wages and prices worked adequately during two war periods; hence there is sufficient evidence, they claim, that controls will be able to cope effectively with rising inflation during peacetime. A variant of this argument holds that short-term controls may be necessary to break the inflationary psychology of both buyers and labor, enabling them to readjust their expectations to lowered levels of price increase, which then may slow down their demand for goods as well as money wage increases.

Radical economists can hardly deny the validity of the distortions argument of the libertarians. Surely controls eventually lead to shortages because they suppress market forces which, however socially irrational, have their own internal coherence in our capitalist system. Who cannot recall seeing baby chicks smothered before TV cameras as irate farmers were caught between frozen sales prices and climbing feed prices in the summer of 1973? Radicals are also quick to point out that Galbraith's harkening back to wartime conditions ignores the realities of today's international trade. The fertilizer and copper examples cited above are evidence not only of allocation problems associated with controls, but also of the impact of international trade. With price controls on copper in World War II, we did not have to contend with copper flights to Germany and Japan, two of the main consumers of our copper in the 1972–74 period. The primary hallmark of the radical analysis is the assertion that controls are aimed at the labor sector to slow down the rate of wage increase in order to enhance the profit position of the corporate sector. Price controls merely are added to make the controls politically palatable and give the impression of impartiality.

The radical contention is supported by the very nature of controls themselves. First, it is easier to control wages than prices, since pricing practices generally are more varied and complex than methods of calculating compensation. Second, prices can be "raised" merely by changing the quantity or quality of the goods or the services associated with the delivery of the goods. Third, price increases usually take place on a continuous basis and may involve differential increases for thousands of individual commodities, while wage changes are often made on a fixed cycle of across-the-board adjustments. Hence wage increases are visible and amenable to control. Fourth, when all employers are under similar restraints and unlikely to compete for a given labor force, built-in cost-reduction incentives guarantee that wage controls will not be evaded.

The views of business and labor leaders help to clarify the substantive issues involved in a critique of wage and price controls. For instance, the business sector strongly supported President Nixon's initiation of controls in 1971. *Fortune* magazine editorialized for controls in the spring of 1970. In October of 1970 the Business Council, composed of top executives of the largest corporations, told Administration representatives that they could not dispel demands for activist intervention by appeals to conservative ideology. These business leaders were obviously concerned about their declining profits, especially evident since 1965. Precedent-setting construction-wage settlements of over 10 per cent in 1970 were also worrisome to business because of the large number of union collective-bargaining contracts coming up for renewal in 1971. As the *Wall Street Journal* expressed it: "Actually, many businessmen never did favor permanent controls. Many just wanted some temporary government intervention to block what they considered to be unreasonable union wage demands" (March 4, 1974, p. 1). Toward the end of the Nixon controls in the spring of 1974, the business community had not experienced the rejuvenation of their profit position as they had expected. Disillusionment with controls was evident. But *Fortune* magazine again editorialized: "The Phase IV fiasco, however, should not be allowed to discredit the idea that restraints on wages and prices can sometimes be useful" (March, 1974, p. 100). The editors noted that in times of slack overall demand for goods and services, controls might be a useful device to apply again to the labor market. The year 1975 certainly qualifies as one of slack demand.

But a contradiction in business attitudes is also apparent. Ideologically, big business maintains a public stance against government intrusion into the market place (unless it is their specific market place and the intrusion is either a subsidy or regulation to restrain aggressive competitors). Business worries that wage and price controls may lead to economic planning and further restraints on independent decision making within the corporate sector. Indeed this might be the case. Thus the contradiction arises between the business community's desire for government help to hold down union wage demands, and so spur declining profits, and the fear of controls leading to unforeseen fetters on the business sector.

The position of the other main protagonist, organized labor, is also ambiguous. Since 1966 the AFL/CIO, actually representing less than one quarter of the labor force but acting as if it were the spokesman for all labor, has publicly stated that it would cooperate with mandatory controls, provided such controls were "even-handed and across-the-board." This position was repeated in a statement issued just two days before the freeze was announced. It is difficult to understand how labor conceived of fair controls emanating from a Republican Administration. Possibly the previous two years' unexpectedly large (by 1960 standards!) price increases of 5.5 and 6 per cent were seen as the cause of the decline in real take-home pay during 1969 and 1970. The AFL/CIO may have felt that with a large number of contract renegotiations coming up in 1971, the key to real increased take-home pay would be achieved through controls on prices. But four days after the announced freeze, the AFL/CIO executive council denounced the freeze as "unequitable, unjust, unfair, and unworkable." Besides lambasting the lack of controls over executive compensation, new products, some agricultural products, interest, profits, and dividends, the council also pointed out that previously negotiated wage hikes due during the freeze were not permitted while employers could enjoy extra profits, since their price structures would already have reflected the negotiated wage increases. Attempts to close some of the "loopholes" cited by the AFL/CIO after the Phase I freeze did not prove either effective or sufficient to satisfy the labor leaders. The naming of manifestly pro-management "public members" to the tripartite wage-monitoring Pay Board also angered labor. By March 1972, all AFL/CIO members had departed from this board.

The leadership of the AFL/CIO may not appreciate the full significance of the present profit crisis and thus initially may have placed too much faith in controls. Profits are very low and declining; there is no self-adjusting process which business can rely upon to make sure that the free enterprise system will restore profits; and the nation is beset by troubles emanating from the international crisis. The end result of this situation may be government economic planning on a broad scale which may ultimately rely upon controls to help bolster corporate profits.

The use of corporate profits as a key analytical tool is another hallmark of the radical economists. However, profit studies are not their province alone, as is exemplified by the recent comprehensive study of profits by William Nordhaus of Yale. The title of his paper, "The Falling Share of Profits," aptly summarizes his findings. These results lend perspective to the wage-price controls issue.

Once nonfinancial corporate profits have been adjusted for a number of factors, Nordhaus' data clearly indicate a secular decline in corporate profits over the postwar period, expressed in a variety of ways. The after-tax rate of return on corporate capital, for instance, has fallen, though not continuously, from 9.7 to 5.4 per cent between 1948 and 1973. It is instructive to note that the cyclical upswing in the corporate rate of return experienced from 1960 to 1965 was dramatically arrested after 1965 through 1970. The year 1971 saw a slight increase in the rate of return, with the following two years again experiencing a decline. The latest figures indicate that the corporate rate of return is just slightly over half of what it was in 1965. Despite the banner headlines announcing record profits, the adjusted data do not paint such a rosy picture.

Nordhaus contends that the long-run decline in the corporate rate of return is due to a response to decreased risk of corporate ventures as the government has learned how to dampen swings in the business cycle via monetary and fiscal policy. Though the present unemployment rate of over 7 per cent may call this reasoning into question, there is other evidence to buttress the idea that there has been a decline in risks taken by entrepreneurs in this advanced capitalist economy. Consider the risk-aversion implications of the Penn-Central bail-out, the Lockheed loan, the recently passed oil-cargo–hauling act, and the recent discussion of reviving the Reconstruction Finance Corporation to buck up companies in dire financial straits. There are some who think that this does not have the ring of free enterprise; others will point out that the function of the state in a capitalist economy is to support the corporate interests—the absence of adequate benefit-cost ratios and "market failures" notwithstanding.

A quick look at some of the factors underlying the profit erosion experienced in the latter half of the 1960's and the first half of the 1970's may shed some light on what might be called the myth of the self-regulating economy. During the first half of the 1960's, increases in labor productivity and increases in prices more than made up for the increases in wages. But as the expansion continued, bolstered by war expenditures, production bottlenecks were encountered, labor-productivity increases slowed down (and actually declined in 1968), and increases in costs could not be passed on in the form of price increases, in part because of the significant increases in imported products. The result was a continuance of the secular (or long-run) profit decline. Conventional thinking predicted that the recession of 1970 (brought about by a leveling off of defense expenditures and a budget surplus) would restore profits, and hence encourage subsequent expansion as a slack in the labor market would mitigate wage demands and labor productivity would pick up. But the Nordhaus data indicate that profits continued their decline except for the year 1971. Wage demands skyrocketed, spurred on by unanticipated increases in the cost of living; labor productivity increased very little after 1970; and interest payments cut deeply into corporate profits. The interest issue is more important than is generally realized, since the ratio of interest payments to corporate profits rose from 3 per cent in 1948 to 24 per cent in 1973. In part this change reflects the expanded share of debt in corporate securities, and in part the increase of nominal interest rates on corporate debt over the postwar period.

Nor was the magnitude of the 1970 recession sufficient to dampen labor's demands. With the political machinery geared to maintaining full employment, unemployment ceases to play its primary role of disciplining the labor force. Thus there is no automatic regulating mechanism governing the corporate profit rate. The corporate sector currently appears caught in the dilemma of the full employment-profit squeeze and recessionary catch-up wage demands. As the present recession rolls on, further profit erosions are anticipated as debt-ridden corporations find it extremely difficult to meet their fixed-interest obligations. The inability of unemployed workers to maintain payments on personal debts will only exacerbate the situation.

Because of the lack of a self-regulating profit mechanism, new tools may be necessary to deal with our own problems. Major decisions along the lines of energy use and recent talk of a revitalized Reconstruction Finance

Corporation are suggestive of economic planning. The planning imperatives for the United States arising from the current crisis only reinforce the existing belief that the superior performance of Japan and West Germany in the 1960's was based in large part on the fact that they relied on planning to a much greater extent than the United States. Wage and price controls would then be one tool in the planner's toolbox. At this point the radical economist is quick to point out that as long as the individuals who are planning are responsive to the interests of the corporate sector, the controls, as well as other programs, will continue to be what they were in the past—in effect, props for corporate profits.

The London *Economist* recently characterized President Ford's new Cost of Living Task Force as "a thin end of a new controls wedge." Recent polls have shown that Americans again want some form of controls. Since incomes policies have never been successfully instituted in situations of excess demand, the recession year 1975 appears ripe for the institution of permanent controls. Radical economists contend that such controls will immediately politicize the income-distribution issue. They point to the following scenario: government determination of the distribution of income between labor and capital; the rationing of final goods, raw materials, and credit; the imposition of anti-strike legislation; the eventual allocation of labor; and an increased level of class and political conflict.

Whatever the exact details of the future when controls are reinstituted, let no one mistake the undeniable class interests masked behind the myth of impartial wage and price controls. Those forgetting the lessons of the first peacetime controls of 1971–74 might ponder the words of Arnold Weber, former executive director of the Cost of Living Council:

Business had been leaning on [Secretary of the Treasury] Schultz and [Chairman of Economic Advisers] McCracken to do something about the economy, especially wages. The idea of the freeze and Phase II was to zap labor, and we did. (*Business Week* [April 27, 1974], p. 108.)

45

Capital vs. Labor: The Current Crisis in the Sphere of Production

David M. Gordon

Everyone is feeling the pinch of the current economic crisis in one way or another. Consumers face soaring prices. Workers face layoffs. Workers' real wages continue to decline. The poor suffer cutbacks in essential social services. Even corporations—oh, pity their impoverished coffers—fear liquidity crises.

Most economic discussions of the current crisis have focused on the *appearances* of the crisis in the sphere of circulation—dealing almost exclusively with the behavior of monetary variables like prices, wages, profits and interest rates. There is another, equally important dimension to the dynamics of the current crisis, hiding beneath the surface of those economic aggregates, underlying policies and strategies, framing the growing struggle between corporations and working people in this country. The crisis *also* involves the struggle between capital and labor in the sphere of *production*. In order to understand the current situation, in order to discuss strategies for defending our own interests, we must focus clearly on these struggles between capital and labor as well.

SEEDS OF STRUGGLE IN THE LATE SIXTIES

Conflict between capital and labor began to sharpen during the sustained boom of the mid-1960's.

From the corporations' perspective, prosperity continued longer than it should have. As the demand for labor tightened after 1965 and as unions bargained more and more strenuously to keep up with rising inflation, corporate profits got squeezed. Corporate profits as a share of national income began to fall and the ratio of profits to wages plunged.[1]

Ordinarily, corporations would have tried to protect their profits by continuing their practices of mark-up pricing, passing on higher costs in continually higher prices, maintaining their margin of profits over average costs.[2] Partly because of increasing international competition, corporations' freedom to raise prices continually was gradually curtailed. Particularly in such industries as auto and steel, which felt the impact of international competition most severely, the limits on continuing price increases were clearly felt.[3] This meant, among other things, that corporations were beginning to find it more and more difficult to salvage retained earnings for continual investment in plants and equipment.

From the traditional Marxian perspective, capitalists will respond to rising wages by trying to substitute capital goods for labor, striving to increase relative surplus value by increasing the productiveness of workers.[4] When profits are squeezed and investment funds begin to dry up, their ability to pursue those strategies is often constrained by the declining in-

---

[1] Absolute profits fell by 4.0 per cent per year (in real terms) from 1965 through 1969. The ratio of profits to wages fell from .165 to .09, and the share of profits in gross corporate product fell from roughly 17 per cent to 10 per cent over the same period. See R. Boddy and J. Crotty, "Class Conflict, Keynesian Policies and the Business Cycle," *Monthly Review* (October 1974); and W. Nordhaus, "The Falling Share of Profits," *Brookings Papers on Economic Activity*, No. 1 (1974).

[2] Nordhaus ("The Falling Share of Profits") provides useful evidence that corporations had been following average cost mark-up pricing throughout the 1950's and the early 1960's.

[3] Nordhaus ("The Falling Share of Profits") also shows, from his own estimations, that the gap between aggregate prices and aggregate estimated "average total normal cost" fell to its lowest point in 1968–69 since the mid-1950's. See Figure 5, p. 196.

[4] This refers to the analysis originally developed by Marx in Vol. I of *Capital*, part V, on the "Production of Absolute and of Relative Surplus-Value."

vestment fund and the high costs of many labor-saving technological innovations.

Many corporations, in the period of continuing boom in the late 1960's, tried to compensate for declining retained earnings by increasing their borrowing, hoping to maintain constant levels of investment in structures and equipment. Corporate indebtedness, having grown rapidly throughout the post–World War II period, grew even more rapidly during the mid- and late 1960's.

External financing of investment does not solve the problem of diminished retained earnings quite so simply, however. Borrowing to finance earnings involves heavy interest payments. By 1973, corporate interest payments had reached fully a quarter of total profits, eight times greater than their share immediately after World War II.[5] Those interest payments, as they grew more and more expensive, represented another kind of drain on profits.

As the 1960's wore on, therefore, corporations were faced with the same kind of problem in either of two forms. Profits were declining. Corporations could either lower their investment, slowing their replacement of labor by labor-saving capital goods, or they could try to maintain their rate of investment by borrowing to finance those investments, incurring increasing interest charges. In the one case they had to try to protect profits by finding some other means of compensating for higher labor costs than replacing labor through automation. In the other case they could continue to replace labor but had to find some way of compensating for the drain on profits from higher interest payments.

In either case, then, the drain on profits remained serious. Marxian theory would predict that corporations would seek to maintain and restore profits in those kinds of situations *by seeking to increase relative surplus value through the intensification of labor*—by trying to *speed up* the pace of production in order to get more output from workers in any given hour of the working day. Employer efforts to speed up production always encounter worker resistance, and such efforts are almost always bound to sharpen capital-labor conflict in production itself.

And by a variety of indications, that was precisely what began to happen in the late 1960's. Especially in those industries suffering increasing international competition, evidence of speed-up and worker resistance abounds.

One interesting indication of speed-up involves industrial accidents. When corporations are trying to substitute capital for labor, industrial accidents appear to fall.[6] Indeed, the incidence of industrial accidents had been falling in this country since World War I, a period during which corporations had been turning more and more to automation.[7] But during

---

[5] Nordhaus, "The Falling Share of Profits," p. 171.

[6] Marx had argued, in Vol. I of *Capital*, that employers' ability to increase relative surplus value through the intensification of labor was indeterminate, in part because workers might get worn out or injured by speed-up too quickly and would have to be replaced. Increasing their productiveness did not suffer that particular indeterminacy.

[7] One consistent series on work injuries in manufacturing extends from 1926 through the early 1960's. The incidence of injuries, measured as hours lost through disabling work accidents over millions of man-hours worked, fell from

the 1960's, as speed-up began to replace or complement labor-saving investment, the rate of industrial accidents began to rise. The rate of industrial
accidents in manufacturing was 27.7 per cent higher in 1970 than it was in
1963.[8]

Workers do not endure such speed-ups and accidents without protest.
They feel it in their muscles and they suffer it when they get hurt. Largely
in response to speed-up, wildcat strikes began to increase during the late
1960's as well. Workers marched out of the plants protesting working conditions. Reflecting their anger, the index of aggregate strike activity began to
climb along with the rate of accidents. By 1968, work time lost through
strikes was 2 1/2 times greater than it had been in 1963. After a brief decline
during the recession of 1969, work time lost through strikes climbed again
in 1970 to 3 1/2 times its 1963 levels.[9]

Corporations began to panic. Their profits were being squeezed and
workers were beginning to resist their efforts at intensification. So we
began to hear the hue and cry of the famous "productivity crisis." America
was losing its position of international economic advantage, we were told,
because our workers weren't working hard enough. All those lazy workers,
taking off Mondays and Fridays! To save America, we all had to work a little
harder. The National Commission on Productivity posted billboards along
the highways, urging us to knuckle down.

The workers' struggles at the Vega plant in Lordstown, Ohio, were
symptomatic of these developments. The General Motors Assembly Division
had taken over management of the Vega plant in 1971. As *Business Week*
had reported, "The need for GMAD's belt-tightening role was underscored
during the late 1960's when GM's profit margin dropped from 10 per cent to
7 per cent." [10] Among its "modernizing" innovations, GMAD increased the

---

its peak in 1926, at the beginning of the series, almost continuously to the early
1960's, when it began to level off at exactly half the 1926 peak. See the U.S.
Bureau of Census, *Historical Statistics of the United States, Colonial Times to
1957* (Washington, D.C., U.S. Government Printing Office, 1960), p. 100, for data
up to 1956; and the *President's Report on Occupational Safety and Health*
(Government Printing Office, 1972), Appendix B, Work-Injury Rates by Industry,
1958–1970, pp. 71 ff., for more recent data.

[8] See the *President's Report on Occupational Safety and Health*, Appendix B.
There is further evidence from that table that the increases in injury rates came
especially in those industries which had previously experienced the most substantial labor displacement through automation. In what Robert Averitt calls
"core industries," those concentrated industries in which market power and
capital/labor ratios are highest, the average increase in the incidence of industrial
accidents between 1963 and 1970 was nearly 50 per cent, or almost twice the
overall increase in manufacturing. See Robert Averitt, *The Dual Economy* (New
York, Norton, 1968), for the distinction between core and peripheral industries,
and David M. Gordon, "Class and Segmentation in the United States: A
Methodological and Empirical Review," New School for Social Research (in
progress 1975), for the empirical distinction between the two sectors.

[9] Further indication of this effect comes from specific data about the purposes of
strikes. The number of workers involved in work stoppages over "speed-up"
increased by 350 per cent from 1965 to 1969, and work time lost through stoppages over "speed-up" increased by 240 per cent during the same years. For aggregate strike data, see the U.S. Bureau of Labor Statistics, *Handbook of Labor
Statistics*, Bulletin #1925 (1974), Table on Work Stoppages in the United States,
1927–1972. For the data on strikes by objective and grievance, see *Handbook of
Labor Statistics*, pp. 373 ff.

[10] Quoted in Stanley Aronowitz, *False Promises* (New York, McGraw-Hill, 1973),
p. 22.

speed of the line from sixty cars per hour to over a hundred. The workers protested and finally struck. The press talked innocently about changes in the workers' attitudes, about some new, mystifying preoccupation with non-monetary issues. The workers talked quite simply about the speed of the line. As the local union president observed, ". . . people refused to do extra work. The more the company pressured them, the less work they turned out. Cars went down the line without repairs." [11]

CONTROLS SHIFT THE TERMS OF STRUGGLE

As the boom continued, as profits eroded, as workers began to resist speed-up, it became more and more obvious to corporations and the government that workers' strength had to be directly attacked. When the Nixon Administration took office in 1969, it moved quickly to cool off workers by trying to cool off the economy, by inducing a recession.

The economy had been booming for so long that a fairly lengthy recession was required to cool it out. The Nixon Administration, beginning to plan the President's re-election campaign in 1971, could not risk continuing unemployment for much longer. Corporations themselves were wary of a lengthy recession; their profits were already very low, and profits normally continue to decline during the first stage of the downswing.

But the Administration could not afford normal expansionary policies, either. The balance-of-payments deficits made normal expansion, with accompanying inflation, much too risky, so controls were the answer. We were told that we needed controls to curb inflation and protect the dollar. However, one of their more fundamental purposes, reflecting the mounting struggle of the late 1960's and the inadequacy of the short-lived recession, was to control wages *and* workers. Their purpose, as the deputy director of the Cost of Living Council later admitted, was to "zap labor."

And they did. Wages were carefully controlled, while prices, more difficult to control, permitted recovery of profits by late 1972. Equally important, wage controls also curbed workers' militance. Strike activity began to fall rapidly as workers recognized the impossibilities of improving their living standard by exercising their right to strike. By the last stage of controls, in early 1974, strike activity had fallen below the levels of the early 1960's. The index of work time lost through work stoppages was less than one-quarter its level during the peak of workers' resistance in 1970.[12]

The timing of controls was important too. Large numbers of major contracts were expiring in late 1971 and early 1972, like the mine workers' contract. By racing to institute controls in August 1971, the government helped corporations forestall a bitter set of bargaining demands at precisely that point when workers' anger was rising most dramatically. For many industries, the timing of the controls bought the corporations a three-year lease on life (most major contracts have three-year terms), a respite during which they were assured of at least wage moderation. It was precisely

---

[11] Quoted, Aronowitz, *False Promises*, p. 42.
[12] Data on work stoppages since 1972 from U.S. Bureau of Labor Statistics, *Current Wage Developments*, Vol. 26, No. 12 (December 1974), p. 32.

during this period that the public relations campaign announcing the productivity crisis reached its peak, seeking to convince workers to settle into
a more intense pace, to tolerate their loss of bargaining power over wages.

CONTROLS ARE LIFTED AND THE CRISIS INTENSIFIES

Controls themselves could not last forever, for many shortages and bottlenecks developed in the economy. When they were lifted in March 1974, the
economic crisis exploded. Many corporations raced to increase their prices
as soon as they were permitted. Workers were beginning to experience the
sharp decline in their real earnings by May, as workers' real earnings fell
back to the levels of 1966 and 1967.

In protest, workers marched out on strike again. By June the index of
work time lost through stoppages had soared to its highest levels since the
late 1940's. Almost 800,000 workers were involved in strikes during the month
of June alone. The index of work time lost rose to four times its level in
1963, a third higher than the previous peak of 1970.

The Administration faced its most serious test. Prices were still soaring.
The balance-of-payments deficits began to spurt again after price controls
were lifted. And workers were beginning to see through the mystifying
rhetoric of "productivity crises" and price "controls."

What to do?

PHASE I OF THE ATTACK: PUBLIC RELATIONS AND RECESSION

The Administration was confused. Corporations were confused. Orthodox
economists were confused, but there was no time for the luxury of confusion. By early summer, corporations were beginning to face an extraordinary period of contract negotiation. During 1974 and the first half of 1975,
contracts covering two-thirds of all workers protected by "major contracts"
were expiring.[13] Many of these contracts, lasting three years, had been
negotiated just after controls had been imposed in August 1971; workers in
those unions were bristling for a fight, anxious to try to compensate for the
real wage losses they suffered during contracts negotiated under the club
of controls.

More specifically, corporations looked ahead in early 1974 to the expiration, among others, of the communications workers' contract in July, the
steelworkers' contract in August, scores of aerospace contracts in October,
the mine workers' contract in November, the railroad contracts in December,
hundreds of construction, utility workers' and food workers' contracts
throughout the early part of 1975.

In many of those negotiations, workers were going to be not only
struggling to make up for past real wage losses but also demanding cost-of-
living escalator clauses which would automatically adjust their contractual

---

[13] For information on contract expiration, see U.S. Bureau of Labor Statistics,
"Wage Calendar, 1974," Bulletin #1810 (1974), p. 2. There were 10.3 million workers in the United States covered by major contracts of 1,000 workers or more
in early 1975.

wages to rises in the cost-of-living index. (As of October 1974, only 45 per cent of workers covered by major contracts were protected by cost-of-living escalator clauses, and none of these clauses provided for a penny-for-penny full adjustment.[14]) The Administration and the mine companies expected that at least the miners would strike and that an expensive settlement in the mines would set the trend for more expensive settlements later on.

If wage controls could not be continued politically, then it must have seemed fairly clear, in the early months of 1974, that another return to a period of recession was necessary, *if for no other reason* than to curb labor's bargaining power during the negotiations in the months ahead. As a British banker admitted during the same period, in arguing for a recession with somewhat more candor than we Americans are accustomed to, "We've got to get some discipline back into this country's work force, and the only way to do it is to make the blokes damn grateful to have any sort of job at all." [15] A leader of the International Brotherhood of Electrical Workers admitted recently, reflecting on the same phenomenon from labor's side, "Layoffs take the steam out of members to a certain degree. They take away the urge to strike." [16]

The Administration could hardly talk openly in such terms, however, and its public relations campaigns built during the summer toward Ford's summit conference. Laying the ground for the deepening recession, already in motion, Ford talked more and more about the need to "bite the bullet," to "tighten our belt buckles" for "mutual self-sacrifice." We were all in this together, and we all had to sacrifice together. Significantly, his only definite statement during the period was that he would not tolerate more wage-price controls. Given the imperatives of curbing workers' anger, that left recession—for however long—as the only other alternative.

So, public relations and recession we got. Unemployment climbed rapidly during the second half of 1974, reaching 7.1 per cent by December. Administration spokespeople talked openly of the recession continuing well into 1975, with unemployment rates potentially reaching as high as 8 per cent. As the recession deepened, the public relations campaigns eventually slackened, for it became increasingly clear that people would not easily accept such "sacrifices" for long.

In the short run, however, the combination of public relations and recession was obviously having its direct effects on worker militance and bargaining power. After strike activity reached its post-controls peaks in June and July of 1974, work stoppages began quickly to plummet. The number of workers involved in strikes fell from almost 800,000 in June to less than 200,000 in November and the index of work time lost through stoppages fell back to its levels during the controls of 1972 and 1973.

More important, the combination of propaganda and recession had an impact on some of the crucial bargaining sessions of the period. The United Mine Workers of America did strike, as expected, in November. Demanding

---

[14] Cost-of-living clause information from "Wage Calendar, 1974," p. 4. Only about 600,000 workers not covered by major contracts have escalator clauses, so that, of all 85 million workers in the United States, only about 4.6 million—or barely more than 5 per cent—receive such protection.

[15] Quoted in the *Wall Street Journal* (November 18, 1974), p. 1.

[16] Quoted, *Wall Street Journal* (December 18, 1974), p. 27.

substantial wage recovery, they were able to win large wage increases. But in the last stages of their negotiations, despite those successes, the union leadership began to soften some of its demands. Many rank-and-file mine workers had been demanding a concrete contractual protection of their right to engage in wildcat strikes. The leadership met several times with the Ford Administration, and according to informal reports, began to wear down under the insistent argument that a prolonged strike would irreparably deepen the recession. We were all in this together, the UMWA leaders heard for the six hundredth time, and the litany softened their determination. Much to the dismay of large blocks of the rank-and-file membership, who actually opposed ratification of the contract, the leadership gave in on the wildcat-strike-protection issue.

It would be a mistake to exaggerate the importance of government policy in dealing with the economic crisis. Structural instabilities in the world economy may bring about a deep and protracted depression despite the apparent Administration efforts, announced in January 1975, to begin an expansionary policy, reversing its anti-inflationary tactics of 1974. It is nonetheless important to be clear about the factors which affect the *timing* of changes in government policies.

As the government anticipated the end of controls in late 1973, it knew that the crucial period of major bargaining was approaching. Given that controls and recession represent the only two available strategies for curbing labor militance, and that controls were politically impossible to continue at that time, recession represented a necessary stage in the evolving government arsenal. By now the Administration can move on to other tactics; after June 1975 the bargaining calendar will be virtually empty for more than a year. Major contracts covering only 500,000 workers, or 5 per cent of workers covered by major contracts, will expire in the second half of 1975. In the first half of 1976, only the Teamsters among major unions will be negotiating, and the Republican Administration has had a cozy relationship with the Teamsters for years. After June 1975 the need for a cool economy to cool workers will have diminished. Combining the velvet glove of moral suasion and the iron fist of recession, corporations and the government will have played out their moves during this phase of the crisis.

FIGHTING RECESSION

The first phase of the corporate and government strategy has represented a direct attack on working people. Profits had been declining, worker militance had been increasing, and it was clear, from the corporations' perspective, that something had to be done.

This strategy has meant that working people in this country have been asked to provide the basis for restoring profits by sacrificing their jobs, their social services, their livelihood and their standard of living.

Recession has had many causes, some of them complicated, but recession has also been permitted and exacerbated by conscious, calculated *political* decisions made at the top. Those of us attacked by those decisions must take direct *political* action to overcome that strategy. While it seems clear that the Administration has begun to move away from its recessionary strategy, we cannot wait to see whether their policies have the impact we would like.

In order to fight the recessionary strategy, we can and must demand

- [ ] no layoffs by corporations unless and until corporations can demonstrate to workers that such layoffs are absolutely required for the continuing solvency of the company;
- [ ] open corporate books and accounts, so that workers can decide for themselves whether corporate layoffs are actually justified by the need to maintain corporate solvency;
- [ ] full, inclusive and uniform unemployment compensation, covering 100 per cent of all workers' salaries, during the course of this recession;
- [ ] the maintenance of (real) social service expenditures at previous levels, with no cutbacks, to guarantee that those who do not work or who need special care do not suffer special hardship during a period of recession and rapid inflation.

Through these demands, we can continue to raise the costs of recessionary strategies. Through support of longer-term efforts to create guaranteed public service employment, we can move steadily toward the day when everyone in this country will be able to work at a decent job.

In the meantime, corporations and the government know that the political costs of a continued recession are too risky. Milton Friedman, the conservative economist, says that we have no choice but to continue the recession in order to restore balance to the economy: "There is no way to avoid living with an abnormally high unemployment rate for the next five to eight years."[17] More realistic corporate executives and bankers, speaking in their own journals, know that the political risks of such a policy would be too great.

But moving out of the recession in the present period would involve increasingly rapid inflation once again. People will resist inflation just as strenuously. So what will happen next?

PHASE II OF THE ATTACK: PUBLIC RELATIONS AND PLANNING

It seems clear, from reading the business press, that corporations will begin to press very quickly for a new kind of economic management in this country. Recession to cool out the economy will be too costly. Normal expansion, in this time of crisis, will involve too much inflation and dislocation. Expansion with price controls will be necessary. But most people admit that the first stage of wage-price controls, from 1971 to early 1974, fell apart at least partly because bottlenecks and shortages developed. This time around, corporations recognize that more extensive management of the economy will be required. Wage and price controls will be insufficient. It will also be necessary to exercise government management over invest-

---

[17] Quoted in *Business Week* (December 7, 1974), p. 88.
[18] See Reading 64 by William K. Tabb on economic planning.

ment policies and credit policies—in short, over the allocation of resources.[18]

It will be important to remember, as we approach that stage of management, that corporations will be seeking planning for their own benefit. And such corporate planning will, as always, have two aspects. One of them will focus on the distribution of income between profits and wages. If prices and wages are controlled, corporations will obviously seek to manipulate the planning process in order to protect profits at the expense of wages. Looking ahead, foreseeing this direction, some unions are racing to negotiate their contracts before phase two begins. Negotiating during recession is bad enough, but negotiating during controls may be worse. The West Coast dock workers, for instance, are requesting early expiration of their contract in order to get a new contract before controls resume. As Harry Bridges, the longshoremen's union leader, explained recently, "We've got to worry about controls because controls won't be equitable." [19]

Another aspect of the struggle in a period of planning will necessarily involve the sphere of production. If prices, wages and profits are controlled during a period of planning, corporations will be seeking—among other tactics—to deepen their control over the production process in order to get as much surplus value out of workers in production as they can. Their degrees of freedom for protecting and improving their profits in the sphere of exchange will be more limited. Correspondingly, they will seek to reorganize and intensify production in order to make up for whatever they may lose under price controls.

Some of these kinds of developments seem to have occurred during the first, more limited stage of wage-price controls from 1971 to 1974. Facing limited price controls, corporations appear to have tried to change work rules in order to get more work out of their employees. During 1972, the first full year of wage-price controls, workers' wildcat strikes over "work rules" grievances soared, climbing to ten times their levels in 1965 and 1966, and almost four times their levels during 1968 in the peak of speed-up.[20]

If and when these contests in production begin, workers will depend fundamentally on their rights to strike over grievances, on their right to protest attacks in production by withholding their labor power. Significantly, one has some reason for fearing that corporations recognize that probability. Slowly but surely, the first signs of an attack on workers' right to strike have begun to appear. Two recent legal decisions provide the barest hint of that attack.

The first involves the right of workers to strike over outstanding issues in contract negotiations. During negotiations in the steel industry last year, the corporations convinced the steelworkers' union leadership to accept a "no-strike agreement," under the terms of which the union agreed not to strike over outstanding bargaining disagreements but to submit them to compulsory arbitration. Rank-and-file steelworkers challenged that agreement in court. The no-strike agreement was upheld by the U.S. district court in which the case was heard. In supporting the corporations and the union, the judge argued that "in any system of self-government, in theory and in

---

[19] Quoted in the *Wall Street Journal* (December 18, 1974), p. 27.
[20] The data on "work rules" stoppages come from *Handbook of Labor Statistics*, pp. 373 ff.

practice, even the most precious of rights may be waived. . . . In denying plaintiffs the relief they seek, this Court does no more than permit the [no-strike] . . . negotiating procedures to proceed as, at least potentially, an evolutionary step forward in labor relations." [21]

The second precedent involves the right to wildcat strike over specific grievances during the term of contract. A Supreme Court decision of 1962 had ruled that federal district courts could *not* issue injunctions against wildcat strikes, even though such strikes represented breach of a no-strike provision in a contract which guaranteed binding arbitration of the dispute. In a potentially historic decision in 1970, the new Nixon Supreme Court over-turned that earlier decision. It argued that district courts could and should issue injunctions halting wildcat strikes in such situations. The intent of the decision was clear. Arbitration must prevail and strikes must not. The majority decision argued that "the very purpose of arbitration procedures is to provide a mechanism for the expeditious settlement of industrial disputes without resort to strikes, lock-outs, or other self-help measures." [22] Since al-most all contracts currently provide for arbitration, the decision potentially provides the basis for court injunctions against all wildcat strikes over any issues *unless* the contract explicitly guarantees, in writing, the workers' right to engage in wildcat strikes. It was such protection which many rank-and-file mine workers sought in their 1974 negotiations—explicitly mindful of the 1970 Court decision—and which they were unable to obtain.

In this context, armed with these kinds of court precedents, employers will undoubtedly press ahead with their public relations campaigns during the stage of planning if and when it arrives. Talk of the "productivity crisis" will undoubtedly resume. Workers will once again be asked to pay the costs of economic crises with their muscle and their sweat in production.

In short, if and when planning comes, workers must recognize that as before, the economic crisis will continue to unfold at two levels. In the sphere of circulation, political struggle will take place over the division be-tween profits and wages through the mechanisms of wage and price controls. In the sphere of production, necessarily, political struggle will take place over how hard workers must labor in the service of employers' surplus value. Through every stage, at every moment, workers must maintain their strength and their militance in both these spheres, at both those levels, to protect their own interests.

---

[21] Huber I. Teitelbaum, "Opinion of Court," Aikens et al. vs. I. W. Abel et al., No. 74–17 Civil Action, in the United States Court for the Western District of Pennsylvania, pp. 22–23.

[22] See Boys Market, Inc. v. Retail Clerks Local 770, 398 U.S. 235, 90 S. Ct. 1583, 26 L. Ed. 2d 199 (1970), opinion reprinted in *Labor Relations Law*, ed. by R. A. Smith et al., 1973 Cumulative Supplement (New York, Bobbs-Merrill, 1973), p. 147.

Equal Opportunity and Full Employment Act of 1976

Augustus F. Hawkins and Henry S. Reuss

DECLARATION OF POLICY

SEC. 2. (a) The Congress hereby declares that all adult Americans able and willing to work have the right to equal opportunities for useful paid employment at fair rates of compensation.

. . .

(f) Such other national economic goals as price stability and a favorable balance of payments shall be pursued without qualifying, limiting, compromising, or undermining the rights and guarantees established in this Act.

LOCAL PLANNING COUNCILS

SEC. 4. . . (b) Section 104 of the Comprehensive Employment and Training Act of 1973 is amended to add a new paragraph to read as follows:

"In addition to its other functions and responsibilities, the planning council shall

"(1) identify local needs for additional employment opportunities, and under guidelines to be established by the Secretary of Labor, shall select and plan projects to provide a reservoir of public service and private employment projects to supplement available employment. Such projects shall include expanded or new goods and services that reflect the needs and desires of the local community, such as social services, community health services, day care facilities, legal aid, public transit, housing, recreation, cultural activities, sanitation, and environmental improvement (including projects listed in clause 4(c)(2) below. . . ."

(c) Each Planning Council (established by section 104 of the Comprehensive Employment and Training Act of 1973 and herein referred to as "local planning council") shall, pursuant to regulations of the Secretary, provide for . . .

(2) the establishment of community public service work reservoirs through action of the community job boards. Such reservoirs shall include, but shall not be limited to, projects for (A) infrastructure construction, repair, and maintenance, (B) assistance to any member or group of individuals mentioned in subsection 5(d), (C) construction, repair, or maintenance of public buildings, (D) combating drug abuse, (E) charitable and educational purposes, (F) public recreation, (G) juvenile delinquency prevention, (H) assistance to the elderly and disabled, (I) environmental control, and (J) such other purposes as the Secretary may designate;

SEC. 5. (a) The United States Employment Service shall henceforth be called the United States Full Employment Service.

(b) In addition to its responsibilities under other statutes, the United

States Full Employment Service under the general direction of the Secretary [of Labor] shall assist in the establishment of, in each labor market area in the country in conjunction with the local planning councils acting under section 4(b), the reservoir of public service and private employment projects.

(c) A Job Guarantee Office is hereby created in the United States Full Employment Office headed by a Job Guarantee Officer whose responsibility is to provide useful and rewarding employment for any American, able and willing to work but not yet working, unable otherwise to obtain work and applying to such office for assistance. The Job Guarantee Office shall carry out its responsibilities under this Act in connection with the implementation of subsection (e) upon the recommendation and approval of the local planning councils. Nothing in this Act shall preclude the Job Guarantee Office from contracting directly with the local planning councils for (1) the administration of individual public service and private employment projects or (2) the overall administration of all or any part of such projects within the jurisdiction of the local planning councils.

(d) Each Job Guarantee Office in carrying out its responsibilities shall insure that among projects planned that adequate consideration be given to such individuals and groups as may face special obstacles in finding and holding useful and rewarding employment and shall provide or have provided through the coordination of existing programs special assistance including but not limited to counseling, training, and, where necessary, transportation and migration assistance. Such individuals and groups shall include (1) those suffering from past or present discrimination or bias on the basis of sex, age, color, religion, or national origin, (2) older workers and retirees, (3) the physically or mentally handicapped, (4) youths to age twenty-one, (5) potentially employable recipients of public assistance, (6) the inhabitants of depressed areas, urban and rural, (7) veterans of the Armed Forces, (8) people unemployed because of the relocation, closing, or reduced operations in industrial or military facilities, and (9) such other groups as the President or the Congress may designate from time to time.

. . .

(f) It is the responsibility of the Job Guarantee Office to insure that any person willing and able to work (a "jobseeker") is provided the opportunity to be employed at a suitable and comparable job (as defined in subsection 6(b)(2) below). For the purpose of fulfilling this responsibility the Job Guarantee Office shall, as appropriate—

(1) refer jobseekers to the private sector and general public sector employment placement facilities of the Full Employment Service (other than as supplemented by this Act);

(2) directly refer jobseekers for placement in positions on projects drawn from the reservoir of public service and private employment projects, and

(3) register jobseekers in the standby Job Corps (as established in subsection 6(a) below).

. . .

(g) For the purposes of this Act, any jobseeker who presents himself or herself in person at the Full Employment Office shall be considered prima facie "willing and able" to work. This specifically includes persons with impairments of sight, hearing, movement, coordination, mental retardation, or other handicaps. . . .

pairments of sight, hearing, movement, coordination, mental retardation, or other handicaps. . . .

(h) The district courts of the United States shall have jurisdiction of any action brought seeking relief pursuant to this Act, including injunctive, declaratory, and other forms of relief as well as damages. Any person deprived of rights secured by this Act shall be entitled in an action brought against the United States to recover damages, together with costs and attorney's fees.

STANDBY JOB CORPS

SEC. 6. (a) There is hereby established a Standby Job Corps which shall consist of jobseekers registered pursuant to clause 5(f)(3) above. Such Corps shall be available for public service work upon projects and activities that are approved as a part of community public service work reservoirs established by community boards pursuant to section 4(c)(2).

(b) The Secretary, by regulation, shall provide for—

(1) a requirement that jobseekers registered in the Standby Job Corps (hereafter called Corps members) maintain a status of good standing, which status shall include attendance and performance standards;

(2) a system of compensation for Corps members which shall:

(A) provide that Corps members shall receive a monthly rated sum based upon their employment at a suitable and comparable job (as defined pursuant to paragraph (B) below);

(B) contain a definition of a "suitable and comparable job" which shall take into account, among other factors, the following:

(i) No Corps member shall be paid less than the minimum wage in effect in the area; and

(ii) Corps members shall receive compensation (a) that bears a positive relationship to their qualifications, experience, and training; and (b) that is such that will effectively encourage them (from an economic standpoint) to advance from the Corps to other employment. . . .

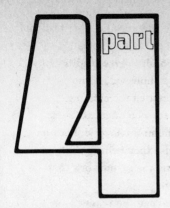

Income, Wealth, and Power

What is a good society? For Karl Marx, the answer was socialism. The vastly expanded productivity of a socialist society would supply the material needs of the people. Class divisions, themselves products of scarcity, would soon disappear, and the state as a ruling-class organ of political repression would "wither away." Some may reject Marx's vision as hopelessly utopian, but few will make the claim that twentieth-century American society approximates an ideal. At the root of America's many problems is the overriding fact of economic and social inequality. The existing distributions of income, wealth, and power belie the democratic rhetoric often used to camouflage a malfunctioning social order.

Unfortunately, the interest of professional economists in income distribution has sharply receded since its heyday a century ago when it was a central concern of Ricardo, Mill, and Marx. Welfare economists, for example—scholars whom ingenuous souls might suppose address themselves directly to the question of economic inequality—merely analyze the benefits and costs of marginal adjustments, given the existing structure of incomes, however unequal. To them, permissible adjustments are generally those that, while improving the fortunes of some, leave no one worse off after the change than he or she was before. Changes that better the lot of some at the expense of others are thought to be products of arbitrary value judgments and therefore ethically invalid. Needless to say, meaningful application of welfare economics is rare.

Of course, many orthodox economists do advocate specific distributional reforms, such as the negative income tax or repeal of tax loopholes. Inequality, after all, is one criterion by which economists have traditionally judged alternative economic systems. Such reforms, however, do not usually challenge the basic institutions that have created the existing distributions of income and wealth. Most economists who advocate such reforms are at once apologetic and curiously utopian: apologetic, because they accept existing class divisions; utopian, because they believe that effective reforms can be made without restructuring the framework that permits huge accumulations of wealth and privilege.

The readings in this section are designed to sharpen the reader's awareness of the process by which contemporary institutions and the market mechanism have created inequalities. For convenience, the readings are divided into three sections: poverty and wealth, capitalism and racism, and sexism and the family. Hopefully, this artificial breakdown of highly interdependent phenomena will not impair our understanding of the processes that determine the distribution of what American society produces.

Poverty and Wealth—Who Gets What and Why

This section documents the fact that extreme inequality of income and wealth is as pervasive in American capitalism today as in years gone by. This is scarcely a revelation, considering the functional design of the system: a competitive rat race in which only a few really win, aligned with a legal system dedicated to preserving the fruits (i.e., property) of their victory. The wealthy begin life with more than just money. They also have social connections, good schooling, and an upbringing conducive to getting ahead. In contrast, the poor—especially blacks, browns, and other Third World peoples—generally have two strikes against them—their poverty and their race. Equality of opportunity is an impossibility within the existing regimen of privilege. Even if it were possible, under capitalist institutions it would lead only to inequality of results. Those dedicated to creating an equitable distribution of income, therefore, must start from the premise that inequality is rooted in our capitalist institutions. These must be totally revamped if genuine equality of both opportunity and outcome is to be achieved.

The eminent conservative economist, Milton Friedman of the University of Chicago, would heartily disagree. He would argue to the contrary that inequality is overstated. Students can better judge the truth of such an assertion after reading some of the empirical findings included in this section. Moreover, Friedman would deny that equality is a worthy social goal. He does not believe that it is either "moral" or legitimate to take from the rich to give to the poor (see Reading 47). Students should be warned that "morality," especially as it pertains to the rights of property, is considerably more complex than in Friedman's simplistic example of the twenty-dollar bill. (Is it really true, as Friedman asserts in his article, that Robinson Crusoe's unwillingness to share his opulence with his poverty-stricken neighbors is "precisely the same situation in a different guise" as the refusal of the lucky finder of twenty dollars to share it with his traveling companions? Perhaps the answer *is* yes: both situations tend to reveal mean-spirited greed!) In addition, there are historical and theoretical reasons for believing that the rich are only rich because of what they took from the poor in the first place. From this perspective, expropriation of wealth is simply elementary justice.

Census Bureau economist Herman Miller, a leading authority on the distribution of income, presents a summary of basic facts. Whatever our interpretive quibbles, we see Miller reveal a static picture of enormous inequality (see Reading 48). Times are certainly not getting better. Radical economist Howard Wachtel examines the lower end of the income spectrum and shows that poverty reflects the social needs of the system. Poor people are generally poor because of characteristics and factors over which they have no control that exist "in markets for labor and capital" (see Reading 49). The penultimate reading is a satiric piece by Cheryl Payer, which tells what happened one day when a secretary, who took courses by night, read the assigned selection from her Samuelson text (see Reading 50).

The final reading in this section is somewhat unusual. Its author, S. Menshikov, is a Soviet citizen who has written a book on the American corporation, its owners, and its managers (see Reading 51). Menshikov's research was largely conducted in the library of the New York Stock Exchange, but he did manage to interview such titans of industry and banking as David Rockefeller, Henry Ford II, and Cyrus Eaton, among others. Menshikov's research confirms or establishes that (a) a wealthy oligarchy of owners, not managers, controls our leading corporations through complex alliances; (b) estate taxes do not prevent those with old wealth from maintaining their fortunes; (c) income taxes have not impeded the rise of new millionaires; and (d) this era of state-monopoly capitalism allows the oligarchs to take more and more direct control of the state apparatus. Two reactions to these disclosures are possible. We can continue to look at wealth with the awe and respect once reserved for royalty and so accept our lot, especially if we can be thankful that others are worse off than we. Or we can face up to the shams and myths of American life and dedicate ourselves to creating a genuinely just and egalitarian democracy based on the common ownership of our great wealth.

47

The Distribution of Income

Milton Friedman

A central element in the development of a collectivist sentiment in this century, at least in Western countries, has been a belief in equality of income as a social goal and a willingness to use the arm of the state to promote it. Two very different questions must be asked in evaluating this egalitarian sentiment and the egalitarian measures it has produced. The first is normative and ethical: what is the justification for state intervention to promote equality? The second is positive and scientific: what has been the effect of the measures actually taken?

THE ETHICS OF DISTRIBUTION

The ethical principal that would directly justify the distribution of income in a free market society is, "To each according to what he and the instruments he owns produces." The operation of even this principle implicitly depends on state action. Property rights are matters of law and social convention. As we have seen, their definition and enforcement is one of the primary functions of the state. The final distribution of income and wealth under the full operation of this principle may well depend markedly on the rules of property adopted.

What is the relation between this principle and another that seems ethically appealing, namely, equality of treatment? In part, the two principles are not contradictory. Payment in accordance with product may be necessary to achieve true equality of treatment. Given individuals whom we are prepared to regard as alike in ability and initial resources, if some have a greater taste for leisure and others for marketable goods, inequality of return through the market is necessary to achieve equality of total return or equality of treatment. One man may prefer a routine job with much time off for basking in the sun to a more exacting job paying a higher salary; another man may prefer the opposite. If both were paid equally in money, their incomes in a more fundamental sense would be unequal. Similarly, equal treatment requires that an individual be paid more for a dirty, unattractive job than for a pleasant rewarding one. Much observed inequality is of this kind. Differences of money income offset differences in other characteristics of the occupation or trade. In the jargon of economists, they are "equalizing differences" required to make the whole of the "net advantages," pecuniary and non-pecuniary, the same.

Another kind of inequality arising through the operation of the market is also required, in a somewhat more subtle sense, to produce equality of treatment, or to put it differently to satisfy men's tastes. It can be illustrated most simply by a lottery. Consider a group of individuals who initially have equal endowments and who all agree voluntarily to enter a lottery with very unequal prizes. The resultant inequality of income is surely required to permit the individuals in question to make the most of their initial equality. Redistribution of the income after the event is equivalent to denying them the opportunity to enter the lottery. This case is far more important in practice than would appear by taking the notion of a "lottery" literally. Individuals choose occupations, investments, and the like partly in accordance with their taste for uncertainty. The girl who tries to become a movie actress rather than a civil servant is deliberately choosing to enter a lottery, so is the individual who invests in penny uranium stocks rather than government bonds. Insurance is a way of expressing a taste for certainty. Even these examples do not indicate fully the extent to which actual inequality may be the result of arrangements designed to satisfy men's tastes. The very arrangements for paying and hiring people are affected by such preferences. If all potential movie actresses had a great dislike of uncertainty, there would tend to develop "co-operatives" of movie actresses, the members of which agreed in advance to share income receipts more or less evenly, thereby in effect providing themselves insurance through the pooling of risks. If such a preference were widespread, large diversified corporations combining risky and non-risky ventures would become the rule. The wild-cat oil prospector, the private proprietorship, the small partnership, would all become rare.

Indeed, this is one way to interpret government measures to redistribute income through progressive taxes and the like. It can be argued that for one reason or another, costs of administration perhaps, the market cannot produce the range of lotteries or the kind of lottery desired by the members of the community, and that progressive taxation is, as it were, a government enterprise to do so. I have no doubt that this view contains an element of truth. At the same time, it can hardly justify present taxation, if only because the taxes are imposed *after* it is already largely known who have drawn the prizes and who the blanks in the lottery of life, and the taxes are voted mostly by those who think they have drawn the blanks. One might, along these lines, justify one generation's voting the tax schedules to be applied to an as yet unborn generation. Any such procedure would, I conjecture, yield income tax schedules much less highly graduated than present schedules are, at least on paper.

Though much of the inequality of income produced by payment in accordance with product reflects "equalizing" differences or the satisfaction of men's tastes for uncertainty, a large part reflects initial differences in endowment, both of human capacities and of property. This is the part that raises the really difficult ethical issue.

It is widely argued that it is essential to distinguish between inequality in personal endowments and in property, and between inequalities arising from inherited wealth and from acquired wealth. Inequality resulting from differences in personal capacities, or from differences in wealth accumulated by the individual in question, are considered appropriate, or at least not so clearly inappropriate as differences resulting from inherited wealth.

This distinction is untenable. Is there any greater ethical justification for the high returns to the individual who inherits from his parents a peculiar voice for which there is a great demand than for the high returns to the individual who inherits property? The sons of Russian commissars surely have a higher expectation of income—perhaps also of liquidation—than the sons of peasants. Is this any more or less justifiable than the higher income expectation of the son of an American millionaire? We can look at this same question in another way. A parent who has wealth that he wishes to pass on to his child can do so in different ways. He can use a given sum of money to finance his child's training as, say, a certified public accountant, or to set him up in business, or to set up a trust fund yielding him a property income. In any of these cases, the child will have a higher income than he otherwise would. But in the first case, his income will be regarded as coming from human capacities; in the second, from profits; in the third, from inherited wealth. Is there any basis for distinguishing among these categories of receipts on ethical grounds? Finally, it seems illogical to say that a man is entitled to what he has produced by personal capacities or to the produce of the wealth he has accumulated, but that he is not entitled to pass any wealth on to his children; to say that a man may use his income for riotous living but may not give it to his heirs. Surely, the latter is one way to use what he has produced.

The fact that these arguments against the so-called capitalist ethic are invalid does not of course demonstrate that the capitalist ethic is an acceptable one. I find it difficult to justify either accepting or rejecting it, or to justify any alternative principle. I am led to the view that it cannot in and of itself be regarded as an ethical principle; that it must be regarded as instrumental or a corollary of some other principle such as freedom.

Some hypothetical examples may illustrate the fundamental difficulty. Suppose there are four Robinson Crusoes, independently marooned on four islands in the same neighborhood. One happened to land on a large and fruitful island which enables him to live easily and well. The others happened to land on tiny and rather barren islands from which they can barely scratch a living. One day, they discover the existence of one another. Of course, it would be generous of the Crusoe on the large island if he invited the others to join him and share its wealth. But suppose he does not. Would the other three be justified in joining forces and compelling him to share his wealth with them? Many a reader will be tempted to say yes. But before yielding to this temptation, consider precisely the same situation in different guise. Suppose you and three friends are walking along the street and you happen to spy and retrieve a $20 bill on the pavement. It would be generous of you, of course, if you were to divide it equally with them, or at least blow them to a drink. But suppose you do not. Would the other three be justified in joining forces and compelling you to share the $20 equally with them? I suspect most readers will be tempted to say no. And on further reflection, they may even conclude that the generous course of action is not itself clearly the "right" one. Are we prepared to urge on ourselves or our fellows that any person whose wealth exceeds the average of all persons in the world should immediately dispose of the excess by distributing it equally to all the rest of the world's inhabitants? We may admire and praise such action when undertaken by a few. But a universal "potlatch" would make a civilized world impossible.

In any event, two wrongs do not make a right. The unwillingness of the rich Robinson Crusoe or the lucky finder of the $20 bill to share his wealth does not justify the use of coercion by the others. Can we justify being judges in our own case, deciding on our own when we are entitled to use force to extract what we regard as our due from others? Or what we regard as not their due? Most differences of status or position or wealth can be regarded as the product of chance at a far enough remove. The man who is hard working and thrifty is to be regarded as "deserving"; yet these qualities owe much to the genes he was fortunate (or unfortunate?) enough to inherit.

Despite the lip service that we all pay to "merit" as compared to "chance," we are generally much readier to accept inequalities arising from chance than those clearly attributable to merit. The college professor whose colleague wins a sweepstake will envy him but is unlikely to bear him any malice or to feel unjustly treated. Let the colleague receive a trivial raise that makes his salary higher than the professor's own, and the professor is far more likely to feel aggrieved. After all, the goddess of chance, as of justice, is blind. The salary raise was a deliberate judgment of relative merit.

THE INSTRUMENTAL ROLE OF DISTRIBUTION ACCORDING TO PRODUCT

The operative function of payment in accordance with product in a market society is not primarily distributive, but allocative. . . . The central principle of a market economy is co-operation through voluntary exchange. Individuals co-operate with others because they can in this way satisfy their own wants more effectively. But unless an individual receives the whole of what he adds to the product, he will enter into exchanges on the basis of what he can receive rather than what he can produce. Exchanges will not take place that would have been mutually beneficial if each party received what he contributed to the aggregate product. Payment in accordance with product is therefore necessary in order that resources be used most effectively, at least under a system depending on voluntary co-operation. Given sufficient knowledge, it might be that compulsion could be substituted for the incentive of reward, though I doubt that it could. One can shuffle inanimate objects around; one can compel individuals to be at certain places at certain times; but one can hardly compel individuals to put forward their best efforts. Put another way, the substitution of compulsion for co-operation changes the amount of resources available.

Though the essential function of payment in accordance with product in a market society is to enable resources to be allocated efficiently without compulsion, it is unlikely to be tolerated unless it is also regarded as yielding distributive justice. No society can be stable unless there is a basic core of value judgments that are unthinkingly accepted by the great bulk of its members. Some key institutions must be accepted as "absolutes," not simply as instrumental. I believe that payment in accordance with product has been, and, in large measure, still is, one of these accepted value judgments or institutions.

One can demonstrate this by examining the grounds on which the internal opponents of the capitalist system have attacked the distribution of income resulting from it. It is a distinguishing feature of the core of central values of a society that it is accepted alike by its members, whether they regard themselves as proponents or as opponents of the system of organization of the society. Even the severest internal critics of capitalism have implicitly accepted payment in accordance with product as ethically fair.

The most far-reaching criticism has come from the Marxists. Marx argued that labor was exploited. Why? Because labor produced the whole of the product but got only part of it; the rest is Marx's "surplus value." Even if the statements of fact implicit in this assertion were accepted, the value judgment follows only if one accepts the capitalist ethic. Labor is "exploited" only if labor is entitled to what it produces. If one accepts instead the socialist premise, "to each according to his need, from each according to his ability"—whatever that may mean—it is necessary to compare what labor produces, not with what it gets but with its "ability," and to compare what labor gets, not with what it produces but with its "need."

Of course, the Marxist argument is invalid on other grounds as well. There is, first, the confusion between the total product of all co-operating resources and the amount added to product—in the economist's jargon, marginal product. Even more striking, there is an unstated change in the meaning of "labor" in passing from the premise to the conclusion. Marx recognized the role of capital in producing the product but regarded capital as embodied labor. Hence, written out in full, the premises of the Marxist syllogism would run: "Present and past labor produce the whole of the product. Present labor gets only part of the product." The logical conclusion is presumably "Past labor is exploited," and the inference for action is that past labor should get more of the product, though it is by no means clear how, unless it be in elegant tombstones.

The achievement of allocation of resources without compulsion is the major instrumental role in the market place of distribution in accordance with product. But it is not the only instrumental role of the resulting inequality. We have noted [elsewhere] the role that inequality plays in providing independent foci of power to offset the centralization of political power, as well as the role that it plays in promoting civil freedom by providing "patrons" to finance the dissemination of unpopular or simply novel ideas. In addition, in the economic sphere, it provides "patrons" to finance experimentation and the development of new products—to buy the first experimental automobiles and television sets, let alone impressionist paintings. Finally, it enables distribution to occur impersonally without the need for "authority"—a special facet of the general role of the market in effecting co-operation and co-ordination without coercion.

FACTS OF INCOME DISTRIBUTION

A capitalist system involving payment in accordance with product can be, and in practice is, characterized by considerable inequality of income and wealth. This fact is frequently misinterpreted to mean that capitalism and free enterprise produce wider inequality than alternative systems and, as a corollary, that the extension and development of capitalism has meant increased inequality. This misinterpretation is fostered by the misleading character of most published figures on the distribution of income, in particular their failure to distinguish short-run from long-run inequality. Let us look at some of the broader facts about the distribution of income.

One of the most striking facts which runs counter to many people's expectation has to do with the sources of income. The more capitalistic a country is, the smaller the fraction of income paid for the use of what is generally regarded as capital, and the larger the fraction paid for human services. In underdeveloped countries like India, Egypt, and so on, something like half of total income is property income. In the United States, roughly one-fifth is property income. And in other advanced capitalist countries, the proportion is not very different. Of course, these countries have much more capital than the primitive countries but they are even richer in the productive capacity of their residents; hence, the larger income from property is a smaller fraction of the total. The great achievement of capitalism has not been the accumulation of property, it has been the opportunities it has offered to men and women to extend and develop and improve their capacities. Yet the enemies of capitalism are fond of castigating it as materialist, and its friends all too often apologize for capitalism's materialism as a necessary cost of progress.

Another striking fact, contrary to popular conception, is that capitalism leads to less inequality than alternative systems of organization and that the development of capitalism has greatly lessened the extent of inequality. Comparisons over space and time alike confirm this view. There is surely drastically less inequality in Western capitalist societies like the Scandinavian countries, France, Britain, and the United States, than in a status society like India or a backward country like Egypt. Comparison with communist countries like Russia is more difficult because of paucity and unreliability of evidence. But if inequality is measured by differences in levels of living between the privileged and other classes, such inequality may well be decidedly less in capitalist than in communist countries. Among the Western countries alone, inequality appears to be less, in any meaningful sense, the more highly capitalist the country is: less in Britain than in France, less in the United States than in Britain—though these comparisons are rendered difficult by the problem of allowing for the intrinsic heterogeneity of populations; for a fair comparison, for example, one should perhaps compare the United States, not with the United Kingdom alone but with the United Kingdom plus the West Indies plus its African possessions.

With respect to changes over time, the economic progress achieved in the capitalist societies has been accompanied by a drastic diminution in inequality. As late as 1848, John Stuart Mill could write, "Hitherto [1848] it is questionable if all the mechanical inventions yet made have lightened the day's toil of any human being. They have enabled a greater population to live the same life of drudgery and imprisonment, and an increased number of manufacturers and others to make fortunes. They have increased the comforts of the middle classes. But they have not yet begun to effect those great changes in human destiny, which it is in their nature and in their futurity to accomplish."[1] This statement was probably not correct

---

[1] *Principles of Political Economy* (Ashley edition; London: Longmans, Green & Co., 1909), p. 751.

even for Mill's day, but certainly no one could write this today about the advanced capitalist countries. It is still true about the rest of the world.

The chief characteristic of progress and development over the past century is that it has freed the masses from backbreaking toil and has made available to them products and services that were formerly the monopoly of the upper classes, without in any corresponding way expanding the products and services available to the wealthy. Medicine aside, the advances in technology have for the most part simply made available to the masses of the people luxuries that were always available in one form or another to the truly wealthy. Modern plumbing, central heating, automobiles, television, radio, to cite just a few examples, provide conveniences to the masses equivalent to those that the wealthy could always get by the use of servants, entertainers, and so on.

Detailed statistical evidence on these phenomena, in the form of meaningful and comparable distributions of income, is hard to come by, though such studies as have been made confirm the broad conclusions just outlined. Such statistical data, however, can be extremely misleading. They cannot segregate differences in income that are equalizing from those that are not. For example, the short working life of a baseball player means that the annual income during his active years must be much higher than in alternative pursuits open to him to make it equally attractive financially. But such a difference affects the figures in exactly the same way as any other difference in income. The income unit for which the figures are given is also of great importance. A distribution for individual income recipients always shows very much greater apparent inequality than a distribution for family units: many of the individuals are housewives working part-time or receiving a small amount of property income, or other family members in a similar position. Is the distribution that is relevant for families one in which the families are classified by total family income? Or by income per person? Or per equivalent unit? This is no mere quibble. I believe that the changing distribution of families by number of children is the most important single factor that has reduced inequality of levels of living in this country during the past half century. It has been far more important than graduated inheritance and income taxes. The really low levels of living were the joint product of relatively low family incomes and relatively large numbers of children. The average number of children has declined and, even more important, this decline has been accompanied and largely produced by a virtual elimination of the very large family. As a result, families now tend to differ much less with respect to number of children. Yet this change would not be reflected in a distribution of families by the size of total family income.

A major problem in interpreting evidence on the distribution of income is the need to distinguish two basically different kinds of inequality; temporary, short-run differences in income, and differences in long-run income status. Consider two societies that have the same distribution of annual income. In one there is great mobility and change so that the position of particular families in the income hierarchy varies widely from year to year. In the other, there is great rigidity so that each family stays in the same position year after year. Clearly, in any meaningful sense, the second would be the more unequal society. The one kind of inequality is a sign of dynamic change, social mobility, equality of opportunity; the other, of a status society. The confusion of these two kinds of inequality is particularly important, precisely because competitive free-enterprise capitalism tends to substitute the one for the other. Non-capitalist societies tend to have wider inequality than capitalist, even as measured by annual income; in addition, inequality in them tends to be permanent, whereas capitalism undermines status and introduces social mobility.

GOVERNMENT MEASURES USED TO ALTER THE DISTRIBUTION OF INCOME

The methods that governments have used most widely to alter the distribution of income have been graduated income and inheritance taxation. Before considering their desirability, it is worth asking whether they have succeeded in their aim.

No conclusive answer can be given to this question with our present knowledge. The judgment that follows is a personal, though I hope not utterly uninformed, opinion, stated, for sake of brevity, more dogmatically than the nature of the evidence justifies. My impression is that these tax measures have had a relatively minor, though not negligible, effect in the direction of narrowing the differences between the average position of groups of families classified by some statistical measures of income. However, they have also introduced essentially arbitrary inequalities of comparable magnitude between persons within such income classes. As a result, it is by no means clear whether the net effect in terms of the basic objective of equality of treatment or equality of outcome has been to increase or decrease equality.

The tax rates are on paper both high and highly graduated. But their effect has been dissipated in two different ways. First, part of their effect has been simply to make the pre-tax distribution more unequal. This is the usual incidence effect of taxation. By discouraging entry into activities highly taxed—in this case activities with large risk and non-pecuniary disadvantages—they raise returns in those activities. Second, they have stimulated both legislative and other provisions to evade the tax—so-called loopholes in the law such as percentage depletion, exemption of interest on state and municipal bonds, specially favorable treatment of capital gains, expense accounts, other indirect ways of payment, conversion of ordinary income to capital gains, and so on in bewildering number and kind. The effect has been to make the actual rates imposed far lower than the nominal rates and, perhaps more important, to make the incidence of the taxes capricious and unequal. People at the same economic level pay very different taxes depending on the accident of the source of their income and the opportunities they have to evade the tax. If present rates were made fully effective, the effect on incentives and the like might well be so serious as to cause a radical loss in the productivity of the society. Tax avoidance may therefore have been essential for economic well-being. If so, the gain has been bought at the cost of a great waste of resources, and of the introduction of widespread inequity. A much lower set of nominal rates, plus a more comprehensive base through more equal taxation of all sources of income could be both more progressive in averaging incidence, more equitable in detail, and less wasteful of resources.

This judgment that the personal income tax has been arbitrary in its impact and of limited effectiveness in reducing inequality is widely shared by students of the subject, including many who strongly favor the use of graduated taxation to reduce inequality. They too urge that the top bracket rates be drastically reduced and the base broadened.

A further factor that has reduced the impact of the graduated tax structure on inequality of income and wealth is that these taxes are much less taxes on being wealthy than on becoming wealthy. While they limit the use of the income from existing wealth, they impede even more strikingly—so far as they are effective—the accumulation of wealth. The taxation of the income from the wealth does nothing to reduce the wealth itself, it simply reduces the level of consumption and additions to wealth that the owners can support. The tax measures give an incentive to avoid risk and to embody existing wealth in relatively stable forms, which reduces the likelihood that existing accumulations of wealth will be dissipated. On the other side, the major route to new accumulations is through large current incomes of which a large fraction is saved and invested in risky activities, some of which will yield high returns. If the income tax were effective, it would close this route. In consequence, its effect would be to protect existing holders of wealth from the competition of newcomers. In practice, this effect is largely dissipated by the avoidance devices already referred to. It is notable how large a fraction of the new accumulations have been in oil, where the percentage depletion allowances provide a particularly easy route to the receipt of tax-free income.

In judging the desirability of graduated income taxation it seems to me important to distinguish two problems, even though the distinction cannot be precise in application: first, the raising of funds to finance the expenses of those governmental activities it is decided to undertake (including perhaps measures to eliminate poverty . . . , second, the imposition of taxes for redistributive purposes alone. The former might well call for some measure of graduation, both on grounds of assessing costs in accordance with benefits and on grounds of social standards of equity. But the present high nominal rates on top brackets of income and inheritance can hardly be justified on this ground—if only because their yield is so low.

I find it hard, as a liberal, to see any justification for graduated taxation solely to redistribute income. This seems a clear case of using coercion to take from some in order to give to others and thus to conflict head-on with individual freedom.

All things considered, the personal income tax structure that seems to me best is a flat-rate tax on income above an exemption, with income defined very broadly and deductions allowed only for strictly defined expenses of earning income. . . . I would combine this program with the abolition of the corporate income tax, and with the requirement that corporations be required to attribute their income to stockholders, and that stockholders be required to include such sums on their tax returns. The most important other desirable changes are the elimination of percentage depletion on oil and other raw materials, the elimination of tax exemption of interest on state and local securities, the elimination of special treatment of capital gains, the co-ordination of income, estate, and gift taxes, and the elimination of numerous deductions now allowed.

An exemption, it seems to me, can be a justified degree of graduation. It is very different for 90 per cent of the population to vote taxes on themselves and an exemption for 10 per cent than for 90 per cent to vote punitive taxes on the other 10 per cent—which is in effect what has been done in the United States. A proportional flat-rate-tax would involve higher absolute payments by persons with higher incomes for governmental services, which is not clearly inappropriate on grounds of benefits conferred. Yet it would avoid a situation where any large numbers could vote to impose on others taxes that did not also affect their own tax burden.

The proposal to substitute a flat-rate income tax for the present graduated rate structure will strike many a reader as a radical proposal. And so it is in terms of concept. For this very reason, it cannot be too strongly emphasized that it is not radical in terms of revenue yield, redistribution of income, or any other relevant criterion. Our present income tax rates range from 20 per cent to 91 per cent, with the rate reaching 50 percent on the excess of taxable incomes over $18,000 for single taxpayers or $36,000 for married taxpayers filing joint returns. Yet a flat rate of 23 1/2 per cent on taxable income as presently reported and presently defined, that is, above present exemptions and after all presently allowable deductions, would yield as much revenue as the present highly graduated rate.[2] In fact, such a flat rate, even with no change whatsoever in other features of the law, would yield a higher revenue because a larger amount of taxable income would be reported for three reasons: there would be less incentive than now to adopt legal but costly schemes that reduce the amount of taxable income reported (so-called tax avoidance); there would be less incentive to fail to report income that legally should be reported (tax evasion); the removal of the disincentive effects of the present structure of rates would produce a more efficient use of present resources and a higher income.

If the yield of the present highly graduated rates is so low, so also must be their redistributive effects. This does not mean that they do no harm. On the contrary. The yield is so low partly because some of the most competent men in the country devote their energies to devising ways to keep it so low, and because many other men shape their activities with one eye on tax effects. All this is sheer waste. And what do we get for it? At most, a feeling of satisfaction on the part of some that the state is redistributing income. And even this feeling is founded on ignorance of the actual effects of the graduated tax structure, and would surely evaporate if the facts were known.

To return to the distribution of income, there is a clear justification

---

[2] This point is so important that it may be worth giving the figures and calculations. The latest year for which figures are available as this is written is the taxable year 1959 in U.S. Internal Revenue Service, *Statistics of Income for 1959.* For that year: Aggregate taxable income reported on

Individual tax returns	$166,540 million
Income tax before tax credit	39,092 million
Income tax after tax credit	38,645 million

A flat rate tax of 23 1/2 per cent on the aggregate taxable income would have yielded (.235) × $166,540 million = $39,137 million.

If we assume the same tax credit, the final yield would have been about the same as that actually attained.

for social action of a very different kind than taxation to affect the distribution of income. Much of the actual inequality derives from imperfections of the market. Many of these have themselves been created by government action or could be removed by government action. There is every reason to adjust the rules of the game so as to eliminate these sources of inequality. For example, special monopoly privileges granted by government, tariffs, and other legal enactments benefiting particular groups, are a source of inequality. The removal of these, the liberal will welcome. The extension and widening of educational opportunities has been a major factor tending to reduce inequalities. Measures such as these have the operational virtue that they strike at the sources of inequality rather than simply alleviating the symptoms.

The distribution of income is still another area in which government has been doing more harm by one set of measures than it has been able to undo by others. It is another example of the justification of government intervention in terms of alleged defects of the private enterprise system when many of the phenomena of which champions of big government complain are themselves the creation of government, big and small.

48

Inequality, Poverty, and Taxes

Herman P. Miller

Income distribution in the United States has remained virtually unchanged for one-quarter of a century. According to government figures, the poorest 20 percent of all families received 5 percent of the cash income in 1947 and they receive the same share today. By contrast, the richest 5 percent received 17 percent of the cash income in 1947 and 16 percent today. If the various types of noncash income that are omitted from the official figures are added to the distribution, the share going to the rich is vastly increased.

Except for the select few in the top 1 percent of the income distribution, there is little if any progressivity in the tax structure. According to a recent report by the Brookings Institution, the same proportion of income is paid in taxes by families at the 20th percentile and at the 99th percentile. Because of high taxes and the high cost of living, very little saving is accumulated by the lower and middle-income groups. About one-third of all the wealth in the United States is owned by the top 1 percent of the families who have a net worth of $200,000 or more.

Our tax policies are in part responsible for the chronic shortage of the funds that are to deal with many social and economic problems. If we were to tax the rich more, it might be possible to do some of those things we now say we cannot afford to do. Our Federal Income Tax laws show that as a society we have a preference for progressive taxation (i.e., for taxing the rich at higher rates than the poor); yet, in practice we do not adhere to this policy. Why? The answer to this question is by no means clear, but it is worth exploring.

The last major attempt to alter the distribution of income in the United States occurred during the 1960s. At that time, the nation rediscovered the fact that, despite the general affluence, large numbers of Americans lived in abject poverty. Programs were instituted to raise the levels of living for the poor and to change those practices which systematically discriminated against ethnic minorities and other disadvantaged groups. Major changes were made in the civil rights laws; training programs were instituted for school dropouts and unskilled workers; and vast expenditures were made to improve the quality of education in low-income areas. Although these changes did not alter the distribution of income very much, they demonstrated widespread awareness and deep concern with the problem at the very highest levels of government.

Today, however, few Americans seem to have much interest in redistributing income. Attention is focused on fuel shortages, inflation, and corruption in government. But even before the onset of these problems, American voters showed strong antagonism to policies designed to alter income distribution. Just a few months prior to the 1972 presidential election, a Harris poll showed that three-fourths of the voters objected to Senator McGovern's proposal "to give each individual in the population $1,000 by sharply increasing taxes on people with incomes of $12,000 and over." There was more objection to McGovern's stand on income redistribution than to any other part of his program, nor is there evidence that attitudes on this subject have changed much since.

The income gap between the rich and the poor in the United States has been narrowed within the lifetime of many who are reading this article. During the depression of the '30s the share of income going to the top 5 percent of the families and individuals dropped sharply; it dropped again during World War II in response to economic forces, which created a great demand for unskilled labor as well as government policies designed to narrow wage differentials between low-paid and high-paid workers. All told, the share of income received by the top 5 percent dropped from nearly one-third of the total income in 1929 to about one-fifth at the end of World War II. Since that time there has been little change in income distribution; however, the average income per family (adjusted to changes in purchasing power) has continued to rise at the rate of 2 percent per year compounded. In other words, the equalization of incomes during the '30s and the early '40s did not diminish the productivity of the economy.

There is no question that equalization of income can be pushed too far. It can destroy incentives to work or invest and thereby become detrimental to the health of the economy. There is little point in changing the percentage of the economic pie received by the poor if it means they will receive a smaller piece. Some socialist countries have found that they have had to widen wage differentials in order to stimulate productivity. But clearly that is not the case in the United States at this time.

All we know from experience is that we had a major redistribution of income 25 years ago and there were no measurable harmful effects. It is entirely possible that we can travel further along the same path without ill effects. We won't know if we don't try; and even if we should try and fail, the action is not irreversible. As a social gamble, such a program is certainly worth serious thought even on the part of the higher income groups who would have to pay the cost. The great majority of the American people have lost faith in their government. They believe that the government serves the interests of the few who are wealthy and powerful rather than the great majority. One way to help change that image would be a major revision of the tax laws, which have long provided a shelter for the rich and have deprived society of the funds needed for income maintenance of the poor, better housing, improved education, and numerous other social and economic programs.

INCOME EQUALITY AND TAXATION

Incomes in the United States are much more unequally distributed than the official figures show. The Census Bureau reports only cash income. No attempt is made to allocate money income that people receive but fail to report. Also excluded are capital gains, undistributed profits, and imputed income. I have attempted to correct this shortcoming by preparing a revised distribution of families by income levels for 1968, which includes the missing income.

The official figures for 1968 are based on a total of $543 billion in cash reported in the census survey. But these figures exclude about $260 billion of unreported cash income, capital gains, undistributed profits, and imputed income, all of which accrue disproportionately to the top-income groups. These items are omitted from the official figures primarily because the procedures that have been developed for distributing them by income levels are regarded as too crude to meet government standards. The income is there, nonetheless. Excluding it from the official figures does not change the economic reality.

According to census statistics, the very small fraction of the consumer units (families of two or more related persons and persons living alone or with nonrelatives) with money incomes over $50,000 in 1968 received 2 percent of the total money income. When the billions of dollars of missing incomes are added, the share going to the top-income group increases to 7 percent. According to the census figures, the 2 percent of the units with incomes over $25,000 received 9 percent of the income; according to my best estimate, they received 18 percent of the total. Changes of this magnitude are not mere technical adjustments. They basically alter the view of income inequality that exists in our society.

For some time now, we have been urged by our leaders to tighten our belts and not to embark on new programs of social reform because we cannot afford them. As a result, we have postponed massive efforts to deal with unemployment and underemployment, decaying central cities, poor schools, inadequate medical care, and pollution.

If the rich have considerably more income than we thought they have, it may be possible, through tax reform, to get them to provide the funds we need for new social programs. These funds cannot come from the middle-income groups. After paying their taxes and the inflated costs for food, shelter, clothing, and other necessities, they have very little left. According to figures published by the Survey Research Center of the University of Michigan, about three-fourths of the families with incomes under $3,000 have liquid assets totaling less than $1,000. (Liquid assets include checking and savings accounts and U.S. savings bonds. They represent, as the name implies, resources that are quickly convertible into cash in the event of an emergency.) The picture was not much better for families somewhat higher on the income scale. At the $3,000–$7,500 income level, two-thirds of the families had less than $1,000 to fall back on in case of emergency.

These figures, perhaps better than any others, portray the sense of terror that must strike the breadwinner in the average poor to middle-class family when faced with the loss of a job. Their resources for sustaining emergencies of even short-range duration are meager indeed. Little wonder that the middle-income groups have reacted so strongly in favor of tax reductions and against new government programs that would have to be paid for by higher taxes. They know that as matters stand the brunt of the burden would fall on their shoulders. They now barely manage to get by from one payday to the next without being able to set much aside for a rainy day. This is certainly not true for the higher-income groups. Much as they complain about taxes, they still do most of the saving in this country.

A recent report prepared by Ben Okner and Joseph Pechman of the Brookings Institution shows the proportion of income paid in taxes by each percentile of the population ranged from lowest to highest according to income. This report presents tax rates based on eight different variants regarding the incidence assumptions of the various kinds of taxes. Shown in the chart [omitted] are the effective rates of federal, state, and local taxes based on the most progressive and least progressive variants; rates based on the other six variants fall somewhere between these two. It is quite apparent that there is little progressivity in the American tax structure. Using the *most progressive* variant, we find that consumer units at the 20th percentile (i.e., the poorest fifth of the units) pay 21 percent of their income in taxes while consumer units at the 80th percentile (i.e., the wealthiest fifth) pay 23 percent of their income in taxes. The tax rates go up to 24 percent for the wealthiest 10 percent of the units and to 25 percent for the wealthiest 5 percent. It is only when we go to the very top of the income pyramid, the wealthiest 1 percent, that tax rates become appreciably progressive and reach 38 percent.

We must remember that these results are based on the *most progressive* assumptions. Using the least progressive assumptions, we arrive at the remarkable conclusions that consumer units at each income level between the poorest 10 percent and the wealthiest 1 percent pay the same share of their income (25 percent) in taxes. Using these assumptions, the share paid by the wealthiest 1 percent rises just slightly to 29 percent.

Nor are these facts new. They have been known for years. They appear in one form or another in elementary economics textbooks. They are taught to anyone who has taken a good introductory course in economics. Why then do Americans overwhelmingly prefer tax cuts and reductions in government spending to tax reforms that would require the rich to pay more? The answer to this question is complicated. For one thing, it takes more than information to change attitudes; it takes a change in feelings. The greatest obstacle to income redistribution and major tax reform is not a lack of evidence that such changes are needed or a lack of knowledge of how to achieve these goals. Rather it is the belief most of us have that such changes are unwise, unfair, and unwarranted, and that some great evil will befall us if they are made. There is little evidence to support these beliefs; they are just ingrained in us by constant repetition in our homes and our schools, on television and in the press. These feelings and attitudes become so much a part of us that we come to assume they are based on facts; but there is no rational basis for such an assumption. Let us look a little closer at the basis for some of our attitudes regarding income redistribution and tax reform.

For years we have been told by conservative economists that we have little to gain by taxing the wealthy more heavily. Such taxation, we are told, would not bring in much revenue, would lead to a reduction in work effort, and would hurt us all in the end. But these economists only know what they believe in their own hearts to be true, and too often, what they know in their hearts is influenced, one way or another, by those who are putting money in their pockets. There is virtually no scientific evidence to support the view that the incentives of the rich to accumulate more would be destroyed if they were taxed more heavily. The few studies that have been made are small and inconclusive. Professor George Break of the University of California summarized the available empirical evidence for a congressional committee. His conclusion was that "income taxes exert relatively little influence on work incentives and when they do they induce greater effort as frequently as they deter it." He cites one study showing that "higher taxes induced more wives of business executives to enter the labor force and in general led executives themselves to postpone their dates of retirement." It is by no means clear that those among the rich who work would stop working if we taxed them more.

Spokesmen for the rich have long tried to persuade the rest of us that they are being pauperized by heavy taxation. We have been led to believe that the great fortunes such as those created by the Mellons, Carnegies, and the Rockefellers are a thing of the past. Nothing could be further from the truth. The rich among us are still flourishing. During the '50s the number of millionaries doubled, increasing from 27,000 to 53,000. According to the best estimates, the number had grown to 200,000 by the end of the '60s. This represents a fourfold increase from the beginning of the decade.

There is little evidence that taxation has dried up the sources of wealth. Table 2 [omitted] shows the distribution of consumer units by the total amount of assets owned. These assets include equity in a home or business, checking and savings accounts, savings bonds and other liquid assets, and bonds and stocks. Debts are subtracted from the market value of each of the above assets, and the result is the estimate of net worth for each consumer unit. These figures show that less than one-half of 1 percent of families and individuals with assets of $500,000 or more own 22 percent of all the wealth in the United States; and 1 percent of the units have wealth of $200,000 or more and own over one-third of the wealth. At the bottom end of the distribution we find that 45 percent of the units have net worth totaling less than $5,000; they own only 2 percent of the wealth. It is also important to recognize that most of the assets of this bottom group are in the form of equity in a home or a car, which are not income-producing but are essential for everyday living. An old home or an old car may show up as an asset on the balance sheet, but they can be a real drag on the family budget. These families have very little, if anything, to fall back on in case of an emergency.

The figures in Table 2 [omitted] pertain to 1962, when the Federal Reserve Board conducted the most recent comprehensive household survey of the distribution of wealth ownership among families in the United States. More recent data based on the analysis of estate tax returns collected by the Internal Revenue Service suggest that there has been no appreciable change in the distribution of wealth ownership since that time.

THE IMPACT OF GOVERNMENT REDISTRIBUTION

The income data described above tell only part of the story. They show how the net national product was distributed before taxes. In 1968, the federal, state, and local governments took one-third of our income in taxes and they gave it back to us in the form of transfer payments, goods, and services. In the reports referred to above [reference omitted], Mr. Herriot and I attempted to distribute the burden of taxation as well as the benefit of government expenditure by income classes. The results are shown in Table 4. The basic procedure required us to make assumptions as to who paid each tax and who benefited from each government service. For many types of services such as education, health, highways, and social welfare it seemed possible to make reasonable assumptions regarding the beneficiaries. The benefits of expenditures on elementary and secondary school education were allocated to families with children in school; benefits from public assistance and social security were allocated to the recipients of these types of income, etc. The big problem was how to allocate the very large fraction of the total that was spent on national defense and related activities. Four different assumptions were used: that the benefits were shared (a) proportionate to income; (b) proportionate to wealth; (c) equally; and (d) one-third according to wealth, one-third to income, and one-third equally.

TABLE 4 □ PERCENTAGE DISTRIBUTION OF INCOME BEFORE AND AFTER GOVERNMENT INTERVENTION: 1968

Money Income Level	Total Income Before Taxes, Transfers, and Government Expenditures	Total Income After Taxes, Transfers, and Government Expenditures *			
		A	B	C	D
Total	100	100	100	100	100
Under $4,000	4	7	8	11	9
$4,000 to $25,000	78	78	75	77	77
$25,000 to $50,000	11	10	10	8	9
$50,000 and over	7	5	7	4	5

* Assumes nonallocatable government expenditures (mostly for national defense) distributed as follows:
  A: total income (each family receives a share proportionate to its income);
  B: total wealth (each family receives a share proportionate to its wealth);
  C: each family receives an equal share;
  D: one-third according to income; one-third according to wealth; and one-third equally.

Presumably the most egalitarian assumption is that we all benefit equally from defense expenditures. This is a valid view if one assumes that we each have one life to save and the same amount of freedom to lose if we should be conquered by an enemy. On this basis the benefits from defense and related activities should be divided equally among all families. Using this assumption we find (from column C in Table 4) that the share of income received by the poorest quarter of the families nearly triples, going from 4 percent to 11 percent; and the share received by the top 3 percent (those making over $25,000) is reduced from 18 percent to 12 percent. This is a sizable reduction of inequality, but it involves a very special and, in my opinion, an unrealistic assumption regarding the distribution of benefits from defense and related expenditures. We spend money for defense to protect our wealth and our income as well as our lives. It is an established principle of law that all lives do not have an equal monetary value. The general rule in wrongful death cases is that the estate can sue for the present value of the expected lifetime earnings of the deceased. According to the Census Bureau reports, for example, the monetary value for an elementary school graduate is about $300,000 and that of a college graduate is over $600,000. These are the amounts that might be asked as payment for damages in wrongful death actions involving persons who had grammar school or college backgrounds. In light of this fact, it seems unreasonable to allocate the benefits of defense expenditures as though we all had an equal share. It would be more reasonable, following the persuasive logic of the law, to make some allowance for the value of our wealth and for our monetary value as human beings.

Table 4 (column B) also shows a distribution based on the assumption that defense expenditures are allocated proportionate to our wealth. This assumption treats defense expenditures as an insurance payment to protect our property. Viewed in this way, the activities of the government cause the share of income going to the bottom quarter of the consumer units to increase at the expense of the middle three-fourths; but the share received by the very small fraction with incomes over $25,000 remains unchanged at about 18 percent. The conclusion based on this interpretation is that the net impact of government intervention on the distribution of income is to transfer income from the middle class to the poor. The rich neither gain nor lose in the process, because most of what is taken away from them in taxes is returned in the form of an insurance benefit designed to protect their property.

Column D shows still another, and perhaps more reasonable, way to allocate expenditures for defense and related activities. Since these expenditures are made to protect our freedom, our lives, and our property, why not divide them into three different components and use a different procedure for each? As a starter, we might assume that one-third of the expenditures are made to protect our freedom and that we all get an equal benefit from that component. Assume also that an additional third is spent to protect our lives. These benefits can be allocated proportionate to the present value of the expected lifetime income of each family. We can assume that the final third is spent to protect our property. This share can be distributed proportionate to our wealth. On this basis we find that the share of income going to families with income under $4,000 is more than doubled, going from 4 percent to 9 percent as a result of the intervention of the government; the

share going to those with incomes between $4,000 and $25,000 is virtually unchanged; and the share going to those with incomes of $25,000 or more is
reduced from 18 percent to 14 percent. The share going to the very wealthy
is cut back from 7 percent to 5 percent based on these assumptions.

CONCLUSION

At one time, income distribution was regarded as fixed. Social scientists
assumed that an inexorable law determined the distribution of income in a
given time and place, and that changes in that distribution could be made
only at great peril to the social order. They even gave this law a name,
"Pareto's Law," in honor of the Italian economist who was among the first to
do empirical work in this field during the latter part of the 19th century.
Some economists went so far as to assert that a sharp rise in income inequality would cause a revolution and a sharp drop would cause a civil war.
It has been argued that the French and Russian revolutions were caused by
undue concentrations of income and wealth whereas the Spanish revolution
of the late 1930s was caused by "socialistic trends" that followed the overthrow of the monarchy and "lowered greatly the ratio of concentration
from its Pareto norm."

Few economists today believe that there are inexorable laws of income
distribution. The fact is that incomes in the United States are more equally
distributed today than they were 40 years ago. Most of the redistribution,
however, took place during the depression of the '30s and during World War
II. There has been little change during the past 25 years. Despite the rhetoric
of the Great Society architects, their programs did not change income distribution very much, if at all. But there is no sound economic reason why we
should not resume the progress that ended one-quarter of a century ago. We
can have a further reduction of inequality and a different distribution of the
tax burden without necessarily hurting the economy. Economists who say
otherwise are going beyond the limits of the knowledge of their profession.
We may not choose to have redistribution as a social goal; but there is no
good *economic* reason that requires us to make such a choice. In short, we
could decide to raise the incomes of poor people and tax the rich more to
help pay for it, if we want to, and not have the feeling that we are violating
some natural law or endangering social order.

For the moment, the nation appears to have lost its interest in income
redistribution. The rallying cry today is, "Balance the Budget." The econo-
mizers are firmly in the saddle. We shall soon see where their policies lead
us. It is comforting to know that we have the wealth to create a better world
if we become disenchanted with their false economics. All we need is the
desire to do so.

49

Looking at Poverty From a Radical Perspective

Howard M. Wachtel

"If the Word was the Beginning,
Then a new Beginning must need another Word."
CARL OGLESBY, FROM "LEMON LIGHT"

Poverty is a condition of society, not a consequence of individual characteristics. If poverty is a condition of society, then we must look to societal institutions to discover the cause of poverty rather than to the particular individual characteristics of the poor. The societal institutions which have been of particular importance for western industrialized countries are the institutions of capitalism—markets in labor and capital, social stratification and class, and the state.

An individual's class status—his or her relationship to the means of production—provides the point of departure for an analysis of income inequalities and low incomes in an absolute sense. If an individual possesses both labor and capital, his chances of being poor or in a low income percentile are substantially less than if only labor is possessed. For individuals earning incomes under $10,000, nearly all income comes from labor. However, for individuals earning between $20,000 and $50,000 (in 1966), only slightly more than half comes from labor; while for individuals with incomes between $50,000 and $100,000 only a third comes from labor. And if you are rich—earning in excess of $100,000—only 15 percent comes from wage and salary earnings while two-thirds comes from capital returns (the balance is composed of "small business" income).

More important than the magnitude of capital income is its unequal distribution in our economy. Were we to redistribute this income, we could alleviate the purely financial aspects of low incomes. A direct transfer of income that would bring every family up to the Bureau of Labor Statistics' "Moderate but Adequate" living standard in 1966 (roughly $9,100) would have required $119 billion. This comes to about 20 percent of total personal income, slightly *less* than the proportion of personal income derived from ownership of capital.

Consequently, any meaningful discussion of the causes of income inequalities or low incomes must start with a discussion of Marx's class categories. The plain fact is that the probabilities of being both a capitalist and poor are slim compared with the opportunities for poverty if labor forms the principal means of acquiring income. And under capitalism, there is no

For their help in preparing this paper, I thank: David Gordon, Richard Edwards, James Weaver, Jim Campen, Stephan Michelson, Frank Ackerman, and Dawn Wachtel. Many of the ideas in this paper have grown out of conversations with Mary Stevenson and Barry Bluestone.

mechanism for sharing the returns from capital—it all goes to the private owners of capital.

The individual's relationship to the means of production is only the starting point in the analysis. The labor market is the next institution of capitalism which must be analyzed to understand the causes of poverty. Given the fact that workers have no capital income, the chances of becoming poor are increased. However, not all workers are poor in any sense of that ambiguous term. This leads us to our next concept in the analysis—*social stratification*. Social stratification refers to the divisions within a social class as distinct from the class itself. In this context, the divisions among workers in the labor market lead to social stratification among the class of workers which has had important implications for the cyclical and secular movements in class consciousness.

The functioning of labor markets, interacting with individual characteristics of workers, determines the wage status of any particular individual in stratified labor markets. The labor market causes poverty in several important ways. Contrary to conventional wisdom, nearly every poor person is or has been connected with the labor market in some way. Poor individuals sift into several categories. First, there are enormous members of *working poor*—individuals who work fulltime and full year, yet earn less than even the government's parsimonious poverty income. These people earn their poverty. Of all poor families attached to the labor force in 1968, about one-third (1.4 million) were fully employed workers. Of the more than 11 million families with incomes under $5,000 in 1968, nearly *30 percent* were headed by a fulltime wage earner. The incidence of the working poor is greater among black poor families and families with female heads. About *22 percent* of all black poor families were headed by an individual working fulltime in 1968. And a *third* of all black families with incomes under $5,000 worked fulltime. The Department of Labor reports that 10 million workers in 1968 (nearly 20 percent of the private nonsupervisory employees) were earning less than $1.60 per hour—the wage rate that yields a poverty income if fully employed.

A second significant proportion of the poor are attached to the labor force but are not employed fulltime. Some of these individuals suffer intermittent periods of employment and unemployment, while others work for substantial periods of time and then suffer severe periods of long-term unemployment.

A third significant portion of the poor are handicapped in the labor market as a result of an occupational disability or poor health. However, these occupational disabilities are themselves related to a person's earlier status in the labor force. There are greater occupational hazards and opportunities for poor health in low wage jobs. Low incomes can contribute significantly to poor health, especially in the American markets for health care, where enormous incomes or proper health insurance are an absolutely essential precondition for the receipt of medical care. Disabilities are widespread throughout the economy. In 1966, nearly *one-sixth* of the labor force was disabled for a period longer than *six months*. Only 48 percent of the disabled worked at all in 1966, while 12 percent of the employed disabled workers were employed only part-time. As a consequence of disability, many households with disabled heads are poor—about 50 percent.

Thus we see that nearly all of these poverty phenomena are endogenous to the system—they are a consequence of the functioning of labor markets in the economy. This argument can be extended to birth defects as well. There is a growing body of evidence which suggests that many forms of birth defects are related to the nutrition of the mother which, in turn, is related to family income (itself dependent upon the class status of the family and the labor market status of the family wage earners). Even with the evidence as tentative as it is, we can say that the probability of birth defects is greater in families with low incomes and the resultant poor nutritional opportunities.

Another category of the poor is not presently attached to the labor market—the aged, the prison population, members of the military, the fully handicapped, and those on other forms of public assistance (principally women with dependent children). Though these individuals are not presently attached to the labor force, in many instances their low income is determined by past participation in the labor force.

STATUS IN THE LABOR FORCE

In broad terms, an individual's wage is dependent upon four types of variables:

1. Individual characteristics over which the individual exercises no control—age, race, sex, family class status, and region of socialization.
2. Individual characteristics over which the individual exercises a degree of control—education, skill level, health, region of employment, and personal motivation.
3. Characteristics of the industry in which the individual is employed—profit rates, technology, product market concentration, relation of the industry to the government, and unionization.
4. Characteristics of the local labor market—structure of the labor demand, unemployment rate, and rate of growth.

One observation is immediately apparent: there are very few variables that lie within the individual's control that affect his labor market status. Even the individual characteristics placed in category two are not completely within the control of the individual. For example, as Coleman, Bowles, and others have shown, education is heavily dependent upon the socioeconomic status of the family, an attribute which lies outside of individual control. Health is partially endogenous to the system as discussed above. Geographic mobility depends upon income and wealth.

This classification scheme is a useful starting point, but a more formal analysis is needed to understand the way in which these several categories of variables interact in the labor market to yield low incomes.

The occupation an individual enters is *associated with* individual characteristics: educational quantity and quality, training skills, and health. These attributes are normally defined as the *human capital* embodied in an individual. The differences in these variables among individuals, which influence their entry into occupations, are dependent upon race, sex, age, and class status of the family. Although human capital is *defined* by the set of characteristics associated with the individual, the *determinants* of the differing levels of human capital among individuals are found in the set of individual characteristics that lie outside of the individual's control.

The story does not end here; the wage is not solely dependent upon the occupation of an individual. The fact that one person is a janitor, another a skilled blue-collar worker, tells us something about the wage that each will receive, but not everything. There is a substantial variation in wage within each of those occupations that is dependent upon the industry and the local labor market in which an individual works. There are a variety of industrial and local labor market characteristics which yield different wages for essentially the same occupation and level of human capital. The wage will be higher for a given occupation in an industry with high profit rates, a strong union, highly productive technologies, a high degree of product market concentration, and a favorable status with the government. A similar type of analysis holds for the impact of local market conditions.

In sum, the individual has very little control over his or her labor force status. If you are black, female, have parents with low socioeconomic status, and dependent upon labor income, there is a high probability that you will have relatively low levels of human capital which will slot you into low-paying jobs, in low wage industries, in low wage labor markets. With this initial placement, the individual is placed in a high risk category, destined to end up poor sometime during her working and nonworking years. She may earn her poverty by working fulltime. Or she may suffer either sporadic or long periods of unemployment. Or she may become disabled, thereby reducing her earning power even further. Or when she retires, social security payments will place her in poverty even if she escaped this fate throughout her working years. With little savings, wealth, or a private pension income, the retiree will be poor.

In contrast with this radical political-economic theory of the causes of poverty, both conservative and liberal political-economic theories look for the cause of poverty in terms of some individual characteristic over which the individual is presumed to exercise control. The conservative theory of poverty relies upon markets in labor and capital to provide sufficient mobility either within a generation or between generations to alleviate poverty. If one does not avail himself of the opportunities for social and economic mobility through the market, the individual is to blame. The poor cause their own poverty and its continuation. The individual is presumed to be master of his own destiny, and individualism will lead any deserving person out of poverty. (Of course, the people who posit these notions are the nonpoor.) For the undeserving poor, only institutionalization of one form or another will do. These people are trapped by their lower class life styles which prevent them from escaping poverty. If the poor would only work, there would be no poverty. The Elizabethan poor laws and their American counterpart considered unemployment a crime for which the penalty was work. Gilbert and Sullivan were appropriate when they said "let the penalty fit the crime."

The liberal (and dominant) theory of poverty grants some recognition to institutions as partial causes of poverty as well as social class as an intergenerational transmitter of poverty. But rather than seeking remedies by altering these social institutions or searching for ways to break class rigidities, liberals concentrate their energies on trying to find ways to use government either to ease the burden of poverty or assist the individual in adapting to prevailing institutions. The liberals reject exclusive reliance upon the market to foster social mobility and attempt to use government to equalize opportunities within the market or assist individuals in coping with their poverty status by direct income transfers. Nonetheless, their commitment to "alleviating" poverty without systemic changes is as deep as any conservative's. Manifestations of this orientation abound. The entire social work profession, borne out of liberal social reform, exists principally to help people cope with a rotten personal or family situation. Hungry people are given nutritional advice rather than access to food, which would involve structural changes in agricultural markets.

The objective of liberal social policy is equal opportunity—a random distribution of poverty—though we are far from that goal today. The radical challenge goes as follows: if you start from a position of inequality and treat everyone equally, you end up with continued inequality. Thus the need to create equality in fact rather than in opportunities.

Manpower programs, educational assistance, and the like are the principal policy results of the contemporary liberal human capital approach to social mobility. All of these programs are based on an essentially *untested* view of the labor market: namely, that personal characteristics over which the individual has control are the major causes of unequal and low incomes. These programs are quite similar in their ideological premise to virtually all the poor laws of capitalist society, starting with the Elizabethan poor laws. Poverty is associated with the absence of work for which work is the cure. The poor are incapable of managing their own affairs so they must be "social worked" to adapt to the rigor and needs of an industrialized and urbanized society.

This view of poverty is wrong in theory, in fact, and in social values. The causes of poverty lie outside the individual's control in markets for labor and capital and class backgrounds. Equally important, something happens both to the people seeking to help the poor and to the poor themselves when we take as our starting point the premise that people are poor because of some manipulable attribute associated with the person.

50

The Lawyer's Typist: Variations on a Theme by Paul Samuelson

Cheryl Payer

Nora, who was Improving her Mind with a night school course in introductory economics, settled down to do her homework. That week's assignment was the chapter on international trade in the textbook for the course (which the instructor had assured the class was The Very Best, being the seventh edition of Paul Samuelson's *Economics: An Introductory Analysis*).

She found it difficult to follow, and therefore boring, until her attention was suddenly caught by a passage which seemed to make more sense than the rest:

> A traditional example used to illustrate this paradox of comparative advantage is the case of the best lawyer in town who is also the best typist in town. Will he not specialize in law and leave typing to a secretary? How can he afford to give up precious time from the legal field, where his comparative advantage is very great, to perform typing activities in which he is efficient but in which he lacks *comparative* advantage? Or look at it from the secretary's point of view. She is less efficient than he in both activities, but her relative disadvantage compared with him is least in typing. Relatively speaking, she has a comparative advantage in typing.
>
> So with countries. Suppose America produces food with one-third the labor that Europe does, and produces clothing with one-half the labor. Then we shall see that America has a comparative disadvantage in clothing—this, despite the fact that America is absolutely efficient in everything. By the same token, Europe has a comparative advantage in clothing. (Samuelson, p. 647)

Nora, you see, was in fact a typist, who worked for one of the partners in a law office. It was natural that she should perk up when she discovered that the difficult concept of comparative advantage in international trade was being explained with an example from her own life. Skipping briefly over the second paragraph, she returned to the first one to read it more slowly and carefully, for she felt an instant empathy with the secretary in the parable.

Too much empathy, perhaps. Her first reaction was an uneasy resentment at the idea that her boss might after all be superior to her in the realm of secretarial skills—the only marketable skill she had. It was bad enough, she thought, that he should know enough about the law to be able to command high fees and to pay her to do his office drudgery—but to deny that she had an absolute superiority in doing that kind of work, why, that was insult added to injury! Even though she kept reminding herself that it was just a story, the sense of humiliation lingered.

Nora turned back to study the paragraph again. "Or look at it from the secretary's point of view. She is less efficient than he in both activities. . . ." At this point Nora snorted. Less efficient in law practice! Nonexistent was a better word. How could one compare efficiency when she'd never even been to law school (even if she had picked up some of the techniques and the jargon through rendering assistance to Mr. Woodbore, her boss).

She stopped laughing and began to think about it. Denigrating as the paragraph in the textbook was to her, it had stirred in her mind the first suggestion of the possibility that perhaps she ought to have the same skills which her boss was exercising, in order to make the example a fair test. What if (she choked with amusement at the idea) she turned out to be a more efficient lawyer than he?

That delicious idea brought a further problem to her mind. Just how could efficiency be tested in such occupations? There were typing and dictation tests, of course, which measured your speed in each of those activities. But that, she knew, was only a small part of the skills which a really good secretary was expected to have; and, confident as she was that she was a good secretary, intelligent and reliable and discreet, she had no idea of how such qualities could ever be quantified.

And how in the world, if she was a lawyer, could her efficiency in that activity be tested and measured against, say, that of Mr. Woodbore? It just wasn't possible to time the preparation of legal briefs the same way one could clock typing speeds with a stopwatch, deducting errors from the total score.

From her previous lessons in the Samuelson textbook, Nora had learned however that there was supposed to be a direct relationship between *price* and efficiency. Perhaps the efficiency of lawyers could be measured by what they earned? But as she thought about Mr. Woodbore, his partners, and the other lawyers that she knew, she was not really satisfied with this hypothesis. She was not convinced that Mr. Woodbore, who was a senior partner and handled a lot of corporation work, was more efficient (for surely efficiency had something to do with intelligence and hard work) than the young lawyers she knew who preferred to handle draft and civil liberties cases—but he certainly earned a lot more. And as for what she knew about the earnings of *women* lawyers (she had met one or two)—well! she was not prepared to accept that as the measure of her efficiency when (if?) she became a lawyer.

She read the passage in the text again. It certainly did imply that Professor Samuelson was equating efficiency with the lawyers' earnings. The first paragraph, however, really didn't go far enough to give her an idea of what comparative advantage would mean if she were a lawyer too, so she read the second paragraph carefully. Then she got out her paper and pencil and began to figure, muttering out loud as she did so:

"Now Mr. Woodbore earns $120 a day while I earn $30. If I am only one third as efficient as a lawyer and only one half as efficient as a secretary, that means I could earn $40 a day as a lawyer and he could earn $60 as a typist. (That's ridiculous, even an inefficient woman lawyer would earn more than an extremely efficient male typist the way things are set up now, but I don't know how else to figure it.) Well, obviously he'd be worse off to be a secretary—but *I'd* be better off to be a lawyer *even* if I was at a relative as well as an absolute disadvantage there!

"But if I have a *relative* advantage as a lawyer, being half as efficient as he is but only one third as efficient as a secretary, then I would be earning $60 as a lawyer while he earns $90 as a secretary (that's even more absurd, no secretary could possibly earn that much—I wonder why not?). I would be better off, but he certainly wouldn't be happy to take the cut in earnings. But Paul Samuelson seems to be saying he ought to! That is, he would have if he'd worked it out as I'm doing.

"But then he can't be correct when he argues that everyone would be better off to do what he or she has a relative advantage doing. Obviously anybody at all would be better off—personally speaking—doing what pays the best (which in this case is practicing law), even if they're not as efficient as somebody else."

But if everybody were a lawyer and nobody did the typing, it would be an impossible situation. For the sake of argument Nora adopted an unselfish point of view and thought about the implications to National Income, rather than to her own salary, of the various combinations she had been playing with. Nora had learned enough economics by now to know that National Income equals the sum of everybody's earnings, so it was a simple exercise.

She discovered that in the case where it was hypothesized that she had the relative advantage as a lawyer, it made no difference at all to the National Income if Mr. Woodbore worked full time as a lawyer at $120 a day and she as a typist at $30 a day; if he worked full time as a typist at $90 a day and she as a lawyer at $60; or if both worked half a day at each task, in which case his daily earnings would be $105 and hers would be $45. The sum in all three cases would be $150.

When she worked out the sums on the opposite assumption—that her relative advantage was as a typist, not a lawyer—then the National Income would fall, if she insisted on working as a lawyer, from $150 a day to $100. But Nora was beginning to suspect by this time that this might have more to do with the absolute level of typists' salaries rather than with the inherent virtues of comparative advantages. After all, lawyers really couldn't produce any faster or more efficiently than the secretarial work relating to their work was done. And Nora did not forget that even when the National Income fell by one third, *her* salary would have gone up by one third if she were a lawyer rather than a secretary.

Nora had decided by the end of the exercise that the absolute disadvantage of being a secretary was a lot more important than any relative advantage to be had doing it efficiently. But Mr. Woodbore flatly refused to take a typing test when she showed her calculations to him the next day, and Nora applied to the local law school. She was accepted in the course because, under pressure of the women's movement, the law school had upped its quota of female students from 5 to 15 percent. Since she has not graduated yet, we do not know whether she will find it to her advantage to hire a secretary to do her typing for her when she begins to practice law.

She will be eternally grateful to Professor Samuelson for showing her (albeit probably against his will) where her true interest lies. She has not, however, opened his textbook since that fateful evening and occasionally still wonders whether the truths she discovered apply also to trade between nations.

51

Millionaires and Managers

S. Menshikov

The American plutocracy exists today, just as it did a quarter or a half a century ago. The old multimillionaire families who made their fortune at the dawn of monopoly capitalism have been preserved in the main and many of them have greatly increased both their wealth and their influence. Relatively few of these families have declined, but their place has been taken by the numerous energetic group of *nouveaux riches*. The share of the national wealth owned by the plutocracy, far from declining, has even increased. The growth of finance capital and the greater domination of the financial oligarchy in political affairs and the ideological sphere have been accompanied by more thorough and carefully devised camouflage on the part of the millionaires and multimillionaires.

It is no easy task to detect a millionaire and ascertain his wealth. . . .

While in 1957 *Fortune* estimated that 45 individuals were worth $100 million or more, in 1968, i.e., only a decade later, the same source easily identified 153 men and women as belonging to this category. This means a more than threefold increase in the number of the super-rich, unprecedentedly high in the history of the United States.

Economic conditions in the U.S.A. after the war were exceedingly favourable for the growth of the biggest fortunes and the replenishment of the ranks of the plutocracy by new multimillionaires. One of the main reasons is the swift development of state-monopoly capitalism. The latter, in combination with other objective tendencies, brought about definite changes in the mechanism of the capitalist cycle. Post-war overproduction crises in the American economy have been less deep and prolonged than in the past. A considerable part of the losses caused by the chronic instability of the economy (slowing down of growth rates in the 1950s, underemployment of productive capacity, etc.) were covered from the federal budget. The monopolies have gained the opportunity to work for the relatively large, stable and definite government market, to make huge new investments on account of direct and indirect government subsidies and to wax fat on the swift advance of certain industries which enjoy especially privileged conditions owing to government support.

THE OLD FORTUNES

F. Lundberg published a list of America's 60 wealthiest families with a personal fortune of $30,000,000 and more. This list was compiled on the basis of tax statistics of the mid-1920s.

Lundberg himself did not consider his list complete and used the term "60 families" in a relative sense. For various reasons he did not include in his list more than 30 multimillionaires whom he named, but could not give even an approximate estimate of their wealth.

Our aim is to trace the fate of these fortunes step by step, as much as possible, and to ascertain what happened to them in the 1960s.

The Rockefellers

In the mid-1920s Lundberg estimated their personal fortune at $1,080 million. At that time it was represented chiefly by the personal capital of John D. Rockefeller, Sr. (he died in 1937 at the age of 97). He owned approximately $900 million and other members of the family $180 million. These estimates were made by an author who was rather critical of the financial oligarchy but most likely they were below the actual figure. J. A. Morris, who wrote a book extolling the Rockefellers, cites a different figure —about $2,000 million. Possibly this figure is closer to the truth. At the beginning of the 20th century, John D. Rockefeller, Sr., himself calculated his fortune with a precision of up to one cent and set it at $815,600,000. A. Nevins, a biographer of Rockefeller, holds that by 1910 his personal capital had exceeded $900 million. From 1910 to 1925, the wealth of the Rockefellers undoubtedly grew substantially and certainly exceeded $1,500 million.

In the mid-1950s, *Fortune* assessed the wealth of the Rockefellers at a minimum of $1,000 million and a maximum of $2,000 million. In addition, philanthropic foundations, set up on their money and fully controlled by them, owned another $1,000 million. Thus, their total capital, according to *Fortune*, amounted from $2,000 million to $3,000 million. At the end of 1957, *Fortune* again published an estimate, this time indicating the capital owned by members of the Rockefeller family. Here are these figures (million dollars).

	Minimum	Maximum
John D. Rockefeller, Jr.	400	700
Mrs. Jean Mauze (Abby Rockefeller) ..	100	200
David Rockefeller	100	200
John D. Rockefeller III	100	200
Laurance Rockefeller	100	200
Nelson Rockefeller	100	200
Winthrop Rockefeller	100	200
Total 1,000		1,900

These figures are incomplete because they do not include the capital of the 22 grandchildren of John D. Rockefeller, Jr., to whom he turned over, just as to his children, part of his fortune prior to his death; the heirs of his sister Edith Rockefeller, who married Harold McCormick, and the brother of his first wife, Winthrop Aldrich, who for a long time was in charge of the Rockefeller family affairs. Together with these additions, the wealth of this family, on the basis of *Fortune*'s estimate, reaches $2,000–$3,000 million.

The will of John D. Rockefeller, Jr., the main provisions of which were made public after his death in May 1960, seems to confirm this estimate. The will shows that during his lifetime he handed over $473 million to various philanthropies, about $600 million–$1,200 million to his children and a large sum to his grandchildren. Lastly, his estate included securities, real property and works of art for a sum of $150 million, also in the main exempt from taxes. Approximately half of this sum was given to his second wife, exempt from taxes up to her death, on the basis of the 1948 law. The other half was bequeathed to the Rockefeller Brothers Fund, i.e., formally also comes into the category of charity. In addition John D. Rockefeller, Jr., presented $5 million to the Lincoln Center of the Performing Arts in New York and bequeathed a number of other gifts.

Thus, *one of the biggest fortunes in America was handed over to the heirs actually without paying taxes.* The lawyers and advisers of the Rockefellers displayed truly demoniacal virtuosity in circumventing the tax laws.

In our opinion, both the estimate of the wealth of John D. Rockefeller, Jr. made in his will and the figures cited by *Fortune* are greatly understated. Victor Perlo, who calculated the value of the stocks belonging to the Rockefellers (as of April 1956), names a figure of $3,500 million. Since stock prices in the United States approximately doubled from 1956 to 1965 this estimate should now be increased at least to $6,000–7,000 million. S. Alsop mentioning the estimate of *Fortune* writes: "Nelson Rockefeller, and all the other Rockefellers, are a great deal richer than they are generally supposed to be. . . . I have never been made privy to the secret financial archives of the Rockefellers. But I should be prepared to eat my boots in béarnaise if those figures are not low." Alsop points out that the increase in the wealth of the Rockefellers from $900 million in 1910 only to $2,000 million at the beginning of 1960 could occur only if it were managed very badly. But actually it was administered by first-class experts. "It is reasonable to suppose," Alsop concludes, "that the total Rockefeller fortune may well amount to several times the accepted figures of between one and two billion dollars. It would not be at all surprising . . . if all the Rockefeller family assets—all the Rockefeller-controlled money as well as the Rockefeller-owned money— came to something like ten billion dollars."

Today, the Rockefeller fortune consists, as it were, of three parts. The first part is the assets inherited by the wife, children and grandchildren of John D. Rockefeller, Jr.; these are mostly the stocks of oil companies and the Chase Manhattan Bank. Under the term of the will, this capital is secured to each member of the family in trust for life. They can use the income but not the capital itself. After their death this part will be inherited by their children, and as American authors consider, will be broken up between them. But even if this prediction comes true, it is clear that the size of the Rockefeller assets will increase because of the mechanism for the self-growth of fictitious capital. At least in the next ten years this wealth will be managed jointly as the combined capital of the quite large financial clan. As for the rates of the self-growth of this part of their capital, it can be judged from the fact that between 1946 and 1958 it increased by 140 per cent owing to the stock market boom.

The second part consists of several philanthropic foundations fully controlled by the Rockefeller brothers. Since this family continues to allot large sums to philanthropy there is every ground for assuming that this part of their capital will continue to increase swiftly.

The third, perhaps most interesting, part of the Rockefeller assets is the capital fully owned by the sons of John D. Rockefeller, Jr. Having no right to spend the inherited capital they utilise for enrichment the income they get from it and also the extensive credit they can receive. In the 1960s, the independent new personal fortune of the children of John D. Rockefeller, Jr., not counting the inherited capital, amounted to not less than $200 million and continued to mount swiftly. In 1968, *Fortune* estimated the total of the capital belonging to the six Rockefeller brothers and one sister at from $1,200 million to $1,800 million. This is a 1.5–2-fold increase as compared to the 1957 estimate.

TABLE I □ THE OLD CORE OF THE AMERICAN PLUTOCRACY

	Personal Wealth, million dollars	
	In the mid-1920s	In the 1960s
Rockefellers	1,000–1,500	6,000–10,000
Du Ponts	100–240	4,000–9,000
Mellons	100–450	3,000–7,500
Mellon's partners—A. V. Davis and R. A. Hunt	—	500–700
Fords	100–660	1,200–4,000
Dorrances	—	100–1,000
Phippses	89–600	500–750
Harknesses	80–450	450–600
Reynoldses	117	500–600
Milbanks	100	400–500
McCormicks-Deerings	260	350–450
Morgans	90	250–400
Whitneys	75–322	400–600
Houghtons	—	350–500
Waggoners	—	300–400
Lehmans	129	250–350
Dukes	—	250–350
Kirby	—	300–350
Astors	30–114	150–300
Bakers	50–200	210–300
Fishers	50–194	200–300
Guggenheims-Strausses	190	200–300
Firestones	—	280–300
Pitcairns	100	230–250
Fricks	—	150–200
Harrimans	—	150–200
Weyerheusers	—	150–200
Pews	—	100–190
Stillmans-Rockefellers	50–102	100–150
Posts-Huttons	—	250–350
Woodruffs	—	150–200
Schiffs	66	75–100
Dodges	—	75–100
Chapmans	—	75–100
George R. Brown	—	75–100
Goulds	34–400	75–100

TABLE 2 □ NEW MULTIMILLIONAIRES

Families or Individuals	Personal Fortune, million dollars in the 1960s	Main Sphere of Enrichment
Getty	1,000–1,500	Oil
H. Hughes	1,000–1,500	Oil equipment, military contracts, aircraft
Cullens	800–1,000	Oil
H. Hunt	800–1,500	Oil
Murchisons	600–700	Oil, investment companies, speculation in securities
S. Richardson	200–600	Oil
Kennedy	200–600	Real estate
Moody	400–500	Banks, real estate, etc.
Upjohns	400–500	Medicines
Kaisers	350–500	Steel, aluminium and others
W. Keck	200–400	Oil
D. Ludwig	500–1,000	Shipping
A. P. Sloan	200–400	Automobile industry
Watsons	150–200	Electronics, military contracts
J. S. Abercrombie	150–200	⎫
J. Blaustein	150–200	⎬ Oil
J. Mecom	100–200	⎪
R. E. Smith	300–500	⎭
G. and H. Brown	150–200	Electrical equipment industry, speculation in securities
W. L. McKnight	300–500	Engineering
J. S. McDonnell	150–200	Aircraft industry
J. D. MacArthur	300–500	Insurance
Ch. Allen, Jr.	200–300	Investment banking
Ch. Engelhard, Jr.	200–300	Mining and metal fabricating
S. Newhouse	200–300	Newspapers
S. Bechtel	100–200	Industrial construction
Dillons	150–200	Banking
Blakley	100–200	Real estate
Land	500–600	Polaroid cameras
L. Corrigan	100–500	Real estate
H. Crown	180–200	Building materials, real estate, military contracts
Ketterings	150–200	⎫
Pratt	100–200	⎬ Automobile industry
C. Mott	300–500	⎭
Meadows	100–200	Oil
C. Eaton	100–150	Iron ore, coal, steel, railways
Cabots	100–150	Chemical industry
Bakalars	70–150	Electronics
Eccles	100–150	Industrial construction, banking
S. Fairchild	200–300	Patent operations, speculation in securities
Olins	100–120	Chemical industry
L. Wolfson	100–120	Engineering, shipbuilding
H. Ahmanson	200–300	Savings associations, real estate
H. Morrison	75–100	Construction
P. and L. Tisch	70–100	Real estate

Note: In addition to the multimillionaires indicated in the table the following persons had in the 1960s an annual income of over $1,000,000 and probably a fortune greater than $50–75 million (the names of the companies they head are given in parentheses): Leon Lewinstein (Lewinstein and Sons—chemicals, textiles); Lewis Rosenstiel (Shenley Industries—alcoholic beverages); Chester Roth (Kayser-Roth Corporation—textiles); Samuel Bronfman (Distillers Corporation—Seagrams Ltd.—alcoholic beverages); N. Milliken (Deering, Milliken and Co.— wholesale trade); Norman Harris (Harris Trust and Savings Bank—commercial bank); Henry Heinz II (H. J. Heinz Co.—food industry); Peter Grace (W. R. Grace and Co.—chemicals); J. F. Cullman III (Philip Morris—tobacco industry); J. E. Jonsson (Texas Instruments— electronics). The following people are frequently mentioned as newcomers to the more than $150-million personal worth category: Leon Hess (Hess Oil and Chemical), William R. Hewlett and David Packard (Hewlett-Packard—machinery), Forrest Mars (Mars candy), Eli Lilly (Eli Lilly and Co.—pharmaceuticals), De Witt Wallace (*Reader's Digest*), Peter Kiewit (construction), S. Mark Taper (finance), and E. C. Robins (drugs).

. . .

Do the top managers really control the leading industrial corporations in America? First, it is clear that when a manager or a group of managers leave a corporation their influence on its affairs drops to a minimum or is even reduced to naught. A study made by Arch Patton shows that in a relatively brief period (1954–59) 47 per cent of the top executives were changed in the leading U.S. corporations. In 60 per cent of the cases at least two or three top executives were replaced. Thus, it may be considered as established that the top management of the U.S. biggest corporations are fully replaced in 10 years on the average and in most cases more frequently.

Second, to demonstrate the control of managers over corporations use is frequently made of data on the composition of the boards of directors which exercise supreme authority in corporations. What are the facts and figures on this score?

In a study published in 1945, R. A. Gordon presented 1935 data on more than 100 of the biggest industrial companies. Of the total number of their directors 43 per cent were hired officials of the given corporation. In 30 out of 84 of the biggest companies (about 36 per cent) hired managers had an absolute majority on the board of directors and in another 15 almost an absolute majority. But notwithstanding such a large number of executives on the boards of directors most of the biggest corporations were actually under the control of several leading financial groups.

Not relying on data of bourgeois authors, we made our own analysis of the composition of the boards of 110 biggest industrial corporations in the U.S.A. (data for 1960–61). Of the 110 companies only 29, or 26 per cent, had a majority of hired executives on their boards.

Thus if Gordon's data are correct then both the proportion of managers on boards of directors and the proportion of corporations with a prevalence of managers *declined* between 1935 and 1960–61 from 43 to 39 per cent and from 36 to 26 per cent respectively.

It would be wrong, however, to consider on the basis of these data that hired managers control the 29 large corporations where they have a formal majority. A concrete analysis of the correlation of forces in these firms produces results which are even more devastating for the "managerial revolution" theory.

In a substantial part of these corporations the numerical "preponderance" of hired officials is explained by the natural desire of the owner of the controlling block of shares to appoint fully obedient men to the board of directors. The result is "paradoxical": according to statistics on directorships, the "managerial revolution" has made the biggest progress in companies where undisputed control belongs to one family. Of the 29 companies in which hired managers predominate on the board of directors, at least 12 are in this category. In another 14 companies the ownership of big blocks of shares by one or several families and also the strong representation of Wall Street bankers preclude any possibility of control by the hired executives. Information about two companies is lacking and only one, Bethlehem Steel, evidently is controlled by the top executives. But this control is of long standing and is not a product of recent decades. Moreover, control of this group has been based for a long time not only on its managerial position but also on the ownership of substantial blocks of stock.

Thus, we can draw a very definite conclusion: *in so far as more than 100 of the biggest U.S. industrial corporations are concerned, they are not controlled by their hired executives and there are no signs of such a tendency.*

The illusion of the supremacy of the managers and their equality and merger with the multimillionaires stems from the very nature of the separation of functioning capital from capital as property. A top executive is appointed by finance-capitalists not in order that he should constantly meddle in their affairs. Such a manager is called upon to replace the proprietor in everything except getting the lion's share of surplus value. A manager cannot discharge his functions successfully unless he is given broad powers and the opportunity to appropriate a definite part of the profit, in other words, unless he can live like a capitalist. Such are the rules of the game and, so long as the manager follows them, he looks like the actual proprietor of the corporation. But this situation remains in force only as long as he "suits" the finance-capitalists and enjoys their confidence.

No case has been recorded in the United States when top managers, acting on their own, have succeeded in wresting control of corporations from financial tycoons. But there have been many instances of tycoons making short shrift of undesirable top managers.

Colbert and other top executives of the Chrysler Corporation who were dismissed from their posts by New York and Pittsburgh bankers, offered no resistance: they lost the battle even before it began.

John J. Hopkins, a Wall Street lawyer, was the organiser and head of General Dynamics. Though he had no big block of shares, Hopkins acted as the company's sole dictator and the New York bankers put no obstacles in his way as long as his management brought them and their clients substantial profits. But as soon as business deteriorated the bankers deposed the "dictator" and put ex-Secretary of the Army Pace in his stead. But the company's business further declined under Pace. When in 1961, Crown, a Chicago tycoon, captured control of General Dynamics, he unhesitatingly removed Pace, notwithstanding the latter's extensive political and business connections. Crown had only one, but decisive, advantage over Pace. He was the owner, while the latter was the executive. And Crown did not stand on ceremony when it was a matter of assuring his profits.

Jeremiah Milbank, a multimillionaire, owned 30 per cent of the stock of Commercial Solvents, of which J. Albert Woods was the chief executive. The Milbanks were not represented on the board of directors and no one, except themselves, knew about their potential control. They were interested only in dividends, which began to drop disastrously in 1958 and 1959. The outraged millionaires decided to intervene. Acting through Harold H. Helm, chairman of the board of the Chemical Corn Exchange Bank, they demanded that the board of directors of Commercial Solvents dismiss Woods at once. "There were no public denunciations or taunts exchanged by the opposing parties," *Fortune* reported in an article aptly entitled "How Well-Bred Investors Overthrow a Management." "They confronted one another behind the closed doors of brokers' and lawyers' offices in downtown Manhattan, and in Commercial Solvents' headquarters on Madison Avenue. Here the sounds of struggle were completely muffled, and the contest was confined to the level of the board of directors. . . . The battle was not prolonged. The decision [to dismiss Woods—*S.M.*] came after five days of hectic negotiation." And this notwithstanding the fact that of the 13 directors 8 were on the side of Woods. The Milbanks clearly showed their managers who was the boss and who was really in charge.[1]

The power of the top executives is quite real, but only so long as they remain obedient tools of the financial oligarchy.

THE ROCKEFELLER GROUP, THE CHASE MANHATTAN BANK, THE CHEMICAL BANK NEW YORK TRUST CO.

The history of the Rockefeller financial group, strictly speaking, began at the time when members of this family, having withdrawn from direct management of the Standard Oil companies, undertook to extend their influence to other spheres, especially banking. John D. Rockefeller I, after retiring as president of Standard Oil, ruled his kingdom from a small office in downtown Manhattan (he died in 1937). His son, John D. Rockefeller II, spent most of his life in supervising the creation of both his financial group and the myth of the Rockefeller benevolence through philanthropic foundations. His brother-in-law Winthrop W. Aldrich headed operations in the banking part of the group. It was only since the end of the 1930s and early 1940s that the Rockefellers returned to direct leadership. The five sons of Rockefeller II act as a well-knit group of finance-capitalists. This system which originated under Rockefeller II continues to function to this day (Rockefeller II died in 1960).

Rockefeller Bros., Inc., founded in 1946, is one of the organisational centres of this system. It administers the capital of the Rockefeller family placed in speculative operations, the buying of small but swiftly growing companies, and so on. Laurance Rockefeller was for a long time president of Rockefeller Bros. He added to the Rockefeller financial group the Eastern Air Lines, Inc., one of the biggest air transport companies, established long-lasting and strong ties between the Rockefeller banks and the McDonnell Aircraft and Martin war-industry companies, and directed the purchase and sale of a number of aircraft, rocket fuel and rare metals companies.

Rockefeller Bros. does not seek to capture outright control of the companies it is interested in. Many small capitalists and executives indebted to

---

[1] How little the situation has changed in the last four decades is demonstrated by the fact that the action of the Milbanks in 1959 was similar to a lesson they administered to the leadership of another company as far back as 1924. At that time the top executives of the Southern Railway had decided, by agreement with the Morgans, not to pay dividends on the stock. The selfsame Jeremiah Milbank did not turn to the executives, considering them to be too small fry. He came to J. P. Morgan, Jr., and his partner Thomas Lamont and asked that the payments of the dividends be continued. Lamont quite cooly replied that they could not satisfy Mr. Milbank's request.

"Milbank, the story goes, said quietly: 'I'm afraid you, gentlemen, misunderstand me. I'm not asking you to pay a dividend. I'm telling you. I own control of the Southern.'

"Lamont and Morgan jumped to their feet. How many shares did Milbank represent?

" 'Five hundred thousand shares,' was the reply.

" 'Mr. Milbank, dividends will be paid on the Southern common,' said Mr. Lamont." (*Fortune*, May 1959, p. 135.)

the Rockefellers for their enrichment or advancement are tied to the chariot of these tycoons to one or another degree. This is a well-conceived line of expanding the Rockefeller group to the utmost in conditions when the existing large corporations have already been divided between the strongest monopoly associations. The policy of the Rockefellers is to create under their aegis a wide coalition with industrialists in the most diverse fields.

Rockefeller Bros. also guides the activity of the International Basic Economy Corporation, set up by Nelson Rockefeller for operations in Latin America. In 1960, the *New York Times* described it as a company engaged in investment, financing and development in all parts of the world. It carries on some of its operations jointly with the Chase Manhattan Bank.

A group of close advisers and assistants to the Rockefellers in their special business interests has crystallised. Rockefeller Bros. is presided over by J. Richardson Dilworth. A former partner of the Kuhn, Loeb investment bank, he became a personal adviser to the Rockefeller family and director of the Chase Manhattan Bank. The International Basic Economy Corporation is headed by Robert W. Purcell, who has served under several masters: he was with White and Case, a Wall Street law firm; acted as a close aide to Robert Young and after the latter's death headed the Investors Diversified Services, Inc., the biggest investment trust in the U.S.A. The advisers of the Rockefellers since 1950 have included Lewis L. Strauss, a former partner of Kuhn, Loeb and ex-chairman of the U.S. Atomic Energy Commission, and leading members of two big law firms—John J. McCloy and John E. Lockwood (of Milbank, Tweed) and Thomas Debevoise (of Debevoise, Plimpton). Thus, the close entourage of the Rockefellers, though it has not been gathered, as in the old J. P. Morgan and Co., "under one roof," consists of past masters in financial operations.

Among the other family organisations of this group mention should be made of:

1. The Rockefeller Center, Inc. In addition to large real estate holdings (a group of skyscrapers in New York), this company with a capital of more than $200 million owns stocks and bonds of banks and industrial corporations. The list of these investments is not made public.

2. Rockefeller Foundation. Besides philanthropic functions it acts as an investment company. More than half of its investments consist of shares of the Standard Oil Co. of New Jersey. John D. Rockefeller III heads the board of trustees, but his functions apparently are limited to general supervision over the philanthropic part of the Foundation's activities. (Such philanthropy is very intimately linked with politics as proven twice in the last 15 years by the appointment of presidents of the Rockefeller Foundation—John Foster Dulles and Dean Rusk—to the post of U.S. Secretary of State.) As for investments, they are directed by a financial committee of five trustees. In 1962, the committee was headed by Lloyd D. Brace, chairman of the board of the First National Bank of Boston. George D. Woods, president of the First Boston Corporation, was one of its members. The Chase Manhattan Bank does the actual work of administering the security holdings. Rockefeller lawyers (Eli W. Debevoise and others) have the final say on stock voting.

3. Rockefeller Brothers Fund, Inc., headed by Laurance Rockefeller. It plays chiefly a political role: draws up statements on questions of foreign

and home policy, subsidises authors who study various aspects of the cold war. In 1959, the nominal value of its assets was $53 million and now it is about $210 million. The fund holds a considerable number of shares of the Chase Manhattan Bank.

But let us go beyond the strictly family establishments of Rockefellers. Chase Manhattan Bank is the most important institution which is under their direct management. It holds first place in the United States for the scale of its network of correspondents, the crediting and financial servicing of the oil, power and aerospace industries. A few years ago all operations related to serving these sectors were handed over to special departments of the bank. Prime importance is also commanded by international financial operations, of which David Rockefeller has been in charge since the end of the 1940s.

At the end of the 1920s, when the Rockefellers, after a long search, picked the Chase National Bank and bought the controlling block of its stock (in exchange for the stock of another bank, Equitable Trust) they took into account both the size of the bank, its clientele and the potentialities of growth. Winthrop W. Aldrich was placed at the head of Chase National. Prior to that he was associated with a Rockefeller law firm and then became chief legal counsellor and president of Equitable Trust. One of his tasks was to train his successor from among the Rockefellers, namely, David Rockefeller. In 1952, John McCloy, also a lawyer, a partner of another law firm close to the Rockefellers, was appointed head of the Chase National Bank and then of the Chase Manhattan Bank. He held that post for the time necessary to complete the schooling of David Rockefeller. In 1962, shortly after his father's death, David was appointed president and head of the bank's executive committee.

The Rockefellers have always had another family representative on the board of Chase National. Under Aldrich it was Bertram Cutler, who was close to John D. Rockefeller, Jr., then Laurance Rockefeller and now it is Richard Dilworth, president of the Rockefeller Brothers. . . .

But this influence cannot be wielded without alliance with other families, groups of capitalists and leaders of big monopolies who may or may not be represented on the bank's directorate. Among such allies we single out the Whitneys and Milbanks and also the banking houses of Kuhn, Loeb and Stone and Webster. The Whitneys are the offspring of Colonel Oliver Paine, who was a Standard Oil partner of Rockefeller I. In time, the capital of this family was shifted to other spheres. The financial "duchy" of the Whitneys now includes a group of magazines and radio stations, Freeport Sulphur, Great Northern Paper, Vitro Corporation of America and interests in Armco Steel, American Smelting and Refining and a number of other companies. Although this group, headed by the J. H. Whitney and Co., a partnership, acts independently of the Rockefellers, allied relations have been preserved between them. Laurance Rockefeller was for a long time a director of Vitro, which is headed by Charles Payson, a brother-in-law of J. H. Whitney. Rockefeller then ceded his place to Purcell, president of the International Basic Economy Corporation. Jean Mauze, a brother-in-law of the Rockefellers, is a director of the Freeport Sulphur Company, which formerly was headed by Whitney himself. The Whitneys undoubtedly helped the Rockefellers to acquire the Bank of Manhattan. As far back as the

1930s James F. Brownlee, a partner of J. H. Whitney and Co., became a director of that bank and then also a director of the merged Chase Manhattan Bank.

The Kuhn, Loeb and the Stone and Webster banking houses had been represented on the directorate of the Bank of Manhattan since the end of the 1920s. The penetration of the Bank of Manhattan by the Rockefellers and the preparations for its merger with the Chase National Bank coincided with two other interesting events. In 1950, Lewis Strauss, a partner of Kuhn, Loeb since the 1930s, became a personal financial adviser to the Rockefeller family and in 1955, Richard Dilworth, another Kuhn, Loeb partner, assumed a similar post. These coincidences are not accidental. It is beyond doubt that at least some of the partners of Kuhn, Loeb helped to bring about the merger of the Bank of Manhattan and Chase National, acting on the side of the Rockefellers. This does not mean that this banking house fully joined the group headed by the Rockefellers. After the retirement of Strauss and Dilworth and some other partners most of the capital of this banking house belongs to John M. Schiff, whose business interests do not always coincide with the Rockefellers. But Kuhn, Loeb services the Eastern Airlines. The solid ties of this banking house with the law firm Cravath, Swaine and Moore and, through it, also with the Chemical Bank New York Trust, makes it part of a broader financial group where Kuhn, Loeb, the Rockefellers and a number of other monopolists generally act as allies.

Another investment bank, Stone and Webster Securities, maintains a direct union with the Chase Manhattan Bank. All its stock belongs to Stone and Webster, Inc., whose head, Whitney Stone, is a director of Chase Manhattan. In its turn, the bank acts as the stock transfer agent of Stone and Webster.

We have mentioned the Milbanks among the families allied with the Rockefellers. Jeremiah Milbank, Sr., was a director of the Chase National Bank from the 1920s to the mid-1950s, and his son, Jeremiah Milbank, Jr., sits on the board of Chase Manhattan to this day. Milbank, Tweed, a law firm founded by Albert G. Milbank, is the chief legal counsellor of the Chase Manhattan Bank and one of its members, John McCloy, headed this bank from 1952 to 1960. The Milbank interests include Allis Chalmers, Corn Products, Commercial Solvents, Borden, Southern Railway and a number of other large companies. The Milbanks do not personally control any commercial bank but hold quite strong positions in Chase Manhattan, Chemical Bank New York Trust and the Bank of New York. Something more than an accidental interlocking of interests exists between these banks.

Prior to the 1920s, an alliance of the Stillmans, Jenningses (from the old Standard Oil of New York), Phippses, Harknesses and Hills dominated the New York Trust Co., which some 40 years later became one of the two components of the Chemical Bank New York Trust. In 1921, the house of Morgan made a coup placing at the head of the New York Trust a new leadership and putting on the directorate three of its partners and also two allies—Grayson Murphy and Charles Hayden. But the era of Morgan domination continued only up to the early 1940s when Morgan partners withdrew from the New York Trust one after another (the last one left in 1943). It was then that the old forces became more active, especially those

TABLE 3 □ COMPOSITION OF THE CHASE MANHATTAN BANK–THE CHEMICAL BANK NEW YORK TRUST GROUP

Name of company	Total Assets, million dollars	Share of Control	Total Controlled Assets, million dollars	Other Groups Participating in Control
Banks				
Chase Manhattan Bank	10,932	1	10,932	—
Chemical Bank New York Trust	5,246	2/3	3,497	Various groups
Bank of New York	776	1/2	388	Sullivan and Cromwell
Metropolitan Life Insurance .	19,596	2/3	13,064	Various groups
Equitable Life Assurance ...	10,824	1/2	5,412	" "
Rockefeller Foundation	554	1	554	—
Rockefeller Center	200	1	200	—
Rockefeller Brothers, Inc. ...	......	1	......	—
Rockefeller Brothers Fund ..	120	1	120	—
International Basic Economy Corporation	......	1	......	—
J. H. Whitney and Co.	......	1	......	—
First Boston Corporation	518	1/4	129	Mellons
Kuhn, Loeb and Co.	7	1/2	3	Schiffs
Stone and Webster Securities	7	1/2	3	Various groups
Milbank, Tweed and Hope ..	......	1	......	—
Debevoise, Plimpton	......	1	......	—
Cravath, Swaine and Moore .	......	1/2	......	Various groups
American Express Co.	877	1/2	439	" "
Industry and Transport				
Eastern Air Lines	329	1	329	—
National Lead	439	1	439	—
Standard Oil Co. of New Jersey	11,488	3/4	8,616	Morgan Guaranty Trust
Borden	503	3/4	377	Various groups
American Airlines	666	2/3	444	" "
Southern Railway	890	2/3	593	" "
Southern Pacific Ry.	2,519	1/2	1,259	" "
Corn Products	504	1/2	252	" "
Mobil Oil	4,136	2/5	1,654	Morgan Guaranty Trust, First National City Bank
International Paper	1,038	2/5	415	Phippses, Morgan Guaranty Trust
Martin-Marietta	554	2/5	222	Mellons
Foremost Dairies	158	1/3	53	California
Sinclair Oil	1,515	1/3	505	Merril, Lynch
International Business Machines	2,112	1/3	704	Morgan Guaranty Trust
Burlington Industries	667	1/3	222	Wacovia Bank
American Smelting and Refining	477	1/3	159	Guggenheims, Morgan Guaranty Trust
American Telephone and Telegraph	26,717	1/4	6,679	Various groups
International Telephone and Telegraph	1,236	1/4	309	First National City Bank and others
Allied Chemical	1,022	1/4	255	" "
Westinghouse Electric	1,516	1/4	379	Mellons
B. F. Goodrich	648	1/4	162	Morgan Guaranty Trust and others
American Electric Power	1,655	1/4	414	" "
Standard Oil Co. (Indiana) ..	3,109	1/4	777	Chicago
Standard Oil Co. (California)	3,358	1/4	838	California, First National City Bank

(TABLE 3, continued)

McDonnell Aircraft	149	1/4	37	St. Louis
U. S. Rubber	686	1/4	171	Du Ponts
American Sugar Refining ...	240	1/5	48	Irving Trust and others
Radio Corporation of America	1,059	1/5	212	Lehman Bros., Lazard Frères
Republic Steel	1,132	1/5	226	Cleveland
Armco Steel	995	1/5	199	First National City Bank, Mellons and others
Youngstown Sheet and Tube	773	1/6	129	Cleveland
Pacific Gas and Electric	2,809	1/6	468	California
Owens-Corning Fiberglass ..	204	1/6	34	First National City Bank, Morgan Guaranty Trust
Goodyear Tire and Rubber ..	1,186	1/6	198	Cleveland, Dillon, Read
Stone and Webster	68	1/2	34	Other groups
Otis Elevator	177	3/4	133	Various New York groups
Vitro Corp.	22	1	22	—
St. Joseph Lead	118	1/3	39	Newmont Mining, St. Louis
West Virginia Pulp and Paper	275	1/4	69	Irving Trust
Great Northern Paper	130	1/2	65	Other New York groups
Freeport Sulphur	182	1/2	91	First National City Bank and others

Total 62,972
   of which
   banking 34,741
   industry and transport 28,231

who in the past were closely associated with the Rockefellers: the Harknesses, Jenningses, Havemeyers and Guggenheims. Towards the end of the 1950s, on the eve of the merger with the Chemical Corn Exchange Bank there were also direct representatives of the Rockefellers on the directorate of the New York Trust: Percy L. Douglas (in the past assistant to Nelson Rockefeller on Latin American affairs, and then president of the Otis Elevator Company and director of the International Basic Economy Corporation) and J. E. Crane (vice-president of the Standard Oil of New Jersey, in the past an adviser to Nelson Rockefeller).

Our summary estimate of the assets of the group (see table [above]) is again smaller than the data of Victor Perlo, although the number of companies in our list is much bigger. While the first divergence is explained, as pointed out earlier, by the method of measuring control, the second reason lies in the consistent policy of expanding the sphere of influence pursued by the Rockefellers, Milbanks, Whitneys and other participants in this monopoly alliance. One outstanding feature is that they no longer keep large controlling blocks in a small number of companies but are trying to penetrate the most diverse sectors. This inevitably leads to wider use of the method of joint control employed long before them by the house of Morgan. Let us note, however, that the latter has a much wider circle of allies than the core of the Rockefeller group. This is the reason why the Morgan banks, together with their coalition, enjoy superiority in a larger number of industrial corporations than their main rival.

COMPOSITION OF THE FINANCIAL OLIGARCHY: A RECAPITULATION

In the first chapter we traced the general evolution of the finance-capitalist and his manager. This evolution inevitably leads to a division of the monopoly bourgeoisie into the millionaires and the top managers serving them. We ascertained the social origin of the managers and revealed their subordinate position in relation to the financial oligarchy proper. But the more detailed analysis of banking monopolies, the forms of finance capital and especially of the financial groups in the United States enables us to add some features to the general set-up of the country's ruling top group.

To begin with, it is clear that economic power is concentrated not in the hands of an abstract finance-capitalist and an abstract manager, but in associations of finance capital. Leadership in these associations is exercised by *definite* combinations of millionaires and managers. Under such circumstances, an executive with a relatively small fortune of his own might head a financial group, while other men holding a *subordinate* position in the given group might be very rich people, at times even multimillionaires.

This millionaire-manager combination, seemingly paradoxical at first glance, assumes the most diverse concrete forms.

In the Morgan group, for example, during a certain period of time, neither the Morgan family nor the families of its partners have produced a man capable, without infringing their own financial interests, to lead the head bank of this group. That is why Henry Alexander, a professional top executive, was made president of the Morgan Guaranty Trust. Finance-capitalists who are in the leadership of this group had to treat him as an equal and in many cases follow his directives because it was he, and not they, who personified the supreme interests of the given group of tycoons.

The Kaiser concern offers another example. The Kaisers are multimillionaires who undoubtedly run all the affairs of the concern, are full dictators in "their own house," including their own corporate bureaucracy. But in financial affairs they for more than 10 years had to heed the opinion of the head of the First Boston Corporation, George Woods, whose fortune is a mere fraction of their own and who in social origin and source of income is a typical chief executive. Why? Because the Mellons and, indirectly also the Rockefellers and Boston millionaires, have entrusted Woods with managing one of the largest U.S. investment banks.

This is not a managerial revolution, and for many reasons. A manager may head a financial group today only if there is no suitable candidate from among the plutocracy itself. Here an analogy with a medieval monarchy can be drawn. If the throne was occupied by a nitwit or an infant, regents ruled the state. The same is true of the financial oligarchy. If the families heading a financial group do not produce a leader from their own midst, the group is ruled by "regents," that is, chief executives.

But the position of the regents is always temporary. Henry Alexander, an executive, was managing the head Morgan bank. But breathing down his neck was Thomas Gates, a rich Morgan partner who had gone through a long political and economic school. The offspring of other Morgan families are also "carefully reared." When Henry Ford I died, Harry H. Bennett, the chief of Ford's private police who ruled in the last years of his master's life, became "regent." But no sooner had Henry Ford II matured than Bennett had to give up the helm.

The National City Bank, in our opinion, furnishes a classical example. From the early 1920s and up to the end of the 1950s, no Stillman-Rockefeller ran the bank. Regents alternated—Vanderlip, Mitchell, Rentschler and

Sheperd. This was the period when one set of executives after another ruled both the bank and the group, and the millionaires obeyed them. But then James Stillman-Rockefeller came on the scene. He is generally considered a rather average banker, but a capable executive. He was made to climb the banking ladder rung by rung so as to compensate by diligence for the lack of special talents. He enjoyed no advantage over his rivals, except the fact that his family, together with its allies, held a big block of the bank's shares. As soon as James Stillman-Rockefeller finished his "schooling" he ascended the "throne" which had been vacant for 30 years. Something similar happened to David Rockefeller in the Chase Manhattan Bank, and to many other representatives of the plutocracy.

In summing up it may be said that the economic power enjoyed by representatives of different segments of the monopoly bourgeoisie depends above all on the place they hold in the main financial groups. Or, to put it differently, the *financial oligarchy*, that is, the group of people whose economic power is based on the disposal of colossal masses of fictitious capital, is limited to that part of the monopoly bourgeoisie which holds a leading position in the main financial groups of the given country. The financial oligarchy draws its personnel from among the finance-capitalists proper, the financial aristocracy and the top managers. The weight of these three components is determined at each given moment by the concrete circumstances, but in all cases the might of all the three rests on the colossal capital of the multimillionaires, which is the foundation of all the main financial groups.

These groups are engaged in constant struggle. Each one intrinsically strives to dominate the other or at least to prevail in an alliance of equals. In the early period of U.S. monopoly capitalism these battles resulted in the establishment of the dictatorship of the Morgan financial group. But in present-day conditions when monopoly capitalism has grown into state-monopoly capitalism, when the role of the state in the capitalist economy has risen to an unusual extent, battles between financial groups for economic power necessarily involve struggle for political power, for predominance in government institutions, and so on. The coalescence of the monopolies with the state furnishes a broad basis on which this struggle is fought in the United States and other capitalist countries.

In present-day conditions the capture of key positions in the central state machine affords the monopolies opportunities to dispose of colossal material and money resources. In brief, in a contemporary capitalist country state power becomes the highest expression of the economic power of the financial oligarchy.

The economic power of the financial oligarchy rests, specifically, on commanding most of the country's money capital. The bank assets controlled by the main financial groups (New York and regional) are twice as large as the annual budget of the U.S. Federal Government. Disposal of these money resources makes it possible to control the political machine: the bosses of the Republican and Democratic parties and government officials.

It would seem that now the political power of the financial oligarchy should be fully guaranteed, but this is not the case. The machine of a contemporary capitalist state is big and cumbersome. Capture of positions in one part does not ensure control over the entire mechanism. The financial oligarchy owns the propaganda machine, is able to bribe politicians and government officials in the centre and the periphery, but it cannot bribe all the people who, notwithstanding all the restrictions of bourgeois "democracy," elect the legislature. The people do not have much of a choice, but without formally abolishing democratic procedures, the financial oligarchy cannot fully guarantee itself against undesirable "accidents."

The financial oligarchy has strong allies in the struggle for political power. These, first, are groups of bourgeois politicians, who, through demagogy and play on national and racial antagonisms, control political power in their particular areas.

Another ally is the local oligarchic cliques of Southern planters who in many cases coalesced with local bankers and with oil millionaires in oil-rich states.

The third ally is the Pentagon militarist clique. Most of its chiefs are not members of the financial oligarchy; their power is rooted in the disposal of colossal state property (armaments, in the first place) and command of a big army.

Thus, while economic rule in the United States is in the hands of the financial oligarchy, in the political field it relies on three extremely reactionary forces: local cliques of corrupted politicians, the oligarchy of Southern racist planters and the Pentagon militarist clique. In practice, this alliance resolves to the following arrangement: the financial oligarchy as the leading force gets control of the Federal Government, while each of its three allies receives the sphere it dominates as its "slice of the pie."

In the struggle for political power the financial oligarchy does not act unitedly; its internal rivalry brings to the foreground now one now another group. To gain the opportunity to dispose of the government's colossal resources it manoeuvres, entering into all kinds of blocs and coalitions. If promises and even real concessions to the petty bourgeoisie or the working class are needed in order to win supreme political power, the tycoons are ready to do so. . . .

The striving of the financial oligarchy for direct administration of the state is one of the most characteristic tendencies of American imperialism in recent decades. That the multimillionaires, who formerly looked upon Washington as a "second-rate city," are now craving for political power, that members of the money "aristocracy" readily turn from a corporation lawyer or investment banker into a member of the Administration or an adviser to the President, is above all a result of the development of state-monopoly capitalism. But that is not the only thing. They are lured by the prospect of deciding the destinies of millions of people, dictating their will to other countries, the possibility of controlling nuclear weapons; they are also driven there by anxiety for the future of the social system which secures them wealth and a seat among the high and mighty.

Such is the logical consummation of the historical evolution of the capitalists in the age when the system of private property and exploitation is increasingly eroded by its general crisis.

Capitalism and Racism

The Constitution of the United States, if we are to believe its preamble, was in part established and ordained to "insure domestic tranquility." No greater threat to domestic tranquillity exists than an outcast minority, denied justice and the blessings of liberty. In the sixties the visible effects of racism were ghetto riots and revolutionary politics; the seventies are increasingly characterized by individualistic acts of illegal expropriation, known familiarly as muggings. Capitalism has thus been transmitted to the ghetto in a deformed variant, highly distasteful to those engaged in socially accepted capitalist practices. (It should be noted, however, that the victims of criminal violence are, as often as not, black residents of the ghetto itself.) By virtue of their urban concentration, blacks, who represent only a fraction more than 10 percent of the population, are just as much the key to contemporary American politics as a century ago, when a civil war was fought to determine their status.

America's future, then, will be determined to a considerable extent by its black minority. Reading 52, by Thaddeus H. Spratlen, reviews black economic progress over the last decade, which a number of writers have termed an era of remarkable development. Spratlen shows these studies to be overstated to the point of distortion. Moreover, since his paper was written the absolute and relative position of black workers has deteriorated under the impact of the current downturn. Usually the last to have been hired (and therefore having no seniority), they are the first to be fired. And because a larger percentage of them are among the poor, astronomical increases in food prices have hit blacks hardest. Depressions are especially damaging, since losses in current income cannot be tided over by drawing upon meager or nonexistent savings. In 1966, for example, a mere 1.1 percent of the money in banks was held by black families; the value of their stock holdings was virtually non-existent at 0.1 percent; and their ownership of other selected assets—in what is most probably an *under*statement of wealth disparity—was only 1.9 percent (see, Robert S. Browne, "Wealth Distribution and Its Impact on Minorities," *Review of Black Political Economy*, Summer 1974, pp. 28–35). These figures confirm what we already knew—blacks do not share in the benefits of American prosperity, and they are much worse off than others when it dwindles. Nor is there evidence that the gap is being closed.

These statistics suggest an important question: Does capitalism tend to erode or to reinforce the pattern of inequality revealed by these studies? In Reading 53, Thomas Sowell dissects the discriminatory features of the marketplace from an orthodox perspective. He acknowledges that there are monopolistic situations where job discrimination is profitable, but in general, he argues, the capitalist market tends to reduce rather than increase discrimination. In contrast to Sowell, Michael Reich points to statistical evidence that capitalists *do* benefit from racism and that white workers lose by it (see Reading 54). Reich shows how the disunity created by racism weakens the bargaining position of labor, and how racial antagonism results in reduced public expenditures for services (particularly education) that most benefit the working class.

The rat-infested, crime-ridden ghettos of our big cities are visible proof of past and present failures. As for the future, American liberalism is faced with a dilemma. If no effort is made to achieve reform, urban blight, with all its social costs—addiction, crime, riots, burgeoning welfare budgets, and, of course, racist backlash—will continue to accelerate. On the other hand, limited but meaningful reforms raise the expectations of black people to a level far beyond the ability of our current society to satisfy. At the same time, these expectations increase the number of articulate black intellectuals. Thus, limited reform tends ironically to make black people more revolutionary, not less. The way out of this quandary is not to deny progress to black people or to restrict their rights, but to restructure American society according to principles that will bring about equality and justice.

52

The Record and Rhetoric of Black Economic Progress

Thaddeus H. Spratlen

COMPARISONS OF BLACK ECONOMIC STATUS

Comparisons of black economic status are based primarily on U.S. Bureau of the Census data. Economic indicators presented include changes with respect to income, poverty, patterns of employment, levels of unemployment, housing characteristics, and ownership of automobiles and household durable goods. Whenever possible data series are presented for the years 1960–1972. In some instances shorter time periods are compared. Attention is focused primarily on two measures: annual percentage changes and changes in the gap or disparity between whites and nonwhites. Absolute quantities are also compared to highlight certain relationships.

Comparisons of Changes in the Income of Blacks

Income comparisons are generally presented for whites and nonwhites. The "nonwhite" grouping, however, results in a general overstatement of conditions for Blacks. Other nonwhites tend to have higher incomes. As an example, for median income the proportion for Blacks is 2–3 percentage points (approximately 3.0 percent–3.5 percent) below that of other nonwhites. The annual median income for Blacks is about $200 less than that of other nonwhites. In addition, the distribution of income tends to be more unevenly distributed for Blacks than for other groups. Thus, relying on Census income data tends to show somewhat more favorable conditions than actually exist for Blacks.

Data on income changes over time for whites and nonwhites are summarized in Tables 1 and 2. The former shows the changing percentage distribution by income level; the latter aggregate income shares of families by quintiles or fifths. The data in Table 1 are used more frequently than that in Table 2 primarily because of the interest in showing the upward movement of family income and income earners. However, because changes are occurring in absolute numbers and points in time, it is difficult to avoid misrepresenting or misinterpreting the changes which have actually occurred.

Table 2 is more appropriate for describing true income gains with respect to inequality and share of aggregate income. It can be seen that the second and fourth quintiles of black families did not change their share of aggregate income between 1960 and 1972. The income share of the lowest quintile increased by 33 percent. However, for white families in the lowest quintile the income share doubled. Interestingly, whereas white families in the highest quintile maintained the percentage share held in 1960 (50.7 percent), the share of income earned by black families in the highest quintile declined from 53.3 percent to 50.2 percent. But the major fact which emerges

TABLE 1 □ TOTAL MONEY INCOME OF FAMILIES AND UNRELATED INDIVIDUALS, UNITED STATES, 1960–1972, BY RACE OF HEAD OF HOUSEHOLD

| | Number (Thousands) | | Per Cent Distribution | | | | | | | | | | | | |
| | | | Under $3,000 | | $3,000–4,999 | | $5,000–6,999 | | $7,000–9,999 | | $10,000–11,999 | | $12,000–14,999 | | $15,000 & Over | |
Year	White	Nonwhite	White	Nonwhite	White	Nonwhite	White	Nonwhite	White	Nonwhite	White	Nonwhite	White	Nonwhite	White	Nonwhite
1972	48,477	5,896	5.9	17.7	8.6	17.5	9.7	14.0	16.7	17.1	11.8	8.6	15.2	9.5	32.2	15.6
1971	47,641	5,655	6.9	19.4	9.3	17.6	10.8	15.2	18.6	17.8	13.0	8.9	15.0	9.0	26.4	12.2
1970	46,535	5,413	7.5	20.1	9.6	16.9	11.3	16.4	20.1	18.2	13.1	8.9	14.8	8.4	23.7	10.8
1969	46,022	5,215	8.1	20.4	9.7	19.3	11.8	17.0	21.9	19.5	13.6	8.1	14.5	7.5	20.6	8.2
1968	45,437	5,074	8.9	22.8	11.0	21.9	14.3	16.5	24.0	17.7	13.0	8.1	13.1	6.6	15.7	6.3
1967	44,814	5,020	10.7	27.2	11.9	21.5	16.0	17.7	25.1	16.9	12.4	6.5	11.2	5.2	12.8	5.0
1966	44,110	4,954	12.2	30.2	12.6	23.3	17.7	17.8	25.4	16.5	12.2	5.9	10.0	4.0	10.1	2.4
1965	43,497	4,782	14.0	35.3	14.4	25.6	19.1	16.3	25.5	13.7	10.7	4.4	8.1	3.3	8.3	1.4
1964	43,081	4,754	15.4	37.3	15.9	25.9	20.1	16.4	24.4	12.1	10.0	4.1	7.3	2.4	6.8	1.8
1963	42,663	4,773	15.8	43.1	17.0	24.4	21.8	16.0	23.8	10.8	9.0	2.5	6.6	1.6	5.9	1.6
1962	42,437	4,561	17.1	44.8	18.4	26.5	23.1	15.4	22.3	8.1	8.1	2.7	5.7	1.6	5.3	0.8
1961	41,888	4,543	18.6	47.5	19.4	24.4	22.7	13.8	22.1	9.0	7.1	2.7	5.0	1.7	5.1	1.2
1960	41,123	4,333	19.2	46.5	19.9	24.5	24.5	15.4	21.3	8.7	6.6	2.7	4.6	1.6	4.1	0.6

TABLE 2 □ PERCENTAGE SHARE OF AGGREGATE INCOME RECEIVED BY EACH FIFTH OF FAMILIES, RANKED BY INCOME, BY RACE OF FAMILY HEAD, 1960–1972

Race of Family Head and Year	Lowest Fifth	Second Fifth	Third Fifth	Fourth Fifth	Highest Fifth	Total	Top 5 Percent
White							
1972	3.4	8.3	13.9	23.8	50.7	100.0	21.5
1971	3.5	8.2	14.0	24.3	50.0	100.0	20.4
1970	3.5	7.9	13.8	24.4	50.5	100.0	20.8
1969	3.3	7.8	13.9	24.2	50.8	100.0	20.8
1968	3.3	7.8	13.9	24.2	50.8	100.0	20.8
1967 [1]	3.1	7.5	13.5	24.6	51.4	100.0	21.1
1966	3.4	7.8	13.8	24.2	50.9	100.0	21.1
1965	2.9	7.5	13.7	25.1	50.8	100.0	20.0
1964	2.5	7.1	12.9	24.4	53.1	100.0	23.2
1963	2.6	7.5	12.9	25.1	51.9	100.0	20.0
1962	2.7	7.5	13.0	24.9	51.9	100.0	20.5
1961	2.3	7.2	13.4	24.9	52.2	100.0	21.5
1960	1.7	7.5	14.0	26.1	50.7	100.0	20.1
Negro and Other Races							
1972	2.8	8.0	13.7	25.0	50.2	100.0	19.0
1971	3.3	8.2	13.4	24.4	50.7	100.0	19.1
1970	3.6	8.1	13.8	25.2	49.4	100.0	17.4
1969	3.5	7.9	14.4	25.0	49.2	100.0	17.7
1968	3.6	8.3	13.7	25.1	49.3	100.0	17.3
1967 [1]	3.0	8.2	13.8	25.4	49.7	100.0	18.1
1966	3.0	8.2	13.7	24.9	50.2	100.0	18.4
1965	2.9	8.4	13.9	25.5	49.3	100.0	17.0
1964	3.1	8.1	13.4	24.7	50.7	100.0	17.0
1963	2.3	8.4	13.9	24.6	50.9	100.0	17.4
1962	2.9	8.7	13.2	22.6	52.7	100.0	20.8
1961	1.9	7.6	12.6	24.3	53.7	100.0	20.1
1960	2.1	7.7	12.0	24.9	53.3	100.0	19.2

[1] Revised

is that the overall distribution of income changed relatively little during the 1960's.

Table 2 is of interest in another respect. It helps to put in perspective the aspect of change and progress. Income redistribution provides a better basis or standard from which to analyze economic gains than comparisons of shifting percentages at given income levels at different points in time.

With respect to total money income it has been reported that for 1959 Blacks earned 6.2 percent of the total for the nation as a whole. The dollar figure was $19.7 billion. For 1972 the proportion was 6.7 percent of $773 billion; in dollars, $51.8 billion. In terms of personal income, then, there was not a marked increase as measured by changes in the proportion of total personal income earned by Blacks.

Income comparisons also focus on the median family income of Blacks and whites. Dollar comparisons are shown in Table 3 along with the income gap which has persisted between the incomes of families and unrelated individuals. An index of percentage changes with 1960 as the base year is also shown.

TABLE 3 □ MEDIAN INCOME OF FAMILIES AND UNRELATED INDIVIDUALS, BY RACE OF HEAD OF HOUSEHOLD, UNITED STATES, 1960–1971

Year	Median Income Amount White	Median Income Amount Nonwhite	Nonwhite Income Gap Amount	Nonwhite Income Gap Percent	Index (1960 = 100) White	Index (1960 = 100) Nonwhite
1972	$11,549	$7,106	$4,443	38.5	198	220
1971	10,672	6,714	3,958	37.1	183	208
1970	10,236	6,516	3,721	36.4	175	202
1969	9,794	6,190	3,604	36.8	171	191
1968	8,937	5,590	3,347	37.5	153	173
1967	8,274	5,141	3,133	37.9	142	159
1966	7,792	4,674	3,118	40.0	134	145
1965	7,251	3,994	3,257	44.9	124	124
1964	6,858	3,839	3,019	44.0	118	119
1963	6,548	3,465	3,083	47.1	112	107
1962	6,237	3,330	2,907	46.6	107	103
1961	5,981	3,191	2,790	46.6	103	99
1960	5,835	3,233	2,602	44.6	100	100

Throughout the thirteen years including 1960 and 1972 the dollar amount of the median income gap between Blacks and whites widened from $2,602 to $4,443, an increase of $1,841 or 70.8 percent. Since it is actual dollars of income which provide purchasing power, this is crucial to any interpretation of change. In actual dollars, then, as shown in Table 3, the black position worsened relative to the median income of whites. The percentage gap in median income did narrow a modest 6.1 percentage points (or 13.7 percent). Yet, the narrowing from 44.6 percent to 38.5 represented an annual percentage change of only 0.47 percent per year. With such a trend increment, the relative gap in median income between Blacks and whites would close in about 77 years.

Relative improvement in median income position is also shown with a median income index, using 1960 as a base year. The median for whites increased 98 percent throughout the period. It more than doubled for nonwhites, with an increase of 120 percent.

Overall, then, income gains have been quite modest. Much disparity remains. Moreover, even with the favorable circumstances which supported black gains during the 1960's, that pace of change would only close the median income gap over the next three-quarters of a century. That is fifteen years more than a black male born in 1968 could expect to live. Thus, to Blacks and the economy as a whole regarding the short-fall in demand, output, and in meeting basic human needs, the record is not one about which we can be jubilant. To be optimistic is to call forth a strong act of faith.

Comparisons of Changes in the Level of Black Poverty

The relatively larger portion of nonwhites at low income levels is further illustrated in the high incidence of poverty. The proportion of nonwhite persons below the low income level increased by 14 percent in the comparison of 1960 and 1972. The pattern of the entire period is shown in Table 4. Another way of viewing the comparisons is to recognize that nonwhites represent approximately 18 percent of the total population. The proportion of nonwhite poor is about twice as high.

TABLE 4 ☐ PERSONS BELOW THE LOW INCOME LEVEL, BY RACE OF HEAD OF HOUSE-
HOLD, UNITED STATES, 1960–1971

Year	Number of Persons (Thousands)		Nonwhite as Percent of All Below Low Income Level	Index of Change in Number of Persons Below Low Income Level (1960 = 100%)	
	White	Nonwhite		White	Nonwhite
1972	16,200	8,300	33.9	56	72
1971	17,780	7,780	30.4	63	67
1970	17,484	7,936	31.2	62	69
1969	16,659	7,488	31.0	59	65
1968	17,395	7,994	31.5	61	69
1967	18,983	8,786	31.6	67	76
1966	20,751	9,673	31.8	73	84
1965	22,496	10,689	32.2	79	93
1964	24,957	11,098	30.8	88	96
1963	25,238	11,198	30.7	89	97
1962	26,672	11,953	30.9	94	104
1961	27,890	11,738	29.6	99	102
1960	28,309	11,542	29.0	100	100

There was, however, a reduction in the overall number of nonwhites as well as whites below the low income level. The percentage changes are also presented as an index series in Table 4. Actually 57 percent as many whites were below the low income level in 1972 as there were in 1960. The proportion was 72 percent for nonwhites.

More specifically with reference to Blacks, data are available only for the years 1966 through 1972. The total number decreased from 8.9 million (31.1 percent of all below the low income level or almost three times the representation in the total population) to 7.7 million. This was a reduction of only 1.2 million or 13.5 percent. The number of whites at this income level decreased by 16.1 percent but on a number base 2.2 times as large.

It is revealing to note that while the aged poor (those 65 years of age and older) make up about one-fifth of whites who are below the low income level, less than 10 percent of nonwhites are poor because of their aged status. In addition, over three times as many black families with male heads of household remained among the poor (16 percent vs. 5 percent in 1972). Over twice as many black households as white below the low income level were headed by a female in 1972 (53 percent vs. 24 percent). Thus, there was a substantially larger proportion of working poor among Blacks than among whites. It should be added that black households headed by women are subject to the compounded restrictions of racism and sexism.

With reference to the percentage of each group that falls below the low income level, the pattern which occurred is presented in Table 5. The incidence of poverty is over three times as great among Blacks as it is among whites. About one-third of the black population still is below the low income level. While this proportion was well over 50 percent in 1960, substantial disparity in the incidence of poverty among Blacks remains.

When comparisons are made between nonwhites and whites over the entire period (1960–1972), the percentage of whites in poverty was reduced by 43 percent; for nonwhites 28 percent. Thus, nonwhites fared rather poorly in comparison with whites in rising above the low income level.

TABLE 5 □ PER CENT DISTRIBUTION OF PERSONS
BELOW THE LOW INCOME LEVEL, BY RACE OF HEAD
OF HOUSEHOLD, UNITED STATES, 1960–1971

Year	Whites	Nonwhites	Blacks
1972	9.0	32.0	33.0
1971	9.9	30.9	32.5
1970	9.9	32.0	33.5
1969	9.5	31.0	32.2
1968	10.0	33.5	34.7
1967	11.0	37.2	39.3
1966	12.2	41.7	41.8
1965	13.3	47.1	NA
1964	14.9	49.6	NA
1963	15.3	51.0	NA
1962	16.4	55.8	NA
1961	17.4	56.1	NA
1960	17.8	55.9	NA

NA—Not Available

Comparisons of Changes in Employment and Occupational Distribution

In terms of broad occupational groups, nonwhites improved their job
status between 1960 and 1972. In most of the ten categories presented in
Table 6, the relative changes were greater for nonwhites than for whites.
The largest percentage increases occurred in two categories: professional,
technical, and kindred workers—148 percent for nonwhites and 49 percent
for whites; and clerical and kindred workers—147 percent for nonwhites and
41 percent for whites. The number of sales workers almost doubled during
the period. Yet this occupation remains as one in which nonwhites are
grossly underrepresented. Table 6 also identifies another pattern of change.
In the lower-paying occupations there were also relatively larger decreases
in the number of nonwhite farmers and farm workers as well as private
household workers—69 percent vs. 35 percent and 41 percent vs. 14 percent,
respectively, for nonwhites and whites.

But such changes in job categories tend to obscure the considerable
disparity which remains. For relative comparisons an index of occupational
representation is presented along with other data in Table 7. Using the overall representation of nonwhites in the employed labor force as a base, the
index indicates relative representation of nonwhites. Thus, there are proportionately only 62 percent as many nonwhite professional, technical, and
kindred workers as there are whites in these occupations. The index is
smallest in the sales and the nonfarm managerial occupations (34 and 38,
respectively). The greatest over-representation occurs among private household workers (384) and other service workers (202). Such disparity remains
after the gains have been measured or allowed for.

As reflected in the indexes of occupational disparity (Table 7) the
pattern is clear: even where appreciable gains have been made substantial
disparity remains. Parity does not exist in any of the occupational groups.
The most favorable index relationship is shown for clerical and kindred
workers and farmers and farm laborers. These are generally not well-paying
job categories (especially in the positions held by nonwhites). Moreover, it
should be recalled that if data for Blacks only were compared (rather than

TABLE 6 □ EMPLOYED PERSONS BY OCCUPATION, UNITED STATES, 1960 AND 1972
(Numbers in Thousands, Annual Averages)

| Occupation | 1960 | | 1972 | | Change 1960 to 1972 | | | |
| | | | | | Number | | Percent | |
	White	Nonwhite	White	Nonwhite	White	Nonwhite	White	Nonwhite
Total	58,850	6,927	73,074	8,628	14,224	1,701	24.2	24.6
Professional, technical, and kindred workers	7,138	331	10,638	821	3,500	490	49.0	148.0
Managers and administrators, except farm	6,889	178	7,711	320	822	142	11.9	79.8
Sales workers	4,123	101	5,161	193	1,038	92	25.2	91.1
Clerical and kindred workers	9,259	503	13,007	1,240	3,748	737	40.5	146.5
Craftsmen and kindred workers	8,139	415	10,061	749	1,922	334	23.6	80.5
Operatives, including transport	10,536	1,414	11,708	1,841	1,172	427	11.1	30.2
Nonfarm laborers	2,602	951	3,367	850	765	-101	29.4	-10.6
Farmers and farm workers	4,335	841	2,806	263	-1,529	-578	-35.3	-68.7
Service workers, except private household	4,836	1,214	7,763	1,766	2,927	552	60.5	45.5
Private household workers	991	982	853	584	-138	-398	-13.9	-40.5

TABLE 7 □ NONWHITE WORKERS AS A PROPORTION OF ALL WORKERS BY OCCUPATION, UNITED STATES, 1960 AND 1972

Occupation	Percent 1960	Percent 1972	Percentage Point Change 1960–1972	Change in Percentage Points Required to Reach 10.6 as of 1972 [1]	1972 Index of Occupational Representation [2]	Index of Occupational Disparity [3] 1960	Index of Occupational Disparity [3] 1972
Total	10.5	10.6	0.1	–	100	84 [4]	85 [4]
Professional, technical, and kindred workers	4.4	6.6	2.2	4.0	62	39	65
Managers and administrators, except farm	2.5	2.0	1.5	6.6	38	22	35
Clerical and kindred workers	5.2	8.7	3.5	1.9	82	46	81
Craftsmen and kindred workers	4.9	6.9	2.0	3.7	65	43	63
Operatives, including transport	11.8	13.6	1.8	(3.0)	(128)	(114)	(123)
Nonfarm laborers	26.8	20.2	-6.6	(9.6)	(191)	(311)	(215)
Farmers and farm workers	16.2	8.6	-7.6	2.0	81	(164)	79
Service workers, except private household	20.1	21.4	1.3	(10.8)	(202)	(213)	(193)
Private household workers	49.8	40.7	-9.1	(30.1)	(384)	(835)	(567)

[1] Proportion of nonwhites in the labor force based on employed and unemployed persons, 1972. Numbers in parenthesis represent excesses or over-representation of nonwhites.
[2] Based on 1972 proportion as 100.
[3] Ratio of the nonwhite to white proportion times 100.
[4] Based on proportion of total employed to total in labor force—employed and unemployed, 10.5 vs. 12.4 in 1960 and 10.6 vs. 12.4 in 1972.

all nonwhites) the extent of disparity would be greater still. Furthermore, such broad groupings obscure the fact that nonwhites in general and Blacks in particular are concentrated in the lower paying, entry-level positions, regardless of occupation.

Comparisons of Changes in the Level of Black Unemployment

Of all the widely used economic indicators of black economic status, the least change has occurred in reducing the level of continual, near-depression levels of black unemployment. Conditions in this critically important dimension of economic life underscore the gaps in the prosperity and improvements which have occurred. The situation is especially bad for nonwhite youth.

It should be noted that whites experienced essentially full-employment levels for several years during the 1960's, black unemployment remained at a ratio of almost consistently twice that of whites. As shown in Table 8, the level in 1972 was only slightly below what it was in 1960.

When viewed in relation to age and sex comparisons rather similar patterns emerge. However, the unemployment gap did narrow considerably for nonwhite adult males. Teenagers fared badly with respect to un-

TABLE 8 □ UNEMPLOYMENT RATES FOR WHITES AND NONWHITES, UNITED STATES, 1960–1972 (ANNUAL AVERAGES)

Year	Whites	Unemployment Index [1]	Nonwhites	Unemployment Index [1]
1972	5.0	114	10.0	227
1971	5.4	123	9.9	225
1970	4.5	102	8.2	186
1969	3.1	70	6.4	145
1968	3.2	73	6.7	152
1967	3.4	77	7.4	168
1966	3.3	75	7.3	166
1965	4.1	93	8.1	184
1964	4.6	105	9.6	218
1963	5.0	114	10.8	245
1962	4.9	111	10.9	248
1961	6.0	136	12.4	282
1960	4.9	111	10.2	232

[1] Based on average rate for whites throughout the period 1960–1972. The base rate is $57.4 - 53 = 4.4$.

employment over the period. The situation worsened for whites as well as nonwhites. The rate was 6.7 times as great for nonwhite teenagers as it was for whites generally; it was 2.4 times as great as that for white teenagers. (See Table 9 for further comparisons.)

Although not presented here in detail, when comparisons are made as to length of period unemployed and location of workers in central cities even greater disparity exists. Thus, nonwhite teenage unemployment in metropolitan areas was 36.1 percent in 1971 (and only 17.5 percent for white teenagers). Whereas 2.4 percent of the nonwhite labor force was unemployed for 13 weeks or more, the proportion for whites was only 1.3 percent —relatively 46 percent less. Thus, the problem of utilizing the available nonwhite population in the workforce is little closer to being relieved or solved now than it was in 1960. Indeed with respect to teenagers and others with limited skills and nonwhites who live in central cities the situation is worse than it was a decade ago.

Using an unemployment index to compare 1960 and 1972, the modest improvement in the level of unutilized manpower is shown in Table 9. The index dropped from 196 to 136 for nonwhite adult men. This amounted to a decline of almost one-third. Note, however, that 89 percent more adult nonwhite males were unemployed than white males.

The relationships involving unemployment clearly illustrate that this indicator shows less improvement than any other area. It would be appropriate to say that progress has been virtually blocked in closing the black unemployment gap. Its added significance lies in the fact that this is the most plentiful and valuable resource available to the black community.

Comparisons of Changes in Housing Conditions

Despite a sizable increase between 1960 and 1970 in the number of dwelling units occupied by Blacks which had complete plumbing facilities, housing conditions remain a major area in which disparity between Blacks and whites continues at a high level. Thus, the incidence of inadequate

TABLE 9 □ EMPLOYMENT RATES BY SEX AND AGE, UNITED STATES, 1960 AND 1972

Group	1960 Whites Rate	1960 Whites Unemployment Index[1]	1960 Nonwhites Rate	1960 Nonwhites Unemployment Index[1]	1972 Whites Rate	1972 Whites Unemployment Index[1]	1972 Nonwhites Rate	1972 Nonwhites Unemployment Index[1]
Total	4.9	100	10.2	208	5.0	100	10.0	200
Adult men	4.2	86	9.6	196	3.6	72	6.8	136
Adult women	4.6	94	8.3	169	4.9	98	8.8	176
Teenagers (Persons 16–19 years old)	13.4	273	24.4	498	14.2	284	33.5	670

[1] Based on overall average rate of total white unemployment in 1960 and 1972, respectively.

plumbing is at least 2.5 times greater than that for whites. Although only about 17 percent of nonwhites (data for Blacks were not reported) lack some or all plumbing facilities in their homes, the figure for whites was only 5 percent. Also, the overall pattern reflected in Table 10 obscures substantial regional differences. As an example, even for 1970, 49 percent of nonwhites living outside of metropolitan areas lacked some or all plumbing facilities. The figure for whites was only 9 percent. It should also be noted that in view of the health and building standards prevailing in the society, the plumbing characteristics indicated could describe dwelling units which are highly inadequate for decent living accommodations.

Another measure of housing conditions pertains to the median value of dwelling units. In 1970 the median value for units occupied by whites was $17,700, for nonwhites $11,700, a difference of $6,000 or 34 percent. In addition, higher proportions of the units occupied by nonwhites have more people per room. Thus, over twice as many of both black owner-occupied and renter-occupied dwelling units have 1.01 or more persons per room than white-owner- or renter-occupied units. But such a number still fails to reveal the actual extent of overcrowding and congestion which characterize the dwelling units occupied by Blacks. Available data on housing also do not reveal the fact that despite a median value two-thirds that of whites, nonwhites have access to only a minute portion of new housing. Further evidence of disparity is suggested by the fact that the reported median value of white homes was 77 percent of estimated existing home cost (at $23,000). The figure for nonwhites was 51 percent.

But as to progress, it must be noted that despite the importance of housing as a basic part of economic well being, available measures of improvements over time do not convey many of the essential aspects of housing quality. To be sure, we can cite the substantial decline in dilapidated

TABLE 10 ☐ NUMBER OF OCCUPIED HOUSING UNITS BY AVAILABILITY OF COMPLETE PLUMBING FACILITIES, UNITED STATES, 1960 AND 1970 (Numbers in Thousands)

	1960		1970	
	Whites	Nonwhites	Whites	Nonwhites
With All Plumbing Facilities [1]	42,190	3,048	53,883	5,139
Percent of Respective Total Occupied Units	88.1%	59.2%	95.3%	83.2%
Percent Increase 1960 to 1970	–	–	27.7%	68.6%
Lacking Some or All Plumbing Facilities [1]	5,689	2,096	2,647	1,041
Percent of Respective Total Occupied Units	11.9%	40.8%	4.7%	16.8%
Percent Decrease 1960 to 1970	–	–	53.5%	50.3%

[1] "Complete (or basic) plumbing facilities" are a flush toilet and a bathtub or shower for the exclusive use of the occupants of the housing unit, and hot piped water. A housing unit is considered "lacking some or all plumbing facilities" if it also does not have one or more of the facilities or if it has plumbing facilities which also are used by the occupants of another unit.

units, or in units lacking certain plumbing facilities. Yet the fact remains that Blacks remain largely underhoused. The housing conditions which existed in the late 1960's prompted the National Commission on Urban Problems to conclude that: "the results achieved thus far under the existing programs related to housing for low- and middle-income families and individuals have fallen far short of objectives. No substantial progress has been made in meeting the backlog of needs."

Comparisons of Automobile and Durable Goods Ownership

Because automobiles and durable goods comprise important areas of ownership, they reflect to a large degree the financial position of households. Actually, wealth comparisons would be more instructive. But, except for data provided through the Survey of Consumer Finances, there are no time series data available for comparing the wealth of black and white households.

In this latter connection it seems worthwhile to call attention to the status of Blacks and whites in terms of wealth. Data for 1967 indicate that black families have about 18.8 percent of the wealth of white families. The range is from a ratio of 16.1 percent for families with incomes between $2,500–4,999 to 47.3 percent for those earning between $15,000–19,999. However, for some asset categories the ratio is shockingly low—a meager 6.2 percent of liquid financial assets (stocks, money in banks, and government bonds); but only 0.7 percent of all financial assets. Clearly, wealth is the most disparate of the key economic indicators of black-white economic status. Whatever the progress that has been made, Blacks still have at least an 80 percent overall wealth gap to close.

In turning to car ownership, which can be compared for a number of years, data are presented in Table 11. Of course, it would be far more instructive to know the figures on equity rather than current expenditures. This would show the greater liabilities, higher credit costs and payments, and generally more unfavorable position than are indicated in the pattern of car purchases. More recent comparisons (for July 1972) showed that the number of cars owned per 100 households was 121 for white households and 72 for Blacks; for new cars the figures were 61 and 25, respectively. There is, then, approximately, a 60 percent (used car) and 40 percent (new car) ratio for Blacks as compared to whites.

TABLE 11 □ MEAN NUMBER OF CARS PURCHASED PER 100 HOUSEHOLDS, UNITED STATES, 1967–1972

Year	Whites	New Cars Blacks	Blacks (100) Whites	Whites	Used Cars Blacks	Blacks (100) Whites
1972	13.6	4.6	33.8%	23.4	14.3	61.1%
1971	13.4	5.1	38.1	23.4	13.4	57.3
1970	11.6	5.5	47.4	20.4	12.0	58.8
1969	13.6	5.7	41.9	21.1	15.8	74.9
1968	13.7	6.4	46.7	22.5	17.5	77.8
1967	12.8	4.0	31.2	22.6	15.8	69.9

TABLE 12 □ MEAN ANNUAL HOUSEHOLD EXPENDITURES ON SE-LECTED DURABLE GOODS, BY RACE OF HEAD OF HOUSEHOLD, UNITED STATES 1967–1972
(In Dollars)

Year	Whites	Blacks	Black Expenditures as Per Cent of Whites
1972	314	227	72.3
1971	285	234	82.1
1970	272	205	75.4
1969	273	201	73.6
1968	273	194	71.1
1967	251	180	71.7

Note: Dollar amounts are sums of quarterly means reported in the sources as indicated.

In light of the importance of household durable goods purchases in the economy, another aspect of black economic status (and progress) can be interpreted from data on household expenditures. As of July 1971, black households comprised 9.8 percent of all households. About 7.7 percent of the total spending for household durables were made by Blacks. But this level of 78.6 percent of the total is a little misleading. On a per-household basis, the mean annual household expenditures are approximately 75 percent, as indicated in Table 12. This is a five-year average for the years 1968 through 1972. For individual product categories, the disparity is even greater. It is probably greatest for central air conditioners in which Blacks have about 20 percent of the number that whites have.

As to progress, average expenditures made by whites for durable goods in the six years between 1967 and 1972 increased 25 percent, those for Blacks increased 26 percent. This points once again to the notion that no real gap-closing occurred. Moreover, since the money income of Blacks was a much smaller proportion than expenditures, considerably more resources must be used to satisfy black demand for household durables. Although data were not available for the early years of the 1960's, it is clear that Blacks only kept pace during the last half of the decade. The ownership position of Blacks did not improve relative to that of whites.

CONCLUSIONS

The record of black economic progress during the 1960's and early 1970's does not support the glowing rhetoric which uses such language as "remarkable," "revolutionary," "mighty strides," and the like to describe the changes which have taken place in black economic status. Such language distorts the real content of the record.

We can see from the evidence presented that just keeping pace with whites will not result in gap-closing progress. Such advancement will ensure the maintenance of black inequality and disparity. Exaggerated interpretations of the record will have many adverse effects. Perhaps most damaging is the resistance it fosters against the massive and special efforts which are still needed to close the gaps of black-white socio-economic status.

A useful point of reference and challenge regarding the record and rhetoric of black economic progress serves as a closing thought. We should keep before us where we have come from on the road to economic progress. That is the factual record. In facing the future we have to reckon with where we are today and judge how far we have to go before we reach the goal of sharing fully and equitably in all the resources and opportunities which exist in the economy. Until this happens any progress necessarily falls short of the need to achieve all the potential gains of parity for Blacks in the economy and society. As an interpretation of the record constructive rhetoric will direct the way to the future, rather than distort the way of the past.

Finally, sound knowledge of the record and clear understanding of the rhetoric are both essential for making realistic decisions about the policies, plans, and programs needed to ensure the continued economic progress of Blacks.

53

Race and the Market

Thomas Sowell

UNPROFITABLE DISCRIMINATION

This analysis tacitly assumes that (1) employers are attracted by prospects of unusually high profits and that (2) there is no effective general collusion against a particular group. If employers were indifferent to opportunities for high profit or if the rate of profit they could earn was externally controlled, then any opportunities to hire members of ethnic groups whose pay was lower than their productivity could be passed up. There is little indication that most employers are unconcerned as between making more money and making less money. What does happen in a number of situations is that they are prevented from earning more by government agencies—regulatory commissions such as the I.C.C., F.C.C., etc.—or may be legally non-profit, as with schools, foundations, hospitals, etc. When this is so, then there is no real opportunity to earn more profit by hiring misjudged minorities or in any other way. In such circumstances, the employer can hire according to his own prejudices without paying any price in terms of foregone profits. This also applies to the government itself as a non-profit employer.

Economic theory would lead to an expectation of more discrimination in markets with externally controlled and externally limited profit rates than in unstructured and uncontrolled competitive markets. In general, this is what is found. The railroad industry, which is tightly regulated by the Interstate Commerce Commission, has long been one of the most discriminatory industries in the United States—hiring *no* Negroes at all, for decades, in many skilled jobs, and hiring substantial numbers only as Pullman porters. In the middle of the nineteenth century, before regulation, Negroes dominated railroad occupations in the South, except for conductors. The communications industry, whose profit is regulated by the Federal Communications Commission and by state regulatory agencies, likewise has a long history of discriminatory hiring far more severe than that in the economy as a whole. Other highly controlled areas of the economy, such as banking, likewise exhibit a pattern of extreme discrimination, not only against Negroes, Jews, and other minorities, but even against non-conformist personality types. It would be hard to explain this pattern by personal prejudice alone, for there is no special reason why employers in regulated industries should happen to have *more* prejudice than other employers in other industries. What is different in the regulated industries is that the *cost* of discrimination is reduced or eliminated.

Regulated industries are of course regulated by politically-appointed commissioners, so that while their hiring policies have fewer *economic* constraints (such as those which force more competitive industries to hire minorities), they are even more subject to *political* constraints. This means that while there is likely to be more racial discrimination in a regulated industry than in an unregulated industry during periods when there is no great public outcry against discrimination, the regulated industries would be forced to make a more sudden about-face on discrimination than the unregulated industries when political forces attack discrimination. An example of this is the telephone industry, a highly regulated industry which has long had an extremely low percentage of Negro employees, even in jobs such as operators and linemen, which require no special education or experience. Yet, when employment discrimination became a major political issue in the 1960's, there were great increases in the hiring of Negroes in the telephone industry—even in occupations where the total number of jobs was declining. In the South, where political pressures were not comparable, there was virtually no increase in the proportion of Negroes hired, even though the industry's employment was growing fastest in the South. In the North, *one-third* of the *new* employees hired between 1966 and 1968 were Negroes. Among electric and gas utilities also, Negro employment gains were concentrated in the North. All these public utilities are primarily *state*-regulated; more so than federally-regulated.

In short, empirical evidence confirms what economic analysis would predict: that regulated industries would have *more* discrimination than unregulated industries when this depended only on economic considerations, but would reverse themselves more rapidly than unregulated industries when discrimination became a political issue.

A legally non-profit organization is in a very similar position to the firm whose profits are limited by a regulation. It too pays no economic cost for discrimination, and could therefore be expected to be more discriminatory than unregulated, profit-seeking organizations—as long as public opinion is not aroused. But since it is typically dependent upon public contributions, grants from the government, or at least needs its tax-exempt status, it too is likely to change more drastically when the climate of opinion changes on racial discrimination. The academic world is a classic example here. In 1936, only three (3) Negro PhD holders were employed by all of the white colleges and universities in the United States. By contrast, more than three hundred (300) Negro chemists alone were employed in private industry in 1940. Just one generation later, after public opinion became aroused against racial discrimination—all this was wholly reversed. White colleges and universities began hiring black faculty members *en masse*—and lectured private industry on the need to end discrimination! It is also significant that black break-throughs in the academic world came first in the money-making part of the college—varsity athletics. Hospitals are another large area of non-profit organizations, and one which, until relatively recent times, practiced extreme exclusion and discrimination against doctors who were Jewish or black. This often extended to patients as well. One bitter irony is that the black scientist who discovered blood plasma and developed its use in transfusions died for lack of a transfusion because the hospital to which he was taken after an auto accident did not treat Negro patients.

A very similar pattern evolved in government employment. Since the government is a non-profit organization racial discrimination is free, except for political repercussions. Historically, the government as an employer was far more discriminatory than private industry, until this became politically impossible, at which point it made extremely rapid increases in minority employment, leading eventually to a higher proportion of minority employment than in private industry. In 1930, Negroes constituted only one percent of public service workers outside the post office. During Reconstruction in the South after the Civil War there had been many Negro office-holders in local government, but these were all driven out with the passing of Reconstruction. During the 1910 to 1930 period, when Negroes were making at least some occupational advances in private industry, the federal government was reducing the number of Negro employees, especially among the few at the higher level (Negro postmasters declined from 153 in 1910 to 78 in 1930), and segregation was introduced into Washington government offices "where it had scarcely occurred before."

This retrogression in the federal government was in keeping with the political trends of the time, including the increase in racial animosity by Whites as Blacks moved into previously all-white jobs in private industry and into previously all-white neighborhoods. Objective hiring by civil service test results was also amended during this period to allow the government hiring official concerned to choose among the top *three* applicants available —and a photograph was also made mandatory. In the military, there were simply no Negroes at all in the Marine Corps during World War II. The Navy, which had had large numbers of Negroes during the Civil War, and substantial numbers even in earlier wars, eliminated the remaining one percent of Negroes in its ranks at the end of World War I, and accepted no more until 1932, when it began accepting Negroes only for kitchen jobs. The Army had only two black combat officers in 1940. For both the Navy and the Army, these were major retrogressions from earlier periods. It would be difficult to find private employers in unregulated nationwide industries who moved backward to such a degree during the same period.

As in the case of public utility hiring, the rise in minority employment followed lines of political development. The number of black postal workers in northern cities tripled during the same 1910 to 1930 period, when the national trend in government employment was the other way—but when the number of black voters in northern cities was growing by leaps and bounds. In these northern states, Negroes were over-represented in the postal service. In New York City, the number of black municipal employees increased from 247 in 1917 to 2,275 in 1929. Other minorities have also been over-represented in government jobs after acquiring political strength. About half the school teachers of New York City are Jews. The Irish have long been over-represented in municipal government jobs after building political power in the nineteenth century.

After civil rights became a great political issue in the 1950's and 1960's, the federal hiring policy underwent a great reversal. In the military, Negroes were slightly over-represented. In the civilian federal agencies, Negroes gained 20 percent of all new employment in a five-year period following the establishment of the equal employment program, with almost a doubling of Blacks in the top six grades during this period, and Blacks often received fancier perquisites than their white counterparts as well.

In short, despite an officially non-racial hiring policy and despite the "merit" principle embodied in civil service systems, government hiring policies have been highly discriminatory, in one direction or the other. Like other non-profit organizations, the government's discrimination has been unconstrained by economic considerations and has varied widely according to public opinion.

In general, job discrimination has a cost, not only to those discriminated against and to society, but also to the person who is discriminating. He must forego hiring some employees he needs, or must interview more applicants in order to get the number of qualified workers required, or perhaps offer higher wages in order to attract a larger pool of applicants than necessary if hiring on merit alone. These costs do not necessarily eliminate discrimination, but discrimination—like everything else—seems to be more in demand at a low price than at a high price. The cost, of course, is of no concern to a businessman who is personally unconcerned about profit, but such businessmen are rare to begin with, and tend to get eliminated through competition, for their financial backers and creditors care about profitability even if they do not. Non-profit organizations, however, can ignore the economic cost of discrimination—though not the cost of antagonizing the public, if the public is actively opposed to discrimination.

PROFITABLE DISCRIMINATION

Under special conditions, discrimination can be made profitable. An extreme example would be if the whole white race organized into one giant monopoly to set the terms and conditions of black employment, housing, and other economic activities—and if it were prepared to retaliate against any individual white employer, realtor, merchant, etc., who violated the terms established. How feasible is this in practice? In many kinds of economic situations, it is not feasible at all. As long as each individual is seeking to maximize his individual gains,—not the collective gains of the group to which he belongs—each individual White has incentives to violate the agreement and can be prevented from doing so only by various means of policing the agreement, of widely varying effectiveness and cost. However, in some special circumstances, the cost of policing and enforcing discriminatory rules may be very small. If there are relatively few Blacks with a certain job skill, and if the mass of white workers with that skill objects to working with Blacks, then the individual employer loses little by refusing to hire Blacks and risks much (in deliberate retaliation and/or lower worker morale) if he does hire a Black. Similarly, if there are very few Blacks who can buy a home in an expensive neighborhood, the realtor or bank who facilitates their doing so may risk a large retaliation for a relatively small gain. Skin color makes policing costs very inexpensive—indeed, word may spread like wildfire when a Negro takes a job or buys a home in a place that has been all-white for many years.

The *cost* of collusion is crucial. An agreement or "understanding" that certain jobs, neighborhoods, or organizations are to be kept 100 percent free of the particular ethnic group can be policed rather cheaply, especially if the excluded groups have distinctive color (Negro, Oriental) or (less effective) distinctive names or accents. It is easy for those most determined to exclude them to tell whether the tacit exclusion is being followed by others. Once the total-exclusion policy is broken, however, it becomes much more difficult and expensive to police an understanding that *only so many* of the excluded group are to be allowed in. One more Negro, Jew, Italian, Oriental, etc., is never as noticeable as the first one, and if there are many independent businessmen involved, each can say that it is not he who is "flooding" in the formerly excluded group.

It is possible for an otherwise competitive industry to behave as a monopolist in racial matters, due to the low cost of exclusion and retaliation sometimes found in racial matters, whereas the cost of collusion and retaliation on the output or prices of the product might be too high to make it worthwhile. However, even racial exclusion requires special conditions to be feasible: that a large proportion of the dominant population feels strongly about excluding a particular group from a particular place or activity, that the cost of identifying the group and policing the "understanding" be low, and that those who feel strongest about this are willing and able to retaliate against individual members of their own group who care less or who find it profitable to violate the exclusion. Once the exclusion has been violated and significant numbers of the excluded group enter despite the exclusion, the cost of keeping out the remainder rises sharply, since the cost of identifying new entrants rises, as does the number of individual members of the dominant group who now have a vested economic interest in keeping the breach open. For these reasons, it is not uncommon for a 100 percent exclusion to last for generations—and then collapse like a house of cards. A certain street may be an iron-clad boundary around a racial ghetto, and, yet, within a few years after the first minority families cross that boundary, the whole neighborhood may be incorporated into the ghetto. In many professional sports, Negroes were totally excluded until after World War II, then once one team began to hire Negro athletes, competitive teams would be risking suicide on the playing field (and therefore at the box office) if they refused to do so.

The feasibility of collusive ethnic exclusion depends not only on conditions within the dominant group, but also on conditions within the excluded minority. The larger the number of minority group members who are *immediately* prepared to enter if the exclusion is broken, the higher the cost to each majority group member who helps maintain the agreement, in terms of his foregone profit-making opportunities. Since the strength of a chain is no greater than that of its weakest link, it is not necessary that the "average" member of the dominant group be prepared to relent in order to increase his personal earnings, but only that one or a few members be prepared to do so. The cost of retaliation, economic or social, is important only *relative* to the profit to be gained by breaching the agreement. Where substantial numbers of the excluded group are both willing and able to enter—a mass of Blacks ready to pay higher prices for better housing, or ready to become star-athletes—then individual profit-seeking is likely to cause the exclusion to give way. A new line of resistance may form elsewhere, at a neighborhood boundary further away or at the occupational level of athletic managers and executives, but how long the new line will hold depends on how long it takes for the same backlog of qualified, excluded individuals to build up.

In situations where long or costly preparations are necessary to be able to enter an excluded area—years of savings to get a down payment on a house, a costly education for a particular profession, years of specialized training to become a skilled craftsman or classical musician, etc.—the very fact that the exclusion exists tends to prevent any backlog or qualified people from building up, and therefore reduces the cost to those who maintain the exclusion. A moderately determined resistance may therefore be effective in maintaining exclusions in such circumstances, whereas an all-out resistance may fail in other areas. Even a long and costly preparation is not an effective barrier, however, where such preparation for a particular excluded field is attained as a by-product of activities in some other fields. Even in times and places where white-collar employment has been closed to Blacks, many jobs, such as school teachers in the segregated educational system, were open, so that great numbers of black women acquired an education, which also qualified them for jobs in white-collar fields in general. This backlog then became a factor in forcing breaches in the wall of exclusion around white-collar jobs. Similarly, large numbers of qualified black athletes were generated by recreational activities, college athletics, and the black professional leagues, even when there was no reason whatsoever for a black man to prepare for a career in major league baseball, football, or basketball.

The Jews are an even more striking example of this. Because they tend to have a high level of education in general, they have the prerequisites for admission to many fields at once, including those in which they may happen to be excluded at a particular time and place. One such excluded field was college and university teaching, until World War II. But once a breach appeared, the economic pressures ripped it wide open, for there were many Jewish scientists, economists, writers, etc., who could also teach their subject in college, at a time when college teachers were in great demand. Because high-quality college and university education prepares an individual for many different fields, a group with such education has a backlog of qualified individuals ready to move into any of a number of fields, and is in a position to break-through many exclusions that would otherwise hold.

This may also explain why Negroes have had far less success in breaking into skilled blue-collar fields than into other fields requiring similar time and expense in preparation. Blue-collar skills are often highly specific, so that only someone who has trained himself for the particular job is likely to be qualified, and no backlog of such persons is likely to develop as long as the exclusion itself is present.

CONSUMER GOODS MARKETS

Numerous studies have indicated that prices of goods tend to be higher and the average quality lower, in low-income ethnic neighborhoods. In addition, numerous schemes to defraud the less knowledgeable people in such neighborhoods have flourished for many years, probably as long as such neighborhoods have existed. In the nineteenth century, the Irish immigrants were cheated and swindled before they even got off the boat, and the process continued on the docks, in the rooming houses in which they usually spent their first day in America, and among travel agents who sold them fraudulent tickets to their destinations. The nineteenth century Italian immigrants were similarly exploited in innumerable ways by travel agents, landlords, bankers, labor contractors, etc. In the twentieth century, the victims are more often Negro, Puerto Rican, or Mexican-American.

In Los Angeles, for example, a clock radio selling for 19 dollars elsewhere in the city is sold for 42 dollars in the Mexican-American community. Gas ranges selling for 110 dollars elsewhere sold for 200 dollars in the Mexican-American community, and a portable television set selling for 230 dollars in the Mexican-American community sold for 270 dollars in Watts. Comparison shoppers in New York found that the same item in the same store sold for different prices to Whites, Puerto Ricans, and Blacks. According to another study, "In East Harlem, there are hardly any 'one price' stores." East Harlem has a variety of ethnic groups, with many individuals being very new to the city. A common feature of fraudulent stores in ethnic neighborhoods is the absence of price tags, for this very reason. In still another study, the Federal Trade Commission found an item selling for 165 dollars in the regular shopping areas of Washington that was selling for 250 dollars in a store specializing in low-income customers.

The question is not whether there is fraud practiced on ethnic minorities, but how much of the price and quality differences in ethnic communities is solely a result of fraud rather than of many other economic factors. What is physically the same product may have very different costs of delivery to the customer, depending upon the conditions of delivery. Supermarkets, for example, are able to operate profitably selling a standard product for less than the price charged at a small grocery store, which may be making little or no profit. This is largely because the *turnover* is faster in the supermarket; the item sits on the shelf a much shorter time before it is sold, so that a given investment in a shelf full of goods earns a return many more times in the course of a year, even if each individual return is slightly lower than in the corner grocery store, where the goods turn over fewer times a year. Low-income ethnic neighborhoods typically have relatively more small grocery stores and relatively fewer major supermarkets. Even if each item sold for the same price in ethnic neighborhood grocery stores as in other grocery stores, and the same price in ethnic neighborhood supermarkets as in other supermarkets, the average price paid in the ethnic neighborhoods would still be higher than elsewhere, simply because the mixture of grocery stores and supermarkets is different in such neighborhoods.

There are reasons why low-income communities have a different mixture of small and large stores. Major supermarket chains have lower costs of delivering goods to the customer because of a higher volume of business for each hour that a store is open—that is, for each hour that they are paying salaries to their employees. The more hours they stay open, the harder it is for them to have as high a volume of business per hour and per employee. Supermarkets are usually not open as many hours per day as the local grocery stores. Obviously they eliminate those hours which bring in the least revenue in proportion to cost. Evening hours are especially costly because of overtime pay or night differential pay for supermarket employees, or because the store may operate less efficiently after the manager has gone home, or because of the higher cost of getting a good manager who is willing to stay in the store extra long hours. Evening hours are also more costly in terms of an increased probability of getting robbed at night.

While there is a demand for supermarket services in low-income ethnic neighborhoods, there are more people in such neighborhoods who cannot rely wholly on supermarkets. People who arrive home in the evening after a day of work—especially at manual labor—may lack the time or energy to get to the supermarket before it closes. A smaller proportion of the families have wives who are at home during the day to do supermarket shopping. A smaller proportion have automobiles, so that the distance to the store is more of a factor. Because of sporadic unemployment and other financial problems, a certain proportion of the residents of low-income ethnic communities use credit in buying grocery items. Supermarkets do a cash business, eliminating the time and paperwork of credit transactions, the cost of collection agencies, and the losses from unpaid debts. Such credit arrangements are left to the small grocery store, or at least to some of them. In short, although the supermarket may deliver the same physical package as the small grocery store, it does not deliver it at the same time, or as close to home, or under the same arrangements, so that the total service that is sold may be very different and have different costs, which are passed on to the consumer. Even when the service is no different, the fact that the goods on the shelf turn over at different rates means that different prices are required to cover operating costs, which are based on time (rent, salaries, electricity, etc.). If a supermarket sells 20 refrigerators full of beer, then it has cost the local grocery store twice as much to refrigerate each can of beer. The same principle applies to operating costs in general.

In addition to different kinds of stores that are represented in low-income ethnic neighborhoods, there are generally different costs for any given kind of store. Insofar as such neighborhoods are less attractive to potential employees or managers (justifiably or not does not matter in cause-and-effect terms), the cost of operating and managing stores tends to rise. Theoretically, this could take the form of paying higher salaries to get the same quality of personnel in the ethnic community stores as in other stores. However, since companies tend to maintain standard salaries, it is more likely to take the form of attracting less efficient employees and managers for the same pay. In either case, the net result is higher costs of operation.

Insurance costs vary greatly with neighborhoods. Where there are higher rates of pilferage, robbery, arson, and civil disorder, insurance companies raise premiums accordingly, and/or reduce the coverage for a given premium, increase the "deductible" level, or otherwise make the policy less valuable. They may require additional security measures by the store as a condition of issuing a policy. Beyond some level of risk, they refuse to issue a policy at all, forcing the individual store to protect itself in various ways: self-insurance if it is part of a chain; or tying up money in a contingency fund if it is not; using more locks, screens, burglar alarms, or guards, or laying out the goods in ways designed to minimize theft, even if these designs are less efficient from other points of view. These costs, whatever form they take, are ultimately paid by the customer in the price of the product. In recent years, a new cost has been added in some ethnic communities— "voluntary" contributions to local "causes," collected by tough young men or by others who speak with the actual or apparent backing of tough young men. Such collections were also common in the nineteenth century ethnic communities, with the collectors being either graft-seeking policemen or gangs of toughs. What is new is the racial ideology associated with such collections. From an economic point of view, however, it is simply one more additional cost of doing business in some low-income ethnic communities, and its net effect is to reduce the number of individuals and institutions willing to work there, and to raise the prices to the consumers.

There is no principle of justice which causes consumers to pay the costs associated with the neighborhood. The bulk of the population, even in crime-ridden areas, are law-abiding people. It is not equity but economics which forces up the prices they pay. The differences in prices between ethnic ghettoes and middle class suburbs cannot be explained by stores charging "all that the traffic will bear" in one case and not in the other. Stores charge all that the traffic will bear in *both* cases. The traffic will just not bear as much in the middle class suburb—and the *reason* for this is that there are so many more *competing* stores. Those businesses are able to operate at lower costs because they can more readily attract efficient workers, management, capital, and low-cost insurance. They are *forced* to operate at lower cost because there are so many firms competing with one another.

For the low-income ghetto working man who has to pay more for the same can of beer chilled to the same temperature as the beer bought by a middle class suburbanite, it may seem like pointless hair-splitting whether the situation is explained economically or is simply called "exploitation." And if he has to pay more money for a lower quality of beer than the suburbanite pays for premium beer, then he may be even more likely to prefer the latter label. The fact is, if he were not Black, or Mexican, or Puerto Rican, etc., he would not have to pay as much for what he buys. Economic analysis is not philosophic justification, nor is that its purpose. What economics can do is help predict the consequences of various possible ways of dealing with the problem. While the term "exploitation" has a variety of shifting meanings, the central idea is that prices exceed cost by some unusual amount (or wages fall short of the worker's contribution to output by some unusual amount). This in turn implies that there is an unusually high rate of profit being made by the businessmen involved. Such opportunities to make profit invariably attract more businessmen and more capital. Yet, low-income ethnic communities are avoided like the plague by many chains of supermarkets, drug stores, restaurants, as well as by the mass of individual businessmen. Many corporations with branches in such neighborhoods are pulling out. If the assumption of unusually high profits were correct, there would also be great opportunities for new businesses run by members of the local ethnic community. Yet, such businesses have had a very high rate of failure. Sometimes these failures are blamed on management, sometimes on inadequate financing by the banks, sometimes on red tape, or a variety of other factors. However, the fact that highly successful supermarket chains, with well-trained and experienced management, and with millions of dollars of their own capital available, have also had to pull out, suggests that the situation itself makes success very difficult to achieve. Far from being a situation of unusually high profits, it is a situation where it is hard to break even, even when charging higher prices.

SUMMARY AND CONCLUSIONS

Discussions of discriminating economic behavior often center on the moral (immoral) aspects of such behavior, rather than on the causal factors which inhibit or intensify the translation of subjective prejudice into overt discrimination. The *cost* of discrimination is crucial—but so too is the extent to which that cost has to be borne by the discriminator, instead of being passed on under cost-plus pricing arrangements (public utilities, government contractors) or absorbed by the taxpayers (the government itself). Equally, prejudiced employers or businessmen may engage in widely differing amounts of actual discrimination, depending upon whether market conditions force them to absorb the cost of discrimination or enable them to escape those costs, partially or totally.

Where the costs of discrimination are cheap, the costs of reversing discrimination may also be cheap—so that a change in the political climate may cause the biggest changes in discriminating behavior among non-profit, profit-constrained, or governmental enterprises. The more competitive, profit-maximizing industries are forced to pay the highest price for discrimination, and therefore tend to have less discrimination than the non-profit sector when both sectors are free of political pressures. However, price controls tend to reduce (or eliminate) the cost of discrimination to competitive, profit-maximizing firms as well. Conversely, when political pressures develop for greater hiring of groups previously discriminated against, the profit-oriented firm tends to accede to such pressures much less than the non-profit enterprises.

Minorities themselves are also a major factor in both the economic and political costs of discrimination. Obviously, an aroused minority raises the political cost of discrimination. Less obviously, but no less decisively, a minority which is well-prepared for areas in which they are discriminated against raises the cost of discrimination to those who are excluding them.

As that cost rises, so too does the probability that the exclusion will give way.

The Economics of Racism

Michael Reich

In the late 1950's and early 1960's it seemed to many Americans that the elimination of racism in the United States was finally being achieved, and without requiring a radical restructuring of the society. The civil rights movement was growing in strength, desegregation orders were being issued, and hundreds of thousands of blacks were moving to Northern cities where discrimination was supposedly less severe than in the South. Government reports seemed to validate the optimism: for example, by 1969 the gap between blacks and whites in median years of schooling for males aged 25 to 29 years old was only one fourth the gap that had existed in 1960.

But by 1970 the optimism of earlier decades had vanished. Despite new civil rights laws, elaborate White House conferences, special ghetto manpower programs, the War on Poverty, and stepped-up tokenist hiring, racism and the economic exploitation of blacks has not lessened. During the past twenty-five years the absolute male black-white income gap has more than doubled, while there has been virtually no permanent improvement in the relative economic position of blacks in America. Median black incomes have been fluctuating at a level between 47 percent and 62 percent of median white incomes, the ratio rising during economic expansions and falling to previous low levels during recessions. Segregation in schools and neighborhoods has been steadily increasing in almost all cities, and the atmosphere of distrust between blacks and whites has intensified. Racism, instead of disappearing, seems to be on the increase.

Racism has been as persistent in the United States in the twentieth century as it was in previous centuries. The industrialization of the economy led to the transformation of the black worker's economic role from one of agricultural sharecropper and household servant to one of urban industrial operative and service worker, but it did not result in substantial relative improvement for blacks. Quantitative comparisons using Census data of occupational distributions by race show that the occupational status of black males is virtually the same today as it was in 1910 (the earliest year for which racial data are available).

This paper presents a radical analysis of racism and its historical persistence in America, focusing on the effects of racism on whites. The paper contrasts the conventional approach of neoclassical economic analysis— with its optimistic conclusions concerning the possibility of eliminating racism—with a radical approach—which argues that racism is deeply rooted in the current economic institutions of America, and is likely to survive as long as they do. A statistical model and empirical evidence are presented which support the radical approach and cast doubt on the conventional approach. The specific mechanisms by which racism operates among whites are also discussed briefly.

THE PERVASIVENESS OF RACISM

When conventional economists attempt to analyze racism, they usually begin by trying to separate various forms of racial discrimination. For example, they define "pure wage discrimination" as the racial difference in wages paid to equivalent workers, i.e., those with similar years and quality of schooling, skill training, previous employment experience and seniority, age, health, job attitudes, and a host of other factors. They presume that they can analyze the sources of "pure wage discrimination" without simultaneously analyzing the extent to which discrimination also affects the factors they hold constant.

But such a technique distorts reality. The various forms of discrimination are not separable in real life. Employers' hiring and promotion practices, resource allocation in city schools, the structure of transportation systems, residential segregation and housing quality, availability of decent health care, behavior of policemen and judges, foremen's prejudices, images of blacks presented in the media and the schools, price gouging in ghetto stores—these and the other forms of social and economic discrimination interact strongly with each other in determining the occupational status and annual income, and welfare, of black people. The processes are not simply additive, but are mutually reinforcing. Often, a decrease in one narrow form of discrimination is accompanied by an increase in another form. Since all aspects of racism interact, an analysis of racism should incorporate all of its aspects in a unified manner.

No single quantitative index could adequately measure racism in all its social, cultural, psychological, and economic dimensions. But, while racism is far more than a narrow economic phenomenon, it does have very definite economic consequences: blacks have far lower incomes than whites. The ratio of median black to median white incomes thus provides a rough, but useful, quantitative index of the economic consequences of racism for blacks as it reflects the operation of racism in the schools, in residential location, in health care—as well as in the labor market itself. We shall use this index statistically to analyze the causes of racism's persistence in the United States. While this approach overemphasizes the economic aspects of racism, it is nevertheless an improvement over the narrower approach taken by conventional economists.

COMPETING EXPLANATIONS OF RACISM

How is the historical persistence of racism in the United States to be explained? The most prominent analysis of discrimination among economists was formulated in 1957 by Gary Becker in his book *The Economics of Discrimination*. Racism, according to Becker, is fundamentally a problem of tastes and attitudes. Whites are defined to have a "taste for discrimination" if they are willing to forfeit income in order to be associated with other whites instead of blacks. Since white employers and employees prefer not to associate with blacks, they require a monetary compensation for the psychic cost of such association. In Becker's principal model white employers have a taste for discrimination; marginal productivity analysis is invoked to show that white employers hire fewer black workers than efficiency criteria would dictate—as a result, white employers lose (in monetary terms) while white workers gain from discrimination against blacks.

Becker does not try to explain the source of white tastes for discrimination. For him, these attitudes are determined outside of the economic system. (Racism could presumably be ended simply by changing these attitudes, perhaps by appeal to whites on moral grounds.) According to Becker's analysis, employers would find the ending of racism to be in their economic self-interest, but white workers would not. The persistence of racism is thus implicitly laid at the door of white workers. Becker suggests that long-run market forces will lead to the end of discrimination anyway—less discriminatory employers, with no "psychic costs" to enter in their accounts, will be able to operate at lower costs by hiring equivalent black workers at lower wages, thus driving the more discriminatory employers out of business.

The radical approach to racism argued in this paper is entirely different. Racism is viewed as rooted in the economic system and not in "exogenously determined" attitudes. Historically, the American Empire was founded on the racist extermination of American Indians, was financed in large part by profits from slavery, and was extended by a string of interventions, beginning with the Mexican War of the 1840's, which have been at least partly justified by white supremacist ideology.

Today, transferring the locus of whites' perceptions of the source of many of their problems from capitalism and toward blacks, racism continues to serve the needs of the capitalist system. Although an individual employer might gain by refusing to discriminate and agreeing to hire blacks at above the going black wage rate, it is not true that the capitalist class as a whole would profit if racism were eliminated and labor were more efficiently allocated without regard to skin color. I will show below that the divisiveness of racism weakens workers' strength when bargaining with employers; the economic consequences of racism are not only lower incomes for blacks, but also higher incomes for the capitalist class coupled with lower incomes for white workers. Although capitalists may not have conspired consciously to create racism, and although capitalists may not be its principal perpetuators, nevertheless racism does support the continued well-being of the American capitalist system.

Capitalist society in turn encourages the persistence of racism. Whatever the origins of racism, it is likely to take root firmly in a society which breeds an individualistic and competitive ethos, status fears among marginal groups, and the need for visible scapegoats on which to blame the alienating quality of life in America—such a society is unlikely magnanimously to eliminate racism even though historically racism may not have been created by capitalism.

Racism cannot be eliminated just by moral suasion; nor will it gradually disappear because of market forces. Racism has become institutionalized and will persist under capitalism. Its elimination will require more than a change of attitudes; a change in institutions is necessary.

We have, then, two alternative approaches to the analysis of racism. The first suggests that capitalists lose and white workers gain from racism. The second predicts the opposite—that capitalists gain while workers lose. The first says that racist "tastes for discrimination" are formed independently of the economic system; the second argues that racism is symbiotic with capitalistic economic institutions.

The two approaches reflect the theoretical paradigms of society from which each was developed. Becker follows the paradigm of neoclassical economics in taking "tastes" as exogenously determined and fixed, and then letting the market mechanism determine outcomes. A radical approach follows the Marxian paradigm in arguing that racial attitudes and racist institutions must be seen as part of a larger social system, in placing emphasis on conflict between classes and the use of power to determine the outcomes of such conflicts. The test as to which explanation of racism is superior is, in some ways, an illustrative test of the relative explanatory power of these competing social paradigms.

The very persistence of racism in the United States lends support to a radical approach. So do repeated instances of employers using blacks as strikebreakers, as in the massive steel strike of 1919, and employer-instigated exacerbation of racial antagonisms during that strike and many others. However, the particular virulence of racism among many blue- and white-collar workers and their families seems to refute the radical approach and support Becker.

THE EMPIRICAL EVIDENCE

Which of the two models better explains reality? We have already mentioned that the radical approach predicts that capitalists gain and workers lose from racism, while the conventional Beckerian approach predicts precisely the opposite. In the latter approach racism has an equalizing effect on the white income distribution, while in the former racism has an unequalizing effect. The statistical relationship between the extent of racism and the degree of inequality among whites provides a simple, yet clear test of the two approaches. This section describes that test and its results.

First we shall need a measure of racism. The index we use, for reasons already mentioned, is the ratio of black median family income to white median family income (B/W). A low numerical value for this ratio indicates a high degree of racism. We have calculated values of this racism index, using data from the 1960 Census, for each of the largest 48 standard metropolitan statistical areas (SMSA's). It turns out there is a great deal of variation from SMSA to SMSA in the B/W index of racism, even within the North; Southern SMSA's generally demonstrated a greater degree of racism. The statistical technique we shall use exploits this variation.

We shall also need measures of inequality among whites. Two convenient measures are (1) S_1, the percentage share of all white income which is received by the top 1 percent of white families, and (2) G_w, the Gini co-efficient of white incomes, a measure that captures inequality within as well as between social classes.

Both of these inequality measures vary considerably among the SMSA's; there is also a substantial amount of variation in these variables within the subsample of Northern SMSA's. Therefore, it is interesting to examine whether the pattern of variation of the inequality and racism variables can be explained by causal hypotheses. This is our first statistical test.

A systematic relationship across SMSA's between racism and white inequality does exist and is highly significant: the correlation coefficient is $-.47$. The negative sign of the correlation coefficient indicates that where racism is greater, income inequality *among whites* is also greater. This result is consistent with the radical model and is inconsistent with the predictions of Becker's model.

This evidence, however, should not be accepted too quickly. The correlations reported may not reflect actual causality, since other independent forces may be simultaneously influencing both variables in the same way. As is the case with many other statistical analyses, the model must be expanded to control for such other factors. We know from previous inter-SMSA income distribution studies that the most important additional factors that should be introduced into our model are (1) the industrial and occupational structure of the SMSA's; (2) the region in which the SMSA's are located; (3) the average income of the SMSA's; and (4) the proportion of the SMSA population which is black. These factors were introduced into the model by the technique of multiple regression analysis. Separate equations were estimated with G_w and S_1 as measures of white inequality.

In all the equations the statistical results were strikingly uniform: racism was a significantly unequalizing force on the white income distribution, even when other factors were held constant. A 1 percent increase in the ratio of black to white median incomes (i.e., a 1 percent decrease in racism) was associated with a .2 percent decrease in white inequality, as measured by the Gini coefficient. The corresponding effect on S_1 was two-and-a-half times as large, indicating that most of the inequality among whites generated by racism was associated with increased income for the richest 1 percent of white families. Further statistical investigation revealed that increases in racism had an insignificant effect on the share received by the poorest whites, and resulted in a small decrease in the income share of whites in the middle-income brackets.

THE MECHANISMS OF THE RADICAL MODEL

Within the radical model, we can specify a number of mechanisms which further explain the statistical finding that racism increases inequality among whites. We shall consider two mechanisms here: (1) total wages of white labor are reduced by racial antagonisms, in part because union growth and labor militancy are inhibited, and (2) the supply of public services, especially in education, available to low- and middle-income whites is reduced as a result of racial antagonisms.

Wages of white labor are lessened by racism because the fear of a cheaper and underemployed black labor supply in the area is invoked by employers when labor presents its wage demands. Racial antagonisms on the shop floor deflect attention from labor grievances related to working conditions, permitting employers to cut costs. Racial divisions among labor prevent the development of united worker organizations both within the workplace and in the labor movement as a whole. As a result, union strength and union militancy will be less, the greater the extent of racism. A historical example of this process is the already mentioned use of racial and ethnic divisions to destroy the solidarity of the 1919 steel strikers. By contrast, during the 1890's, black-white class solidarity greatly aided mineworkers in building militant unions among workers in Alabama, West Virginia, Illinois, and other coalfield areas.

The above argument and examples contradict the common belief that an exclusionary racial policy will strengthen rather than weaken the bargaining power of unions. But racial exclusion increases bargaining power only when entry into an occupation or industry can be effectively limited. Industrial-type unions are much less able to restrict entry than craft unions or organizations such as the American Medical Association. This is not to deny that much of organized labor is egregiously racist. But it is important to distinguish actual discrimination practice from the objective economic self-interest of union members.

The second mechanism we shall consider concerns the allocation of expenditures for public services. The most important of these services is education. Racial antagonisms dilute both the desire and the ability of poor white parents to improve educational opportunities for their children. Antagonism between blacks and poor whites drives wedges between the two groups and reduces their ability to join in a united political movement pressing for improved and more equal education. Moreover, many poor whites recognize that however inferior their own schools, black schools are even worse. This provides some degree of satisfaction and identification with the status quo, reducing the desire of poor whites to press politically for better schools in their neighborhoods. Ghettos tend to be located near poor white neighborhoods more often than near rich white neighborhoods; racism thus reduces the potential tax base of school districts containing poor whites. Also, pressure by teachers' groups to improve all poor schools is reduced by racial antagonisms between predominantly white teaching staffs and black children and parents.

The statistical validity of the above mechanisms can be tested in a causal model. The effect of racism on unionism is tested by estimating an equation in which the percentage of the SMSA labor force which is unionized is the dependent variable, with racism and the structural variables (such as the SMSA industrial structure) as the independent variables. The schooling mechanism is tested by estimating a similar equation in which the dependent variable is inequality in years of schooling completed among white males aged 25 to 29 years old.

Once again, the results of this statistical test strongly confirm the hypotheses of the radical model. The racism variable is statistically significant in all the equations and has the predicted sign: a greater degree of racism results in lower unionization rates and greater amounts of schooling inequality among whites. This empirical evidence again suggests that racism is in the economic interests of capitalists and other rich whites and against the economic interests of poor whites and white workers.

However, a full assessment of the importance of racism for capitalism would probably conclude that the primary significance of racism is not strictly economic. The simple economics of racism does not explain why many workers seem to be so vehemently racist, when racism is not in their economic self-interest. In extra-economic ways, racism helps to legitimize inequality, alienation, and powerlessness—legitimization which is necessary for the stability of the capitalist system as a whole. For example, many whites believe that welfare payments to blacks are a far more important factor in their high taxes than is military spending. Through racism, poor whites come to believe that their poverty is caused by blacks who are willing to take away their jobs, and at lower wages, thus concealing the fact that a substantial amount of income inequality is inevitable in a capitalist society.

Racism also provides some psychological benefits to poor and working-class whites. For example, the opportunity to participate in another's oppression may compensate for one's own misery. The parallel here is to the subjugation of women in the family: after a day of alienating labor, the tired husband can compensate by oppressing his wife. Furthermore, not being at the bottom of the heap is some solace for an unsatisfying life; this argument was successfully used by the Southern oligarchy against poor whites allied with blacks in the inter-racial Populist movement of the late nineteenth century.

In general, blacks as a group provide a convenient and visible scapegoat for problems that actually derive from the institutions of capitalism. As long as building a real alternative to capitalism does not seem feasible to most whites, we can expect that identifiable and vulnerable scapegoats will always prove functional to the status quo. These extra-economic factors thus neatly dovetail with the economic aspects of racism discussed in the main body of this paper in their mutual service to the perpetuation of capitalism.

Sexism and the Family

The contemporary movement for women's liberation is now almost a decade old. Men may appear to treat some feminist demands more seriously, but progress toward equality has been either slow or nonexistent. Professor Barbara Bergmann of the University of Maryland, the first president of the newly founded Eastern Economics Association, evaluates from a mainstream but feminist point of view the factors that keep "women from gaining an equal place in economic life" (see Reading 55). Bergmann concludes that sex discrimination does not pay, or rather that it does not pay the capitalist, although male employees may benefit. But her analysis of sex bias is basically the same as Becker's arguments on race, which have been trenchantly criticized by Michael Reich (see Section *b*, Reading 54). For, although certain groups of workers enjoy special monetary advantages under a racist or sexist system, the capitalist ultimately benefits from the resulting divisions that weaken the working class as a whole.

An extensive profile of women workers, one that documents their increasing importance in the labor force, is provided in Reading 56 by Carolyn Jacobson, a staff member of the Bakery and Confectionery Workers. Both Bergmann and Jacobson emphasize one of the most important barriers to equality—the fact that women who do enter the labor force are largely confined to low-status jobs at the bottom of the income pyramid.

Ultimately, the status of women reflects the role of the nuclear family in capitalist society. In a recent article, the eminent orthodox theorist, Professor Gary Becker of the University of Chicago, relates the division of labor within marriage to the market forces of supply and demand. Becker argues that discrimination and "brainwashing" may not be at the root of this division of labor. Instead, he implies that it may follow from the fact that women are "intrinsically more productive in the nonmarket sector, especially with regard to child care." One wonders whether Professor Becker would list dishwashing, dusting, and shopping as other "productive" activities in the nonmarket area. The argument is by no means convincing even on the question of child care, as logic and anthropological evidence make clear. The maverick bourgeois economist, John Kenneth Galbraith (see Reading 57), is more realistic when he identifies women's role in the household and in society as "servile." As consumption management—the running of the household—women's work permits a vast expansion of aggregate consumption. In this fashion the nuclear family buttresses the capitalist system, which is dependent on the profitable expansion of consumer goods production.

Moreover, the nuclear family promotes incredible waste. Our durable goods—automobiles, washing machines, household equipment—stand idle most of the time. Waste could be substantially reduced if people lived communally or in family clusters with sharing as a way of life. The efficiency in consumption that communal ownership (or sharing) makes possible could simultaneously reduce the work week and ecological disorders. Under capitalism, however, such developments would only bring the disaster of a depression. (Ironically, depressions induce a greater degree of sharing

as friends and relatives help each other out. But the "forced" sharing of hardship is not the same as the beneficial sharing of efficient communal living.)

Increased sales are only one example of how the nuclear family serves the needs of the capitalist order. Another is the labor disunity maintained by the isolation of family members from the larger work force. Alternative living arrangements, for example, threaten profits in more ways than one. When one lives as part of an economic community, one is freer to stand up to oppression. How many times have workers not struck (or been forced to concede) because of family obligations? Above all, the threat to capitalism lies in the solidarity of the working class. How much easier it is for the bosses to maintain labor discipline, break unions, and resist radical demands if each night workers retreat to isolated living quarters, there to make plans independent of their neighbors and fellow workers! Isolated workers are no match for the power of capital. For this reason, the evolution of new living styles among young people is one of the most exciting *political* developments of our day.

This section concludes with an article by Carol Lopate of Staten Island Community College that raises the question of whether women should be paid for the housework they do (see Reading 58). In explaining why she opposes this, Lopate illuminates some of the constraints society places on women (the "brainwashing" that Becker alludes to). She thereby raises the level of our understanding in ways that orthodox economics rarely does, given its unwillingness to study the social origins and functions of our so-called tastes. Like racism, sexism is not about to disappear in capitalist America. Radicals assert that the structure of capitalist society makes sexism (and racism) functionally useful to those in power. Only by transforming our society into one in which genuine social equality is considered the paramount goal can we eradicate evils of this kind.

55

The Economics of Women's Liberation

Barbara R. Bergmann

WHAT'S BLOCKING WOMEN'S LIBERATION?

Aside from inertia, there are four factors that have been alleged to be at work to keep women from gaining an equal place in economic life: (1) discrimination against women in employment and promotion due to male prejudice or malevolence; (2) inferior job performance by women; (3) the disinclination of many women to enter into what they view as men's roles; and (4) the profits to be made by business from keeping women in their present roles. Although not all of these factors are of equal importance, as we shall see, they tend to reinforce each other.

When we speak of employer prejudice against women we generally do not mean feelings of hatred or a desire to refrain from association with them. After all, most men are very glad to have a woman secretary right outside their office door. The most important manifestation of employer prejudice against women is a desire to restrict them to spheres that are viewed as proper for them. Everybody knows which jobs are "fit" for women: domestic and light factory work for the least educated ones; clerical and retail sales work for the high school graduates and even some of the college graduates; and teaching, nursing, and social work for those with professional inclinations. We must look to the future researches of psychologists and sociologists to tell us why human beings enjoy enforcing and conforming to occupational segregation along sex (and racial) lines, and how the occupations "belonging" to each group are selected. But the enjoyment is clearly there. In Aldous Huxley's *Brave New World*—a novel truly remarkable for the number of ominous tendencies to which it correctly called attention—each occupation is performed by genetically identical persons in identical uniforms. Huxley was satirizing not only the misuse of science and the inhumanity of the drive for efficiency but also the strong human liking for castes in economic life.

The economist Victor R. Fuchs of the National Bureau of Economic Research, who is one of the pioneers in research in women's role in the labor market, finds occupational segregation by sex to be far more extreme than occupational segregation by race. He says, ". . . one of the most striking findings is how few [detailed] occupations employ large numbers of both sexes. Most men work in occupations that employ very few women and a significant fraction of women work in occupations that employ very few men." Fuchs attributes occupational segregation and the low pay for women it entails largely to the conditioning of women by society to avoid certain fields. . . .

Up to now, the relative importance of discrimination in filling these high-paying jobs and the relative importance of women's failure to compete for them in explaining occupational segregation by sex have not really been carefully measured by anyone. In the end, it may prove statistically impossible to separate out the precise importance of the various factors. However, there is considerable evidence that discrimination is far from a negligible factor. Much of the evidence is anecdotal, but no less real for being so.

The economic results of occupational segregation for women are low wages. Women are relegated for the most part into those occupations where experience adds very little to the status and productivity of the worker as she advances in age. After a year or two a secretary is about as good as she will ever be, while her junior executive boss, who may have the same formal education as she, continues to gain in confidence, knowledge, and expertise, and of course makes commensurate advances in pay.

Because the boundaries separating the men's occupational preserve from the women's are—economically speaking—artificial and not easily changed, the women's preserve may tend to get overcrowded, especially if the proportion of women in the labor force increases. This is exactly what has been occurring. Between 1950 and 1970, the number of men working increased by 15%, while the number of women working increased by 70%.

Into what kinds of jobs did these women go? Because of employer discrimination and their own limited horizons millions of them went into the traditional women's preserve—clerical work. In that 20-year period, there was a very great increase in the number of women clerical workers: They more than doubled their numbers. . . . There was no change in the nature of the economy to require such a dramatic upsurge in clerical employment. On the contrary, computerization tends to reduce the demand for clerks. These extra women were absorbed through the classic mechanism of a flexible economy—clerks lost ground in pay and took on lower priority work. That clerical jobs of a type filled by women became relatively overcrowded is shown by the fact that during this period, wage rates in this relatively poorly paid occupation lagged still further behind all other occupational groups for men and women [1] . . . .

Interestingly, some progress apparently was made in the professional and technical group and the service worker group during the fifties and sixties. Women increased their representation in these occupations substantially, yet enjoyed better than average increases in pay rates. I take this as evidence of expanding demand for women in these fields, possibly involving some desegregation of employment in the detailed occupations that make up these two large occupational groups.

---

[1] While clerical workers have probably been in plentiful supply in the last two decades, "crowding" in an occupation in the sense we have used it here is not inconsistent with a "shortage" in the occupation. A shortage of nurses exists because the pay of nurses moves up sluggishly when demand gets ahead of supply. At the going price, nurses are hard to get because the number of nurses people want to hire exceeds the supply. But what supply there is of nurses has undoubtedly been increased artificially by the general exclusion of all but a handful of women from the medical schools and from administrative positions. If the pay of nurses were raised so as to equalize supply and demand, and thus eliminate the "shortage," that higher pay would still be considerably below what white males of equivalent talents and educational investment would get.

Allegations concerning women's inferior job performance center in the lower commitment of some women to the labor market. Many women do leave jobs for prolonged periods to give birth to and take care of babies, or to follow their husbands to another city. At any given age they have less work experience than have men of the same age on the average. A great deal has been made about women's relative lack of experience, but the truth is that in the kinds of jobs women are mostly consigned to, experience counts for very little in terms of skill or pay.

Women have been quitting jobs at an only slightly higher rate than men (the latest 1968 figures show quit rates of 2.6% per month for women in manufacturing and 2.2% for men). But calculations by Isabel Sawhill of Goucher College indicate that about half of the gap in quit rates is due to the fact that women are heavily employed in the kinds of occupations where both men and women tend to quit more often, whereas the men are heavily employed in the kinds of jobs in which stability of employment is rewarded.

Of course, there are drop-out women, and they give all women a bad name on the labor market. Unless the liberationists can succeed in making normal maternity leaves of more than 3 weeks unfashionable (as the bearing of 3 or more children has recently become unfashionable), the women who do want equality with men are going to continue to suffer guilt by association. There will also have to be a decrease in the propensity of men to accept a job in another city without consideration of the effect on the wife's career.

We come finally to the allegation, usually made by radicals out to discredit capitalism, that women's subjection is all a capitalist plot. Who benefits financially from the maintenance of the status quo? The most obvious beneficiaries of prejudice against women are male workers in those occupations in which women are not allowed to compete. This lack of competition raises pay and in certain circumstances may reduce unemployment in the occupation largely reserved for males. Of course, those wives who have a stay-at-home ideology also gain when women are excluded from their husbands' occupations. This undoubtedly accounts for some of the social pressure against women's liberation.

It is not the male workers or their wives who do the discriminating, though. The employers of the male workers (almost entirely males themselves) are the ones who do the actual discriminating, although of course they are cheered on in their discriminatory ways by their male employees. The employers may tend to lose financially, because profits are lowered when cheap female help is spurned in favor of high-priced male help. Thus, good strategy for the women's movement might be to fight against the exclusion of women from "men's jobs" and leave the equal-pay-for-equal-work battle until the former fight was won, by which time the pay issue might have solved itself. Whatever losses there are to discriminating employers are in all probability not very large. It is unlikely that profits to discriminating employers from discriminatory hiring are an important roadblock in the way of nondiscriminatory treatment for women.

Will capitalism collapse if women don't stay home and spend their time purchasing consumer goods? In fact, women who stay home are a poorer market for capitalist enterprise's products than are women who go to work. Women who stay at home bake cakes and make dresses. Women who go to work more often patronize bakeries and dress shops. A woman who leaves the home for a job will undoubtedly spend less time thinking about and seeking the detergent that will leave her clothes whiter than white, but she will probably buy the same amount of detergent, unless she starts patronizing a commercial laundry, in which case it will be the laundry that buys the detergent. Some nonworking women do make a career out of shopping and spend a great deal of money on items of doubtful utility, but the spending tendencies of most of these women would probably not be significantly reformed if they went to work. It is true that they would have to spend more dollars per hour, but they and their spendthrift male counterparts would have plenty of time, as the average workweek would tend to fall if more women took paid jobs.

To sum up, discrimination against women is an important factor in keeping women segregated by occupation and earning low pay. This discrimination does not by and large serve the economic ends of those who do the discriminating, although it does benefit male employees. The financial gains to those who do the discriminating are low or negative. The major cause served is psychological (it feels so good to have women in their "place"). The cavalier attitudes and low expectations of many women themselves concerning their paid work are also probably important and may help to rationalize some employer taboos against hiring women for occupations (such as executive) for which a considerable investment in on-the-job training by the employer is demanded. In short, for the post-liberation world to arrive, women's attitudes must be liberated, employers' attitudes must be liberated, but we may be able to do without a revolution that overthrows capitalism.

Women Workers: Profile of a Growing Force

Carolyn J. Jacobson

More American women are working today than ever before. They work largely for the same reasons men do—because they have to. In 1972, 47 percent of working women were single, widowed, divorced, separated or living with husbands who had incomes of $3,000 to $7,000. Clearly, the notion that women work only for "pin money" is not valid. Their employment is vital to the support of themselves and their families.

In 1972 there were 53.3 million families in the United States; 22 percent of these households were headed by women. Of these households headed by women, over half of the women work and are the only source of family income.

The income for these female-headed families is low. The median income in 1972 was $5,380 compared to $12,070 for husband-wife families and $10,350 for families headed by men who were divorced, separated or widowed. The disparity can be traced to fewer job opportunities for women and the lower pay women receive in general. The results of the historic discrimination against women are mirrored in these statistics.

Two in every five women working today are married. In March 1973 for every two married men in the labor force, one married woman was also working; these women, too, work out of economic necessity.

Women today spend a considerable part of their lives working. Nine of 10 American women will work at some point in their lives and more than half work at any given time. The average working woman is 38 years old, married and employed in any number of occupations and plays a major role in the American economy. This is somewhat of a contrast to 1920, when the average working woman was 28, single and limited to factory and clerical positions.

The 1970 census figures reveal that there are 33.3 million women workers in the United States, ranging in age from 16 to 70. Forty-three percent of the total American female population is working and two out of every five American workers are women. Thirteen million new jobs were available in the 1960s and women filled over 60 percent of them.

The rapidly rising inflation, an increasingly service-oriented economy, decreasing family size and legislation outlawing discrimination are factors that have prompted women to pursue careers outside the home—and emergence of the women's movement has accented this trend because of a higher female consciousness of career potentials.

Despite the influx of women into the labor force in recent years, however, their position in the labor force still does not equal men's. Their earnings continue to fall behind men's, averaging only 57.9 percent of male income. They are still in a relatively small number of occupations, most in traditionally "women's occupations" and those who do make it into other occupations find themselves in low-level jobs with limited futures.

Women are by no means newcomers to the American labor force. When the first settlers arrived in America, labor was scarce and women worked out of necessity and contributed to the survival of the community. As industrialization expanded in America, so did the female labor force, especially in manufacturing in the latter 18th and 19th centuries.

The Civil War years opened new jobs for women as men went off to the battlefields. They filled jobs as teachers, nurses and clerical workers, produced war supplies in factories and did most of the farm work. Over 50 years later, during World War I, women again entered the factories in such industries as steel, rubber, copper and oil, staffing blast furnaces as well as the sewing machines, producing uniforms and other war materials. After the war women went back to the kitchen, replaced by the returning men, only to be called out again to work in heavy industry producing war materials for World War II. At the end of the war women made up 36.1 percent of the labor force.

When peace was restored men replaced women in the factories, as had happened after previous wars. However, in 1947 almost one-third of all adult

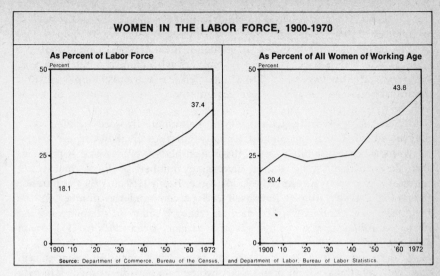

WOMEN IN THE LABOR FORCE, 1900-1970

As Percent of Labor Force

37.4

18.1

1900 '10   '20   '30   '40   '50   '60 1972

Source: Department of Commerce. Bureau of the Census.

As Percent of All Women of Working Age

43.8

20.4

1900 '10   '20   '30   '40   '50   '60 1972

and Department of Labor. Bureau of Labor Statistics.

women remained in the labor force. This trend of increased women's participation in the labor force continued to the 1970 census figure of 33.3 million women workers and the Bureau of Labor Statistics predicts that by 1980 there will be 39.2 million working women.

In 1972 there were 45.8 million husband-wife families in the United States. Of these, 1.3 million husbands were unemployed and looking for employment while 6.6 million had given up in their attempt to find jobs. Consequently, 607,000 wives of unemployed husbands and nearly 1.5 million wives whose husbands were not in the labor force were employed or looking for employment. Many of these women were their family's sole support.

Low-income women are not the only wives who work and contribute to the family's income. It is estimated that a wife contributes approximately one-fourth to one-third of the family income. The 1970 census revealed that the median income of a family of four, with the wife not working, was $9,175; with the wife working part-time or part of the year the family income rose to $11,940; and with the wife working full-time, all year, the family income reached $13,960.

Working mothers have accounted for the largest rise in women in the workforce. From 1940 to 1972 the labor force participation rate of mothers rose almost five times—from 9 to 42 percent. In contrast, the rate for all women workers rose only one and a half times—from 28 to 43 percent. Mothers have been entering the labor force since 1948 at a rate of one percent per year, despite the decline in the total population of children since 1970. In March 1973, U.S. families had 1.5 million fewer children under age 18 than the year before, but 650,000 more mothers were working.

It is clear that women with school aged children are more likely to work both full- and part-time than women with children under age 6. In March 1973 one-third of mothers with children from age 6 to 17 were employed. However, there has been a sharp rise in the number of mothers with preschool children in the labor force. The rate of working mothers with children ages 3 to 5 increased by 13.2 percent to 38.3 percent from 1960 to 1973. The participation rate of mothers with children under 3 rose by 29.4 percent over the same period.

The husband's income seems to influence the work behavior of mothers with children. In 1970, 56.9 percent of mothers with children under 6 whose husbands earned between $5,000 to $10,000 per year were also employed. But, where husbands earned $10,000 per year or more, only 23 percent of wives with small children worked.

As a class, divorced women, even including divorced women with children under 3, had the highest employment rate of all women.

As in the case of white women, the reason black women work is financial —to support their families. An increasing number of black and other minority women are entering the labor force. From 1960 to 1969 the number of employed black women increased 28.5 percent and the number in the labor force rose 25 percent. The median wage or salary of minority women employed full-time, year round rose 50 percent from 1960 to 1971—from $2,372 to $4,674.

Still progress has been limited for minority women. Differences still exist between the position of minority women and white women. Minority women are more likely than white women to be in the labor force. Approximately 50 percent of all minority women were working in 1971 as compared to 43 percent of all white women.

Minority women workers are also more likely than white women workers to be working wives or mothers. They tend to have less formal education, higher unemployment rates and lower incomes than white working women. They are also more likely to be in lower skilled and lower wage occupations. Compared to minority men, their unemployment rates are higher and generally their earnings are lower.

A growing number of black women are becoming marginal workers, that is, working part-time, usually in dead end jobs. Many work to supplement their husbands' incomes; others want to work at full-time jobs but cannot. Either there is no work available or they have the burden of caring for their families while less able to afford child care.

Despite the increasing number of women entering the labor force and recent legislation outlawing discrimination in hiring and promotion, they are still segregated by occupation and are being relegated to lower level jobs in both the public and private sectors. This is a tremendous loss of talent since 7 out of 10 women workers have at least a high school education and 1 out of 9 is a college graduate.

Since the beginning of the century women have been employed in so called "women's occupations." In 1910, over 30 percent of employed women were working as domestics and household workers and nearly 50 percent could be found in three other occupations—farm laborers, dress makers and seamstresses and teachers. In 1960, one-third of the women employed in the United States were in just seven occupations—secretarial, saleswomen in retail trade, general household workers, teachers in elementary schools, bookkeepers, waitresses and nurses. In 1970 more than a third of the working women in America were still concentrated in these occupations. In 1900 and 1960 over half of all working women were employed in jobs in which 70 percent or more of the workers were women.

Working women today are found predominantly in white-collar occupations, but only a very small percentage of them in prestigious white-collar jobs. According to the 1970 census, 15 percent of all working women were in professional and technical fields, 50 percent were in clerical jobs and less than 5 percent were managers and administrators. This represents only a slight increase over 1950.

There are relatively few professional women in most fields, with the exception of traditionally "women's professions," such as nursing and teaching. In the field of architecture 1,981 are women out of 56,000. Of 1.2 million engineers, less than 20,000 are women. Only 8.4 percent of doctors and dentists are women, while women comprise only 4.8 percent of lawyers and judges. They make up only 13 percent of the life and physical scientists, 19 percent of the social scientists and only 33 percent of the writers, artists and entertainers.

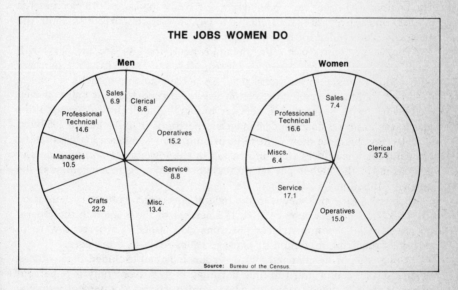

THE JOBS WOMEN DO

Source: Bureau of the Census.

The proportion of women in the total workforce varies only slightly by regions. In 1971 in the four regions in the United States, the North Central region had the lowest proportion of women in the labor force—38 percent—and the South had the highest proportion—39 percent.

Over half of all women workers in 1971 were in the 10 large states for which data were available. California and New York had the most women—3.2 and 2.9 million, respectively. For these states, the proportion of women in the total workforce ranged from 36 percent in Michigan to 40 percent in Massachusetts. Approximately one-half of all minority women workers were in the South. Three-quarters of the others were in equal proportions in the Northeast and North Central regions. The West accounted for the other one-quarter.

The occupational distribution of minority women has improved somewhat in recent years, but they still lag behind their white counterparts. The proportion of minority women workers in professional and technical occupations increased from 6 to 11 percent from 1960 to 1971 and in clerical fields from 9 to 22 percent. During the same period, the proportion in service occupations in private households decreased from 35 to 17 percent.

The 1974 Manpower Report of the President found that in comparing white and black women who began in the same occupational categories, black women experienced less upward mobility and more downward mobility than white women.

Unemployment rates can be viewed as a barometer of economic status —and women fare worse than men. Traditionally they are among the highest groups of unemployed. The annual unemployment rate for women in 1973 was 6 percent compared with 4.1 percent for men.

The unemployment rate for black women, as one would expect, is considerably higher than it is for white women or for black men. The annual unemployment rate for black women over age 20 in 1973 was 8.2 percent. The comparable rates were 5.7 percent for black males and 4.3 percent for white women over 20. This reflects a lack of job opportunities and the necessary skills called for in the labor market.

The women hardest hit by unemployment, though, are mothers with young children. The most recent figures, March 1973, reveal that mothers with children under three experienced 8.6 percent unemployment.

The 1972 Manpower Report of the President reported that more women were working in lower-paying service, blue-collar and clerical occupations and fewer in professional and managerial positions in 1970 than in 1950 and 1960. During this time their relative position to men was changing drastically, for while their numbers were increasing in the lower paid occupations and decreasing in the higher paying professions, men were moving in just the opposite direction.

Statistics for employment in the federal government reflect the situation in the economy as a whole. In 1971, 18.5 percent of the women in the federal government held administrative positions. The other 81.5 percent were in positions requiring minimum or average education and experience.

Along with being channeled into certain jobs and excluded from others, women's year round and full-time earnings in 1972 were only 57.9 percent of men's. This is down from 1955 when women earned 63.9 percent as much as men. In 1972 the median income for men and women working full-time and year round was $10,202 and $5,593, respectively. Pay differentials based on sex are greater than those based on race or national origin.

A study published in the January 1973 *American Journal of Sociology,* "Income Differences Between Men and Career Women," found in a sample of technical and professional women who had been working most of their lives ". . . earned only 66 percent of the male average in these occupations. A similar comparison made for clerical workers showed that career women earned 79 percent as much as men and among operatives and service workers . . . only half as much as men."

Many reasons have been advanced for the lower salaries women receive and the lower-skilled and lower levels of occupations they find themselves in. Many employers still hold the attitude that women's role is to complement men and thus look for women to fill only these types of positions. Some employers still believe that it is a waste of money to hire women, who they believe have a much higher turnover and absentee rate than men. A 1967 Public Health Service study, however, showed little difference between male and female turnover and absentee rates.

Seniority systems also hamper advancement opportunities for women. Seniority which keeps women in separate departments also excludes them from the higher paying jobs. In addition, women with higher seniority than men, but in a different department, can be laid off first, because of this system.

Another explanation for women's position in the labor force is the informal communications systems in which men pass along information about job openings and advancement opportunities, bypassing women colleagues.

Women's position in the labor force is often tied to lack of education, which tends to be true to some extent. The courses women take in college differ widely from men. This is partially due to the typical socialization of women who were brought up to think of themselves entering the "traditional women's fields." On the undergraduate and graduate levels women are still more likely to be found in English, languages and fine arts while their male counterparts are more likely to be studying technical subjects that have a much higher income potential.

Both men and women workers today have completed a median of 12.4 years of school. But the average female college graduate today earns only slightly more than a man who has completed the eighth grade. The average female college graduate makes $7,930, just a little over half of what a male college graduate makes—$13,320.

In 1973 congressional testimony, Barbara Bergmann, professor of economics at the University of Maryland, placed the blame for lower wages

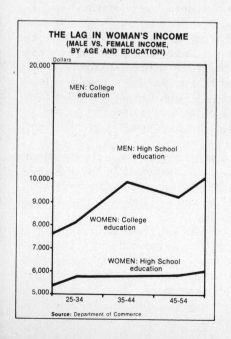

THE LAG IN WOMAN'S INCOME
(MALE VS. FEMALE INCOME, BY AGE AND EDUCATION)

Dollars

MEN: College education

MEN: High School education

WOMEN: College education

WOMEN: High School education

25-34   35-44   45-54

Source: Department of Commerce

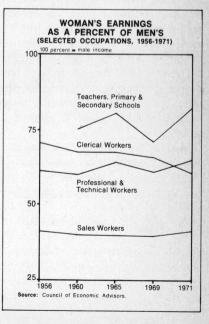

WOMAN'S EARNINGS
AS A PERCENT OF MEN'S
(SELECTED OCCUPATIONS, 1956-1971)

100 percent = male income

Teachers, Primary & Secondary Schools

Clerical Workers

Professional & Technical Workers

Sales Workers

1956   1960   1965   1969   1971

Source: Council of Economic Advisors.

and higher unemployment for women on "overcrowding in the women's occupations." She explained that by virtually excluding women from certain fields, the demand for women is kept artificially low, thereby increasing the supply in the new fields where they are welcome.

The 1974 Manpower Report of the President reports that over the course of their work lives, career women show little positive change in their occupational status. Women aged 30 to 44 with children experienced a greater amount of downward mobility between their first and second jobs than upward mobility. The "never married" group, however, a relatively stable group as far as occupational attachment, did experience more upward than downward mobility.

Clearly, the interruption of work for child bearing and family obligations inhibits the progress of working mothers. But even for white women with continuous work experience "the percentage who were upwardly mobile (30 percent) was only about half that for men workers (57 percent) covered in the parallel survey of men aged 45–49."

Whatever the reason, discrimination exists. The President's Council of Economic Advisors estimated an earnings differential of 20 percent attributable to sex discrimination alone, after adjusting for differences in education, work experience and level of employment.

In recent years women have made significant gains largely through organization and federal legislation passed with AFL-CIO support. The two legislative pillars are the Equal Pay Act of 1963 and the Civil Rights Act of 1964. More progress will be attained with ratification of the Equal Rights Amendment.

The Equal Pay Act was the first piece of federal legislation to outlaw discrimination against women. The act, an amendment to the Fair Labor Standards Act, prohibits discrimination on the basis of sex in the payment of wages (wages meaning all remuneration, including holiday and vacation pay, health, shift differentials, bonuses, incentive pay, etc.), requiring equal pay for equal work. The Department of Labor enforces the act, which defines equal work as equal skill, effort, responsibility and performance under similar working conditions. In Wirtz vs. Wheaton Glass, a landmark case, the U.S. Court of Appeals in New Jersey held in 1970 that a woman performing work which is "substantially equal to that of a man" is entitled to receive equal pay. An important provision of the act requires that salaries are not to be lowered to equalize pay, but that everyone should receive the higher salary.

Labor organizations are prohibited under the act from causing an employer to discriminate against an employee in violation of the pay provisions. The law, however, does not prohibit wage differences on a seniority or merit system established by an employer for measuring productivity on a factor other than sex. . . .

Title VII of the 1964 Civil Rights Act makes it illegal to discriminate in employment based on sex, race, color, religion or national origin. The Equal Employment Opportunity Commission was established to enforce this section of the law. The law itself is broader than the Equal Pay Act in that it forbids discrimination in all aspects of employment. . . .

The 1972 amendments to the act expanded women's employment rights by stating that benefits from health insurance plans for sickness or temporary physical disability must be extended to women employees disabled by pregnancy, miscarriage, abortion, childbirth or recovery from any of these conditions. There is a large backlog of cases under both the Equal Pay Act and Title VII. Some complaints are not even processed for one or two years. Because of this bureaucratic red tape women often get discouraged from even filing, or give up midway through the case.

Sex discrimination by federal contractors and subcontractors was outlawed by Executive Order 11246, as amended in 1968. . . .

Success under this order has been limited. Since each compliance agency is independent, inconsistencies in policies exist. Compliance agencies, such as the Defense Department, have done little in the direction of affirmative action. Similarly, in the private sector, compliance in such industries as construction, in which there are almost 11,000 women carpenters, 32,000 women riveters and flame cutters and almost 10,000 women construction laborers, has been limited.

The minimum wage law and its amendments throughout the years have helped women as well as men. The new amendments, effective on May 1, 1974, extend coverage for the first time to domestic household workers, an occupation composed mainly of women. The act also extends to federal employment the prohibitions against discrimination on account of age, a provision especially important to women who re-enter the labor force after raising families.

The Equal Rights Amendment, a vital step forward insuring full equality for American women, was endorsed by the 1973 AFL-CIO convention, pledging full support of ERA which will guarantee "equality of rights under the law shall not be denied or abridged by the United States or any state on account of sex." Discrimination on the basis of sex will then be unconstitutional when based on any action taken by local, state or federal government. The ERA now must be ratified by three-fourths of the state legislatures.

In March 1974 over 3,200 trade union women convened in Chicago for the founding conference of the Coalition of Labor Union Women (CLUW) to work within the union structure to better the position of working women in America.

These women came together in Chicago because the time was right—women trade unionists were ready to respond in their own terms to the women's liberation movement—and wanted to play a more meaningful role within the trade union movement.

Although union members earn an average $1,500 a year more than their non-union counterparts, out of 33.3 million working women in 1972, only 4.2 million were unionized. The proportion of female union membership is growing, however. From 1958 to 1970 female union membership increased by one million, an increase of 30 percent. Male membership increased by 1.7 million over the same period. The two-year period between 1970 and 1972 witnessed the smallest gain in trade union membership since 1962, yet women's membership grew at a much faster rate.

Of the AFL-CIO's 13.5 million members, about 25 percent are women. In national and international unions they now hold less than 5 percent of the key leadership positions. In recent years more women are being elected to national union executive boards. Women do hold more positions, however, on local and shop levels, but here many still assume the "traditional women's jobs" of secretaries and trustees rather than presidents or vice presidents.

CLUW's main goal is to develop action programs to bring more women into unions; to achieve active, affirmative action in the work places; to encourage women to run for political office; and to strengthen their own participation in unions.

The organization's legislative proposals include a major effort to adopt the Equal Rights Amendment; full employment and job opportunities for women; shorter work week without loss of pay; extension of "truly protective legislation for all workers" (both men and women); improved maternity and pension benefits; child care; and stronger job safety and health standards and enforcement.

In sum, women, like all workers, must be free of all types of discrimination. Now, with the organizing of CLUW, women are expressing their determination to take positive, collective action.

57

Consumption and the Household

John Kenneth Galbraith

I

In the neoclassical system consumption is a generally flawless thing to be maximized by any honest and socially benign means. It is also a curiously trouble-free enjoyment. Thought must be given to the selection of goods and services. No problems arise in their use. None of this is true, and what is omitted from view deeply shapes the patterns of individual, family and social life. This omission, and the circumstances which lie back of this myopia, must now be examined. They are matters of no small consequence.

Beyond a certain point the possession and consumption of goods becomes burdensome unless the tasks associated therewith can be delegated. Thus the consumption of increasingly elaborate or exotic food is only rewarding if there is someone to prepare it. Otherwise, for all but the eccentric, the time so required soon outweighs whatever pleasure is derived from eating it. Increasingly spacious and elaborate housing requires increasingly burdensome maintenance and administration. So also with dress, vehicles, the lawn, sporting facilities and other consumer artifacts. If there are people to whom responsibility for administration can be delegated and who, in turn, can recruit and direct the requisite servant labor force, consumption has no limits. Otherwise the limits on consumption are severe. In looking at the great houses of seventeenth-, eighteenth- and nineteenth-century England, the first thought is of the wealth of the inhabitants. Often it was modest by modern standards. More should be attributed to the ability to delegate administrative responsibility for consumption to a large, willing and disciplined servant class.

Personal service has always been threatened by the more attractive labor opportunities provided by industrial development. It is also made more necessary by the wealth that such development provides. Not surprisingly, therefore, much effort has been devoted in the past hundred years to finding ways of preserving it or in finding surrogates for it or in devising substitutes. The search for surrogates has led generally to women and the family. It has made use of a pervasive force in the shaping of social attitudes—one that has often been sensed but rarely described. A name for it is needed, and it may be called the Convenient Social Virtue.

The convenient social virtue ascribes merit to any pattern of behavior, however uncomfortable or unnatural for the individual involved, that serves the comfort or well-being of, or is otherwise advantageous for, the more powerful members of the community. The moral commendation of the community for convenient and therefore virtuous behavior then serves as a substitute for pecuniary compensation. Inconvenient behavior becomes deviant behavior and is subject to the righteous disapproval or sanction of the community.

The convenient social virtue is widely important for inducing people to perform unpleasant services. In the past it has attached strongly to the cheerful, dutiful draftee who, by accepting military service at rates of pay well below the market, appreciably eased the burden of taxes on the relatively well-to-do taxpayer. Anyone resistant to such service was condemned as deeply unpatriotic or otherwise despicable. The convenient social virtue has also helped obtain the charitable and compassionate services of nurses, custodial personnel and other hospital staff. Here too the resulting merit in the eyes of the community served as a partial substitute for compensation. (Such merit was never deemed a wholly satisfactory substitute for remuneration in the case of physicians.) Numerous other tasks for the public good—those commonly characterized as charitable works—are also greatly reduced in cost by the convenient social virtue. But the convenient social virtue has been most useful of all in solving the problem of menial personal service.

In the last century and earlier in the present one the household domestic was regularly pictured as a person uniquely worthy of esteem. Nothing reflected more admirably on a person than diligent and enduring service to another. The phrase "old family retainer" suggested merit only slightly below that of "wise and loving parent." The phrase "good and faithful servant" had recognizable scriptural benediction. In England a large and comparatively deft literature associated humor, conversational aptitude, social perception and great caste pride with a servant class. None of this, however, stemmed the erosion to industrial employments. The ultimate success of the convenient social virtue has been in converting women to menial personal service.

In preindustrial societies women were accorded virtue, their procreative capacities apart, for their efficiency in agricultural labor or cottage manufacture or, in the higher strata of the society, for their intellectual, decorative, sexual or other entertainment value. Industrialization eliminated the need for women in such cottage employments as spinning, weaving or the manufacture of apparel; in combination with technological advance it greatly reduced their utility in agriculture. Meanwhile rising standards of popular consumption, combined with the disappearance of the menial personal servant, created an urgent need for labor to administer and otherwise manage consumption. In consequence a new social virtue came to attach to household management—to intelligent shopping for goods, their preparation, use and maintenance and the care and maintenance of the dwelling and other possessions. The virtuous woman became the good housekeeper or, more comprehensively, the good homemaker. Social life became, in large measure, a display of virtuosity in the performance of these functions—a kind of flair for exhibiting comparative womanly virtue. So it continues to be. These tendencies were already well advanced in the upper-income family by the beginning of the present century. Thorstein Veblen noted that "according to the ideal scheme of the pecuniary culture, the lady of the house is the chief menial of the household."

With higher income the volume and diversity of consumption increase and therewith the number and complexity of the tasks of household management. The distribution of time between the various tasks associated with the household, children's education and entertainment, clothing, social life and other forms of consumption becomes an increasingly complex and demanding affair. In consequence, and paradoxically, the menial role of the woman becomes more arduous the higher the family income, save for the small fraction who still have paid servants. The wife of the somewhat senior automobile executive need not be intellectually alert or entertaining, although she is required to be conventionally decorative on occasions of public ceremony. But she must cook and serve her husband's meals when he is at home; direct household procurement and maintenance; provide family transport; and, if required, act as charwoman, janitor and gardener. Competence here is not remarked; it is assumed. If she discharges these duties well, she is accepted as a good homemaker, a good helpmate, a good manager, a good wife—in short, a virtuous woman. Convention forbids external roles unassociated with display of homely virtues that are in conflict with good household management. She may serve on a local library board or on a committee to consider delinquency among the young. She may not, without reproach, have full-time employment or a demanding avocation. To do so is to have it said that she is neglecting her home and family, i.e., her *real* work. She ceases to be a woman of acknowledged virtue.

The conversion of women into a crypto-servant class was an economic accomplishment of the first importance. Menially employed servants were available only to a minority of the preindustrial population; the servant-wife is available, democratically, to almost the entire present male population. Were the workers so employed subject to pecuniary compensation, they would be by far the largest single category in the labor force. The value of the services of housewives has been calculated, somewhat impressionistically, at roughly one fourth of total Gross National Product. The average housewife has been estimated (at 1970 wage rates for equivalent employments) to do about $257 worth of work a week or some $13,364 a year. If it were not for this service, all forms of household consumption would be limited by the time required to manage such consumption—to select, transport, prepare, repair, maintain, clean, service, store, protect and otherwise perform the tasks that are associated with the consumption of goods. The servant role of women is critical for the expansion of consumption in the modern economy. That it is so generally approved, some recent modern dissent excepted, is a formidable tribute to the power of the convenient social virtue.

As just noted, the labor of women to facilitate consumption is not valued in national income or product. This is of some importance for its disguise; what is not counted is often not noticed. For this reason, and aided by the conventional pedagogy as presently observed, it becomes possible for women to study economics without becoming aware of their precise role in the economy. This, in turn, facilitates their acceptance of their role. Were their economic function more explicitly delineated in the current pedagogy, it might invite inconvenient rejection.

The neoclassical model has, however, a much more sophisticated disguise for the role of women. That is the household. That the model emphasizes the role of individual decision in the economic system has been sufficiently stressed. This moral sanction would be seriously eroded if that decision depended on the facilitating toil of women—and if the decision-making role of women were seen to be subordinate to that of men.

These difficulties are elided by the concept of the household. Though a household includes several individuals—husband, wife, offspring, sometimes relatives or parents—with differing needs, tastes and preferences, all neoclassical theory holds it to be the same as an individual. Individual and household choices are, for all practical purposes, interchangeable.

The household having been made identical with the individual, it then distributes its income to various uses so that satisfactions are roughly equal at the margin. This, as observed, is the optimal state of enjoyment, the neoclassical consumer equilibrium. An obvious problem arises as to whose satisfactions are equated at the margin—those of the husband, the wife, the children with some allowance for age or the resident relatives, if any. But on this all accepted theory is silent. Between husband and wife there is evidently a compromise which accords with the more idyllic conception of the sound marriage. Each partner subordinates economic preference for the greater pleasures of propinquity and the marriage bed. Or only individuals with identical preference schedules marry. Or in a hitherto unnoticed instrument of the marriage sacrament these schedules are made equal thereafter. Or, if the preference schedules do differ, divorce ensues, and the process continues until persons with identical schedules are mated. Or the woman, who in practice does much of the buying, equalizes her preferences at the margin, and her husband contrives to live in a lesser state of satisfaction. Or the husband, as the dominant member of the family, makes the decisions in accordance with his preference schedule, and his wife, however resignedly, goes along.

In fact the modern household does not allow expression of individual personality and preference. It requires extensive subordination of preference by one member or another. The notion that economic society requires something approaching half of its adult members to accept subordinate status is not easily defended. And it is not easily reconciled with a system of social thought which not only esteems the individual but acclaims his or her power. So neoclassical economics resolves the problem by burying the subordination of the individual within the household, the inner relationships of which it ignores. Then it recreates the household as the individual consumer. There the matter remains. The economist does not invade the privacy of the household.

The common reality is that the modern household involves a simple but highly important division of labor. With the receipt of the income, in the usual case, goes the *basic* authority over its use. This usually lies with the male. Some of this authority is taken for granted. The place where the family lives depends overwhelmingly on the convenience or necessity of the member who makes the income. And both the level and nature or style of expenditure are also extensively influenced by its source—by whether the recipient is a business executive, lawyer, artist, accountant, civil servant, artisan, assembly-line worker or professor. More important, in a society which sets store by pecuniary achievement, a natural authority resides with the person who earns the money. This entitles him to be called the *head* of the family.

The administration of the consumption resides with the woman. This involves much choice as to purchases—decisions as between different cake mixes and detergents. The conventional wisdom celebrates this power; it is women who hold the purse strings. In fact this is normally the power to implement decisions, not to make them. Action, within the larger strategic framework, is established by the man who provides the money. The household, in the established economics, is essentially a disguise for the exercise of male authority.

This household could not be better designed to facilitate consumption. The broad decisions on the general style of life rest with the husband and can be made without personal concern for the problems of administration that are involved. These are the business of his wife. Most things, including consumption, are more enjoyed if the work associated therewith is performed by someone else.

Women acquiesce normally in the crypto-servant functions of consumption administration—in arranging maintenance and repair of the house and of the household machinery and of the automobile and other equipment, in procurement and preparation of food, in supervision of the consumption of the young, in organization and management of social enjoyments, in participation in competitive social display. Such tasks are taken to be the natural responsibilities of the sex. It will be urged that there is no cause here for comment or complaint; most women perform these functions contentedly and even happily.

In a more comprehensive view the acceptance and happiness are an impressive tribute to the social conditioning to which people are subject. It is a prime tenet of modern economic belief—one that is central to the established economics and powerfully reinforced by advertising and salesmanship—that happiness is a function of the supply of goods and services consumed. This point having been established, how better can a woman contribute to her own happiness and that of the family she loves than by devoting herself to the efficient and energetic administration of the family consumption? Her service to the economy thus hitchhikes on her sense of duty and her capacity for affection. And, as with other economic needs, it is affirmed in the convenient social virtue. This celebrates as uniquely moral the woman who *devotes* herself to the well-being of her family; is a gracious helpmate; is a good manager; or who, at lesser levels of elegance, is a good housekeeper or real homebody. By comparison mere beauty, intellectual or artistic achievement or sexual competence is in far lower repute. And qualities that are inconsistent with good and acquiescent household administration—personal aggressiveness, preoccupation with personal interests to the neglect of husband and family and, worst of all, indifferent housekeeping—are strongly deplored.

In few other matters has the economic system been so successful in establishing values and molding resulting behavior to its needs as in the shaping of a womanly attitude and behavior. And, to summarize, the economic importance of the resulting achievement is great. Without women to administer it, the possibility of increasing consumption would be sharply circumscribed. With women assuming the tasks of administration, consumption can be more or less indefinitely increased. In very high income households this administration becomes, as noted, an onerous task. But even here expansion is still possible; at these income levels women tend to be better educated and better administrators. And the greater availability of divorce allows of a measure of trial and error to obtain the best. Thus it is women in their crypto-servant role of administrators who make an indefinitely increasing consumption possible. As matters now stand (and for as long as they so stand), it is their supreme contribution to the modern economy.

II

> To effect her complete emancipation and make her the equal of men it is necessary for housework to be socialized and women to participate in common productive labour. Then women will occupy the same positions as men enjoy.
>
> (*Lenin*, The Emancipation of Women)

The modern economy, we have seen, requires for its success a crypto-servant class. This class makes possible the more or less indefinite expansion of consumption in face of the considerable administrative tasks involved. One of the singular achievements of the planning system has been in winning acceptance by women of such a crypto-servant role—in making acquiescence a major manifestation of the convenient social virtue. And in excluding such labor from economic calculation and burying the separate personality of the woman in the concept of the household, where her sacrifice of individual choice goes unnoticed, neoclassical pedagogy has contributed competently to concealing this whole tendency even from the women concerned. It is now possible for most women to study economics without discovering in what manner they serve economic society—how they are being used.

However the acceptance by women of their major economic role is not completely secure. In recent years in all industrial countries there has been a measure of restlessness, even of minor revolt, among women. Again we have the validating reaction that shows the problem we are discussing to be real. As usual what is lacking is a clear view of the underlying economic circumstance. And again emancipation of belief is itself a consequential reform. For once women perceive their role as instruments for expanding consumption on behalf of the planning system, their acquiescence in this role will surely diminish. Or so one may hope.

The reasonable goal of an economic system is one that allows all individuals to pursue socially benign personal goals regardless of sex. There should be no required or conditioned subordination of one sex to another. This, with the techniques by which such rights are presently denied to women, requires a substantial change in the way decisions on consumption are made within the household. These, at a minimum, ought to be appraised for their administrative cost to the participants. This means that the woman, as the administrator, should have the decisive voice on the style of life, for she shoulders the main burden. Or, if decisions are made jointly, the tasks of administration—cleaning, maintenance and repair of dwelling, artifacts, vehicles or planning and management of social manifestations—should also be equally shared. Either convention could, if adopted, bring a drastic change in present consumption patterns.

However the more plausible solution involves an attack on a more fundamental cause. That, at the deepest level, involves the concept of the family in which one partner provides the income and the other supervises the details of its use. To a substantial though unmeasurable extent the family is derived from economic need. For agriculture and handicraft production it was a highly convenient unit, one that involved firmly centralized responsibility for decisions on production and consumption and a useful division of labor on various tasks associated with both the production and use of goods. The man did the heavier field work or the more heroic tasks of the hunt or predation; the woman managed the poultry and made the clothes. With industrialization and urbanization men and women no longer share in tasks of production in accordance with strength and adaptability. The man disappears to the factory or office, the woman concentrates exclusively on managing consumption. This is a conventional arrangement, not an efficiently necessary division of labor; at a simple level of consumption it is perfectly possible for one person to do both. Without denying that the family retains other purposes, including those of love, sex and child-rearing, it is no longer an economic necessity. With higher living standards it becomes, increasingly, a facilitating instrument for increased consumption. The fact that, with industrialization and with higher living standards, family ties increasingly weaken strongly affirms the case.

It follows that, with economic development, women should be expected and encouraged to regard marriage not as a necessity but as a traditional subordination of personality, one that is sustained by custom and the needs of the planning system. It should be the choice of many to reject the conventional family in return for other arrangements of life better suited to individual personality.

This means also, as a practical matter, that women, if they are to be truly independent, must have access to income of their own. This is obviously necessary for survival outside the traditional family. And it makes possible an independent existence—for shorter or longer periods—within the context of the family.

With such income goes increased power over household decisions. With it also goes work which reflects, in some measure at least, the individual's preference as to how her days should be spent. Even if not satisfactory, as work for many is not, the choice is not preordained as is domesticity (meaning the administration of consumption) by marriage. Marriage should no longer be a comprehensive trap. A tolerant society should not think ill of a woman who finds contentment in sexual intercourse, child-bearing, child-rearing, physical adornment and administration of consumption. But it should certainly think ill of a society that offers no alternative—and which ascribes virtue to what is really the convenience of the producers of goods.

Equal access to jobs requires the support of law. It also requires a series of companion reforms. Not all of these are of great novelty, for the instinct for solving problems has, as usual, anticipated the clear diagnosis of the ill. Four things are of particular importance:

(1) Provision for professional care for children. The importance of this requires no comment. It is also, by the most orthodox measures of efficiency, a very great economic bargain. In a child care center one person cares professionally for numerous children; in the family one person cares unprofessionally for one or a very few. Thus there can be few institutions so directly designed to increase the productivity of labor.

(2) Greater individual choice in the work week and work year. That women need provision, as men do not, for maternity leave will be generally agreed. Their transition into the working force also requires flexibility. What could be accomplished gradually is excluded if abrupt reorganization of traditional household practices is thought to be required. A three- or four-day week, or a fifteen- or twenty-hour week, may make the transition possible for many women where immediate commitment to a normal working week would be an insuperable barrier.

(3) An end to the present monopoly of the better jobs in the technostructure by males. . . .

(4) Provision of the requisite educational opportunity for women. . . .

The consequence of the emancipation of women—and the rationalization of the household—will be a substantial change in patterns of life. Thus suburban life—as a wealth of commonplace comment affirms—is demanding in the administrative requirements of its consumption. Vehicle maintenance, upkeep of dwellings, movement of offspring, extirpation of crabgrass, therapy of pets, the heavy demands of social intercourse involving competitive display of housewifely competence are among the innumerable cases in point. Were all of these tasks shared by the male, there would be an urgent reconsideration of the advantages of suburban life. Urban multiple-dwelling units are much less demanding in their administration. Here, not surprisingly, wives of independent purpose in life are now generally to be found.

Lesser changes may be assumed. There will be more professionally prepared food. There will be less home cooking, the quality of which, though often dubious, is ardently celebrated in the convenient social virtue. Similarly there will be increased reliance on external services rather than home-installed machinery—on laundries, professional housecleaning and public transport instead of wife-operated and -maintained washing machines, housecleaning apparatus and automobiles. Professional entertainment will replace the social intercourse associated with exhibition of womanly talent in food preparation, home decoration, gardening and the dispensation of alcohol. Plausibly there will be an increased resort to the arts. The arts, unlike, for example, competitive display of social craftsmanship, are relatively undemanding in administration, and they involve tasks which are themselves interesting and preoccupying.

A final observation is in order. Economic production divides between services and goods or things. With *many* exceptions services are supplied by the market system; things come, in the main, from the planning system. The rendering of services is geographically dispersed and associated with the personality of the individual performing them, both factors that lend themselves badly to organization and thus to the planning system. Manufacturing of goods is pre-eminently a function of the planning system—the great majority of the large corporations are manufacturing enterprises. The consumption of goods, in most cases, requires administration—preparation, cleaning, maintenance, repair, disposal. The consumption of services does not usually require administration; they are, in effect, used up in the act of service. And a very large number of services—those of laundries, garages, plumbers, snow removers—have, as their purpose, the easing of the tasks of administration associated with the use or consumption of goods, including real property.

It follows that, if women are no longer available for the administration of consumption and the administrative task must thus be minimized, there will be a substantial shift in the economy from goods to services. This means, pari passu, a shift in the economy from the planning system to the market system. This, at least subjectively, could be sensed. It is, or could be, another reason why producers of goods ascribe virtue to the present role of women.

There are few matters on which the mind can dwell more appreciatively than on the changes that would occur if women were emancipated from their present service to the consumer society and the planning system. But it is the emancipation itself that is the present concern. Its further effects can now be left to others to envisage and to history to reveal.

58

Pay for Housework?

Carol Lopate

The idea of paying people to do housework has been around for some time. Recently it has begun to receive serious consideration among feminist groups here, largely as a result of the publication in February 1973 of the English version of Mariarosa Dalla Costa's pamphlet *The Power of Women and the Subversion of the Community*.[1] Dalla Costa's analysis comes out of the Italian women's movement and was first introduced to American women through her article "Women and the Subversion of the Community," which appeared in *Radical America*.[2]

THE PAY-FOR-HOUSEWORK ARGUMENT

Briefly, the pay-for-housework argument goes like this. Traditional analyses of the working class have excluded women because their work has not been considered "productive"—or, more commonly, has not been considered at all. These analyses have called women "oppressed" but not "exploited," because exploitation would imply that surplus value is extracted from their labor. In contrast, Dalla Costa and other feminists say that it is clear that women as housewives produce and reproduce capitalism to at least as great a degree as any other working sector. But, say these feminists, women's work in the home produces "use value" rather than "exchange value" and is thus a remnant of a precapitalist structure existing within capitalism. Still, the work of women in the home forms the basis for all other labor, from which, in turn, surplus value is extracted. Women help reproduce capitalism through both childbirth and socialization; they keep capitalism running smoothly by servicing its current (and future) workers with food, clothes, and sex. Thus, although women in the home are part of the working class, they are not recognized as such because they are unpaid. Producing only use value, they remain part of a precapitalist structure. To legitimize women as part of the working class and free them financially from men, they must produce exchange value. The subsequent demand proceeds directly from the analysis: women should be paid for housework.

The attraction of this theory is not difficult to understand. First, in a brief and efficient manner, it analytically integrates women into the working class. Second, a platform for concrete action flows directly from the analysis. Moreover, this demand can be readily understood as emerging from a com-

---

[1] Published jointly by the Falling Wall Press, Ltd., 79 Richmond Rd., Montpelier, Bristol B56 5EP, England, and a group of individuals from the women's liberation movement in England and Italy.
[2] Vol. 6, no. 1 (January/February 1972).

prehensive theoretical framework, a fact which may attract the large numbers of women who have not as yet been drawn into such piecemeal feminist demands as abortion and child care. Finally, given a capitalist society in which personal autonomy as well as status are gained through money, women do need to be wage earners in order to achieve the self-reliance and self-esteem which are the first steps toward equality.

THE CASE AGAINST PAY FOR HOUSEWORK

But the attraction of pay for housework is not unlike the attraction of union demands for better wages, shorter hours, increased benefits. All of these are far easier to conceptualize and communicate to workers than the demand to change the nature of work itself—a goal which, even when packaged as "workers' control," is comparatively utopian and hard for people to visualize. Just as unions have generally pushed only quantitative demands and have become reformist institutions for integrating workers into the system, feminist concentration on pay for housework can only serve to further drive women (and men) into the clutches of capitalism.

Before going further, I want to make it clear that I am not against reformist demands as such—that is, I'm not automatically opposed to demands whose goals are to ameliorate rather than change the basic structure and relations of society. For example, it is irrelevant to me that capitalism may have accepted abortion reform only because *its* need for workers no longer requires such a high birth rate. I support abortion reform because I believe that the right to decide whether or not to have a child *frees* women. In a similar vein, I am not opposed to pay for housework simply because it is a reformist, quantitative demand that the system could accept at some point in the future. (And, given the rising unemployment and the increased usage of the state to ameliorate economic conditions in all areas, pay for housework might well become a logical step. In fact, it would probably be far less threatening to the capitalist order than creating real jobs outside the home for all women on an equal basis with men.) I am against pay for housework because instead of freeing women, it will serve to rigidify the sexual and other forms of oppression that we are already fighting against. In the following pages I will elaborate on why I am opposed to feminists spending their energies on the pay-for-housework demand.

The Trivialization of Home Life

The women who support pay for housework say, quite rightly, that work outside the home is often glamorized and held out as a false carrot. Women in the home are made to lust after paid jobs whose daily actuality is at least as grubby as housework. But such jobs do provide social networks with men and women which reach far beyond what any housewife has access to. Moreover, these networks are different qualitatively: the housewife's networks, as far as they may range, never flow into lines of power. Jobs also provide an existence autonomous of the family, whatever the control exercised by a boss. And they also provide money—which is where the pay-for-housework alternative comes in.

But I don't believe that sufficient attention has been paid to the quality of life inside the home. The lives of most housewives have undergone major changes over the past 30 years or so. As men increasingly commute to work, women's days have become more and more separate from those of their husbands. The greatly accelerated geographic mobility among both blue- and white-collar workers has left women also bereft of continuity and community with neighbors, and, with the decline of the extended family, without the support of relatives who once provided both friendship and assistance. With the increase in crime and the vastly increased fear of it, women are locked inside their houses to an unprecedented extent: even such once hoped-for guests as the Avon lady or the Fuller Brush man are now regarded with suspicion, and the door is often not opened to them.

The decrease in house size and the mechanization of housework have meant that the housewife is potentially left with much greater leisure time; however, she is often kept busy buying, using, and repairing the devices and their attachments which are theoretically geared toward saving her time. Moreover, the trivial, manufactured tasks which many of these technological "aids" perform are hardly a source of satisfaction for housewives. Max-Pacs may give "perfect coffee every time," but even a compliment about her coffee can offer little more than fleeting satisfaction to the housewife. Finally, schools, nurseries, day care, and television have taken away from mothers much of their responsibility for the socialization of their children. While much of the early childhood development literature of the fifties and sixties stressed the importance of the mother in developing the child's emotional growth or IQ, and women took up slack time from housework to "work" with their children, at the same time women found their control over their children's development increasingly preempted by educational institutions and the media. Few women today can feel that their children's upbringing is really in their hands.

Instead of simply paying women to do increasingly trivialized work, we need to re-evaluate which tasks are actually necessary to keep a house going. We need to discover which "time- and laborsaving" devices are truly useful and which ones merely cause a further degradation of housework. We need to investigate the isolated way in which work is done in the home and look for new, possibly communal, organizations for doing housework, even when living arrangements are not communal. Finally, we need to re-evaluate mothers' (and fathers') roles in bringing up children, as well as the roles which now exist for day care, nurseries, public schools, and the media.

Women and the Working Class

The Dalla Costa demand for pay for housework originated in Italy, where the overwhelming majority of women in all classes still remain at home. In the United States, over half of all women *do* work for wages outside the home. The women who stay at home are predominantly the very poor, usually welfare mothers who in a sense are already being paid by the state to work in the home (or to stay out of the labor market, however one wishes to conceive of it), and women of the upper-middle class. The wives of blue- and white-collar workers usually do not stay home, even when they have children. They work.

The project of bringing American women into the working class is therefore not merely a question of material conditions but of ideology. Women who work in America are still seen largely in terms of their husbands' or fathers' class designation; women themselves remain classless no matter what they do or do not do for a living.

The women who support the pay-for-housework demand argue that merely proposing that women be paid for their work in the home will raise their consciousness and help them to see themselves as part of the working class. Some go so far as to argue that they are not even interested in the demand being met; that the posing of it is in itself an important method for helping women to understand their connection with other workers and their role in keeping capitalism running smoothly. Whatever the contradictions (and moral dilemmas) of demanding something which one does not, in fact, want, the proposal to pay women for housework does not deal with the fact that the preconditions for working-class solidarity are networks and connections which arise from working together. These conditions do not occur when isolated women work in their separate homes—whether or not they are being paid for their housework.

Financing Payment for Housework

The financial aspects of payment for housework are highly problematic. Under our present system of corporate capitalism, pay for housework would not lead to any significant redistribution of income or wealth from the rich to the poor. Instead, the money to pay for housework would come from an already overtaxed working class, either through direct taxation or through special corporate taxes which would in turn be passed on to consumers. Moreover, since most men's incomes are at least partially determined on the basis of their being "family incomes," removal of all women from financial dependence on men in terms of a family unit would probably lower the income standards for male work. Concentration on the demand for pay for housework without acknowledgment of the effect on other segments of society would have the same devastating effect on any long-range strategy for alliance and solidarity between men and women workers that the demand for compensatory education and social welfare programs for Blacks during the 1960s had on relations between whites and Blacks. Workers knew that they, not the corporations, ended up paying for those programs. Although from one point of view women ought not plan their strategies with male acceptance in mind, it is somewhat ironic to use a strategy whose overt goal is working-class solidarity and yet at the same time has such an obvious undertow in the opposite direction.

The question of how one would evaluate what houseworkers ought to earn has provoked some alternatives that are almost funny, if one has a morbid sense of humor. For example, in Canada in the late 1960s, a plan actually brought before the government proposed that women be paid according to their educational background; that is, Ph.D.s would get the highest rate for doing housework and high-school dropouts the lowest. The use of this salary scale for creating interclass solidarity and interclass antagonisms among women is not difficult to imagine!

A second proposal which I have seen suggests that a composite of all the activities included in housework be made up with their respective average salaries (nursery care at x amount, sweepers at y, dishwashers at z, etc.), and that a final salary be based on the proportion of time generally spent in each of these activities. Since the only job on the list with any financial status is nursery teacher, houseworkers' wages would be very low.

Finally, a third means of allocating payment might be to make housework competitive with what the woman (or man) could make on the outside. Naturally, this would again create a hierarchy of pay among women, with some women able to make $30 an hour for washing the dishes, while others would do their dishes for the minimum wage. Obviously, almost any man would receive a higher wage for his participation in the home than any women he might be living with. Needless to say, it would be rather uneconomical for the state or any other paying agent to ask men to stay home and do housework while women went out to work.

Another question that arises is how houseworkers' work would be judged, and by whom. If the woman (or man) did not sweep behind the couch, would she (or he) be docked? Would there be increases for taking the kids to the dentist (or demerits for forgetting to take them)? If the children cleaned their own rooms, would they get paid? Obviously, there would have to be some kind of institutionalized supervisor to investigate the cleanliness of homes and the health of children, since otherwise pay for housework would merely be welfare or a minimum standard income. Would there be a weekly visit by the housecleaning supervisor? A daily one? Such visits would smack of yet another form of welfare investigators or inspectors, of yet another arm reaching in from the state.

Housework as a Commodity

The elimination of the one large area of capitalist life where all transactions do not have exchange value would only serve to obscure from us still further the possibilities of free and unalienated labor. The home and family have traditionally provided the only interstice of capitalist life in which people can possibly serve each other's needs out of love or care, even if it is often also out of fear and domination. Parents take care of children at least partly out of love, and children are nourished by the knowledge that the care they are being given is rendered at least partly on that basis. I even think that this memory remains with us as we grow up, so that we always have in mind a kind of utopia in which the work and caring come out of love rather than being based on financial reward. It seems to me that if children grew up knowing that every bit of attention they demanded and received was calculated by their mothers and then charged to the state, then some of our last, ever more flimsy notions of humanity would be blown away like dust.

I can imagine at least two counterarguments against keeping the family, or whatever living unit, in the private sphere: (1) the distinction between public and private should be erased, and (2) the lovely domain of "free giving" that I am defending has always been at the expense of women. I don't want to go into a long argument in favor of the private sphere. Let me say merely that I believe that it is in our private worlds that we keep our souls alive, and this is so not merely because we live in a capitalist world but would be equally necessary under socialism. The problem raised by capitalism is that it is difficult to keep the private sphere alive when it is constantly battered down by the commercialization of everyday life and by the constant threats to it posed by the mass media. But we must fight this encroachment and not simply abandon our last bastion under the guise of liberating women.

Neither women nor men have to transform all their labor into a commodity in order to be considered an intrinsic part of the working class or to be part of the struggle for human liberation. The commodity form is an alienated form, and bringing housework into the area of commodities will simply be perpetuating and increasing that alienation.

As I have said, I think women in our society have to work for money in order to gain the autonomy and self-esteem that is part of liberation. However, I do not believe in the inevitability of the stages which Dalla Costa's argument implies. The proposition that women must enter the commodity form in order to liberate themselves stems implicitly from a theory which regards capitalism as the inevitable transition stage between feudalism and socialism. Thus women must first be paid for their labor power if they are to move on to the next stage. In contrast, it seems to me that women might easily move directly into a stage of social and economic relations that we can't even conceive of without ever having to pass a capitalist stage. Moreover, to look at housework as a vestige of feudalism is to see it merely from one viewpoint. The separation between use value and exchange value is itself part of the capitalist stage of development. Unfortunately, in fact, attempts to bring underdeveloped sectors into the capitalist sector have done just that and nothing more. The revolutionary project is quite another matter.

Division of Labor by Sex

I have left for the end what I feel is the most obvious objection to the pay-for-housework demand: it does nothing to solve the sexual division of labor. Because I believe that feminist goals must be integrated into a total theory of revolution, I would not struggle for a feminist goal which sought to undermine the sexual division of labor if it did not at the same time seek to undermine the commodity form. But conversely, I am not interested in revolutionary projects which do not include a constant attack on the sexual division of labor.

I have already shown how pay for housework would make it cheaper (for the employer) to have women work in the home. It is highly likely that the institution would also solidify the nuclear family. No bureaucracy, whether public or private, would be likely to allow pay for communal houseworkers, pay for a man in a homosexual couple, pay for one of two women living together, or even pay for a man and a women living in a nuclear situation but out of wedlock. Free life-styles, changing life and living situations, and job and task rotations would all be made cumbersome if not impossible by the bureaucratic controls that would be required.

The demand for pay for housework is clearly an easier one to move on than is the call to abolish the sexual division of labor. The latter would involve a total restructuring of private work, as well as of work outside the home. Most women who have fought for such a restructuring of our lives have fallen into periodic despair. First, there were the old habits—the men's and ours—to break. Second, there were the real problems of time: many of us have lived with men who work an eight- or ten-hour day, while we have found ourselves preferring or finding less consuming jobs which have left us more time for housecare. Ask any man how difficult it is for him to arrange part-time hours or special time schedules so he can be involved equally in child care! Finally, as we have argued and struggled with the men we have chosen to live with, we have found ourselves with little other than moral imperatives to bolster our side. I have noticed the relief of women in meetings when talking about the Dalla Costa analysis: it gives scientific validity to our struggle for equality; we need no longer resort to the moral imperative of convincing men to be "good" people.

CONCLUSION

But let us go back to the analysis of housework as production, from which the demand of pay for housework derived. There has been an argument in circles of left or Marxist feminists over whether the importance to capitalism of woman's role within the family lies in her role as producer/reproducer or as consumer. The argument for women as consumers is obvious, given the advertisements and commodities which are structured around the created needs of women. And yet, as most feminist Marxists like to point out, production is a more deeply essential category than consumption. The rhetorical battle goes back and forth, in my experience, with a lot of anger on each side. There is almost an unstated presupposition that if women can be shown to be the unrealized "producers," the spine of capitalism, then they will also be the "vanguard of the revolution."

I do not have my own analysis to propose, nor do I have a concrete, radical platform for feminist-socialist action. But I do have one insight which I hope can become part of a framework for analysis which I and others will do in the future, and on which I and other women—and men—will act. This is that we women must stop borrowing categories from the Marxist world. We are not a class, since all individuals of a class have a specific relationship to the means of production, and we vary greatly in this respect. We are not a caste, as a caste is an endogamous (self-reproducing) group, often also characterized by a specific economic niche, and there is no way—as yet—that women can be endogamous. Even if we use sperm banks or other forms of mechanized reproduction, the sperm will come from the outside. Some of us may be doing work that has use value but that does not have exchange value, and many of us, including those who receive exchange value for our labor power, may be suffering from an ideology which still attributes to women the power and status of a second sex. The essential thing to remember is that we are a *sex*. That is really the only word as yet developed to describe our commonalities. But what do the differences in our daily lives mean for theory and for practice? What does being female actually mean; what, if any, specific qualities necessarily and for all time adhere to that characteristic? I believe that if, as revolutionary feminists, we want to be clear about where we are going, we must also be clear about the terms we borrow from the Marxist analysis. It is a quick way to legitimize ourselves on the left, but it is not a long-range strategy. What we may, in fact, have to do is to devise our own new terms. We may have to decide that housework is neither production nor consumption. We may have to be hazy in our visions. After all, a total reordering of sex and sexual roles and relationships is not easy to describe.

part 5

American Capitalism at the Crossroads

How often in the past have we seen cartoons lampooning some odd-looking character carrying a sign stating The End of the World Draws Nigh? Today, we may see, not a religious fanatic or quack, but well-known ecologists and distinguished citizens relaying a similar message—similar but not the same. For few of the pessimists have given up all hope. Instead their warnings are carefully couched: there will be no future unless . . . One "unless" is the attainment of a zero GNP growth. This debate is included in section a, Economic Growth and Ecological Constraints. Ecological issues "belong" to both micro- and macroeconomics. However, they are included here, in a final division of the book—one pointing to the future—since it is clear that ecological considerations will be central to any future that still remains.

In the last analysis, the alternatives will be, as they are today, capitalism or socialism. Radical critics have insisted not only that capitalism is unjust but that it is no longer a viable system of social organization. In the final section of this book, socialism is examined in more detail. Included are various views on what it is, how we can get there, and what life will be like once it is achieved. However, socialists differ among themselves, both in their definitions of socialism and in the tactics one must employ to achieve it. More precise definitions of goals and means will ultimately develop, as they should, out of the concrete struggles that socialists are making for the establishment of a just and humane social order.

Economic Growth and Ecological Constraints

John Maynard Keynes, the most influential economist of the twentieth century, once wrote, "In the long run we are all dead." His exasperation was directed at economists who shrugged off short-run dislocations by pointing to hypothetical long-run equilibriums. In the contemporary context of severe ecological dislocation, Keynes' jibe assumes a new and disturbing meaning. The "we" may include not only our own generation but also those that succeed it. It follows that the "long run" may point to a new type of economic "equilibrium," one totally bereft of human beings.

Ecological disaster is being projected everywhere with alarming regularity. There is the M.I.T. computer study of Jay Forrester and his associates, sponsored by the group of businessmen and "distinguished citizens" known as the Club of Rome. Among ecologists, there is Paul Erlich. Economist Robert Heilbroner paints pictures of such unrelenting gloom that we are reduced to making a morbid

choice between starvation and nuclear fallout. In an impressive overview, S. R. Eyre, former president of the British Association for the Advancement of Science, argues that we have reached what is known in biology as a "swarming stage" situation, which, if not checked, leads inevitably to mass morbidity (see Reading 59). Ultimately, the issue boils down to economic growth: can it be sustained or not? (Those media sources creating the impression that the problem is one of sloppy housekeeping— litter in the streets, and so forth —do us a great disservice.) Professors Peter Passell and Leonard Ross of Columbia University assert in Reading 60 that it can: "Don't knock the $2-trillion economy," they tell us.

On the other hand, radical economist John Hardesty argues that growth cannot be sustained. He points out some of the limits and inequities that necessarily result from mainstream solutions to the problems of pollution (see Reading 61). Hardesty argues that ecological imperatives require that economic growth cease. The stationary state he calls for "must be founded not on production for profit and private ownership but on production for social benefit and social ownership."

Some of the issues dividing the advocates of growth from their critics need to be emphasized. Eminent mainstream economists, like Walter Heller, recognize the problem of nonlinearity (that is, at some juncture a point of no return is reached and irrevocable changes occur). But they offer no useful solution. Since we do not know where the tip-off point is, cautious economists find themselves in the uncomfortable position of risking all for the sake of the dubious advantages of growth. Passell and Ross sum up these so-called advantages: "Twenty more years of growth could do for the poor what the Congress won't do." One wonders if such optimism about the future is based on the sterling accomplishments of the past. Rather than face the enormously difficult task of restructuring society to achieve equality, liberals like Passell and Ross choose a course they no doubt believe to be reasonable. Such practicality, to use a phrase from Robert Heilbroner, is what ecological Armageddons are made of.

Passell, Ross, and other orthodox economists would leave to a series of taxes functioning within the market pricing system much of the burden of ecological reform. But what price does one charge when the effects are unknown? In the case of nuisances like noise, errors may be painful—even fatal— but society continues. With DDT and mercury it may not; here, the pricing system is clearly not applicable. Orthodox economists doubt that such cases will multiply rapidly, but our ecological knowledge is limited. Advocates of growth gamble, not with our money, but with our lives! In short, free market economists who insist that reform is only a matter of internalizing external costs have nothing to offer in a world where real costs are unknown.

Finally, Passell and Ross deny that resources will run out. "The technology of substituting plentiful materials for scarce ones grows every day. Silicates made from sand replace copper and silver radio circuitry . . . [and] the power of the hydrogen bomb could provide all the energy we would need for several billion years." What Passell and Ross overlook is that these new processes are themselves the primary cause of pollution. Moreover, they require a vast increase in energy input per unit of final product with unknown dire effects on ocean life and climate. Liberal economics cannot repeal the laws of thermodynamics; endless growth is simply impossible.

Students should realize, however, that radical economists are not of one mind on the issue of growth. All would agree that resources have been atrociously misallocated. But some radicals believe that science and technology could be used wisely to increase production still further if growth were directed by a socialist government for the good of the people. On the other hand, even if planned socialist growth is presumably less destructive than its capitalist counterpart, the antigrowth arguments of ecologists Eyre, Commoner, Erlich, and others still seem to apply, independent of social organization.

One reason some radicals are hostile to the notion of zero GNP growth (or its variants) is that they fear it might become the official rationale for the brutal extermination of vast numbers of "excess" people. Such genocidal policies, whether in the form of starvation or war, must obviously be opposed. World poverty, of course, will not easily be eradicated. Solutions consistent with ecological sanity call for reduced numbers both here and abroad. More important, such curbs on population must simultaneously be part of a socialist recon-struction of a world distorted, damaged, and disrupted by capitalist development. Smaller numbers are suggested for the United States if we are not to usurp the world's limited resources or suffer extensive reductions in our standard of living. That is, the United States can reduce its GNP (and hence its yearly usage of resources) and still maintain its output per

capita—a rough measure of living standards—if total numbers diminish. To be sure, the eradication of cyclical and structural unemployment along with other forms of economic waste, such as missiles and conspicuous consumption, can theoretically enable an *existing* population to maintain its living standards with greater leisure, a smaller GNP, and consequently a lower level of pollution. Still, the exigencies of conservation and ecological health strongly compel reductions in the populations of countries that use more than their share of resources. As a result, sharing (as discussed in the introduction to section 4c) may then apply not only to automobiles, washing machines, and toasters, but even to the rearing of children. If the latter notion seems somewhat bizarre or unnatural, it would seem considerably less so if ethnocentric Americans were more aware of other modes of social organization, such as the tribal life of the Naskapi, a Labradorian hunting people.

One final note. In their efforts to save whales, polar bears, and alligators, ecologists have often been said to be unconcerned about people; these accusations are grossly unfair. It is out of respect for *human* life that ecologically minded individuals make their protest. Ecological Armageddon does not mean the end of life—just human life. Bacteria, roaches, and algae would doubtless survive. A new ecological balance would then be achieved. But it would be one without people. Is there justification, it may then be asked, for preferring that the human species survive? The answer, in my opinion, is Yes— not on the basis of religion, but on that of evolution. Billions of years were needed to create human life, and with it, consciousness and toolmaking. The eradication of human life would re-create the circumstances from which human beings originally evolved—it would not be an alternative but an immeasurably tragic setback.

59

Man the Pest: The Dim Chance of Survival

S. R. Eyre

The present state of the whole of the human species in relation to its total environment is so vast a topic that cautious and discriminating people might well avoid it as the subject of a single, short paper. It is, after all, a major area of concern for many sciences—social, biological, and technological. I take it as my subject here not, I hope, because I am incautious or undiscriminating, but because the ecology of any species, no matter how complex its behavior, can justifiably be regarded as unitary, and should therefore be reviewed as a whole from time to time. Furthermore, I would hold that the predicament of our species at the present time makes such a review not only desirable but vital.

THE SWARMING STAGE OF THE HUMAN SPECIES

Following an evolution of hundreds of millennia, Homo sapiens emerged on the post-glacial scene as a dominant species with almost world-wide distribution. Clearly his numbers had increased only very slowly over this vast period of time, and it was not until around A.D. 1810 that a world population of one billion was first achieved. Only just over a century then elapsed before the species had added just as many again to its numbers, the two billion mark being passed just after 1920. Then, in less than forty years, another increment of the same magnitude was added by the end of 1960.

If the growth rate of the decade 1950–60 were to be continued up to A.D. 2000, projection indicates the addition of further increments of one billion by the years 1975, 1984, 1992, and 1998, and a total of 7.41 billion by the end of the century. In fact it seems unlikely that such a growth rate could be sustained. Nevertheless, realistic projections made in 1963 still indicated a vast population increase by the year 2000; projections for that year varied between 5.30 billion and 6.83 billion according to the assumptions made, but medium assumptions indicated a population of four billion by about 1977, five billion by about 1990, and 5.96 billion by the end of the century. Furthermore, there are now clear indications that, in the absence of disasters on a world scale, these 1963 medium estimates will be far exceeded and that the world population in A.D. 2000 will be more than double that in 1960.

A biologist presented with this graph of population increase would diagnose a "swarming stage" situation. This is frequently observed both in nature and in the laboratory when a population of a particular species experiences favorable environmental conditions in the absence of some of the environmental controls to which it has normally been subjected throughout its evolution. The stage is inevitably short-lived and may be terminated in a number of ways: there may be mass neurosis owing to overcrowding, as has been suggested for the Scandinavian lemming; there may be a great increase in predators; or there may occur that concatenation of events which is so well demonstrated in a laboratory culture of bacteria, where the population gradually expands to occupy the whole medium and then rapidly declines from the original focus outward, partly through food shortage and partly poisoned by its own waste products. Whatever the end may be, the inevitable outcome is mass mortality.

Social scientists have largely been very unwilling to view the increase of our own species on so cataclysmic a plane. They have held that man has evaded the inexorable operation of the Malthusian law (and other biological controls) by his creation of a technology which can be handed on from generation to generation with increasing refinement and elaboration. In the minds of many people, however, doubts are beginning to develop. Even for one who has almost boundless faith in technological advancement, though it may be possible to contemplate with equanimity a world population of over six billion in A.D. 2000, it becomes progressively more difficult to be optimistic about twelve billion in 2035, twenty-five billion by 2065, and fifty billion by around the end of the twenty-first century.

FALLACIES ABOUT ECONOMIC GROWTH

Because rational projections can produce figures such as these, for a point in time only four generations ahead, an increasing number of social scientists are concluding that some kind of population limitation program will have to be formulated. Unfortunately, those who have begun to recognize the need for such a limitation often seem to betray a lack of appreciation of the complexity of the whole problem: indeed their recommendations are often misleading if not actually contradictory. Thus we read:

Increasing rates of economic growth and slowing rates of population growth are both essential to rising levels of living. . . .

Statements such as this must be regarded as misleading since they may leave the reader with the impression that, unlike population growth, economic growth may well be infinite. And yet the very reason why population increase must cease is *because* economic growth is *finite*. Although "growth" has become the cornerstone of our technological society, nevertheless any vision of its continuance into the indefinite future is based on illusion. All the evidence suggests that the earth's resources, renewable and nonrenewable, cannot possibly sustain technological and agricultural expansion for very much longer.

AGRICULTURAL FOOD PRODUCTION

In order to justify this statement fully, it would be necessary to review the whole of the earth's resources alongside the population projections already given. Clearly this is impossible in the space available, but examination of a selection of critical facts and basic issues provides sufficient indication of the gravity of the human situation. The rapid rate of population increase in many of the technology-deficient nations is one of the most striking features of the world population picture. It is particularly obvious in the countries of southern and eastern Asia where, on the basis of the medium projection, a 1970 population of some two billion will increase to some 3.40 billion by A.D. 2000.

We are concerned here then with more than half of the world's population. Work that has been done on the rates of increase in food production in this area provides no grounds whatever for optimism. One set of projections for India indicated that while the population would have increased 2.9 times by the end of the fifty-year period following 1961, the available food supply would be capable of increasing only 2.74 times. Furthermore this estimate was assuming the realization of the "full potential of increased agricultural production . . ." making the best possible use of known technology and allowing for little administrative or cultural waste. It should also be noted that, even if this level of productivity were achieved, production would still fall short of a satisfactory nutrition level by something like 20 percent. In fact, during the five years following the publication of these projections, agricultural production in India fell far short of the rate prescribed for it: there is no indication whatever that the near-miracle of technological application and administrative efficiency can possibly be achieved.

Working on similar assumptions, Sukhatme estimated that the Far East would require an increase in food supplies of 286 percent between 1960 and 2000 in order to achieve an adequate nutritional standard, and that the developing countries as a whole would require an increase of 261 percent. He went on to make the point that, with considerable effort, food production in the developing countries might be increased by 70 percent by 1980, but that food demands (taking into account population increase and a modest improvement in diet) will have risen by 100 percent. He emphasized, of course, that these broad figures conceal a variety of conditions, and that it is in Asia that the great difficulties will develop.

It seems most unlikely therefore that food production in Asia, even on the basis of the most optimistic assumptions regarding technological application and social adjustment, will be able to keep pace with population increase; and with any kind of climatic, economic, or social cataclysm, the shortfall will be enormous. Indeed it appears only reasonable to anticipate the necessity to obtain sufficient food for something like 700 million people in monsoon Asia by A.D. 2000, and if technical improvement and innovation proceed no faster than they have been doing during the past twenty-five years, much greater deficits will have developed.

Food imports on a vast scale would be necessary to counterbalance deficits of this size. Whether or not these could materialize would depend upon two things: first, the existence of commensurate food surpluses elsewhere in the world, and secondly the long-term ability of the Asian peoples to purchase them. With regard to the first point, any attempt to provide a simple answer would be hazardous; nevertheless some commonly held views on the agricultural potential of the earth require closer scrutiny.

It is certainly true that the best lands of Europe and eastern North America are, at the present time, capable of producing large agricultural surpluses—indeed overproduction has been a frequent problem. In the work already cited, Sukhatme estimates that by 1980 this surplus could amount to about 10 percent of world food production and that this would approximately balance the food deficit in Asia and elsewhere. Whether the volume of this food transfer could go on progressively up to the year 2000 is very problematical: the projected population increase in the developed countries would certainly take care of a lot of surpluses, and the attitudes of the taxpayers in the producing countries would become a not inconsiderable factor should the transfer be effected as aid rather than through trade.

THE POTENTIAL PRODUCTIVITY OF VIRGIN LANDS

It is also important to examine some of the fairly deep-rooted misconceptions regarding the large, sparsely populated areas of the earth. Quite a large percentage of these are arid deserts, mountain ranges, and cold tundras which could only be made productive with a capital input which would be prohibitive even for a rich, technologically developed nation. At first glance, however, suggestions regarding the potential productivity of the Amazon and Congo basins, Borneo, and the coastlands of New Guinea are more beguiling: these, after all, are well-watered tropical areas with high temperatures throughout the year.

A review of the present man/land ratio in Indonesia puts this problem in a proper perspective. A quarter of a century ago Mohr pointed out that it was no mere accident that Java had about sixty million people on thirty million acres, whereas Borneo, with four times that area, supported only about three million people. Three quarters of the soils of Java are developed in recent base-rich andesitic lavas or in colluvial and alluvial deposits derived from such lavas, and most of the remainder are formed in marls and limestones with some addition of volcanic ash.

Most of Borneo's soils on the other hand are on older sedimentary rocks; the igneous rocks that are to be found there are of the rhyolite and dacite groups—base-deficient and inherently infertile. In an area with around 100 inches mean annual precipitation and no dry season, there must also be very rapid leaching. In other words, the agricultural potential of Borneo is very similar to that found over much of the Amazon and Congo basins and many other smaller areas in the humid tropics which remain sparsely populated. In such areas the clay-humus complex is often less than 5 percent base-saturated as compared to the 70 percent required for a moderately productive soil.

This is not to say that the application of artificial fertilizer, if generously and scientifically applied, could not produce a harvest, but as Mohr has pointed out:

. . . if we stop to figure out how much calcium, potassium, magnesium and phosphorus we would have to add—it would be quite impossible to develop an agriculture which would pay.

If agriculture in these areas would not pay, clearly they could never become either a source of food for export to impoverished countries or places to which mass immigration could take place. It might also be added that if large-scale food production from such soils were attempted without the necessary capital input, the resulting erosion, laterization, and general degradation would create more of a Pandora's Box than an Open Sesame.

The basic unrealism of any agricultural philosophy that visualizes a great increase in the use of mineral fertilizers by the underdeveloped countries is underlined by the pattern of phosphate consumption at the present time. Of all the mineral fertilizers, phosphates are the most important: they not only contain one of the vital elements for plant nutrition but also are essential for the rapid incorporation of atmospheric nitrogen into the nutrient cycle through the medium of leguminous plants. And yet mineral phosphates in economically exploitable deposits are of very restricted distribution: over the past decade 90 percent of world production has come from the US, the USSR, Morocco, and Tunisia, and world reserves are of very limited extent.

Furthermore, in the year 1968–69, out of a world consumption of 17.3 million metric tons (P_2O_5 from all sources), Anglo-America, the USSR, and Europe accounted for 13.1 m.m.t. and the agriculture of the whole of Africa, Latin America, and Asia (less Japan and mainland China) less than 2.2 m.m.t. The agriculture of West Germany (population 60 million) consumed twice as much as the combined agricultural systems of India, Pakistan, and Indonesia (population over 700 million). One must doubt the feasibility of so expensive a commodity being made available in vast quantities to poor countries.

FOOD FROM THE OCEANS

The oceans have often been presented as a limitless source of food with which to supplement terrestrial production, but recent estimates have shown this to be very unrealistic. Precision is impossible at the present time, but the fact that estimates based on two independent approaches have produced very similar answers does indicate that we now have a sound notion of the total productivity of the earth's water bodies.

A summation of the productivity of the upper trophic levels of marine life has produced answers of between 300 and 320 m.m.t. per annum, of which no more than half—150–160 m.m.t.—are harvestable at a sustained yield. When we recollect that the total world catch of aquatic products in 1966 was already in the vicinity of 60 m.m.t., it becomes patently obvious that here is no limitless supply. It would certainly be possible to push production up to 100 m.m.t. by A.D. 2000 if the capital were made available, but this would only be a 66 2/3 percent increase on the present and there is reason to believe it could only be achieved by a total physical investment in ships and equipment of three times that of the present (an increase of 200 percent). If an attempt were then made to push production to its probable limit of about 150 m.m.t., this might well require six times the present investment.

This is obviously not an inexpensive way by which impoverished nations can supplement their food supplies. It is equally clear that any attempt to increase marine production by mass harvesting of the lower trophic levels of the food pyramid, such as the plankton and small plankton feeders, would be even more costly per unit of production, quite apart from the fact that conventional fishing would then become less profitable as the basis of fish subsistence was removed.

It has also been suggested that the productivity of the oceans could be increased by raising the nutrient status of the water. This is undeniably feasible but its implementation begs so many of the questions that have already been raised that it cannot seriously be entertained as a substantial contribution to world food problems over the next twenty-five to fifty years. Indeed, there is every indication that population increase and human technology on the land masses are far more likely to *decrease* the productivity of the water bodies than the reverse. Methyl mercury in the oceans, the eutrophication of Lake Erie, and the deleterious effects of chlorinated hydrocarbons on marine plankton—these are all now well-worn themes.

Furthermore, concentrated pollution of the more insidious kind is being discharged into the marine ecosystems, at the present time, by a relatively small percentage of the world's rivers—primarily those of North America and Europe. If, in an effort to raise agricultural productivity, the other peoples of the world begin to apply biocides to the land in anything like the same concentration, the effect could be very serious. If these peoples also expand their industrial capacity and begin to emit industrial waste in materially greater quantities, then the results could be catastrophic.

WORLD CONSUMPTION OF MINERALS

For reasons I am about to give, there may well be no chance of such world-wide industrialization. From the viewpoint of the ultimate ecological health of the world this could be one of the most fortunate facets of the human situation, but one cannot expect the technology-deficient nations to take this view: at the present time it is the lack of a capacity to produce industrial goods that is regarded as the main criterion of "underdevelopment," and those impoverished nations with large food deficits will obviously attempt to expand industrial production as one means of increasing their economic flexibility and exchange capability.

At the present time, although a large percentage of the world's industrial raw materials are extracted in underdeveloped countries, these materials are largely consumed by the manufacturing industries of Europe and North America. This applies not only to obvious commodities such as iron ore but to almost the whole range of mineral materials which are indispensable to the functioning of a modern industrial complex. Detailed and accurate statistics for the *consumption* of such commodities are notoriously difficult to obtain, but a few examples make the broad picture clear enough.

In 1965, out of a world smelter production of about six million tons of metallic copper, the industries of Europe, the USSR, and the US (total population about 850 million) consumed well over 75 percent while the industries of the whole of Asia, Africa, and Latin America (population about 2.50 billion) consumed far less than 25 percent. Indeed if the very considerable copper consumption of Japan and the Union of South Africa is deducted, an almost insignificant amount is left to the underdeveloped world.

More precise figures are available for the world consumption of tin. In 1967 the industries of the noncommunist world (along with Yugoslavia) consumed 166,000 short tons of which almost 75 percent was absorbed by Western Europe and Anglo-America alone and less than 10 percent by Southern Asia, Africa, and Latin America. And in the case of aluminum the contrast between the developed and the underdeveloped world is even more striking: out of a world production of 7,415,000 short tons in 1965, Europe, Anglo-America, and the USSR consumed about seven million tons and Japan a further 300,000 tons. Even in the absence of exact consumption figures for the technology-deficient countries it is obvious that their industries can have consumed only a negligible amount.

Some measure of the contrast between the technologically developed and the technology-deficient countries is obtained from the fact that the industries of the US consume 50 percent of the annual world production of aluminum, 25 percent of the smelted copper, about 40 percent of the lead, over 36 percent of the nickel and zinc, and about 30 percent of the chromium. But it is perhaps even more salutary to realize that the industries of the Netherlands (population 13 million) consumed more tin than the whole of the Indian subcontinent (population 600 million) in 1967, and nearly twice as much as the whole of Africa (population 280 million).

It is against this background that we should view the future of living standards in underdeveloped countries. Many social scientists seem to regard it as axiomatic that these countries should industrialize at the maximum possible rate, presumably with a view to achieving Western levels ultimately. Before one commits oneself to this view, however, consideration should be given to the *amounts* of raw materials that would be required to achieve the Western scale of industrialization in technology-deficient areas.

During the century from 1860–1960, in which its population grew from about 31 million to 180 million, the US consumed an estimated 45 million short tons of primary copper. If the population of the Indian subcontinent, *given no increase whatever*, were to use primary copper at the same rate per capita as did that of the US in the 1960s, during the coming century it would consume 450 million tons. If the remainder of the technology-deficient countries were to do the same thing, they would consume about 1.25 billion tons. Inevitably the question arises whether there is so much copper available in the earth's crust; are there the amounts of lead, tin, zinc, cobalt, manganese, and tungsten for their rates of extraction to be raised commensurately? And if there are enough metals, are there sufficient power supplies to drive the machines that would be manufactured?

Unfortunately there are, as yet, no precise answers to these questions, but increasingly intensive and comprehensive exploration is beginning to provide some indication of the size of many mineral reserves. The problem is not merely one of geological exploration however; nearly all elements are *present* in nearly all rocks, but usually in such small proportions as to make them economically unexploitable. In the case of many metals, relatively rich ores are of very limited extent and will soon be worked out; from then onward cost will make them unavailable to all but the richest nations.

Since 1940 technology has consumed more primary metal than during the whole of previous history. During the past ten years world production of industrial metals has been increasing at a rate of more than 6 percent per annum. The situation is already an urgent one with regard to certain scarce metals which, though only used in small quantities, are nevertheless vital to industrial complexes. The world production of mercury in 1969 stood at about 275,000 flasks (76 lbs.) per annum, and the US Bureau of Mines estimated world reserves, at $200 per flask, to be no more than 3,160,000 flasks. At this price and with world demand rising at no more than half its present rate, far more mercury would have to be mined over the next twenty years than is present on the basis of this estimate. If world prices were to rise to over $1,000 per flask, leaner ores could be exploited and world production might be maintained for fifty years; but the future of industrial development in technology-deficient countries is obviously in great jeopardy if prices rise in this way.

To a greater or lesser degree one can speak of the imminent exhaustion of the reserves of a large number of essential metals; the time scale with which the crisis is concerned is to be measured in decades rather than centuries. One can appreciate why so eminent a figure as the former Director of the US Bureau of Mines, Walter Hibbard, should have reached the conclusion that the time is rapidly approaching when indifference could be disastrous. The all too prevalent notion that mineral resources are to all intents and purposes inexhaustible must be discarded with the least possible delay.

ENERGY PROBLEMS

A recent review of the world's energy resources reinforces Hibbard's statement. Technology today is very dependent on fossil fuels, particularly coal and oil. Although, given time, these could be substantially supplemented and partially replaced by other sources of energy, contemporary solar energy, direct and indirect, cannot be harnessed to the extent that it could supply total requirements, even with the present world population. The vista of a great world industrial complex supplied by tidal power and vast batteries of photoelectric cells is an illusion, and potentialities for hydroelectric generation, though much greater, are nevertheless subject to certain limitations: although total world *potential* is certainly equal to the present world consumption of energy, it is very unequally distributed, and the great majority of impounded reservoirs do, after all, become silted up during the course of a century or two.

Nor can nuclear sources be regarded as a certain future source of almost unlimited, cheap energy as has so frequently been assumed. Apart from problems of waste disposal, it is by no means certain that power from fusion reaction will ever be available and, indeed, the whole future of fission energy is now in dire jeopardy: consumption of the relatively rare uranium-235 in non-breeder reactors could result in its complete exhaustion in relatively cheap deposits in a mere fraction of a century, resulting in a situation where nuclear power would be *more* expensive than power from fossil fuels and water.

One point is salient in this general picture: world reserves of petroleum —the mineral upon which world industry (particularly its transport sector) leans so heavily—are running out very rapidly. Evaluations from a range of estimates indicate quite clearly that the oil reserves of the US (excluding Alaska) had been reduced by half by about the year 1968, and that only 10 percent will remain by about the year 1990. Equivalent estimates of world resources show that they will have been halved by a point in time somewhere between 1988 and A.D. 2000 with 90 percent exhaustion somewhere between the years 2020 and 2030. The main corollary is that world oil production will begin to fall at the turn of the century if not well before it.

The prospect of an almost doubled world population along with a decreasing supply of petroleum in a mere thirty years' time should be a daunting one for any technologist; indeed the shortness of the time interval is the most disconcerting point of all. When one considers the small amount of fundamental change in the resource basis of industry that has occurred in the past quarter of a century and compares it with the enormous revolution that appears to be necessary over the next quarter, the tasks ahead seem insuperable.

The case of the hydrocarbon fuels illustrates the point very well. It is true that the earth's reserves of tar sands and bituminous coal are sufficient to supply requirements for several centuries, given the present rate of expansion. But the costs of transport and plant conversion that would be necessary to distill a large percentage of the earth's supply of liquid fuels from such materials would be enormous. Furthermore, such rapid developments can usually only be achieved with the accumulated capital and technical skills of an already developed country; again, the technology-deficient countries will be at a great disadvantage, and one can visualize this being particularly serious if it coincided with a great increase in the cost of nuclear energy.

OPTIMISM

With a hazard of these dimensions looming ahead one might expect that our species, unique in the animal kingdom for its capability for logical anticipation, would already be caught up in a near-frenzy of conservationist activity. In reality it is difficult to find serious public warnings, much less any sign of action. It is as though mankind has developed a blind faith in the immortality of the Industrial Revolution: ever since the great expansion began over a century and a half ago materials have been available, and it is unthinkable that this should not always be the case! Technology is taken to be omniscient, and even if resources are used up, substitutes will inevitably be found!

It is this faith in unspecified future technological innovation that is perhaps the most disturbing feature of our current social philosophy. It is completely unscientific and should certainly be deprecated by a body such as the British Association for the Advancement of Science. Any planning policy whose main prop rests upon unknowns rather than on rational assessment of what is known and understood indulges in nothing better than foolish optimism; its standpoint is exactly analogous to that of Mr. Micawber, but the evidence suggests that it has far less chance than he that something will actually turn up.

PESSIMISM

Before us there is a vision of what intellectual and material emancipation we, mankind, might achieve, and there is no technological reason why this should not materialize were *we* not so numerous. Indeed, just what might become possible, given time, cannot be imagined: a minority of mankind has already profited enormously after a mere century of development. But the press of numbers gives us so little time, and the door will inevitably close on the vast range of options open to mankind unless a revolution of unprecedented speed in attitudes and activities takes place within the next generation.

If the door does close, it will do so on an organism that is then forced into the position of having to destroy the remaining fertility of the planet in a vain effort to survive. The last precious resources will be used up carelessly and the very material that should be carefully husbanded will continue to contaminate the environment and vitiate the situation. As with the bacterial culture already referred to, an ultimate population crash to very low levels will be inevitable. Even if our species survives, the struggle back to a technological civilization will be subject to far greater restrictions than was originally the case. Nearly all easily accessible minerals will have been exhausted and the gene pool of the earth's ecosystems will be enormously reduced as compared to that which was available to man when he set out on his hunting and collecting forays in Paleolithic times.

This is no fanciful excursion into science fiction: given a continuation of present trends it is probably the most optimistic way of speaking of man's future. When the swarming stage is reached in nature, mass mortality is inevitable. But in nature, because of limited mobility, predators, and weather fluctuations, the effect of the swarm is rarely more than very local and the scars wrought by the temporary imbalance are soon healed. Because of his mobility and other aspects of his technology, man will be the first species to achieve the swarming stage simultaneously over the whole earth: from the point of view of all the other organisms in all the earth's ecosystems, man is becoming a "pest" everywhere at the same time. Furthermore, as a technological animal, he is more of a pest than other organisms that reach the swarming stage because he uses up non-renewable resources and produces inorganic by-products, whereas a non-technological species consumes mainly renewable resources and produces only organic waste.

If Homo sapiens, as a reasoning organism, is to have a chance of avoiding the population crash, he must simultaneously, and with the greatest speed, dramatically reduce his consumption of primary mineral material and he must cease to increase his numbers. There cannot be the slightest chance of the former unless the latter is achieved, since recycling any substance with 100 percent efficiency is an impossible goal, and even if achievable, could only cater for the present population at the present level of industrialization.

Three further doublings would produce a world population of 30 billion, and with the kind of birth rates and death rates experienced in the mid-twentieth century, this could easily be achieved in less than a century from now. And yet responsible estimates of the maximum sustained yield of world food supply have indicated that little more than three doublings are theoretically possible. It should be noted also that these estimates assume that all renewable assets are used with maximum efficiency and that the economic and social systems of the earth are rigorously managed as a unit with no major disruptions or mistakes.

Furthermore, the product of this almost inconceivable feat of organization would be a vast population at a chronic level of near starvation for the great majority and with personal choice and freedom of action reduced to a level far below that which obtains at present even in the under-privileged countries. Nor would there be any possibility whatsoever of any further population increase: those who might have continued to oppose birth control up to that point would no longer be able to do so without implicitly condemning people to certain death by starvation.

In the face of this prospect it is small wonder that the final policy statement of the Committee on Resources and Man of the United States Academy of Sciences contains the following recommendation:

That efforts to limit population increase in the nation and the world be intensified by whatever means are practicable, working towards a goal of zero rate of growth by the end of the [twentieth] century.

But even if this demographic miracle can be achieved, it will only be a short first step. Mere contemplation of the intricacies of the human ecological problem is depressing enough, but it is when one begins to consider the measures that are necessary for a long-term solution that one plumbs the depths of pessimism. In a world where politicians, economists, industrialists, and trade unions—capitalist and communist—are in almost universal agreement that an increased rate of growth is the panacea for nearly all our ills, how can a rapid and complete revolution in thought be possible? When the power of politicians and the wealth of business are ultimately dependent on the number and wealth of constituents and customers, how can it ever be possible to gain voluntary acceptance for a philosophy whose central theme is conservation and contraction?

It is not as though solid economic benefits can be offered as a reward to our children and grandchildren: a contracting economy would, of itself, create problems, and a new race of economists would have to be born to cater to a progressively aging population over two or three generations. In the Western countries in particular it is barely conceivable that any administration could persuade the population to accept a drastic reduction in standard of living so that conservation policies of world-wide scope could be effected and so that a much larger percentage of resources could be diverted to technology-deficient peoples.

In the present world, dogged by political and economic nationalism, racial tension, and conflicting political and religious ideologies, there seems to be no glimmer of hope that these problems of unprecedented magnitude can be solved in a mere quarter to half a century. It is small wonder that some have already reached the conclusion that *all* optimism is no more than foolish optimism, and that mankind (to use the words of Paul Ehrlich) may be "too far into the tube already" for any planned solution to be a practical possibility.

Perhaps those who anticipate the end of the road in this way are wrong, and some way out can be found. If so, it can only be through an unimaginable transference of our total scientific effort from exploitation to conservation. It is certainly to be hoped that those who have plumbed the depths of pessimism will not cease to urge constructive action along these lines in order to try to avert what they feel to be almost inevitable.

TASKS FOR THE PLANNER

Although the problems facing mankind have been presented here as essentially global ones, it should not be inferred that local effort in one's own community is pointless. Politicians must certainly be provided with the information necessary for a global strategy, but this cannot possibly succeed if human ecology on the local scale is not intensively studied to provide a basis for realistic planning. As pressures grow and shortages develop, a constant surveillance of man-land relationships in all kinds of environments will be a necessity. Indeed the need for analyzing developing land-use problems is so great that the efforts of planners of all kinds should surely not be misdirected and squandered as they are at the present time.

In a situation where so much effort is needed, trained social scientists and technologists must surely forsake many of the purely academic and fruitless exercises to which they are at present devoting their lives. As our cities swell and crumble about our ears, and as our agricultural lands deteriorate and disappear beneath bricks and mortar, it seems incredible that countless academics—be they civil engineers, architects, economists, geographers, or the rest—should sit in their university departments or municipal offices devising theoretical models of cities and transport networks for the year A.D. 2000. There can be no more pointless exercise if the former are to lack the bare necessities of subsistence and the latter are to have no power for traction.

Planning there must certainly be, indeed I am calling for planning at the most fundamental level. But any planning that ignores either of the two fundamentals in the equation—amounts of people and amounts of raw materials—must be baseless. Practitioners of superficial planning are wielding their bows in competition with Nero, and the developing conflagration promises to be a holocaust.

Don't Knock the $2-Trillion Economy

Peter Passell and Leonard Ross

"Wealth," wrote John Kenneth Galbraith in "The Affluent Society," "is not without its advantages and the case to the contrary, although it has been made, has never proved widely persuasive." But times have changed since 1958. We have become a richer nation but not, by common agreement, a happier one. The Gross National Product has gone up 64 per cent; but what of the gross national pleasure?

. . . "You could very comfortably have stopped growing after the first World War," the British economist Ezra J. Mishan recently said . . . "There was enough technology to make life quite pleasant. Cities weren't overgrown. People weren't too avaricious. You hadn't really ruined the environment as you have now, and built up entrenched industries so you can't go back."

That, in a nutshell, is the case against growth: more is less. More automobiles, cassette recorders and cook-in-a-pouch vegetables. Less satisfaction in the quality of the common life.

The case sounds simple, but it is really a sheaf of complaints misleadingly wrapped as one. Antimaterialism tells us that we have so much now that more can't really make us happier, while élitism confides that mushrooming incomes for the masses can only dilute the pleasures of those on top. Ecological conservatism says that the process of growth ruins our environment and may even risk the extinction of life. Antimaterialism warns that prosperity in the rich nations is hewn from the hides of other countries' poor.

Actually the sharp contrast in living standards between the United States and the rest of the industrialized world suggests the obvious virtues of the trillion-dollar economy. The average factory worker in Britain, earning half the wage of his Yankee counterpart, may in many respects lead an adequate existence. But he does it living with his wife and children in a three-room apartment, often without a refrigerator. The chances are good that his family shares a bathroom at the end of the hall. There is plenty of food on his dinner table, but too much of it is starch. To save money, his annual vacation is spent at a cheap seashore hotel a hundred miles from home. His kids cannot afford to go to college or, often, even to finish school.

Of course, none of this really proves that Englishmen are less happy than Americans. England may enjoy a less materialist culture than ours, and its poorly paid factory workers may be less prone to base their self-esteem on making money. To critics of growth, this cultural difference is far from accidental. Growth itself, they say, speeds up the treadmill of industrial life, creating the acquisitive values necessary to sustain it. . . .

Growth, then, often reflects some unappetizing values. But for the most part it does not create those values. American materialism and German regimentation could survive decades of economic stagnation. The low-growth Eisenhower years did not wean Americans from their dependence on tangible signs of success nor soften them up for an eventual change of consciousness. . . .

Even if America could remake her culture by reducing her growth rate, it is not clear that the trade would be worth making. English values, for example, are not unambiguously preferable to our own. . . .

Luckily, the question need not be answered. For better or worse, most Americans unambiguously cherish middle-class comforts. And the process of slowing growth is more likely to cause unnecessary ulcers than it is to alter our materialistic values. Thanks to the enormous capacity of the U.S. economy, Americans have since World War II lived better than the English live today. But the average working man is still far from achieving affluence. His take-home pay, after taxes, is about $110 a week. That suffices to keep the wolf from the door (especially if his wife also works) but buys few real luxuries. Our typical wage-earner knows quite well what to do with extra cash. He could use money for roomier housing to make the presence of his children less harassing; money for movies and restaurants and baby sitters as an alternative to Saturday night in front of the television set; money to support aging parents under a different roof.

The only way he has to get those things is through growth. The economic pie just is not big enough to go around, no matter how we choose to slice it. A reasonable growth rate, however, could easily double the average American's income in the next 25 years.

The *dolce vita* image of overabundance does not fit the facts—only 10 per cent of all families make $15,000 after taxes. . . .

. . . The obvious fact that a three-car garage and ski weekends in Switzerland don't guarantee happiness is a less than convincing reason for denying aspirants a chance at bourgeois living.

A less charitable interpretation of upper middle-class criticism of growth is that the élite understands it has more to lose than gain from the diffusion of the bourgeois standard throughout the United States. Wealth in America provides membership privileges in a rather exclusive club. And like most clubs, the tangible and intangible benefits of membership decline as the club expands.

Nature lovers grieve for their loss of privacy in national parks as more people can afford to make the trip. Skiers must endure endless lift lines and reckless adolescents on busy slopes where they once schussed in peace. Hit plays sell out months in advance; opera tickets are unpurchasable; *grand cru* Burgundy prices are bid up by *nouveaux* wine enthusiasts; vacationers must wait for hours to pick up mail at the London American Express.

· · ·

Intangible status losses accompany these very real losses in comfort and serenity. One of the virtues of a winter vacation in the Caribbean used to be the uniqueness of sporting a tan in January. Now this sign of affluence is shared with a half-million secretaries who can afford a week at the Montego Bay Holiday Inn. What is the purpose of shopping at Tiffany's or Neiman-Marcus if everybody else does too?

Such are the rules of a democratic society that this loss of privilege is only rarely marshaled as an argument against growth. The point is transformed into generalized *Angst* about materialist values, concern for the environment, an enthusiasm for population control. Automobiles are cast as the villains of a physically and spiritually depleted society with no recognition of the mobility they symbolize for most Americans. . . .

It would be unfair to tar all the opponents of growth as élites securing their room at the top. Economic growth has real costs which must be weighed against the benefits. Few of us are immune from the irritation of pollution linked to prosperity. River water used as a coolant by thousands of factories is dumped back, warmed and reeking with chemicals. Insecticides washed off millions of farms into the national water supply threaten to make fish toxic to man. Electric power plants, garbage incinerators and automobiles defile the air with gases slicing years off the lives of city dwellers.

It is even plausible, though not very convincing, that these side effects of prosperity have completely canceled out the benefits of further material accumulation. By this reasoning, a proper accounting would show that a billion-dollar increase in output creates more than a billion dollars' worth of damage from extra pollution. Put another way, the argument implies that growth is an illusion. Each new kilowatt of electricity has less value than the house paint and human lungs destroyed by the accompanying smoke. . . .

Economists have little quarrel with the need to weigh the costs of prosperity against the benefits, but they don't believe that the solution requires a slackening of growth. Pollution, they say, doesn't come from growth but from our perverse system of incentives to industry. Today firms aren't charged for using the biosphere as a dumping ground, so they poison the air and foul the water. Any resource for which no charge is made would likewise be overused by business. If precious metals were free, every steam shovel would be made of platinum. Since nobody is charged for using the environment, its value is ignored. The answer is not to stop aiming for growth but to start charging for pollution.

If Con Ed were forced to pay for its abuse of the air, the management would learn how to clean up its own mess. . . .

A corollary to the environment arguments against growth is the notion that fuel for the economic machine is finite; the more rapidly we grow, the more we hasten the day when the earth will be stripped of all usable raw materials. This natural-limit theory of growth is at the core of the elaborate computer simulation of the world created by engineer Jay Forrester of the Massachusetts Institute of Technology, which predicts economic collapse within a few generations. As a disciple, Anthony Lewis of The Times, writes: "Growth is self-defeating . . . the planet cannot long sustain it. . . . To ignore that tendency, to predict that growth can go on forever, is like arguing that the earth is flat. Only the consequences are more serious."

The fallacy in this reasoning is the assumption that raw materials will always be used in the future as they are today: when the last drop of oil is burned, the last truck will sputter to a halt. But the history of technology gives us every reason to believe that long before we run out of Arabian oil we will begin extracting petroleum from the vast reserves of oil-shale rocks and tar sands. And long before we run out of those reserves, cars will be powered with other sources of energy.

Appeals to faith in technical change are more than a cheap debating technique to counter the Forrester school. The technology of substituting plentiful materials for scarce ones grows every day. Silicates made from sand replace copper and silver radio circuitry; European cattle feeds are enriched with nutrients made of natural gas converted by bacteria; mattresses are filled with polyurethane which never was closer to a Liberian rubber tree than Bayonne, N.J. Among long-range prospects is the controlled-fusion reaction. This capture of the power of the hydrogen bomb could provide all the energy we would need for several billion years. Technology, of course, is neither entirely benign nor entirely predictable. But it would be foolish to act on the assumption that science has nothing more to offer.

Critics have used similar arguments about raw materials to link growth with our drive for economic and political domination of the Third World. . . .

This assault on growth raises two quite separate questions: Is American growth dependent on foreign raw materials? If so, does our consumption of these resources hurt the nations in which they are found?

. . . The American economy does use an increasing amount of the world's minerals. But that does not mean that we are becoming more dependent on them. Today, raw materials brought in from abroad constitute less than 1 per cent of the U.S. Gross National Product, and with few exceptions these materials can be found in North America (though at somewhat higher cost).

Of course, in the process of the expansion of world trade, American companies like Anaconda, Alcoa and Gulf have developed private stakes in the control of foreign resources. Corporate interests can more than occasionally be translated into American foreign policy; at its bleaker moments, the U.S. State Department has been the drone of Wall Street. But growth itself is not the villain and actually serves to weaken the rationale for imperialism. Gunboat diplomacy makes even less sense now for the United States than it did in 1906.

Nor is it true that American economic growth is necessarily injurious to the Third World. Underdeveloped countries need dollars to buy industrial products more than they need their own raw materials. Chile has more use for turbines and tractor parts than for mountains of copper ore. The only way it can buy these goods is through trade. A slowdown in American growth would simply mean reduced American demand for most of the products of the world's poorer nations.

So far we have spoken only of the arguments against growth—the fruits of progress, it seems to us, need not be electric can openers, sulphurous rivers and castrated banana republics. But rapid growth as a national policy has a *raison d'être* more pressing than the extension of the good life beyond Scarsdale. Quite simply, growth is the only way in which America will ever reduce poverty.

The attraction of growth is that nobody gets to vote on the slice of its benefits saved for the poor. While the relative share of income that poor people get seems to be frozen, their incomes do keep pace with the economy. It's more lucrative to wash cars or wait on tables today than 20 years ago. Even allowing for inflation, the average income of the bottom 10th of the population has increased about 55 per cent since 1950. Twenty more years of growth could do for the poor what the Congress won't do.

Growth is not a romantic goal, nor is it a military or strategic imperative. It offers at most a partial substitute for the measures which America should take to create a humane society. We do not argue for growth as an obsession or an object of heroic sacrifice, but simply as a sober undertaking for a nation in which scarcity is not for many a thing of the past.

Economic Implications of Environmental Crisis

John Hardesty

There are two fundamentally opposed positions on the environment that are held by economists today: the orthodox position and the stationary-state position. Evidence heavily supports the latter viewpoint, and social and political implications weigh heavily on the overall situation.

The orthodox and stationary-state positions involve a close interrelationship yet distinction between resource depletion and environmental destruction. Resource depletion is the total usage of nonreplaceable mineral resources and fossil fuels. Environmental destruction, on the other hand, is the filling of environmental sinks and pollutable reservoirs with gaseous, liquid, and solid wastes—a serious disruption of natural ecosystems vital to the continuance of life. The stress should be on survival in a livable world. Unfortunately, there are too many economists who see the problem as simply too much dirt in the air or water, and an unsightly mess here or there.

The orthodox position of the environmental situation holds that there can be no problem of resource depletion because these nonreplaceable resources are appropriable by the individual firm. This means that they will be owned by some individual or company and will be sold at a market price reflecting both the availability of the resource and the consumer need. Walter Heller, former economic advisor to Lyndon Johnson, claimed that, "intensive scientific research and technological development—responding partly to the alarms . . . but mostly to the signals sent out by the pricing system—resulted in the upgrading of old resources, the discovery of new ones, the development of substitutes, and the application of more efficient ways of utilizing available resources and adjusting to changes in relative availabilities."

The orthodox faith in the pricing system falters on the issue of environmental destruction, however, because it is realized that environmental sinks such as the atmosphere and bodies of water are not appropriable; they cannot be privately owned. Here the market mechanism fails altogether since private firms, in their effort to maximize profit by minimizing their own costs, will tend to impose excessive costs on the natural environment, the work environment, and on nearby communities. In order to minimize private costs of production, they will maximize the social costs of production that all must bear.

One feasible solution is the government levying of taxes on the guilty products equal in amount to the dollar value of the social costs of pollution imposed on society. This will naturally increase prices to the consumers of the products and lower the resulting quantity in demand. At this point, the remaining pollution is considered optimal from the point of view of economic welfare. Furthermore, polluting firms are seen as having an incentive to clean up, and, in addition, the government may use the pollution tax revenues to aid this process.

A few of the more conservative economists take this nonappropriability argument to its logical conclusion, pointing out that all would be well if only there was a way to sell the atmosphere over Richmond to Standard Oil of California or Lake Erie to U.S. Steel. Then, if Exxon or Bethlehem wants to pollute, they will have to pay for it—thus internalizing the social costs of pollution, making them private costs to the firm.

The stationary-state position maintains that the chief cause of both resource depletion and environmental destruction is exponential growth. Linear growth is an absolute amount of increase per unit of time. Exponential growth is a percentage increase per unit of time. National and world economies grow exponentially. An all-important characteristic of exponential growth is suddenness.

The stationary-state position argues that exponential economic growth inevitably requires exponential resource depletion and that the suddenness factor may soon be upon us. For support they point to a whole range of nonrenewable resources that are becoming increasingly scarce. They illustrate the impact of exponential depletion by comparing a static index— one that gives the number of years known reserves would last if present world use did not increase—with an exponential index—one that shows the number of years remaining, given current growth trends. For example, the static index for coal is around 2,300 while the exponential index is only 111. In the case of all-important crude oil, the exponential index is only 24, and even a doubling of known crude reserves will add only 12 years.

The stationary-state position on environmental destruction maintains that all power pollutes and all production does also. Trying to attempt to produce more services and less of the supposedly more destructive manufactured goods at most delays the inevitable as long as exponential growth continues. The same is true for less environmentally destructive technologies. For example, hydrocarbon emissions may be reduced for each car, but if the total automobile population continues to grow exponentially, then the reductions will eventually be overwhelmed and hydrocarbon pollution will continue to increase. According to the MIT *Limits to Growth* study, ". . . on the basis of the physical constraints of the planet . . . the growth phase cannot continue for another one hundred years. . . . if the global society waits until those constraints are unmistakably apparent, it will have waited too long."

The stationary-state position also offers some specific criticisms of the orthodox view. First, the orthodox position assumes a precision in determining social costs that we simply do not have. Ecologists have warned that their science is relatively new and still largely descriptive. They simply cannot accurately predict what current or future effect a new product or production process will have on natural systems. Second, there is the problem of the rate at which we discount the interests of future generations. People tend to value what happens today more than next year. Third, even if social costs could be quantified, they are likely to be found to be huge, particularly when the quality of human life as well as natural ecosystems are included. To impose equivalent taxes on particular products could be outrageous. Think of the price of an automobile if it included a tax equal in amount to all the social disruption, misery, death, and natural destruction for which it is responsible. Certainly only a few of the corporate and political elite would even be able to afford one.

A fourth criticism is already implicit—such taxes on pollution are extremely regressive because they hit the lower incomes the hardest and the higher incomes the least. Here criticisms of environmental elitism heard from working and poor people are well founded.

Fifth, the international elitism implicit in the orthodox position must also be pointed out. The natural response of a profit-maximizing firm faced with a stringent pollution tax would be to consider relocating abroad in a less-developed nation that does not have such a program. The runaway-shop phenomenon is already underway on a large scale in response to tax advantages and lower wage scales available in less-developed countries. The effect of this is not only to take jobs away from U.S. workers but also to relocate environmental destruction from the rich to the poor countries (while, of course, the profits return to the U.S.). This is hardly a solution to the worldwide problems of the physical constraints of the growth phase.

A final criticism of the orthodox position concerns its assumption of continuous (exponential) growth of technology to offset exponential growth of the economy and resource depletion. The stationary-state advocates point out that taking past rates of growth of technology and projecting them into the future is a very risky business. The most optimistic technological assumptions imaginable today find that this only adds a few years to the period before ultimate disaster occurs. The *Limits to Growth* study has stated that, "Technology can relieve the symptoms of a problem without affecting the underlying causes."

On resource depletion, the standard reply is that if natural resources were indeed growing scarcer it would be expected that the price of such commodities would increase. In fact they have not. Resource prices have been more or less constant over the past 100 years when adjusted for general inflation.

On the *Limits to Growth* study, the sustained abuse has been such that one can only conclude that the supporters of the orthodox position must feel extremely threatened. When academic economists use extremely emotional language, they are really upset.

To specific criticisms, the orthodox reply is, first, that even if we cannot determine the exact amount of social costs, any pollution tax will be better than none at all. We will manage to bumble through the environmental crisis as we have others. Second, the orthodox position denies the assertion that social costs of production are huge. Two well-known economists set the level of environmental disadvantages associated with the growth of the Gross National Product at only $35 billion in 1965, approximately five percent of the GNP. The same study shows that when these social costs are subtracted from the GNP along with certain other regrettables, such as police services and defense expenditures, the adjusted measure continues to grow at an average rate of 1.1 percent per year. Thus economic growth does add to our well-being—so they maintain.

Finally, in response to the charge of environmental elitism, the orthodox economists reverse the accusation by maintaining that economic growth is needed not only to provide resources to clean up the environment but also to provide the means to eliminate poverty, cleanse urban ghettos, and fight crime. This, apparently, is based on some kind of ideal conception rather than on real world experience, for the decade of the 1960s was one of unprecedented economic growth accompanied by declining environmental and social conditions.

The findings of two excellent technical studies carried out by researchers not identified with either extreme position provide helpful settlement of this matter. On the issue of resource depletion, Robert U. Ayres and Allen V. Kneese, a physicist and an economist respectively, make several key points. They indicate that it has been largely through the use of increasingly large-scale operations and high-cost technology that it has been possible to exploit ores of declining quality without corresponding price increases. This implies that we must expect diminishing returns to this process and that it will not be able to continue indefinitely.

Second, part of the increased output of the extractive industries in the last century can be attributed to the opening up of previously unexplored areas such as Canada, Siberia, Australia, Africa, and Brazil. Third, lower quality ores in some important minerals do not necessarily exist in exploitable quantities, for example, lead and zinc. The prices of mineral resources, a fourth point, have not reflected the social costs arising from pollution and waste disposal and these costs can be expected to increase rapidly in the future. Additionally, some government policies such as depletion allowances have in effect subsidized lower prices.

Finally, the developed countries are rapidly using up their domestic high-grade sources of minerals and fossil fuels and becoming increasingly dependent on less-developed countries. In the future we can expect, according to Ayres and Kneese, to see more of these countries banding together to protect their natural resources and to extract higher prices for what they do sell. Of course, the success of the Organization of Petroleum Exporting Countries is exactly along these lines.

Key technical questions in favor of the stationary-state position are increasingly settled: resources are becoming increasingly scarce; social costs of production (imposed on the environment) are pervasive, large, and related to output of goods and services; and fundamental change rather than ad hoc taxes are required to deal with the problem.

Economist-environmentalists have discussed the necessary framework. Here the economy-environment nexus is viewed as a flow process whereby raw materials are extracted from the natural environment; processed into goods and services with the aid of labor, machinery, and energy; and then discharged back into the environment as solid waste along with the other emittances from production and consumption.

To orthodox economics this flow-through process is an end in itself. The happy economy is the economy that can produce the greatest flow (GNP). This economic flow is more properly viewed as a means to an end. The end, of course, is human well-being. Human well-being is a level or a stock, not a *flow*. A rational society would determine (democratically) the most desirable quality of life (or stock of material and mental well-being) for its members, then minimize the economic flow necessary to maintain this optimal level. This means, for example, eliminating wasteful consumption that merely makes money for some business interests, designing essential products to be durable rather than profitable, and getting rid of the excess baggage of military spending. Adjustments in the level of human welfare could be made up or down as the community desired, but for any given level the economic flow would be minimized. It hardly needs pointing out that this is also ecologically rational—under these conditions both resource depletion and environmental destruction would be minimized. It is worth adding that while recycling is no panacea (it requires energy, labor, and capital inputs), it should be utilized wherever feasible.

The environmental imperative requires the following:

(1) A nongrowing, minimum Gross National Product economy (the stationary state).
(2) Systematic and coherent nationwide programs for environmental quality management to include provision of efficient, available, and low-cost mass transit and other public investment programs.

Yet this is not only unbearable but impossible under current economic institutions. It is no accident that orthodox economists see maximum economic flow as an end in itself. The private enterprise economy of capitalism is based on economic growth. Growth is inherent to the system, and the present economic system cannot survive without it. The individual corporation's reason for existence is to maximize profits and sales. Profit maximization requires socially irrational practices such as planned obsolescence and wasteful consumption. General Motors could not survive if automobiles lasted 25 years instead of five. At an even more fundamental level, the capitalist firm, in order to survive and increase profits, must reinvest its profits and expand; it must conduct an unending search for new products and new markets. Adding together these firms give us an economy that must grow in order to provide jobs and profits. It is important to understand that, while this is socially and environmentally irrational, it is economically rational within the capitalist framework. Governmental efforts to modify the search for profits, to create soulful corporations, merely increase the economic irrationality of the capitalist system—on this the conservative economists are correct.

On a macroeconomic or national level, the federal government is committed to use its taxing, spending, and monetary powers to assure economic growth, for without it, under capitalist institutions, recessions or depressions would result. Minimizing economic flow in our present economy would mean people out of work, profits dropping sharply and abruptly, and stock markets crashing. Thus we are faced with a choice of two evils—economic growth on the one hand, or unemployment and economic disaster on the other.

The environmental imperative requires the following institutional framework:

- ☐ A stationary state for the U.S. and world but for the U.S. first and foremost, and not for the less-developed nations for some time to come. This implies an investment rate equal to the rate of depreciation of the capital stock; a birthrate equal to the death rate; and that these rates, representing flows, be minimized consistent with the desired level of human well-being. Included must be a relentless effort to minimize the differences in living standards between the over-developed and the less-developed countries, perhaps by including in our constant flow a certain quantity of output to be transferred to those nations whose resources helped us become over-developed in the first place.
- ☐ The stationary-state economy must be founded not on production for profit and private ownership but on production for social benefit and social ownership.
- ☐ Resources must be allocated and tasks coordinated and carried out through the use of decentralized, democratic planning and the voluntary social motivation of people as opposed to the individualistic personal-gain incentives of the market.
- ☐ In a nongrowing economy there must be essential income and wealth equality with differentials based primarily on need as contrasted with the present system that is based, by definition, on a substantial inequality that is irremediable (that is, a few own the means of production and most do not).
- ☐ Economic self-sufficiency of communities and nations must be stressed. This is particularly important in order to conserve national

resources by making use of uneconomic local reserves. This should help to prevent over-exploitation of internal regions and less-developed nations. It should also encourage substitution of small-scale energy technologies (wind and solar power especially) for those based on fossil and nuclear fuels.

These changes would necessitate economic, political, and social decentralization. Particularly important would be the replacement of our very large urban conglomerations with human-sized, human-oriented, and ecologically sound communities distributed more evenly across the land. Such diversification is necessary to counter the simplification of society, economy, and ecosystems now occurring that do not add to human happiness and, in fact, create an ecologically untenable future.

Toward a Socialist Alternative

The deepening crisis of modern life has placed capitalism on trial. Its defenders often reject the socialist alternative on what they believe to be practical grounds. They may admit that socialism is an interesting idea, or even a desirable goal, but they insist that it cannot work because it does not take human nature into account. Yet recent events have shown the by-products of capitalism to include racism, war, inequality, and alienation—inevitable in a society rooted in economic self-interest, with its means of production privately owned. Such a system will never allow the best traits of human beings to emerge, and is thus incompatible with the creation of a good society. Under socialism, Marx insisted, "we shall have an association, in which the free development of each is the condition for the free development of all." Socialism has as its goal the construction of institutions dedicated to equality, humanity, and community—in other words, to the creation of a classless society. It is the socialist belief

that if the pernicious institutions that have hitherto governed us are destroyed and replaced by others more compatible with basic human needs, there are no limits to the possibilities for humankind. Capitalist intellectuals are, on the other hand, hopelessly utopian (in the pejorative sense of that term), for they believe that perverse institutions can somehow create "good" societies. There is no guarantee, of course, that statism and bureaucracy can be avoided under socialism. But capitalist America, as well as Soviet Russia, has created a Leviathan State; and bureaucracy already exists in America's mammoth corporate structures. There is reason to believe that the Soviet pattern would *not* be duplicated by American socialism; the Russian Revolution took place, after all, in a backward agricultural country surrounded by hostile capitalist powers.

Moreover, American tradition, however violated in practice, abhors bureaucracy and centralization. The radical movement in this country reflects this tradition, repudiating not only the Stalinist bureaucracy of the Soviet Union, but also the proliferation of manipulative practices, the undemocratic imposition of bureaucratic programs from above, and the tightening restrictions on personal freedoms here in America. Bureaucracy, then, may be less of a problem in a socialist society in which the administrative ethos has been inspired by both Marx and Jefferson. Still, dehumanizing bureaucratic practices, deeply entrenched, are not easily eradicated and will vex the new socialist society for many years to come.

The readings in this final section of the book deal with this and other problems. In Reading 62, Professor Thomas Sowell contrasts the alternatives of capitalism and socialism from a mainstream point of view. A radical statement of what distinguishes capitalism from socialism is provided in Reading 63 by Professor William K. Tabb of Queens College (CUNY).

American socialism, should it occur, will naturally draw upon American traditions and reflect our level of economic development. Nonetheless, socialist experiments elsewhere, especially in China, are not without lessons and interest. Professor John Gurley of Stanford University, former editor of *The American Economic Review*, sheds new light on Maoist economics (see Reading 64). Gurley is sharply critical of bourgeois sinologists for their biased, shallow, and incompetent analysis of the People's Republic of China. Finally, in the last piece included in this volume, Marxist economist Paul Sweezy tries to pull together these and other considerations and to set up a general theoretical framework in which the transition from capitalism to socialism may be considered (see Reading 65).

The preceding essays indicate what humans can hope ultimately to achieve through socialism. However, many short-run problems of socialism remain unsolved, and detailed plans to follow once power is assumed have not yet been formulated. There is no socialist consensus, for example, on how much of the market mechanism should be retained. Should all productive private property be taken over, and, if so, how fast should this be accomplished? Should incomes immediately be made equal? These and other economic problems of the transition will be truly formidable. No blueprint for their solution is proffered here, but I am convinced that, when expenditures on armaments are terminated, the resources released will so advance the rate of productivity that the transition to a prosperous socialist society can be speedily accomplished. Many other problems that plague America should be similarly short-lived. Assuming that black people would be part of the coalition bringing about a socialist revolution, it is not hard to envision discrimination wiped out by fiat (as happened in Cuba) and, in time, a new generation free of racist attitudes.

In the development of the socialist human being, three obstacles of exceptional difficulty may be encountered. The first involves the relationship between men and women. The need to dominate or be dominated is a deep-rooted neurosis. It is not known to what extent neuroses and insecurity are conditioned responses to economic and social exploitation. Socialists believe that in a more rationally constructed society the tensions that produce neuroses in general and male supremacism in particular will be greatly reduced. No longer, for example, will women be treated as sex objects in the interests of commercialism.

Women—even working women —are now assigned household chores. Responsibility for cooking, cleaning, shopping, and child-rearing must be fundamentally altered. Apart from bearing and nursing children, sexual division of labor is a social convention. There is no physiological reason that prevents men from doing most jobs now performed by women, and vice versa. A socialist ethic will permit other alternatives because it will recognize *social* responsibility for many tasks now assumed individually. For example, public nurseries and inexpensive dining facilities

might be set up. No one, however, has any reason to be dogmatic about either this form of child care or the future of the family. These decisions will be freely made by those involved, and much room for healthy variation is possible.

The second problem is closely related to the first. The globe cannot support increased numbers of people: *population must be curbed*. Abortions, for instance, must be not only legalized but encouraged. But, of course, not all births take place because people are ignorant of the means of prevention or are legally constrained from using them. Individuals become parents for many reasons, including the need to exert power over other human beings, the desire to avoid the loneliness of old age, the need to prove one's manliness or womanliness, and the more positive wish to give and receive love. With the emancipation of women and the development of a new social ethic—one that stresses social responsibility—control of population may prove less difficult than many believe.

Finally, society must come to grips with the problems created by technology. We are within reach of a life free from drudgery and toil. But indiscriminate use of technology has also brought humankind to the brink of disaster. It must be controlled. We are all painfully aware of the destruction of our natural surroundings. Pavement inexorably replaces open land, streams are polluted, and foul air is almost taken for granted. Few of us are aware of the fear of ecologists that the carbon dioxide-oxygen balance, upon which life itself depends, may be tipping. At the same time that the oxygen content of the atmosphere is threatened by the destruction of plant life, expanding technology increases the number of users of combustion engines, adding greater quantities of carbon dioxide to the atmosphere. Constraints on technology are desperately needed. We must therefore seek, not ever-increasing material wealth, but rather, incomes merely high enough to meet basic human needs. This must not be construed as a call to leap backward into poverty; existing technology, properly used, makes possible a high degree of comfort for all. I do, however, urge a more modest concept of affluence. Ultimately, we must be induced to prefer leisure to goods, learning and spiritual growth to acquisition.

Karl Marx believed that the precondition to a meaningful, spiritual life was freedom from the necessity to perform coerced labor, and that technology would allow humankind to triumph over nature. Capitalism, in Marx's view, stood in the way of true freedom because it fettered the development of production and technology. Marx was only partly right; technological development is necessary, but it is not sufficient to effect human liberation. The primary barriers to human development created by capitalism are psychological, rather than material. We are induced to buy goods we do not need and things that bring us no spiritual joy; in so doing, we perpetuate our enslavement. The achievement of liberty requires an ethical commitment to leisure, learning, and reflection. Ecological considerations preclude endless growth for its own sake. We have no alternative but to accede to these natural considerations, for in the final analysis nature itself determines what we are free to do.

62

Capitalism Versus Socialism

Thomas Sowell

"Capitalism" usually means private ownership not only of direct consumer goods but also of the means of production, including investment channels, and a system in which the allocation of resources responds to prices on a profit-maximization principle. "Socialism" typically implies national collective ownership of the means of production, including investment channels, and resource allocation according to priorities established by a political process.

So-called "market socialism" would enforce governmentally determined priorities indirectly, by arranging personal income distribution in whatever way was considered desirable, and by special taxes and subsidies on goods whose output was to be given special restriction or encouragement—but would allow a market to function along profit-maximization lines, though the profits might go to a particular enterprise or to the government treasury rather than to the head or owner of each firm. By contrast, "central planning" socialism would directly allocate resources and distribute output in physical units or in value units *not* determined by supply and demand in the market, but according to the decisions made by the central government. Socialism as a political movement has always stressed a need for a more equal personal distribution of income than that which exists under capitalism, so this may be considered an important goal under both market socialism and central planning socialism.

Market socialism as a pure type differs from capitalism as a pure type only in the absence of private ownership of the means of production and of investment channels. This would permit a socialist government to do the following:

1. Eliminate monopolistic or oligopolistic pricing, and other practices which prevent the kind of optimal results achievable under perfect competition.
2. Internalize external costs by judging the profitability of an enterprise (and the rewards of its managers) according to "shadow prices," which include the external social costs and benefits not collectible in the market process.
3. Reduce and eliminate depressions and unemployment brought on by uncoordinated production in which each capitalist knows only his own production plans but not those of his fellow producers, who may be, altogether, overstocking or understocking the market.
4. Correct personal income distribution inequities resulting from the mere historical accident of ancestors' differential access to natural resources or other advantages, which were an artifact of existing social arrangements rather than a result of any personal contribution to national economic well-being.

5. Enable government regulation of business to be redirected to the public interest rather than becoming dominated by the regulated industry, whose owners' wealth makes them politically influential.
6. Eliminate mutually canceling activities, such as competitive advertising by advertisers who offset one another's claims.

Critics of socialism have argued that not only may some of these problems be corrected under capitalism, but that the distinguishing feature of socialism—the absence of capital ownership—is also the key weakness of its market mechanism. Resources must be allocated, not only among competing uses at a given time, but also between present uses and future uses, via the investment process. Iron ore may go into the current production of typewriters or into the production of machines that will produce future typewriters. In the first case, there will be more typewriters during the current period, and in the second case more typewriters in the future.

How much more output in the future can be obtained by how much sacrifice of present consumption is a technical question, and how much preference there is for present over future consumption depends upon people's taste. A government commission may be able to estimate the former, but the latter requires that people actually be faced with the alternatives—a safe 8 percent return on investment in a new typewriter plant, versus a less certain 12 percent return on investment in an unproven new product, versus spending the money for a trip instead of investing it at all. Merely *asking* people what they prefer, in a polling booth or in public opinion surveys, is no substitute for actually confronting them with the concrete alternatives. Pulling a lever or checking a box costs virtually nothing, but committing your hard-earned money is something to stop and think about.

In addition to determining how much total investment is optimal for the economy in the light of people's time preferences, a capital market determines *who* will get control of how much of the available investment resources—and can take these resources away if either the existing managers' efficiency falls below expectations or if potentially *more* efficient managers come along. Where capital assets are salable to the highest bidder and bids and acceptances are based on profit maximization, the more efficient potential users, who by definition have a higher prospective income stream from the same physical assets than do their current owners, can afford to pay the latter more than the assets' present value under present ownership and management, and to profit by the remaining difference between the two values. Property is transferred every day for precisely this reason, and the same principles apply to everything from vacant lots to multi-billion-dollar corporations.

Under administrative allocation, both the original assignment of capital assets and any future transfers would be based on the judgments of political officials responsible for a wide range of complicated economic decisions, and who suffer no personal penalty from wrong decisions and make no personal gain from correct decisions.[1] By contrast, capital transfers through a market

---

[1] If the decision maker is "wrong" in a way which can be readily seen or demonstrated by everyone, there can be political repercussions, but the bulk of economic decisions may be right or wrong in terms of alternatives which the

involve people with specialized knowledge of the particular industry and assets involved, who stand to personally gain or lose by the correctness of their decisions. Insofar as the capital market mechanism is functioning competitively, this means that powerful incentives are at work to produce a decision which is *socially* optimal, though based only on the individual self-interest of current owners and potential bidders.

Believers in fully centralized social planning also criticize market socialism—for not going further in that direction. Market socialism appears to them as essentially capitalism with the technical difference that deeds of ownership are in government hands instead of in private vaults. Pure market socialism which depended on the labor market to place people at the various tasks that need doing would end up with the same wage and salary differentials as would capitalism—or would pay the penalty of reduced output because of inefficient allocation if it did not. When central planners have the legal authority to place people where their work is most needed, according to the planners' judgment, there is no need for wage differentials. But freedom of choice of occupations and locations for the individual means that the government's choices are restricted to (1) providing whatever wage and salary differentials are necessary to get people where they ought to be, or (2) accepting lower total output in the interest of more equal income distribution by failing to provide as large differentials as needed.

The same reasoning applies to allocation over time. An individual who is free to invest or not to invest current time and effort in acquiring work skills for the future will make that investment only to the extent that the future return is sufficiently greater—in pay differentials for skill—that it repays his current loss of time and effort, with sufficient "profit" to overcome his time preference. Only if people can be assigned to tasks—and work just as efficiently when assigned as when voluntarily working for a salary differential—can skilled work, including management, be kept from earning as large a differential under socialism as in a competitive capitalist market.

Central planning differs from both capitalism and market socialism in replacing the variety of individual consumer preferences and priorities with one governmental set of preferences and priorities. Sometimes the establishment of government priorities is based on the belief that the government understands the alternatives better than the public, meaning that it makes the same decision which the public would have made in the light of its own pattern of preferences, if it had possession of the necessary knowledge and expertise. This argument can of course be used in practice to conceal the fact that the government officials' preferences are different, and that the cost of satisfying them is being externalized to the public via the governmental process.

Another argument is that the government's preferences are different in a nobler direction—including the interest of unborn generations who are

---

public neither knows nor understands. This lack of *general* knowledge and understanding of the economic system as a whole does no great damage as long as each individual is reasonably aware of his own alternatives and preferences in a market situation, but to monitor central planners requires training and knowledge of a much higher order.

not around to vote their interests in the marketplace or in the political process. This argument is stronger politically than economically, since the future use of currently available resources competes in a capitalistic market with their current uses through the investment markets and through speculation in land and natural resources.

Two of the major government priorities which can be imposed under central planning are in income distribution and in the division of current output into consumer goods and capital investments. The former involves a high and highly visible cost, in lost incentives to locate and acquire skills where and in the amounts needed. Early attempts to equalize pay right after the Bolshevik revolution in Russia had to be reversed by Lenin to restore the economy to a functioning level, and Stalin raised pay differentials even more (above those of capitalist countries in many cases) in his industrialization plans.

The power to set income differentials according to social philosophy rather than economic principles is one which can be exercised in practice only at a cost in reduced output that many socialist countries have refused to pay when confronted with the concrete choice. The great socialist theoreticians, including Karl Marx,[2] saw this long ago, but the moral fervor behind this idea in the socialist tradition has led to its being attempted again and again, in disregard of the experience of previous socialists. Sometimes the feeling has been that only selfish, capitalist-formed men need such income inequalities to make them do what is necessary, but that a more unselfish breed of men, reared in socialist surroundings, would not. This then becomes a question of (1) the degree of malleability of human nature, (2) the length of time necessary to accomplish the change, and (3) an estimate of where we stand in this respect at a given moment. These are all empirical questions in principle, though perhaps unanswerable in practice, and thus far the bias shown in efforts to equalize pay has been toward overoptimism as to immediate results.

The ability of a centrally planned economy to increase its rate of investment above that which normally occurs in a market economy has been a striking feature of socialist economies, notably in the rapid industrialization of the Soviet Union, which has captured the imagination of many poor, preindustrial nations. Here central planners simply substitute their time preferences for those of individuals, causing those individuals to consume less than otherwise and to invest more. There are no *visible* losses from this process analogous to the losses of output from lack of sufficient pay incentives, because the loss suffered is in subjective disutility, whatever its magnitude.

Another way of viewing this process might be to regard it as the purchase of ideological satisfaction and/or national prestige by government officials at costs externalized to the public. This possibility is not inherent in socialism but in centrally directed economic growth under any form of economy with a government not removable by the voting public. A czarist ministry, long before Stalin, adopted the slogan "Let us starve but export!" as a means of forced industrialization. This particular advantage or dis-

---

[2] Karl Marx, *Critique of the Gotha Program,* Sections 1–3.

advantage of centrally planned socialism is in reality a function of the insulation of political decision makers from voter reprisal rather than a distinguishing feature of socialism or capitalism as such.

In the absence of voter reprisal or of an articulate opposition, the grossest inefficiencies may be concealed where they take the form of a lesser total satisfaction than that possible from given resources—even if it is less by vast amounts—when people are in desperately poor circumstances. Ironically, many inefficiencies of central planning in the Soviet Union became manifest enough for corrective measures to be taken only after a sufficient level of economic well-being had been reached for the public to stop buying certain goods that did not fit their preferences. In poorer times, everything was so badly needed that no goods piled up on the shelves to embarrass the central planners. Although losses of efficiency are harder on the public when they are desperately poor, they are harder on the central planners after prosperity is achieved. Various economic reforms in the Soviet Union in recent years, relaxing the degree of central control on consumer goods, are a product of the now accepted view that central planning has its limitations.

Capitalism, like socialism, can be centrally planned as well as operating with a market. Fascist states have typically allowed private property to exist, though controlling its use in accordance with the plans of the national government. The superficial resemblance of this arrangement to traditional socialist ideals caused the German fascists to call themselves National Socialists—shortened to Nazis. Under fascism, the right to receive income from property is retained but the right to allocate it to uses determined by market supply and demand is canceled. However, the extreme limit of planning is incompatible with private ownership of capital, just as the extreme limit of a market economy—including a capital market—is incompatible with socialism. In between, all sorts of combinations exist.

Capitalist State Planning Is Not Socialism

William K. Tabb

There is increasing talk in this country about a gradual, relatively painless transition to socialism. This is dangerous and foolish talk, especially when it comes from self-professed socialists who should know better. In its approach it is very close to the "greening of America" notions of the 1960's, which deny the central point of class contradictions and thus presume away the strength of the obdurate forces which preserve the system. The issue is not being faced.

Liberal theorists see the state as above the rest of society, mediating between different interest groups. In the pluralist model, many voices are heard and some compromise which accords with the "public interest" is developed. It is assumed that different views exist, coalitions are built, and while conflicts do arise, it is in everyone's interest to compromise. After hard bargaining each accepts the outcome, at least for that round. In place of the liberal's question, "Given a certain class structure, how will the various classes, with their divergent and often conflicting interests, manage to get along together?," the question might be posed as: "How did a particular class structure come into being, and by what means is its continued existence guaranteed?" Radicals drawing on the Marxist conception might well say: "It is clear that the state exists as the creation of the most powerful class or classes in a given historical epoch and is used in their interests." The assertion that the state stands above individual interests is a weak reed on which to place the burden of a serious argument. While the desires of the dominant group are put forward as if they were in the interest of all of society's members, too much evidence exists to lead to easy acceptance of such a notion. Consider the implications of a situation in which the disadvantaged classes held state power; attempts would surely be made to establish a social order more favorable to their own interests. Why can't the same presumption be made about the rich and powerful who, after all, hold office in government? The dominant class has every interest in seeing that its representatives hold public office, that its ideology be widely accepted and that its preferences appear to be naturally correct. The most important aim of the state under capitalism is to preserve property relationships—the right of some to own the factories, mines and other capital, and the necessity of most people who do not own such assets to work for them. Under the guise of protecting individual rights to own a home, a car, etc. (assets which do not allow further accumulation), capitalists encourage workers to defend the power of banks, large corporations and capitalist relations more generally. But private property and capitalist property are not one and the same thing. The latter requires a relationship of exploitation, the former does not imply class domination.

As Paul Sweezy, a leading Marxist theorist, writes: "Capitalist private property does not consist in things—things independently of their ownership—but in a social relation between people. Property confers upon its owners freedom from labor and the disposal over the labor of others, and this is the essence of all social domination whatever form it may assume."

There is no secret conspiracy involved in the government's protecting of capital. The government is staffed by corporate executives and lawyers who have spent their lives in the service of corporations. The relation between most members of the Cabinet and Congress and our large corporations is an intimate one. There are few production workers in Congress, and consumer advocates are unlikely to be invited to sit in the Cabinet. Yet, who would doubt that a representative chosen from the plant floor in open debate and by free ballot would not serve working people and consumers generally better in government than do the lawyers, corporate officials and other representatives of wealth who now dominate government?

This is not to say that gains cannot and have not been made under capitalism. By winning the right to vote and by struggling to form unions, working people have won important weapons. It is too facile to say that there is no one to vote for who can realistically win, that unions act as agencies to control worker militancy. While both statements may in many, even most instances be true, the working class is better off because it can to a greater extent than previously make its demands effective. Short of seizing state power, it must use whatever weapons it can, no matter how inadequate. The task is to build organizations which genuinely serve working-class interest.

PLANNING AND THE STATE

The difficulty with pushing reformist solutions so far that they break asunder the bounds of the old order is that the way in which the reform is implemented is not decided by the mass movement raising the demand and pressuring for its acceptance, but instead by those controlling the dominant societal institutions. Even control through an electoral upset, enlightened court precedent or the appointment of honorable officials can never be extended to the point of qualitative transformation. Short of socialist victory, such institutional vehicles can never be secure or be expected to be strong enough.

As early as in the nineteenth century Rosa Luxemburg, a leader of the militant German left, expressed this point in the following manner: "The institutions which are democratic in form are in substance instruments of the dominant class interests. This is most obvious in the fact that as soon as democracy shows a disposition to deny its class character and to become an instrument of the real interests of the people, the democratic forms themselves are sacrificed by the bourgeoisie and their representatives in the state."

From Chile to Greece to South Korea to Brazil, such has actually been the pattern. When advanced capitalist classes are threatened, the same has happened—witness Nazi Germany and Fascist Italy. In the present crisis, such a threat hangs over many of the nominally democratic nations of the world. It is in this light that we must look again at the notion of planning.

Liberal leaders neglect to point out that the question is one of *Who does the planning and in whose interests is the planning done?* If we assume a national unity, then planning is done for everyone, for the general welfare. However, if planning is done *by the powerful, for the powerful*—as it has been and will continue to be if "unity" is allowed to act as a cover for privilege—then we should expect that the dominant class, with the minor participation of "responsible" labor statesmen, will plan in the interests of those very corporations which liberals admit already have too much power. The government will be used by giant corporations to do the kind of colluding (planning) which they can't do as well by themselves. Concretely, this means that the right to strike will be taken away from labor. The logic is clear enough. First, planners' decisions made "in the national interest" will require an uninterrupted flow of goods and services—especially in key sectors such as steel, coal, other basic industries (where, it happens, trade unions are strongest)—and second, unless planners' decisions are legally enforced, the planning system will quickly break down. Strikes then become an impediment to the "public interest."

Simultaneously, capital will be allowed to move freely in order to equalize wage rates as a method of lowering costs. Put differently, it will become part of the logic of planning to encourage corporations to move plants to low-wage nonunionized areas at home and abroad.

By the same logic, it follows that the powers of the government will be used to provide, through forced savings, for the investment needs of the private sector's more risky ventures. Funds will be provided collectively, but profits will continue to be enjoyed privately.

Once the outlines of the planned economy of monopoly capitalism are spelled out, they resemble more and more the *economic* policy of the fascist state. These policies need not be accompanied by the full political manifestations we identify with Hitler's Germany or Fascist Italy. For the polity to move toward fascism, it is necessary for the democratic forces to be discredited to the point of being, for all intents and purposes, dead.

The economic form of fascism has been described by Paul Sweezy in the following terms: "Under fascism, control over the economic system is centralized, conflicts between the different branches of capital are largely suppressed in the interests of capital as a whole, and heavy risks are pooled through the instrumentality of the state. We have here what Nazi economists have appropriately called a 'steered economy.'"

Historically, fascism has also led to war when economic expansion could not be continued on any other basis. National chauvinism, race bigotry, suppression of trade unions and forced cartelization and state planning may not be preferred by individual capitalists; but as crisis deepens and a left movement develops, fascism may be the preferable choice. The militarization and crude fascism of the Chilean junta may be an evil omen of what is possible elsewhere today.

Maurice Dobb's view is that "If one is to summarize shortly the historical preconditions of Fascism, one can speak, I think, of three factors as pre-eminent: a despair on the part of Capital of finding a normal solution for the impasse created by the limitations of the investment-field; considerable and depressed 'middle class' or declassé elements, ripe in the absence of an alternative rallying-point, to be recruited to the Fascist creed; and a working class, privileged enough to be resistant to normal pressure on its standard of life, but insufficiently united or non-class-conscious (at least in its political leadership) to be *politically* weak in asserting its power or in resisting attack."

Fascism projects a dream of reconstruction, of glory, mixed with appeals to racial hatred and national chauvinism. How many of these elements are present in the United States in the mid-1970's?

Those who consider themselves progressives should feel a sense of urgent concern over such possibilities and take a closer look at what national planning would mean in our historical context. People who stress the benign potential of planning and see it as a way toward full employment and the re-establishment of American affluence, and possibly even the greening to a humanitarian socialism, see only one of two possible directions such planning may lead us.

The relation between forms of state planning and the ultimate creation of socialism has a twofold nature. It raises the possibility of a planned economy, but as Ernest Mandel, the Belgian Marxist, notes, it is really in its essence capitalist. Mandel maintains: "Increasing state intervention in the economy, the growth of a 'public' sector, and even nationalization of certain unprofitable branches do not amount to 'socialism.' An economy can no more be a 'little bit socialist' than a woman 'a little bit pregnant.' State intervention, management of the economy, operate within the framework of capitalism in order to consolidate capitalist profits, or at least those of the decisive sections of the capitalist monopolies. . . . The idea of planning is accepted and applied by the bourgeoisie; indeed, one can even say that it is of bourgeois origin. But the bourgeoisie accept and adopt it only to the extent that it does not imperil the *profit motive*, does not embrace the whole of economic life, substituting production to meet need for production for profit."

Further, at this point in world capitalist history, the question is not only one of theoretical possibilities. Instead, it is unlikely that the adoption of state planning can in fact overcome the contradictions which are rooted in the very nature of capitalism. Rather like a junkie, capitalism seeks new highs through finding new opiates. It must take higher and higher doses— of militarism, consumerism and credit. The contradiction between the needs of capital and labor, the interclass struggle and the intraclass conflicts among the capitalists themselves cannot be papered over through a disinterested planning. The struggles are simply moved to a higher level. The outcome will depend on two types of developments: the degree to which irreconcilable interests can compromise and temporarily moderate the tendencies toward collapse, and the degree to which an alternative vision of society that seems desirable and possible can be developed in the very act of struggling to actualize itself.

Maoist Economic Development

John G. Gurley

The Maoists' disagreement with the capitalist view of economic development is profound. Their emphases, values, and aspirations are quite different from those of capitalist economists. To begin with, Maoist economic development occurs within the context of central planning, public ownership of industries, and agricultural cooperatives or communes. While decision-making is decentralized to some extent, decisions regarding investment vs. consumption, foreign trade, allocation of material inputs and some labor supply, prices of goods and factors—these and more are essentially in the hands of the State. The profit motive is officially discouraged from assuming an important role in the allocation of resources, and material incentives, while still prevalent, are down-graded.

But perhaps the most striking difference between the capitalist and

Maoist views is in regard to goals. Maoists believe that while a principal aim of nations should be to raise the level of material welfare of the population, this should be done only within the context of the development of human beings and of encouraging them to realize fully their manifold creative powers. And it should be done only on an egalitarian basis—that is, on the basis that development is not worth much unless everyone rises together; no one is to be left behind—either economically or culturally. Indeed, Maoists believe that rapid economic development is not likely to occur *unless* everyone rises together. Development as a trickle-down process is therefore rejected by Maoists, and so they reject any stronger emphasis on profit motives and efficiency criteria that lead to lopsided growth. Their emphasis, in short, is on man rather than on "things."[1]

EMPHASIS ON MAN

In Maoist eyes, economic development can best be attained by giving prominence to man. "In building up the . . . country, we—unlike the modern revisionists who one-sidedly stress the material factor, mechanization, and modernization—pay chief attention to the revolutionization of man's thinking and through this, command, guide, and promote the work of mechanization and modernization."[2] The Maoists' stress on this point most sharply distinguishes their thinking on the subject of economic development from that of capitalist economists. For Maoists, correct ideas can be transformed into a tremendous material force to push socialist construction to ever-higher levels. "Once Mao Tse-tung's thought is grasped by the broad masses, it will become an inexhaustible source of strength and an infinitely powerful spiritual atom bomb."[3] If, on the other hand, one concentrates on machinery, techniques, and things, economic development will proceed at a snail's pace. There can be big leaps forward only by putting man at the center, and so releasing his huge reservoir of energy, creativity, and wisdom, which up to now have been submerged by bourgeois society and by the ideas and behavior patterns it generates.

Capitalist economists have recently stressed the importance for economic growth of "investment in human capital"—that is, investment in general education, job training, and better health. It has been claimed that ex-

---

[1] This has been expressed by Maoists in many ways. As Mao Tse-tung has put it: "Of all things in the world, people are the most precious." ("The Bankruptcy of the Idealist Conception of History," in *Selected Works of Mao Tse-tung*, Vol. IV [Peking, Foreign Languages Press, 1961 & 1965], p. 454.) The *Peking Review* adds: "Whatever we do, we give prominence to the factor of man and put man at the centre" (November 11, 1966, pp. 19–20). And: "Chairman Mao's teaching to 'be resolute, fear no sacrifice and surmount every difficulty to win victory' means, in the last analysis, to give emphasis to the human factor." (*Peking Review*, March 17, 1967, p. 12.) With regard to national defense, Lin Piao has stated: "For our armed forces, the best weapon is not aircraft, heavy artillery, tanks or the atom bomb. It is Mao Tse-tung's thought. The greatest fighting power is the men who are armed with Mao Tse-tung's thought." (Quoted in *Peking Review*, March 17, 1967, pp. 12–13.) Mao has expressed the same idea: "Weapons are an important factor in war, but not the decisive factor; it is people, not things, that are decisive." ("On Protracted War," in *Selected Works*, Vol. II, pp. 143–44.)
[2] Mao Tse-tung, quoted in *Peking Review* (November 11, 1966), pp. 19–20.
[3] *Peking Review* (December 23, 1966), p. 7.

penditures in these directions have had a large "pay-off" in terms of output growth. The Maoists' emphasis, however, is quite different. First of all, while they recognize the key role played by education and health in the production process, their emphasis is heavily on the transformation of ideas, the making of the Communist man. Ideology, of course, may be considered as part of education in the broadest sense, but it is surely not the part that capitalist economists have in mind when they evaluate education's contribution to economic growth. Moreover, ideological training does not include the acquisition of particular skills, or the training of specialists—as education and job training in capitalist countries tend to do. The Maoists believe that economic development can best be promoted by breaking down specialization, by dismantling bureaucracies, and by undermining the other centralizing and diverse tendencies that give rise to experts, technicians, authorities, and bureaucrats remote from or manipulating "the masses." Finally, Maoists seem perfectly willing to pursue the goal of transforming man even though it is temporarily at the expense of some economic growth.[4] Indeed, it is clear that Maoists will not accept economic development, however rapid, if it is based on the capitalist principles of sharp division of labor and sharp (unsavory, selfish) practices.

THE MAKING OF COMMUNIST MAN

The proletarian world view,[5] which Maoists believe must replace that of the bourgeoisie, stresses that only through struggle can progress be made; that selflessness and unity of purpose will release a huge reservoir of enthusiasm, energy, and creativity; that active participation by "the masses" in decision-

---

[4] For 3,000 years the Chinese have paid much more attention to human relations than to conquering nature. Mao Tse-tung, as a Chinese, *and* as a Marxist, cannot help but follow in this tradition. But, as a Chinese, he wishes to make China powerful in the eyes of the world, and, as a Marxist, through socialism. The world views power in terms of GNP and nuclear weapons, not in terms of perfection in human relations. So Mao has to go in both directions at the same time, and the two goals often conflict with one another, at least in the short run.

This conflict was especially prominent in the latter half of the nineteenth century when some Chinese advocated using Western techniques but retaining Chinese culture and human relations. At that time and later, the adoption of Western techniques subverted Chinese culture. This conflict can perhaps be stated in terms of the "quantity of life" vs. the "quality of life."

Mao, of course, does not wish to preserve the "old ways," but he is interested in "man" and in human relations in an industrial society. Thus, just like his nineteenth century predecessors, Mao is faced with the conflict between developing "good" human beings and attaining rapid economic development.

[5] Mao Tse-tung follows Marxism-Leninism in adopting the world outlook of dialectical materialism, which is a philosophy of human and natural change and interaction. Changes in society, for example, according to Mao, are not due chiefly to external causes but instead to internal ones—to the internal contradictions between the productive forces and the relations of production, between classes, etc. There is internal contradiction in every single thing, and it is the development of the contradiction that gives rise to changes; eventually to qualitative changes. External causes by themselves could explain only changes in quantity or scale, but they could not explain qualitative or "leap" changes. "The development of things should be seen as their internal and necessary self-movement, while each thing in its movement is interrelated with and interacts on the things around it." (See Mao Tse-tung, "On Contradiction," *Selected Works*, Vol. I, p. 313.)

making will provide them with the knowledge to channel their energy most productively; and that the elimination of specialization will not only increase workers' and peasants' willingness to work hard for the various goals of society but will also increase their ability to do this by adding to their knowledge and awareness of the world around them.

Struggle

It is an essential part of Maoist thinking that progress is not made by peace and quietude, by letting things drift and playing things safe, or by standing for "unprincipled peace, thus giving rise to a decadent, philistine attitude. . . ." [6] Progress is made through struggle, when new talents emerge and knowledge advances in leaps. Only through continuous struggle is the level of consciousness of people raised, and in the process they gain not only understanding but happiness.

Mao sees man engaged in a fierce class struggle—the bourgeoisie against the proletariat—the outcome of which, at least in the short run, is far from certain. The proletarian world outlook can win only if it enters tremendous ideological, class struggles.

In China, although in the main socialist transformation has been completed with respect to the system of ownership, and although the large-scale and turbulent class struggles of the masses characteristic of the previous revolutionary periods have in the main come to an end, there are still remnants of the overthrown landlord and comprador classes, there is still a bourgeoisie, and the remoulding of the petty bourgeoisie has only just started. The class struggle is by no means over. The class struggle between the proletariat and the bourgeoisie, the class struggle between the different political forces, and the class struggle in the ideological field between the proletariat and the bourgeoisie will continue to be long and tortuous and at times will even become very acute. The proletariat seeks to transform the world according to its own world outlook, and so does the bourgeoisie. In this respect, the question of which will win out, socialism or capitalism, is still not really settled. [7]

Selflessness

Maoists believe that each person should be devoted to "the masses" rather than to his own pots and pans, and should serve the world proletariat rather than reaching out with "grasping hands everywhere to seek fame, material gain, power, position, and limelight." [8] They think that if a person is selfish, he will resist criticisms and suggestions and is likely to become bureaucratic and elitist. Such a person will not work as hard for community or national goals as he would for narrow, selfish ones. In any case, a selfish person is not an admirable person. Thus, Maoists de-emphasize material incentives, for they are the very manifestation of a selfish, bourgeois society.

---

[6] Mao Tse-tung, "Combat Liberalism," *Selected Works*, Vol. II, p. 31.
[7] Mao Tse-tung, "On the Correct Handling of Contradictions Among the People," in *Quotations of Mao Tse-tung* (Peking, Foreign Languages Press, 1966), pp. 17–18.
[8] *Peking Review* (March 10, 1967), p. 22.

Active Participation

While selflessness is necessary to imbue man with energy and the *willingness* to work hard, this is not sufficient, for man must also have the *ability* as well. And such ability comes from active participation—from seeing and doing. As Mao has written in a famous essay:

If you want to know a certain thing or a certain class of things directly, you must personally participate in the practical struggle to change reality, to change that thing or class of things, for only thus can you come into contact with them as phenomena; only through personal participation in the practical struggle to change reality can you uncover the essence of that thing or class of things and comprehend them. . . . If you want knowledge, you must take part in the practice of changing reality. If you want to know the taste of a pear, you must change the pear by eating it yourself. . . . All genuine knowledge originates in direct experience. . . . There is an old Chinese saying, "How can you catch tiger cubs without entering the tiger's lair?" This saying holds true for man's practice and it also holds true for the theory of knowledge. There can be no knowledge apart from practice.[9]

To gain knowledge, people must be awakened from their half slumber, encouraged to mobilize themselves and to take conscious action to elevate and liberate themselves. When they actively participate in decision-making, when they take an interest in State affairs, when they dare to do new things, when they become good at presenting facts and reasoning things out, when they criticize and test and experiment scientifically, having discarded myths and superstitions, when they are aroused—then "the socialist initiative latent in the masses [will] burst out with volcanic force and a rapid change [will take] place in production."[10]

I noted above that both attributes of selflessness and active participation were necessary for the making of the Communist man. For a selfish person, who has nevertheless become fully aware and knowledgeable through correctly combining theory and practice, will be given to sharp practices for his own ends and will become bureaucratic and divorced from the masses. A passive, unknowing person who has nevertheless become selfless, will be well-meaning but largely ineffective, for he will not be able to use his energies productively. In fact, it is likely that in the long run "selfless" and "active" cannot exist separately, only together. If one is not active, he will eventually revert to selfish behavior; if one is selfish, he will eventually become passive, bureaucratic, and unable to gain true knowledge.[11]

---

[9] Mao Tse-tung, "On Practice," *Selected Works*, Vol. I, pp. 299–300. Mao holds to the dialectical-materialist theory of knowledge, the theory of unity and knowing and doing—theory and practice. He believes that truth can be discovered by starting from perceptual knowledge, actively developing it into rational knowledge, and then going out into the world of revolutionary practice to test the knowledge. "Practice, knowledge, again practice, and again knowledge. This form repeats itself in endless cycles, and with each cycle the content of practice and knowledge rises to a higher level." (*Selected Works*, Vol. I, p. 308.)

[10] *Peking Review* (February 24, 1967), p. 22.

[11] Lenin implies that to reach the Marxian goal, "From each according to his ability, to each according to his needs," people will have to become selfless *and* highly productive. If each person is to take freely according to his needs, he cannot be

Finally, if men become "selfless," there will be discipline and unity of will, for these "cannot be achieved if relations among comrades stem from selfish interests and personal likes and dislikes." [12] If men become "active," then along with extensive democracy they will gain true consciousness and ultimately freedom, in the Marxian sense of intelligent action.[13] Together, selflessness and active participation will achieve ideal combinations of opposites:

a vigorous and lively political situation . . . is taking shape throughout our country, in which there is both centralism and democracy, both discipline and freedom, both unity of will and personal ease of mind.[14]

It is important to note the "discipline" and "unity of will." So far as the basic framework of Marxism-Leninism is concerned, Maoists believe that everyone should accept it, and they are quick to "work on" those who lag behind or step out of line. But, within this framework, the Maoists energetically and sincerely promote individual initiative, "reasoning things out and not depending on authorities or myths," "thinking for oneself," etc. Outside of this framework, an individual stands little chance; inside the framework, an individual is involved in a dynamic process of becoming "truly free," in the sense of being fully aware of the world around him and being an active decision-maker in that world. Mao's thought is meant to lead to true freedom and to unity of will based on a proletarian viewpoint. So everyone must think alike—the Maoist way—to attain true freedom!

Non-Specialization

For Marx, specialization and bureaucratization were the very antitheses of Communism. Man could not be free or truly human until these manifestations of alienation were eliminated, allowing him to become an "all-round" Communist man.[15] Maoists, too, have been intensely concerned with this

---

selfish. If there is to be enough for everyone, people will have to be highly productive. The latter is achieved by active participation, by seeing and doing, by theory and practice. See V. I. Lenin, "The State and Revolution," in *Selected Works*, Vol. 2 (New York, International Publishers, 1967), pp. 340–41.

[12] *Peking Review* (January 6, 1967), p. 13.

[13] Marxian freedom is real knowledge of a subject, intelligent action. A free individual "is no longer history's pawn, no longer condemned by the blind mechanics of social and economic forces to the mere suffering of history, but one who is a maker of history, who, knowing the nature of these forces, becomes, by choice and action, a part of them, thus changing them, and changing, too, himself, thus guiding both along those paths where each may live its fullest fruitfulness and history become at last appropriate to the best that human nature can become." (Vernon Venable, *Human Nature: The Marxian View* [New York, Meridian Books, 1969], p. 204.)

[14] *Peking Review* (December 23, 1966), p. 21.

[15] Vernon Venable sums up the position of Marx and Engels on this point when he writes: "by forcing men into a specialization of function that becomes more and more narrow, less and less interesting, less and less inclusive of his various potentials of ability, it has had the effect of stunting him, dehumanizing him, reducing him to a mere fragment of a man, a crippled monstrosity, an appendage to a machine." (Venable, *Human Nature*, pp. 123–24.) For further views by Marx on specialization, see *The Economic and Philosophic Manuscripts of 1844*, Struik (ed.) (New York, International, 1964) pp. 110, 161; *Capital* (New York, Modern Library), pp. 397–98.

goal, specifying it in terms of eliminating the distinction between town and countryside, mental and manual labor, and workers and peasants. The realization of the universal man is not automatically achieved by altering the forces of production, by the socialist revolution. Rather it can be achieved only after the most intense and unrelenting ideological efforts to raise the consciousness of the people through the creative study and creative use of Mao's thought. Old ideas, customs, and habits hang on long after the material base of the economy has been radically changed, and it takes one mighty effort after another to wipe out this bourgeois superstructure and replace it with the proletarian world outlook. This transformation of the "subjective world" will then have a tremendous impact on the "objective world."

Intellectuals, party and administrative cadres, and other mental workers are prodded into taking part in physical labor—in factories and out in the fields. This will not only

encourage the initiative of the workers and peasants in production and uproot the ingrained habit of bureaucracy, but even more important, it can ensure that leading cadres work among the people like ordinary laborers, and opens up a way for the gradual integration of mental and manual work.

Physical labor by intellectuals will eventually get rid of men whose "four limbs do not move and [who are] unable to distinguish the five grains."[16] And laborers should become intellectuals.

The characteristic feature of these efforts has been, and remains, a massive attack on the notion that culture, science and technology are attributes of intellectuals . . . the widely propagated rallying cry is that the "masses must make themselves masters of science and culture." For example, the purpose of "half-work and half-study" programs is proclaimed to be to develop "red and expert socialist laborers who can grasp the principles of science and technology . . . and who are both mental workers as well as people who can go to factories and field to engage in industrial and agricultural productions," thus refuting the notions of bourgeois intellectuals who "oppose mental labor to physical labor and who hold that physical labor is the task of workers and peasants while only they themselves can engage in mental labor."[17]

MAOIST IDEOLOGY AND ECONOMIC DEVELOPMENT

In many ways, then, Maoist ideology rejects the capitalist principle of building on the best, even though the principle cannot help but be followed to some extent in any effort at economic development. However, the Maoist departures from the principle are the important thing. While capitalism, in their view, strives one-sidedly for efficiency in producing goods, Maoism, while also seeking some high degree of efficiency, at the same time, in nu-

---

Marx saw a better day when each man could pursue not any one occupation but a variety of activities. Now a crippled fragment, man should become "the fully developed individual . . . to which the different social functions he performs are but so many modes of giving free scope to his own natural and acquired powers." (Marx, *Capital*, p. 534.)

[16] Quoted in Maurice Meisner, *Ascetic Values and Utopian Goals in Chinese Communist Ideology* (Mimeo., May 1967), p. 76.

[17] Meisner, *Ascetic Values and Utopian Goals*, pp. 77–78.

merous ways, builds on "the worst." Experts are pushed aside in favor of decision-making by "the masses"; new industries are established in rural areas; the educational system favors the disadvantaged; expertise (and hence work proficiency in a narrow sense) is discouraged; new products are domestically produced rather than being imported "more efficiently"; the growth of cities as centers of industrial and cultural life is discouraged; steel, for a time, is made by "everyone" instead of by only the much more efficient steel industry.

Maoists build on the worst not, of course, because they take great delight in lowering economic efficiency, but rather to involve everyone in the development process, to pursue development without leaving a single person behind, to achieve a balanced growth rather than a lopsided one. If Maoism were only that, we could simply state that, while Maoist development may be much more equitable than capitalist efforts, it is surely less efficient and thus less rapid; efficiency is being sacrificed to some extent for equity. But that would miss the more important aspects of Maoist ideology, which holds that the resources devoted to bringing everyone into the socialist development process—the effort spent on building on "the worst"—will eventually pay off not only in economic ways by enormously raising labor productivity but, more important, by creating a society of truly free men, who respond intelligently to the world around them, and who are happy.[18]

UNITED STATES STUDIES OF CHINESE ECONOMIC DEVELOPMENT

The sharp contrast between the economic development views of capitalist economists and those of the Chinese Communists cannot be denied; their two worlds are quite different. The difference is not mainly between being Chinese and being American, although that is surely part of it, but rather between being Maoists in a Marxist-Leninist tradition and being present-day followers of the economics first fashioned by Adam Smith and later reformed by J. M. Keynes. Whatever the ignorance and misunderstanding on the Chinese side regarding the doctrines of capitalist economics, it is clear

---

[18] This emphasis on man was expressed by Marx in many ways, including the following: "A critique of religion leads to the doctrine that the highest being for man is man himself, hence to the categorical imperative to overthrow all relationships in which man is humbled, enslaved, abandoned, despised." (Karl Marx, "Zur Kritik der Hegelschen Rechtsphilosophie," in Marx and Engels, *Der Historische Materialismus; Die Fruhschriften,* Vol. I [Leipzig, Alfred Kroner Verlag, 1932], p. 272. Quoted in Alfred G. Meyer, *Marxism: The Unity of Theory and Practice* [Ann Arbor, Univ. of Michigan Press, 1963], p. 51.) Or, as Friedrich Engels saw man in the new society: "Man, at last the master of his own form of social organization, becomes at the same time the lord over nature, his own master—free." (Friedrich Engels, "Socialism, Utopian and Scientific," in W. O. Henderson [ed.], *Engels: Selected Writings* [Harmondsworth, Penguin, 1967], p. 225.) The aim of socialism, for Marx, was not the production of more things but the self-realization of man. It is easy to forget, Marx wrote, "that the production of too many useful things results in too many useless people." (Karl Marx, *The Economic and Philosophic Manuscripts of 1844,* p. 151.) This humanist strain, this dislike of anything that makes man a mere fragment of himself, runs through all of Marx's writings. "Marx is thoroughly and consistently humanist. A positive image of man, of what man might come to be, lies under every line of his analysis of what he held to be an inhuman society." (C. Wright Mills. *The Marxists* [New York, Dell, 1962], p. 25.)

that many Western economic experts on China have shown little interest in and *almost no understanding of Maoist economic development.* . . .

CRITICISM OF ECONOMIC RESEARCH

Economic research on China suffers from an ailment common to most of economics: a narrow empiricism. . . . Each economist tills intensively his small plot, gaining highly specialized knowledge in the process, finally ending up an expert in his cramped quarters. There are not many economists in the China field who try to see Chinese economic development as a whole, as "the comprehensive totality of the historical process." If the truth is the whole, as Hegel claimed, most economic experts on China must be so far from the truth that it is hardly worthwhile listening to them.

Moreover, it is often painful. . . . [The] biases [in this research] show up in a variety of ways, from such trivial things as changing Peking to Peiping (à la Dean Rusk), which reveals a wish that the Communists weren't there; to the frequent use of emotive words (e.g., the Communists are not dedicated but "obsessed"; leaders are "bosses"; a decision not to release data is described as "a sullen statistical silence"; the extension of the statistical system becomes "an extension of its tentacles farther into the economy"); to the attribution of rather sinister motives to ordinary economic and cultural policies (e.g., education and literacy are promoted for the purpose of spreading evil Marxian doctrines; economic development is pursued for the principal purpose of gaining military strength for geographical expansion—which is the theme of W. W. Rostow's book on *The Prospects for Communist China*); to dire forecasts of imminent disasters which are based on little more than wishful thinking; to data manipulation of the most questionable sort.

This strong propensity to treat China as The Enemy has led, in my opinion, to some grossly distorted accounts of China's economic progress. The picture that is presented by these studies as a whole is one in which China, while making some progress for a time in certain areas, is just barely holding on to economic life. It is a picture of a China always close to famine, making little headway while the rest of the world moves ahead, being involved in irrational economic policies, and offering little reason for hope that the lives of her people will be improved. Our China experts, furthermore, know what is wrong, and that in a word is Communism. They seldom fail to pass judgment on some aspect or other of Chinese economic development, and this judgment is almost invariably capitalist-oriented. Thus, national planning and government-controlled prices cannot be good because they do not meet the criteria of consumer sovereignty and competitive markets; communes violate individualism and private property; ideological campaigns upset order and harmony; the de-emphasis on material incentives violates human nature and so reduces individual initiative and economic growth; the breakdown of specialization lowers workers' productivity. This sort of thing pervades much of the economic literature on China.

The truth is that China over the past two decades has made very remarkable economic advances (though not steadily) on almost all fronts. The basic, overriding economic fact about people in China is that for twenty years they have all been fed, clothed, and housed, have kept themselves healthy, and have educated most. Millions have *not* starved; sidewalks and streets have *not* been covered with multitudes of sleeping, begging, hungry, and illiterate human beings; millions are *not* disease-ridden. To find such deplorable conditions, one does not look to China these days but rather to India, Pakistan, and almost anywhere else in the underdeveloped world. These facts are so basic, so fundamentally important, that they completely dominate China's economic picture, even if one grants all of the erratic and irrational policies alleged by her numerous critics. The Chinese, all of them, now have what is in effect an insurance policy against pestilence, famine, and other disasters. In this respect, China has outperformed every under-developed country in the world; and, even with respect to the richest one, it would not be far-fetched to claim that there has been less malnutrition due to maldistribution of food in China over the past twenty years than there has been in the United States.[19]

If this comes close to the truth, the reason lies not in China's grain out-put far surpassing her population growth, for it has not, but rather in the development of institutions to distribute food evenly among the population. It is also true, however, that China has just had six consecutive bumper grain crops (wheat and rice) which have enabled her to reduce wheat im-ports and greatly increase rice exports. On top of this, there have been large gains in the supplies of eggs, vegetables, fruits, poultry, fish, and meat. In fact, China today exports more food than she imports. As I have indicated, the Chinese are in a much better position now than ever before to ward off natural disasters. There has been significant progress in irrigation, flood con-trol, and water conservancy; the use of chemical fertilizers is increasing rapidly, the volume of which is now over ten times that of the early 1950's; there have been substantial gains in the output of tractors, pumps, and other farm implements; and much progress has been made in the control of plant disease and in crop breeding.

In education, there has been a major breakthrough. All urban children and a great majority of rural children have attended primary schools, and enrollments in secondary schools and in higher education are proportion-ately large compared with pre-Communist days. If "school" is extended in meaning to include these as well as part-time, part-study education, spare-time education, and study groups organized by the communes, factories, street organizations, the army, then there are schools everywhere in China; then China may be said to be just one great big school.

China's gains in the medical and public health fields are perhaps the most impressive of all. The gains are attested to by many recent visitors to China. For example, a Canadian doctor a few years ago visited medical col-leges, hospitals, and research institutes, and everywhere he found good equipment, high medical standards, excellent medical care; almost all com-parable to Canadian standards.[20] A member of the United States Public

---

[19] Much of the material in this paragraph was suggested by John Despres, but he is not responsible for my interpretations of his remarks.

[20] G. Leslie Willcox, "Observations on Medical Practices," *Bulletin of the Atomic Scientists* (June, 1966), p. 52. See also William Y. Chen, "Medicine and Public Health," in *Sciences in Communist China*, pp. 384, 397–99.

Health Service, a few years ago, stated that "the prevention and control of many infections and parasitic diseases which have ravaged [China] for generations" was a "most startling accomplishment." He noted, too, that "the improvement of general environmental sanitation and the practice of personal hygiene, both in the cities and in the rural areas, was also phenomenal." [21]

While all these gains were being made, the Chinese have devoted an unusually large amount of resources to industrial output. China's industrial production has risen on the average by at least 11 per cent per year since 1950, which is an exceptionally high growth rate for an underdeveloped country. And industrial progress is not likely to be retarded in the future by any lack of natural resources, for China is richly endowed and is right now one of the four top producers in the world of coal, iron ore, mercury, tin, tungsten, magnesite, salt, and antimony. In recent years, China has made large gains in the production of coal, iron and steel, chemical fertilizers, and oil. In fact, since the huge discoveries at the Tach'ing oil field, China is now self-sufficient in oil and has offered to export some to Japan.

From the industrial, agricultural, and other gains I have outlined, I would estimate that China's real GNP has risen on the average by at least 6 per cent per year since 1949, or by at least 4 per cent on a per capita basis. This may not seem high, but it is a little better than the Soviet Union did over a comparable period (1928–40), much better than England's record during her century of industrialization (1750–1850) when her income per capita grew at one-half of 1 per cent per year, perhaps a bit better than Japan's performance from 1878 to 1936, certainly much superior to France's 1 per cent record from 1800 to 1870, far better than India's 1.3 per cent growth during 1950 to 1967, and much superior to the post-war record of almost all underdeveloped countries in the world.

This is a picture of an economy richly endowed in natural resources, but whose people are still very poor, making substantial gains in industrialization, moving ahead more slowly in agriculture, raising education and health levels dramatically, turning out increasing numbers of scientists and engineers, expanding the volume of foreign trade and the variety of products traded, and making startling progress in the development of nuclear weapons. This is a truer picture, I believe, than the bleak one drawn by some of our China experts. [22]

The failure of many economic experts on China to tell the story of her economic development accurately and fully is bad enough. But even worse, I think, has been the general failure to deal with China on her own terms, within the framework of her own goals and methods for attaining those goals, or even to recognize the possible validity of those goals. Communist China is certainly not a paradise, but it is now engaged in perhaps the most interesting economic and social experiment ever attempted, in which tremendous efforts are being made to achieve an egalitarian development, an

---

[21] Chen, "Medicine and Public Health."
[22] The above account of China's recent economic progress is largely taken from my testimony before the Joint Economic Committee. See *Mainland China in the World Economy Hearings*, Joint Economic Committee, Washington, D.C., April 5, 10, 11, and 12, 1967, pp. 184–88.

industrial development without dehumanization, one that involves everyone and affects everyone. But all those efforts seem not to have affected Western economists, who have proceeded with their income accounts and slide rules, and their free enterprise values, to measure and judge. One of the most revealing developments in the China field is the growing belief among the economic experts that further research is hardly worthwhile in view of the small amount of economic statistics that have come out of China since 1958. Apparently it does not matter that 775,000,000 people are involved in a gigantic endeavor to change their environment, their economic and social institutions, their standard of living, and themselves; that never before have such potentially important economic and social experiments been carried out; that voluminous discussions of these endeavors by the Maoists are easily available. No, if GNP data are not forthcoming, if numbers can't be added up and adjusted, then the economy is hardly worth bothering about!

SOME SUGGESTIONS AND CONCLUSIONS

. . . A thoughtful consideration of Maoism means paying proper attention to Marxism-Leninism as well as to the Chinese past of the Maoists. The Maoists' Marxist-Leninist goal of the Communist man within a classless society in which each person works according to his ability and consumes according to his needs, should be taken seriously in any economic analysis of what is now going on.

I mentioned earlier, when discussing the core of the development theory that would probably be accepted by both the capitalist and Maoist sides [omitted] that economic growth can be attained by increasing the amounts of labor, capital goods, and land used in production; by improving the quality of these factors of production; by combining them in more efficient ways and inspiring labor to greater efforts; and by taking advantage of economies of scale. Now, Maoism undoubtedly affects every one of these ingredients of economic growth, and often in ways quite different from the capitalist impact. For example, it is likely that Maoist ideology discourages consumption and encourages saving and investment, and so promotes the growth of the capital stock. It does this by preventing the rise of a high-consuming "middle class," by fostering the Maoist virtues of plain and simple living and devoting one's life to helping others rather than to accumulate "pots and pans."

As another example, it is possible that Maoist economic development, by de-emphasizing labor specialization and reliance on experts and technicians, reduces the quality of the labor force and so slows the rate of economic growth. On the other hand, as Adam Smith once suggested, labor specialization, while increasing productivity in some narrow sense, is often instituted at the expense of the worker's general intelligence and understanding. For, "The man whose whole life is spent in performing a few simple operations . . . generally becomes as stupid and ignorant as it is possible for a human creature to become." [23] The difference between the most dissimilar of human beings, according to Smith, is not so much the cause of

---

[23] Adam Smith, *The Wealth of Nations*, Book V, Ch. I, Part III.

division of labor as it is the effect of it. Consequently, while an economy might gain from the division of labor in some small sense, it could lose in the larger sense of creating men who are little more than passive and un-reasoning robots. A major aim of the Maoists is to transform man from this alienated state into a fully aware and participating member of society. The emphasis on "Reds" rather than experts is just one part of this transformation which, it is felt, will release "an atom bomb" of talents and energy and enable labor productivity to take great leaps.

In addition to this argument, which is based on Maoist interpretation of their own history and experience, particularly during the Yenan period, it is also possible that the "universal man" in an underdeveloped economy would provide more flexibility to the economy. If most people could perform many jobs moderately well, manual and intellectual, urban and rural, the economy might be better able to cope with sudden and large changes; it could with little loss in efficiency mobilize its labor force for a variety of tasks. Further, since experience in one job carries over to others, a person may be almost as productive, in the job-proficiency sense, in any one of them as he would be if he specialized on it. A peasant who has spent some months in a factory can more easily repair farm equipment, and so on. Finally, a Maoist econ-omy may generate more useful information than a specialist one and so lead to greater creativity and productivity. When each person is a narrow special-ist, communication among people is not highly meaningful: your highly specialized knowledge means little to me in my work. When, on the other hand, each person has a basic knowledge of many lines of activity, the ex-periences of one person enrich the potentialities of many others.

The point is that this topic—which, I should stress, includes not only labor productivity, the development of material things by human beings, but also the development of human beings themselves—this topic of generalists vs. specialists, Reds vs. experts, the masses vs. bureaucrats, or whatever, is not a foolish concept to be laughed away, as it had been in effect by some China experts. How men, in an industrial society, should relate to machines and to each other in seeking happiness and real meaning in their lives has surely been one of the most important problems of the modern age. There is also another basic issue here: whether modern industrial society, capi-talist or socialist, does in fact diminish man's essential powers, his capacity for growth in many dimensions, even though it does allocate him "effi-ciently" and increase his skills as a specialized input. Is man Lockean in nature, reactive to outside forces, adjusting passively to unbalancing forces from without? Or is he essentially Leibnitzian, the source of acts, active, capable of growth, and having an inner being that is self-propelled? If the latter, how are these powers released?

The Maoists claim that the powers exist and can be released. If they are right, the implications for economic development are so important that it would take a bunch of absolute dunces on this side of the Pacific to ignore them.

65

Toward a Program of Studies of the Transition to Socialism

Paul M. Sweezy

To discuss intelligently the transition to socialism, we must have a clear idea of what we mean by "socialism." Unfortunately, there is no general agreement, not even among those who consider themselves to be socialists. Without straining after precise definitions, I will focus on two conceptions of socialism and try to trace some of the main questions they raise for the problem of transition.

First, let me say that I shall remain within what may be called a Marxist universe of discourse. And for all Marxists, socialism is not the end of the road: it is itself a way station on the journey from capitalism to communism. As far as the latter is concerned, there would probably be pretty general agreement on its main features: under communism, classes have disappeared; the state has withered away; crippling forms of the division of labor have been overcome; distinctions between city and country and between manual and mental labor have been abolished; distribution is according to need, etc. But there would also be pretty general agreement that it is impossible to move directly from capitalism to communism, that the two are separated not by years or even decades but by a whole historical epoch, or perhaps even more than one historical epoch. In the meantime there must be a concrete target which a society setting out on the journey from capitalism to communism can aim at, can orient its policies toward, and by reference to which it can measure its advances or retreats. This target we call socialism, and here the disagreements begin.

But before we come to the different conceptions of socialism, there is one more preliminary. For Marxists it is impossible to set out on the journey at all unless or until a preliminary condition has been fulfilled: state power must first be transferred from the bourgeoisie to the working classes, i.e., to the proletariat and the peasantry. This means not only that the leading governmental offices must be occupied by representatives of the working classes: that by itself is not enough, as numerous historical experiences of social democratic and popular-front governments have proved. What is necessary is that the state apparatus, and above all its armed forces, should be a loyal and reliable instrument in the hands of the representatives of the masses. Here it is enough to recall the famous statement of Marx that "the working class cannot simply lay hold of the ready-made state machinery and wield it for its own purposes," and of Lenin's interpretation, undoubtedly correct, that "Marx's idea is that the working class must *break up*, *smash* the 'ready-made state machinery,' and not confine itself merely to laying hold of it."

There could certainly be a question about the interpretation of "break up" and "smash," but no one could very well deny that the real point here is that in one way or another the bourgeois state apparatus, which has been fashioned and long used as an instrument of bourgeois rule, must be effectively and definitively transformed into an instrument of *anti*-bourgeois rule. And this can be accomplished only through far-reaching changes in both structure and personnel. (The specific nature of these changes has varied, and will continue to vary, according to particular historical circumstances. But certain general requirements are bound to recur, e.g., the replacement of bourgeois legislatures and judicial systems by popular assemblies and courts, the staffing of the armed forces—including the police—at all levels of command by thoroughly trustworthy leaders chosen for their political rather than their professional qualifications, the drastic overhaul of elite-oriented educational systems, etc.) When Marxists speak of a revolution's having occurred, they mean that this process of transferring power from the bourgeoisie to the working classes, with the closely related (and indispensable) transformation of the state apparatus, has been accomplished. Historically, all revolutions in this sense have been violent processes, but violence is not the essence of the matter and there is nothing irrational in seeking to carry through a revolutionary process without violence. It needs only to be added that the greater the strength of the revolutionaries and the more evident their ability and willingness to meet counterrevolutionary violence with overwhelming revolutionary violence, the greater the chance that violence can be avoided.

Once the initial barrier has been cleared and the new regime has set out on the journey to socialism and communism, the question already alluded to of the meaning of socialism must be squarely faced.

One school of thought, to which I myself once belonged, holds that the distinguishing characteristics to socialism are, first, state ownership of the decisive means of production, and second, comprehensive planning of the economy. The assumption, more often implied than spelled out, is that once socialism in this sense has been firmly established, *its own inner dynamic will automatically propel it forward on the next leg of the journey to communism.* The reasoning here is superficially similar to that which leads Marxists to conclude that once competitive capitalism has been established, it must inevitably develop into monopoly capitalism. No one, however, has succeeded in explaining what the "law of motion" of socialism (in the sense indicated) is supposed to be. With respect to capitalism, on the other hand, Marx was very clear and explicit about the system's law of motion which leads from competitive to monopoly capitalism. And, as we shall see, there is in fact no reason to suppose that state ownership and comprehensive planning must produce forward movement in the direction of communism.

If this first conception of socialism—state ownership and planning—is adhered to, it has certain implications for the policies of a regime seeking to negotiate the transition to socialism and to establish the new system on firm foundations. Here we can usefully draw on the experience of the Soviet Union.

It was impossible to move directly from revolution to state ownership and planning in the Soviet Union. True, the so-called commanding heights (large industry, banking, railroads, etc.) were immediately incorporated into the state sector and became subject to a rudimentary kind of planning. But by far the larger part of the country's economy was in the hands of peasants, small producers, and private traders, all engaged in the production and circulation of commodities and hence subject to the law of value. Far from being suppressed or taken over in the early period after the revolution, this vast commodity-producing sector had to be stimulated and expanded under Lenin's New Economic Policy, a course which in the circumstances was absolutely essential to the physical survival of the people. Thereafter the effort to achieve socialism took on the form of a struggle between the planned state sector and the commodity-producing private sector, the former seeking to expand and achieve ever greater control both internally and over its rival, the latter resisting incursions and following a more or less "normal" path of expanded reproduction. (The classic study of this process is Preobrazhensky's *New Economics.*)

The tension between the two sectors finally became so great that it required what has often been called a "second revolution," this time from the top, to resolve it. With the collectivization of agriculture and the launching of the first Five Year Plan, the state sector triumphed over the private sector, and the Soviet Union became—not only in the eyes of its own leaders but also in those of its supporters and many others everywhere—the world's first socialist society.

Having completed this part of the journey to communism, the Soviet leadership under Stalin saw as its primary task the promotion of maximum growth of the socialist economy. This was considered necessary to enable the country to defeat its foreign capitalist enemies, and to provide the material base in both production and consumption for the further advance to communism. This meant putting economics in command. All policies had to be judged by reference to their effect on economic growth: all were good that contributed to rapid growth, all bad that hindered it. *The advance to communism would be an automatic by-product of economic growth and need not be a direct concern of policy-makers.*

Guided by this perspective, Stalin put into effect what could be called his own New Economic Policy. In addition to an extremely high rate of investment, major features of this policy were: (1) Concentration of authority at the top, not only in government and party but also in economic enterprises. Workers were deprived of any role in the decisions affecting their lives, and in their work were subjected to wholesale regimentation and harsh discipline. (2) Complementary to this was the unbridled use of material incentives to secure maximum effort and productivity. All manifestations of egalitarianism—such as the provision enacted in Lenin's time, which prohibited party members, no matter what positions they held, from receiving more than skilled laborers—were wiped out, and Stalin himself waged a bitter ideological campaign against the very ideal of equality, calling it a "reactionary, petty bourgeois absurdity worthy of a primitive sect of ascetics but not a socialist society organized on Marxian lines."

These policies did indeed produce a rapid rate of growth, but they also resulted, I believe inevitably, in an increasing stratification of society and a progressive depoliticization of the masses. Not only were these trends in and of themselves contrary to development toward communism; even more important, they made it relatively easy for the privileged groups in the bureaucracy, in the management of economic enterprises, and in the professions to consolidate their position in society and to pass their advantages along to their children. In other words, Stalin's policies made it possible for those in positions of political and economic power to constitute themselves as a new ruling *class*. (This is a complicated problem which cannot be discussed in detail in the present context: suffice it to say that ownership and inheritance of property is not the only way that class position can be transmitted from one generation to the next. Systematic differential access to educational opportunities is another way and probably the most important one in the Soviet Union today.) Following Charles Bettelheim, I call this new ruling class a "state bourgeoisie." It rules not through private ownership of the means of production, as in capitalist society, but through occupying the decision-making positions in the party, the state, and the economy; and it is a class and not simply a stratum because its sons and daughters have a much better chance of occupying the same positions of power than do the children of the rest of the population.

Here we must say a few words about value, prices, commodities, money, etc., in a socialist society of the type of the Soviet Union. . . .

. . . For reasons which I believe were related to the rise of the new state bourgeoisie and the depoliticization of the masses, the system of centralized administrative planning entered a period of crisis during the 1950s and 1960s. In seeking a way out, the countries of Eastern Europe, led by Yugoslavia, turned increasingly to the methods of capitalism. Since all the necessary forms were still there, not having been replaced by any specifically socialist forms, this was an easy course to follow. The content which had been injected into these forms in the earlier period was now gradually drained off and slowly replaced by a "new" content, which in reality was the old pre-revolutionary content.

Some Marxists reject this analysis on the ground that it is impossible for true value relations to exist as long as state ownership of the means of production prevails. Since to examine this position in depth would take us far beyond the confines of this paper, I must be content with suggesting the lines along which such an examination ought to proceed. According to one student of the Yugoslav economy:

The traditional socialist principle of distribution—"to each according to his work"—has been revised by the Yugoslavs, becoming "to each according to the factors supplied by the human agent or to which the human agent has access, as valued on the (imperfect) market." This principle is scarcely distinguishable from that of private enterprise.

What has happened in Yugoslavia is that the social ownership of productive factors has been eroded and private ownership has been established. The concept of social ownership of productive factors, always vague, in fact proved vacuous. Gradually, certain members of society acquired effective property rights which prevailed over social property. . . . Although title to the asset remains in the name of society, the exclusive rights granted enterprise members amount to private property rights, albeit in group rather than individual form.[1]

---

[1] Deborah Milenkovitch, "Which Direction for Yugoslavia's Economy?" *East Europe* (July 1969), p. 17. The kind of "socialist" results which this system makes possible is well illustrated by an Associated Press dispatch, datelined Cacak, Yugoslavia, which appeared in the *New York Times* of September 1, 1971. Here is the complete text: "A clothing factory was threatened with bankruptcy, until it began making hot pants. Profits burgeoned and workers' wages were doubled."

It may be said, of course, that this relates only to Yugoslavia and that the situation in the Soviet Union is quite different. That differences do exist is quite true, and it would require more knowledge than I have to establish how fundamental they are. Nevertheless, I think the Yugoslav case shows what is *possible* and underlines the warning expressed by Bettelheim that "it is precisely very dangerous, for the development of the socialist economy, to rely on the idea that, given the existence of state property in the means of production, the value form and the commodity form could have no more than a 'formal existence,' i.e., that they would be in some way 'forms' of the 'second degree.' " [2]

I conclude that "socialism" defined as a society characterized by state ownership of the means of production and comprehensive planning is not *necessarily* a way station on the journey from capitalism to communism, and that reliance on the theory that such a society must automatically develop toward communism can lead to movement in the exact opposite direction, i.e., to the reconstitution of class rule. Whether this reconstituted class society represents the restoration of capitalism, as the Chinese maintain, is an interesting and important question, but one which we cannot attempt to deal with here. For our present purposes it is enough to know that this traditional conception of socialism is altogether inadequate as a target and criterion of achievement for a revolutionary government setting out on the long march to communism.

This does not mean that we must reject state ownership and comprehensive planning. Without them, it is obviously impossible to leave capitalism behind and take even the first steps on the long march. But state ownership and planning are not enough to define a viable socialism, one immune to the threat of retrogression and capable of moving forward on the second leg of the journey to communism. Something more, indeed much more, has to be added.

What is this "something more"? Since the great dangers to be guarded against are the emergence of a new state bourgeoisie and retrogression to class rule under which the actual producers, as under capitalism, are exploited for the benefit of others, it seems obvious that what is needed is, in Bettelheim's words, "domination by the immediate producers over their conditions of existence and therefore, in the first instance, over their means of production and their products." The question, however, is what this means and, perhaps equally important, what it does *not* mean. There are no ready-made answers to this question and (to the best of my knowledge) very few studies bearing upon it. Here, surely, is one of the areas most in need of intensive investigation in any serious program of studies of the transition to socialism.

To begin with, we must be careful not to confuse Bettelheim's formula-

---

[2] In considering this question, one should bear in mind that the idea that property forms can conceal as well as articulate real social relations is in no sense foreign to Marxism. See, for example, Marx's statement: "In England, serfdom had practically disappeared in the last part of the fourteenth century. The immense majority of the population consisted then, and to a still larger extent in the fifteenth century, of free peasant proprietors, *whatever was the feudal title under which their right of property was hidden.*" (*Capital*, vol. 1, chap. 27, emphasis added.)

tion with the traditional syndicalist conception of workers' control. It is perfectly possible, as the Yugoslav experience proves, for control in economic enterprises to be formally and legally vested in the workers without changing anything fundamental. If the system as a whole is dominated by value relations, the effect of workers' control is simply to transform the workers (or rather an inner core of privileged workers) in each enterprise into a sort of collective capitalist. For the workers as a class this situation is in many ways even worse than capitalism, since it divides the workers and pits them against each other in a most destructive way. This does not mean that workers should have no part in the control and management of enterprises; it only means that such participation, which in fact should be constantly increasing, must take place within the context of a system which *as a whole is moving away from every kind of stratification and toward a situation in which the entire population constitutes a single homogeneous working class.* (The end result of this process, of course, is the disappearance of all classes and hence of the working class itself.) I believe that this provides us with the best possible criterion for judging and even measuring progress in a socialist (and communist) direction. To explore its implications should be, I believe, the central task of a program of studies of the transition to socialism. What follows are no more than a few tentative suggestions.

1. We must decisively reject the idea, expressed in the quotation from Stalin above, that egalitarianism is foreign to "a socialist society organized on Marxian lines." This idea is in fact an ideological rationalization for privilege and ultimately class rule. It is necessary to proclaim, on the contrary, that egalitarianism is the most fundamental principle of a socialist society organized on Marxian lines. But egalitarianism must not be interpreted in a purely material sense, i.e., as the mere equalization of incomes. This would be a superficial form of equality, correcting only one manifestation of the much more profound inequality engendered by centuries of capitalism, and leaving largely untouched stubborn roots from which all forms of inequality could, and in due course probably would, sprout again. For basically the inequality of capitalism springs not only from the circumstance that workers own no means of production but also from their lack of the knowledge and understanding necessary to operate the means of production. . . .

As long as this situation exists, as it certainly does exist on the morrow of the revolution, genuine equality is an impossibility, and any approaches that may be made in the direction of equality must remain precarious and reversible. And the overcoming of this situation can come about not only from changes in the legal ownership of the means of production but from profound changes in many other aspects of society, including the entire educational system and the forms of organization of production and government. The realization of these changes will necessarily be a long process and will involve bitter struggles which, precisely because of the nature of the capitalist heritage, will have the character of class struggles. Real equality will not come of itself, nor as a gift from the advantaged to the disadvantaged. It must be constantly fought for, and there must be willingness to pay even a high price in terms of immediate output or efficiency for advances toward greater equality.

2. Just as workers should participate in management, so managers should participate in work. It should never be forgotten that the aim is to abolish all such distinctions, and in the meantime concrete steps must be taken to move in that direction.

3. All producers must have complete freedom of discussion and criticism.

4. Agriculture and industry must be combined. Modern technology makes possible a radical decentralization of industrial production, allowing an increasing proportion of the population to live in a healthful setting offering a great variety of different kinds of work. At the same time, the monstrous urban agglomerations which the capitalist era has spawned and which are fertile sources of social pathology must be broken up and dispersed.

5. It is essential that work should be treated not as a mere means of acquiring income and consumer goods but as life's most important creative activity. Human beings have a need for work just as much as they have for food, clothing, shelter, culture, leisure, etc. It is of the utmost importance that all these needs should be brought into balance with each other and with society's natural resources and environment. The absurd and ultimately disastrous bourgeois notion of insatiable wants must be decisively repudiated.

6. To these ends a crucially important means would be the complete elimination of the entire system of distribution through the earning and spending of money incomes. This can be begun immediately with the free provision of such services as health care and education, and can be gradually extended to other categories of goods and services, ending with completely free distribution according to need. This of course implies the end of all value and commodity relations, even as mere forms of calculation, and the substitution of what Bettelheim calls *calcul économique social*. A society which has already made substantial progress in this direction and is clearly and measurably moving forward rather than backward could be called fully socialist and well on the way to communism.

The foregoing list could be endlessly expanded and/or subdivided, but I think it is enough to indicate the kinds of problems that are involved in a genuine process of transition toward socialism. Their study can and must proceed along both theoretical and empirical lines. Apart from the works of Bettelheim, there is a remarkable scarcity of significant theoretical work in this area. And in the absence of adequate theoretical tools, much of the empirical work on the various societies which have set out on the journey to socialism during the last half century has been singularly unenlightening. The time has come, I think, for great strides forward on both the theoretical and the empirical fronts. This is the more important because the number of transition societies is sure to increase as time goes by, and it is the more possible because we now have before us the extraordinarily rich experience of the Great Proletarian Culture Revolution in China, an event which I believe future generations will look back upon as a turning point in mankind's struggle to achieve a more rational and humane society.